# Family Therapy
## History, Theory, and Practice
### Third Edition

## Samuel T. Gladding
### Wake Forest University

Merrill
Prentice Hall

Upper Saddle River, New Jersey
Columbus, Ohio

**Library of Congress Cataloging-in-Publication Data**

Gladding, Samuel T.
    Family Therapy : history, theory, and practice / Samuel T. Gladding.—3rd ed.
        p.    cm.
    Includes bibliographical references and index.
    ISBN 0-13-016720-7
    1. Family psychotherapy.    I. Title.
RC488.5.G535    2002
616.89'156—dc21

2001030700

**Vice President and Publisher:** Jeffery W. Johnston
**Executive Editor:** Kevin M. Davis
**Associate Editor:** Christina M. Kalisch
**Production Editor:** Linda Hillis Bayma
**Copy Editor:** Lorretta Palagi
**Photo Coordinator:** Valarie Schultz
**Design Coordinator:** Diane C. Lorenzo
**Text Designer:** Marilyn Paselsky
**Cover art:** SuperStock
**Cover Designer:** Thomas Mack
**Production Manager:** Laura Messerly
**Electronic Text Management:** Marilyn Wilson Phelps, Karen L. Bretz, Melanie N. Ortega
**Illustrations:** Christine Marrone
**Director of Marketing:** Kevin Flanagan
**Marketing Manager:** Amy June
**Marketing Coordinator:** Barbara Koontz

This book was set in Goudy Old Style by Prentice Hall and was printed and bound by R.R. Donnelley & Sons Company. The cover was printed by The LeHigh Press, Inc.

**Photo Credits:** Scott Cunningham/Merrill, pp. 84, 114, 198, 218, 264, 288, 314, 342, 394; Mike Gallitelli/PH College, p. 58; Rhoda Sidney/PH College, p. 30; Teri Leigh Stratford/PH College, p. 170; Todd Yarrington/Merrill, p. 366; Shirley Zeiberg/PH College, pp. 2, 144, 240.

Prentice-Hall International (UK) Limited, *London*
Prentice-Hall of Australia Pty. Limited, *Sydney*
Prentice-Hall Canada, Inc., *Toronto*
Prentice-Hall Hispanoamericana, S.A., *Mexico*
Prentice-Hall of India Private Limited, *New Delhi*
Prentice-Hall of Japan, Inc., *Tokyo*
Prentice-Hall Singapore Pte. Ltd.
Prentice-Hall do Brasil, Ltda., *Rio de Janeiro*

10 9 8 7 6 5 4
ISBN: 0-13-016720-7

*To my family,*
  *especially my parents,*
    *Gertrude Barnes Templeman Gladding*
      *and*
    *Russell Burton Gladding,*
*who taught me by example*
  *how to handle adversity,*
    *give love,*
      *and work for the greater good.*

# About the Author

Samuel T. Gladding is professor of counselor education, director of the counselor education program, and the associate provost at Wake Forest University in Winston-Salem, North Carolina. He has been a practicing counselor in both public and private agencies since 1971. His leadership in the field of counseling includes service as

- president of the Association for Counselor Education and Supervision (ACES),
- president of the Association for Specialists in Group Work (ASGW),
- president of Chi Sigma Iota (international academic and professional counseling honor society),
- vice president of the Counseling Association for Humanistic Education and Development (C-AHEAD), and
- president of the Alabama Association of Marriage and Family Therapists.

Dr. Gladding is the former editor of the *Journal for Specialists in Group Work* and the ASGW newsletter. He is also the author of more than 100 professional publications. In 1999, he was cited as being in the top 1% of contributors to the *Journal of Counseling and Development* for the 15-year period from 1978 to 1993. Some of Gladding's most recent books include *The Counseling Dictionary* (2001); *Counseling: A Comprehensive Profession,* Fourth Edition (2000); *Group Work: A Counseling Specialty,* Third Edition (1999); *The Creative Arts in Counseling,* Second Edition (1998); and this edition of *Family Therapy: History, Theory, and Practice* (2002).

Dr. Gladding's previous academic appointments have been at the University of Alabama at Birmingham, Fairfield University (Connecticut), and Rockingham Community College (Wentworth, North Carolina). He was also director of Children's Services at the Rockingham County (North Carolina) Mental Health Center. Gladding received his degrees from Wake Forest (B.A., M.A. Ed.), Yale (M.A.R.), and the University of North Carolina–Greensboro (Ph.D.). He is a National Certified Counselor, a Certified Clinical Mental Health Counselor, and a Licensed Professional Counselor (North Carolina). He is a former member of the Alabama Board of Examiners in Counseling and a current member of the Research and Assessment Corporation for Counseling (RACC).

Dr. Gladding is the recipient of numerous honors, including

- the Chi Sigma Iota Thomas J. Sweeney professional Leadership Award,
- the Counseling Association for Humanistic Education and Development Joseph W. and Lucille U. Hollis Outstanding Publication Award,
- the Association for Counselor Education and Supervision Professional Leadership Award, and
- the Association for Specialists in Group Work Eminent Career Award.

He is also a Fellow of the Association for Specialists in Group Work.

Dr. Gladding is married to the former Claire Tillson and the father of three children—Ben, Nate, and Tim. Outside of counseling, he enjoys tennis, swimming, and humor.

# Preface

## Philosophy

Therapeutic work with families is a recent scientific phenomenon but an ancient art. Throughout human history, designated persons in all cultures have helped couples and families cope, adjust, and grow. In the United States, the interest in assisting families within a healing context is both a twentieth and twenty-first century movement. Family life has always been of interest, but because of economic, social, political, and spiritual values, outsiders made little direct intervention, outside of social work, into ways of helping family functioning until the 1920s. Now, there are literally thousands of professionals who focus their attention and skills on improving family dynamics and relationships.

In examining how professionals work to assist families, the reader should keep in mind that there are as many ways of offering help as there are families. However, the most widely recognized methods are counseling, therapy, educational enrichment, and prevention. The general umbrella term for remediation work with families is *family therapy*. This concept includes the type of work done by family professionals who identify themselves by different titles including counselors, psychologists, psychiatrists, social workers, nurses, and clergy.

*Family therapy* is not a perfect term; politically it gets bandied about by a number of professional associations such as the American Association for Marriage and Family Therapy (AAMFT), the American Counseling Association, the American Psychological Association (APA), and the National Association of Social Workers. Physicians who treat families also debate this term, as well as whether as doctors they are "family therapists" or engaged in the practice of medicine and therefore "family medical specialists." For purposes of this book, the generic term *family therapy* is used because of its wide acceptance among the public and professionals who engage in the practice of helping families. Within this term, some aspects of educational enrichment and prevention are included.

## Organization

As a comprehensive text, this book focuses on multiple aspects of family therapy. Part One introduces the reader to the various ways in which families develop and the characteristics of healthy and dysfunctional families. Part Two examines the rationale and history of family therapy, its general processes, and the main theoretical approaches to working therapeutically with families: Adlerian/psychodynamic, Bowenian, experiential, behavioral and cognitive-behavioral, structural, strategic, systemic (Milan), solution focused, and narrative. Each theoretical chapter emphasizes the major theorists of the approach, premises, techniques, process/outcome, and unique aspects of the theory. A case illustration is provided also.

Part Three examines issues and dynamics in working with special family forms—single-parent families, remarried families, culturally diverse families, and addictive/abusive families—as well as the different therapeutic approaches used, according to family type and background. Finally, Part Four discusses ethical, legal, and professional issues in being a family therapist. It also explores research and assessment in family therapy.

## New to This Edition

The third edition of *Family Therapy* has been thoroughly updated with new and relevant sources. It has been strengthened to include a greater emphasis on family health, a more complete integration of issues related to diversity and gender, and an expanded discussion of professional identity and ethics. Another added feature is a new chapter on working with families who suffer from substance-related disorders, domestic violence, and child abuse. A student workbook, *Exercises in Family Therapy* by Mark E. Young, Monserrat Casado, and Scott Rasmus, now accompanies the text. It includes case studies, structured exercises, and questions to help the student reflect on material presented in the book.

## A Personal Note

In undertaking the writing of this work, I have been informed not only by massive amounts of reading in the rapidly growing field of family therapy but also by my own experiences during the past 25 years of therapeutically working with families. Both my family of origin and current family of procreation have influenced me as well. In addition, because I belong to the AAMFT, the International Association for Marriage and Family Counseling, and Division 43 (Family Psychology) of the APA, I have tried to view families and family therapy from the broadest base possible. Readers should find information within this work that will help them gain a clear perspective on the field of family therapy and those involved with it.

Like the authors of most books, I truly hope you as a reader enjoy and benefit from the contents of this text. It is my wish that when you complete your reading you will have gained a greater knowledge of family therapy, including aspects of therapy that affect you personally as well as professionally. If such is the case, then you will have benefited and possibly changed, and I, as an author, will have accomplished the task I set out to do.

## Acknowledgments

I am grateful to the reviewers who spent many hours critiquing the first edition of this book: James Bitter, California State University at Fullerton; Donald Bubenzer, Kent State University; Harper Gaushell, Northeast Louisiana University; J. Scott Hinkle, University of North Carolina at Greensboro; Gloria Lewis, Loyola University of Chicago; Donald Mattson, University of South Dakota; Eugene R. Moan, Northern Arizona University; and Tom Russo, University of Wisconsin, River Falls.

I also gratefully acknowledge the contributions of time and insightful suggestions from reviewers for the second edition: Charles P. Barnard, University of Wisconsin–Stout; Peter Emerson, Southeastern Louisiana University; and Eugene R. Moan, Northern Arizona University.

Reviewers for the third edition of the book who provided me with valuable input were Michael Carns, Southwest Texas State University; Thomas A. Cornille, Florida State University; Merith Cosden, University of California, Santa Barbara; Vonda Jump, Utah State University; and Jeffrey M. Smith, Kent State University.

I especially thank Virginia Perry of Summit School, my graduate assistants, Michele Kielty and Jenny Cole, and the program manager of the Counselor Education Program, Pamela Karr, all of Wake Forest University, for their constructive and positive input and for the painstaking way they helped me assemble this text. I am also indebted to my editor at Merrill/Prentice Hall, Kevin Davis, for his tireless effort, support, and assistance on my behalf.

This text is dedicated to my family, especially my parents. My father died in April 1994, at the age of 84, shortly after I completed the first edition of this text. My mother died more recently in August 2000, two months short of turning 90, just as I was finishing up this third edition of the book. The love and courage of both my parents along with the legacy left to me by previous generations of my family have affected me positively. I know I am most fortunate.

Finally, I am grateful for the support, encouragement, and comfort of my wife, Claire, who has insisted throughout this effort that we talk and build our marriage. She has employed all of her communication skills, including a generous dose of humor, to help me be a better spouse. She has also been throughout these years my partner, friend, and lover in the raising of our three children: Benjamin, Nathaniel, and Timothy.

*Samuel T. Gladding*

# Discover the Companion Website
# Accompanying This Book

## The Prentice Hall Companion Website:
## A Virtual Learning Environment

Technology is a constantly growing and changing aspect of our field that is creating a need for content and resources. To address this emerging need, Prentice Hall has developed an online learning environment for students and professors alike—Companion Websites—to support our textbooks.

In creating a Companion Website, our goal is to build on and enhance what the textbook already offers. For this reason, the content for each user-friendly website is organized by topic and provides the professor and student with a variety of meaningful resources. Common features of a Companion Website include:

## For the Professor—

Every Companion Website integrates **Syllabus Manager**™, an online syllabus creation and management utility.

- **Syllabus Manager**™ provides you, the instructor, with an easy, step-by-step process to create and revise syllabi, with direct links into the Companion Website and other online content without having to learn HTML.
- Students may log on to your syllabus during any study session. All they need to know is the web address for the Companion Website and the password you've assigned to your syllabus.
- After you have created a syllabus using **Syllabus Manager**™, students may enter the syllabus for their course section from any point in the Companion Website.
- Clicking on a date, the student is shown the list of activities for the assignment. The activities for each assignment are linked directly to actual content, saving time for students.
- Adding assignments consists of clicking on the desired due date, then filling in the details of the assignment—name of the assignment, instructions, and whether or not it is a one-time or repeating assignment.
- In addition, links to other activities can be created easily. If the activity is online, a URL can be entered in the space provided, and it will be linked automatically in the final syllabus.
- Your completed syllabus is hosted on our servers, allowing convenient updates from any computer on the Internet. Changes you make to your syllabus are immediately available to your students at their next logon.

## For the Student—

- **Counseling Topics**—17 core counseling topics representing the diversity and scope of today's counseling field
- **Annotated Bibliography**—seminal foundational works and key current works
- **Web Destinations**—significant and up-to-date practitioner and client sites
- **Professional Development**—helpful information regarding professional organizations and codes of ethics
- **Electronic Bluebook**—send homework or essays directly to your instructor's email with this paperless form
- **Message Board**—serves as a virtual bulletin board to post—or respond to—questions or comments to/from a national audience
- **Chat**—real-time chat with anyone who is using the text anywhere in the country—ideal for discussion and study groups, class projects, etc.

To take advantage of these and other resources, please visit the *Family Therapy: History, Theory, and Practice,* Third Edition, Companion Website at

**www.prenhall.com/gladding**

# Contents

## Chapter 7: Behavioral and Cognitive–Behavioral Family Therapies

**171**

# PART ONE

# Understanding Families

# C H A P T E R 1

# Individual and Family Life Cycles

He was as nervous as a cat
in a room full of rockers
stiffly dressed in formal black
uptight, and afraid of moving quickly
lest he break a button or the mood from the organ music.

She was serene
as if living a dream from childhood
dressed in layers of white with a lilac bouquet
unable to conceal her contentment
she remained poised amid the quiet
of assembled excitement.

Together they exchanged formal wedding vows,
homemade bands, and brief, expectant glances.

Then numbed, as if by novocaine,
they slowly greeted guests and themselves anew
as they whispered good-bye to innocence
and hello to the opening of a marriage.

*Gladding, 1993*

**F**amilies have historically played an important part in the life and development of people and nations. The origin of families "dates back to prehistoric times when our hominid ancestors developed the original family unit. Although the family has evolved, it has maintained many of its original functions. It produces and socializes children, acts as a unit of economic cooperation, gives us significant roles as children, husbands, wives, and parents, and provides a source of intimacy" (Strong & DeVault, 1986, p. 4). Furthermore, a family provides some of the deepest and most satisfactory emotional experiences of life, such as love, devotion, attachment, belonging, fun, and joy (Framo, 1996). The family can also be therapeutic with members listening, sympathizing, assisting, and reassuring each other (Sayger, Homrich, & Horne, 2000).

The early Egyptians considered the royal family so important that they encouraged marriages among kin. In Chinese dynasties, family life was crucial to the accrual of power and survival of empires; consequently, marriages were arranged. In medieval Europe, powerful families intermarried in order to rule and maintain wealth. As a result, certain families, such as the Hapsburgs, enjoyed great success in accumulating wealth and power (Klein, 1992).

Throughout time, social and economic factors have forced modifications in the customs governing family life. New rules have been established and/or abandoned as a result of societal changes resulting from such events as revolutions, economic turmoil, or natural disasters. For example, in the late 1800s the United States underwent a major transition from an agricultural society to an industrial one. This socioeconomic change altered the lives of American families:

> Industrial workers of agricultural backgrounds exchanged their rural "freedom" of flexible schedules, lack of control over environmental uncertainties on their work effort, and social isolation of rural living for regimented time schedules, lack of control over extreme and tedious work conditions, and city living. . . . In large measure, this shift resulted in an exchange of independence and economic self-reliance for social and economic dependence within families. (Orthner, Bowen, & Beare, 1990, p. 18)

In examining families and how to work with them, a professional must explore historical, societal, economic, and governmental factors that have had an impact on family life over time. This knowledge includes seeing the systemic interaction of personalities, communities, and events. It involves an appreciation of the tension that exists within the structure of families for dealing with outside environmental forces and internal relationship difficulties. After all, "families do not dance alone or in isolation" (Stevenson, 1994, p. 39). Take, for example, the following case.

━━━━━━━━━━━━━━━ **CASE ILLUSTRATION** ━━━━━━━━━━━━━━━

### THE HARDY FAMILY

The Hardy family requested family therapy because of a promiscuous and defiant teenage daughter. Upon further investigation, the therapist found that the father lost his job 2 years ago, and since then the family has been strapped for money. Currently, they are receiving food stamps and live in public housing. In addition, the family has moved from a small town to a large city, where they know very few people. The mother's health has declined to the point that she is now almost an invalid. In addition, the younger brother of the identified patient has taken on a star student role and is the antithesis of his sister, who is being teased by her classmates in high school about her looks, poor dress, and lack of ability.

If the family therapist makes the mistake of ignoring the economic, social, health, and historical factors the Hardy family brings into therapy, he or she may not be able to offer them any meaningful help. Only when the therapist takes all of the family's interactive variables into account and looks at how each member influences the other and the family as a whole can a useful intervention be designed and delivered. Basically, families are **systems** in which the individuals within them stand in interaction with each other and the family unit as a whole. The movement of each person in and outside the family environment has an impact on every family member and the way the family functions. The interrelatedness of the family, which is governed by rules, sequences, and feedback, is known as **cybernetics** (Bateson, 1971). It is artificial to try to isolate individual and family life cycles from one another or to separate interactions in a "freeze-frame" fashion.

In essence, understanding the various developmental and systemic nuances of family life is the first step in the process of becoming a family therapist. The second step involves becoming knowledgeable about the dynamics of individual and family life cycles. Families share universal and unique functions. Universally, they provide a structure for sexual, reproductive, economic, and educational endeavors (Cavan, 1969). Defining and appreciating the global and essential components of families in various contexts is essential. This process includes assessing the family's behavior patterns and the make-up and functioning of the family's **subsystems** (i.e., smaller units of the family system, such as parents or children, logically grouped together by age or function). Families attend to the specific needs of all or some of their members for better or worse.

This chapter tackles the task of exploring how a family's form and context play a part in its well-being. Life cycles are examined from both a developmental and a systems perspective. An attempt is made to interconnect aspects of growth and interaction among family members.

# What Is a Family?

Ideas about what a family is and how it should be structured vary across cultures and are constantly changing (Coontz, 1992, 1997). In America, "families have been changing since the first settlers arrived on the shores of the new world" (Bird & Sporakowski, 1992, p. xiv). For some groups, such as many Americans of European descent, the family includes only blood-related kin and is "nuclear." For other groups, such as many African Americans, the family tends to focus on a "wide informal network of kin and community" (Hines, Preto, McGoldrick, Almeida, & Weltman, 1999, p. 70). In such cases, the family includes anyone who is psychologically connected, such as close long-term friends (Hines & Boyd-Franklin, 1996). For yet others, such as some Asian Americans, the family includes ancestors and all descendants. In essence, the definition of a family is not monolithic. It varies according to cultural groups. Reaching a consensus on what constitutes a family is difficult at best.

Thus, in formulating a definition of a family, inclusive as well as exclusive elements need to be considered. The U.S. Bureau of the Census (1993) defines a family as "a group of two or more persons related by birth, marriage, or adoption and residing together in a household" (p. 5). This broad definition includes people who never marry, those who marry and never have children, those whose marriages end in divorce or death, and a variety of nontraditional family arrangements. In essence, this definition of a family is one that is geared toward one's family of origin, that is, the family in which a person grew up. The definition, however, excludes some forms of living arrangements that a number of people consider a family too, such as gay or lesbian couples, close friends, or ancestors. Therefore, in this book, the definition of a family will be kept broad in order to promote an understanding of the different forms of family life available. A **family** here is considered to be those persons who are biologically and/or psychologically related whom historical, emotional, or economic bonds connect and who perceive themselves as a part of a household. By broadly defining a family, we hope an appreciation of persons in family units will be gained, and insight into the ways families govern themselves will be obtained.

Overall, families in whatever form they come in are characterized by economic, physical, social, and emotional functions. There is a dual emphasis on fostering the development of individuals within families while simultaneously offering family members stability, protection, and preservation of the family unit structure (Burr, Hill, Nye, & Reiss, 1979; Strong, DeVault, & Sayad, 1998). An example of these emphases and what they foster can be seen in the Temple family. The Temple family is composed of a stepfather, a biological mother, and two daughters, ages 11 and 9. Both the mother and stepfather work outside the home to provide economic and physical support for themselves and the children. In addition, the mother makes sure the daughters behave properly by monitoring the time and people with whom she allows them to socialize. She listens and reflects with them as well and has enrolled them in gymnastics and music classes. The family routine of supper, homework, and television is run by the clock and strictly monitored. However, the parents take a night out once a week to bowl and enjoy themselves as a couple. Although there are disagreements in the family, there is also balance.

# Types of Families

As pointed out earlier, many alternative family lifestyles have emerged and are now competing for recognition as legitimate and healthy lifestyles. "It no longer makes sense to refer to a typical American family life. Accuracy requires us to consider various types of families, with diverse organizational patterns, styles of living, and living arrangements" (Goldenberg & Goldenberg, 1998, p. 7). Consequently, in discussing the term *family*, an appreciation of differences works best. Among the many family forms, the following are the most prevalent:

- **Nuclear family:** A core family unit of husband, wife, and their child(ren). The nuclear family has traditionally been seen as the main provider of socialization for the young and as a preserver of cultural traditions. This family type has also been viewed as the social grouping in which society sanctions sexual relationships. The traditional nuclear family household is shrinking in both number and percentage.
- **Single-parent family:** A family that includes one parent, either biological or adoptive, who is solely responsible for care of self and child/children (see Chapter 11).
- **Remarried** (*i.e., blended, step*) **family:** A family created when two people marry and at least one of them has been married previously and has a child/children (see Chapter 12).

Other frequently mentioned family forms that are often variations on one of the three family forms just cited are as follows:

- **Dual-career family:** Those families in which both marital partners are engaged in work that is developmental in sequence and to which they have a high commitment (Gilbert, 1994). The acronym **DINK** (dual income, no kids) is one that is used to describe a portion of this population. Balancing the dual career and family life can lead to satisfaction as well as conflict (Thomas, 1990). Learning new skills, staying flexible, and continually assessing and revising work and family life are necessary if dual-career couples are to thrive.
- **Childless family:** Couples who consciously decide not to have children or who remain childlessness as a result of chance (such as marrying late) or biology (infertility). Childless couples have opportunities and advantages, such as having less stress, more discretionary income, and greater options to serve in the community; but they face pressures and may be stigmatized if they elect to be childless. Childless couples may also have difficulty in mourning the children they never had or in coming to terms with the choices they made not to have children (McGoldrick & Walsh, 1999).
- **Gay/lesbian families:** These types of families are made up of same-sex couples without children or with children from a previous marriage or as a result of artificial insemination. Census data suggest that partners of gays and lesbians are better educated and have higher incomes than heterosexual couples, which partially explains their varied lifestyles. Almost all gay/lesbian couples face some form of discrimination and prejudice in the communities in which they live (Johnson & Colucci, 1999).
- **Aging family:** A family headed by those 65 years old and above. The focus of this family type is on health, transition to retirement, widowhood, sexual dysfunction, dealing with adult children, grandparenting, imparting wisdom, and long-lived marriages (Walsh, 1999). Aging families are involved with the launching or relaunching of their young adult children and sometimes in the care of their grandchildren.
- **Multigenerational family:** Households that include a child, a parent, and a grandparent (Harrigan, 1992) are considered multigenerational families. "By the year

2020, the typical family will consist of at least four generations" (Goldenberg & Goldenberg, 1998). Two factors, the economy and medical advancement, are influencing the increase in the number of these families.

# Individual and Family Development

**Development** (i.e., predictable physical, mental, and social changes over life that occur in relationship to the environment) is a powerful factor in individuals and in families. The process is often uneven, with alternating times of growth and regression. In examining the concept of development, the factors of time and stages must be addressed. In the broadest sense, development is a "life course." As such, it refers to three different time dimensions in human life: individual time, social time, and historical time (Elder, 1975). **Individual time** is defined as the span of life between one's birth and death. Notable individual achievements are often highlighted in this perspective, for example, being recognized as "employee of the year." **Social time** is characterized by landmark social events such as marriage, parenthood, and retirement. Family milestones are a central focus here. **Historical time** is the era in which people live, that is, the culture. It consists of forces that affect and shape humanity at a particular point in time, such as during economic depression or war. For example, a Vietnam veteran may still be angry about government decisions involving the Vietnam War, and a survivor of the Great Depression may still hoard money and be distrustful of banks. In both cases, memories of time influence present lifestyles (see Figure 1.1).

Everyone is influenced by the three dimensions of time, both concurrently and sequentially. The term **life cycle** is used in this text to describe life events. A life cycle presents

**Figure 1.1**
Three different time dimensions in human life.

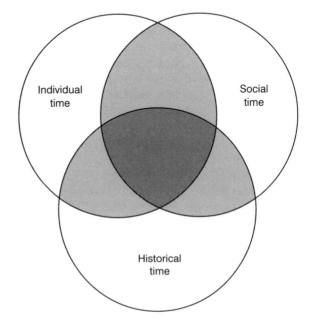

Individual time

Social time

Historical time

an active way to conceptually picture time in human development because it denotes the continuous development of people over time in multiple contexts of their lives.

Life cycles have been formulated for both individuals and families. Neither people nor families develop or interact in isolation from each other or from the society in which they live (Schwartz, 1999). Rather, life cycles often juxtapose and intertwine within a particular social framework. Interactions with family members, both living and dead, influence the course of one's life (Bowen, 1978; Okun, 1984). For example, the choice of career and professional development is frequently connected with one's family life and history. Take the case of a 39-year-old single woman who was named after her maiden aunt, a former schoolteacher. This woman has always valued education. She turned down dates in college in order to devote more time to her studies. Now her primary focus has paid off. She has been promoted to a full professor at a major university. Her life up to this point parallels her aunt's. In examining her life after her latest academic achievement, she continues to take her cues from the life of her namesake. She may wonder about marriage or adopting a child. If she were to elect either of these routes, she would deviate from the life pattern she set in motion. Such a change would not be impossible but would require more effort because she has no family role model to follow.

## Individual Life Cycle Development

Up until the 1970s, the word *development* usually referred to an individual. Part of the reason is attributable to the popularization of Erik Erikson's (1950, 1959, 1968) theory on human growth and development. Erikson was a pioneer in describing human life in terms of **stages,** sequential developmental occurrences. Following Erikson's lead, Daniel Levinson (1978), Roger Gould (1972, 1978), and Gail Sheehy (1977, 1981) proposed adult developmental stages that focus on the individual. Indirectly reinforcing this personal emphasis has been the concentration in the helping professions on counseling individuals. With the exceptions of social work and marriage and family therapy, most helpers have traditionally worked on a one-to-one basis (Gladding, 2000).

From an individual point of view, people face predictable **developmental crises** (i.e., times of turmoil and opportunity) throughout their lives. These times involve such events as aging, retirement, birth, and marriage. The therapist should recognize how people handle and adjust to these events. The early and later phases of life and the tasks that are faced during these times result in either failure or success on many levels. Erikson's (1950, 1959, 1968) first five stages specifically focus on the formation of the person into a competent individual with adequate skills and identity. These stages are sequential, with individuals having to achieve a percentage of accomplishment in one stage before they can proceed to take on the goals of the next (Allen, 1990). The stages and their tasks are as follows:

| Stage | Age | Task |
|---|---|---|
| 1. Trust vs. mistrust | 1st year | Emphasis on satisfying basic physical and emotional needs |
| 2. Autonomy vs. shame/doubt | 2–3 years | Emphasis on exploration and developing self-reliance |

| | | |
|---|---|---|
| 3.  Initiative vs. guilt | 4–5 years | Emphasis on achieving a sense of competence and initiative |
| 4.  Industry vs. inferiority | 6–12 years | Emphasis on setting and attaining personal goals |
| 5.  Identity vs. role confusion | 12–18 years | Emphasis on testing limits, achieving a self-identity |

Gilligan (1982), McGoldrick and Carter (1999), and feminist family therapists have criticized this conceptualization of development because they believe it is centered more on men than women and that it leaves out the importance of relationships and connectedness in individuals' lives. Their points are well made and need to be considered in evaluating Erikson's model.

The last three stages of Erikson's developmental scheme are more interpersonally based and until recently have not been elaborated on much. The processes involved in these final stages are intimacy, generativity, and wisdom. They are tied to and dovetail with family life processes. The satisfaction people receive from intimate relationships goes a long way in influencing what they will do to help prepare the way for the next generation. Intimacy and generativity consequently relate to the total quality of life and how persons integrate overall life experiences in a healthy or unhealthy manner (Allen, 1990). Briefly, these stages can be described as follows:

| Stage | Age | Task |
|---|---|---|
| 6.  Intimacy vs. isolation | 18–35 years | Emphasis on achieving intimate interpersonal relationships |
| 7.  Generativity vs. stagnation | 35–65 years | Emphasis on helping next generation, being productive |
| 8.  Integrity vs. despair | 65+ years | Emphasis on integration of life activities, feeling worthwhile |

According to Erikson (1968), other factors, in addition to the initial achievement of identity, are also important to the formation of a family. These factors, which typically increase as a person matures, are intimacy, productivity, and integration. As individuals grow into adulthood, they are challenged and tested by new conflicts that must be mastered. These conflicts come in the form of interactions with others in leisure and work settings.

## Family Life Development

The **family life cycle** is the term generally used to describe developmental trends within the family over time (Carter & McGoldrick, 1999). This model includes all dimensions of the individual life course but emphasizes the family as a whole. Inherent in this model is tension between the person as an individual and the family as a system. Like other views, the family life cycle emphasizes some stages and aspects of life more than others. Note that what is considered an *appropriate* family life cycle is a social/cultural variable. Therefore, the family life cycle of many families in the United States that is outlined here is not universally accepted worldwide and is subject to change as society changes.

The initial version of the family life cycle was proposed by Evelyn Duvall (1977) in 1956. This model has lost some of its potency over the years as the traditional nuclear families exemplified in it have decreased in number and influence. New models have replaced Duvall's original concept and are more relevant for conceptualizing family life today. Among these are the life cycle of the intact middle-class, nuclear family; the life cycle of the single-parent family; and the life cycle of the blended family. The life cycle of the intact middle-class, nuclear family is highlighted here. (The life cycles of single-parent families and blended families are discussed in Chapters 11 and 12, respectively.)

Carter and McGoldrick (1999) outline a six-stage cycle of the intact middle-class, nuclear family that begins with the unattached adult and continues through retirement. It includes (1) single young adults, leaving home; (2) the new couple; (3) families with young children; (4) families with adolescents; (5) families launching children and moving on; and (6) families in later life. Each of the stages of this life cycle involves key adjustments, tasks, and changes that must be accomplished if the individual, family as a whole, and specific family members are going to survive and thrive. Not all intact nuclear families go through all of the stages in this model. Yet for those who do, the crucial aspects of their lives and the issues they face that might bring them into family therapy can be conceptualized as follows.

## Single Young Adults: Leaving Home

The proportion of single young adults in the United States (i.e., those 18 years and over) is rising. According to the U.S. Census Bureau (1993), approximately 10% of the total population in the United States is composed of never-married adults, a level last reached in the early 1940s. Never marrieds, together with a large number of divorced and widowed persons, make singles a significant part of the adult population in the United States (approximately one third of all people over age 18).

With an increase in singlehood, lifestyles within society are changing with a greater emphasis on individual events. Societal institutions that have been bastions for family-sponsored activities, such as churches, are being reshaped to be more accommodating to singles. The field of family therapy must change by necessity in response to the steady rise of singles. For instance, the importance of treating the individual from a family systems perspective will take on increased importance.

Being a single young adult and leaving home is one stage that individual and family life cycle theorists both emphasize. A major task of this period is to disconnect and reconnect with one's family on a different level while simultaneously establishing one's self as a person (Haley, 1980). Developing such an identity—what Murray Bowen (1978) calls "a 'solid self' (i.e., a sense of one's own beliefs and convictions that are not simply adaptive to others)"—is difficult at best and requires emotional maturity (Gerson, 1995, p. 96).

Being single requires a person to strike a balance between a career and/or marriage ambitions and a desire for personal autonomy. An increasing number of young adults in recent years have tried to achieve such a balance through **cohabitation,** that is, living together without being married. For instance, in 1998 there were 4.2 million couples cohabitating (Bryant, 2000). In fact, at the beginning of the new millenium "more than 50% of opposite-sex couples tying the knot lived together first" (Peterson, 2000b, p. D1).

Cohabitation as an alternative to marriage has both positives and negatives. On the positive side, it allows young adults the freedom to leave a relationship that is not working without becoming involved or embroiled in the legal system. It also allows more individual freedom for the persons involved in the relationship because there is no legal commitment to it. On the negative side, however, cohabitation can undermine marriage. In fact, couples who cohabitate and then marry are more likely to divorce than those who do not (Peterson, 2000b). Regardless, the trend appears to be that cohabitation is going to remain a lifestyle choice of young adults.

Another alternative is remaining single, which is now more accepted than it was in the past. Like cohabitation, its popularity as a lifestyle appears to be growing. Indeed, "the number of never-married men and women doubled or tripled in various age groups since 1970; for example, among people 35 to 39 years old, the rate more than doubled for women (from 5 percent to 13 percent) and tripled for men (from 7 percent to 19 percent)" (Carter & McGoldrick, 1999, p. 13). At the same time only 61% of adult Americans were married compared with a record high of 74% in 1960 (Usdansky, 1992). In 1995, more than 24 million Americans lived alone, and the number is expected to increase to 31 million by 2010 (Carey & Bryant, 1996a).

Singlehood is a viable alternative to marriage. Indeed, singles are usually the second-happiest group (married couples being the happiest), ranking above homosexual couples, unmarried couples, and others. Singlehood can be as fulfilling as marriage, depending on the needs and interests of the individual. Being single and mentally healthy requires that individuals establish social networks, find meaning in their work or avocations, and live a balanced life physically and psychologically. Singles must also develop coping strategies so as not to become distressed (Kleinke, 1991). Living a healthy single life in the United States requires making adjustments to cultural demands and realizing that culture is a phenomenon that one must accommodate.

A major challenge for singles is overcoming internal and external pressures to marry. They must also find ways to deal with loneliness. On the other hand, the personal freedom to choose one's actions is a major attraction and benefit to this style of life.

Issues that are likely to prompt singles to seek family therapy are those connected with:

- a weak personal sense of self
- the inability to emotionally and/or physically separate from one's family of origin
- a lack of social skills to establish significant relationships with others

### The New Couple: Joining of Families Through Marriage

The new-couple relationship begins with courtship, the period when individuals test their compatibility with others through dating. This process may involve a number of partners before one commits to marriage. Secure men tend to become involved with secure women, and anxious women tend to become involved with less committed and more disengaged men (Lopez, 1995). Generally, individuals tend to be most comfortable with others who are at the same or similar developmental level (Santrock, 2000). That is one reason why relationships between dissimilar people rarely last. Environmental, psychological, and situational factors can also hinder people's adjustment to marriage (see Figure 1.2).

In marriage, men seem to benefit the most; their mental health generally improves. However, for women the reverse may occur. Single women, as a rule, have better mental

**Figure 1.2**

Factors that negatively influence marriage.

From *The Changing Family Life Cycle: A Framework for Family Therapy* (2nd ed.) by B. Carter and M. McGoldrick, 1988, Boston: Allyn & Bacon. Copyright © 1988 Allyn & Bacon. Reprinted by permission.

1. The couple meets or marries shortly after a significant loss.
2. One or both partners wish to distance from family of origin.
3. The family backgrounds of each spouse are significantly different (religion, education, social class, ethnicity, age, etc.).
4. The couple has incompatible sibling constellations.
5. The couple resides either extremely close to or at a great distance from either family of origin.
6. The couple is dependent on either extended family financially, physically, or emotionally.
7. The couple marries before age 20 or after age 30.
8. The couple marries after an acquaintanceship of less than 6 months or after more than 3 years of engagement.
9. The wedding occurs without family or friends present.
10. The wife becomes pregnant before or within the first year of marriage.
11. Either spouse has a poor relationship with his or her siblings or parents.
12. Either spouse considers his or her childhood or adolescence as an unhappy time.
13. Marital patterns in either extended family were unstable.

and physical health than their married counterparts (Apter, 1985). The reason is related to a number of variables including the fact that some women who are emotionally unstable may marry, a phenomenon that is not as likely to occur with emotionally unstable men since women do the choosing of marriage partners. In addition, newly married women may cater to the wishes of their husbands at the expense of meeting their own needs.

In general, the early stages of a couple relationship are characterized by idealization. Both men and women in marriage initially idealize each other and relate accordingly. This phenomenon is likely to dissipate naturally to some degree over the course of a marriage. However, some evidence indicates that individuals who report a high level of marital satisfaction also maintain a high level of idealistic distortion about their marriages and spouses—that is, they report them to be better than they actually are (Fowers, Lyons, & Montel, 1996). This quality of seeing each other positively, or through "rose-colored glasses," helps married couples endure. It is just the opposite of those most likely to divorce who see each other through "fogged lenses" and are cynical and unable to say good things about each other (Peterson, 2000a).

Overall, the new-couple stage of the family life cycle is one of adjustment and adaptation. For example, new couples must learn how to share space, meals, and work, leisure, and sleep activities. They must accommodate each other's wishes, requests, and fantasies. This process takes time, energy, goodwill, and the ability to compromise. For example, Bill must understand that his new wife, Maria, takes longer to get dressed than he does. At the same time, Maria must take into consideration that Bill is more meticulous about the upkeep of the house than she is.

It is not surprising that this stage of marriage is one of the most likely times for couples to divorce due to an inability of individuals to resolve differences. It is also often seen as a time of life when couples experience the greatest amount of satisfaction, especially if they later have children (Glenn & McLanahan, 1982). The new couple is free to experiment with life and to engage freely in a wide variety of activities. Financial and time constraints are the two main limitations for couples at this time.

Issues that are likely to prompt new couples to seek family therapy are those connected with:

- the inability to adjust to living as a couple instead of as an individual
- difficulty with relatives, either family of origin or in-laws
- the inability to work through interpersonal issues, such as developing adequate or optimal communication patterns

### Families with Young Children

Becoming a parent is a physical, psychological, and social event that alters a couple's lifestyle dramatically. The arrival of a child has an impact on a couple's lifestyle (e.g., place of residence), marital relationship (e.g., sexual contact), and paternal/maternal stress (e.g., new demands) (Hughes & Noppe, 1991). When a newborn enters a family, the family becomes unbalanced, at least temporarily. Couples have to adjust the time they spend working outside the house, socializing with friends, and engaging in recreational activities. They also have to arrange between themselves who will take responsibility for the child, as well as when, where, and how this responsibility will be met. A crucial task in caring for an infant is ensuring that an enduring attachment bond is created (Bowlby, 1988). In the process of caregiving, a rebalancing occurs between husbands and wives in regard to their investment of time, energy, and focus (Carter, 1999).

After attachment is achieved, families in this stage must accomplish other important tasks, such as those connected with meeting the physical and psychological demands involved in having preschool children. This challenge becomes especially great when both partners within a marriage are working outside the home, which is the case with more than 50% of the couples in the United States with children under the age of 6 (Carter, 1999). In such arrangements, husbands are more involved in child care than the norm, but it is women who still carry the burden of being the primary caregivers (Darling-Fisher & Tiedje, 1990).

Other aspects of family life where adjustments must be made include relationships with extended family, demands of work, use of leisure, and finances. Often there are strains and tension in one or more of these areas. "The strength of the marital bond (i.e., marital satisfaction) goes a long way toward mediating stress and time constraints associated with the presence of children and work" (Giblin, 1994, p. 50). Overall, marital satisfaction tends to go down with each child that is added to a family (see Figure 1.3) (Mattessich & Hill, 1987).

Issues that are likely to prompt families with young children to seek family therapy are those connected with:

**Figure 1.3**

Stressors, strains, and well-being across the family life cycle.

From "Life Cycle and Family Development" by P. Mattessich and R. Hill, in *Handbook of Marriage and the Family* (p. 447), edited by M. Sussman and S. K. Steinmetz, 1987, New York: Plenum. Copyright Plenum Press. Reprinted by permission.

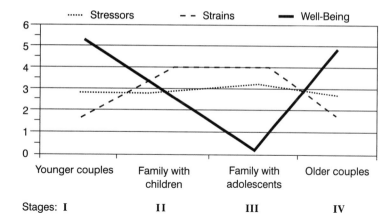

- "the fallout that accompanies the necessary reorganization of relationships and activities" of the married couple
- "the establishment of controls" for a young child (Minuchin, 1995, p. 115)

### Families with Adolescents

Couples who have adolescents must take care of themselves, their relationship, their teenagers, and often their aging parents (Hughes & Noppe,1991). Because of the squeeze they may be in psychologically and physically, they are sometimes referred to as the **sandwich generation.** This is one of the most active and exciting times in the family life cycle. It is filled with turbulence that varies across families (Ellis, 1986). Some families may have trouble setting limits, defining relationships, and taking adequate care of one another. Others do just fine.

The most obvious sign of stress in families with adolescents is seen in the number and kinds of disagreements between parents and teens. Increased family conflict and tension often occur during the time adolescents are in the family (Worden, 1992). The reasons for this increased conflict and tension are numerous. For one,

> . . . in families with adolescents, there seems to be a difficulty on the part of parents to make a distinction between what they want for their youngsters and what their youngsters want for themselves. This leads to parents' unwillingness to let youngsters make decisions for themselves even if they are good decisions. (Dickerson & Zimmerman, 1992, p. 341)

A second reason for the rise of tension in these families is related to the process of adolescence itself. At this time of life, young adults express more of a desire and an assertiveness to be autonomous and independent (Collins, Newman, & McKenry, 1995; Fishman, 1988). Peer groups and siblings become more important for them, and parental influence decreases as conflicts with parents increase. Yet, because adolescents are limited in experience, "they are restrained from seeing the multitude of possibilities available to them and are vulnerable to others' ideas . . . [which they] fight against" (Dickerson & Zimmerman,

1992, p. 344). In response to this situation, families "must establish qualitatively different boundaries. . . . Parents can no longer maintain complete authority" (McGoldrick & Carter, 1982, p. 183). Families with adolescents also need to facilitate the recognition and acceptance of differences of family members.

If all goes well during this time in the family life cycle, adolescents develop what is known as a **planful competence**, which entails having a reasonably realistic understanding of their intellectual abilities, social skills, and personal emotional responses in interrelationship with others (Clausen, 1993). No environmental influence in the preadolescent years is as important to the development of adolescent planful competence as parenting. "Significant influences include parents paying attention to the child, providing intellectual stimulation, being supportive rather than abusive, involving the child in decision making, and conducting consistent disciplining" (Nurse, 1994, p. 36). Fathers who are as involved with their adolescents as mothers help raise psychologically healthier children who exhibit less delinquent behavior and who obtain more education (Elias, 1996).

Yet, parenting may change during this stage as the couple relationship changes. "In the early afternoon of life—the forties, usually—many couples' relationships undergo a kind of sea change. [Either] the partners start to move closer, in ways that were not possible earlier in the marriage, or a huge amount of emotional distance begins to develop" (Scarf, 1992, p. 53). This change is related to the aging process and heightened feelings of vulnerability, "hers, about her desirability and attractiveness; his, about his virility and about physical survival itself" (Scarf, 1992, p. 53). If the couple treat each other with tenderness, empathy, and understanding, they become stronger partners and comfort each other. If, on the other hand, the couple misread each other and do not understand the physiological changes occurring, they are likely to be rejecting and hostile toward each other.

Issues that are likely to prompt families with adolescents to seek family therapy are those connected with:

- conflict between parents and their teenage offspring, such as the setting of limits and the expression of opinions
- detachment or anger over the couple relationship as partners age developmentally and psychologically and realize dreams and opportunities are slipping away
- stress related to the care of aging parents and/or the demands of work and family life

### Launching Children and Moving On

As children leave home for college, careers, marriage, or other options, parents face the so-called **empty nest**—life for couples without child-rearing responsibilities. The percentage of empty nesters is increasing in the United States and will include 59% of all families by 2010, with the aging Baby Boomer generation fueling the trend (Carey & Rechin, 1996b). This time is ideal for couples to rediscover each other and have fun together. It is also a stage of vulnerability where couples may split up.

Most middle-aged women at this stage "are likely to be energetically attending to their own interests and thankful for the freedom to pursue them at last" (Scanzoni & Scanzoni, 1988, p. 535). For some women, who have mainly defined themselves as mothers and invested heavily in their children, the empty nest can be a time of sadness. In such situations, depression, despondency, and divorce may occur (Strong et al., 1998).

For men, the empty nest usually corresponds to midlife. At this time, men may focus on "their physical bodies, marriages, and occupational aspirations," as well as the new changes in the behaviors of their wives (Scanzoni & Scanzoni, 1988, p. 540). Because few studies have focused on men and the empty nest period, few data are available that report on how these men feel about the launching of their children. However, factors that correlate negatively for the happiness of men at the time of launching children are having few children, being older at the time of their children's leaving, experiencing unsatisfactory marriages, and being nurturant as fathers (Lewis, Freneau, & Roberts, 1979).

In recent years, we have seen the trend develop in which children remain with their families of origin for longer periods of time. This failure to leave is usually due to financial problems, unemployment, or an inability or reluctance to grow up (Clemens & Axelson, 1985). When children do not leave home, the result is often increased tension between parents and the young adult. Overall, as pointed out by Haley (1973), pathological behaviors tend to surface at points in the family life cycle when the process of disengagement of one generation from another is prevented or delayed.

Issues that are likely to prompt empty nesters to seek family therapy are those connected with:

- a sense of loss in regard to oneself, a marriage, or the moving out of a child
- a sense of conflict with a child who is not becoming independent enough
- a sense of frustration or anger in regard to one's marriage or career ambitions

### Families in Later Life

The family in later life is usually composed of a couple in their final years of employment or in early retirement. The age range is from about 65 years and above. This stage of family life can cover a span of 20 or 30 years depending on the health of those involved. Within this group are three groups: "the **young old** (65–74), the **old old** (75–84), and the **oldest old** (85 and after)" (Anderson, 1988, p. 19).

A general trend in these families is physical decline and dependency (Goldin & Mohr, 2000). One of the major concerns of some members of this group is finances. Elderly couples often worry about whether they will have enough money to take care of their needs. This concern is heightened when retirement occurs. It may be especially crucial to men who stop working or women who live long lives.

A second equally important concern of elderly couples involves the loss of a spouse. "Only about half of the men and women over sixty-five are married; most of the others are widowed" (Strong et al., 1998). Recovering from the loss of a spouse is a difficult and prolonged process. It is one that women are more likely to face than men. The absence or presence of extended family at such times can make a difference in how one adjusts. The preservation of a coherent sense of self in the midst of loss is the best predictor of psychological and physiological resilience for the elderly (Kaufman, 1986).

A third concern of the aging and their families is chronic illness:

> Among seniors age 65 to 84, arthritis, high blood pressure, and heart disease are most prevalent. For people over 85, the risk of cancer and the extent of disabilities increase, combined with intellectual, visual, and hearing impairment. Physical and mental dete-

rioration may be exacerbated by depression and helplessness, reverberating with the anxiety of family members. (Walsh, 1999, p. 312)

Keeping healthy is a major task of this group.

The aging family also has advantages. One of them is being a grandparent or foster grandparent. Interacting with their children's children or other children heightens the sensitivity of many aging couples and helps them become more aware of the need for caring (Mead, 1972). The ability to do what one wants at one's pace is another advantage of this family stage. The family of later life, like the newly married couple, has the most freedom to come and go as they wish. Finally, the aging family can experience the enjoyment of having lived and participated in a number of important life cycle events. This is a time when couples can reflect on the activities they were too busy with previously.

Issues that are likely to prompt families in later life to seek family therapy are those connected with:

- a lack of meaning or enjoyment related to the loss of actively working or caring for children or the death of a spouse
- a concern over adjustments in aging, such as diminished energy or facing one's own mortality
- an inability to establish good relationships with children, in-laws, or grandchildren

A summary of family life cycle phases, stages, and crises is given in Table 1.1.

# Unifying Individual and Family Life Cycles

At first glance it would appear difficult to unite individual and family life cycles in more than a superficial way. The reason is that, outwardly, stages in the individual life cycle do not always parallel and complement those within a family's development (e.g., Erikson, 1959; Gilligan, 1982; Levinson, 1978, 1986; Sheehy, 1977). The two life cycle concepts are unique because of the number of people involved in them, the diversity of tasks required in each, and gender distinctions. Yet, the differences in these ways of viewing life may not be as sharp or contrasting as they first appear.

One unifying emphasis of both the individual and family life cycle is the focus within each on growth and development. In most types of growth there is "change in the direction of greater awareness, competence, and authenticity" (Jourard & Landsman, 1980, p. 238). Within individuals and families, growth can be a conscious process that involves **courage**, that is, the ability to take calculated risks without knowing the exact consequences. When planned strategies and activities are outlined and accomplished as a part of growth, persons understand the past more thoroughly, live actively and fully in the present, and envision possibilities of the future more clearly.

A second unifier of individual and family life cycles is that they can both be viewed from a systemic perspective. **Systems theory** focuses on the interconnectedness of elements within all living organisms, that is, systems. It is based on the work of Ludwig von Bertalanffy (1968), a biologist, who proposed that to fully understand how a living creature operates, it is necessary to see the interfunctioning of the entire unit. A person and a

**Table 1.1**
Family Life Cycle Phases, Stages, and Crises

| Phases | Family Life Cycle Stage | Practical Challenges | Emotional Challenges | Relational Challenges | Potential Crises |
|---|---|---|---|---|---|
| Coupling | Unattached young adult | Financial independence<br>Caretaking of self | Secure sense of self<br>Feelings of competency | Differentiation of self from family of origin | Failure to grow up |
| | Family formation through coupling | Finding potential mate<br>Economic partnership<br>Domestic cooperation<br>Compatibility of interests | Commitment<br>Balancing needs and expectations of self and partner | Form stable marital unit<br>Shifting allegiances from family of origin to new family | Failure to find a mate or commit<br>End of "honeymoon"<br>In-law conflict |
| Expansion | Family with young children | Financial obligations<br>Organizing household for raising children | Accepting new members<br>Nurturance<br>Parental responsibilities | Maintaining marital unit<br>Integrating grandparents and other relatives | Marital dissatisfaction<br>School and behavior problems |
| | Family with adolescents | Less predictable routines and schedules<br>Adolescent unavailability | Flexibility with change<br>Sense of irrelevance<br>Loss of control | Maintaining contact between parents and adolescent<br>Caring for elderly parents | Adolescent rebellion |
| Contraction | Launching children and moving on | Financial burdens (college, weddings, etc.)<br>New financial resources<br>Refocus on work | Loss of family life with children<br>Aging and death of parents | Reestablishing primacy of marriage<br>Adult relationship with children | "Empty nest"<br>Children returning home |
| | Family in later life | Uncertainties of old age: economic insecurities<br>Medical care | Coping with loss<br>Maintaining dignity despite decline | Maintaining adequate support systems<br>Reconciliation | Retirement<br>Illness and death |

From "The Family Life Cycle: Phases, Stages, and Crises" by R. Gerson, in *Integrating Family Therapy* (p. 96), edited by R. H. Mikesell, D.-D. Lusterman, and S. H. McDaniel, 1995, Washington, DC: American Psychological Association. Copyright © 1995 by the American Psychological Association. Reprinted with permission.

family are more than the separate parts that compose them. They are a whole—a system that expresses itself through an organization, rules, and repetitive patterns.

Therefore, in working with individuals and families, therapists must emphasize **circular causality,** the idea that actions are a part of "a causal chain, each influencing and being influenced by the other" (Goldenberg & Goldenberg, 1998, p. 21). For instance, a mother overprotects her awkward and shy daughter, who stays awkward and shy due to a lack of opportunities to do otherwise, which leads to continued overprotection, which results in more awkwardness and shyness, and so forth. This idea is the opposite of **linear causality,** in which forces are seen as moving in one direction with each action causing another. In linear causality, a mother's overprotection would be targeted as the cause of her daughter's awkwardness and shyness (see Figure 1.4).

A third unifying aspect of the individual and family life cycles is that they are complementary and competitive (McGoldrick, Gerson, & Shellenberger, 1998). People within each cycle go through experiences for which they are usually developmentally ready. For example, children enter school at age 5 or 6. Most couples become parents in their late 20s or early 30s. Likewise, from interacting with their environments, the majority of individuals and families become aware of their skills and abilities. For example, from his play with peers, an adolescent may realize he is not as gifted an athlete as he previously thought. Similarly, family members may appreciate each other more from having survived a natural trauma, such as an earthquake, a hurricane, or a fire (Figley, 1989).

In the competitive realm, the needs and desires of individuals within the family and the needs of the family to sustain itself often differ. For example, a young couple might want to visit friends or relatives, but are distracted by the demands of their toddler who might prefer running around their host's house. A second area of conflict involves launching young people into the world. Sometimes these individuals are hesitant to go and resist leaving home (Haley, 1980). Both the family and the young adults suffer in the struggle that ensues.

# Implications of Life Cycles for Family Therapy

Life cycles have a number of implications regarding family therapy. Some are more subtle than others, but all are important.

**Figure 1.4**
**Linear versus circular thinking.**

Linear causality

Circular causality

## Match of Life Cycles Between Family and Therapist

The "fit" between a family's and a therapist's life cycles plays a major role in the process of helping a family change. Fit is an ever changing variable that fluctuates according to the ages and stages of all involved in the therapeutic process. If a therapist "brings unresolved issues from a past or current life cycle stage into the clinical work with a family that is struggling to navigate the same life cycle stage, predictable problems may emerge" (Lerner, 1999, p. 512). Basically, the life cycles of a therapist and family can combine in three major ways: "(1) the therapist has not yet experienced the family's stage; (2) the therapist is currently experiencing the same stage of the life cycle as the family; and (3) the therapist has already been through that stage of the life cycle" (Simon, 1988, p. 108). While each of these global factors presents its own unique challenge, specific variables have an impact too. "The match between the therapist and the clinical family on variables such as race, ethnicity, gender, class, sibling position, and sexual orientation" must be considered for they also "influence the degree to which the life cycle issues become emotionally loaded in therapy" (Lerner, 1999, p. 513).

Particular problematic areas include the ability to express empathy and understanding, or to establish rapport. These difficulties may be especially prevalent in cases where the therapist has not yet experienced the family's stage of development or where the therapist lacks awareness of matters related to variables such as ethnicity, class, or sexual orientation. Contempt, anxiety, or jealousy may interfere with therapists whose life cycles parallel families with whom they work or who may be of the same race or gender. On the other hand, "fit with families gets a little easier" as therapists get older and past crucial life stages (Simon, 1988, p. 110). In such circumstances, families may feel that therapists recognize and understand their problems better. However, on the downside, therapists who are beyond the life stage of their client families may have difficulties in regard to acting too knowledgeable, being out of touch with current realities, dealing with ghosts of their own pasts, and being "distant, cynical, or patronizing" (Simon, 1988, p. 111).

To compensate for a lack of fit between themselves and the families they are working with, therapists of all ages and backgrounds can do several things. First, they can work on increasing their sensitivity to particular families and issues with such families. Each family differs, and therapists, regardless of age and background, can usually be helpful if they are attuned to the specific concerns of a family. Second, therapists who do not ideally fit certain families can have their work supervised. Often, through peer consultation and clinical supervision, family therapists learn ways to overcome their deficits. Finally, a lack of fit can be addressed by continuing education programs that give therapists greater knowledge and skill in dealing with specific types of families or variables.

## Ethnicity and Life Cycles

The ethnic background of families influences their concept of life cycles and their behaviors in regard to life events. It is important for clinicians to evaluate families in relation to their ethnic background and to not judge them from a limited cultural perspective (Hines et al., 1999). For example, different ethnic groups place more value on certain events and rituals, such as funerals, weddings, and transitions from childhood to adulthood. Types of interaction dominant in a majority culture, such as among Americans of European descent, may not be considered appropriate in a minority culture, such as among African Americans or Asian Americans.

In therapeutic situations, families become more attuned to their ethnic backgrounds and values. In family therapy it is important to encourage families to use their life cycle transitions to strengthen individual, family, and cultural identities (Hines et al., 1999). Through such a process, families and their members gain a greater appreciation of and sensitivity to their heritage and the role of the past in present-day life.

Family therapists, regardless of their cultural backgrounds, can work with a variety of families if they attune themselves to learning about the culture and the circumstances from whence these families came. Therapists must acquire special skills as well, through both formal training and continuing education. Finally, therapists must realize that, regardless of their best efforts, gender and ethnicity differences between themselves and their clients may enhance or detract from the therapeutic experience, at least initially (Gregory & Leslie, 1996).

## Illness and Life Cycles

The onset of an illness in a family member can disrupt life cycles temporarily or permanently. If the illness is acute and of short duration, the person and family may suffer only a mild setback. However, if the illness is more severe, such as AIDS or cancer, the family and its members may be adversely affected. Therefore, in examining illness and life cycles, therapists must examine the onset of the disorder, its course, the outcome, and its degree of incapacitation, if any (Rolland, 1999). For example, a progressive and chronic disease, such as Alzheimer's, can put a major strain on caretakers within a family and the family as a whole. The result may be the delay of life cycle transitions, such as marriage, and the blockage of unfinished business.

Therapeutically, it is imperative that those who work with families help them assess present ways of functioning in relationships as compared with past coping strategies (Rolland, 1999). For example, a therapist may explore with family members how they previously dealt with a family illness. Thus, therapists may better understand present family behaviors and the individuals within them. Therapists may also assist families in resolving the developmental disruptions that occur in dealing with diseases. There is a growing movement in family therapy to focus on mental and physical issues in families (Wynne, Shields, & Sirkin, 1992). To work best in this domain, family therapists must prepare themselves through direct educational and supervisory experiences.

## Poverty, Professionalism, and Life Cycles

As indicated throughout this chapter, individuals and families are affected by economic as well as social factors. Dual-career professional families and low-income families do not go through life cycle stages in the same way or at the same rate as other families. There is an "extreme elongation of the process of forming the family in the professional class and an extreme acceleration in the lower class" (Fulmer, 1988, p. 548).

Poverty and professionalism have several implications for family therapy. One of the most obvious is for therapists to realize that the structure of these two types of families differs. *Fam-*

*ilies in poverty* are generally larger, more dependent on kin, and maternal. Continuing poverty pushes fathers away from their children and families because these men are often working two or three jobs and are simply not available (Elias, 1996). In contrast, *families of professionals* are generally smaller, dependent on hired help, and often more individual or career focused. They can afford to buy services and engage in a number of enriching activities.

In addition to structural differences, symptom formation differs, with symptoms in poor families often connected with sudden shifts and changes in life cycle events and symptoms in professional families often connected with delays in reaching developmental mile-stones. The comparison of family life stages for these two types of families from ages 12 to 35 is shown in Table 1.2, as outlined by Fulmer (1988). Therapists must acquaint themselves with the issues of both types of families. To be of assistance to each, they must cognitively and psychologically learn to address their unique problems and possibilities.

**Table 1.2**
Comparison of Family Life Cycle Stages

| Age | Professional Families | Low-Income Families |
|---|---|---|
| 12–17 | a. Prevent pregnancy<br>b. Graduate from high school<br>c. Parents continue support while permitting child to achieve greater independence | a. First pregnancy<br>b. Attempt to graduate from high school<br>c. Parent attempts strict control before pregnancy; after pregnancy, relaxation of controls and continued support of new mother and infant |
| 18–21 | a. Prevent pregnancy<br>b. Leave parental household for college<br>c. Adapt to parent–child separation | a. Second pregnancy<br>b. No further education<br>c. Young mother acquires adult status in parental household |
| 22–25 | a. Prevent pregnancy<br>b. Develop professional identity in graduate school<br>c. Maintain separation from parental household; begin living in serious relationship | a. Third pregnancy<br>b. Marriage—leave parental household to establish stepfamily<br>c. Maintain connection with kinship network |
| 26–30 | a. Prevent pregnancy<br>b. Marriage—develop nuclear couple as separate from parents<br>c. Intense work involvement as career begins | a. Separate from husband<br>b. Mother becomes head of own household within kinship network |
| 31–35 | a. First pregnancy<br>b. Renew contact with parents as grandparents<br>c. Differentiate career and child-rearing roles between husband and wife | a. First grandchild<br>b. Mother becomes grandmother and cares for daughter and infant |

From "Lower-Income and Professional Families: A Comparison of Structure and Life Cycle Process" by R. H. Fulmer, in *The Changing Family Life Cycle: A Framework for Family Therapy* (2nd ed., p. 551), edited by B. Carter and M. McGoldrick, 1988, Boston: Allyn & Bacon. Copyright © 1988 Allyn & Bacon. Reprinted by permission.

# Summary and Conclusion

This chapter has examined the family from an historical and contemporary viewpoint. Historically, families have been around since before recorded time. They have served a number of functions including social, economic, and reproductive—many of the same purposes served by contemporary families. Yet, today there are more family forms (dual career, gay/lesbian, aging, etc.) and more opinions on what constitutes a family. A family may be considered in its broadest context those persons who are biologically and/or psychologically related whose historical, emotional, or economic bonds connect and who perceive themselves as a part of a household. The three most prevalent family forms are nuclear, single parent, and remarried.

Different models of individual and family life cycles have been constructed over the years to explain tasks and potential problems of people and family units. Erik Erikson first popularized the idea of an individual life cycle through his research and writings on the eight stages of life. His work has been praised for its innovation but criticized for its limited focus on males. The idea of a family life cycle was first proposed by Evelyn Duvall, only a few years after Erikson's model was introduced. Duvall's model was based on the nuclear family of the 1950s. In more recent years, as families in the United States have become more diverse, varied models of family life cycles have been proposed. The cycles of Carter and McGoldrick (1999), which cover many different forms of family life, are among the most useful. This chapter presented the six-stage model of the intact, middle-class nuclear family. This model is used for comparison with other life cycle models, including Erikson's individual life cycle model.

Individual and family life cycles intertwine at times. Events in one impact those in the other. Individual and family life cycles are similar in their emphasis on growth, development, and systemic interaction. However, they often differ in emphasis, with individual life cycles focused more narrowly and family life cycles focused more systemically. Family therapists must be aware of individual issues, as well as family issues, that are brought before them.

As a rule, family therapists should be aware of how their own individual and family life stages compare with those of their clients. They must also be sensitive to health, ethnic/cultural, and socioeconomic issues as they relate to families. A general systems perspective of individuals and families allows for such a broad-based view. It permits therapists to observe dynamics within the system of the person and family without blaming or focusing on unimportant micro-issues. Family therapists can study and receive supervision to overcome deficits they may have in regard to issues surrounding a particular type of family. Overall, the family life cycle and the variables that compose it are exciting to study and complex entities with which to work.

# Summary Table

## Individual and Family Life Cycles

Families date back to prehistoric times and have played an important part in the development of persons and nations.

Social and economic forces, wars, national policies, and natural disasters have modified the structure and governance of families.

Families must be worked with from a developmental, systemic, and historical perspective. The dynamics of external and internal pressures and interactions should be taken into consideration.

## What Is a Family?

The definition of a family varies across cultural settings and often changes. However, despite definitions, the family is a system with members impacting one another in an interactive and circular way.

The U.S. Bureau of the Census (1993, p. 5) gives a broad definition of a family as "a group of two or more persons related by birth, marriage, or adoption and residing together in a household." However, this definition excludes some relationships that people consider families.

For this text, a family is defined broadly as those persons who are biologically and/or psychologically related whom historical, emotional, or economic bonds connect and who perceive themselves as a part of a household.

Overall, families are characterized by economic, physical, social, and emotional functions. They foster development and offer stability.

Among the different types of families are nuclear, single parent, remarried, dual career, childless, gay/lesbian, aging, and multigenerational.

## Individual and Family Development

Development is an uneven and powerful factor in families.

Three different time dimensions affect personal and family life: individual time, social time, and historical time.

The term *life cycle* is used to describe personal and family life development. These two life cycles intertwine and are interactional. Dealing with them in isolation would be artificial.

Individual life cycle development has been popularized in the work of Erikson and others who describe human life in terms of stages. People face developmental crises in each of these stages.

The first five stages Erikson describes deal with the formation of a person as a competent individual. His final three stages are more interpersonally based.

Developmental theories have focused mainly on men, but are slowly being formulated for women as well.

The family life cycle is a social/cultural phenomenon that was first proposed by Duvall in 1956. It has been modified over the years, and currently life cycles are available that describe many types of families.

A family life cycle for middle-class, nuclear families proposed by Carter and McGoldrick outlines the following six stages:

1. *Single young adults—tasks:* to develop personal autonomy, leave home, establish a career, and develop a support group

2. *The new couple—tasks:* to adjust and adapt, and learn to share with partner
3. *Families with young children—tasks:* to adjust time, energy, and personal schedules to take care of child[ren], self, and other relationships
4. *Families with adolescents—tasks:* to physically and psychologically take care of self, couple relationship, child[ren], and aging parents, and successfully handle increased family tension and conflict
5. *Families launching children and moving on—tasks:* to rediscover each other as a couple, deal with midlife events, and let child go
6. *Families in later life—tasks:* to adjust to aging, loss of a spouse, and decreased energy

### Unifying Individual and Family Life Cycles

Individual and family life cycles are characterized by:

- growth and development
- systemic interconnectedness of people
- complementary and competitive experiences occurring within a societal context

### Implications of Life Cycles for Family Therapy

Life cycles impact family therapy through:

- the matching or fitting of the therapist's life stage(s) with that of the family
- the understanding, or lack thereof, between the therapist's ethnic background and that of the family
- the influence of the unexpected, such as an illness, on the stage development of the family/individual
- the uniqueness of poverty or professionalism on the rate of recovery and the resources of the family as therapy progresses

Family therapists can overcome developmental or systemic handicaps in regard to families through education, supervision, consultation, and experience.

# References

Allen, B. P. (1990). *Personal adjustment.* Pacific Grove, CA: Brooks/Cole.

Anderson, D. (1988, July/August). The quest for a meaningful old age. *Family Therapy Networker, 12,* 16–22, 72–75.

Apter, T. (1985). *Why women don't have wives.* New York: Schocken.

Bateson, G. (1971). The cybernetics of "self": A theory of alcoholism. *Psychiatry, 34,* 1–18.

Bertalanffy, L. von (1968). *General systems theory: Foundation, development, and application.* New York: Braziller.

Bird, G., & Sporakowski, M. J. (1992). Introduction. In G. Bird & M. J. Sporakowski (Eds.), *Taking sides: Clashing views on controversial issues in family and personal relationships* (pp. x–xv). Guilford, CT: Dushkin Publishing.

Bowen, M. (1978). *Family therapy in clinical practice.* New York: Jason Aronson.

Bowlby, J. (1988). *A secure base: Parent/child attachment and healthy human development.* New York: Basic Books.

Bryant, W. (2000, April 18). Number of unmarried couples cohabitating continues to increase. *USA Today,* p. D1.

Burr, W. R., Hill, R., Nye, F. I., & Reiss, I. L. (1979). *Contemporary theories about the family.* New York: The Free Press.

Carey, A. R., & Bryant, W. (1996a, June 25). Living alone. *USA Today,* p. A1.

Carey, A. R., & Rechin, K. (1996b, July 5). Nation of "empty nests." *USA Today*, p. A1.

Carter, B. (1999). Becoming parents: The family with young children. In B. Carter & M. McGoldrick (Eds.), *The expanded family life cycle* (3rd ed., pp. 249–273). Boston: Allyn & Bacon.

Carter, B., & McGoldrick, M. (1999). *The expanded family life cycle* (3rd ed.). Boston: Allyn & Bacon.

Cavan, R. S. (1969). *The American family* (4th ed.). New York: Thomas Y. Crowell Co.

Clausen, J. A. (1993). *American lives*. New York: Free Press.

Clemens, A., & Axelson, L. (1985). The not-so-empty-nest: The return of the fledgling adult. *Family Relations, 34*, 259–264.

Collins, W. E., Newman, B. M., & McKenry, P. C. (1995). Intrapsychic and interpersonal factors related to adolescent psychological well-being in stepmother and stepfather families. *Journal of Family Psychology, 9*, 433–445.

Coontz, S. (1992). *The way we never were: American families and the nostalgia trap*. New York: Basic Books.

Coontz, S. (1997). *The way we really are: Coming to terms with America's changing families*. New York: Basic Books.

Darling-Fisher, C. S., & Tiedje, L. B. (1990). The impact of maternal employment characteristics on fathers' participation in child care. *Family Relations, 39*, 20–26.

Dickerson, V. C., & Zimmerman, J. (1992). Families with adolescents: Escaping problem lifestyles. *Family Process, 31*, 341–353.

Duvall, E. (1977). *Marriage and family development* (5th ed.). Philadelphia: Lippincott.

Elder, G. H., Jr. (1975). Age differentiation and the life course. *Annual Review of Sociology, 1*, 165–190.

Elias, M. (1996, August 22). Teens do better when dads are more involved. *USA Today*, p. D1.

Ellis, G. F. (1986). Societal and parental predictors of parent–adolescent conflict. In G. K. Leigh & G. W. Peterson (Eds.), *Adolescents in families* (pp. 155–178). Cincinnati: South-Western Publishing.

Erikson, E. H. (1950). *Childhood and society*. New York: Norton.

Erikson, E. H. (1959). *Identity and the life cycle: Psychological issues*. New York: International Universities Press.

Erikson, E. H. (1968). *Identity: Youth and crisis*. New York: Norton.

Figley, C. R. (1989). *Helping traumatized families*. San Francisco: Jossey-Bass.

Fishman, H. (1988). *Treating troubled adolescents*. New York: Basic Books.

Fowers, B. J., Lyons, E. M., & Montel, K. H. (1996). Positive marital illusions: Self-enhancement or relationship enhancement? *Journal of Family Psychology, 10*, 192–208.

Framo, J. L. (1996). A personal retrospective of the family therapy field: Then and now. *Journal of Marital and Family Therapy, 22*, 289–316.

Fulmer, R. H. (1988). Lower-income and professional families: A comparison of structure and life cycle process. In B. Carter & M. McGoldrick (Eds.), *The changing family life cycle* (2nd ed., pp. 545–578). New York: Gardner.

Gerson, R. (1995). The family life cycle: Phases, stages, and crises. In R. H. Mikesell, D. Lusterman, & S. H. McDaniel (Eds.), *Integrating family therapy* (pp. 91–112). Washington, DC: American Psychological Association.

Giblin, P. (1994). Marital satisfaction. *The Family Journal, 2*, 48–50.

Gilbert, L. A. (1994) Current perspectives on dual-career families. *Current Directions in Psychological Science, 3*, 101–105.

Gilligan, C. (1982). *In a different voice: Psychological theory and women's development*. Cambridge, MA: Harvard University Press.

Gladding, S. T. (1993). *Nervous beginnings*. Unpublished manuscript.

Gladding, S. T. (2000). *Counseling: A comprehensive profession* (4th ed.). Upper Saddle River, NJ: Merrill/Prentice Hall.

Glenn, N., & McLanahan, S. (1982). Children and marital happiness: A further specification of the relationship. *Journal of Marriage and the Family, 43*, 63–72.

Goldenberg, H., & Goldenberg, I. (1998). *Counseling today's families* (3rd ed.). Pacific Grove, CA: Brooks/Cole.

Goldin, E., & Mohr, R. (2000). Issues and techniques for counseling long-term, later-life couples. *The Family Journal, 8*, 229–235.

Gould, R. L. (1972). The phases of adult life: A study in developmental psychology. *American Journal of Psychiatry, 129*, 521–531.

Gould, R. L. (1978). *Transformations*. New York: Simon and Schuster.

Gregory, M. A., & Leslie, L. A. (1996). Different lenses: Variations in clients' perception of family therapy by race and gender. *Journal of Marital and Family Therapy, 22*, 239–251.

Haley, J. (1973). *Uncommon therapy: The psychiatric techniques of Milton Erickson, M.D.* New York: Norton.

Haley, J. (1980). *Leaving home*. New York: McGraw-Hill.

Harrigan, M. P. (1992). Advantages and disadvantages of multigenerational family households: Views of three generations. *Journal of Applied Gerontology, 11*, 457–474.

Hines, P., & Boyd-Franklin, N. (1996). African American families. In M. McGoldrick, J. Giordano, & J. K. Pearce (Eds.), *Ethnicity and family therapy* (2nd ed.). New York: Guilford.

Hines, P. M., Preto, N. G., McGoldrick, M., Almeida, R., & Weltman, S. (1999). Culture and the family life cycle. In B. Carter & M. McGoldrick (Eds.) *The expanded family life cycle* (3rd ed., pp. 69–87). Boston: Allyn & Bacon.

Hughes, F. P., & Noppe, L. D. (1991). *Human development across the life span*. Upper Saddle River, NJ: Merrill/Prentice Hall.

Johnson, T. W., & Colucci, P. (1999). Lesbians, gay men, and the family life cycle. In B. Carter & M. McGoldrick (Eds.), *The expanded family life cycle* (3rd ed., pp. 346–361). Boston: Allyn & Bacon.

Jourard, S. M., & Landsman, T. (1980). *Healthy personality* (4th ed.). New York: Macmillan.

Kaufman, S. R. (1986). *The ageless self: Sources of meaning in later life.* Madison, WI: University of Wisconsin Press.

Klein, W. (Ed.). (1992). *Austria.* Singapore: Hofer Press.

Kleinke, C. L. (1991). *Coping with life challenges.* Pacific Grove, CA: Brooks/Cole.

Lerner, S. (1999). Interactions between the therapist's and client's life cycle stages. In B. Carter & M. McGoldrick (Eds.), *The expanded life cycle* (3rd ed., pp. 512–519). Boston: Allyn & Bacon.

Levinson, D. J. (1978). *The seasons of a man's life.* New York: Knopf.

Levinson, D. J. (1986). A conception of adult development. *American Psychologist, 41,* 3–13.

Lewis, R., Freneau, P., & Roberts, C. (1979). Fathers and the postparental transition. *Family Coordinator, 28,* 514–520.

Lopez, F. G. (1995). Attachment theory as an integrative framework for family counseling. *The Family Journal, 3,* 11–17.

Mattessich, P., & Hill, R. (1987). Life cycle and family development. In M. B. Sussman & S. K. Steinmetz (Eds.), *Handbook of marriage and the family* (p. 447). New York: Plenum.

McGoldrick, M., & Carter, E. A. (1982). The family life cycle. In F. Walsh (Ed.), *Normal family processes* (pp. 167–195). New York: Guilford.

McGoldrick, M., & Carter, B. (1999). Self in context. In B. Carter & M. McGoldrick (Eds.), *The expanded family life cycle* (3rd ed., pp. 27–46). Boston: Allyn & Bacon.

McGoldrick, M., Gerson, R., & Shellenberger, S. (1998). *Genograms in family assessment* (2nd ed.). New York: Norton.

McGoldrick, M., & Walsh, F. (1999). Death and the family life cycle. In B. Carter & M. McGoldrick (Eds.), *The expanded family life cycle* (3rd ed., pp. 185–201). Boston: Allyn & Bacon.

Mead, M. (1972). *Blackberry winter.* New York: Morrow.

Minuchin, P. (1995). Children and family therapy: Mainstream approaches and the special care of the multicrisis poor. In R. H. Mikesell, D. Lusterman, & S. H. McDaniel (Eds.), *Integrating family therapy* (pp. 113–140). Washington, DC: American Psychological Association.

Nurse, A. R. (1994, Spring). A 60-year study of normals through time: Implications for practice. *The Family Psychologist, 10,* 35–36, 38.

Okun, B. F. (1984). *Working with adults: Individual, family, and career development.* Pacific Grove, CA: Brooks/Cole.

Orthner, D. K., Bowen, G. L., & Beare, V. G. (1990). The organization family: A question of work and family boundaries. *Marriage and family review, 15,* 15–36.

Peterson, K. S. (2000a, March 30). Sweet nothings help marriages stick. *USA Today,* p. A1.

Peterson, K. S. (2000b, April 18). Changing the shape of the American family. *USA Today,* pp. D1, D2.

Rolland, J. S. (1999). Chronic illness and the family life cycle. In B. Carter & M. McGoldrick (Eds.), *The expanded family life cycle* (3rd ed., pp. 492–512). Boston: Allyn & Bacon.

Santrock, J. W. (2000). *Life-span development.* New York: Brown & Benchmark.

Sayger, T. V., Homrich, A. M., & Horne, A. M. (2000). Working from a family focus. In A. M. Horne (Ed.)., *Family counseling and therapy* (pp. 12–40). Itasca, IL: F. E. Peacock.

Scanzoni, L. D., & Scanzoni, J. (1988). *Men, women, and change* (3rd ed.). New York: McGraw-Hill.

Scarf, M. (1992, July/August). The middle of the journey. *Family Therapy Networker, 16,* 51–55.

Schwartz, R. C. (1999). Narrative therapy expands and contracts family therapy's horizons. *Journal of Marital and Family Therapy, 25,* 263–267.

Sheehy, G. (1977). *Passages.* New York: Bantam.

Sheehy, G. (1981). *Pathfinders.* New York: Bantam.

Simon, R. M. (1988). Family life cycle issues in the therapy system. In B. Carter & M. McGoldrick (Eds.), *The changing family life cycle* (2nd ed., pp. 107–117). New York: Gardner.

Stevenson, H. C. (1994, Spring). Research on African-American family life: Learning to interpret the dance. *The Family Psychologist, 10,* 38–40, 46.

Strong, B., & DeVault, C. (1986). *The marriage and family experience* (3rd ed.). St. Paul, MN: West Publishing.

Strong, B., DeVault, C., & Sayad, B. W. (1998). *The marriage and family experience: Intimate relationships in a changing society* (7th ed.). Belmont, CA: Wadsworth.

Thomas, V. G. (1990). Determinants of global life happiness and marital happiness in dual-career black couples. *Family Relations, 39,* 174–178.

U.S. Bureau of the Census. (1993). *Statistical abstract of the United States, 1993* (113th ed.). Washington, DC: U.S. Government Printing Office.

Usdansky, M. L. (1992, July 17). Wedded to the single life. *USA Today,* p. 8A.

Walsh, F. (1999). Families in later life: Challenges and opportunities. In B. Carter & M. McGoldrick (Eds.), *The expanded family life cycle* (3rd ed., pp. 307–326). Boston: Allyn & Bacon.

Worden, M. (1992). *Adolescents and their families.* New York: Haworth Press.

Wynne, L. C., Shields, C. G., & Sirkin, M. I. (1992). Illness, family theory, and family therapy: I. Conceptual issues. *Family Process, 31,* 3–18.

# Healthy and Dysfunctional Characteristics of Families

Amid the white sterility of intensive care
and the cries of incubated newborns
I watch your parents struggle in the quiet realization
that your life hangs by a thread too thin to sustain it.

Tenuously you fight to hold onto every breath
until peacefully, in your father's arms,
you give up in exhaustion
and with a final release, almost like a whisper,
air leaves your lungs forever.

Your mother has said her gentle good-byes
only hours after your birth
with her dreams turning into nightmares
as she contemplates her loss in the thought
of going home to silence.

Life, like faith, is sometimes fragile
best personified in newness and simple acts of courage.

*Gladding, 1992*

**F**amily life is constantly changing, and what is considered functional and healthy in one era is not necessarily seen the same way later. For instance, in the 1890s, there was widespread agreement among white, middle-class Americans within urban centers in the United States that a healthy and functional family was patriarchal (Footlick, 1990). Fathers were bread winners and rule makers; mothers were bread makers and caregivers. This type of picture is still attractive to some people, but realistically there are, and always have been, various forms of functional families (Coontz, 2000). In fact, what were once considered nontraditional family forms (e.g., single-parent and remarried) now outnumber nuclear families.

Regardless of form, the health of families varies over their life spans. The fact that a family is healthy at one stage of life of its existence is no guarantee that it will remain that way (Carlson & Fullmer, 1992; Carter & McGoldrick, 1999). In fact, achieving and maintaining health demands constant work for members of a family unit as well as the family as a whole.

Numerous events can throw families into new or unexpected ways of functioning. When such events occur, family relationships are altered and the family as a whole is shaken up. "Destabilizing events create stress to which family systems can react in different ways. Some systems respond by transforming the rules under which they operate, thereby allowing new, more functional behaviors. In other systems, rather than changing shape, a medical or psychological symptom emerges" (Fishman, 1988, p. 15). Healthy families reorganize their structure and relationships to accommodate new circumstances. This type of readjustment keeps these families from becoming chaotic (Cuber & Harroff, 1966).

This chapter examines qualities associated with healthy and dysfunctional families. First, the family as a living system will be explored in regard to its well-being and growth. This exploration will be followed by a discussion of the qualities of healthy families. Next family stressors, both expected and unexpected, are looked at in regard to their impact on families, and the influence of family structure on functionality is considered. Coping strategies for dealing with family stress are highlighted, too. Finally, the implications of health (especially mental health) in working with families are featured.

# The Family System and Health

As briefly examined in Chapter 1, systems theory is the basis on which most family therapists view families and around which they organize their clinical work. The theory was refined and developed by Ludwig von Bertalanffy (1934, 1968), a biologist, in an attempt to explain how organisms thrive or die in accordance with their openness or closedness to their environments (Kaplan, 2000). Bertalanffy "saw the essential phenomena of life as individual entities called 'organisms'" (Okun & Rappaport, 1980, p. 6). He defined an

**organism** as a form of life "composed of mutually dependent parts and processes standing in mutual interaction" (Bertalanffy, 1968, p. 33). As such, an organism was primarily motivated behaviorally by internal mechanisms. From Bertalanffy's work, social scientists conceptualized that all living systems, including families, operate on a similar set of principles, that is, they are internally interdependent.

Therefore, in a family, members are constantly interacting and mutually affecting one another as they are in relationship to each other. When change or movement occurs in any of the members or circumstances that make up the family system, all aspects of the family are affected for better or worse. Thus, the family's well-being and ability to function are influenced by the health of all of its members.

From a healthy systems perspective, families are continuously changing and reconstituting themselves. Those that stay healthy are open and self-regulating. They are also interactive within larger social systems. The family stabilizes and changes by using negative **feedback** loops (morphostasis) (see Figure 2.1). These loops, like a thermostat in a home heating system, allow family expansion and contraction within the limits of a range of behaviors. If for some reason the negative feedback loops do not work, the family becomes out of control and dysfunctional. Times of stability and homeostasis are temporary, and a major task for families is to maintain a balance between change and stability. If there is too much of either, the family and those within it suffer:

> Viewing families as systems involves recognizing that the relationships formed among family members are extremely powerful and account for a considerable amount of

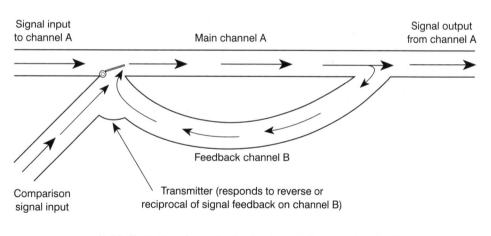

Signal input to channel A

Main channel A

Signal output from channel A

Feedback channel B

Comparison signal input

Transmitter (responds to reverse or reciprocal of signal feedback on channel B)

In this illustration of negative feedback, part of a system's output is reintroduced into the system as information about the output, thus governing and correcting the process. A negative signal from channel A, fed back to the sender through channel B, alters the signal in A. Feedback loops characterize all interpersonal relationships.

**Figure 2.1**
Negative feedback loops.
From "The Nature of Living Systems" by J. G. Miller, 1971, *Behavioral Sciences, 16,* p. 293. Reprinted by permission of the Mental Health Research Institute.

human behavior, emotion, values, and attitudes. Moreover, like strands of a spider web, each family relationship, as well as each family member, influences all other family relationships and all other members. (Figley, 1989, p. 4)

# Qualities of Healthy Families

Studies reveal that functional families are able to adapt to change, set appropriate boundaries, develop relationships through open communication, promote responsibility, express confidence in themselves and their children, and are optimistic about their future (Cutler & Radford, 1999). Yet, there is still disagreement as to all of the qualities of ideal healthy families. In fact, there is even a fundamental disagreement about what the word *health* means. **Health** is an interactive process associated with positive relationships and outcomes (Wilcoxon, 1985). In families health involves ethical accountability, such as when good relationships exist and there is a balance of give and take among members (Boszormenyi-Nagy & Ulrich, 1981). Most families experience times of both healthy and unhealthy interactions during the family life cycle.

In regard to health, one cannot assume that healthy individuals necessarily come from continuously healthy families (Wolin & Wolin, 1993). In fact, highly resilient individuals who successfully overcome adversities do best in life (Walsh, 1995). However, being in a healthy family environment is an advantage for learning productive relationships and is more helpful than not.

As a group, *healthy families* have a number of characteristics in common. Families that are most successful, happy, and strong are balanced in a number of ways. For example, they seem to know what issues to address and how to address them. Furthermore, they do not operate from either an extreme cognitive or emotional framework. They exert the right amount of energy in dealing with the matters before them, and they make realistic plans. Overall, in families with a sense of well-being, multiple forces and factors interact in complex but positive ways. One of the most vital of these factors is the strength of the marital unit (Beavers, 1985; Lavee, McCubbin, & Olson, 1987). A healthy marriage is intimate, flexible, and even synergistic (Olson & Olson, 2000). In such a relationship, partners adapt to and promote the individual growth of each other. If couples get along and work at keeping the marriage exciting and open, chances are greatly improved that the family will be well and do well, too.

A number of aspects seem to distinguish healthy families from those who function less well (McCoy, 1996). According to research (Krysan, Moore, & Zill, 1990; Stinnett & DeFrain, 1985), healthy families include the following characteristics:

- commitment to the family and its individuals
- appreciation for each other (i.e., a social connection)
- willingness to spend time together
- effective communication patterns
- high degree of religious/spiritual orientation
- ability to deal with crisis in a positive manner (i.e., adaptability)
- encouragement of individuals
- clear roles

The following sections address these characteristics, along with the importance of structure and development within families.

## Commitment

At the core of healthy family functioning is the idea of commitment. "In strong families, members are devoted not only to the welfare of the family but also to the growth of each of the members" (Thomas, 1992, p. 62). A commitment to the family is the basis for family members giving their time and energy to family-related activities.

Commitment involves staying loyal to the family and its members through both good and adverse life events. It is based on both emotion and intention. Couples and individuals who have not thought through their commitment to one another or who are ambivalent about how committed they are have difficulty staying in a marriage and working with each other. The result is often infidelity (Pittman, 1991).

## Appreciation

The commitment that family members have toward one another is strengthened when they verbally or physically express their appreciation. In healthy families, "the marital partners tend to build the self-esteem of their mates by mutual love, respect, [and] compliments" (Thomas, 1992, p. 64). Other family members do likewise with each other. They avoid fights that take the form of personal attacks or violence (Wills, Weiss, & Patterson, 1974).

## Willingness to Spend Time Together

Healthy families spend both quantitative and qualitative time together. "The time they spend together needs to be good time; no one enjoys hours of bickering, arguing, pouting, or bullying. Time also needs to be sufficient; quality interaction isn't likely to develop in a few minutes together" (Stinnett & DeFrain, 1985, pp. 83–84).

Events that encompass both qualitative and quantitative time abound. They range from family picnics to overnight campouts, to vacations, to special nights out that involve entertainment such as a play, ball game, or concert. They also encompass rituals and traditions such as celebrating birthdays and anniversaries, family interactions at mealtimes, and observing rites of passage together such as graduations, weddings, and funerals (Giblin, 1995). The idea behind spending time together is sharing thoughts, feelings, and identities. In the process, family members come to think of themselves as a cohesive unit and not just a random group of individuals.

## Effective Communication Patterns

"Communication is concerned with the delivery and reception of verbal and nonverbal information between family members. It includes skills in exchanging patterns of information within the family system" (Brock & Barnard, 1999, p. 36). When families are healthy, members attend to the messages from one another and pick up on subtle as well as obvious points. Within these families there is support, understanding, and empathy (Giblin, 1994). There is no competition for "air time" or silence. Messages are sent and received in a sensitive or caring manner.

Brock and Barnard (1999, p. 36) have delineated characteristics of *optimal family communication situations.* They state that in the best of circumstances, communication within families is of a high volume and includes seeking and sharing patterns. The messages between family members are clear and congruent. In addition, healthy families deal with a wide range of topics and are open to talking rather than remaining silent. When there is conflict, these families seek to work it out through discussion. Family members seek to problem solve. They are more likely than not to communicate in a positive tone.

## Religious/Spiritual Orientation

A religious/spiritual orientation to life is a characteristic of "the vast majority of the world's families" (Prest & Keller, 1993, p. 137). Involvement in the religious/spiritual dimension of life also correlates with an overall sense of marital and family health and well-being and helps families find meaning and moral principles by which to live (Griffith & Rotter, 1999). According to research, religion and spirituality have traditionally played an important part in the lives of some groups more than others. For example, collective faith has been the cornerstone by which African Americans were supported and sustained from the "oppression of slavery" to the "civil rights movement" (Hampson, Beavers, & Hulgus, 1990, p. 308).

An orientation still exists toward the religious/spiritual in regard to both organized and unorganized efforts. The elderly and adolescent, to say nothing of those in middle age, are frequently involved in life matters that can best be described as religious/spiritual (Campbell & Moyers, 1988). In addition, members of families often deal as a group with religious/spiritual questions during certain events, for example, deaths, births, and marriages. Couples who share a common faith or orientation toward religious matters and who are intrinsically motivated in their religious/spiritual orientation report more satisfaction in their relationships than those who are divided on these issues (Anthony, 1993).

## Ability to Deal with Crisis in a Positive Manner

A number of different types of crises affect families over their life span. Usually the most common type of crisis is an expected event, which is active. An **expected event** is one that is predictable and actually occurs, for example, leaving one's family of origin to make a life for oneself, finding employment, or getting married. In these situations the general nature of the event is known but the specifics are always unique, hence the crisis. Families that function well in these times use such coping strategies as negotiating, seeking advice from those who are more experienced, rehearsing, using humor, and expressing emotions to deal with such transitions (Schlossberg, Waters, & Goodman, 1996).

There are also **nonevents**, which are passive in the sense that they are events that do not happen as envisioned or expected (Schlossberg et al., 1996). Examples of a nonevent might be the failure of a couple to have healthy children or to reach their financial goals in life. In such circumstances, families are thrown into a crisis that may or may not be recognized by others. Healthy families deal with these situations by expressing their emotions and supporting one another.

## Encouragement of Individuals

Because families work as systems, they are only as strong as their weakest members. Therefore, it behooves families to encourage the development of talents and abilities within their individual members. Such a process is generally done systemically and is carried out over the family life cycle (Carter & McGoldrick, 1999).

Encouragement is especially important at certain times in the life cycle. Among the most crucial times encouragement is needed are

- with school-age children as they engage in the educational process
- with adolescents as they cope with physical changes and peer groups
- with young adults as they move from their parents' houses into their own psychological and physical spaces filled with dreams and possibilities. (Lambie & Daniels-Mohring, 1993)

## Clear Roles

Roles are prescribed and repetitive behaviors involving a set of reciprocal activities with other family members (Steinhauser, Santa-Barbara, & Skinner, 1984). Roles in healthy families are clear, appropriate, suitably allocated, mutually agreed on, integrated, and enacted (Minuchin, 1974). Some roles are necessary, such as the provision of material resources. Others are unique and/or unnecessary, such as the acquiring of coins for a coin collection.

The exact roles within families are determined by such factors as age, culture, and tradition. Healthy families strive to make roles as interchangeable and flexible as possible.

## Growth-Producing Structure and Development Patterns

Healthy families are organized in a clear, appropriate, and growth-producing way (Lewis, Beavers, Gossett, & Phillips, 1976; McGoldrick, Gerson, & Shellenberger, 1999; Napier & Whitaker, 1978). There are no intergenerational coalitions (e.g., mother and daughter against everyone else in the family) or conflictual **triangles** (e.g., mother and father arguing over and interacting with their rebellious son) as the basis for keeping the family together. Instead, parents are in charge (or, in the case of single-parent families, the single parent is in charge). Subsystems, such as those composed of family members logically grouped together because of age or function (e.g., parents), carry out needed tasks (e.g., parenting). Because the structure is clear, the boundaries (physical and psychological lines of demarcation) are, too, and growth can take place. When a family member steps out of bounds, family pressure brings him or her back into line. This process takes place through **homeostasis**—the tendency to resist change and keep things as they are. For instance, if a teenager violates a curfew, the parents may "ground" the young person for a week or until responsibility is taken for coming home on time.

Other salient features of healthy families that center around structure are those connected with the formation and display of symptoms. Some individual dysfunctions, such as depression (Lopez, 1986), career indecisiveness (Kinnier, Brigman, & Noble, 1990), and substance abuse (West, Hosie, & Zarski, 1987), are related to family structure. In these situations, families are usually too tightly or too loosely organized, a matter that is discussed more fully later in this chapter.

# Family Life Stressors

Stress is a part of every family's life. As with individuals, families attempt to keep stressful events from becoming distressful, that is, overwhelming so that the family cannot function (Selye, 1976). They do this through a variety of means, some of which are more healthy (such as planning ahead) than others. Sometimes families cope with stressors according to whether they are prepared to deal with the situations or not.

Carter and McGoldrick (1999) have placed family stressors into two categories: vertical and horizontal (see Figure 2.2). **Vertical stressors** are those that bring past and pre-

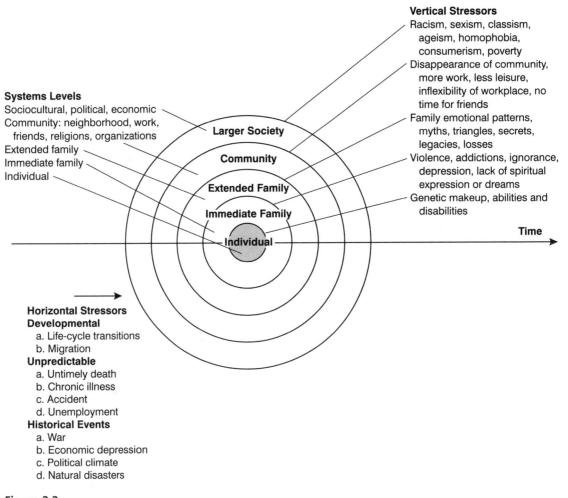

**Systems Levels**
Sociocultural, political, economic
Community: neighborhood, work,
   friends, religions, organizations
Extended family
Immediate family
Individual

**Larger Society**
**Community**
**Extended Family**
**Immediate Family**
**Individual**

**Time**

**Vertical Stressors**
Racism, sexism, classism,
   ageism, homophobia,
   consumerism, poverty
Disappearance of community,
   more work, less leisure,
   inflexibility of workplace, no
   time for friends
Family emotional patterns,
   myths, triangles, secrets,
   legacies, losses
Violence, addictions, ignorance,
   depression, lack of spiritual
   expression or dreams
Genetic makeup, abilities and
   disabilities

**Horizontal Stressors**
**Developmental**
   a. Life-cycle transitions
   b. Migration
**Unpredictable**
   a. Untimely death
   b. Chronic illness
   c. Accident
   d. Unemployment
**Historical Events**
   a. War
   b. Economic depression
   c. Political climate
   d. Natural disasters

**Figure 2.2**
Flow of stress through a family.

From "Overview: The Expanded Family Life Cycle" by B. Carter and M. McGoldrick, in *The Expanded Family Life Cycle* (3rd ed., p. 6), edited by B. Carter and M. McGoldrick, 1999, Boston: Allyn & Bacon. Copyright © 1999 Allyn & Bacon. Reprinted with permission.

sent issues to bear reciprocally such as family attitudes, expectations, secrets, and legacies. These stressors are historical and inherited from previous generations. They are the hand we were dealt. **Horizontal stressors** are aspects of our lives that relate to the present. They are developmental and unfolding. Many are predictable such as life cycle transitions (e.g., the transition from being a new couple to being a couple with a new child). Others are unpredictable, such as an untimely death, chronic illness, or the loss of a job.

The occurrence and impact of some developmental stressors can be predicted for the future. For example, the structure of the family and its vertical and horizontal stressors shift over time. This transition occurs in several ways, but one prevalent way is with the addition of an extra generation to the life of the family (e.g., having aging parents come and live with their grown children). Such a change tilts the family as a whole from a more horizontal to a more vertical emphasis. Likewise, if couples in the United States continue to have fewer children, "individuals in upcoming generations will have fewer siblings and cousins (horizontal dimension) and more relatives in the older generations (vertical dimension). . . . Divorces and remarriages by children may multiply the vertical lines of the family" (Shields, King, & Wynne, 1995, p. 141).

Overall, the Carter and McGoldrick model of family life stressors is systemic and in line with how most family therapists view families. However, families are unique in their timing of transition events. For example, families plan for their children to grow up, leave home, and start families, but British-American families usually expect a much faster shift in these events than Italian-American families. Anticipating when events may happen helps family members prepare mentally and physically for changes. Sometimes family life stages and individual life stages complement each other (Bowen, 1978); however, at other times, families and individuals may become distressed and dysfunctional.

## Expected Life Stressors

As mentioned earlier, families can expect a number of stressors regardless of their level of functioning. As indicated, some are **developmental stressors** (i.e., age and life-stage related), and others are **situational stressors** (i.e., interpersonal, such as dealing with feelings) (Figley, 1989). Some stressors are related to present events such as work, school, and social functions (Kaslow, 1991). Others are more historical in nature (i.e., they have family life heritage).

When surveyed, family members frequently cite prevalent stressors in their families as those associated with (1) economics and finances, (2) children's behaviors, (3) insufficient couple time, (4) communicating with children, (5) insufficient personal time, and (6) insufficient family play time (Curran, 1985). Clearly, some of these everyday stressors deal with deficiencies, such as not having enough time. In these types of stress situations families can resolve problems through planning ahead, lowering their expectations, or both. They are then better able to cope. The flip side of this solution-based stress relief is that families and their members may experience stress from not accomplishing enough of what they planned and from overscheduling family calendars.

## Unexpected Life Stressors

Some family life situations take family members by surprise or are beyond their control. If life events come too soon, are delayed, or fail to materialize, the health, happiness, and well-being of all involved may be affected (Schlossberg et al., 1996). Intensified emotionality and/or behavioral disorganization in families and their members is likely to occur as a result (Roberto, 1991).

Timing is crucial to the functioning of families and their members, especially when dealing with the unexpected. Struggle results if timing is off, or families are "off-time" (Neugarten, 1979). For example, if a first wedding is either relatively early or late in one's life (e.g., before age 20 or after age 40, respectively), the difficulty of accepting or dealing with the circumstances surrounding the event, such as interacting with the new spouse, is increased for both the persons marrying and their families (Carter & McGoldrick, 1999). Also, if grandparents assume the task of raising their grandchildren because of unexpected circumstances, such as the incarceration of the biological parents, greater risks for all are involved (Pinson-Milburn, Fabian, Schlossberg, & Pyle, 1996). Risks for the grandparents include increased psychological stress, financial difficulties, and health problems. Children in such circumstances are likely to suffer from a lack of consistent parenting and discipline and thus may do less well academically and socially.

Another crucial variable in dealing with the unexpected is **family development and environmental fit** (Eccles et al., 1993). Some environments are conducive to helping families develop and resolve unexpected crises. Others are not. For example, despite its best effort, a family living in an impoverished environment that experiences the loss of its major wage earner may not recover to its previous level of functioning. Such would probably not be the case with a family experiencing the same circumstance but living in a more affluent and supportive environment.

In addition to the situations just cited, families may have special difficulty in handling the following unexpected events in their life cycles (McCubbin & Figley, 1983):

1. *Happenstance and chance:* One unpredictable aspect of the life cycle is happenstance and chance (Bandura, 1982; Seligman, 1981). It is impossible to gauge when a person or an event may have a major impact on an individual or family that alters the style and substance of their existence. For example, members of a family on vacation may become friends with members of another family because they were housed in adjoining motel rooms. The results may be a marriage of their children, a business deal that produces wealth/frustration, or extended visits to each other's homes. Another chance event that may have a major impact on a family is the birth of a child with a disability. Such a child may strain the psychological and financial resources of a family and increase stress and, at the same time, reduce pleasant interactions and communications within the family (Seligman & Darling, 1997). It may also draw the family closer together physically and emotionally.

2. *Physical/psychological trauma:* People can be traumatized by experiencing natural events such as hurricanes, earthquakes, or fires, as well as by experiencing violent crime and physical abuse. These events may happen singularly or collectively. They share in common the fact that they are sudden, overwhelming, and often dangerous, either to one's self or significant other. These experiences are usually horrific in nature.

Regardless of the form or circumstances, traumatic experiences have an impact on families. "Traumatized families are those who are attempting to cope with an extraordinary stressor that has disrupted their normal life routine in unwanted ways" (Figley, 1989, p. 5). Trauma can upset the family's organizational ability and adaptability. The greater the distress of the victim(s), the greater the distress within the family as a whole. For instance, an adolescent girl may find it impossible to have a relationship with the brother who raped her. Similarly, a mother and children may be unable to reorganize themselves into a functional family unit after the untimely death of the husband/father. Symptoms displayed by families in these circumstances include role reversals, somatization of experiences, interruption of normal developmental life cycles, alienation, and inappropriate attempts at control, such as emotional withdrawal.

3. *Success and failure:* In his poem "If," Rudyard Kipling describes success and failure as "impostors" that should be treated just the same. Indeed, success and failure are both unsettling events for individuals and families. For example, a family that wins a lottery or sweepstakes may find its members disagreeing over how the monies will be spent. Family members may also find themselves besieged with solicitations. In another example, a family that acquires fame and notoriety may become isolated from routine interactions with friends or colleagues, thereby cutting off a social system of support and comfort.

The results of success or failure can leave people who experience them with mixed and volatile feelings ranging from depression to elation. The outcome may be progression or regression. Consequently, emotions and behaviors may be directed at increasing intimacy, physical or psychological distancing, or the adoption of a new set of values. In any such scenarios, lifestyles and life cycle events are altered.

When anyone or anything either enters or leaves the family system, members within the family become unsettled. This point is seen graphically in the Social Readjustment Rating Scale (Holmes & Rahe, 1967). Of the 43 life-stress situations listed in the scale, 10 of the top 14 involve gaining or losing a family member.

In general, events such as illness, loss of a job, or inheriting a substantial amount of money are unpredictable and stressful. These occurrences add tension to the family system because of their newness, demands, and the changes they require of family members (Carter & McGoldrick, 1999). "Dysfunctional family behaviors develop when unexpected crises unbalance the system beyond its natural ability to recover" (Burgess & Hinkle, 1993, p. 134). Even in the best circumstances, certain events can cause families to behave in dysfunctional ways.

# Family Structure and Functionality

In addition to stress, another factor that contributes to the health or dysfunctionality of families is structure/organization. As seen in Chapter 1, a variety of family forms are present in society (Bubenzer, West, & Boughner, 1994). Some work better than others in handling life events. For example, a family that is rigidly structured may respond best in a crisis situation, and one that is loosely organized may do best in recreational circumstances. The roles family members enact make a difference in regard to family health. For instance, "organized cohesiveness, sex role traditionalism, role flexibility, and shared roles" are correlated with husbands' health, and "organized cohesiveness and differentiated sharing" are correlated with wives' health, in middle-class families (Fisher, Ransom, Terry, & Burge, 1992, p. 399). Three common family organizational forms are (1) symmetry/complementary, (2) centripetal/centrifugal, and (3) cohesive/adaptable.

## Symmetrical/Complementary Families

In Western society, families vary in the way they function. Although some are mainly symmetrical and others are mainly complementary, most successful couples show an ability to use both styles of interaction (Main & Oliver, 1988). In symmetrical families the relationship is based on similarity of behavior. At its worst, family members—especially the couple subsystem members—act alike. For example, if she screams, he screams back. At its best, a **symmetrical relationship** is one where each partner tries to become competent in doing necessary or needed tasks (Watzlawick, Beavin, & Jackson, 1967). Members within these units are versatile. For example, either a man or a woman can work outside the home or take care of children. The major time of difficulty in a symmetrical relationship is when partners do not minimize differences and instead compete with each other or when one member of the relationship is not skilled in performing a necessary task (Sauber, L'Abate, & Weeks, 1985).

In **complementary relationships,** family member roles are defined more rigidly and differences are maximized. For example, one is either dominant or submissive, logical or emotional. If members fail to do their tasks, such as make decisions or nurture children, other members of the family are adversely affected. As long as the prescribed roles in these relationships dovetail with each other and there is no change in the status quo, complementary families do fine.

Overall, both symmetrical and complementary forms of family life will work as long as at least two conditions are met. First, members in the relationships must be satisfied with and competent in their roles. Second, there must be a sufficient interrelationship of roles so that necessary tasks are accomplished. In these cases, harmony results and the family functions adequately. However, it is not always possible to meet these two conditions, and thus families, especially the couples in them, do best if they practice **parallel relationships** (Main & Oliver, 1988). In parallel relationships, both complementary and symmetrical exchanges occur as appropriate.

## Centripetal/Centrifugal Families

The term **centripetal** (directed toward a center) is used to describe a tendency to move toward family closeness. The term **centrifugal** (directed away from a center) is used to describe the tendency to move away from the family (i.e., family disengagement). In all families, periods of both closeness and distance occur during the individual and family life cycles. Some of these periods "coincide with shifts between family development tasks that require intense bonding or an inside-the-family focus" such as families with young children, and tasks, that emphasize "personal identity and autonomy" such as launching children (Rolland, 1999, p. 500).

One of the strongest models that outlines the natural tendencies of three-generational families to be close to or distant from each other has been formulated by Lee Combrinck-Graham (1985) (see Figure 2.3). It relates strength and health to the developmental state of the family and its individuals. It also stresses the importance of working through transitions in the family.

The work of Robert Beavers and associates at the Timberlawn Psychiatric Center in Dallas, Texas, shows that extremes in either a centripetal or centrifugal style of family

**Figure 2.3**
Density of the family over time.

From "A Developmental Model for Family Systems" by L. Combrinck-Graham, 1985, *Family Process, 24,* p. 142; permission conveyed through Copyright Clearance Center, Inc.

interaction as a lifestyle are likely to produce poor family functioning (Lewis et al., 1976). Figure 2.4 describes the relationship between family interaction style and family health. Families with a centripetal style have members who "view their relationship satisfactions as coming from inside the family" (Nichols & Everett, 1986, p. 77). They tend to produce children who are too tightly held by the family and who are prone to be antisocial, irresponsible, and egocentric. "Certain types of symptoms in teenagers, such as eating disorders and schizophrenia, indicate centripetal forces at work in the family" (Thomas, 1992, p. 105). Also, young adults who are unable or unwilling to leave home are the products of such families (Haley, 1980).

Families with a centrifugal style "are characterized by the tendency to expel members and view their relationship satisfactions as coming from outside the family" (Nichols & Everett, 1986, p. 77). They are likely to produce children who become socially isolated, disorganized, or withdrawn. "Adolescents who run away from home after enduring rejection or neglect and who remain on the street as casual, prematurely independent runaways would come from families in which centrifugal forces are dominant" (Thomas, 1992, p. 105).

## Cohesion/Adaptability

Regardless of timing, all families have to deal with **family cohesion** (i.e., emotional bonding) and **family adaptability** (i.e., the ability to be flexible and change) (Olson, 1986; Strong, DeVault, & Sayad, 2001). In the Circumplex Model of Marital and Family Systems shown in Figure 2.5, cohesion and adaptability are highlighted. These two dimensions each have four levels (Olson, 1986). Adaptability ranges from a low to high dimen-

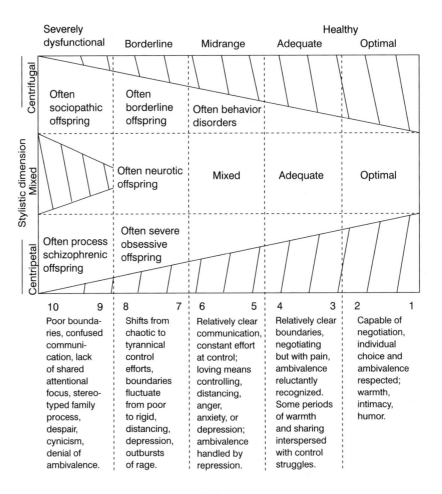

**Figure 2.4**
Beavers's concept of family health.

From *Successful Marriage, A Family Systems Approach to Couples Therapy* by W. Robert Beavers, M.D., 1985. Copyright © 1985 by W. Robert Beavers. Reprinted by permission of the author.

sion on the categories characterized as (1) rigid, (2) structured, (3) flexible, and (4) chaotic. The structured and flexible categories are the two most moderate levels of functioning. Cohesion ranges from low to high on these four levels: (1) disengaged, (2) separated, (3) connected, and (4) enmeshed. Hypotheses have been advanced that high levels of enmeshment or low levels of cohesion in the form of disengagement may be problematic for families. For example, a lack of family cohesion, along with poor discipline, appears to raise the risk for serious delinquency in adolescents (Gorman-Smith, Tolan, Zelli, & Huesmann, 1996). Overall, the two dimensions of adaptability and cohesion are curvilinear. "Families that apparently are very high or very low on both dimensions seem dysfunctional, whereas families that are balanced seem to function more adequately" (Maynard & Olson, 1987, p. 502).

LEVELS OF FLEXIBILITY

**CHAOTIC**
- Lack of leadership
- Dramatic role shifts
- Erratic discipline
- Too much change

**FLEXIBLE**
- Shared leadership
- Democratic discipline
- Role sharing change
- Change when necessary

**STRUCTURED**
- Leadership sometimes shared
- Somewhat democratic discipline
- Roles stable
- Change when demanded

**RIGID**
- Authoritarian leadership
- Strict discipline
- Roles seldom to change
- Too little change

○ BALANCED  ◑ MIDRANGE  ■ UNBALANCED

COHESION — Low —— High

FLEXIBILITY — High (top) to Low (bottom): CHAOTIC, FLEXIBLE, STRUCTURED, RIGID

|  | DISENGAGED | SEPARATED | CONNECTED | ENMESHED |
|---|---|---|---|---|
| **CHAOTIC** | CHAOTICALLY DISENGAGED | CHAOTICALLY SEPARATED | CHAOTICALLY CONNECTED | CHAOTICALLY ENMESHED |
| **FLEXIBLE** | FLEXIBLY DISENGAGED | FLEXIBLY SEPARATED | FLEXIBLY CONNECTED | FLEXIBLY ENMESHED |
| **STRUCTURED** | STRUCTURALLY DISENGAGED | STRUCTURALLY SEPARATED | STRUCTURALLY CONNECTED | STRUCTURALLY ENMESHED |
| **RIGID** | RIGIDLY DISENGAGED | RIGIDLY SEPARATED | RIGIDLY CONNECTED | RIGIDLY ENMESHED |

| LEVELS OF COHESION: | DISENGAGED | SEPARATED | CONNECTED | ENMESHED |
|---|---|---|---|---|
| I-We Balance: | I | I-we | I-We | I-WE |
| Closeness: | Little closeness | Low-moderate | Moderate-high | Very high closeness |
| Loyalty: | Little loyalty | Some loyalty | High loyalty | Very high loyalty |
| Independence/ Dependence: | High independence | Interdependent (More independence than dependence) | Interdependent (More dependence than independence) | High dependence |

**Figure 2.5**
Circumplex model of family systems.

From "Circumplex Model of Family Systems: Integrating Ethnic Diversity and Other Social Systems" by Dean M. Gorall and David H. Olson, in *Integrating Family Therapy* (p. 219), edited by R. H. Mikesell, D.-D. Lusterman, and S. H. McDaniel. Copyright © 1995 by the American Psychological Association. Reprinted with permission.

As previously seen from the Combrinck-Graham diagram (1985) (Figure 2.3) and as recently acknowledged by Olson, the degree of adaptability and cohesion within families is dependent on their life cycle stage and their cultural background. Therefore, caution must be exercised when stressing these two dimensions of family life in isolation from other factors.

# Coping Strategies of Families

The coping strategies of healthy and dysfunctional families vary both quantitatively and qualitatively. According to Figley and McCubbin (1983), families that are generally able to cope with stress have most of the following characteristics (p. 18):

- ability to identify the stressor
- ability to view the situation as a family problem, rather than a problem of one member
- solution-oriented approach rather than blame
- tolerance for other family members
- clear expression of commitment to and affection for other family members
- open and clear communication among members
- evidence of high family cohesion
- evidence of considerable role flexibility
- appropriate utilization of resources inside and outside the family
- lack of physical violence
- lack of substance abuse

Hill's (1949) ABCX model illustrates whether an event is a crisis. In Hill's model, "A" represents the stressor event that happens to the family, "B" represents the resources at the family's disposal, and "C" represents the meaning or interpretation the family attaches to the experience. "X" is the combined effect of these factors (i.e., the crisis itself). This model highlights that the same type of event may be handled differently by different families. For instance, consider two families in each of which a person has lost a job. In an affluent family, this event may have little impact or meaning because the family has a number of outside contacts that will readily find the person who lost the job a new one. However, the same event in a poor family may provoke a considerable crisis because members do not have access to outside employment resources and the family was dependent on the income from the lost job for daily necessities.

The process that a family goes through in adjusting to a crisis is illustrated in what is sometimes referred to as the "check mark diagram" (see Figure 2.6). Families at first become disorganized and usually experience a period where they do not function well. That period stops and recovery begins once the crisis has ended. How well a family recovers depends on both the resources they have available and how well they use the resources.

Families that are unable to adjust to new circumstances try the same solutions over and over again (Watzlawick, 1978) or intensify nonproductive behaviors. In this process they fail to make needed adjustments or changes and thus become stuck or exacerbate their symptoms (Burgess & Hinkle, 1993). For example, a husband, concerned about his wife's weight, may tease or criticize her in an attempt to get her to lose pounds. If this strategy does not work, he may tease or criticize her more or he may yell at her. These

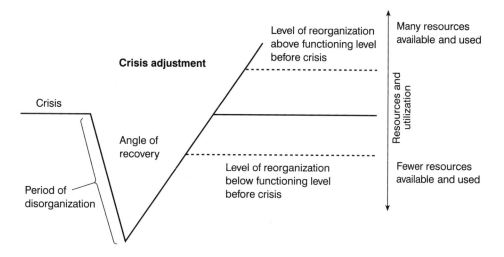

**Figure 2.6**
Check mark diagram: A model of a family's reaction to crisis.
From *Families Under Stress: Adjustment to the Crisis of War, Separation, and Reunion* by R. Hill, 1949, Westport, CT: Greenwood Press.

behaviors ultimately result in hurt feelings, resentment, anger, frustration, and a lack of effort to change.

In making changes we should stress that there are two levels of change that can work for families but they need to be employed at different times for different situations. One type of change is referred to as **first-order change** (Watzlawick, Weakland, & Fisch, 1974) and is characterized by its superficial nature. For instance, dinner may be moved from being served at 6 P.M. to being served at 8 P.M. if a mother's work schedule is shifted or a father's train runs late. This type of change is appropriate in such situations. Dinner is still served. However, a first-order change that simply delays an argument from 6 P.M. to 8 P.M. is usually not going to be productive unless new ways of resolving the disagreement are found in that 2-hour span of time. Otherwise, the argument and its results still happen.

The opposite of first-order change is **second-order change**. The dynamics surrounding second-order change are those that result in a **metachange**, that is, a changing of rules sometimes referred to as a "change of change" (Watzlawick et al., 1974). In this process, a new set of rules and behaviors is introduced into the existing behavioral repertoire, often in an abrupt way (Burgess & Hinkle, 1993). The outcome is that a qualitatively new type of behavior appears.

In the previous example, a second-order change would occur if the family members engaging in the fight brought in a mediator or agreed beforehand to work on possible solutions rather than to just voice grievances. If such changes were made, better communication would be fostered because power struggles would no longer be a part of the agenda, and divisiveness would thereby be prevented.

A study of 78 French-Canadian couples who had been living together an average of 13 years further illustrates the difference between first- and second-order change. According to the result of this investigation, "when compared to nondistressed spouses, distressed spouses showed less problem solving confidence, a tendency to avoid different problem solving activities, and poor strategies to control their behavior" (Sabourin, Laporte, & Wright, 1990, p. 89). In other words, first-order change spouses were stuck in repetitive, nonproductive behaviors, but their counterparts engaged in new, productive behaviors.

Other dysfunctional patterns in families, such as sexual abuse of children, also show first-order change patterns. In families where there is incest, for instance, the family is "typically a closed, undifferentiated and rigid system primarily characterized by sexualized dependency" (Maddock, 1989, p. 134). In these families the same pattern of abuse is repeated because the family unit is "insulated from critical social feedback that might influence their behavior" (Maddock, 1989, p. 134).

Other coping strategies that relieve stress in well-functioning families include:

- recognizing that stress may be positive and lead to change
- realizing that stress is usually temporary
- focusing on working together to find solutions
- realizing that stress is a normal part of life
- changing the rules to deal with stress and celebrating victories over events that led to stress (Curran, 1985)

# Implications of Health in Working with Families

Studying healthy families is a complicated process (Smith & Stevens-Smith, 1992). It requires that researchers invest considerable time and effort in observing and calculating the multiple impact of numerous interactions that occur in families, such as speech and relationship patterns. In addition, to study the health of families, researchers must overcome "the individually oriented, linear causation thinking of psychopathology" as represented in the *Diagnostic and Statistical Manual of Mental Disorders* of the American Psychiatric Association (Huber, 1993, p. 70). Family therapists have "typically worked with clients experiencing stress and crisis in relationships, a viewpoint indicating transient dysfunctioning" (Sporakowski, 1995, p. 61). Both the complexity of families and the bias toward researching individuals inhibits many clinicians from carefully investigating families. Yet, knowledge about the health of families can assist family therapists in a number of ways.

First, through studying the literature on family health, therapists can appreciate the multidimensional aspects of family life and how members influence each other systemically (Wilcoxon, 1985). This knowledge and awareness can be useful to practitioners as they interact with families experiencing difficulties. For instance, if a family member abuses alcohol, estimated by Treadway (1987) to be a factor in possibly half of the cases treated, the therapist can work to identify the problem and break the dysfunctional pattern of secrecy and silence by working in a confrontive but caring way.

A second benefit for therapists in examining healthy families is the realization that even dysfunctional families have areas of adequate or above-average performance. Because novice therapists tend to "overpathologize" client families, knowledge of healthy families is essential in gaining a balanced perspective (Barnhill, 1979). A knowledge of healthy families can be useful because it, for example, provides insight into the developmental aspects of enmeshment and disengagement that occur over the family life cycle (Combrinck-Graham, 1985). This type of information can help therapists become aware of what is normal and healthy behavior and thereby focus on situations that are not normal and healthy.

A third advantage of exploring characteristics of healthy families is the realization that health and pathology are developmental (Wilcoxon, 1985). For example, in midlife, couples may grow together and function with less conflict and stress as they launch their children (Blacker, 1999; McCullough & Rutenberg, 1988). Similarly, couples who maintain positive interactions during this time may be less susceptible to premature death from such disorders as hypertension, stroke, and coronary heart disease (Lynch, 1977). This type of knowledge helps clinicians realize more fully that change is possible and probable if proper therapeutic interventions are made.

A fourth implication of studying healthy families is that through such a focus, therapists can delineate areas of deficiency and strength (Huber, 1993). Healthy families have weaknesses and dysfunctional families have strengths. Secrets, conflict, jealousy, guilt, and scapegoating, as well as openness, cooperation, admiration, understanding, and accepting of responsibility, may occur on occasions in almost any family (Framo, 1996). Realizing the range and extent of behaviors in families gives therapists an awareness of how to potentially deal in an effective way with severely stressed families as well as an understanding of how healthy families develop.

Tomm (1989) has conceptualized how transitions lead to pathology or wellness. His model provides a basis for helping family therapists realize the dynamics of family situations and plan constructive and effective interventions. In this wellness and dysfunctionality cycle, acronyms have been assigned that stand for patterns of functioning among family members and in the family itself. These acronym patterns are characterized as follows:

| | | |
|---|---|---|
| PIPS | = | Pathologizing Interpersonal Patterns (such as failure to speak or communicate effectively) |
| HIPS | = | Healing Interpersonal Patterns (such as support or understanding) |
| TIPS | = | Transforming Interpersonal Patterns (such as using psychological resources or material resources) |
| Slips | = | Events that trigger HIPS back to PIPS (such as cutting oneself off from the family physically or psychologically) |
| DIPS | = | Deteriorating Interpersonal Patterns (such as accidentally or intentionally avoiding a member of the family) |
| WIPS | = | Wellness Interpersonal Patterns (such as honest and open communication) |

Taken together, Tomm's cyclical model of transition looks like the following:

For example, in the case of the marriage of a new couple, a wife might feel verbally misunderstood by her husband (Slip) after a pattern of open communication (WIP) had been established. The result on her part would be sullenness and silence (DIP), followed by avoidance (PIP). If the husband were to ask her to help him understand her behavior and, after her reply, to understand and seek to rectify the situation (TIP), a new trusting environment might be created in which each member of the couple system would understand the other one better (HIP). In such an atmosphere, the couple might work even harder on being effective communicators (WIP).

Another example of the Tomm system is a situation in which a parent deviates from her general understanding behavior (WIP) and yells (Slip) at an adolescent for telling the truth about getting into trouble. This results in the adolescent hiding facts from his parent the next time (DIP) and continuing to do so on future occasions (PIP). If the parent were to apologize for yelling (TIP), the adolescent might feel psychologically closer to the parent (HIP) and reestablish trust and understanding with her (WIP).

Tomm's model is useful as a way of understanding how systems, such as families, change with time, events, and circumstances. Expected events and unusual circumstances may become more or less stressful depending on how family members and families as a whole react to them.

A final implication for studying healthy families is educational. An awareness of potential stressors in life can help therapists prepare a family and its members to deal with situations in advance. For instance,

> . . . those struggling to recover from traumatic events appear to need to resolve five fundamental questions: (1) What happened? (2) Why did it happen? (3) Why did I and others act as we did then? (4) Why did I and others act as we did since then? (5) If something like this happened again, would I be able to cope more effectively? (Figley, 1989, p. 14)

Only by directly addressing these questions can a person or a family realize to the greatest extent possible the effect of a trauma on them and their life cycle development.

Education concerning healthy families also emphasizes the values of previously tried solutions (O'Hanlon & Weiner-Davis, 1989). Families and their members sometimes do not deal appropriately with events because they fail to examine strategies they could employ or have utilized at exceptional times for reaching successful resolutions. By focusing on universal or unique strategies that enable them to deal with stress, families may become healthier and more satisfied with themselves and their environments.

Knowledge is not a guarantee that families will handle changes in their life cycles without turmoil and crisis. However, through educating themselves and the families they work with about potential difficulties, family therapists and families are given a choice as to what they do and when. One of these choices is to seek enrichment services.

# Strengthening Families Through Enrichment

The idea of **marriage and family enrichment** is based on the concept that couples and families stay healthy or get healthier by actively participating in certain activities, usually in connection with other couples (Mace & Mace, 1977). There are more than two dozen enrichment organizations in the United States operating at the national level, and the material in this field has mushroomed (Mace, 1987).

Recommended ways to achieve health in families include involvement in couple and family retreats, interactive cooperative activities, and family councils. Research shows that enrichment can be helpful to couples and families who are not in distress.

A part of marriage and family enrichment involves self-help and couple help. This type of help is often in the form of couples and family members participating in structured exercises that theoretically and practically bring them closer together through sharing information and experiences (Calvo, 1975; Guerney, 1977). Such experiences also help couples renew their closeness as well as confront areas of conflict (Eckstein & Jones, 1998). For instance, couples may learn to give and receive nonverbal and verbal messages and reflect on positive times in their life together. They may also be able to give and receive feedback on important relationship topics such as sexuality, finance, parenting, and household chores (Johnson, Fortman, & Brems, 1993).

# Summary and Conclusion

Exploring aspects of healthy families is important from a conceptual, ethical, and treatment basis. Clinicians can become more competent and also preempt personal and legal criticism by describing their model of healthy family functioning (Brendel & Nelson, 1999). One aspect of family life that stands out is that families go through periods of transition and develop according to general and specific milestones. Families that work best are those that plan and use their time wisely in setting up and implementing positive activities around expected and unexpected events in their lives.

This chapter examined multiple aspects of family health. First, the nature of the family as an interactive relationship system was discussed in regard to family health. Next the nature of healthy families was explored in regard to characteristics and behaviors. Healthy families are in a cycle that, when unbalanced, eventually changes in order to accommodate new situations. Family stressors were also examined. Stressors come in many forms, such as vertical and horizontal, present and past. Handling expected stressful situations, through such techniques as time management, is difficult for many families. More troublesome is the management and recovery from unexpected life stressors, such as traumas from natural disasters like a hurricane or unexpected death.

Another area explored was family structure. Families organize themselves in many different ways. However, families that are primarily symmetrical, versus those that are predominantly complementary, will vary in their ability to achieve tasks. A parallel family structure, which depends on flexibility and appropriateness of couples, seems to be most successful. Centripetal and centrifugal families differ in the ways in which they address family matters. Centripetal families depend more on other members for help, and centrifugal families focus outwardly. Both are appropriate ways for families to be structured at different times in the life cycle. A final characteristic of structure is cohesion and adaptability. Again, both of these qualities differ in families depending on their cultural background and stage of life. The point is that family therapists need to realize that there are preferred family structures at various times in the family life cycle. Therapists also need to know how family structure influences family system dynamics.

The final three sections of this chapter dealt with coping strategies of families, the implication of understanding health as it pertains to family therapy, and couple and family enrichment. Generally, families cope the best they can. Families that are able to make second-order changes, that is, try totally new responses, do a better job of marshaling their resources than those who repeat old patterns or make incremental changes regardless of the situation (first-order changes). By studying healthy families, family therapists educate themselves to the complexity of family life and change. They also become sophisticated in realizing the developmental aspects of health. Therefore, they tend to be appropriately cautious in their assessment and treatment procedures. This type of knowledge gives therapists and the families they work with more choice in regard to what they do and how, thereby empowering all concerned in the process of change. With such information, family therapists "can take a leadership role in helping society come to terms with what is needed to create strong [and healthy] families" (Arnold & Allen, 1996, p. 84) and promote enrichment activities as well.

# Summary Table

## Healthy and Dysfunctional Characteristics of Families

### The Family System and Health

Families are systemic in nature. Their health varies over their life span.
Healthy families readjust their rules and structure in dealing with crises and change.

### Qualities of Healthy Families

Healthy families interact in a productive manner. They are characterized by:

- commitment of family members
- spending of qualitative and quantitative time together
- effective communication patterns
- a religious/spiritual orientation to life
- dealing with crises in a positive and effective manner
- clear roles and encouragement of members
- an appropriate structure and organization

### Family Life Stressors

Stress is a part of family life. It may be vertical (i.e., historical) or horizontal (i.e., current), predictable (e.g., aging) or unexpected (e.g., death).
Expected life stressors are developmental and situational. They revolve around issues associated with economics, children, time, and behavior.
Unexpected life stressors are beyond a family's control and include happenstance and chance, physical/psychological trauma, and success/failure. Timing and environmental fit are crucial factors in dealing with unexpected stress.
Stress events initially unbalance the family.

### Family Structure and Functionality

The way in which a family is structured affects its ability to respond.
Three common ways families organize are

- symmetry/complementary
- centripetal/centrifugal
- cohesive/adaptable

### Coping Strategies of Families

The ability of families to cope is both a qualitative and quantitative process. Coping is characterized by:

- an ability to identify a stressor
- viewing a problem from a family perspective
- adopting a solution-oriented approach
- showing tolerance for other family members
- establishing clear communication patterns
- high family cohesion and role flexibility
- appropriate utilization of resources
- lack of physical violence and substance abuse
- use of second-order change strategies
- recognizing that stress is normal and may lead to change
- celebrating victories over events that led to stress

### Implications of Health in Working with Families

Studying family health helps family therapists:

- appreciate the complexity of families
- realize that health is developmental and situational
- be less prone to pathologizing families
- be aware of families' strengths and deficits
- be more educational in assisting families with problems

### Strengthening Families Through Enrichment

By participating in enrichment activities couples and families take positive action to promote their health and well-being.
Various forms of enrichment are available and becoming more important to couples and families.

# References

Anthony, M. (1993). The relationship between marital satisfaction and religious maturity. *Religious Education, 88*, 97–108.

Arnold, M. S., & Allen, N. P. (1996). Andrew Billingsley: The legacy of African American families. *The Family Journal: Counseling and Therapy for Couples and Families, 3*, 77–85.

Bandura, A. (1982). The psychology of chance encounters and life paths. *American Psychologist, 37*, 747–755.

Barnhill, L. R. (1979). Healthy family systems. *Family Coordinator, 28*, 94–100.

Beavers, W. R. (1985). *Successful marriage.* New York: Norton.

Bertalanffy, L. von (1934). *Modern theories of development: An introduction to theoretical biology.* London: Oxford University Press.

Bertalanffy, L. von (1968). *General systems theory: Foundation, development, and application.* New York: Braziller.

Blacker, L. (1999). The launching phase of the life cycle. In B. Carter & M. McGoldrick (Eds.), *The expanded family life cycle* (3rd ed., pp. 287–306). Boston: Allyn & Bacon.

Boszormenyi-Nagy, I., & Ulrich, D. N. (1981). Contextual family therapy. In A. S. Gurman & D. P. Kniskern (Eds.), *Handbook of family therapy* (pp. 159–186). New York: Brunner/Mazel.

Bowen, M. (1978). *Family therapy in clinical practice.* New York: Jason Aronson.

Brendel, J. M., & Nelson, K. W. (1999). The stream of family secrets: Navigating the islands of confidentiality and triangulation involving family therapists. *The Family Journal: Counseling and Therapy for Couples and Families, 7,* 112–117.

Brock, G. W., & Barnard, C. P. (1999). *Procedures in marriage and family therapy* (3rd ed.). Boston: Allyn & Bacon.

Bubenzer, D. L., West, J. D., & Boughner, S. R. (1994). Michael White and the narrative perspective in therapy. *The Family Journal: Counseling and Therapy for Couples and Families, 2,* 71–83.

Burgess, T. A., & Hinkle, J. S. (1993). Strategic family therapy of avoidance behavior. *Journal of Mental Health Counseling, 15,* 132–140.

Calvo, G. (1975). *Marriage encounter: Official national manual.* St. Paul, MN: Marriage Encounter, Inc.

Campbell, J., & Moyers, B. (1988). *The power of myth.* New York: Doubleday.

Carlson, J., & Fullmer, D. (1992). Family counseling: Principles for growth. In R. L. Smith & P. Stevens-Smith (Eds.), *Family counseling and therapy* (pp. 27–52). Ann Arbor, MI: ERIC/CAPS.

Carter, B., & McGoldrick, M. (1999). *The expanded family life cycle* (3rd ed.). Boston: Allyn & Bacon.

Combrinck-Graham, L. (1985). A developmental model for family systems. *Family Process, 24,* 139–150.

Coontz, S. (2000). *The way we never were: American families and the nostalgia trap.* New York: Basic Books.

Cuber, J., & Harroff, P. (1966). *Sex and the significant Americans.* Baltimore: Penguin.

Curran, D. (1985). *Stress and the healthy family.* San Francisco: Harper & Row.

Cutler, H. A., & Radford, A. (1999). Adult children of alcoholics: Adjustment to a college environment. *The Family Journal: Counseling and Therapy for Couples and Families, 7,* 148–153.

Eccles, J. S., Midgley, C., Wigfield, A., Buchanan, C. M., Reuman, D., Flanagan, C., & MacIver, D. (1993). Development during adolescence: The impact of stage-environment fit on young adolescents' experiences in schools and families. *American Psychologist, 48,* 90–101.

Eckstein, D., & Jones, J. E. (1998). Thirty-three suggestions for relationship renewal. *The Family Journal: Counseling and Therapy for Couples and Families, 6,* 334–336.

Figley, C. R. (1989). *Helping traumatized families.* San Francisco: Jossey-Bass.

Figley, C. R., & McCubbin, H. (1983). *Stress and the family: Vol. 2: Coping with catastrophe.* New York: Brunner/Mazel.

Fisher, L., Ransom, D., Terry, H. E., & Burge, S. (1992). The California family health project: IV. Family structure/organization and adult health. *Family Process, 31,* 399–419.

Fishman, C. H. (1988). *Treating troubled adolescents.* New York: Basic Books.

Footlick, J. K. (1990, Winter/Spring). What happened to the family? *Newsweek,* pp. 15–20.

Framo, J. L. (1996). A personal retrospective of the family therapy field: Then and now. *Journal of Marital and Family Therapy, 22,* 289–316.

Giblin, P. (1994). Marital satisfaction. *The Family Journal: Counseling and Therapy for Couples and Families, 2,* 48–50.

Giblin, P. (1995). Identity, change, and family rituals. *The Family Journal: Counseling and Therapy for Couples and Families, 3,* 37–41.

Gladding, S. T. (1992). *On the death of Paul.* Unpublished manuscript.

Gorman-Smith, D., Tolan, P. H., Zelli, A., & Huesmann, L. R. (1996). The relation of family functioning to violence among inner-city minority youth. *Journal of Family Psychology, 10,* 115–129.

Griffith, B. A., & Rotter, J. C. (1999). Families and spirituality: Therapists as facilitators. *The Family Journal: Counseling and Therapy for Couples and Families, 7,* 161–164.

Guerney, B. (1977). *Relationship enhancement.* San Francisco: Jossey-Bass.

Haley, J. (1980). *Leaving home: The therapy of disturbed young people.* New York: McGraw-Hill.

Hampson, R. B., Beavers, W. R., & Hulgus, Y. (1990). Cross-ethnic family differences: Interactional assessment of white, black, and Mexican-American families. *Journal of Marital and Family Therapy, 16,* 307–319.

Hill, R. (1949). *Families under stress: Adjustment to the crisis of war, separation, and reunion.* Westport, CT: Greenwood.

Holmes, T. H., & Rahe, R. H. (1967). The social readjustment rating scale. *Journal of Psychosomatic Research, 2,* 213–228.

Huber, C. H. (1993). Balancing family health and illness. *The Family Journal: Counseling and Therapy for Couples and Families, 1,* 69–71.

Johnson, M. E., Fortman, J. B., & Brems, C. (1993). *Between two people: Exercises toward intimacy.* Alexandria, VA: American Counseling Association.

Kaplan, D. M. (2000). Who are our giants? *The Family Digest, 12*(4), 1,6.

Kaslow, F. W. (1991). The art and science of family psychology. *American Psychologist, 46,* 621–626.

Kinnier, R. T., Brigman, S. L., & Noble, F. C. (1990). Career indecision and family enmeshment. *Journal of Counseling and Development, 68,* 309–312.

Krysan, M., Moore, K. A., & Zill, N. (1990). *Identifying successful families: An overview of constructs and selected measures.* Washington, DC: Child Trends.

Lambie, R., & Daniels-Mohring, D. (1993). *Family systems within educational contexts.* Denver, CO: Love.

Lavee, Y., McCubbin, H. I., & Olson, D. H. (1987). The effects of stressful life events and transitions on family functioning and well-being. *Journal of Marriage and the Family, 49,* 857–873.

Lewis, J. M., Beavers, W. R., Gossett, J. T., & Phillips, V. A. (1976). *No single thread: Psychological health in family systems.* New York: Brunner/Mazel.

Lopez, F. G. (1986). Family structure and depression: Implications for the counseling of depressed college students. *Journal of Counseling and Development, 64,* 508–511.

Lynch, J. J. (1977). *The broken heart: The medical consequences of loneliness.* New York: Basic Books.

Mace, D. (1987). Three ways of helping married couples. *Journal of Martial and Family Therapy, 13,* 179–186.

Mace, D., & Mace, V. (1977). *How to have a happy marriage: A step-by-step guide to an enriched relationship.* Nashville, TN: Abington.

Maddock, J. W. (1989). Healthy family sexuality: Positive principles for educators and clinicians. *Family Relations, 38,* 130–136.

Main, F., & Oliver, R. (1988). Complementary, symmetrical and parallel personality priorities as indicators of marital adjustment. *Journal of Individual Psychology, 44,* 324–332.

Maynard, P. E., & Olson, D. H. (1987). Circumplex model of family systems: A treatment tool in family counseling. *Journal of Counseling and Development, 65,* 502–504.

McCoy, C. W. (1996). Reexamining models of healthy families. *Contemporary Family Therapy, 18,* 243–256.

McCubbin, H. I., & Figley, C. R. (1983). Bridging normative and catastrophic family stress. In H. I. McCubbin & C. R. Figley (Eds.), *Stress and the family.* New York: Brunner/Mazel.

McCullough, P. G., & Rutenberg, S. K. (1988). Launching children and moving on. In B. Carter & M. McGoldrick (Eds.), *The changing family life cycle* (2nd ed., pp. 285–309). New York: Gardner.

McGoldrick, M., Gerson, R., & Shellenberger, S. (1999). *Genograms: Assessment & intervention.* New York: Norton.

Minuchin, S. (1974). *Families and family therapy.* Cambridge, MA: Harvard University Press.

Napier, A. Y., & Whitaker, C. A. (1978). *The family crucible.* New York: Harper & Row.

Neugarten, B. L. (1979). Time, age, and the life cycle. *American Journal of Psychiatry, 136,* 887–894.

Nichols, W. C., & Everett, C. A. (1986). *Systemic family therapy.* New York: Guilford.

O'Hanlon, W. H., & Weiner-Davis, M. (1989). *In search of solutions: A new direction in psychotherapy.* New York: Norton.

Okun, B. F., & Rappaport, L. J. (1980). *Working with families: An introduction to family therapy.* North Scituate, MA: Duxbury.

Olson, D. H. (1986). Circumplex model VII: Validation studies and FACES III. *Family Process, 25,* 337–351.

Olson, D. H., & Olson, A. (2000). *Empowering couples: Building on your strengths.* Minneapolis: Life Innovations Inc.

Pinson-Milburn, N. M., Fabian, E. S., Schlossberg, N. K., & Pyle, M. (1996). Grandparents raising grandchildren. *Journal of Counseling & Development, 74,* 548–554.

Pittman, F. (1991). *Private lies: Infidelity and betrayal of intimacy.* New York: Norton.

Prest, L. A., & Keller, J. F. (1993). Spirituality and family therapy: Spiritual beliefs, myths, and metaphors. *Journal of Marital and Family Therapy, 19,* 137–148.

Roberto, L. A. (1991). Symbolic-experiential family therapy. In A. S. Gurman & D. P. Kniskern (Eds.), *Handbook of family therapy* (Vol. II, pp. 444–476). New York: Brunner/Mazel.

Rolland, J. S. (1999). Chronic illness and the family life cycle. In B. Carter & M. McGoldrick (Eds.), *The expanded family life cycle* (3rd ed., pp. 492–510). Boston: Allyn & Bacon.

Sabourin, S., Laporte, L., & Wright, J. (1990). Problem solving self-appraisal and coping efforts in distressed and nondistressed couples. *Journal of Marital and Family Therapy, 16,* 89–97.

Sauber, S. R., L'Abate, L., & Weeks, G. R. (1985). *Family therapy: Basic concepts and terms.* Rockville, MD: Aspen.

Schlossberg, N. K., Waters, E. B., & Goodman, J. (1996). *Counseling adults in transition: Linking practice with theory* (2nd ed.). New York: Springer.

Seligman, D. (1981, November 16). Luck and careers. *Fortune,* pp. 60–75.

Seligman, M., & Darling, R. B. (1997). *Ordinary families, special children* (2nd ed.). New York: Guilford.

Selye, H. (1976). *The stress of life* (2nd ed.). New York: McGraw-Hill.

Shields, C. G., King, D. A., & Wynne, L. C. (1995). Interventions with later life families. In R. H. Mikesell, D. Lusterman, & S. H. McDaniel (Eds.), *Integrating family therapy* (pp. 141–160). Washington, DC: American Psychological Association.

Smith, R. L., & Stevens-Smith, P. (1992). A critique of healthy family functioning. In R. L. Smith & P. Stevens-Smith (Eds.), *Family counseling and therapy* (pp. 3–13). Ann Arbor, MI: ERIC/CAPS.

Sporakowski, M. J. (1995). Assessment and diagnosis in marriage and family counseling. *Journal of Counseling & Development, 74,* 60–64.

Steinhauser, P. D., Santa-Barbara, J., & Skinner, H. (1984). The process model of family functioning. *Canadian Journal of Psychiatry, 29,* 77–88.

Stinnett, N., & DeFrain, J. (1985). *Secrets of strong families.* Boston: Little, Brown.

Strong, B., DeVault, C., & Sayad, B. W. (2001). *The marriage and family experience* (8th ed.). Belmont, CA: Wadsworth.

Thomas, M. B. (1992). *An introduction to marital and family therapy: Counseling toward healthier family systems across the life span.* Upper Saddle River, NJ: Merrill/Prentice Hall.

Tomm, K. (1989). *PIPS, TIPS, HIPS, and Slips: A heuristic alternative to DSM-III?* Paper presented at the AAMFT annual conference, San Francisco.

Treadway, D. (1987, July/August). The ties that bind. *Family Therapy Networker, 11,* 16–23.

Walsh, F. (1995). From family damage to family challenge. In R. H. Mikesell, D.-D. Lusterman, & S. H. McDaniel (Eds.), *Integrating family therapy* (pp. 587–606). Washington, DC: American Psychological Association.

Watzlawick, P. (1978). *The language of change.* New York: Basic Books.

Watzlawick, P., Beavin, J. H., & Jackson, D. D. (1967). *Pragmatics of human communication.* New York: Norton.

Watzlawick, P., Weakland, J. H., & Fisch, R. (1974). *Change: Principles of problem formation and problem resolution.* New York: W. W. Norton.

West, G. D., Hosie, T. W., & Zarski, J. J. (1987). Family dynamics and substance abuse: A preliminary study. *Journal of Counseling and Development, 65,* 487–490.

Wilcoxon, S. A. (1985). Healthy family functioning: The other side of family pathology. *Journal of Counseling and Development, 63,* 495–499.

Wills, T. A., Weiss, R. L., & Patterson, G. R. (1974). A behavioral analysis of the determinants of marital satisfaction. *Journal of Consulting and Clinical Psychology, 42,* 802–811.

Wolin, S. J., & Wolin, S. (1993). *The resilient self: How survivors of troubled families rise above adversity.* New York: Villard.

# PART TWO

# Therapeutic Approaches to Working with Families

# CHAPTER 3

# Rationale and History of Family Therapy

In the lighting of candles and exchanging of vows
we are united as husband and wife.

In the holiday periods of non-stop visits
we are linked again briefly to our roots.

Out of crises and the mundane
we celebrate life
appreciating the novel
and accepting the routine
as we meet each other anew
amid ancestral histories and current reflections.

Families are a weaver's dream
as unique threads from the past
are intertwined with the present
to form a colorful tapestry
of relationships in time.

*Gladding, 1991*

The practice of family therapy is relatively new "dating back only a few decades" (Sayger, Homrich, & Horne, 2000, p. 12). Its theoretical and clinical beginnings were hammered out in the 1940s, 1950s, and 1960s while its real growth as a legitimate form of therapy occurred in the 1970s, 1980s, and 1990s (Foley, 1989; Kaslow, 1991). Family therapy differs from individual and group counseling both in its emphasis and in its clientele (Hines, 1988; Trotzer, 1988). Family therapy concentrates on making changes in total life systems; individual and group counseling focus on select intrapersonal and interpersonal changes.

The rise of family therapy as a practice and then as a profession closely followed dramatic changes in the form, composition, and structure of the American family. These variations were a result of the family's shift from a primarily nuclear unit to a complex and varied institution, for example, single parents, remarried families, and dual-career families (Pickens, 1997). Family therapy has also been connected to the influence of creative, innovative, and assertive mental health practitioners who devised and advocated new ways of providing services to their clients (Nichols, 1993).

Although some of the theories and methods employed in family therapy are similar to those used in other settings, many differ. This chapter examines the genesis and development of family therapy. The emphasis is on the people, events, and interactional processes that most contributed to the formation of the field. Before examining these historical events, the rationale for working with families and reasons for working with families instead of individuals is highlighted.

# The Rationale for Family Therapy

One reason for conducting family therapy is the belief that most life difficulties arise and can best be addressed within families. In this view, families are seen as powerful forces that work for either the good or the detriment of their members. Because an interconnectedness exists among family members, the actions of the members affect the health or dysfunctionality of each individual and the family as a whole.

Another reason for working therapeutically with families is the proven effectiveness of such treatment. In a landmark issue of the *Journal of Marital and Family Therapy*, edited by William Pinsof and Lyman Wynne (1995), a meta-analysis was conducted on more than 250 studies. The results showed that various forms of family therapy worked better than no treatment at all and no study showed negative or destructive effects. In addition, family and couple therapy had a positive effect in treating such disorders as adult schizophrenia, adult alcoholism and drug abuse, depression in women who were in distressed marriages, adult hypertension, dementia, adult obesity, adolescent drug abuse, anorexia in young adolescent females, childhood conduct disorders, aggression and noncompliance in children with attention deficit disorders, childhood autism, chronic physical illnesses in adults and children, and couple distress and conflict. While couple and family therapy was not in itself sufficient to treat a number of severe and chronic mental disorders, for example, unipolar and bipolar affective disorders, it "significantly enhances the treatment packages for these disorders" (Pinsof & Wynne, 2000, p. 2).

A final rationale for family therapy concerns client satisfaction. In a national survey of family therapists and their clients, Doherty and Simmons (1996) found that over 97% of clients were satisfied with the services they received from marriage and family therapists and rated these services good to excellent. In addition, an equally large percentage of clients reported that the services they received from marriage and family therapists helped them deal more effectively with their problems; that is, they got the help they wanted.

In summary, given the nature and origin of family troubles, as well as the effectiveness and satisfaction with forms of family therapy, it is little wonder that this form of treatment has gained and is continuing to achieve recognition and status in the mental health field.

# Reasons for Working with Families as Opposed to Working with Individuals

In addition to the rationale for family therapy, there are a number of advantages to working with entire families as a unit rather than just the individuals within them. First, family therapy allows practitioners to "see causation as circular as well as, at times, linear" (Fishman, 1988, p. 5). This type of view enables clinicians to examine events broadly and in light of their complexity. It keeps therapists from being overly simplistic when offering help to those with whom they work. For example, a circular view of the problem of anorexia nervosa considers the friction within the whole family, especially the couple relationship. With this perspective, the inward and outward social pressures of the young person displaying obvious symptoms of the disorder are examined, but in a much broader interactive context.

A second advantage family therapy has over individual therapy is that it involves other real, significant individuals as a part of the process. There are no surrogate substitutes or "empty chairs" who act as significant people in a client's life. Instead, therapists deal directly with the family members involved. In other words, most family therapy does not depend on role plays or simulations. Therefore, if a young man is having difficulty with his parents or siblings, he is able to address them in person as he strives toward resolution. This type of emphasis usually cuts through to the reality of a situation more quickly and more efficiently than indirect methods.

Third, in family therapy, all members of a family are given the same message simultaneously. Thus, they are challenged to work on issues together. This approach eliminates "secrets" and essentially makes the covert overt. The result is an increase in openness and communication within the family. For example, if a couple is fighting, the issues over which there is tension are discussed within the family context. In this setting, family members become aware of what is involved in the situation. They deal with conflict directly. They also have the opportunity to generate ideas on what might be most helpful in bringing their situation to a successful resolution.

Fourth, family therapy usually takes less time than individual counseling. Many family therapists report that the length of time they are engaged in work with a family can literally be as brief as a few sessions (Fishman, 1988; Gilbert & Shmukler, 1997). In fact, some family therapy approaches, notably those connected with strategic and solution-focused family therapy, emphasize contracting with client families for limited amounts of time (usually no more than 10 sessions). The stress on time is motivational for therapists and families because it tends to maximize their energy and innovation for creating resolutions.

Finally, the approaches utilized in working with families focus on interpersonal instead of primarily intrapersonal relationships. This type of difference is comparable with seeing the forest instead of just the trees. The larger scope by which family therapy examines problematic behavior enables practitioners to find more unique ways to address difficulties.

Having examined the reasons for using family therapy as opposed to individual therapy, it is important to understand how it developed. The following sections trace the development of family therapy over time.

# Family Therapy Through the Decades

Family therapy is an extension of the attempt by people throughout history to cure emotional suffering. "Over 2,000 years ago the first written accounts of an integrative system of treating mental illness were recorded" (Kottler, 1991, p. 34). Prehistorical records indicate that systematic attempts at helping were prevalent even before that time. Family members throughout history have tried to be of assistance to each other. This help initially took two forms:

1. Elders gave younger members of family clans and tribes advice on interpersonal relationships.
2. Adult members of these social units took care of the very young and the very old (Strong & DeVault, 1998).

Despite this history of care, family therapy is one of the newer methods of professional helping, with its roots in the 20th century.

Even though it is relatively recent in its formal development, multiple events have influenced and shaped the profession of family therapy. Although all of the facts and personalities mentioned here had some impact on the growth of the field, some were more pivotal than others. The exact importance of particulars sometimes changes according to who is recounting events. The order in which these developments occurred, however, can be charted chronologically, and some historical facts and figures stand out regardless of one's historical orientation.

## Family Therapy: Before 1940

### Inhibitors of the Development of Family Therapy

Prior to the 1940s, family therapy in the United States was almost a nonentity. Three social influences contributed to this phenomenon. The first involved myth and perception. The myth of rugged individualism was the predominant deterrent to the genesis of family therapy. Healthy people were seen as adequate to handle their own problems.

Rugged individualism stemmed from the settling of the United States, especially the American West. Individuals were expected to solve their own problems if they were to survive. Intertwined with this myth was the perception handed down from the Puritans and other religious groups that those who prospered were ordained by God (Strong & DeVault, 1998). To admit one had difficulties, either inside or outside of a family context, was to also admit that one was not among the elect.

A second social factor that deterred the development of family therapy was tradition. Historically, people usually confided with clergy, lawyers, and doctors, rather than with mental health professionals, when they discussed their marital and family concerns. These professionals knew the families in question well because they usually lived with them in a shared community over many years. Seeking advice and counsel from these individuals was different from talking to a professional family specialist.

A third factor that prevented family therapy from evolving before the 1940s was the theoretical emphases of the times. The major psychological theories in the United States in the early part of the 20th century were psychoanalysis and behaviorism. Both were philosophically and pragmatically opposed to dealing with more than individual concerns. Proponents of psychoanalysis, for instance, believed that dealing with more than one person at a time in therapy would contaminate the transference process and prevent depth analysis from occurring. Likewise, behaviorists stressed straightforward work with clients, usually in the form of conditioning and counterconditioning. The social and political climate required for family therapy to develop and grow was almost nonexistent.

### Catalysts for the Growth of Family Therapy

Despite this inhospitable environment, four factors combined to make family therapy accepted and eventually popular. The first was the growth of the number of women enrolled in colleges and their demand for courses in family life education (Broderick & Schrader, 1981). Educators from a number of disciplines responded to this need. Among the most noteworthy was Ernest Groves, who taught courses on parenting and family living at Boston University and the University of North Carolina. Groves later became instrumental in founding the American Association of Marriage Counselors in 1942 (Broderick & Schrader, 1991).

The second event that set the stage for the development of family therapy was the initial establishment of marriage counseling. In New York City, Abraham and Hannah Stone were among the leading advocates for and practitioners of marriage counseling in the late 1920s and 1930s. Emily Mudd began the Marriage Council of Philadelphia in 1932, which was devoted to a similar endeavor. Meanwhile, in California, Paul Popenoe established the American Institute of Family Relations, which was in essence his private practice. Popenoe introduced the term *marriage counseling* into the English language. He popularized the profession of marriage counseling by writing a monthly article, "Can This Marriage Be Saved?" in the *Ladies Home Journal*—a practice that began in 1945 and continues today (Broderick & Schrader, 1991).

A third impetus to the genesis of family counseling was the founding of the National Council on Family Relations in 1938 and the establishment of its journal, *Marriage and Family Living,* in 1939. This association promoted research-based knowledge about family life throughout the United States. Through its pioneer efforts, and those of the American Home Economics Association, information about aspects of family life were observed, recorded, and presented.

The fourth favorable event that helped launch family therapy as a profession was the work of county home extension agents. These agents began working with families educationally in the 1920s and 1930s and helped those they encountered to better understand the dynamics of their family situations. Some of the ideas and advice offered by agents were advocated by Alfred Adler, who developed a practical approach for working with families that became widespread in the United States in the 1930s (Dinkmeyer, Dinkmeyer, & Sperry, 2000; Sherman, 1999).

## Family Therapy: 1940 to 1949

Several important events took place in the 1940s that had a lasting impact on the field of family therapy. One of the most important was the establishment of an association for professionals working with couples. As mentioned earlier, the American Association of Marriage Counselors (AAMC) was formed in 1942 by Ernest Groves among others. Its purpose was to help professionals network with one another in regard to the theory and practice of marriage counseling. It also devised standards for the practice of this specialty.

A second landmark event of the 1940s was the publication of the first account of concurrent marital therapy by Bela Mittleman (1948) of the New York Psychoanalytic Institute. Mittleman's position stressed the importance of object relations in couple relationships. It was a radical departure from the previously held intrapsychic point of view.

A third significant focus during the 1940s was the study of families of schizophrenics. One of the early pioneers in this area was Theodore Lidz, who published a survey of fifty families. He found that the majority of schizophrenics came from broken homes and/or had seriously disturbed family relationships (Lidz & Lidz, 1949). Lidz later introduced into the family therapy literature the concepts of **schism,** the division of the family into two antagonistic and competing groups, and **skew,** whereby one partner in the marriage dominates the family to a striking degree, as a result of serious personality disorder in at least one of the partners.

The final factor that influenced family counseling in the 1940s was World War II and its aftermath. The events of the war brought considerable stress to millions of families in the United States. Many men were separated from their families because of war duty. Numerous women went to work in factories. Deaths and disabilities of loved ones added further pain and suffering. A need to work with families suffering trauma and change became apparent. To help meet mental health needs, the National Mental Health Act of 1946 was passed by Congress. "This legislation authorized funds for research, demonstration, training, and assistance to states in the use of the most effective methods of prevention, diagnosis, and treatment of mental health disorders" (Hershenson & Power, 1987, p. 11). Mental health work with families would eventually be funded under this act.

## Family Therapy: 1950 to 1959

Some family therapy historians consider the 1950s to be the genesis of the movement (Guerin, 1976). Landmark events in the development of family therapy in the 1950s centered more on people than on organizations, because of the difficulty of launching this therapeutic approach in the face of well-established opposition groups, such as psychiatrists.

**Important Personalities in Family Therapy in the 1950s**

A number of professionals contributed to the interdisciplinary underpinnings of family therapy in the 1950s (Shields, Wynne, McDaniel, & Gawinski, 1994). Each, in his or her own way, contributed to the conceptual and clinical vitality as well as the growth of the field.

Nathan Ackerman was one of the most significant personalities of the decade. Although he advocated treating the family from a systems perspective as early as the 1930s (Ackerman, 1938), it was not until the 1950s that Ackerman became well known and prominent. His strong belief in working with families and his persistently high energy influenced leading psychoanalytically trained psychiatrists to explore the area of family therapy. An example of this impact can be seen in Ackerman's book *The Psychodynamics of Family Life* (1958), in which he urged psychiatrists to go beyond understanding the role of family dynamics in the ethology of mental illness and to begin treating client mental disorders in light of family process dynamics. To show that his revolutionary ideas were workable, he set up a practice in New York City, where he could show his ideas had merit through pointing out results in case examples.

Another influential figure of the time was Gregory Bateson, in Palo Alto, California. Bateson, like many researchers of the 1950s, was interested in communication patterns in families of schizophrenics. He obtained several government grants for study and, with Jay Haley, John Weakland, and eventually Don Jackson, Bateson formulated a novel, controversial, and influential theory of dysfunctional communication called the **double-bind** (Bateson, Jackson, Haley, & Weakland, 1956). This theory states that two seemingly contradictory messages may exist on different levels and lead to confusion, if not schizophrenic behavior, on the part of some individuals. For example, a person may receive the message to "act boldly and be careful." Such communication leads to ignoring one message and obeying the other or to a type of stressful behavioral paralysis where one does nothing because it is unclear which message to follow and how.

Bateson left the field of family research in the early 1960s, and the Bateson group disbanded in 1962. However, much of the work of this original group was expanded on by the Mental Research Institute (MRI), which Don Jackson created in Palo Alto in 1958. Jackson was an innovative thinker and practitioner who helped lead the family therapy field away from a pathology-oriented, individual illness concept of problems to one that was relationship oriented (Ray, 2000). Among the later luminaries to join MRI with Jackson were Virginia Satir and Paul Watzlawick. A unique feature of this group was the treatment of families, which was resisted by Bateson. In fact, the MRI established **brief therapy,** an elaboration of the work of Milton Erickson and one of the first new approaches to family therapy (Haley, 1976).

A third leading professional in the 1950s was Carl Whitaker. Whitaker "risked violating the conventions of traditional psychotherapy" during this time, by including spouses and children in therapy (Broderick & Schrader, 1991, p. 26). As chief of psychiatry at Emory University in Atlanta, Whitaker (1958) published the results of his work in **dual therapy (conjoint couple therapy)**. He also set up the first conference on family therapy at Sea Island, Georgia, in 1955.

A fourth key figure of the 1950s was Murray Bowen. Beginning in the mid-1950s, under the sponsorship of the National Institute of Mental Health, Bowen began holding therapy sessions with all family members present, as part of a research project with schizophrenics (Guerin, 1976). Although he was not initially successful in helping family members constructively talk to each other and resolve difficulties, Bowen gained experience that would later help him formulate an elaborate theory on the influence of previous generations on the mental health of families.

Other key figures in family therapy who began their careers in the 1950s were Ivan Boszormenyi-Nagy, at the Eastern Pennsylvania Psychiatric Institute (EPPI), and his associates, including James Framo and Gerald Zuk. The work of this group eventually resulted in the development of Nagy's contextual therapy. "At the heart of this approach is the healing of human relationships through trust and commitment, done primarily by developing loyalty, fairness, and reciprocity" (Anderson, Anderson, & Hovestadt, 1993, p. 3).

## Family Therapy: 1960 to 1969

The decade of the 1960s was an era of rapid growth in family therapy. During this time, the idea of working with families was embraced by more professionals, a number of whom were quite charismatic. Four of the most prominent of these figures were Jay Haley, Salvador Minuchin, Virginia Satir, and Carl Whitaker. Other family therapists who began in the 1950s, such as Nathan Ackerman, John Bell, and Murray Bowen, continued contributing to the concepts and theories in the field. Another factor that made an impact at this time was the widespread introduction of systems theory. Finally, in the 1960s, training centers and academic programs in family therapy were either started, strengthened, or proposed.

### Major Family Therapists of the 1960s

Numerous family therapists emerged in the 1960s. They came from many interdisciplinary backgrounds and, like their predecessors of the 1950s, most were considered "mavericks" (Framo, 1996). The following therapists are discussed here because of their significant impact in shaping the direction of family therapy.

Jay Haley was probably the most important figure in family therapy in the 1960s. During this time, Haley had connections with most of the important figures in the field, and through his writings and travels, he kept professionals linked and informed. Also during this time, he began to formulate what would become his own version of strategic family therapy. Haley relied most on expanding and elaborating on the work of Milton Erickson (Haley, 1963). He shared with Erickson an emphasis on gaining and maintaining power during treatment. Like Erickson, Haley often gave client families permission to do what they would have done naturally (e.g., to withhold information). Furthermore, Haley used directives, as Erickson had, to get client families to do more within therapy than merely gain insight.

From 1961 to 1969, Jay Haley edited *Family Process*, the first journal in the field of family therapy. Through it, he helped shape an emerging profession. In the late 1960s, Haley moved from Palo Alto to Philadelphia to join the Child Guidance Clinic, which was under the direction of Salvador Minuchin. His move brought two creative minds together and helped generate new ideas in the minds of both men and the people with whom they worked and trained.

Salvador Minuchin, the psychiatrist with whom Haley collaborated in 1967, first began his work with families at the Wiltwyck School for Boys in New York State in the early 1960s. He used his own form of family therapy with urban slum families he encountered because it reduced the recidivism rate for the delinquents who comprised the population of the school. The publication of his account of this work, *Families of the Slums* (Minuchin, Montalvo, Guerney, Rosman, & Schumer, 1967), received much recognition and led to his appointment as director of the Philadelphia Child Guidance Clinic and to the formulation of a new and influential theory of family therapy: structural family therapy.

Like most pioneers in the field of family therapy (e.g., Whitaker, Haley), Minuchin did not have formal training in how to treat families. However, he did have an idea of what healthy families should look like in regard to a hierarchy, and he used this mental map as a basis on which to construct his approach to helping families change. Another innovative idea he initiated at the end of the 1960s was the training of indigenous members of the local black community as paraprofessional family therapists. He believed this special effort was needed because cultural differences often made it difficult for white middle-class therapists to understand and relate successfully to urban blacks and Hispanics. Overall, Minuchin began transforming the Philadelphia Child Guidance Clinic from a second-rate and poor facility to the leading center for the training of family therapists on the East Coast of the United States.

Virginia Satir was the most entertaining and exciting family therapist to emerge in the 1960s. Satir, as a social worker in private practice in Chicago, started seeing family members as a group for treatment in the 1950s (Broderick & Schrader, 1991). However, she gained prominence as a family therapist at the Mental Research Institute. There she collaborated with her colleagues and branched out on her own. Satir was unique in being the only woman among the pioneers of family therapy. She had "unbounded optimism about people . . . and her empathic abilities were unmatched" (Framo, 1996, p. 311). While her male counterparts concentrated on problems and building conceptual frameworks for theories and power, she touched and nurtured her clients and spoke of the importance of self-esteem, compassion, and congruent expression of feelings.

Satir gained national recognition with the publication of her book *Conjoint Family Therapy* (1964). In this text, she described the importance of seeing both members of a couple together at the same time, and she detailed how such a process could and should occur. Her clear style of writing made this book influential. Overall, "Satir's ability to synthesize ideas, combined with her creative development of teaching techniques and general personal charisma, gave her a central position in the field" of family therapy (Guerin, 1976, p. 8).

Carl Whitaker can be described in many ways. He dared to be different and at his best was creative as well as wise (Framo, 1996). He was never "conventional." Whitaker, a psychiatrist, became interested in working with families in the 1940s. As already mentioned, he was chair of the psychiatry department of Emory University in the early 1950s. In 1955, he resigned to begin a private practice.

His main influence and renown in the field, however, came following his move to become a professor of psychiatry at the University of Wisconsin in 1965. It was at Wisconsin that Whitaker was able to write and lecture extensively. Beginning in 1965, his affectively based interventions, which were usually spontaneous and sometimes appeared outrageous, gained notoriety in the field of family therapy. In the 1960s, Whitaker also nurtured the field of family therapy by connecting professionals with similar interests.

### Continuing Leaders in Family Therapy During the 1960s

Nathan Ackerman continued to be a leader of the family therapy movement throughout the 1960s. In 1961, with Don Jackson, he cofounded *Family Process,* the first journal devoted to family therapy and one that is still preeminent in the field. One of Ackerman's most significant books during this decade was *Treating the Troubled Family* (1966). In this text, he elaborated on how to intervene with families and "tickle the family's defenses" through being involved with them, being confrontative and bringing covert issues out into the open.

John Bell, like Carl Whitaker, began treating families long before he was recognized as a leader in the field of family therapy. Bell's work began in the 1950s when he started using group therapy as a basis for working with families (Gurel, 1999; Kaslow, 1980). He published his ideas about **family group therapy** a decade later (Bell, 1961) and proposed a structured program of treatment that conceptualized family members as strangers. Members become known to each other in stages similar to those found in groups.

Bell taught his natural family group approach at the University of California, Berkeley, in 1963 in one of the first graduate courses on family therapy ever offered in the United States. From 1968 to 1973, he directed the Mental Research Institute in Palo Alto. It was Bell's belief that "all children 9 years or older and all other adult family members living in the home should be included in family therapy and should be present for all sessions" (Nichols & Everett, 1986, p. 43). Bell's ideas were unique and received considerable criticism, thus generating a good deal of discussion about family therapy (Hines, 1988).

Murray Bowen gained considerable insight into the dynamics and treatment of families during the 1960s. Part of the reason was that he was able to successfully deal with problems within his own family of origin. Another reason was that he began to see a connectedness between working with families that had a schizophrenic member and working with families that had other problems.

One of his most significant discoveries was the "emotional reactivity" of many troubled families when brought together to solve problems. In these situations, family members had difficulty maintaining their identities and their actions. They would often resemble what Bowen (1961) called an **undifferentiated family ego mass**. In working with these families, Bowen found that by being cognitive and detached, he could help them establish appropriate relationship boundaries and avoid projecting (or **triangulating**) interpersonal dyadic difficulties onto a third person or object (i.e., a scapegoat).

### Systems Theory

With the emergence of new ideas came a novel theoretical perspective on which to center these concepts: **systems theory** (Bertalanffy, 1968). In systems theory, a **system** is a set of elements standing in interaction with one another. Each element in the system is affected by whatever happens to any other element. Thus, the system is only as strong as its weakest part. Likewise, the system is greater than the sum of its parts. Whether the system is a human body or a family, it is organized in a particular manner with boundaries that are more or less open (i.e., permeable) depending on the amount and type of feedback received.

By viewing the family in this manner, clinicians in the 1960s focused away from linear causality (direct cause and effect) and more on circular causality (the idea that events are related through a series of interacting loops or repeating cycles). Subsequently, family therapists began to claim their role as specialists within therapy. This position was reinforced in 1963, when the first state licensure law regulating family counselors was passed in California. This legislation was just the beginning of family therapy's increasing prominence.

### Institutes and Training Centers

In addition to the rise of personalities and systems theory, in the decade of the 1960s, training institutes and centers also came into prominence. In California, the Mental Research Institute in Palo Alto flourished even after Jay Haley's departure for Philadelphia in 1967 and Don Jackson's death in 1968. Likewise, the Family Institute of New York (headed by Ackerman) thrived during this time, as did the Albert Einstein College of Medicine in New York City and the affiliated Bronx State Hospital (Broderick & Schrader, 1991).

In Philadelphia, the Philadelphia Child Guidance Clinic opened its facilities to surrounding neighborhoods and to aspiring family therapists. Innovative techniques, such as the "bug in the ear" form of communication, were devised at the clinic during this time. In 1964, the Family Institute of Philadelphia emerged. This institute was a merger of the EPPI and the Philadelphia Psychiatric Center and fostered such notable practitioner/theorists as Gerald Zuk and Ross Speck (Broderick & Schrader, 1991).

Meanwhile, in Boston, the Boston Family Institute was established in 1969 under the direction of Fred Duhl and David Kantor (Duhl, 1983). This institute focused on expressive and dramatic interventions and originated the technique of family sculpting.

Overseas, the Institute for Family Studies in Milan was formed in 1967. This institute was based on the MRI model and came into prominence in the 1970s with many innovative, short-term approaches to working with families (Selvini Palazzoli, Boscolo, Cecchin, & Prata, 1978).

## Family Therapy: 1970 to 1979

The 1970s were marked by several nodal events in regard to family therapy. These events centered around many activities, including a major membership increase in the American Association for Marriage and Family Therapy (AAMFT), the founding of the American Family Therapy Association (AFTA), the refinement of theories, the influence of foreign therapies and therapists (especially the Milan Group), the growth of family enrichment, and the introduction of feminism into the family therapy field.

### Membership in the American Association for Marriage and Family Therapy

In 1970, the membership of the AAMFT stood at 973. By 1979, membership had increased more than 777% to 7,565 (Gurman & Kniskern, 1981). The dynamic growth of the association can be explained in many ways including that it was recognized by the Department of Health, Education, and Welfare in 1977 as an accrediting body for programs granting degrees in marriage and family therapy. Also, at about the same time, the association changed its name from the American Association of Marriage and Family Counselors to the American Association for Marriage and Family Therapy.

In addition, more focus was placed on families and therapeutic ways of working with them as a result of the upheavals in family life in the 1960s. Furthermore, many of the pioneers of the family therapy movement, such as Virginia Satir, James Framo, Carl Whitaker, Salvador Minuchin, Jay Haley, and Florence Kaslow, began making a greater impact on therapists across the nation with their workshop presentations and writings. To add to this impact, in 1974, the AAMFT began publishing its own professional periodical, the *Journal of Marital and Family Therapy*, with William C. Nichols, Jr., as the first editor, and made plans late in the decade to move its headquarters from Claremont, California, to Washington, D.C. (an event that actually transpired in 1982).

### Establishment of the American Family Therapy Association (AFTA)

AFTA was founded in 1977 by a small group of mental health professionals who were active during the early years when the field of family therapy was emerging. Initially, it strove to represent "the interests of systemic family therapists as distinct from psychodynamic marriage counselors" (Sauber, L'Abate, & Weeks, 1985, p. 180). Leaders of AFTA included Murray Bowen and James Framo. As a "think tank," AFTA's annual meeting brings together professionals to address a variety of clinical, research, and teaching topics.

In 1981, a joint liaison committee made up of AAMFT and AFTA representatives was formed to address the respective roles of the two organizations within the profession. AFTA was identified as an academy of advanced professionals interested in the exchange of ideas; AAMFT retained government recognition for its role in providing credentials to marriage and family therapists.

### Refinement of Family Therapy Theories

The 1970s marked the growth and refinement of family therapy theories outside the psychoanalytical tradition. It is ironic and symbolic that Nathan Ackerman, who carried the banner of psychoanalytical family therapy, died in 1971 (Bloch & Simon, 1982). It is also interesting to note that the works of Salvador Minuchin (structural family therapy), Gerald Patterson (behavioral family therapy), Carl Whitaker (experiential family therapy), and Jay Haley (strategic family therapy) increased in frequency, scope, and influence during this decade. The newness of ideas generated in the 1960s bore fruit in the 1970s.

One major example of this phenomenon was the work of Salvador Minuchin. In a clearly articulated book, *Families and Family Therapy*, Minuchin (1974) outlined a practical guide for conducting structural family therapy. He followed this publication, later in the decade, with a complementary coauthored text entitled *Psychosomatic Families: Anorexia Nervosa in Context* (Minuchin, Rosman, & Baker, 1978), which showcased in a dramatic way the power of the therapy he had created. These writings, combined with his well-staffed training center in Philadelphia, made structural family therapy a major theoretical force in family therapy circles in a relatively brief period of time.

### Influence of Foreign Therapies and Therapists

In Europe, in the late 1960s and early 1970s, the development of family therapy grew rapidly. By the mid-1970s, theories and theorists, especially in Italy and Great Britain, became influential in the United States. The influx of non-U.S. family therapists' ideas led many American professionals to question "particular ethnocentric values about what is good and true for families" (Broderick & Schrader, 1991, p. 35).

Particularly influential was the Milan (Italy) Group headed by Mara Selvini Palazzoli and staffed by three other psychoanalytically trained psychiatrists: Gianfrano Cecchin, Giulana Prata, and Luigi Boscolo. Their book, *Paradox and Counterparadox* (1978), was influenced by the work of Bateson and Watzlawick in Palo Alto. However, it was original in its emphasis on **circular questioning** (asking questions that highlight differences among family members) and **triadic questioning** (asking a third family member how two others members of the family relate). The Milan approach emphasized developing a hypothesis about the family before their arrival. Furthermore, it prescribed homework assignments that were often ritualistic and difficult.

Two British leaders in the helping profession who influenced the development of family therapy in the United States were R. D. Laing and Robin Skynner. Laing (1965) coined the term **mystification** to describe how some families mask what is going on between family members by giving conflicting and contradictory explanations of events. His complicated but interesting book, *Knots* (1970), further enhanced his status as an original thinker in understanding universal family dynamics in dysfunctional families. Skynner (1981) developed a brief version of psychoanalytic family therapy in the 1970s that helped complement and enrich the work done by Ackerman and Boszormenyi-Nagy.

### Growth of Marriage/Family Enrichment

The exact date of the launching of preventive programs for family enhancement is difficult to trace, but credit is often given to David and Vera Mace. The Maces were pioneers of marriage counseling in England. After they moved to the United States in the early 1960s, they began leading retreats for couples and developing enrichment programs (Mace, 1983). On their 40th wedding anniversary, in July 1973, they established the Association of Couples for Marriage Enrichment (ACME).

At about the same time as the Maces were initiating their efforts in marriage enrichment, a Catholic priest, Father Gabriel Calvo, began leading retreats for married couples in Barcelona, Spain. His efforts later evolved into the Marriage Encounter Movement.

Other pioneers in marriage/family enrichment were Bernard G. Guerney, Jr., (1977) and his four-basic-skill relationship enhancement approach, and the staffs of the Family and Children's Service in Minneapolis and the University of Minnesota Family Study Center, who developed the Couples Communication Programs (Miller, Nunnally, & Wackman, 1977, 1979).

### Feminist Theory and Family Therapy

"Feminist thinking explicitly entered the family therapy field in the 1970s and has increasingly influenced the theory and practice of family therapy" (Framo, 1996, p. 303). As an approach, **feminist family therapy** "is an attitude, a lens, a body of ideas about gender hierarchy and its impact rather than a specific model of therapy or a grab bag of clinical techniques. Feminists recognize the overriding importance of the power structure in any human system" (Carter, 1992, p. 66). They question among other things whether some concepts in family therapy, such as complementarity, circularity, and neutrality, are oppressive to women (May, 1998). Table 3.1 lists some characteristics of gender-sensitive family therapy.

**Table 3.1**
Characteristics of Gender-Sensitive Family Therapy

| Nonsexist Counseling | Empowerment/Feminist/<br>Gender-Aware Counseling |
|---|---|
| Does not reinforce stereotyped gender roles. | Helps clients recognize the impact of social, cultural, and political factors on their lives. |
| Encourages clients to consider a wide range of choices, especially in regard to careers. | Helps clients transcend limitations resulting from gender stereotyping. |
| Avoids allowing gender stereotypes to affect diagnoses. | Recognizes the degree to which individual behaviors may reflect internalization of harmful social standards. |
| Avoids use of sexist assessment instruments. | Includes gender-role analysis as a component of assessment. |
| Treats male and female clients equally. | Helps clients develop and integrate traits that are culturally defined as "masculine" and "feminine." |
| Avoids misuse of power in the counseling relationship. | Develops collaborative counselor–client relationships. |

From "Gender Sensitivity and Family Empowerment" by J. Lewis, 1993, *Family Psychology and Counseling, 1,* 1–7. Used with permission of Judith Lewis.

The challenge to family therapy by feminist theory began in 1978, when an article by Rachel Hare-Mustin entitled "A Feminist Approach to Family Therapy" was published in *Family Process.* Hare-Mustin took the position that family therapy discriminated against women because it basically promoted the status quo that women were unequal in regard to their duties and roles within families.

After Hare-Mustin's paper was published, a number of other pieces on the adequacy of family therapy from a systemic perspective began to be published. Among the most consistently voiced views, from feminist therapists' perspectives, is that historic sexism and structural inequalities cannot be corrected through improving relationships among family members or creating a new family hierarchy. Rather, the goals of working with a family are "to facilitate the growth of a strong, competent woman who has enhanced control over resources" and "to increase the ability of women to work together politically to change society and its institutions" (Libow, Raskin, & Caust, 1982, p. 8).

Although feminist family therapists "represent a wide range of theoretical orientations," they are "drawn together by their recognition that sexism limits the psychological well-being of women and men, by their advocacy of equality in relationships and society, and by their refusal to use any counseling methods or explanatory concepts that promote bias" (Enns, 1992, p. 338). Training models developed by feminist family therapists that place gender at the heart of educating family therapists have been and will continue to be developed (e.g., Storm, 1991).

# Family Therapy: 1980 to 1989

Several important events marked the emergence of family therapy in the 1980s. One was the retirement or death of some of the leading pioneers in the movement and the emergence of new leaders. A second was the growth in the number of individuals and associations devoted to family therapy. A third was an increase in research in family therapy (Miller, 1986) and an explosion in publications devoted to family therapy. Finally, further recognition of marriage and family therapy came about on a national level.

### Change in Family Therapy Leadership

In the 1980s, new leadership began to emerge in family therapy circles. One reason was the aging of the initial pioneers in the field. Another reason was the maturity of clinicians who studied in the 1960s and 1970s with the founders of the movement. The second and third generations of family therapists had new ideas and abundant energy (Kaslow, 1990). They basically preserved the best of the founders while forging out in different directions. Some of the more established leaders in the field, such as Jay Haley, switched emphases at this time and maintained their leadership roles.

Within the growth of this movement, many women came to the forefront. Among them were Monica McGoldrick, Rachel Hare-Mustin, Carolyn Attneave, Peggy Papp, Peggy Penn, Cloe Madanes, Fromma Walsh, and Betty Carter. These women began to create novel theories and to challenge older ones. Cloe Madanes was especially prolific and creative during the last part of the 1980s. Overall, the work of new women leaders in family therapy contributed much to the profession. Many of these women realized the need to "include women's voices and experiences" within the family therapy field in order to gain a richer and more evenly balanced perspective on family life and to discern what changes are needed in families (Carter, 1992, p. 69). The Women's Project in Family Therapy (Walters, Carter, Papp, & Silverstein, 1988) was a major undertaking of these researchers and practitioners who sought to emphasize the absence of gender in the formation of systems theory. Their presence and prominence altered the view that a professional panel of family therapists consisted of four men and Virginia Satir.

### Growth in the Profession of Family Therapy

Family therapy grew significantly as a profession in the 1980s. The membership of the AAMFT, for instance, almost doubled to a total of 14,000 members. At the same time, two new associations devoted to the study and practice of family therapy were formed. The first was the Division of Family Psychology, which was established within the American Psychological Association (APA) in 1984. The division was established because of the desire by some family practitioners to maintain their identity as psychologists (Kaslow, 1990). Such noted individuals as James Alexander, Alan Gurman, Florence Kaslow, Luciano L'Abate, Rachel Hare-Mustin, Duncan Stanton, and Gerald Zuk were among those who became affiliated with this division.

The second new professional association formed in the 1980s was the International Association of Marriage and Family Counselors (IAMFC), which was established initially as an interest group within the American Counseling Association (ACA) in 1986. The

IAMFC grew from an initial membership of 143 in 1986 to more than 4,000 in 2001. In 1990, IAMFC became a division of ACA.

The initial goals and purposes of the IAMFC were to enhance marriage and the family through providing educational programs, conducting research, sponsoring conferences, and establishing interprofessional contacts, and by examining and removing conditions that create barriers to marriages and families. Since its formation, the IAMFC has broadened its vision to include work in promoting ethical practices, setting high-quality training standards, helping families and couples cope successfully, and using counseling knowledge and systemic methods to ameliorate the problems confronting marriages and families (Maynard & Olson, 1987). Overall, the IAMFC provides a base for training, research, collaboration, and support for counselors who work with families (Pietrzak & L'Amoreaux, 1998).

### Development of Research Techniques in Family Therapy

Until the 1980s, research techniques and solid research in family therapy were scarce. It was implicitly assumed that other research methodologies could be translated to the family therapy field or that case study reports were sufficient in validating the impact of family therapy. In the 1980s, however, this changed.

A forewarning of the increased emphasis on family research came when a 1982 edition of the *Journal of Marriage and the Family* devoted an entire issue to family research methodologies. A parallel event occurred in the *Journal of Family Issues* in 1984 (Miller, 1986). In addition, a research methods book by Adams and Schvaneveldt (1991) was among the first to use examples involving families. A breakthrough in research in the 1980s came when studies indicated that certain forms of family therapy, e.g., behavioral and systems approaches, were effective in working with families (Gurman, Kniskern, & Pinsof, 1986).

### Publications in Family Therapy

The growth in the number of individuals and associations involved in family therapy was paralleled by an increase in publications in this area. Some major publishing houses, such as Guilford Press and Brunner/Mazel, began to specialize in books on family therapy. Almost all publishers of texts in counseling, psychology, and social work added books on marriage and family therapy. In addition, new periodicals were established, and older ones grew in circulation.

The *Family Therapy Networker*, a periodical with a subscription list of over 50,000, was the success story of the 1980s. The success of the *Networker* is attributable to its timely and interesting articles and its journalistic (as opposed to scholarly) form of writing. Its magazine format and featured information on professional conferences across the country were undoubtedly additional factors in its success.

### National Recognition of Family Therapy

The main national event for family therapy in the 1980s was the listing of the profession as one of the four core mental health professions eligible for mental health traineeships (Shields et al., 1994). This action occurred as a part of the Public Health Service Act, Title III, Section 303(d)(1). It basically placed the profession, in the eyes of the federal government, on a par with other professions vying for federal training grants, such as psychology and psychiatry.

# Family Therapy: 1990 to the Present

The 1990s continued to be an exciting time in the field of family therapy. One reason was that new theories and specialty areas emerged. Another reason was that the number of professionals who primarily identify themselves as family therapists continued to grow. Still another reason was that academic curriculums and experiential components in family therapy were being continually refined. The term *family therapist* is now definable in regard to course work, competencies, and clinical experience. Furthermore, there are now a number of well-respected and researched theories practitioners can claim (Piercy & Sprenkle, 1996). The issues of the 1990s and into the 21st century concerned professional affiliation, accreditation, and licensure, that is, matters related to power and influence. They also involved identification and influence specifically regarding whether family therapy would continue to be interdisciplinary or if it would be "marginalized" (Shields et al., 1994).

## New Theories and Specialties Within Family Therapy

The 1990s and early 2000s saw a number of new theories of family therapy either emerge or gain added attention. Feminist family therapy, for instance, gained increased recognition as a powerful trend in the field and issues surrounding the importance of gender grew (Norsworthy, 2000). Family therapy also began concentrating more on examining "gender-sensitive issues in therapy" rather than feminine or masculine issues per se (Smith & Stevens-Smith, 1992). Thus, differences in genders were recognized in a less emotionally or politically volatile way. Solution-focused and narrative theories developed in the Midwest by Steve deShazer (1988) and Bill O'Hanlon (O'Hanlon & Weiner-Davis, 1989) and in Australia and New Zealand by Michael White and David Epston (1990), respectively, also received much publicity. These theories are characterized by their brevity and creativity and are covered in Chapter 10 of this text.

Other emerging theories for the treatment of families in the 1990s and early 2000s were

- the reflecting team approach of Tom Andersen (1991)
- the therapeutic conversations model of Harlene Anderson and Harry Goolishian (Anderson, 1994)
- the improvisational therapy model of Bradford Keeney (1990)
- the psychoeducational model of Carol Anderson (1988), and
- the internal family systems model of Richard Schwartz (1994)

Of these new family theories, some are radically different from their forerunners because they are based on **social constructionism,** a philosophy that states that our experiences are a function of how we think about them instead of objective entities. This viewpoint is opposed to systemic assumptions and has caused many family therapists to reexamine their basic assumptions (Piercy & Sprenkle, 1990).

Related to these developments in theory and emphasis was the Basic Family Therapy Skills Project, which was established in 1987 and has focused on determining, defining, and testing "the skills essential for beginning family therapists to master for effective therapy practice" (Figley & Nelson, 1990, p. 225). Four basic family therapy skills research reports have been prepared. In these reports, structural, strategic, brief, and transgenerational family therapies have been examined from the perspective of distinctive and generic skills critical for beginning therapists (Nelson, Heilbrun, & Figley, 1993). The identified skills generated from this project will continue to be researched and refined in future years as educators, practitioners, and researchers seek to determine what therapeutic interventions are most important and when.

Along with the work in specific theories was an increased emphasis on the **new epistemology**—the idea that the cybernetic approach of Bateson (1972, 1979) and others must be incorporated in its truest sense into family therapy. Among other things, the new epistemology emphasizes **second-order cybernetics**—the cybernetics of cybernetics—which stresses the impact of the family therapist's inclusion and participation in family systems (Keeney, 1983). On its most basic level, second-order cybernetics emphasizes positive feedback in system transformation. It extends first-order cybernetics foci beyond the homeostatic and adaptive properties of family systems in general. The new epistemology also concentrates on the importance of family belief systems in treatment and on **ontology** (i.e., a view of the world) that stresses the circularity and autonomy of systems (in contrast to linear causality).

Equally pervasive in the 1990s and at present has been the redirection of the family therapy education field from a focus on producing narrowly trained theory-specific clinicians to a focus on training practitioners who know how to work with special types of families (Broderick & Schrader, 1991). This shift has produced a plethora of new books and an emphasis on distinct types of family problems and families. For instance, books have been written and specialized courses offered on working with families comprised of individuals who abuse drugs, alcohol, food, or other family members. In addition, literature and academic offerings have become available for treating single-parent families, remarried families, aging families, and families with young children, adolescents, or members with disabilities. Further, opportunities for reading about or studying culturally diverse families, as well as gay and lesbian families, have emerged.

### Growth in Number of Family Therapists

The major professional associations for family therapists (i.e., AAMFT, IAMFC, AFTA, and Division 43 of APA) continue to attract members. The largest (more than 22,000 members) and most organized association is the AAMFT. The second largest association, the IAMFC, grew to a membership of approximately 4,000 members by the beginning of the new millennium. It had the distinction during this time of being one of the fastest growing associations for family therapists. The third association, Division 43 (Family Psychology), increasingly brought psychologists into working with family systems but at a rate slower than the first two groups because of its APA membership requirement. Likewise, the AFTA, with its strict experiential requirement, grew slowly.

These associations were competitive for status and recognition on a state-by-state level. However, under the regulations published in the *Federal Register* (Vol. 57, No. 14), marriage and family therapists officially became the fifth "core" mental health profession, along with psychiatrists, psychologists, social workers, and psychiatric nurses (Shields et al., 1994).

### Accreditation and Licensure of Family Therapists

Two associations currently accredit programs in family therapy: AAMFT and IAMFC. Both do so under accrediting commissions that operate independently from their associations. The AAMFT standards are drawn up and administered by the Commission on Accreditation for Marriage and Family Therapy Education (CAMFTE). Those for IAMFT are similarly handled through the Council for Accreditation of Counseling and Related Educational Programs (CACREP) (Hollis, 2000). A minimum of a masters degree is required as the credential for entering this specialty, although there is debate over the exact content and sequencing of courses.

Both the AAMFT and IAMFC worked hard in the 1990s and early 2000s to increase the number of programs they accredited. Making these programs more rigorous was a goal for these associations. The health reform agenda of the decade influenced educational programs and the work of family therapists regardless of their professional setting. Being recognized as a core mental health provider was crucial to the well-being of educational programs in family therapy and the profession as a whole.

In regard to licensure and recognition, 43 states now either license or certify family therapy professionals. The number of states that regulate family therapy is likely to increase in the 21st century. Such a practice is designed to protect the public from unscrupulous and unqualified practitioners with minimal costs because regulating boards are self-governing.

# Summary and Conclusion

This chapter examined the rationale for conducting family therapy and the reasons for working with families instead of individuals. It also gave a brief history of family therapy. Both the reasons for working with families and the traditions and methods employed with such groups have expanded with time.

The rationale for conducting family therapy is based on a systems viewpoint of personality disorders. From a systems perspective, people's mental health and difficulties are based more on interpersonal dynamics than on an intrapersonal struggle. Because families, like other living organisms, are only as healthy as their weakest members, it makes logical and empirical sense to treat individuals within a family context, so that the power and resources of families and their members can be supportively maximized. This is a macro, as opposed to a micro, viewpoint of dysfunctionality and one that has an increasing amount of research support.

Parallel to the rationale for family therapy is the history of this movement, primarily seen in this chapter from the perspective of its development within the United States. Notable events in the life of family therapy have been traced through the decades. Before the 1940s, this form of treatment was virtually nonexistent, because of prevailing beliefs within the culture of the United States that stressed the importance of the individual. A further factor prohibiting the development of family therapy was historic tradition. Individuals in need of assistance in their relationships consulted first with other family members, then with clergy and physicians.

Family therapy grew, however, due to a number of events such as the growth of the number of women in higher education and increased demand for more courses in family life. Likewise, the founding of associations (e.g., the National Council of Family Relations), the pioneer work in marriage counseling, the growth in the role of county home extension agents, and World War II influenced the formation of the profession.

The 1940s saw the formation of the American Association for Marriage Counselors and initial treatment of schizophrenics through treating their families. The 1950s saw the emergence of strong personalities who advocated for family therapy, such as Nathan Ackerman, Gregory Bateson, Don Jackson, Carl Whitaker, and Murray Bowen. Their work was expanded on in the 1960s, and new important figures that became pioneers at this time were Jay Haley, Salvador Minuchin, Virginia Satir, and John Bell. In retrospect, all of these professionals began their therapeutic journeys in the 1950s, but some came into prominence before others.

In the 1970s, family therapy became more respectable, and the American Association for Marriage and Family Therapy grew rapidly and was recognized by government agencies. New journals and books appeared on a range of family therapy topics. In addition, established family therapies were refined, and practitioners from Great Britain and Italy began to have greater influence. Complementing these developments was an emerging emphasis on marriage and family enrichment, the rise of feminist theory influence in family therapy, and the development of assessment techniques geared to families.

In the 1980s, 1990s, and early 2000s the number of professionals involved in working with couples and families has increased. Two new associations were established in the mid-1980s: Division 43 (Family Psychology) of the American Psychological Association and the International Association for Marriage and Family Counselors, an affiliate of the American Counseling Association. Amidst the excitement, growth, and continuing governmental recognition of family therapy, turf wars between associations regarding recognition and accreditation have begun.

Family therapy appears to be basically healthy. More women have emerged as leaders, and feminist theory has grown in its influence and impact to make the entire field reexamine itself anew. As in the 1970s, the proliferation of publications in family therapy has increased, with the most widely read periodical being the *Family Therapy Networker*. New theoretical approaches, such as solution-focused and narrative family therapies, are also having an impact. Licensure efforts are growing. Health care reform has become an issue. Yet, considering everything, the outlook for family therapy is promising.

# Summary Table

## Rationale and History of Family Therapy

Most life difficulties arise and are best addressed in families.
Family therapy is effective in treating a number of disorders.
Client families express satisfaction with family therapy.
Family therapy allows the therapist to see and treat interpersonal dynamics in a systemic and more timely way than does individual therapy.

### Family Therapy Through the Decades
*Before 1940*

Cultural beliefs stress the individual, the use of community resources, and psychoanalytic theory.

Ernest Groves, Alfred Adler, and county home extension agents teach family living/parenting skills.

Abraham and Hannah Stone, Emily Mudd, and Paul Popenoe begin marriage counseling.

National Council on Family Relations is founded (1938).

### 1940 to 1949

The American Association of Marriage Counselors (AAMC) is established (1942).

Milton Erickson develops therapeutic methods that will later be adopted by family therapy.

First account of concurrent marital therapy is published by Bela Mittleman (1948).

Theodore Lidz and Lyman Wynne study schizophrenic families.

World War II brings stress to families.

The National Mental Health Act of 1946 is passed by Congress.

### 1950 to 1959

Nathan Ackerman develops a psychoanalytical approach to working with families.

Gregory Bateson's group begins studying patterns of communication in families.

Don Jackson creates the Mental Research Institute (1958).

Carl Whitaker sets up the first conference on family therapy at Sea Island, Georgia (1955).

Murray Bowen begins the National Institute of Mental Health (NIMH) project of studying families with schizophrenics.

Ivan Boszormenyi-Nagy begins work on contextual therapy.

### 1960 to 1969

Jay Haley refines and advocates therapeutic approaches of Milton Erickson. He moves from Palo Alto to join the Philadelphia Child Guidance Clinic (1967).

*Family Process*, the first journal in family therapy, is cofounded by Nathan Ackerman and Don Jackson (1961).

Salvador Minuchin begins development of structural family therapy at Wiltwyck School and continues at the Philadelphia Child Guidance Clinic. He coauthors *Families of the Slums*.

John Bell publishes the first ideas about family group therapy (1961).

Virginia Satir publishes *Conjoint Family Therapy* (1964) and gains a national following.

Legislation authorizing community mental health centers is passed by Congress (1963).

First state licensure law regulating family counselors is passed in California (1963).

Nathan Ackerman publishes *Treating the Troubled Family* (1966).

Carl Whitaker moves to the University of Wisconsin. He begins to write and lecture extensively.

General systems theory, formulated by Ludwig von Bertalanffy (1934/1968), becomes the basis for most family therapy.

Murray Bowen begins to formulate his own theory.

Training centers and institutes for family therapy are established in New York, Philadelphia, and Boston.

### 1970 to 1979

Membership in the American Association for Marriage and Family Therapy grows by 777% to 7,565 members.

Nathan Ackerman dies (1971).

Association of Couples for Marriage Enrichment is established by David and Vera Mace (1973). The marriage/family enrichment movement grows.

The *Journal of Marital and Family Therapy* is founded (1974).

*Families and Family Therapy* and *Psychosomatic Families* are published by Salvador Minuchin and associates.

The *Family Therapy Networker* is created (1976).

The American Association of Marriage and Family Counselors becomes the American Association for Marriage and Family Therapy (1979). Its degree-granting programs are recognized by the Department of Health, Education, and Welfare.

The American Family Therapy Association is created (1977).

*Paradox and Counterparadox* is published by the Milan Group (1978). European family therapists become influential in the United States.

Feminist theorists, led by Rachel Hare-Mustin, begin questioning the premises of family therapy.

Jay Haley publishes *Uncommon Therapy* (1973) and *Problem Solving Therapy* (1976).


### 1980 to 1989

Membership in the AAMFT grows to 14,000.

Division 43 (Family Psychology) of the American Psychological Association is established (1984).

The International Association of Marriage and Family Counselors within the American Counseling Association is established (1986).

New leaders in family therapy emerge.

Research procedures in family therapy are developed and refined.

Publications in family therapy increase. *Family Therapy Networker* reaches a circulation of 50,000.

Virginia Satir dies (1988).


### 1990 to the Present

Solution-focused family therapies of deShazer and O'Hanlon and narrative approach of White and Epston become popular.

Other new theories are developed, including constructionist theories, challenging systems thinking.

The integration and merger of family therapy theories occurs, with less emphasis on specialization.

The new epistemology, which involves second-order cybernetics, emphasizes positive feedback in system transformation.

The Basic Family Therapy Skills Project focuses on determining, defining, and testing the skills necessary for novice therapists to master, generically and specifically.

Professional membership grows in AAMFT, IAMFC, AFTA, and Division 43 of APA.

Accreditation of programs and licensure efforts at the state level increase.

Health care reform and mental health care provider status become increasingly important.

Tension between professional associations in family therapy developed.

# References

Ackerman, N. (1938). The unity of the family. *Archives of Pediatrics, 55,* 51–62.

Ackerman, N. (1958). *The psychodynamics of family life.* New York: Basic Books.

Ackerman, N. (1966). *Treating the troubled family.* New York: Basic Books.

Adams, G. R., & Schvaneveldt, J. D. (1991). *Understanding research methods* (2nd ed.). London: Pearson Education.

Andersen, T. (1991). *The reflecting team: Dialogues and dialogues about dialogues.* New York: W. W. Norton.

Anderson, C. M. (1988). Psychoeducational model different than paradigm. *Family Therapy News, 19,* 10–12.

Anderson, H. (1994). Rethinking family therapy: A delicate balance. *Journal of Marital & Family Therapy, 20,* 145–149.

Anderson, R., Anderson, W., & Hovestadt, A. J. (1993, May/June). Family of origin work in family therapy: A practical approach. *Family Counseling and Therapy, 1,* 1–13.

Bateson, G. (1972). *Steps to an ecology of mind.* New York: Ballantine.

Bateson, G. (1979). *Mind and nature: A necessary unity.* New York: E. P. Dutton.

Bateson, G., Jackson, D. D., Haley, J., & Weakland, J. (1956). Toward a theory of schizophrenia. *Behavioral Science, 1,* 251–264.

Bell, J. E. (1961). *Family group therapy.* Public Health Monograph #64. Washington, DC: U.S. Government Printing Office.

Bertalanffy, L. (1934). *Modern theories of development: An introduction to theoretical biology.* London: Oxford University Press.

Bertalanffy, L. (1968). *General systems theory.* New York: George Braziller.

Bloch, D., & Simon, R. (1982). *The strength of family therapy: Selected papers of Nathan W. Ackerman.* New York: Brunner/Mazel.

Bowen, M. (1961). Family psychotherapy. *American Journal of Orthopsychiatry, 31,* 40–60.

Broderick, C. B., & Schrader, S. S. (1981). The history of professional marriage and family therapy. In A. S. Gurman & O. P. Kniskern (Eds.), *Handbook of family therapy* (pp. 5–38). New York: Brunner/Mazel.

Broderick, C. B., & Schrader, S. S. (1991). The history of professional marriage and family therapy. In A. S. Gurman & O. P. Kniskern (Eds.), *Handbook of family therapy, II* (pp. 3–40). New York: Brunner/Mazel.

Carter, B. (1992, January/February). Stonewalling feminism. *Family Therapy Networker, 16,* 64–69.

deShazer, S. (1988). *Clues: Investigating solutions in brief therapy.* New York: Norton.

Dinkmeyer, D. C., Dinkmeyer, D. C., Jr., & Sperry, L. (2000). *Adlerian counseling and psychotherapy* (3rd ed.). Upper Saddle River, NJ: Merrill/Prentice Hall.

Doherty, W. J., & Simmons, D. S. (1996). Clinical practice patterns of marriage and family therapists: A national survey of therapists and their clients. *Journal of Marital and Family Therapy, 22,* 9–25.

Duhl, B. S. (1983). *From the inside out and other metaphors.* New York: Brunner/Mazel.

Enns, C. Z. (1992). Dilemmas of power and equality in marital and family counseling: Proposals for a feminist perspective. In R. L. Smith & P. Stevens-Smith (Eds.), *Family counseling and therapy* (pp. 338–357). Ann Arbor, MI: ERIC/CAPS.

Figley, C. R., & Nelson, T. S. (1990). Basic family therapy skills II: Structural family therapy. *Journal of Marital and Family Therapy, 16,* 225–239.

Fishman, C. H. (1988). *Treating troubled adolescents.* New York: Basic Books.

Foley, V. D. (1989). Family therapy. In R. J. Corsini & D. Wedding (Eds.), *Current psychotherapies* (4th ed., pp. 455–502). Itasca, IL: F. E. Peacock.

Framo, J. L. (1996). A personal retrospective of the family therapy field: Then and now. *Journal of Marital and Family Therapy, 22,* 289–316.

Gilbert, M., & Shmukler, D. (1997). *Brief therapy with couples: An integrative approach.* New York: Wiley.

Gladding, S. T. (1991). *Present vows and memories.* Unpublished manuscript.

Guerin, P. J., Jr. (1976). Family therapy: The first twenty-five years. In P. J. Guerin, Jr. (Ed.). *Family therapy: Theory and practice* (pp. 2–22). New York: Gardner.

Guerney, B. G., Jr. (1977). *Relationship enhancement.* San Francisco: Jossey-Bass.

Gurel, L. (1999, June). John Elderkin Bell (1913–1995). *American Psychologist, 54,* 434.

Gurman, A. S., & Kniskern, D. P. (1981). Preface. In A. S. Gurman & D. P. Kniskern (Eds.), *Handbook of family therapy* (pp. xiii–xviii). New York: Brunner/Mazel.

Gurman, A. S., Kniskern, D. P., & Pinsof, W. (1986). Research on the process and outcome of marital and family therapy. In S. L. Garfield & A. E. Bergin (Eds.), *Handbook of psychotherapy and behavior change* (3rd ed.). New York: Wiley.

Haley, J. (1963). *Strategies of psychotherapy.* New York: Grune & Stratton.

Haley, J. (1976). Development of a theory: A history of a research project. In C. E. Sluzki & D. C. Ransom (Eds.),

*Double-bind: The foundation of the communication approach to the family.* New York: Grune & Stratton.

Hare-Mustin, R. T. (1978). A feminist approach to family therapy. *Family Process, 17,* 181–194.

Hershenson, D. B., & Power, P. W. (1987). *Mental health counseling: Theory and practice.* New York: Pergamon Press.

Hines, M. (1988). Similarities and differences in group and family therapy. *Journal for Specialists in Group Work, 13,* 173–179.

Hollis, J. W. (2000). *Counselor preparation 1999–2001.* Bristol, PA: Taylor & Francis.

Kaslow, F. W. (1980). History of family therapy in the United States: A kaleidoscopic overview. *Marriage and Family Review, 3,* 77–111.

Kaslow, F. (1990). *Voices in family psychology.* Newbury Park, CA: Sage.

Kaslow, F. W. (1991). The art and science of family psychology. *American Psychologist, 46,* 621–626.

Keeney, B. (1983). *The aesthetics of change.* New York: Guilford.

Keeney, B. (1990). *Improvisational therapy.* St. Paul, MN: Systemic Therapy Press.

Kottler, J. A. (1991). *The compleat therapist.* San Francisco: Jossey-Bass.

Laing, R. D. (1965). Mystification, confusion, and conflict. In I. Boszormenyi-Nagy & J. L. Framo (Eds.), *Intensive family therapy: Theoretical and practical aspects.* New York: Harper & Row.

Laing, R. D. (1970). *Knots.* New York: Pantheon.

Libow, J. A., Raskin, P. A., & Caust, B. L. (1982). Feminist and family systems therapy: Are they irreconcilable? *American Journal of Family Therapy, 10,* 3–12.

Lidz, R. W., & Lidz, T. (1949). The family environment of schizophrenic patients. *American Journal of Psychiatry, 106,* 332–345.

Mace, D. (1983). *Prevention in family services.* Beverly Hills, CA: Sage.

May, K. M. (1998). A feminist and multicultural perspective in family therapy. *The Family Journal, 6,* 123–124.

Maynard, P. E., & Olson, D. H. (1987). Circumplex model of family systems: A treatment tool in family counseling. *Journal of Counseling and Development, 65,* 502–504.

Miller, B. C. (1986). *Family research methods.* Beverly Hills, CA: Sage.

Miller, S., Nunnally, E., & Wackman, D. B. (1977). *Couple communication instructor's manual.* Littleton, CO: Interpersonal Communication Programs.

Miller, S., Nunnally, E. W., & Wackman, D. B. (1979). *Couple communication: Talking together.* Littleton, CO: Interpersonal Communication Programs.

Minuchin, S. (1974). *Families and family therapy.* Cambridge, MA: Harvard University Press.

Minuchin, S., Montalvo, B., Guerney, B. G., Rosman, B. L., & Schumer, F. (1967). *Families of the slums.* New York: Basic Books.

Minuchin, S., Rosman, B. L., & Baker, L. (1978). *Psychosomatic families: Anorexia nervosa in context.* Cambridge, MA: Harvard University Press.

Mittleman, B. (1948). The concurrent analysis of married couples. *Psychoanalytic Quarterly, 17,* 182–197.

Nelson, T. S., Heilbrun, G., & Figley, C. R. (1993). Basic family therapy skills, IV: Transgenerational theories of family therapy. *Journal of Martial and Family Therapy, 19,* 253–266.

Nichols, W. C. (1993). *The AAMFT: 50 years of marital and family therapy.* Washington, DC: AAMFT.

Nichols, W. C., & Everett, C. A. (1986). *Systemic family therapy: An integrated approach.* New York: Guilford.

Norsworthy, K. L. (2000). Feminist family therapy. In A. M. Horne (Ed.), *Family counseling and therapy* (3rd ed., pp. 515–538). Itasca, IL: F. E. Peacock.

O'Hanlon, W., & Weiner-Davis, M. (1989). *In search of solutions: A new direction in psychotherapies.* New York: Norton.

Pickens, M. E. (1997, January). Evolving family structures: Implications for counseling. *Counseling and Family Development, 29,* 1–8.

Piercy, F. P., & Sprenkle, D. H. (1990). Marriage and family therapy: A decade review. *Journal of Marriage and the Family, 52,* 1116–1126.

Pietrzak, D., & L'Amoreaux, N. (1998). Robert Smith. *The Family Journal, 6,* 159–162.

Piercy, F. P., & Sprenkle, D. H. (1996). *Family therapy sourcebook* (2nd ed.). New York: Guilford.

Pinsof, W., & Wynne, L. (Eds.). (1995). Special issue: The effectiveness of marital and family therapy. *Journal of Marital and Family Therapy, 21*(4), 339–613.

Pinsof, W. M., & Wynne, L. C. (2000). Toward progress research: Closing the gap between family therapy practice and research. *Journal of Marital and Family Therapy, 26,* 1–8.

Ray, W. A. (2000). Don D. Jackson—A re-introduction. *Journal of Systemic Therapies, 19*(2), 1–6.

Satir, V. (1964). *Conjoint family therapy.* Palo Alto, CA: Science and Behavior Books.

Sauber, S. R., L'Abate, L., & Weeks, G. R. (1985). *Family therapy: Basic concepts and terms.* Rockville, MD: Aspen.

Sayger, T. V., Homrich, A. M., & Horne, A. M. (2000). Working with a family focus. In A. M. Horne (Ed.), *Family counseling and therapy* (3rd ed., pp. 12–40). Itasca, IL: F. E. Peacock.

Schwartz, R. (1994). *Internal family systems therapy.* New York: Guilford.

Selvini Palazzoli, M., Boscolo, L., Cecchin, G., & Prata, G. (1978). *Paradox and counterparadox.* New York: Jason Aronson.

Sherman, R. (1999). Family therapy: The art of integration. In R. E. Watts & J. Carlson (Eds.), *Interventions and strategies in counseling and psychotherapy* (pp. 101–134). Philadelphia: Francis & Taylor.

Shields, C. G., Wynne, L. C., McDaniel, S. H., & Gawinski, B. A. (1994). The marginalization of family therapy: A historical and continuing problem. *Journal of Marital and Family Therapy, 20,* 117–138.

Skynner, A. C. R. (1981). An open-systems, group-analytic approach to family therapy. In A. S. Gurman & D. P. Kniskern (Eds.), *Handbook of family therapy* (pp. 39–84). New York: Brunner/Mazel.

Smith, R. L., & Stevens-Smith, P. (1992). Future projections for marriage and family counseling and therapy. In R. L. Smith & P. Stevens-Smith (Eds.), *Family counseling and therapy* (pp. 435–440). Ann Arbor, MI: ERIC/CAPS.

Storm, C. L. (1991). Placing gender at the heart of MFT masters programs: Teaching a gender sensitive systemic view. *Journal of Marital and Family Therapy, 17,* 45–52.

Strong, B., & DeVault, C. (1998). *The marriage and family experience* (7th ed.). Belmont, CA: Wadsworth.

Trotzer, J. P. (1988). Family theory as a group resource. *Journal for Specialists in Group Work, 13,* 180–185.

Walters, M., Carter, B., Papp, P., & Silverstein, O. (1988). *The invisible web.* New York: Guilford.

Whitaker, C. A. (1958). Psychotherapy with couples. *American Journal of Psychotherapy, 12,* 18–23.

White, M., & Epston, D. (1990). *Narrative means to therapeutic ends.* New York: Norton.

# CHAPTER 4

## The Process of Family Therapy

My son, Benjamin, rolls over in his crib
to the applause of his mother and delight of himself
while I catch an afternoon flight to Saint Paul
to conduct a counseling seminar.

These are milestones in our lives
marking steps in family development
as we reach out to touch
and are changed through our behaviors.

At 33,000 feet, I drift in and out of sleep,
aware that in the process, but on a different level,
my wife and child do the same.

In the depth of thought and images
we attempt in special ways
to bridge the gap of distance.

*Gladding, 1988*

The process of conducting family therapy is predictable, regardless of one's theoretical approach. All schools of family therapy have a theoretical commitment to working with family interactions. Despite outward appearances, different systems of family therapy are more alike in practice than their theories would suggest. For example, family therapists of all persuasions are concerned with processes involved in clarifying communications among family members, overcoming resistance, and rectifying dysfunctional behaviors. Consequently, family therapists have many common concerns and procedures that transcend their different theoretical emphases. In fact, surveys indicate that the dominant theoretical orientation to family therapy is eclectic (e.g., Rait, 1988).

Therefore, it is important for family therapists to be aware of the universal methods of working with families. By being so attuned, they are better able to communicate with a variety of professionals. They are also better able to realize the uniqueness of the theories under which they work. Such knowledge gives them a flexibility and common bond to others in the helping professions.

This chapter covers the importance of the personhood of the therapist in working with families as well as potential problems encountered by family therapists. Along with this material are guidelines for appropriate processes in helping families and expected procedures for the main stages of family therapy. Although this material is targeted toward new family therapists, it is applicable to experienced therapists as well.

# The Personhood of Family Therapists

In the process of therapy, the personhood of family therapists is quite important (Aponte, 1992; Satir, 1987). "Research on counseling outcome consistently reports that the beneficial effects of counseling are related more to the personal characteristics of the counselor than to any specific intervention or approach" (Kier & Lawson, 1999, p. 118). Not everyone who is bright, articulate, and attuned to systems theory and the process of change should enter the profession of family therapy. Indeed, individuals who have had negative family of origin experiences may find that they cannot deal successfully with or do not wish to work with families (Bowen, 1978; Kier & Lawson, 1999). In addition, persons who treat difficult families must often engage in a considerable amount of therapy for themselves on an individual and family level (Wilcoxon, Walker, & Hovestadt, 1989). Being a family therapist and staying psychologically healthy is not an easy task.

Major stressors for family therapists include increased depression from listening to a client family's problem, less time for one's own family because of work demands, unrealistic expectations of one's own family, and psychological distancing from one's family because of professional status (Duncan & Duerden, 1990; Wetchler & Piercy, 1986).

However, not all of the impact from working with families is negative. Enhancers for family therapists include an increased ability to solve one's own family problems, an acceptance of one's part in contributing to family dysfunctionality, a deeper appreciation of one's own family, and a greater ability and desire to communicate effectively (Duncan & Duerden, 1990; Wetchler & Piercy, 1986). Being a family therapist is clearly a multifaceted process.

Overall, a family therapist "should be a healer: a human being concerned with engaging other human beings therapeutically, around areas and issues that cause them pain, while always retaining great respect for their values, areas of strength, and esthetic preferences" (Minuchin & Fishman, 1981, p. 1). To achieve the role of a healer requires dedication, awareness, and stable mental health. It is the exceptional person who can achieve this balance. Those who are best suited in nature to be helpers of families most often have artistic qualities, that is, they are intuitive and feeling in regard to interpersonal relationships (Brammer & MacDonald, 1999). It is these individuals who some educators recommend for training in the field of family therapy. Regardless, it takes time for people to develop to the point of seeing themselves as competent professionals, often reaching such a point only after 5 or 6 years of experience (Kral & Hines, 1999).

# Common Problems of Beginning Family Therapists

Several problems are germane to family therapists in general when they are just beginning to work with families. These common concerns must be addressed if the therapeutic process is to have a significant impact. Some therapists' downfalls are a result of an overemphasis, while others are the result of underemphasis.

## Overemphasis

Family therapists can overemphasize and try to do too much. The following subsections discuss some common ways in which overemphasis is expressed.

### Overemphasis on Details

Two primary components of family therapy are content and process. When families come for treatment, they are usually focused on a content issue, for example, a husband may want a divorce, a child may refuse to go to school, or a wife may be wrestling with depression. **Content** involves details and facts. **Process** focuses on how information is dealt with. Sometimes content is essential. Knowledge of past patterns and the sequencing of family interaction is helpful in breaking up dysfunctional forms of relating. At other times, facts get in the way of helping families make necessary changes. In such cases, the therapist might concentrate on the trees instead of the forest. For example, if a family therapist says to a woman, "Tell me about every time your husband has yelled at you," the therapist might be focusing too closely on a specific behavior and not enough on the significance of the behavior. In such a circumstance, the family therapy is limited.

A good rule to follow in dealing with facts is to ask "how" questions along with "what," "where," and "when" queries. For example, "How does your husband's behavior affect your ability to relate to him?" Such a question helps get to the heart of the relationship between the individuals involved.

### Overemphasis on Making Everyone Happy

Sometimes family therapists become concerned or overconcerned when families leave their offices in a state of tension. The reason for their disturbance is an illogical belief, the essence of which is that if they were competent, the family would be able to resolve its difficulties. While therapists can do a great deal to help families, friction is sometimes unavoidable. Furthermore, friction can be productive. It can motivate individuals to try new behaviors and break out of old patterns.

When clients leave a session in turmoil, the therapist can paradoxically ask them to stay that way until next session or instruct the family to "go slow" in coming to a resolution of the difficulty. The end result in such a case is usually that the family resolves the conflict fairly quickly and either returns to a previous homeostatic balance or moves on to a more functional set of behaviors. Regardless of whether the family resolves the issue or not, the therapist can use the next session to ask each member of the family what the family tried in response to their discomfort. Using this information, the family and the therapist will gain a clearer perspective on the processes the family employs in creating strategies. Then new or varied themes can be explored.

### Overemphasis on Verbal Expression

Well-chosen words can have a therapeutic effect on families. For example, if the therapist can verbally assure the family that what they have been through and the strategies they have tried in the past are normal, the family might be open to new ways of working on their present situation. However, in most cases, the exact words said by a therapist are not remembered. A helpful way of understanding the limited impact of a therapist's words is to think about what words or advice you most remember in your life. For the majority of people, the list of such remarks is short and the people involved are few.

Therapists must work with families in a number of ways. They instruct, comment, and inquire; but they also model behavior, use role plays, and assign homework. In other words, therapists recognize and utilize teachable moments. It is what the family and therapist do and when, as well as what is said, that makes a difference. For example, a therapist could use hand signals like a traffic officer at a crucial time in a family's therapy to indicate who may talk. Although the family might not remember all of what was said, the use of the therapist's nonverbal directions can leave a lasting impression and message about the art of effective communication.

### Overemphasis on Coming to an Early or Too Easy Resolution

There is a tendency in therapy for families to "fly into health." After a couple of sessions, for example, a family might report that they are doing better and are ready to terminate therapy. Although this might be true for a few families, most who report feeling better quickly are experiencing the euphoria that often comes out of discussing a situation rather than actually changing it. Therefore, flights into health and early or easy resolutions of family problems seldom succeed. Families involved in such processes rarely examine the dynamics in their problems.

From all theoretical perspectives, the conducting of family therapy is an ongoing process. Consequently, families need to be initially advised of how long the process of therapy generally takes and what will be expected from them. For example, a brief theory therapist might say: "We will be working together on your situation for ten sessions. It is crucial that you define what you wish to change as soon and as concretely as possible."

### Overemphasis on Dealing with One Member of the Family

When family therapists concentrate on just one member of a family, they fall into the same trap that has caused the family difficulty—that is, they scapegoat (select one person as the cause of difficulties). Family problems are not linear in nature, and one person does not cause a family to be dysfunctional. It is crucial that beginning family therapists recognize the dynamics within families and the power of homeostasis in keeping families operating at a certain level, even if it is dysfunctional. Only when therapists consider the relationships among everyone in the family can meaningful interventions be made. It is imperative that family therapists periodically remind themselves and their client families about the importance of examining interpersonal dynamics in regard to dysfunctionality.

In working with a couple who bring their adolescent in for breaking curfew, the therapist might say: "While Jane's behavior is of concern, in our sessions we will look at the behaviors of everyone. I have found that when one person in a family is having difficulties, others usually are as well." By alerting the family to this systemic view of family relations, the therapist makes it easier for everyone to become more aware of their actions and how they personally contribute to the family's well-being or lack thereof.

## Underemphasis

Underemphasis can be as bad as overemphasis. By underemphasizing and failing to make an intervention at a strategic time, a therapist might subtly suggest that the family's interaction is adequate when, in fact, nothing could be further from the truth. Underemphasis takes several forms. Among the most prominent are the following.

### Underemphasis on Establishing Structure

If family therapy is to achieve a positive outcome, it helps to start the process properly. The struggle to establish the parameters under which therapy is conducted is referred to as the **battle for structure** (Napier & Whitaker, 1978). This battle must be won by the therapist, otherwise the family members could attempt to run the therapy sessions in the same nonproductive manner in which they conduct their family life.

A key component in winning the battle for structure is for the therapist to delineate the conditions under which treatment will occur. "Clients have both a right and a need to know about fees and payment schedules, your theoretical framework and treatment approach, rules about appointments, how and when they are allowed to contact you, rules about confidentiality, and your educational background and training" (Kaplan & Culkin, 1995, p. 33). Much of this information can be provided to families through a **professional self-disclosure statement** (see Figure 4.1) (Gladding, 2000). Such a disclosure statement should be written because verbal statements can be misunderstood or misinterpreted. The statement should be read by the family and feedback from family members should be solicited as well. Incorporated into the self-disclosure statement can be an **informed consent brochure** (Kaplan, 2000a). Such a piece includes all the information in a self-disclosure statement, but goes

*The Nature of Family Therapy*

There are many approaches to family therapy, and different clinicians utilize a number of theories and techniques in their practice. Some work only with the individual or couple, while others insist that the whole family be seen. I have prepared this brief professional self-disclosure form to inform you how I conduct sessions.

*My Qualifications*

I am a graduate of Purdue University's marriage and family therapy doctoral program. I have been in practice for the past 10 years in the Philadelphia area. I am licensed as a marriage and family therapist by the state of Pennsylvania. I am a clinical member of the American Association for Marriage and Family Therapists. I also belong to the International Association of Marriage and Family Counseling and Division 43 (Family Psychology) of the American Psychological Association.

I have done extensive work with families under supervision at the Philadelphia Child Guidance Clinic. I am not a physician and cannot prescribe medicine. However, if medical treatment seems warranted, I consult with a psychiatrist and can make a referral.

*Family Therapy as a Process*

Family therapy is a process that requires a considerable investment of time. I prefer to work with the entire family, and I realize that this style may make one or more of you uncomfortable. Although each family is unique, there are some common stages you can expect.

The first stage is the beginning session(s) where we will work to clarify your concerns and difficulties. This process will require observation on my part and verbalization/behavior on your parts. My belief is that there is no one single cause of or cure for a family's problems.

The second stage is the working sessions in which we will concentrate on helping you make changes that will work for you and make your relationships and family life better. During this time, I will ask you to be active as problem solvers.

The final stage is termination, in which we will complete the process of change and end our sessions. It is at this time when you may wish to be most reflective.

*Length of Family Therapy and Fees*

Family therapy sessions are 50 minutes in length once a week. They begin on the hour. The fee is $75 per session and payment is expected at the end of each session. I will work to help you file insurance, if you wish. Although no one can guarantee how many sessions a particular family may need, I have found the range to be between 10 and 30.

*Your Rights*

As a consumer of therapeutic services, you have a right to be treated with dignity, respect, and in a professional manner. You have the right to ask me questions about your therapeutic concerns at any time.

*Emergency*

There is someone from the office on call 24 hours a day. Although you will probably not need this service, the number for emergencies is 814–555–8309.

**Figure 4.1**
Sample professional disclosure statement.

one step further in that the family signs off that they understand the policies and procedures of therapy. They are given a copy of what they have signed as a reminder.

In addition to setting guidelines, the therapist must also physically structure the room so that therapeutic interactions can take place. This includes arranging the furniture so that family members can talk directly with each other. The structure should also be flexible, so the therapist can move family members closer to or farther away from each other.

### Underemphasis on Showing Care and Concern

Most families enter counseling with some trepidation. Their anxiety might be increased if family members think they are being treated as objects and not persons, or if they perceive the therapist as rigid and distant. Effective family therapists follow the guidelines of other helping professionals; they are caring, open, sensitive, and concerned; and they are empathetic and show it.

Family therapists can convey this professional care by demonstrating the skills in the acronym *SOLER* (Egan, 1998). The *S* stands for facing the client or family squarely, either in a metaphorical or literal manner. The *O* is a reminder to adopt an open posture that is nondefensive, such as avoiding crossing one's arms or legs. The *L* indicates that the therapist should lean forward toward the client family to show interest. A therapist can overdo this procedure and must gauge what is appropriate for each family. The *E* represents good eye contact. One way of letting family members know they are cared about is by looking at them when appropriate. Finally, *R* stands for relaxation. Working with families is an intense process, but therapists need to feel comfortable.

Effective family therapists also make brief disclosure statements (when appropriate). For example, in response to a parent who reports having been previously married, a therapist might briefly reveal that he or she is also a stepparent. Therapists might also show concern by using self-effacing humor that indicates to family members their awareness of the difficulties families encounter (Piercy & Lobenz, 1994). For instance, a therapist might briefly recount a time in his or her own family when the family struggled in a futile but serious way, such as trying to make it to church on time the day after daylight savings time ended, with family members waking up late and having to rush, only to find they were hassled, haggled, irreverent, and an hour early!

### Underemphasis on Engaging Family Members in the Therapeutic Process

Engaging family members in therapy includes attending to each one personally. For example, shaking hands, bowing, or establishing eye contact are three ways this connection can be made (Olkin, 1993). If a family member feels slighted, chances are increased that this person will overtly refuse to participate or will sabotage the therapeutic process in some subtle manner. Although personally soliciting the participation of all family members takes time, it pays off in the long run.

When therapists meet new families and their members, it is crucial that they spend some time with each person. They should concentrate on the interests and dislikes of each individual for a few moments. For example, therapists might talk to children about school and to parents about different aspects of work and family life. In so doing, therapists help build rapport and create an atmosphere of cooperation through acknowledging each person's importance to the family.

### Underemphasis on Letting the Family Work on Its Problems

Just as the family therapist must win the battle for structure, the family must win the **battle for initiative** (Napier & Whitaker, 1978). This battle centers around the family becoming motivated to make changes. A family that does not see any benefit in altering its behaviors is likely to either drop out of therapy or simply go through the motions. On the opposite side is the effect of initiative on family therapists. When families are not working well, some family therapists mentally take these families home, much to their own distress (Guy, 1987).

Therapists can help families win the battle for initiative by helping them envision how their lives can become healthier collectively and individually. Such a process means that therapists must be enterprising and sell the family a set of possibilities (Holland, 1973). For example, the therapist might ask a family that is constantly fighting these questions: How would it be for you to be able to live in peace with one another? Think for a moment what you really want from this family. Can you envision some ways that you could settle your differences and get on with your lives?

### Underemphasis on Attending to Nonverbal Family Dynamics

Nonverbal messages are a major part of any therapeutic process (Egan, 1998). These messages include eye glances, hands folded across one's body, and even the distancing of people through the arrangement or rearrangement of chairs. The most frequent nonverbal cues are facial. However, facial and other body movements often are combined. For example, when clients are describing feelings about an object or event, they may exhibit increased animation of the face and hands (Cormier & Hackney, 1999).

Family therapists who do not pay attention to the nonverbal aspects of family dynamics will only partially decipher what is being conveyed among family members (Brock & Barnard, 1999). The result might be that crucial issues within the family are not addressed and change is limited. For instance, if a daughter tells her father she loves him but does so in a trembling voice and with a look of fear, the therapist would be wise to pursue what the relationship between these two family members is really like.

# Appropriate Process

The process of family therapy can be conducted in a variety of ways, but some vital aspects of it must be included. If therapists do not plan properly, they are likely to fail. A keystone of proper planning in working with families encompasses a consideration of ways to conduct sessions based on one's impression of a family, one theoretical position, and one's clinical skills (Rickert, 1989).

## Pre-Session Planning and Tasks

Family therapy "begins the moment of the first interaction" between the family and therapist (Olkin, 1993, p. 32). Initial contact is generally made by a family member's telephone call to a therapist. Also, the individuals who initiate the phone calls are usually "the most interested in change and may be the most open to engaging in therapy" (Weber & Levine, 1995, p. 54). Some calls are handled by an intermediary (e.g., a secretary); but the family and the therapist are better served if calls are directed to and handled by the therapist (Brock & Barnard, 1999). One reason is that the therapist can directly answer questions about who should attend the sessions and how the sessions will be structured. A second reason is that through the phone conversation, the therapist gains an opportunity to establish rapport and a cooperative alliance with the family member (Weber, McKeever, & McDaniel, 1992). Finally, in answering calls, therapists have an opportunity to demonstrate their own competency and credibility.

Regardless of who answers calls, it is essential during this first contact to obtain certain information and establish a professional but cordial atmosphere (Snider, 1992). Essential information to be gathered includes the name, address, and phone number of the caller. A concise statement of the problem to be addressed is also helpful, even if it is modified or changed later. Other information that is useful includes the referral source, history of previous treatment, and preferred method of payment (if relevant).

The tone and type of speech used by the secretary or therapist can either help or hinder the decision of the family to engage in the treatment process. If the receiver of the call is supportive, caring, and talks in a manner that conveys respect and receptivity, an appointment is more likely to be made and kept. Whenever possible, the initial appointment should be made within 48 hours of the call. The reason is that most families who call for help are ready to begin the process. Delaying an appointment can cause some members to reconsider their decision to attend or to resist coming.

When evaluating intake information, hypotheses about dynamics within the family should be made, especially if the therapist is operating from a problem-oriented position (Weber et al., 1992). One source to consider in making such speculations is the family life cycle (Duvall, 1977; Carter & McGoldrick, 1999). Therapists need to ask themselves what issues are to be expected from a family in a certain stage of life. Some transitional difficulties are natural and some are not. The ethnic/cultural background of the family is also a consideration. In some traditional Italian families, for example, an unmarried daughter leaving home might bring about a crisis that would not develop in a traditional British family.

A final pre-session task is to form a preliminary diagnosis of what is happening within the family (Rickert, 1989). For example, in a family where an adolescent male is becoming a delinquent, the therapist might hypothesize that the boy and his father are **disengaged** and cut off from each other physically as well as psychologically. Similarly, in the case of child who refuses to attend school, the therapist might hypothesize that the child and the family are enmeshed and that the child's actions are somehow being reinforced or supported.

Engaging in this diagnostic exercise, which is a hallmark of the Milan approach, requires that the therapist spend time thinking about possible linkages within the family and the development of persons and systems. The payoff for this investment in time is that the therapist can hone in on issues more quickly and effectively. Through diagnostic procedures, therapists are more likely to "work within the limits of their training and experience" (Carlson, Hinkle, & Sperry, 1993, p. 309). The therapist is also in a good position to formulate a treatment plan that is communicable to other mental health professionals. Finally, diagnosis is a way for family therapists to comprehend more thoroughly what is happening with family members as well as with the family as a whole.

## Initial Session(s)

Research points out that the first few sessions, not just the first session, are the most critical in terms of successful therapy (Odell & Quinn, 1998). Both structuring (e.g., teaching, directing) and supportive (e.g., warmth, caring) behaviors make a difference in whether client families return. Therefore, in conducting therapy with families, clinicians should realize that the first session is not usually a determinant of whether a family returns for treatment. Rather most families suspend judgment for a few sessions in order to give the treatment a chance to work and the therapist a chance to prove his or her competence. Nevertheless, therapist should work hard from the beginning to make treatment as effective as possible and set the stage for success.

Before an initial session begins, the therapist should know who is coming; for instance, is just the marital couple coming or the whole family? In some traditions, such as Bowen family therapy, the couple is the unit of treatment, whereas in other schools of family therapy, including strategic, systemic, behavioral, and experiential, children are encouraged to attend treatment and become actively engaged in the therapeutic process (Sweeney & Rocha, 2000). In a study of clinical members of the AAMFT on the inclusion of children in family therapy, Johnson and Thomas (1999) found that "half of the therapists excluded children on the basis of their comfort" with them (p. 117). Children were included most often in sessions where they were prone to be internalizing (i.e., quiet) as opposed to externalizing (i.e., aggressive). Children were also more likely to be seen in family sessions with single-parent (as opposed to two-parent) families and when the presenting problem was child focused.

During the initial session(s), in order to be successful with the family, the therapist must achieve a number of crucial tasks. Some of the goals of the initial session(s) must be accomplished simultaneously and others sequentially. As with other stages of family therapy, "timing is everything." Some of the most important tasks in the first session are as follows.

### Join the Family: Establishing Rapport

The first step in helping a family during the initial session(s) is for therapists to establish a sense of trust between themselves and the members of the family. This stage is referred to as **joining** (Haley, 1976; Minuchin, 1974). It is a crucial component of family therapy and requires therapists to meet, greet, and form a bond with family members in a rapid but relaxed and authentic way. Therapists must make the family comfortable through social exchange with each member.

If a therapist fails to join with a family, its most disengaged members, or the family as a whole, could leave treatment either physically or psychologically. It is usually the least involved member of a family who has the most power in deciding whether the family stays in therapy or not (Mark Worden, personal communication, 1982). A weak alliance with family members is a frequently cited reason for treatment not working (Coleman, 1985).

### Inquire About Members' Perceptions of the Family

When making inquiries of family members, family therapists must challenge old perceptions. Individuals within families usually have a problem, person, or situation framed in a certain manner. A **frame,** a concept originated by Bateson (1955), is a perception or opinion that organizes one's interactions so that "at any given time certain events are more likely to occur and certain interpretations of what is going on are more likely to be made" (Coyne, 1985, p. 338).

By challenging the perception (or frame), therapists can get family members to define problems, persons, or situations differently, as well as "look for different solutions" (Olkin, 1993, p. 33). Such a change sets up the opportunity for success.

## Observe Family Patterns

Families, like individuals, have unique personalities. They come into therapy and display these personalities both in a verbal and nonverbal manner, a phenomenon referred to as the **family dance** (Napier & Whitaker, 1978). Some systematic ways of observing family interactions are helpful for novice and experienced therapists. The following questions are among those that Resnikoff (1981) advised family therapists to ask themselves in regard to how a family functions:

- "What is the outward appearance of the family?" (p. 135) For example, how far do members sit from each other and who sits next to whom?
- "What is the cognitive functioning in the family?" (p. 136) For example, how specifically and straightforwardly do family members communicate? Is there much give and take in the communication patterns?
- "What repetitive, non-productive sequences do you notice?" (p. 136) For instance, do parents scold or praise their children in certain ways after special behaviors?
- "What is the basic feeling state in the family and who carries it?" (p. 136) All families have a variety of feelings, but often one member conveys the overall affect of the family. For example, a depressed child might indicate a depressed family.
- "What individual roles reinforce family resistances and what are the most prevalent family defenses?" (p. 136) Individuals and families sometimes have characteristic responses to stress, such as anger or denial. It is crucial to recognize these responses and to be sensitive and innovative in responding to them.
- "What subsystems are operative in this family?" (p. 137) Almost all families have subsystems, that is, members who because of age or function are logically grouped together, such as parents or siblings. It is important to identify these subsystems and how they function. Some work well, but others end up with someone being scapegoated or triangulated (i.e., focused on as a way of relieving tension between two other family members). It is crucial for the therapists to recognize and work through subsystems so that families can relate in a more open and healthy manner.
- "Who carries the power in the family?" (p. 137) Persons who have power in families make the rules and decisions. They might act in a benign manner, but what they say or do is adhered to by others. For instance, a mother who acts as the family spokesperson probably has considerable power. Families that operate in a functional way have flexibility in regard to rules and the balance of power.
- "How are the family members differentiated from each other and what are the sub-group boundaries?" (p. 137) In some families, **enmeshment** (overinvolvement either

physically and/or psychologically) occurs, and in others **distancing** (isolated separateness, either physically and/or psychologically) occurs. In healthy families, a balance exists between these two extremes. Therapists need to be aware of family members' degrees of separation and individuation.

- "What part of the family life cycle is the family experiencing and are the problem-
  solving methods stage appropriate?" (p. 138) For example, is a family treating its 18-
  year-old like an 8-year-old? Family therapists need to check on how well a family
  deals with current developmental reality.
- "What are the evaluator's own reactions to the family?" (p. 138) Reactions to families are made on both an emotional and cognitive level. Sometimes, the therapist
  might see the family in light of his or her own family of origin and confuse the issues
  to be worked on. Such a perception is not in the service of the family or the therapist. To truly be helpful to a family, a therapist must be aware of the root of his or her
  reaction, and must know how to respond appropriately.

### Assess What Needs to Be Done

The family therapist needs to assess what changes should be made or can be made in
order to help the family function better (L'Abate & Bagarozzi, 1993). This assessment can
mean the employment of specific diagnostic instruments (West, 1988). In most cases,
however, this procedure can also be conducted more informally, such as through observation. In assessing what needs to be done, family therapists must be aware not only of the
family but about biases they hold because of a client's sociodemographic characteristics.
For example, Pals, Piercy, and Miller (1998) found that "a therapist's decision to break
confidence appears to depend in part on the therapist's background characteristics" (p.
470). Such may also be the case in assessing what needs to be done and therapists must be
sure they are proceeding in this area as objectively as possible.

### Engender Hope for Change and Overcome Resistance

Many family members need assurance that their situations can get better. Hope motivates
them to work and make difficult changes and choices. Essential elements of hope can be
given in direct or indirect ways. For instance, a family therapist might say: "Your situation
did not get this way overnight, and it will not change overnight. But, I think if you work
hard it will change." This type of comment directly addresses the family's plight and possibilities. Other less formal statements, such as "I think you might be able to do something more
productive," can also be encouraging and foster a positive attitude in family members.

Further, family therapists can engender hope that change can take place within families by helping them identify their assets and strengths. Most families know their liabilities.
However, discovering strengths, such as that they live in a supportive neighborhood, helps
families recognize they have more potential than they might have previously thought.

Regardless of the therapist's words of encouragement or the identified family strengths,
almost all families exhibit some form of **resistance** to treatment (Anderson & Stewart,
1983). Resistance comes in many forms, such as "members attempting to control sessions,
absent or silent members, refusal of family members to talk to each other in sessions, hostility, and failure to do homework" (Olkin, 1993, p. 33). Other forms of resistance include

being late to sessions, denying reality, rationalizing, insisting that one family member is the problem, and challenging the therapist's competence. If treatment is to be successful, family therapists have to understand the nature of resistance and overcome it without alienating family members. "When therapists . . . intervene, their choice of a type of intervention, and whether to attempt to overcome, avoid, or use resistance to produce change, will be based on their theoretical orientation and their understanding of where on the compliance/defiance continuum a family or family member is at any given time" (Anderson & Stewart, 1983, p. 38).

One way to overcome resistance is to create boundaries for the family (Jaffe, 1991). For instance, all family members must be present for a session to occur, or there will be no name calling in or outside the therapy sessions. Through the use of boundaries, members and the family as a whole can feel safe and begin opening up to one another. Another strategy is to interpret positively the actions associated with resistance as ways the family copes or protects itself. This is a type of reframing: "the art of attributing different meaning to behavior so the behavior will be seen differently by the family" (Constantine, Stone Fish, & Piercy, 1984). Thus, a therapist might commend family members who refuse to participate in a session for being "rightfully cautious" about opening themselves or the family up to new situations. A final way to deal with this phenomenon is to endorse it. For example, the therapist might say, "Go slow." This strategy is called a paradox, or a form of treatment in which therapists give families permission to do what they were going to do anyway. This type of directive allows a family to be more flexible in their responses and to deal with matters in a more open manner.

## Make a Return Appointment and Give Assignments

At the end of a first session, some beginning therapists make the mistake of waiting to see if a family wishes to make another appointment. Although it is appropriate to let the family make a decision regarding future sessions, it is equally important that the therapist offer to see the family again. For instance, the therapist can propose that the family come for a set number of additional sessions, say, four. After the additional sessions have taken place, the family can evaluate them and decide what progress has been made. This approach relieves the therapist and the family of the burden of dealing with the question of future sessions after each appointment. However, regardless of whether the number of sessions is agreed to ahead of time or session by session, the therapist needs to take the lead in giving the family options.

If future sessions are agreed to, then the next step in the process is to assign the family **homework** (i.e., tasks to do outside the therapy session), if theoretically appropriate. For example, the structural, strategic, Bowen, and behavioral types of family therapy emphasize working between sessions. Haley (1987) cites three reasons for giving homework. First, it helps families behave and feel differently. Many families need practice in order to be comfortable with new or prescribed ways of interacting. Second, homework assignments intensify the relationship between the therapist and the family. Finally, homework gives the therapist an opportunity to see how family members relate to each other. Therefore, homework or directives can be a way to help families help themselves and assist the therapist in deciding what course of action to take next.

In assigning homework, family therapists should make it clear to their families the specifics of what they are to do, as well as when and how often they are to do it (Keim, 2000). A "trial run" should be conducted in the therapist's office, if time allows. For some families, a time should be scheduled to talk over and process what they did; for others, simple action is enough. An example of a homework assignment would be for family members to practice listening to one another, and then for each member to paraphrase what another family member said before making a statement of his or her own.

### Record Impressions of Family Session Immediately

Impressions of particular families are fleeting, especially if therapists are busy. The result is that information about a family or a session can become unintentionally distorted over time (Gorden, 1992). Thus, it is crucial that those who work with families record their impressions in the form of *clinical notes* as soon as possible after sessions. Historically, clinical notes have been more content oriented than process oriented. However, family therapists have a choice as to what they record and how they do so. A balance between noting the process and the content of sessions probably works best.

In writing clinical notes, therapists accomplish three vital tasks. First, clinical notes can be studied over time in regard to patterns or processes that may evolve. This type of "paper trail" is invaluable because it helps therapists remember nonverbal interactions and occurrences. Clinical notes lend themselves to future use (Gorden, 1992).

Second, clinical notes give therapists the opportunity to be reflective and objective, and to pull away from the seductive power of becoming a family member (Mark Worden, personal communication, 1982). Families are powerful and can easily engulf outsiders into their ways of thinking.

Finally, clinical notes can help therapists probe in a specific way by reminding them of what has been previously said or dealt with. Many families are theme oriented and talk about behaviors and events in some detail. By referring to notes, therapists can avoid going over the same material twice (Gorden, 1992).

A unique way of recording clinical notes, used by Michael White and other narrative family therapists, is through the practice of writing a letter to the family about what occurred during the session. The letters then become the clinical record—that is, the clinical notes.

## Middle Phase of Treatment

If rapport, structure, and initiative have been fostered in the initial sessions of family therapy, the middle phase of treatment can begin. During this phase, family therapists push family members and the family as a whole to make changes and breakthroughs. To do so, the therapist should employ the procedures discussed in the following subsections.

### Involve Peripheral Family Members

A family is only as productive as its least involved member. Therefore, in most orientations to family therapy, the middle phase of treatment emphasizes making sure that all family members are committed to and working toward a common goal. If a family member is not involved in the process of therapy, the therapist can invite him or her in one or more of three ways (Barker, 2001).

The first way is to invite the uninvolved family member to be an observer of the family. In this role, he or she begins to participate by giving the family feedback on what has transpired in their interaction. He or she acts as a reporter, summarizing what has occurred, at the end of a session.

The second way to get the uninvolved family member to participate is through the Milan therapy technique of circular questioning. In this procedure, the detached family member is asked to give his or her impressions about the different interactions of other family members. For example, the therapist might ask: "How does your father act when *that* happens? How does your mother respond?" The process, in itself, elicits involvement and helps the family recognize the uniqueness of the individuals within it. Circular questioning "can and does trigger therapeutic change" (Tomm, 1987, p. 5).

The third way to entice an uninvolved family member is to use the power of the family group as a whole. This could mean that the uninvolved person is literally carried into the session. However, most often it involves physical reassurance and verbal insistence that the reluctant member be present for the session.

### Seek to Connect Family Members

A second goal of the middle phase of family therapy is to link members of the family together in an appropriate manner. This objective is especially noticeable in structural family therapy in which boundaries are emphasized (Minuchin & Fishman, 1981). However, the proper joining and separating of family members from one another is not owned by any theoretical position.

Making sure of linkage between individuals (e.g., siblings) whose generational interests and concerns are common is crucial at this time. Similarly, breaking up inappropriate intergenerational coalitions that are formed against other members of the family, while supporting those that are formed for connection, closeness, and growth, is a must (Milstein & Baldwin, 1997). An example of the former type of coalition occurs when a mother and daughter form an alliance against a father. On the other hand, the latter type of coalition, if considered from a feminist perspective, might be a mother and teenage daughter alliance that provides "strength and a source of comfort during what can be a confusing and painful developmental period" (p. 129).

### Establish Contracts and Promote Quid pro Quo Relations

A third dimension of the middle phase of family therapy is to foster "payoffs" in relationships, especially in newly formed connections. This procedure can be done through the use of contracts, a type of **quid pro quo** (something for something) relationship in which family members begin to benefit from their involvement with each other. For instance, in return for doing chores on Saturday morning, parents make Saturday dinner "pizza time." In such a circumstance, household tasks are completed more easily (a benefit for the parents), and the children enjoy a special treat while also taking on appropriate responsibilities.

### Emphasize Some Change Within the Family System

The process of change is difficult for most individuals, let alone families. In helping families consider change, therapists must assist families in understanding what is currently happening in their lives, what options are available, what the consequences are for change, and what new skills they will have to acquire if they change (Snider, 1992). Sometimes change is best approached in small steps. Using this strategy, families can begin to get used to behaving differently. For example, suppose family members have difficulty clearly communicating with one another in the morning because they are so rushed. A small change might be to start getting up 15 minutes earlier and then moving the clock back in 5-minute segments each day until the family arises 30 minutes earlier than before. A similar small change might be a husband and wife who agree to concentrate on listening to each other exclusively for 15 minutes each day.

Emphasizing contracts and small changes is helpful because these procedures are relatively nonthreatening. In addition, they help everyone envision future happenings in a concrete way.

### Reinforce Family Members for Trying New Behaviors

Family members and the family as a whole need to be reinforced when they take risks and attempt new behaviors. Such a policy encourages families to try different ways of interacting. For example, when children ask parents if they can have candy instead of just taking it, they should be rewarded (possibly with candy). Similarly, if a man appropriately asks his estranged spouse if she would sit and talk with him about their relationship, he should be rewarded.

Family therapists can use many different means to reinforce family members, but probably the most simple and effective, in most cases, is a brief verbal acknowledgment of what has been done. For example, therapists can say "good" or "nice work" to clients immediately after learning about the risks they have taken. The goal of this procedure is for the therapist's role of giving awards to gradually be taken over by the family members or for the process of reward to become internalized by the family.

### Stay Active as a Therapist

Being a family therapist means being mentally, verbally, and behaviorally active (Friedlander, Wildman, Heatherington, & Skowron, 1994). Few approaches to working with families are passive. Therapists are expected to be involved; otherwise, they will probably fail. On the importance of being active, Haley (1969) offers "the Five B's, which guarantee dynamic failure" (p. 61):

- Be passive
- Be inactive
- Be reflective
- Be silent
- Beware

The case for focusing on behavior and action in family therapy is based on the observation that people often do not change even though they understand why and how they should. For instance, individuals may know they need to lose weight, stop smoking, or spend time with their children, yet they do not (Nichols & Schwartz, 2001). Promoting insight in people may help them understand themselves better and freely act in their own best interest; but family therapists do not, as a rule, count on this happening. Instead, the therapist invests a great deal in bringing about change in families and does not wait for insight or spontaneous remission of symptoms.

### Link Family with Appropriate Outside Systems

Family therapy is limited in time and scope. It is important that families and their members learn to link up with outside groups whenever possible. For example, when families are working to overcome problems related to alcohol abuse, it may be helpful if members connect with Alcoholics Anonymous (AA) and Al-Anon. By so doing, they can receive the additional necessary support and knowledge they need in order to cope and change.

Linkage between families and agencies should be made during the middle phase of family therapy. Consequently, family therapists avoid making hasty and often ineffective referrals to outside agencies at the end of treatment. The importance of outside groups to the health and well-being of families is highlighted in the writings of Boszormenyi-Nagy (1987), who stresses that healing and growth for families take place best when the total context in which families operate is included in treatment.

### Focus on Process

Family therapy is a continuous process, and when changes are made in families, it is usually because therapists have focused on the process instead of just the content. Those who practice family therapy must realize that just as "one swallow does not a summer make," one change or even several within the family does not indicate that the family is ready to be discharged from treatment. Rather, changes occur over time and tend to be affective, behavioral, and cognitive, with affective changes among family members being especially significant (Friedlander et al., 1994).

In many cases, family members make their easiest adjustments first. Consequently, family therapists must keep unbalancing, or disturbing, the family when it resists dealing with difficulties or focuses on one person instead of on systemic changes. This requires that the therapist engage the family continuously in a therapeutic alliance of collaboration (Friedlander et al., 1994).

### Interject Humor When Appropriate

Many families enter therapy with the perception that life is a tragedy. As a result, they struggle, suffer profoundly, and feel alone and unable to change. Although some events and circumstances in life are tragic, most families who seek therapy are not in such a state. Therefore, it is appropriate at times, especially in the middle phase of family therapy, to help families become more aware of and even enjoy the folly of their existence. In doing so, families might see how they have painted themselves into corners or acted in absurd ways.

Caution must be taken to not make fun of families but rather to let them have fun and simultaneously gain insight. As Frank Pittman (1995) says: "In my therapy, I don't eschew laughter, but the patients have most of the funny lines" (p. 39). For example, if a mother is obsessed with the fact that her 12-year-old daughter will not pick up her clothes, the therapist might have the mother project the concern into future years and events. In this exercise the mother might imagine her daughter getting married and never being able to have romantic times with her spouse because of her inability to wade through the sea of clothes she has habitually tossed on the floor. Although such an example is absurd, it helps illustrate a point and aids the mother and daughter in sharing a moment of levity. Again, as Pittman (1995) says:

> We can bear far more in comedy than in tragedy, because in comedy we don't have to be perfect, we are not alone in our suffering, and we get to change in time to not die from our hopeless emotional position. If we are fully embedded in our comic perspective then we can bear all the reality life has to offer. (p. 40)

### Look for Evidence of Change in the Family

If therapy is going well, it will become evident. Therefore, therapists need to closely observe the family system to see if it is accommodating to new experiences and input data from therapy. Many subtle and many blatant signs usually appear to indicate that changes are occurring. For example, family members might appear to be more relaxed with one another and to talk more directly with one another; or conflict and defensiveness might lessen, and humor and goodwill might increase.

When family therapists discover these changes along with families, it then becomes evident that the work of the middle phase of therapy is winding down. In such cases, families and clinicians move their focus and efforts to termination.

## Termination

"Progress in family therapy moves in a circular direction. The potential for reaching new goals depends on the growth that has occurred previously. If one understands systems to be open and changing, it is hard to define the conclusion of family therapy simply in terms of accomplished goals, for the goals themselves may change over the course of therapy" (Nichols & Everett, 1986, p. 266). Nevertheless, family therapy reaches a point in which either the family or the therapist or both agree that it is time to end. The family and the therapist are more likely to benefit if termination is handled in a planned and systematic way, rather than in an abrupt manner.

The termination process has four steps: (1) orientation, (2) summarization, (3) discussion of long-term goals, and (4) follow-up (Epstein & Bishop, 1981):

1. *Orientation.* Just as with other therapeutic processes, the subject of termination is best raised before it is actually implemented. This is accomplished in the orientation step of termination. Orientation commences when therapists realize that families have reached their goals or will be concluding their contracted sessions.

2. *Summarization.* After the family has become oriented to the fact that therapy will be ending, the therapist goes over with the family what has occurred during their sessions together. This process can replace the therapist as chief spokesperson, or it can involve both the therapist and family taking equal responsibility for summarizing their time and experiences together.

3. *Discussion of Long-Term Goals.* The discussion of long-term goals is a means by which families can be helped during termination to anticipate, avoid, or modify potentially troublesome situations. For example, a therapist may ask a family how they are going to avoid yelling at each other when they get tired. In raising such an issue, the therapist and family

have an opportunity to identify resources both within and outside the family system that may be helpful to them in the future.

4. *Follow-Up.* The idea behind follow-up is that family therapy is a never-ending process; it continues long after the therapist and family have finished their formal work. Such a premise considers therapy and termination "open ended," that is, the family may need to return (Nichols & Everett, 1986, p. 266). It also acknowledges that some families do better over time when they know someone will check up on their progress. In essence, follow-up is a paradox. It is the last step in family therapy, but it can lead to more family therapy.

As far as the mechanics go, one of the simplest ways to achieve termination is to reduce the frequency of sessions. This may be implemented informally or formally, over a number of months. One suggestion for bringing family therapy to a close is through a *three-session termination process*—that is, setting the date, a next-to-the-last session, and the final farewell session (Thomas, 1992). The use of rituals and tasks can be especially meaningful during termination and can remind family members of what they have achieved and of behaviors they need to continue (Imber-Black, Roberts, & Whiting, 1989). For example, in a final session, members of a family can give each other wishes for the future in a written form that can be revisited later. The family can also plan a celebration of who they have become and symbolically lay to rest in a mock funeral the family that originally entered therapy.

Overall, the process of termination, like the therapeutic process itself, is more complicated than it seems (Lebow, 1995). If conducted over time and with sensitivity, it can help families and family members recognize their growth and development during treatment. It can also help families and their members recognize and accept their feelings, thoughts, behaviors, failures, and accomplishments. Unfortunately, termination is often premature, and about 40% to 60% of families who begin treatment drop out before therapy is finished (Kazdin, Stolar, & Marciano, 1995). The result is a loss of benefits for families and a lost opportunity for family therapists to work with those in need of mental health services.

Therefore, careful attention must always be paid to all aspects of the therapeutic process. Termination should not be treated as the highlight of the therapeutic experience, but it should certainly be a goal (Hackney & Cormier, 2001). Although termination can help bring the therapeutic process to a logical and positive conclusion, it is only one part of the entire system of family therapy. If possible, termination should take into account the family's progress in therapy, including skills they have learned that can be applied later (Lebow, 1995).

# Adlerian Family Therapy: An Example of Appropriate Process

Although any of a number of family therapies could be used to illustrate appropriate process, Adler's model is used here for two reasons. First, it is one of the oldest forms of family therapy having been in use in this way since the 1920s (Sherman, 1999). "Adler was the first to understand and emphasize the importance of a family's influence on an individual's development" as he brought "the focus of family dynamics into the mainstream" (Kaplan, 2000b, p. 1). Second, the model is not easily categorized although it has a systems and social orientation (LaFountain & Mustaine, 1998). Therefore, it can be employed in a variety of settings.

## Background of Adlerian Theory

Adlerian family therapy is an offshoot of the socially oriented and pragmatically focused treatment approach developed by Alfred Adler (1870–1937). It has been perpetuated in the United States by individuals such as Rudolph Driekurs, Don Dinkmeyer, Robert Sherman, Roy Kern, and Thomas Sweeney, as well as organizations such as the Alfred Adler Institute of Chicago and the North American Society of Adlerian Psychology. Some journals, such as the *Journal of Individual Psychology*, are devoted to publishing Adlerian-based research and practice articles.

A major premise of Adlerian theory is that "individuals and social systems are holistic and indivisible in nature, that behavior is purposeful and interactive, and that the individual seeks significance by belonging within a social system" (Walsh & McGraw, 1996, p. 103). The family is seen as the prototype of a social system.

Another premise of this theory is that perception is subjective, and individuals create their own meaning from experiences. The meaning of life and life's roles and responsibilities are influenced by the family atmosphere in which one grows up (Watts, 2000). A family that is nurturing and democratic may help produce a child with a positive self-concept whose behaviors are purposeful and goal directed. On the other hand, a family that is authoritarian is more likely to foster a feeling of inferiority in a child that leads to unproductive or even destructive behaviors such as aggression and violence (Smith, Mullis, Kern, & Brack, 1999).

Birth order, sibling rivalry, and gender roles are also important. A child's ordinal position (i.e., first, second, middle, youngest, or only) may impact the way that child responds to his or her family and society in general. For instance, firstborn are often achievement oriented, and youngest are often socially oriented. Sibling rivalry, such as that between firstborn and second-born children, can also make a difference, with second-born children seeking to pursue roles taken by firstborns and firstborns striving to avoid being "dethroned." In addition, gender roles and the expectations associated with them may either enhance behaviors within a family or lead to conflict.

These underlying assumptions are considered by Adlerian family therapists in the preplanning stage of family therapy, because theory is the basis for therapy. Inattention to one or more of these basic assumptions can lead to actions that are incongruent with therapeutic purposes. Overall, "the general goal of Adlerian family counseling is to encourage change in family members, as well as the family as a whole" (LaFountain & Mustaine, 1998, p. 193).

## Initial Session(s)

Unlike Adlerian family counseling, which focuses on parent education and prevention, Adlerian family therapy is directed toward changing family interactions (Walsh & McGraw, 1996). Therefore, it requires that entire families be present in sessions.

Within initial sessions, joining and establishing rapport with a family is accomplished by making contact with each family member and listening to his or her concerns. Family dynamics are directly observed, especially in regard to **power** (i.e., decision making, manipulation, negotiation), **boundaries** (i.e., physical and emotional closeness), **coalitions** (i.e., two or more people joined together for support), **roles** (i.e., behaviors members expect from one another), **rules** (i.e., implicit or explicit guidelines that determine behaviors of family members), and **patterns of communication** (i.e., double messages, withholding information, and overgeneralizing).

In addition to viewing family patterns, an Adlerian family therapist might ask family members to give self-reports about how the family functions. One way of doing this is for family members to talk about a typical day in the life of their family. Inventories and assessment techniques, such as the recalling by family members of their earliest recollections, are also employed.

With this material in hand, Adlerian family therapists can engender hope that change can take place within the family by reframing problems to have more positive connotations and working with the family to formulate appropriate goals. Resistance may be dealt with by renegotiating goals, confronting the family with the fact that it is resisting and thus making them aware of their behaviors, assigning a positive connotation to the resistance to avoid a power struggle, and joining the resistance and even exaggerating it so that to resist, the family has to be more cooperative (Walsh & McGraw, 1996).

## Middle Phase of Treatment

In the middle phase of treatment, an Adlerian therapist would concentrate on helping family members become more aware of their behaviors and to reorient (i.e., change what they are doing). Awareness is increased through such processes as examining individual versus family goals, exploring life styles and types of communication between family members, and making explicit the needs and wants of the family as a whole, as well as of its individual members. Through such an understanding, families may become more motivated to want to try new behaviors and ways of interacting.

Reorientation and change can take place by simultaneously addressing several areas of difficulty (Sherman & Dinkmeyer, 1987). Among the most important of these areas are

- changes in perceptions, beliefs, values, and goals
- changes in the structure and organization of the family
- changes in the skills and social behavior of the family through teaching
- changes in the way direct and indirect power are employed in the family

## Termination

Termination is initiated in Adlerian family therapy when a family and a therapist agree that change has occurred and that the family is making progress or has made the type of progress initially agreed on. Measuring progress comes through observation of family interactions, self-reports, and various assessment techniques. In initiating termination, the Adlerian family therapist reinforces newly learned skills or ways of behaving. Because Adlerian theory has a strong teleological (i.e., futuristic) component, a family during termination is encouraged to project ahead to problems that might arise and discuss how they would handle such difficulties.

Finally, during termination, a family's strengths and abilities to continue their success are reiterated by the Adlerian family therapist. The family is then followed up through a variety of means at a predetermined time. At follow-up, the family is again reinforced by the therapist in regard to competencies and ability to maintain or continue change.

# Managed Health Care and the Process of Therapy

In ending this chapter on process, the influence of managed health care must be considered because of the impact this phenomenon has had and continues to have on family therapy. **Managed health care** began to emerge in the late 1980s when businesses perceived the predominantly fee-for-service health care system characterized by overutilization and little accountability to be hurting them financially. For example, in 1992, General Motors "spent more on employee health care than it did on steel" (Hutchins, 1995, p. 15). Thus, to reduce overall health care costs to their companies, businesses contracted with managed care organizations. In 2000, approximately 60% of Americans enrolled in health care programs were covered by a managed care contract and that number continues to increase.

The issue of managed health care is of importance to family therapists for a number of reasons. For example, it has an impact on private practitioners and agency clinicians in regard to the number of practitioners available to see families, the length over which treatment occurs, the type of treatment received, and the compensation received for their services (Adams, 1987). While a "guild" model has arisen in some areas to combat the influence of managed health care (Bittner, Blalek, Nathiel, Ringwald, & Tupper, 1999), the fact remains that this type of care is still a dominant force in the health care field.

Managed mental health care (MMHC) is a branch of managed health care that focuses on mental health services, such as family therapy. In MMHC limits are placed "on the amount and type of services, by monitoring services intensely, and by changing the nature of services" (Foos, Ottens, & Hill, 1991, p. 332). One common component of MMHC is called the **utilization review (UR)**:

> UR entails the practitioner submitting a written justification for treatment along with a comprehensive treatment plan. The justification and plan are reviewed by a utilization reviewer, who, if the plan is approved, typically allocates a specific number of sessions; further sessions are subject to reapplication and approval by the reviewer. Only under these conditions can claims be reimbursed. (Huber, 1995, p. 42)

Another emerging managed care method of cutting costs is the **capitated contract** "in which providers . . . agree to provide treatment for a population for a per person per year fee. In essence, providers become their own case managers" (Hutchins, 1996, p. 7).

The most prevalent managed care organizations are preferred provider organizations (PPOs) and health maintenance organizations (HMOs) (Levitan & Conway, 1990). With government as well as private interest in the health care field growing, there continues to be a high demand "to minimize the number of sessions available for reimbursement" (West & MohdZain, 2000, p. 293). Therefore, brief family therapy approaches have become quite popular (Fleming & Rickord, 1997). Solution-focused, narrative, and strategic forms of family therapy seem especially well suited for managed health care programs. Overall, "in a managed care setting, providers must be able to draft a treatment plan, follow it, and provide documentation that it is being followed and, most importantly, that treatment is effective" (Hutchins, 1995, p. 15). Thus, the process as well as the theoretical approaches practiced in family therapy stand to be influenced for years to come.

# Summary and Conclusion

This chapter focused on the personhood of the therapist as well as on universal aspects in the process of conducting family therapy. It gave an example of the process of therapy using an Adlerian-based treatment model of a case. It also dealt briefly with the influence of managed care on the practice of family therapy.

What type of person a potential family therapist is becomes crucial to the success of that individual as a clinician. There are certain family-of-origin backgrounds and personal dispositions that are more congruent to one becoming a family therapist. Simply being intelligent, articulate, and motivated is not enough.

Specific topics that were addressed in the appropriate process section of the chapter included the initial session(s), the middle phase of therapy, and termination. Within each of these three topics numerous points were discussed.

During the initial session(s) the task of the therapist is to create a structure in which change can take place. This "battle for structure" process begins on the phone and/or in studying background material. Through such involvement, the family therapist establishes rapport and structure. He or she also hypothesizes what is happening within the family (i.e., makes a diagnosis) from a developmental and systemic frame of reference. It is hoped that during the initial session(s), families will become more motivated and win what has been defined as the "battle for initiative." It is important that families win this battle because the best success in any clinical setting is seen when families are motivated to accomplish goals.

During the middle phase of family therapy, most of the work of therapy takes place. If family therapy is like a play, then the middle phase contains the most action. It is crucial in this phase that clinicians pay as much attention to the processes within families as they do to the content. It is also important that families be helped or encouraged to make links to support groups and resources within their communities. It is during the middle phase that family therapists are extremely involved in helping families overcome natural and artificial barriers that keep them from achieving their goals.

Finally, the process of termination is the last part of the therapeutic cycle. Termination works best when client families are prepared for it. The results are usually better when it is agreed to by both the therapist and family. Termination is not the highlight of therapy, but if conducted properly, it can help families reflect on what they have accomplished and learned. It can motivate families and their members to continue new behaviors, especially if follow-up is included.

Adlerian family therapy was introduced as an example of how a theory is implemented in the process of working with a family. The Adlerian approach is one of the oldest in the field of family therapy and is socially and pragmatically based. Like other forms of therapy, the Adlerian approach is driven by its theoretical presuppositions about how families function. From the theory, Adlerian family therapists focus on certain aspects of the family as shaping a treatment process that includes initial sessions, a middle or working phase, and then, finally, termination and follow-up.

In the final section of the chapter, the influence of managed health care on the practice of family therapy was discussed. Managed care is a present reality and impacts what treatment will be received by families, using what theory, and for how long. While guilds and other alternatives are springing up to challenge managed health care, it continues to dominate the field.

# Summary Table

## The Process of Family Therapy

### The Personhood of Family Therapists

The personhood of family therapists is important to the process of family therapy.
Major stressors and enhancers for family therapists continue to be highlighted and evaluated in regard to one's readiness to practice in the profession.

### Common Problems of Beginning Family Therapists

*Overemphasis*

Beginning therapists can overemphasize details.
They can overemphasize making everyone happy.
They can overemphasize verbal expression.
They can overemphasize coming to early or easy resolution.
They can overemphasize dealing with one member of the family.

*Underemphasis*

Beginning therapists can underemphasize the establishment of structure (use of self-disclosure statements can avoid this problem).
They can underemphasize showing care and concern.
They can underemphasize the engagement of family members in the therapeutic process
They can underemphasize letting the family work on its problems, that is, win their battle for initiative.
They can underemphasize and thus not attend well to nonverbal family dynamics.

### Appropriate Process

*Pre-Session Planning and Tasks*

Establish initial professional relationship with referral source/person.
Collect essential information about the family.
Make arrangements to see the family (within 48 hours if possible).
Hypothesize about dynamics within the family (from family life cycle literature).
Form a preliminary diagnosis (e.g., distancing, cutoffs, enmeshment, disengagement, friction, denial, enabling, unresolved grief).

*Initial Session*

Make the family comfortable through social exchange with each member, that is, establish rapport and join with the family.

Ask each member for his or her perception of the family.

Observe family patterns, that is, the "family dance" (who speaks to whom and how, what is the outward appearance of family, what is the family mood, etc.).

Assess what needs to be done (e.g., treatment, referral, testing, and so forth).

Engender hope for change and overcome resistance.

Break dysfunctional patterns through words and actions congruent with one's theoretical perspective (if appropriate).

Make a return appointment and assignments.

Write impressions of family and session immediately after the session ends.

*Middle Phase of Treatment*

Involve peripheral family members in the therapeutic process, (e.g., use circular questioning).

Seek to connect family members with appropriate generational interests and concerns (i.e., break up intergenerational coalitions).

Promote quid pro quo (something for something) relationships so that family members begin to think they are benefiting from the therapeutic process.

Emphasize progress or change within family system however small.

Reinforce family members for taking risks and trying new behaviors.

Stay active as a therapist by continuing to probe, direct, and suggest.

Link family members with appropriate outside support systems if needed.

Focus on process.

Look for evidence of change in the family (i.e., utilize all of the techniques within your approach that are germane to the family with whom you are working).

*Termination*

Plan with the family for a mutually agreed-on termination.

Consider termination "open ended" (i.e., the family may need to return).

Reduce the frequency of sessions.

Follow the four-step termination process: (1) orientation, (2) summarization, (3) discussion of long-term goals, and (4) follow-up.

Formally bring family therapy to a close (i.e., discuss what was learned and achieved during family therapy).

Celebrate and/or resolve grief.

## Adlerian Family Therapy: An Example of Appropriate Process

*Background of Adlerian Theory*

The theory was created by Alfred Adler (1870–1937).

Adlerian theory is socially oriented and pragmatically focused.

Social systems are indivisible and holistic; a family is a prototype of a social system.

Perception is subjective; individuals create their own meaning from experiences.

A family atmosphere either promotes or inhibits positive social behaviors.

Birth order, sibling rivalry, and gender roles either enhance or detract from behaviors in families and societies.

Therapists must consider these underlying assumptions of Adlerian theory in the preplanning stage.

### Initial Session(s)

The whole family is seen in therapy.

After joining and initial rapport building, the therapist observes family dynamics related to power, boundaries, coalitions, roles, rules, and patterns of communication. Also, self-reports are received.

Adlerian family therapists engender hope for change, reframe problems, and work with family to formulate appropriate goals.

Resistance is dealt with in a number of ways, including confrontation and joining.

### Middle Phase of Treatment

Therapist helps families become more aware of their behaviors and to reorient (i.e., make changes).

Individual and family goals are compared and contrasted.

Several areas of change may be addressed at once, for example, perceptions, beliefs, social skills, family structure, and power.

### Termination

Termination is initiated when the therapist and family mutually agree concerning progress and goals.

New skills and ways of behaving are reinforced.

Potential future problems are addressed.

Family strengths are reinforced.

A time for follow-up is planned.

## Managed Health Care and the Process of Therapy

Managed health care in the form of PPOs and HMOs is likely to increase in the future and severely impact the services and processes of family therapy.

Briefer forms of family therapy will most likely be more in demand as managed health care becomes more pervasive.

Guilds and other alternatives to managed health care are being formed.

# References

Adams, J. (1987). A brave new world for private practice? *Family Therapy Networker, 11,* 18–25.

Anderson, C. M., & Stewart, S. (1983). *Mastering resistance: A practical guide to family therapy.* New York: Guilford.

Aponte, H. J. (1992). Training the person of the therapist in structural family therapy. *Journal of Martial and Family Therapy, 18,* 269–281.

Barker, P. (2001). *Basic family therapy* (4th ed.). New York: Bladewell Science Inc.

Bateson, G. (1955). A theory of play and fantasy. *Psychiatric Reports, 2,* 177–193.

Bittner, S., Blalek, E., Nathiel, S., Ringwald, J., & Tupper, M. (1999). An alternative to managed care: A "guild" model for the independent practice of psychotherapy. *Journal of Marital and Family Therapy, 25,* 99–111.

Boszormenyi-Nagy, I. (1987). *Foundations of contextual therapy.* New York: Brunner/Mazel.

Bowen, M. L. (1978). *Family therapy in clinical practice.* New York: Jason Aronson.

Brammer, L. M., & MacDonald, G. (1999). *The helping relationship: Process and skills* (7th ed.). Boston: Allyn & Bacon.

Brock, G. W., & Barnard, C. P. (1999). *Procedures in marriage and family therapy* (3rd ed.). Boston: Allyn & Bacon.

Carlson, J., Hinkle, J. S., & Sperry, L. (1993). Using diagnosis and DSM-III-R and IV in marriage and family counseling and therapy: Increasing treatment outcomes without losing heart and soul. *The Family Journal, 1,* 308–312.

Carter, B., & McGoldrick, M. (Eds.). (1999). *The expanded family life cycle* (3rd ed.). Boston: Allyn & Bacon.

Coleman, S, (1985). *Failures in family therapy.* New York: Guilford.

Constantine, J. A., Stone Fish, L. S., & Piercy, F. P. (1984). A systematic procedure for teaching positive connotation. *Journal of Marital and Family Therapy, 10,* 313–316.

Cormier, L. S., & Hackney, H. (1999). *Counseling strategies and interventions* (5th ed.). Boston: Allyn & Bacon.

Coyne, J. C. (1985). Toward a theory of frames and reframing: The social nature of frames. *Journal of Marital and Family Therapy, 11,* 337–344.

Duncan, S. F., & Duerden, D. S. (1990). Stressors and enhancers in the marital/family life of the family professional. *Family Relations, 39,* 211–215.

Duvall, E. (1977). *Marriage and family development* (5th ed.). Philadelphia: Lippincott.

Egan, G. (1998). *The skilled helper* (6th ed.). Pacific Grove, CA: Brooks/Cole.

Epstein, N. B., & Bishop, D. S. (1981). Problem centered systems therapy of the family. *Journal of Marital and Family Therapy, 7,* 23–31.

Fleming, J. S., & Rickord, B. (1997). Solution-focused brief therapy: One answer to managed mental health care. *The Family Journal, 5,* 286–294.

Foos, J. A., Ottens, A. J., & Hill, L. K. (1991). Managed mental health: A primer for counselors. *Journal of Counseling and Development, 69,* 332–336.

Friedlander, M. L., Wildman, J., Heatherington, L., & Skowron, E. A. (1994). What we do and don't know about the process of family therapy. *Journal of Family Psychology, 8,* 390–416.

Gladding, S. T. (1988). *Milestones.* Unpublished manuscript. Winston-Salem, NC.

Gladding, S. T. (2000). *Counseling: A comprehensive profession* (4th ed.). Upper Saddle River, NJ: Merrill/Prentice Hall.

Gorden, R. (1992). *Basic interviewing skills.* Itasca, IL: F. E. Peacock.

Guy, J. D. (1987). *The personal life of the psychotherapist.* New York: Wiley.

Hackney, H., & Cormier, L. S. (2001). *The professional counselor: A process guide to helping* (4th ed.). Boston: Allyn & Bacon.

Haley, J. (1969). *The power tactics of Jesus Christ and other essays.* New York: Grossman.

Haley, J. (1976). *Problem-solving therapy.* San Francisco: Jossey-Bass.

Haley, J. (1987). *Problem solving therapy* (2nd ed.). San Francisco: Jossey-Bass.

Holland, J. L. (1973). *Making vocational choices: A theory of vocational personalities and work environments* (3rd ed.). Sarasota, FL: Psychological Assessment Resource.

Huber, C. H. (1995). Counselor responsibility within managed mental health care. *The Family Journal: Counseling and Therapy for Couples and Families, 3,* 42–44.

Hutchins, J. (1995, December). Industry downsizing, increased provider risk, and niche marketing are trends, say experts. *Family Therapy News, 26,* 15.

Hutchins, J. (1996, April). Beyond office sharing: Starting a group practice. *Family Therapy News, 27,* 7, 22.

Imber-Black, E., Roberts, J., & Whiting, R. (1989). *Rituals in families and in family therapy.* New York: Norton.

Jaffe, D. T. (1991). *Working with the ones you love.* Berkeley, CA: Conari Press.

Johnson, L., & Thomas, V. (1999). Influences on the inclusion of children in family therapy. *Journal of Marital and Family Therapy, 25,* 117–123.

Kaplan, D. M. (2000a). Using an informed consent brochure to help establish a solid therapeutic relationship. In R. E. Watts (Ed.), *Techniques in marriage and family counseling* (pp. 3–10). Alexandria, VA: American Counseling Association.

Kaplan, D. M. (2000b). Who are our giants? *The Family Digest, 12*(4), 1, 6.

Kaplan, D., & Culkin, M. (1995). Family ethics: Lessons learned. *The Family Journal, 3,* 335–338.

Kazdin, A. E., Stolar, M. J., & Marciano, P. L. (1995). Risk factors for dropping out of treatment among white and black families. *Journal of Family Psychology, 9,* 402–417.

Keim, J. (2000). Strategic family therapy: The Washington School. In A. M. Horne (Ed.), *Family counseling and therapy* (3rd ed., pp. 170–207). Itasca, IL: F. E. Peacock.

Kier, F. J., & Lawson, D. M. (1999). A comparison of family-of-origin perceptions of doctoral student psychotherapists with doctoral students in other fields: Implications for training. *The Family Journal, 7,* 118–124.

Kral, R., & Hines, M. (1999). A survey study on developmental stages in achieving a competent sense of self as a family therapist. *The Family Journal, 7,* 102–111.

L'Abate, L., & Bagarozzi, D. (1993). *Sourcebook of marriage and family evaluation*. New York: Brunner/Mazel.

LaFountain, R. M., & Mustaine, B. L. (1998). Infusing Adlerian theory into an introductory marriage and family course. *The Family Journal, 6*, 189–199.

Lebow, J. (1995). Open-ended therapy: Termination in marital and family therapy (pp. 73–86). In R. H. Mikesell, D.-D. Lusterman, & S. H. McDaniel (Eds.), *Integrating family therapy*. Washington, DC: American Psychological Association.

Levitan, S. A., & Conway, E. A. (1990). *Families in flux*. Washington, DC: Bureau of National Affairs.

Milstein, K., & Baldwin, C. (1997). Coalitions in primary triads: Reexamining the theoretical constructs from a feminist perspective. *The Family Journal, 5*, 125–131.

Minuchin, S. (1974). *Families and family therapy*. Boston: Harvard.

Minuchin, S., & Fishman, H. C. (1981). *Family therapy techniques*. Boston: Harvard.

Napier, A. Y., & Whitaker, C. (1978). *The family crucible*. New York: Bantam Books.

Nichols, M. P., & Schwartz, R. C. (2001). *Family therapy: Concepts and methods* (5th ed.). Boston: Allyn & Bacon.

Nichols, W. C., & Everett, C. (1986). *Systemic family therapy: An integrative approach*. New York: Guilford.

Odell, M., & Quinn, W. H. (1998). Therapist and client behaviors in the first interview: Effects on session impact and treatment duration. *Journal of Marital and Family Therapy, 24*, 369–388.

Olkin, R. (1993, Winter). Teaching family therapy to graduate students: What do we teach and when do we teach it? *Family Psychologist, 9*, 31–34.

Pals, S., Piercy, F., & Miller, J. (1998). Factors related to family therapists' breaking confidence when clients disclose high-risks-to-HIV/AIDS sexual behaviors. *Journal of Marital and Family Therapy, 24*, 457–472.

Piercy, F. P., & Lobenz, N. M. (1994). *Stop marital fights before they start*. New York: Berkeley Press.

Pittman, F. (1995, November/December). Turning tragedy into comedy. *Family Therapy Networker, 19*, 36–40.

Rait, D. (1988). Survey results. *Family Therapy Networker, 12*, 52–56.

Resnikoff, R. O. (1981). Teaching family therapy: Ten key questions for understanding the family as patient. *Journal of Marital and Family Therapy, 7*, 135–142.

Rickert, V. (1989). *The initial family interview*. Presentation at the annual convention of the American Association for Marriage and Family Therapy, San Francisco, CA.

Satir, V. (1987). The therapist story. *Journal of Psychotherapy and the Family, 3*, 17–25.

Sherman, R. (1999). Family therapy: The art of integration. In R. E. Watts & J. Carlson (Eds.), *Interventions and strategies in counseling and psychotherapy* (pp. 101–134). Philadelphia: Taylor & Francis.

Sherman, R., & Dinkmeyer, D. (1987). *Systems of family therapy: An Adlerian integration*. New York: Brunner/Mazel.

Smith, S., Mullis, F., Kern, R. M., & Brack, G. (1999). An Adlerian model for the etiology of aggression in adjudicated adolescents. *The Family Journal, 7*, 135–147.

Snider, M. (1992). *Process family therapy*. Boston: Allyn & Bacon.

Sweeney, D. S., & Rocha, S. L. (2000). Using play therapy in assessing family dynamics. In R. E. Watts (Ed.), *Techniques in marriage and family counseling* (pp. 33–47). Alexandria, VA: American Counseling Association.

Thomas, M. B. (1992). *An introduction to marital and family therapy*. Upper Saddle River, NJ: Merrill/Prentice Hall.

Tomm, K. (1987). Interventive interviewing: Part 1. Strategizing as a fourth guideline for the therapist. *Family Process, 26*, 3–13.

Walsh, W. M., & McGraw, J. A. (1996). *Essentials of family therapy*. Denver, CO: Love.

Watts, R. E. (2000). Using the how I remember my family questionnaire in couples counseling. In R. E. Watts (Ed.), *Techniques in marriage and family counseling* (pp. 53–56). Alexandria, VA: American Counseling Association.

Weber, T., & Levine, F. (1995). Engaging the family: An integrative approach. In R. H. Mikesell, D.-D. Lusterman, & S. H. McDaniel (Eds.), *Integrating family therapy* (pp. 45–71). Washington, DC: American Psychological Association.

Weber, T., McKeever, J. E., & McDaniel, S. H. (1992). A beginner's guide to the problem-oriented first family interview. In R. L. Smith & P. Stevens-Smith (Eds.). *Family counseling and therapy* (pp. 202–212). Ann Arbor, MI: ERIC/CAPS.

West, J. D. (1988). Marriage and family therapy assessment. *Counselor Education and Supervision, 28*, 169–180.

West, P. L., & MohdZain, A. Z. (2000). Marriage counseling and the TFA model: An application. *The Family Journal, 8*, 293–299.

Wetchler, J. L., & Piercy, F. P. (1986). The marital/family life of the family therapist: Stressors and enhancers. *American Journal of Family Therapy, 14*, 99–108.

Wilcoxon, S. A., Walker, M. R., & Hovestadt, A. J. (1989). Counselor effectiveness and family-of-origin experiences: A significant relationship? *Counseling and Values, 33*, 225–229.

# CHAPTER 5

# Psychodynamic and Bowenian Family Therapies

I walk thoughtfully down Beecher Road
at the end of a summer of too little growth,
the autumn wind stirring around me
orange remnants of once green leaves.

I am the son of a fourth-grade teacher
and a man who dabbled in business,
a descendant of Virginia farmers
and open-minded Baptists,
the husband of a Connecticut woman,
the father of preschoolers.

Youngest of three, I am a trinity:
counselor,
teacher,
writer.

Amid the cold, I approach home,
midlife is full of surprises.

*Gladding, 1993*

Psychodynamic and Bowenian family therapies began developing in the 1950s. Their founders, Nathan Ackerman in New York and Murray Bowen in Washington, D.C., were both known for their strong personalities and loyal followings.

They originally were educated to utilize Freud's (1940) psychoanalytic theory with individual clients. Indeed, the tenets of psychoanalysis are a shared source from which psychodynamic and Bowenian family therapies sprang. However, Ackerman and Bowen, because of their interests and circumstances, took liberties to apply Freud's theory to families and stressed the development of interpersonal as well as intrapersonal relationships.

This chapter examines the main aspects of psychodynamic and Bowenian family therapies. In identifying themselves as either psychodynamic or Bowenian family therapists, clinicians are distinct in emphasizing specific theoretical techniques and factors associated with each theory (e.g., who is worked with, as well as how and when treatment occurs). At the heart of treatment, from both viewpoints, is a belief that changes in families and their members occur best when the family is examined in the context of its history and development. Conscious and unconscious processes are collectively and individually the focus of therapeutic interventions.

On the surface, psychodynamic and Bowenian family therapies have much in common. This is particularly true in regard to numerous premises and beliefs. For instance, psychodynamic and Bowenian family treatments are based on conceptual models that are comprehensive in scope. They also have applied techniques that have developed from both research and practice (e.g., Papero, 1990; Titelman, 1987).

Another unifying feature that psychodynamic and Bowenian family therapies share is the belief that in family therapy an emphasis should be placed on the fact that "the past is active in the present" (Smith, 1991, p. 24). These two approaches stress the importance of social and historical data in the lives of families. For example, early childhood experiences (i.e., the past), whether consciously maintained or not, can have an impact on an individual and a family now (i.e., the present) and for years to come. Initial experiences associated with bonding and connectedness are particularly relevant. The memories and patterns of interaction established during these moments continue to influence present levels of functioning in multiple ways (Gibson & Donigian, 1993). For example, a couple's struggle over emotional and physical closeness might be a renewal of difficulties each had in forming relationships early in life.

A further common denominator of these theories is their focus on how intrapersonal and interpersonal aspects of life impact on each other. Basically, the way people relate to themselves influences how they interact with others. Similarly, the way in which people have been reacted to by others in the past affects how they perceive and treat themselves. For instance, an 11-year-old girl who withdraws from social activities may be expressing her feelings about her inadequacy in a family and minimizing her risk of being ridiculed.

Those associated with psychodynamic and Bowenian family therapies have created their own specific descriptors of interactions as well. A number of phrases from each theory characterize family dynamics. Psychodynamic theorists, for instance, have coined terms such as **marital schism, marital skew** (Lidz, Cornelison, Fleck, & Terry, 1957), and **pseudomutuality** (Wynne, Ryckoff, Day, & Hirsh, 1958) to describe dysfunctional relationships within families. Bowenian family therapists have invented other words or phrases such as differentiation, fusion, and emotionally cut off (Kerr & Bowen, 1988).

A final premise these two theories share is their view that change is usually gradual and requires hard work with a heavy investment of time and resources. Bowen and Ackerman, as psychodynamically trained psychiatrists, did not let their theories stray far from an in-depth treatment perspective. Although Bowenian family therapy may sometimes achieve good results in as few as 5 or 10 sessions, families using either of these two approaches generally require 20 to 40 sessions (Bowen, 1975). Members within families usually examine their relationships in regard to themselves and others before they risk trying new patterns of behavior.

# ◼ Psychodynamic Family Therapy ◼

Psychodynamic family therapy encompasses more than traditional psychoanalytic theory applied to families. Rather, it is composed of a number of approaches, such as object relations theory, that are offshoots of Freud's basic tenets.

## Major Theorists

The most prominent professionals associated with psychodynamic family therapy are Nathan Ackerman, Ivan Boszormenyi-Nagy, James Framo, Theodore Lidz, Norman Paul, Donald Williamson, Robin Skynner, and Lyman Wynne. However, Ackerman is generally credited as the founder of psychodynamic family therapy.

### Nathan Ackerman

Nathan Ackerman (1908–1971) became a family therapist over an extended period of time. Initially, he was educated as a child psychiatrist and followed the traditional psychoanalytic approach of seeing one patient at a time. However, in the 1930s Ackerman became interested in families and their influence on mental health/illness (Ackerman, 1937). This interest was sparked by his observations about the effect of unemployment on men and their families in a mining town in western Pennsylvania and about how families seemed to change more rapidly when all members were interviewed together (Broderick & Schrader, 1991). In his initial clinical work at the Menninger Clinic in Topeka, Kansas, he began treating whole families and sending his staff on home visits (Guerin, 1976). He was especially interested in the psychosocial dynamics of family life and in applying psychoanalytical principles to family units.

In the 1950s and 1960s, Ackerman was even more heavily involved in his work with families and, consequently, became the leading family therapist on the East Coast. He opened the Family Mental Health Clinic at Jewish Family Services in New York in 1957 and established the Family Institute in New York in 1960. In 1961, he became the cofounder of *Family Process,* the first journal in family therapy (Kaplan, 2000). This publication, along with Ackerman's earlier landmark text, *The Psychodynamics of Family Life* (1958), gave credibility and credence to the field of family therapy. Ackerman remained staunchly psychodynamic in outlook throughout his professional career.

Ackerman made many contributions to the field of family therapy. His overall success as a therapist is especially noteworthy. Ackerman documented many of his sessions with families by publishing transcripts of them (Kaplan, 2000). He was also an excellent theorist who made unique contributions to the literature in the field of family therapy through articulating arguments that were based on principles and filled with passion. His writings and practice documented the principles by which he operated. Finally, Ackerman had a strong, charismatic personality, which helped attract interest in what he was doing (Bloch & Simon, 1982). He was a fighter for what he believed in. "Innumerable minor skirmishes and border wars" that Ackerman engaged in "were never chronicled but clung to the man's reputation like the leathery scars of an old warrior chief" (Bloch & Simon, 1982, pp. xv–xvi). He has been described as feisty, brilliant, charming, and a gadfly.

Ackerman influenced many psychodynamically oriented practitioners, as well as other professionals, to treat individuals and families together as a system. He helped open the field of psychoanalysis to nonmedical specialists by establishing the American Academy of Psychoanalysis in 1955.

Ackerman defined the difference between family psychotherapy and psychoanalysis (Ackerman, 1962). His conceptualizations of families and presentations about them were creative and thought provoking. For instance, Ackerman published transcripts of family therapy sessions that contained interpretive comments in the margins, such as "Therapist contrasts father's quiet way with Alice's noisy aggressiveness" (Ackerman, Beatman, & Sherman, 1961, p. 139). Ackerman is recognized as being the initiator of or at least the one who emphasized such concepts as scapegoating, tickling of defenses, complementarity, focus on strengths, interlocking pathology, and live history.

Overall, Nathan Ackerman was a leading pioneer in family therapy. His work ethic and sense of responsibility to the field of family therapy advanced the field considerably. Unfortunately, his early death, at the age of 63, deprived the field of a crusader and innovative thinker.

# Premises of the Theory

Psychodynamic family therapy is based on the classic work of Sigmund Freud, as interpreted, modified, and applied to family life. Freud viewed human nature as one based on drives (e.g., sexuality and aggression). Mental conflict arises when children learn—and mislearn—that expressing these basic impulses will lead to punishment. Conflict is signaled by unpleasant affect: anxiety or depression. In other words, to resolve conflict one of two actions must occur: There must be a strengthening of defenses against a conflicted wish, or defenses must be relaxed sufficiently to permit some gratification.

In addition to Ackerman, several other theorists and practitioners helped apply Freud's individually focused approach to families, including Heinz Kohut (1977), James Framo

(1981), and Ivan Boszormenyi-Nagy (1987). However, Ackerman took the lead by setting up a training and treatment center for this purpose, the Family Institute (now known as the Ackerman Institute, 149 East 78th Street, New York, NY 10021). This facility provided a place where professionals could come and observe his work. He also wrote prolifically on the diagnosis and treatment of families (e.g., Ackerman, 1958). As a psychodynamically oriented therapist, he initiated a new way of thinking about individuals and families and advocated that an accurate understanding of an individual's unconscious requires an understanding of its context. One of the primary contexts is the reality of family interactions. The importance of context in the treatment of families has continued to be stressed by Boszormenyi-Nagy (1987).

Ackerman (1956) clearly articulated the concept of **interlocking pathology** to explain how families and certain of their members stay dysfunctional. In an interlocking pathology, an unconscious process takes place between family members that keeps them together. If members violate the unwritten family rules, then the members either make a conscious decision to leave the family and become healthier or they are drawn back into the familiar family pattern by other members and continue to function in a less than ideal manner. For example, a young adult who has not adequately separated from his parents may move into an apartment. If the young adult gets an adequate job and makes new friends in his or her age group, he or she may avoid being pulled back into the family and may begin to establish a new identity and way of life.

A more recent focus of psychodynamical theory is **object relations theory** (Kohut, 1977; Scharff, 1989; Slipp, 1988). Object relations theory is the bridge between classical Freudian theory, with its emphasis on individual drives, and family therapy, with its emphasis on social relationships. An **object** is something that is loved, usually a person. Therefore, the term *object relations* means "relations between persons involved in ardent emotional attachments. These attachments can exist in the outer world of reality or as residues of the past—that is, inner presences, often unconscious, that remain vigorous and very much alive within us" (Scarf, 1995, p. xxxvii).

Through object relations theory, relationships across generations can be explained. According to this theory, human beings have a fundamental motivation to seek objects, that is, people in relationships, starting at birth (Fairbairn, 1954; Klein, 1948). In this case, an object is a significant other (e.g., a mother during infancy) with whom children form an interactional, emotional bond. As they grow, children will often internalize (interject) good and bad characteristics of these objects within themselves. Over time, these interjects form the basis for how individuals interact and evaluate their interpersonal relationships with others, especially those with whom they are close.

This process of evaluation occurs at its lowest level through an unconscious procedure known as **splitting** (Kernberg, 1976). In splitting, object representations are either all good or all bad. The result is a projection of good and bad qualities onto persons within one's environment. Through splitting, people are able to control their anxiety and even the objects (i.e., persons, within their environment) by making them predictable. However, the drawback to splitting is that it distorts reality. When splitting occurs, children (and later their adult counterparts) fail to integrate their feelings about an object (a person) into a realistic view (Hafner, 1986). For example, in a couple relationship, each spouse might project unrealistic patterns of behavior onto the other. In addition to distorting the relationship, this type of projection causes conflict and confusion. Individuals who operate in this way have trouble dealing with the complexity of human relationships and may be immature in their interactions (Kernberg, 1976; Kohut, 1971).

The importance of object relations theory in family therapy is that it provides a way for psychodynamic clinicians to explain reasons for marital choices and family interactional patterns (Dicks, 1963). It stresses the value of working with unconscious forces in individuals and families beyond Freud's metaphorical concepts of id, ego, and superego. Unconscious and unresolved early object relations that adults may bring into their marriage relationships can result in the development of dysfunctional patterns in which persons cling to each other desperately and dependently (Ackerman, 1956; Napier & Whitaker, 1978). These patterns keep repeating themselves until one or both spouses (or in some cases their children) become more aware, take actions to differentiate themselves from past objects, and in the process, learn to act in new and productive ways.

# Treatment Techniques

In psychodynamic family therapy, considerable emphasis is placed on the unconscious, early memories and on object relations. The therapeutic techniques used include transference, dream and daydream analysis, confrontation, focusing on strengths, life history, and complementarity.

## Transference

**Transference** is the projection onto a therapist of feelings, attitudes, or desires. This technique is employed in individual analysis to help clients work through their feelings by viewing the therapist as a significant other with whom relationships are unresolved (Ellis, 2000). Transference is utilized in family therapy in order to understand dominant feelings within a family unit and delineate which emotions are being directed toward what people.

In cases where transference occurs, clients in the family form a bond with the therapist and act toward the therapist as they would toward people with whom they are having difficulties. Thus, they benefit through the expression of pent-up emotion (i.e., catharsis) and through self-discovery, insight, and the learning of new ways to interact. For example, family members who are angry with each other and frustrated with social service agencies might say to a family therapist such words as:

- "I don't see what good you are going to do us."
- "What's the use of talking to you."
- "I'm really mad that this family is going down the tubes and all we are doing is talking to you. When are we going to get some real help?"

By treating these sentences in a nondefensive and understanding way, the family therapist can help a family get through dealing with unproductive emotions and move on toward the task of working on important issues in their lives.

## Dream and Daydream Analysis

The objective of having family members discuss their dreams or daydreams is to analyze what needs within the family are not being met. For example, if a father has a recurring dream of being abandoned, he may be expressing a need for greater affiliation with family members. Strategies are then developed to meet members' deficits. For instance, in the case of the father, family outings or dinners could be planned to help tie the father closer to other members in a pleasant way.

Overall, dream analysis may be quite useful for some families in helping them see areas that need attention. However, dream analysis can become problematic if the number of family members participating is large.

## Confrontation

In **confrontation** procedures, the therapist points out to families how their behaviors contradict or conflict with their expressed wishes (Ackerman, 1966). For example, a father who protests that he wishes to spend more time with his wife and children, yet who continues to work late at his office on a consistent basis, may be confronted by the therapist as follows:

> George, I see you voluntarily working at your business all hours of the night and day. Yet, I hear you want to spend more time with your family. Help me understand what you are doing to get what you say you want.

The idea behind confrontation is to help family members become more aware of what they are doing and to change their strategies for coping and becoming functional.

## Focusing on Strengths

As with other therapeutic endeavors, psychodynamic family therapists are aware that most families come to treatment because they are focused on perceiving and dealing with weaknesses in themselves and their families. By concentrating on strengths, family therapists help change the family's focus. For instance, the therapist may point out to a family that they all seem quite willing and capable of breaking past patterns of interaction by saying:

> I have heard from each of you how you would like for your family to work. Bill, I am impressed with your strong commitment to doing whatever it takes. Sue, I am equally struck by the fact that you have stated you are willing to make any sacrifice necessary for the family to run more smoothly. Likewise, Chip, even though you are only fourteen years old, I am aware that you are mature and willing to work with your parents to bring about needed changes.

As a consequence of focusing on strengths, structured activities can be designed to promote cooperation and break dysfunctional patterns of behaving. For instance, a family can be asked to plan an event that will utilize the abilities of all family members.

## Life History

By taking and assessing a family's life history, psychodynamical family therapists can report present and past patterns of interaction within the family. This process also affirms to family members that they are valued and accepted regardless of their backgrounds. Taking a family life history promotes trust in the therapist and also provides family members with insight. The history can be written in a narrative or an abbreviated form.

## Complementarity

**Complementarity** is the degree of harmony in the meshing of family roles. For example, if a husband and wife agree that her role should be planning the family budget and his should be balancing the checkbook, they have established a complementarity relationship in regard to financial roles. When roles dovetail, as in the previous example, family life is likely to be satisfactory. One task of the therapist is to help family members provide and receive satisfaction from their relationships. It may mean asking members what they want and what they are willing to do in return.

# Role of the Therapist

In psychodynamic treatment, the therapist plays several roles. One is that of a teacher. It is crucial that family members understand how influences in their past, especially those that were unconscious, have an impact on them now. Therefore, it is essential that family members learn basic psychoanalytic terms and how these terms apply on a personal and interpersonal basis.

A second role the therapist might play is that of a **good enough mother** (Winnicott, 1965). A good enough mother is one whose infant feels loved and cared for and, thus, is able to develop trust and a true sense of self. This role might call for the therapist to actually nurture the family member by providing encouraging behaviors that were absent at earlier developmental stages. In this role, the therapist might involve family members in interactions with one another that help them make up for past deficits. This behavior could take the form of anything from pats on the back to the giving of compliments.

A final role the psychodynamic therapist might play is that of a catalyst who moves into the "living space" of the family and stirs up interactions. Ackerman (1966) was a master of engaging families in this manner. The result was that families in treatment would often have a meaningful emotional exchange. In the role of a catalyst, the therapist activates, challenges, confronts, sometimes interprets, and helps integrate family processes. Such a role requires high energy and stamina.

In fulfilling any of these roles, but especially the last one, the therapist must be careful to emphasize family as well as individual interactions. It is crucial that family members have extensive and free-flowing interchanges and that the therapist not become overly involved or central in the process. Such a stance is easier to describe than to implement.

# Process and Outcome

A major goal of psychodynamic family therapy is to free family members of unconscious restrictions. This outcome is sometimes achieved through the therapist's interpretation of events and insight on the part of family members regarding events. Interpretation is best offered by the therapist on a preconscious level, that is, on material that family members are almost aware of. When insights are achieved in such an endeavor, they must be **worked through**, that is, translated into new and more productive ways of behaving and interacting.

Once unconscious restrictions are worked through, family members are able to interact with one another as whole, healthy persons on the basis of current realities rather than unconscious images of the past. When this goal is achieved, the results are usually manifested in changes that are described by the term **differentiation.** The idea behind differentiation is that individuals have reached a level of maturity in which they can balance their rational and emotional selves and in which they can separate themselves from others in a nonanxious way. When this dynamic occurs, family members can interact thoughtfully as persons. They can participate in the family fully and can also be themselves. Furthermore, they do not get caught up in dysfunctional interactions with other family members.

Sometimes the achievement of differentiation is not possible. In such cases, professionals often opt for **crisis resolution**, which is similar to that of other treatment modalities and basically involves a reduction in symptoms. Therapists in these circumstances focus more on supporting defenses and clarifying communication than on analyzing defenses and uncovering repressed needs and impulses.

# Unique Aspects of Psychodynamic Family Therapy

## Emphases

A major emphasis of psychodynamic family therapy is that it concentrates on the potency of the unconscious in influencing human behavior. How the unconscious influences interpersonal and intrapersonal relationships, such as those found in marital and family living, is a focus. This method of treatment can increase family members' awareness of how forces within themselves and others, such as **invisible loyalties** to their parents, either bring them closer to each other or influence their distancing (Boszormenyi-Nagy & Spark, 1973).

The psychodynamic approach examines basic defense mechanisms and the part they play in family relationships. This is a unique contribution to the literature on family dynamics and helps make interactions among some family members more understandable (Skynner, 1981). For example, abused children who stay loyal to their parents may be seen from this perspective as employing the Freudian defense mechanism of identification with the aggressor (see Table 5.1).

A third novel aspect of psychodynamic family therapy is its emphasis on historical origins of dysfunctionality and the treatment of persons and families so affected. By working with a family or an individual, therapists get to the roots of problems formulated in childhood. They are then able to help families resolve troublesome issues by exploring past ways the family, as a unit, acted during troublesome times.

Finally, psychodynamic family theory, especially object relations, helps explain how persons form attachments and how family members function as a result. This emphasis on the genesis of family relationships is something no other approach to working with families explores in as much depth.

**Table 5.1**
Basic Psychoanalytic Defense Mechanisms

| | |
|---|---|
| Repression | The most basic of the defense mechanisms, repression is the unconscious exclusion of distressing or painful thoughts and memories. All other defense mechanisms make some use of repression. |
| Denial | In this process, a person refuses to see or accept any problem or troublesome aspect of life. Denial operates at the preconscious or conscious level. |
| Regression | When individuals are under stress, they often return to a less mature way of behaving. |
| Projection | Instead of stating what a person really thinks or feels, he or she attributes an unacceptable thought, feeling, or motive onto another. |
| Rationalization | This defense mechanism involves giving an "intellectual reason" to justify doing a certain action. The reason and the action are only connected in the person's mind after the behavior has been completed. |
| Reaction Formation | When an individual behaves in a manner that is just the opposite of how he or she feels, it is known as a "reaction formation." This type of behavior is usually quite exaggerated, such as acting especially nice to someone whom one dislikes intensely. |
| Displacement | This defense is a redirection of an emotional response onto a "safe target." The substitute person or object receives the feeling instead of the person directly connected with it. |

From *Group Work: A Counseling Specialty* (3rd ed., p. 344) by S. T. Gladding, © 1991. Reprinted by permission of Prentice-Hall, Inc., Upper Saddle River, NJ.

## Comparison with Other Theories

As opposed to most family therapies, psychodynamically oriented family therapy is linear, that is, it focuses on cause-and-effect interactions. This quality of the theory has resulted in criticism of it. Although Ackerman and others attempted to make psychodynamic theory applicable to family systems, they only partially succeeded. Too often this type of treatment is either limited to an individual or not broadened to family life (Perosa, 1996).

A second comparison of psychodynamic family therapy to other approaches is its expense in regard to financial and time commitments. Psychodynamically based approaches are demanding in the investment they require of their participants. Individuals and families must be prepared to explore the roots of their difficulties, including early childhood/parent interactions. Most cannot afford to take the time or afford the price.

A third comparison that can be made between psychodynamic family therapy and other approaches is that psychodynamic treatment generally requires higher than average intellectual ability. Psychodynamic theory may not be appropriate for families that are concrete in handling situations or become impatient with the abstract. These families want immediate results and cannot cope well with abstract concepts, such as the unconscious.

Finally, compared with most family therapy approaches, especially recently developed ones, psychodynamic treatment lacks empirical research (Shields, Wynne, McDaniel, &

Gawinski, 1994). Instead, psychoanalysis has a strong preference for nonempirical and nonquantitative studies such as case examples. Such an emphasis "has contributed to the near demise of psychoanalysis as a recommended therapy" (Shields et al., 1994, p. 121).

## CASE ILLUSTRATION

### THE CASA FAMILY

Maria Casa is a 39-year-old single parent with a 13-year-old daughter, Gloria, and an 11-year-old son, Juan. She has been divorced for 5 years, but before her divorce was married for 10 years. Her husband, Roberto, kept in touch with the children for about 2 years after the divorce, but then moved to a distant city, and last year quietly remarried. The children hear from him only at Christmas, when he sends them each a present and a card.

Maria works as an executive assistant to a vice president of a major local employer. Earlier, she had been on the company assembly line, so she appreciates her position because of its greater benefits and flexibility. Yet, she resents having to dress well for the job and to occasionally stay late at the office to finish reports. She feels she is losing touch with her children because of her work responsibilities.

Recently, Juan has started using profanity and being disrespectful to his mother and sister. He does a poor job on family chores, such as cutting the grass. In addition, he has begun to hang out after school with a group of boys Maria considers undesirable. Gloria, on the other hand, is making good grades in school and working especially hard to please her mother by doing extra tasks Maria does not have time for, such as sweeping the walk. Maria is angry at Juan and proud of Gloria. She is worried that both children may get stuck in patterns that will ultimately not benefit them. She is particularly concerned about Juan.

### Conceptualization of Family: Psychodynamic Perspective

On an unconscious level, this family appears to be enacting roles that are noncomplementary. Maria and Gloria are acting out heroine roles; Juan is the rebel. Underneath all of their public behaviors are feelings, most likely anger, about their life condition and the desertion of their father, Roberto. Juan is playing the role of the scapegoat to bring the family into treatment. Interestingly, all members of the family are seeking some social interaction—either with other family members (e.g., Gloria and Maria) or with a group (e.g., Juan and his gang). Defense mechanisms, such as sublimation by Gloria, are also evident.

### Process of Treatment: Psychodynamic Family Therapy

To help the family, a psychodynamic therapist need not bring all members of the present family into treatment. However, to understand the family thoroughly, it would be beneficial to have all members present, including Roberto if he would agree to come. After taking time to join with the family, a therapist should take a history of the family up to and after the time of the mother–father divorce. Nodal points in the family's history before and after that time should be assessed. In taking the family history, the therapist should observe the similarities and discrepancies voiced by the members of the family and the feelings associated with particular events, people, and times.

From this point on, a psychodynamic therapist has several choices. First, the therapist can try to get family members to engage in transference and ventilate their feelings about their situation and themselves. Through such a collective process, catharsis could be promoted. Second, the therapist can look for and utilize opportunities to confront family members in regard to their present behaviors and the behaviors they claim they want. This type of confrontation may be especially helpful to Juan because of the nature of his aggressive actions. Such a confrontation starts with the therapist saying: "Juan, I hear you really want to be close to others, such as your mother and sister. Yet, I notice you are cursing at them and staying away from them. Help me understand how what you are doing is helping you."

A third option for the therapist is to examine cultural and unique family/individual patterns related to the current crisis. Psychodynamic theory is not culturally specific, but a therapist should view a family in light of its cultural background regardless of the theory being utilized. The Casas are Hispanic/Latino, and as pointed out in a later chapter, there are general cultural influences that impact on family life from this tradition.

A fourth option that may come up immediately, later, or concurrently through treatment is exploring the unconscious. It is the task of a psychodynamically oriented family therapist to help family members delve into themselves intrapersonally as well as interpersonally. Unconscious material may surface and can be handled through dream analysis or through dealing with memories. The idea is that through handling aspects of the unconscious, family members will gain insight into themselves and others. They can then use this knowledge to change their behavior.

Overall, a psychodynamic therapist's work with families, such as the Casas, is to identify and utilize individual and family unit strengths. It is hoped that through the therapeutic process, unconscious aspects of family life that keep members apart will surface and be resolved.

# ◼ Bowenian Family Therapy ◼

Bowenian family therapy has the distinction of being among the first, if not the first, systemically based approaches for working with families. It has an historical overtone but is simultaneously geared toward the present.

## Major Theorists

Murray Bowen and Michael Kerr have been the chief architects and advocates of Bowenian family therapy. However, the major originator of this approach was Murray Bowen. Bowen formulated the ideas that resulted in a distinct theory of family therapy. The theory and its techniques have been popularized by authors such as McGoldrick, Gerson, and

Shellenberger (1999) (*Genograms: Assessment and Intervention*) and Friedman (1985) (*Generation to Generation: Family Process in Church and Synagogue*).

## Murray Bowen

The oldest of five children, Murray Bowen (1913–1990) grew up in a tightly knit family that for several generations resided in a small town in Pennsylvania. After growing up, Bowen moved away and kept a formal distance from his parents. He maintained family relations on a comfortable but superficial level. Bowen, like Nathan Ackerman, was a psychiatrist who became interested in working with families while employed at the Menninger Clinic. As early as 1951, he began to require that mothers of disturbed children live in the same hospital setting as their offspring (Guerin, 1976). From this experience, he became interested in studying "mother–patient symbiosis," that is, the intense bond that develops between a parent and child that does not allow for either to differentiate themselves from the other (Bowen, 1960, 1961).

In 1954, Bowen moved to join Lyman Wynne at the National Institute of Mental Health (NIMH), where he continued to be involved in studying the dynamics of families with schizophrenic children. As a part of the treatment, Bowen worked with the research team at NIMH on a pilot project to hospitalize and treat all members of such families. He recognized during this time that the characteristics exhibited by a schizophrenic family were similar to symptoms in many dysfunctional families. A few years later he moved to Georgetown University, where he researched family dynamics and developed his therapeutic approach until his death.

During his years at Georgetown, especially in the 1970s, Bowen completed his most productive personal and professional work. Personally, he detriangulated himself from his parents by returning home and reacting cognitively and neutrally to a number of emotional issues family members presented to him (Anonymous, 1972). Professionally, he clarified his theory (Bowen, 1978); began the Georgetown Family Center Symposium; expanded the Georgetown Family Center to new, off-campus quarters; and initiated the founding of the American Family Therapy Association (AFTA), "in order to restore a serious research effort in family therapy" (Wylie, 1991, p. 77).

# Premises of the Theory

For Bowen, therapy and theory are part of the same fabric and cannot be separated without doing a disservice to each. Bowen preferred to think of himself as a theorist. He saw himself as one who stood alone in conceptualizing "the family as a natural system . . . which could only be fully understood in terms of the fluid but predictable processes between members" (Wylie, 1991, p. 26). Bowen was a scientist in search of universal truths. "Bowen theory constantly strives to make continuous what other theories dichotomize" (e.g., nature/nurture, male/female, and physical illness/emotional illness) (Friedman, 1991, p. 136). However, sometimes Bowen's writings about the continuity and connection between theory and therapy are criticized for their complex and convoluted nature (Kaplan, 2000).

Bowen was influenced by events in his own life history, especially his difficulties with his own family of origin. Thus, his personal situation had a major impact on what he proposed (Anonymous, 1972; Papero, 1991). Basically, Bowen stated that unless individuals examine and rectify patterns passed down from previous generations, they are likely to repeat these behaviors in their own families (Kerr, 1988). The possibility of repeating certain behaviors in interpersonal relations is particularly likely if family members, especially between the generations, are characteristically either **emotionally overinvolved** (i.e., fused) with each other or **emotionally cut off** (psychologically or physically) from each other. Bowen concerned himself with the family's emotional system.

A key element of Bowenian family therapy is "that there is a chronic anxiety in all of life that comes with the territory of living" (Friedman, 1991, p. 139). This anxiety is both emotional and physical and is shared by all protoplasm. Some individuals are more affected than others by this anxiety "because of the way previous generations in their families have channeled the transmission" of it to them (Friedman, 1991, p. 140).

If anxiety remains low, few problems exist for people or families. In such cases, the family emotional system is undisturbed. However, in the midst of anxiety, some predictable patterns occur. According to Greene, Hamilton, and Rolling (1986, p. 189):

> Lower scale [undifferentiated] people are vulnerable to stress and are much more prone to illness, including physical and social illness, and their dysfunction is more likely to become chronic when it does occur. Higher scale people can recover emotional equilibrium quickly after the stress passes.

To address chronic anxiety and emotional processes in families and society, Bowen emphasized eight basic concepts. Through understanding these concepts, a therapist understands and successfully treats a family. These basic concepts are (Bowen, 1978; Kerr, 1981):

- Differentiation
- Emotional system
- Multigenerational transmission process
- Nuclear family emotional system
- Family projection process
- Triangles
- Sibling position
- Societal regression

Differentiation refers to the ability of persons to distinguish themselves from their family of origin on an emotional and intellectual level, to balance the intrapsychic and interpersonal dimensions of the self (Bowen, 1978). There are two counterbalancing life forces: togetherness and individuality. People vary as to the level of self-differentiation that they achieve at any one time, and the concept itself denotes a process (Bowen, 1965). The level of differentiation is on a continuum, from **autonomy** at one end (which signals an ability to think through a situation clearly) to undifferentiated on the other end (which implies an emotional dependency on one's family members, even if living away from them). In such cases, the relationship is described as being fused or as an undifferentiated family ego mass (Bowen, 1965).

"Theoretically, at least four factors influence a person's level of differentiation: emotional reactivity, emotional cutoff, fusion with others, and the ability to take an 'I-position'" (Tuason & Friedlander, 2000, p. 27). It is through the process of differentiation that families and the individuals in them change (see Figure 5.1).

In a fused situation, family members may exhibit dysfunctional behaviors such as bulimia. In these cases, family therapists should try to help family members (usually young women) increase their degree of self-differentiation. Procedures that are sometimes used include assertiveness training, building healthier family boundaries, enhancing cognitive communication skills, and finding new coping behaviors for stress (Levy & Hadley, 1998).

Coping strategies and patterns of coping with stress tend to be passed on from generation to generation, a phenomenon known as the **multigenerational transmission process.** Families who present a problem have had the forces of several generations shaping and carrying the symptom. In marriage, people tend to select partners at their own level of differentiation (Bowen, 1976). In these unions, a nuclear family emotional system evolves.

Spouses with equally high levels of identity are able to establish and maintain clear individuality "and at the same time to have an intense, mature, nonthreatening, emotional closeness" (Bowen, 1965, p. 220). Indeed, research shows that couples who are less reactive, cutoff, or fused and are able to relate from an I-position "experience the greatest levels of marital satisfaction" (Skowron, 2000, p. 233). Such is particularly true if the male partner remains emotionally present and available. On the other hand, spouses with equally low levels of differentiation have difficulty establishing intimacy because they have developed only **pseudo-selves,** that is, "pretend" selves (Kerr, 1988, p. 43). The pseudo-selves fluctuate according to situations and usually result in the **fusion** of these selves into a "common self with obliteration of ego boundaries between them and loss of individuality to the common self" (Bowen, 1965, p. 221). Couples tend to produce offspring at the same level of differentiation as themselves, a process Bowen describes as **family projection** (Kilpatrick, 1980).

To rid themselves of anxiety, spouses who are low on differentiation of self keep an emotional distance from each other. Thus, when anxiety becomes too great, it is frequently manifested in one of four ways: (1) marital conflict, (2) physical or emotional ill-

**Figure 5.1**
Bowen's continuum of self-differentiation.

From *Working with Families: An Introduction to Family Therapy, 1st edition,* by B. Okun and L. Rappaport © 1980. Reprinted with permission of Wadsworth, an imprint of the Wadsworth Group, a division of Thomson Learning. Fax 800-730-2215.

ness in one spouse, (3) projection of the problem to the children, or (4) a combination of these (David, 1979).

Bowenian family therapists look for triangles when working with couples. Triangles can occur between people or between people and things. They consist of a state of calm between a comfortable twosome and an outsider (Anonymous, 1972). A triangle is "the basic building block of any emotional system and the smallest stable relationship system" (Kilpatrick, 1980, p. 168). Some triangles are healthy, others are not. In the latter case, triangles are a frequent way of dealing with anxiety in which tension between two persons is projected onto another object. The original triangle is between a child and parents. In stressful situations, anxiety spreads from one central triangle within the family to interlocking triangles outside the family, especially in work and social systems (Kerr, 1988).

Given this background, it is understandable why Bowenian family therapists work to help people, especially couples, separate their feelings from their intellect and in the process **detriangulate**. They do this through asking questions about thoughts and constructing a type of family tree (which is explained later) called a *multigenerational genogram* (McGoldrick et al., 1999). They also give homework assignments that require individuals to visit their families in order to learn through questioning (Bowen, 1976). Furthermore, Bowenian therapists examine sibling positions; people can develop fixed personality characteristics based on their functional birth order in the family (Toman, 1961). The more closely a marriage replicates a couples' sibling positions in the family of origin, the better the chance for success. For example, if a youngest son marries an oldest daughter, both have much to gain from the arrangement because the youngest son will most likely enjoy "being taken care of," and the oldest daughter will probably enjoy "taking care of" someone.

By examining the processes just mentioned, family members gain insight and understanding into the past and are freed to choose how they will behave in the present. Similarly, they gain a perspective on how well society as a whole is doing. If a society is under too much stress (e.g., population growth, economic decline), **societal regression** will occur, because of too many toxic forces countering the tendency to achieve differentiation.

# Treatment Techniques

Bowenian family therapy focuses on the promotion of differentiation (in regard to self/family and intellect/emotion). This approach is not technique oriented, because of the tendency to get caught up and overpowered by particular techniques at particular times. However, among those techniques most often employed are genograms, going home again, detriangulation, person-to-person relationships, differentiation of self, and asking questions.

## Genograms

A **genogram** is a visual representation of a person's family tree depicted in geometric figures, lines, and words (Sherman, 1993) (see Figure 5.2). Genograms include information related to a family and its members' relationships with each other over at least three generations. A genogram helps people gather information, hypothesize, and track relationship changes in the context of historic and contemporary events (Dunn & Levitt, 2000). "From this simple diagram, counselors and clients alike are able to view simultaneously

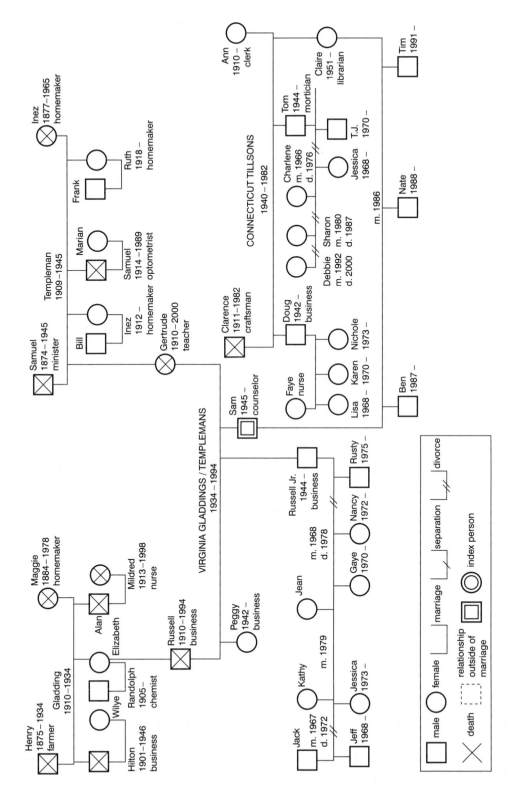

**Figure 5.2**
Gladding family genogram.

family composition, gender, age, ethnicity, dates of birth, marriages, divorces, deaths, and other important family events" (Frame, 2000, p. 69).

The tangibility and nonthreatening nature of making a genogram helps family clinicians gather a large amount of information in a relatively short period of time. Furthermore, genograms can increase "mutual trust and tolerance" among all involved in their construction (Sherman, 1993, p. 91). Bowenian family therapy "advises people to go 'back, back, back; and up, up, up' their family tree to look for patterns, 'recycling,' getting not just information but a feel for the context and milieu that existed during each person's formative years" (White, 1978, p. 25–26). This process promotes the shift from emotional reactivity to clear cognitions.

Genograms can be color coded to indicate everything from substance abuse to forms of spirituality (Frame, 2000). They can also be multicultural in nature and include an assessment of worldview and cultural factors that influence the behaviors of family members (Thomas, 1998). Data in a genogram is scanned for

1. "repetitive patterns," such as triangles, cutoffs, and coalitions
2. "coincidences," such as the death of members or the age of symptom onset
3. "the impact of change and untimely life cycle transitions," such as "off-schedule" events (e.g., marriage, death, and the birth of children) (McGoldrick et al., 1999)

## Going Home Again

In **going home again,** the family therapist instructs the individual client or family members to return home in order to better get to know their family of origin (Bowen, 1976). The idea behind this technique is that with this type of information, individuals can differentiate themselves more clearly. Such a process allows persons to operate more fully within all family contexts of which they are a part. Before returning home, clients may need to practice learning how to remain calm (Bowen, 1976).

## Detriangulation

The concept of **detriangulation** involves "the process of being in contact and emotionally separate" (Kerr, 1988, p. 55). It operates on at least two levels. On one level, a person resolves his or her anxiety over family situations and does not project feelings on to another. At a second level, Bowenian therapists help individuals separate themselves from becoming a focus when tension or anxiety arises in the family. In this procedure, persons do not become targets or scapegoats for others who may be overcome with anxiety. For example, if a usually triaded person stays rational during times of emotional stress, he/she will seldom become the attention of two other people (Bowen, 1972). On both levels, families and their individuals are free to voice their concerns and try out new ways of acting.

## Person-to-Person Relationships

In the person-to-person relationships, two family members "relate personally to each other about each other; that is, they do not talk about others (triangling) and do not talk about impersonal issues" (Piercy & Sprenkle, 1986, p. 11). For instance, a father may say to his son: "Your actions remind me of myself when I was your age." In return the son may say: "I really don't know much about you when you were a boy. Please tell me about what you did and how you felt when you were my age." Such a process helps promote individuation (autonomy) and intimacy.

## Differentiation of Self

"Differentiation of self has to do with the degree to which a person is able to distinguish between the subjective feeling process and the more objective intellectual (thinking) process" (Gibson & Donigian, 1993, p. 28). This procedure may involve all of the preceding techniques plus some confrontation between family members and the therapist. A failure to differentiate results in fusion in which "people are dominated by their automatic emotional system." In such circumstances, they have "less flexibility, less adaptability, and are more emotionally dependent on those around them" (Sauber, L'Abate, & Weeks, 1985, p. 43). Over generations, children most involved in family fusion move toward a lower level of differentiation of self (Bowen, 1972).

## Asking Questions

In each of the techniques in Bowenian family theory, an underlying aspect is to ask questions. In fact, from this perspective, asking questions is deemed the "magic bullet" and is a main tool of Bowenian therapists. Nodal events such as deaths, births, and marriages have an impact on families. For instance, death of family members disturbs the equilibrium of a family, and "emotional shock waves" can be expected as a result (Bowen, 1976). By asking questions, people involved in Bowenian family therapy learn to understand the reactions of those in their families better.

# Role of the Therapist

In the Bowenian model, the differentiation of the therapist is crucial. The Bowenian family therapist must maintain a calm presence and be differentiated from his/her family of origin (Friedman, 1991). Objectivity and neutrality are important behavioral characteristics for therapists to display. To be able to work with families, the therapist must first undergo an emotional change (Kerr, 1981). The idea is that if those who do treatment do not first undergo changes important in family therapy, those they work with will not experience healthy shifts either.

As someone who has personally resolved family-of-origin concerns, the Bowenian therapist is usually involved in coaching and teaching. These activities occur on more cognitive levels, initially with family members, primarily individuals or couples, talking to the therapist or to one another through the therapist so that emotional issues do not cloud communication messages.

> According to Bowen, therapists should not encourage people to wallow in emotionalism and confusion, but teach them to transcend it by setting examples as reasonable, neutral, self-controlled adults. Therapy should be, in fact, just like a Socratic dialogue, with the teacher or "coach" calmly asking questions, until the student learns to think for him- or herself. (Wylie, 1991, p. 27)

In the process of therapy, there is concern with boundary and differentiation issues from an historical perspective. The therapist instructs individuals to search for "clues" as to where the various pressures on the family have been expressed and how effectively the family has adapted to stress since its inception. One way of obtaining this information is for individuals to draw a genogram or to visit their family of origin. Through examining the dynamics in these experiences, therapists become interpreters with their clients in assessing and working through multigenerational patterns of fusion and cutoffs. Unresolved areas of difficulty become resolved.

# Process and Outcome

One of the primary outcomes of successful treatment with families from a Bowenian standpoint is that family members will understand intergenerational patterns and gain insight into historical circumstances that have influenced the ways they currently interact (Learner, 1983). Furthermore, it is expected that accompanying this knowledge is a focus on changing "intergenerational inferences operating with the current family" (Smith, 1991, p. 25). Changes such as these occur when therapists help family members differentiate from each other and become more diverse and fluid in their interactions (Bowen, 1978). At the end of treatment, issues related to fusion and unconscious relationship patterns should be cleared up. Individuals should be able to relate on an autonomous, cognitive level, and projective patterns of blame should be changed (Kerr & Bowen, 1988). There should be a greater self-differentiation among nuclear family members.

In Bowenian family therapy, the chief focus and place where change is emphasized is the individual or couple. The whole family is usually not seen. Instead, individuals are often targeted for treatment even though the emphasis in this approach is systemic. "A theoretical system that thinks in terms of family, with a therapeutic method that works toward improvement of the family system, is 'family' regardless of the number of people in the sessions" (Kerr, 1981, p. 232). Therefore, by changing one person, a family may be directly influenced for the better.

"Since the two spouses are the two family members most involved in the family ego mass, the most rapid family change occurs when the spouses are able to work as a team in family psychotherapy" (Bowen, 1965, p. 220). The family can improve its functioning when spouses become more cognitively based, although in this process, the therapist may work "with all involved family members present, with any combination of family members present, or with only one family member present" (Bowen, 1965, p. 220).

# Unique Aspects of the Bowenian Family Therapy Approach

## Emphases

Bowenian theory calls attention to family history and the importance of noticing and dealing with past patterns in order to avoid repeating these behaviors in interpersonal relationships. The use of the genogram in plotting historical linkages is a specific tool developed for this purpose. The genogram is increasingly being used by theorists of all persuasions in assessing their client families.

The theory and the therapy of Murray Bowen are extensive, complex, and intertwined. The theory is a blueprint for therapy. Therefore, therapy is consistent with and inseparable from theory. Family therapists are indebted to Bowen for intertwining these two aspects of his approach. He was also insightful and detailed in suggesting the course of working with families. The Georgetown Family Center (4400 MacArthur Boulevard N.W., Suite 103, Washington, D.C. 20007-2521), which he established for educating practitioners in his method, ensures the Bowenian approach will continue to be learned and used.

Bowenian family therapy is systemic in nature, controlled in focus, and cognitive in practice, thereby giving clinicians and their clients a way of concretely evaluating progress (Bowen, 1975). Unlike many other systemic family approaches, Bowenian family therapy can be used extensively with individuals or couples.

## Comparison with Other Theories

Bowenian family therapy is a well-established and heuristically appealing approach. Its strong emphasis on theory as well as its practical nature make it attractive. However, the theory is vulnerable to criticism is in its failure to support the intergenerational hypothesis (Tuason & Friedlander, 2000). While there is evidence that differentiation is a concept applicable on a multicultural level, for example, in Filipinos and North Americans, "psychological well-being in adulthood may well be affected by factors outside of the family, such as peer relationships, employment, or societal influences" (Tuason & Friedlander, 2000, p. 33).

Nevertheless, Bowen's stress on the importance of the past encourages some families or family members to examine their history rather than deal immediately with present circumstances. Such a process promotes insight before action. Client families in which there is severe dysfunctioning or low differentiation of self may benefit most from this emphasis.

Another aspect of Bowenian family therapy that makes it unique compared with other approaches is that the theory underlying the approach is its own paradigm (Friedman, 1991). Thus, setting up research questions to refute or verify this way of working with families is a challenging task of the highest order. One way theoretical research is being conducted is by exploring the significance of family-of-origin experiences (Hovestadt, Anderson, Piercy, Cochran, & Fine, 1985).

A final unique angle in regard to Bowenian family therapy is the time and, consequently, the money it requires of its clients. Most people cannot afford to invest as heavily in this process as is necessary. As with psychodynamically oriented therapy, the number of people who can benefit from this approach is limited.

### CASE ILLUSTRATION

## THE COBB FAMILY

The Cobb family is a three-generational family composed of the father, David, age 45; mother, Juanita, age 42; son, James, age 16; daughter, Anita, age 12; and maternal grandmother, Lilly, age 65. The maternal grandfather, John, a farmer, died 3 years ago of a heart attack. The paternal grandparents, Dan, a retired banker, age 70, and Ruth, a homemaker, age 68, live in a nearby city. The couple, David and Juanita, have been married for 20 years. Like his father, David is emotionally withdrawn from his family and overinvolved with his job.

In terms of family background, David comes from a middle-class background. He has an older sister, Daisy, who was 3 years his senior. His father has a history of high blood pressure, but his mother is in good health. Juanita was an only child. After 20 years of marriage, her mother, Lilly, almost divorced her father, when Juanita was 13 years old. Juanita and her mother have had a close but conflictual relationship since that time, with Lilly coming to live with her daughter after the death of John. At present, Juanita and Lilly take care of the house and children, and David works as a salesperson for a cleaning supply company.

The problem for which the Cobb family has requested help centers around James. Instead of doing well academically and socially, James is failing all his subjects and staying out late at night. He has been arrested once for vagrancy, and David and Juanita suspect he is drinking alcohol and doing drugs. Money from Juanita's purse has been stolen twice in recent weeks. Lilly has written James off as a delinquent. Interestingly enough, he has the same first name as her former lover who almost ended her marriage. Anita simply ignores James whenever possible. Although she is a good student, her relationship with her mother is conflictual.

### Conceptualization of Family: Bowenian Perspective

The Cobb family is notable from a Bowenian family perspective for several reasons. For one, there is a repeated pattern of mother/daughter conflict over the generations. For another, there is a tendency for men in the family to be emotionally cut off from other family members through withdrawing or rebelling. It is also striking that James has the same name as his maternal grandmother's lover, who almost broke up her marriage of 20 years when Juanita was 13 years old. It appears to be more than coincidental that during the 20th year of Juanita's marriage, another James has created turmoil in the family's life.

### Process of Treatment: Bowenian Family Therapy

Treatment of any family from a Bowenian family therapy perspective usually involves either an individual or a couple. In the case of the Cobbs, initially, the therapist might help the marital unit make a genogram (see Figure 5.3). The genogram would then be examined by the therapist and the family to denote patterns such as those mentioned previously.

After analysis of family life patterns, the therapist might concentrate with the couple on issues involving detriangulation. For instance, there is a triangle between Lilly, Juanita, and James that works in a dysfunctional way. Likewise, the issue of emotional disengagement would be addressed, such as the ones Dan and David have exemplified. Their lack of involvement in the family has created a parenting void. It is most likely associated with James' present rebellious behavior. Therefore,

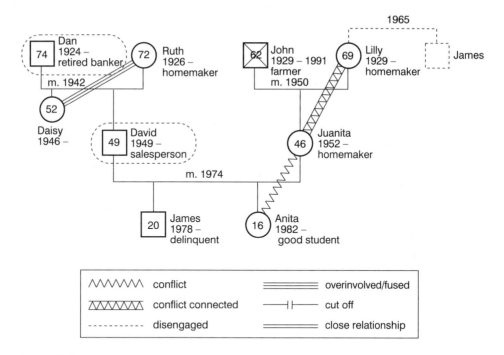

**Figure 5.3**
Cobb family genogram.

parenting skills and ways of interacting in parent/child relationships might be stressed, especially as they relate to previous family-of-origin patterns.

To help the Cobb family break out of its present condition, the therapist could have the couple engage in person-to-person conversations on a dyadic basis. This might begin with David and Juanita talking to each other about their marriage. Other person-to-person relationships might be conducted outside of the treatment sessions, with James and Juanita, or Lilly and Juanita, talking with each other. In these exchanges, the asking of cognitively based questions would be encouraged, especially about topics not discussed previously, such as Lilly's affair.

Overall, through these procedures, the family would begin to engage in new behaviors that were less blaming, conflictual, or withdrawn. Appropriate ways of interrelating could then be set in motion, with family members interacting from a position of differentiation.

# Summary and Conclusion

Psychodynamic and Bowenian family therapies are two of the most established approaches to working with families. Psychodynamic family therapy was first developed by Nathan Ackerman, who applied the principles of individual psychoanalysis to families. In doing so, he made the treatment of families more respectable and prevalent among psychiatrists. Murray Bowen, a psychoanalytically trained psychiatrist, devised his own approach to working with families, especially couples, based in part on his life experiences and in part on psychoanalytic theory.

Both psychodynamic theory and Bowenian theory emphasize the importance of unconscious forces in family life. Psychodynamically oriented family therapy, however, is an eclectic mix of psychoanalysis and systems concepts that sometimes make it more linear in its stress on working with individuals in families. Bowenian theory is systemic, although its primary clients are individuals and couples. It emphasizes the importance of looking at historical intergenerational patterns. The Bowenian approach uses a cognitive strategy to help couples and family members differentiate; psychodynamic family therapy is insight oriented. In both approaches, the therapist acts as a coach, a teacher, and a catalyst, although the content and unit of treatment, as well as final end results, differ.

Overall, both approaches are in depth and concentrate on long-term results. They emphasize the unconscious and require a considerable investment of time and resources. Bowenian theory is concrete in outcome and gives its clients a way to recognize dysfunctional patterns transmitted across generations (i.e., a genogram). On the other hand, psychodynamic theory provides its recipients with a way to work through issues that frees them from relying on defense mechanisms. Each theory can be beneficially utilized by some client families/individuals.

# Summary Table

## Psychodynamic and Bowenian Family Therapies

### Common Characteristics of Psychodynamic and Bowenian Theories

Both theories are conceptual and comprehensive. They emphasize the importance of historical, social, and childhood experiences and stress the significance of unconscious forces in the lives of families.

The founders of the two approaches were trained as psychoanalytical therapists.

Each theory has developed its own terminology.

Both treatments may be long term (over 20 sessions).

### Psychodynamic Family Therapy

*Major Theorists*

| | | |
|---|---|---|
| Sigmund Freud | Nathan Ackerman | Ivan Boszormenyi-Nagy |
| James Framo | Theodore Lidz | Norman Paul |
| A. C. Robin Skynner | Donald Williamson | Lyman Wynne |

*Premises of the Theory*

Unconscious processes link family members and influence individuals in the decisions about who they marry. Objects—significant others in one's life—are identified with or rejected.

Unconscious forces must be worked through and "interlocking pathologies" must be broken up.

*Treatment Techniques*

The individual or the individuals within a family are the units of treatment.

The goals of treatment are to break dysfunctional interactions within the family based on unconscious processes and to resolve individual dysfunctionality.

The therapeutic techniques include transference, dream analysis, confrontation, focusing on strengths, and life history.

*Role of the Therapist*

The therapist is the teacher (especially of terms), "good enough mother" (or "parent"), and interpreter of experience.

*Process and Outcome*

Help family members work through unconscious restrictions and insights.

Assist family members to interact on the basis of current realities.

*Unique Aspects of Psychodynamic Family Therapy*

The psychodynamic approach emphasizes:

- the potency of the unconscious in influencing human behavior
- defense mechanisms and the part they play in family relations
- an in-depth historical perspective on the development of problems and a treatment of dysfunctionality that is thorough
- an attachment of people to objects (i.e., other people)

*Comparison with Other Theories*

Compared with other approaches, psychodynamic therapy:

- offers a treatment that is primarily linear and limited more to individuals than families
- offers a treatment that is expensive in regard to both time and money
- is not appropriate for concrete-thinkers or those who want immediate results
- lacks traditional empirical research and is reliant on case history reports

## Bowenian Family Therapy

*Major Theorists*

Murray Bowen               Michael Kerr               Ed Friedman

*Premises of the Theory*

Theory and therapy are the same.

Family patterns are likely to repeat.

It is important to differentiate oneself from one's family of origin.

Uncontrolled anxiety results in family dysfunctionality.

The formation of triangles is a key manifestation of uncontrolled anxiety.

*Treatment Techniques*

The individual or the couple are the units of treatment.

The goals of treatment are to prevent triangulation and help couples and individuals relate more on a cognitive, as opposed to an emotional level, and to stop dysfunctional, repetitive, intergenerational patterns of family relations.

The therapeutic techniques include genograms, going home again, detriangulation, person-to-person relationships, differentiation of self, and asking of questions.

### Role of the Therapist

The therapist is a differentiated person who acts as a coach and teacher and concentrates on boundary and differentiation issues.

### Process and Outcome

Help family members to become more differentiated and fluid in their interactions.

Assist family members in therapy to be more cognitive and understand intergenerational patterns better.

### Unique Aspects of the Bowenian Family Therapy Approach

The Bowenian approach emphasizes:

- intergenerational relationships and the nature of repeating patterns
- an in-depth theory of family relationships
- a systemic and cognitive theory that provides a concrete evaluation of progress

### Comparison with Other Theories

Compared with other approaches, Bowenian therapy:

- stresses the importance of the past, thereby encouraging some families or family members to examine history and not deal with present circumstances
- is difficult to research
- requires a high degree of investment in time and money

# References

Ackerman, N. (1937). The family as a social and emotional unit. *Bulletin of the Kansas Mental Hygiene Society, 12.*

Ackerman, N. (1956). Interlocking pathology in family relations. In S. Rado & G. Daniels (Eds.), *Changing concepts of psychoanalytic medicine* (pp. 135–150). New York: Grune & Stratton.

Ackerman, N. (1958). *The psychodynamics of family life.* New York: Basic Books.

Ackerman, N. (1962). Family psychotherapy and psychoanalysis: The implications of difference. *Family Process, 1,* 30–43.

Ackerman, N. (1966). *Treating the troubled family.* New York: Basic Books.

Ackerman, N. W., Beatman, F. L., & Sherman, S. N. (1961). *Exploring the base of family therapy.* New York: Family Service Association of America.

Anonymous. (1972). Differentiation of self in one's family. In J. L. Framo (Ed.), *Family interaction.* New York: Springer.

Bloch, D. A., & Simon, R. (Eds.). (1982). *The strength of family therapy: Selected papers of Nathan W. Ackerman.* New York: Brunner/Mazel.

Boszormenyi-Nagy, I. (1987). *Foundations of contextual therapy: Collected papers of Ivan Boszormenyi-Nagy.* New York: Brunner/Mazel.

Boszormenyi-Nagy, I., & Spark, G. M. (1973). *Invisible loyalties: Reciprocity in intergenerational family therapy.* New York: Brunner/Mazel.

Bowen, M. (1960). A family concept of schizophrenia. In D. Jackson (Ed.), *The etiology of schizophrenia.* New York: Basic Books.

Bowen, M. (1961). Family psychotherapy. *American Journal of Orthopsychiatry, 31,* 40–60.

Bowen, M. (1965). Family psychotherapy with schizophrenia in the hospital and in private practice. In I. Boszormenyi-Nagy

& J. T. Framo (Eds.), *Intensive family therapy* (pp. 213–243). Hagerstown, MD: Harper & Row.

Bowen, M. (1972). Toward the differentiation of self in one's family of origin. In F. D. Andres & J. P. Lorio (Eds.), *Georgetown Family Symposia* (pp. 70–86). Washington, DC: Georgetown University.

Bowen, M. (1975). Family therapy after twenty years. In S. Arieti, D. X. Freedman, & J. E. Dyrud (Eds.), *American handbook of psychiatry V: Treatment* (2nd ed.). New York: Basic Books.

Bowen, M. (1976). Theory in the practice of psychotherapy. In P. J. Guerin (Ed.), *Family therapy: Theory and practice* (pp. 42–90). New York: Gardner Press.

Bowen, M. (1978). *Family therapy in clinical practice.* New York: Jason Aronson.

Broderick, C. B., & Schrader, S. S. (1991). The history of professional marriage and family therapy. In A. S. Gurman & D. P. Kniskern (Eds.), *Handbook of family therapy* (Vol. II, pp. 3–40). New York: Brunner/Mazel.

David, J. R. (1979). The theology of Murray Bowen or the marital triangle. *Journal of Psychology and Theology, 7,* 259–262.

Dicks, H. V. (1963). Object relations theory and marital studies. *British Journal of Medical Psychology, 36,* 125–129.

Dunn, A. B., & Levitt, M. M. (2000). The genogram: From diagnostics to mutual collaboration. *The Family Journal: Counseling and Therapy for Couples and Families, 8,* 236–244.

Ellis, A. (2000). Rational-emotive behavior marriage and family therapy. In A. M. Horne (Ed.), *Family counseling and therapy* (3rd ed., pp. 489–514). Itasca, IL: F. E. Peacock.

Fairbairn, W. R. (1954). *An object-relations theory of personality.* New York: Basic Books.

Frame, M. W. (2000). Constructing religious/spiritual genograms. In R. E. Watts (Ed.), *Techniques in marriage and family counseling* (pp. 69–74). Alexandria, VA: American Counseling Association.

Framo, J. L. (1981). The integration of marital therapy with sessions with family of origin. In A. S. Gurman & D. P. Kniskern (Eds.), *Handbook of family therapy.* New York: Brunner/Mazel.

Freud, S. (1940). An outline of psychoanalysis. In *The standard edition of the complete psychological works of Sigmund Freud* (Vol. 23, pp. 139–171). London: Hogarth Press.

Friedman, E. H. (1985). *Generation to generation: Family process in church and synagogue.* New York: Guilford.

Friedman, E. H. (1991). Bowen theory and therapy. In A. S. Gurman & D. P. Kniskern (Eds.), *Handbook of family therapy* (Vol. II, pp. 134–170). New York: Brunner/Mazel.

Gibson, J. M., & Donigian, J. (1993). Use of Bowen theory. *Journal of Addictions and Offender Counseling, 14,* 25–35.

Gladding, S. T. (1993). *Beecher Road.* Unpublished manuscript.

Greene, G. J., Hamilton, N., & Rolling, M. (1986). Differentiation of self and psychiatric diagnosis: An empirical study. *Family Therapy, 8,* 187–194.

Guerin, P. J. (1976). Family therapy: The first twenty-five years. In P. J. Guerin (Ed.), *Family therapy: Theory and practice* (pp. 2–22). New York: Gardner.

Hafner, R. J. (1986). *Marriage & mental illness.* New York: Guilford.

Hovestadt, A. J., Anderson, W. T., Piercy, F. P., Cochran, S. W., & Fine, M. (1985). A family of origin scale. *Journal of Marital and Family Therapy, 11,* 287–297.

Kaplan, D. M. (2000). Who are our giants? *The Family Digest, 12*(4), 1, 6.

Kernberg, O. F. (1976). *Object-relations theory and clinical psychoanalysis.* New York: Jason Aronson.

Kerr, M. (1981). Family systems theory and therapy. In A. S. Gurman & D. P. Kniskern (Eds.), *Handbook of family therapy.* New York: Brunner/Mazel.

Kerr, M. E. (1988). Chronic anxiety and defining a self. *The Atlantic Monthly, 262,* 35–37, 40–44, 46–58.

Kerr, M. E., & Bowen, M. (1988). *Family evaluation: An approach based on Bowen theory.* New York: W. W. Norton.

Kilpatrick, A. C. (1980). The Bowen family intervention theory: An analysis for social workers. *Family Therapy, 7,* 167–178.

Klein, M. (1948). *Contributions to psychoanalysis, 1921–1945.* London: Hogarth Press.

Kohut, H. (1971). *The analysis of self.* New York: International Universities Press.

Kohut, H. (1977). *The restoration of the self.* New York: International Universities Press.

Learner, S. (1983). *Constructing the multigenerational family genogram: Exploring a problem in context* (videotape). Topeka, KS: Menninger Video Productions.

Levy, P. A., & Hadley, B. J. (1998). Family-of-origin relationships and self-differentiation among university students with bulimic-type behavior. *The Family Journal: Counseling and Therapy for Couples and Families, 6,* 19–23.

Lidz, T., Cornelison, A., Fleck, S., & Terry, D. (1957). The intrafamilial environment of schizophrenic patients. II: Marital schism and martial skew. *American Journal of Psychiatry, 114,* 241–248.

McGoldrick, M., Gerson, R., & Shellenberger, S. (1999). *Genograms: Assessment and intervention.* New York: W. W. Norton.

Napier, A., & Whitaker, C. A. (1978). *The family crucible.* New York: Bantam.

Papero, D. V. (1990). *Bowen family systems theory.* Boston: Allyn & Bacon.

Papero, D. V. (1991). The Bowen theory. In A. M. Horne & J. L. Passmore (Eds.), *Family counseling and theory* (2nd ed., pp. 47–76). Itasca, IL: F. E. Peacock.

Perosa, L. (1996). Relations between Minuchin's family model and Kohut's self-psychology constructs. *Journal of Counseling & Development, 74,* 385–392.

Piercy, F. P., & Sprenkle, D. H. (1986). *Family therapy sourcebook.* New York: Guilford.

Sauber, S. R., L'Abate, L., & Weeks, G. R. (1985). *Family therapy: Basic concepts and terms.* Rockville, MD: Aspen.

Scarf, M. (1995). *Intimate worlds: Life inside the family.* New York: Random House.

Scharff, J. (Ed.). (1989). *The foundations of object relations family therapy.* New York: Jason Aronson.

Sherman, R. (1993). The intimacy genogram. *The Family Journal: Counseling and Therapy for Couples and Families, 1,* 91–93.

Shields, C. G., Wynne, L. C., McDaniel, S. H., & Gawinski, B. A. (1994). The marginalization of family therapy: A historical and continuing problem. *Journal of Marital and Family Therapy, 20,* 117–138.

Skowron, E. A. (2000). The role of differentiation of self in marital adjustment. *Journal of Counseling Psychology, 47,* 229–237.

Skynner, A. C. R. (1981). An open-systems, group analytic approach to family therapy. In A. S. Gurman & D. P. Kniskern (Eds.), *Handbook of family therapy.* New York: Brunner/Mazel.

Slipp, S. (1988). *The technique and practice of object relations family therapy.* New York: Aronson.

Smith, R. L. (1991). Marriage and family therapy: Direction, theory, and practice. In J. Carlson & J. Lewis (Eds.), *Family counseling* (pp. 13–34). Denver, CO: Love Publishing.

Thomas, A. J. (1998). Understanding culture and worldview in family systems: Use of the multicultural genogram. *The Family Journal: Counseling and Therapy for Couples and Families, 6,* 24–32.

Titelman, P. (1987). *The therapist's own family: Toward the differentiation of self.* Northvale, NJ: Jason Aronson.

Toman, W. (1961). *Family constellation: Its effects on personality and social behavior.* New York: Springer.

Tuason, M. T., & Friedlander, M. L. (2000). Do parents' differentiation levels predict those of their adult children? and other tests of Bowen theory in a Philippine sample. *Journal of Counseling Psychology, 47,* 27–35.

White, H. (1978). *Exercises in understanding your family.* In *Your family is good for you.* New York: Random House.

Winnicott, D. W. (1965). *The maturational processes and the facilitation of environment.* London: Hogarth Press.

Wylie, M. S. (1991, March/April). Family therapy's neglected prophet. *Family Therapy Networker, 15,* 24–37, 77.

Wynne, L., Ryckoff, I., Day, J., & Hirsh, S. (1958). Pseudomutuality in the family relations of schizophrenics. *Psychiatry, 21,* 205–220.

# C H A P T E R 6

# **Experiential Family Therapy**

My father tells me
my mother is slowing down.

He talks deliberately and with deep feelings
as stoop-shouldered he walks to his garden
behind the garage.

My mother informs me
about my father's failing health.
"Not as robust as before," she explains,
"Lower energy than in his 50s."

Her concerns arise as she kneads dough for biscuits.

Both express their fears to me
as we view the present from the past.

In love, and with measured anxiety,
I move with them into new patterns.

*Gladding, 1992*

**T**he experiential branch of family therapy emerged out of the humanistic-existential psychology movement of the 1960s. It was most popular when the field of family therapy was new. Some of its proponents and creators drew heavily from Gestalt therapy, psychodrama, client-centered therapy, and the encounter group movement of the time. The emphasis has been on immediate, here-and-now experience as opposed to historical information. Therefore, concepts such as encounter, process, growth, spontaneity, and action are emphasized. Theory and abstract factors are minimized. The quality of ongoing experiences in the family is the criterion for measuring psychological health and for deciding whether to make therapeutic interventions.

Experiential family therapy emphasizes **affect**, that is, emotions. Awareness and expression of feelings are considered the means to both personal and family fulfillment. Professionals who operate from this perspective consider the expression of affect to be a universal medium in which all can share. Therefore, the expression of feelings in a clear and effective way is encouraged (Kane, 1994). A healthy family is a family that openly experiences life with each other in a lively manner. Such a family supports and encourages a wide range of emotions and personal encounters. In contrast, dysfunctional families resist taking affective risks and are rigid in their interactions.

# Major Theorists

A number of professionals have contributed significantly to the development of experiential family therapy. Among the most notable are David Kantor, Fred Duhl, Bunny Duhl, Virginia Satir, Carl Whitaker, Bernard Guerney, Louise Guerney, Walter Kempler, August Napier, Leslie Greenberg, Susan Johnson, and David Keith. Virginia Satir and Carl Whitaker are examined here as representatives of this approach.

## Virginia Satir

Virginia Satir (1916–1988) was born and raised on a farm in Wisconsin. She was extraordinarily different from others even at an early age. At 3, she had learned to read, and "by the time she was 11, she had reached her adult height of nearly six feet" (Simon, 1989, p. 37). Although she was sickly and missed a lot of school, she was a good student and began her college experience after only 7½ years of formal education. Her initial goal, which she achieved, was to become a schoolteacher. "Growing up a big, awkward, sickly child, Satir drew from her experience of being an outsider" an acute sensitivity for others (Simon, 1989, p. 37). This quality eventually led her from the classroom to social work with families.

Satir entered private practice as a social worker in 1951 in Chicago. This venture came after 6 years of teaching school and 9 years of clinical work in an agency. Her unique approach to working with families evolved from her treatment of a schizophrenic young woman whose mother threatened to sue her when the young woman improved. Instead of becoming defensive, Satir invited the mother to join the therapy and worked with them until they reached communication congruence (Satir, 1986). She then invited the father and oldest son into treatment until the family had achieved a balance.

Satir was influenced by Murray Bowen's and Don Jackson's work with schizophrenic families, and in 1959 she was invited by Jackson and his colleagues to help set up the Mental Research Institute (MRI) in Palo Alto, California. From her clinical work and interaction with other professionals there, she refined her approach to working with families, which was simultaneously folksy and complex. "Satir was the prototypical nurturing therapist in a field enamored with experience-distant concepts and tricky strategic maneuvers. Her warmth and genuineness gave her a tremendous appeal and impact . . . " (Nichols & Schwartz, 1995, pp. 289–290). At the core of Satir's approach was "her unshakable conviction about people's potential for growth and the respectful role helpers need to assume in the process of change" (Simon, 1989, p. 38).

Satir gained international attention in 1964 with the publication of her first book, *Conjoint Family Therapy*. The clarity of her writing made the text a classic and put Satir in demand as a workshop presenter. She continued to write and demonstrate her "process model of therapy" (Satir, 1982) until her death. Among her many contributions were a strong, charismatic leadership (Beels & Ferber, 1969); a simple but eloquent view of effective and ineffective communication patterns (Satir, 1972; Satir & Baldwin, 1983); and a humanistic concern about building self-worth and self-esteem in all people. "She also pioneered the concept of actively engaging couples and families in exercises during and between sessions" (Kaplan, 2000, p. 6). She conducted much of her work using structured experiential exercises (Woods & Martin, 1984).

Satir is often described as a master of communication and even as an originator of family **communications theory** (an approach that focuses on clarifying transactions among family members). During her lifetime she worked with more than 5,000 families and demonstrated her skills and her approach before hundreds of audiences (Satir & Bitter, 2000).

## Carl Whitaker

Carl Whitaker (1912–1995) grew up on a dairy farm in upstate New York. With few exceptions, his nuclear family was his "entire social existence" (Simon, 1985, p. 32). He was shy, and when his family moved to Syracuse in 1925, he felt awkward and out of place. He attributed his ability to stay sane and adjust to two "cotherapists"—two fellow students with whom he made friends, one the smartest and the other the most popular in the school (Whitaker, 1989).

Whitaker entered medical school in 1932, penniless but with a sound work ethic and a bent toward public service. He had originally planned to specialize in obstetrics and gynecology, but a tragic operation on a patient who died even though his surgery was perfect proved to be a turning point in Whitaker's life. It influenced him to switch to psychiatry during the last year of his residency and to concentrate his attention on working with schizophrenics. Toward the end of his medical training in 1937, Whitaker married and later fathered six children.

Whitaker developed the essence of his approach to therapy while assigned to Oak Ridge, Tennessee, during World War II (Whitaker, 1990). There he saw as many as 12 patients a day in half-hour sessions. He did not have any mentors and basically taught himself psychiatric procedures. From his experience, he realized he needed a cotherapist in order to be effective. He also experimented during this time with the technique of using the spontaneous unconscious in therapy (Whitaker & Keith, 1981).

"The turning point in Whitaker's career came in 1946 when he was named chairman of the Department of Psychiatry at Emory University" at age 34 (Simon, 1985, p. 33). It was at Emory that Whitaker hired supportive colleagues, increased his work with schizophrenic patients, and began developing his own free-wheeling style. He was dismissed from Emory in 1956 and went into private practice with his colleagues in Atlanta. In 1965, he accepted a faculty position at the University of Wisconsin's Department of Psychiatry, where he stayed until his retirement in 1982. During the Wisconsin years, Whitaker devoted his efforts almost entirely to families and served as a mentor to young practitioners, such as Augustus Napier, who coauthored with him one of the best selling books in the field of family therapy, *The Family Crucible* (1978). Also during this time, Whitaker traveled extensively, giving workshops on family therapy.

"More than with most well-known therapists, it is difficult to separate Whitaker's therapeutic approach from his personality" (Simon, 1985, p. 34). As a family therapist, Whitaker was quite intuitive, spontaneous, and unstructured. His surname, derived from *Witakarlege* (meaning a wizard or witch) has prompted at least one writer (Keith, 1987) to put Whitaker in a class of his own. Yet, Whitaker focused on some therapeutic elements that are universal. His main contribution to family therapy was in the uninhibited and emotional way he worked with families by teasing them "to be in contact with their absurdity" (Simon, 1984, p. 28). He used the term **absurdity** to refer to half-truthful statements that are silly if followed out to their natural conclusion (Whitaker, 1975). He likened the use of absurdity to the Leaning Tower of Pisa, which if built high enough would eventually crash.

Whitaker accomplished his tasks in family therapy by being spontaneous, especially in dealing with the unconscious, and by highlighting the absurd. He influenced family members to interact with each other in unique and new ways. For example, Whitaker once encouraged a boy and his father, who were having a dispute over who had the most control in the family, to arm wrestle, with the winner of the match becoming the winner of the argument. Obviously, the flaw in such a method, that is, its absurdity, was crucial to Whitaker in helping the family gain insight and tolerance.

Regardless of what he suggested on the spur of the moment, Whitaker refused to become involved in giving families overt directives for bringing about change. He was a "Don Quixote" who challenged people to examine their own view of reality and the idea that they can be in control of their lives apart from others in the family (Simon, 1984, p. 28).

Overall, Whitaker (1989) emphasized uncovering and utilizing the unconscious life of the family. In this respect, he related to some of the psychoanalytic dimensions of other family therapy pioneers. However, in contrast to this connection, Whitaker focused on helping the family live more fully in the present. Since 1988 his approach has been labeled **experiential symbolic family therapy**. In this position, he assumed that

> experience, not education . . . changes families. The main function of the cerebral cortex is inhibition. Thus, most of our experience goes on outside of our consciousness.

We gain best access to it symbolically. For us "symbolic" implies that some thing or some process has more than one meaning. While education can be immensely helpful, the covert process of the family is the one that contains the most power for potential changing. (Keith & Whitaker, 1982, p. 43)

Whitaker died at age 83 on April 21, 1995, after an illness of 2 years (Andolfi, 1996).

# Premises of the Theory

The underlying premise of the experiential approach is that individuals in families are not aware of their emotions, or if they are aware of their emotions, they suppress them. Because of this tendency not to feel or express feelings, a climate of **emotional deadness** is created that results in the expression of symptoms within one or more family members. In this type of atmosphere, family members avoid each other and occupy themselves with work and other nonfamily activities (Satir, 1972). These types of behaviors perpetuate the dysfunctionality of the family further in a downward spiral.

The resolution to this situation is to emphasize sensitivity and feeling-expression among family members and within the family itself. This type of expression can come verbally, but often it is expressed in an affective or behavioral nonverbal manner. For instance, family members may represent the distance they wish to maintain between themselves and other family members by using role play, mime, or even arranging physical objects such as furniture in a particular way.

Regardless of how relationships are enacted or represented, it is crucial that emphasis be placed on the present. Overall, the experiential family therapy approach concentrates on increasing self-awareness among family members "through action in the here-and-now" (Costa, 1991, p. 122). Interpersonal skills are also taught directly and indirectly. The theoretical roots of this treatment are humanistic and phenomenological in origin. Theory is always secondary to process in attempts to bring about change.

# Treatment Techniques

Experiential family therapists "can be divided into two groups in regard to therapeutic techniques" (Costa, 1991, p. 121). A number of therapists (e.g., Virginia Satir, Peggy Papp, Fred and Bunny Duhl, Bernard and Louise Guerney) employ highly structured activities, such as sculpting and choreography. A few clinicians (e.g., Carl Whitaker) rely more "on their own personality, spontaneity, and creativity" (Costa, 1991, p. 121). It is probably safe to say that most experiential family therapists take a middle road between these two positions. They use techniques that are most often extensions of their personalities. In such cases, the effectiveness of experiential family therapy depends on the personhood of the therapist (Kempler, 1968).

Experiential family therapists employ many different processes. Even therapists who do not consider techniques important may advocate at least a few of these processes. For instance, according to Whitaker (Keith & Whitaker, 1982), seven different interventions aid the therapeutic process:

1. *Redefining symptoms as efforts for growth.* By viewing symptoms in this way, therapists help families see previously unproductive behaviors as meaningful. Families and therapists are able to evaluate symptoms as ways families have tried to more fully develop.

2. *Modeling fantasy alternatives to real-life stress.* Sometimes change is fostered by going outside the realm of the expected or conventional. Modeling fantasy alternatives is one way of assessing whether client families' ideas will work. The modeling may be done through role play by either therapists or families.

3. *Separating interpersonal stress and intrapersonal stress.* Interpersonal stress is generated between two or more family members. Intrapersonal stress is developed from within an individual. Both types of stresses may be present in families, but it is important to distinguish between them because there are often different ways of resolving them (e.g., face-to-face interactions versus muscle relaxation exercises).

4. *Adding practical bits of intervention.* Sometimes family members need practical or concrete information to make needed changes. For example, adolescents may find it beneficial to know that their fathers struggled in achieving their own identity. Such information helps teenagers who are confused feel more "normal." They may be further assisted through finding that there are career tests they can take to help them sort out their preferences.

5. *Augmenting the despair of a family member.* Augmenting the despair of a family member means to enlarge or magnify his or her feelings so that other family members, and the family as a whole, understand them better. When families have difficulties, they often deny that any of their members are in pain. In addition, family members may suppress their feelings. Augmenting despair prevents the occurrence of such denial or suppression.

6. *Affective confrontation.* As mentioned earlier, a major premise of the experiential approach and those associated with it is its emphasis on the *primacy of emotion.* Therefore, in confronting, therapists will often direct family members to examine their feelings before exploring their behaviors.

7. *Treating children like children and not like peers.* A major emphasis of the experiential approach is to play with children and treat them in an age-appropriate manner. Therefore, although children are valued as a part of the therapeutic process, they are treated differently from the rest of a family.

Among the most widely used structured therapeutic responses are the employment of questions, empathic responses, humor, games, clarification, directives, and modeling of effective communication procedures (Satir, Stachowiak, & Taschman, 1975). Family sculpting and choreography are also frequently employed in order to increase family members' awareness and thereby alter their relationships (Duhl, Kantor, & Duhl, 1973; Jefferson, 1978). In addition, experiential family therapists use the techniques of family drawing (Bing, 1970) and family puppet interviews (Duhl et al., 1973).

A discussion follows of some of the most widely used technical procedures employed by experiential family therapy.

## Modeling of Effective Communication Using "I" Messages

In dysfunctional families, members often speak in the first-person plural (i.e., "we"); give unclear and nonspecific messages; and tend to respond to others with monologues (Stoltz-

Loike, 1992). For example, in response to her daughter, a mother might drone on about her daughter's behavior by saying: "Someone is going to get angry unless you do something good quickly."

To combat such ineffective and indirect communication patterns, experiential family therapists insist that family members take "I" positions when expressing their feelings. For example, in response to the situation just given, a mother might say to her daughter: "I feel discouraged when you do not respond to my requests."

"I" statements involve the expression of feelings in a personal and responsible way and encourage others to express their opinions. This type of communication also promotes **leveling** or congruent communication, in which straight, genuine, and real expressions of one's feelings and wishes are made in an appropriate context. When leveling and congruence occur, communication increases, stereotyping decreases, and self-esteem and self-worth improve (Satir, 1972). When leveling does not occur, Satir states that people adopt four other roles: blamer, placater, distractor, and computer (or rational analyzer). These four roles are used by most individuals at one time or another. They can be helpful in some situations, but when they become a consistent way of interacting, they become problematic and dysfunctional.

### Blamer

A **blamer** is one who attempts to place the focus on others and not take responsibility for what is happening. This style of communication is often done from a self-righteous stance. A blamer's might make this type of statement: "Now, see what you made me do!" or "It's your fault." In blaming, a person may also point his or her finger in a scolding and lecturing position.

### Placater

A **placater** is one who avoids conflict at the cost of his or her integrity. This type of stance is one that originates out of timidity and an eagerness to please. For example, a placater might say in response to something with which he or she disagrees, "That's fine," or "It's ok."

### Distractor

A **distractor** is one who says and does irrelevant things. This type of person does not seem to be in contact with anything that is going on. For instance, when a family is talking about the importance of saving money and being thrifty, a distractor might try to tell a joke, say something flippant, or even walk around looking out the windows and calling the family over to look at a stray cat or a passing car.

### Computer (or Rational Analyzer)

A **computer** (or **rational analyzer**) is one who interacts only on a cognitive or intellectual level. This type of person avoids becoming emotional and stays detached. In a situation where the person playing this role is asked how he or she feels, the response might be: "Different people have different feelings about this circumstance. I think it is difficult to say how one feels without first looking at what one's thoughts are."

To help family members level and become congruent, Satir (1988) sometimes incorporated a technique known as the **communication stance.** In this procedure, family members are asked to exaggerate the physical positions of their perspective roles. For example, a blamer may be asked to make an angry face, bend over as in scolding, and point a finger at the person he or she is attacking. This process promotes an increase in awareness of what is being done and how it is being conveyed. Feelings may surface in the process. The result may be a conversation on alternative ways of interacting, which could lead to practicing new ways of opening up.

## Sculpting

In **sculpting,** "family members are molded during the therapy session into positions symbolizing their actual relationships as seen by one or more members of the family" (Sauber, L'Abate, & Weeks, 1985, p. 147). In this process, past events and patterns that affect the family now are perceptually set up. The idea is to expose outgrown family rules and clarify early misconceptions so that family members and the family can get on with life. For example, an historic scene of a father's involvement with a television program and his neglect of his son might be shown through having the father sit close to an imaginary television and the son sit isolated in a corner. The point is that in this "still life portrait of time," family members and the therapist gain a clearer view of family relationships. Often the therapist plays the part of the person setting up the scene. Sculpting consists of four steps and their accompanying roles (Duhl et al., 1973; Moreno & Elefthery, 1975):

1. *Setting the scene.* The therapist helps the sculptor identify a scene to explore.
2. *Choosing role players.* Individuals are chosen to portray family members.
3. *Creating a sculpture.* The sculptor places each person in a specific metaphorical position spatially.
4. *Processing the sculpture.* The sculptor and other participants derole and debrief about experiences and insights acquired through engaging in this exercise.

## Choreography

In **choreography,** family members are asked to symbolically enact a pattern or a sequence in their relationship to one another. This process is similar to mime or a "silent movie." Through it, family members come to see and feel alliances and distances that are not obvious through merely discussing problem situations (Papp, 1976).

For instance, in a family with an overinvolved mother and an underinvolved father, members may be asked to act out a typical scene showing this dynamic at a certain time of the day, for example, breakfast. Each family member then takes a turn positioning other family members in certain spatial relationships to one another. In such a scenario, a daughter might have her father turn the pages of a newspaper and sit away from her while her mother heaps cereal into the daughter's bowl and/or straightens the daughter's hair or dress while the daughter leans toward her father and pushes away her mother.

Such scenes should be reenacted three or four times so that family members get a good feeling for what certain experiences are like from the perspectives of other family members. Then, the family and the therapist can sit down and discuss what has occurred and what family members would like to have happen. In many cases, new scenes are created and acted out (Papp, 1976).

## Play Therapy

**Play therapy** is a general term for a variety of therapeutic interventions that use play media as the basis for communicating and working with children (Johnson, Bruhn, Winek, Krepps, & Wiley, 1999). In child-centered play therapy, which is based on the humanistic theory of Carl Rogers, the therapist accepts the child unconditionally and allows the child complete freedom of expression. In this process the child explores feelings and relationships with the therapist and comes to resolution of troubling matters in his or her life over time.

## Filial Therapy

**Filial therapy**

> is a hybrid form of child-centered play therapy in which parents (or other primary caregivers) engage in play therapy with their own children. The aim of filial therapy is to address the child's problems in the context of the parent–child relationship, effecting changes in parent–child interactions. (Johnson et al., 1999, p. 170)

In filial therapy, the family therapist can work with parents in groups where parents can give and receive feedback and suggestions (Guerney, 1991) or they can work with individual families (VanFleet, 1994).

Research on filial therapy shows that it is effective in training parents to "acquire reflective listening skills, to allow children self-direction, to demonstrate involvement in children's emotional expression and behavior" and to maintain these positive changes long term (Johnson et al., 1999, p. 171). Overall, filial therapy equips parents to handle emotional expression and problems with their children better and to reduce parenting stress for couples.

## Humor

Creating humor within a family therapy session is a risky proposition. If successful, humor will reduce tension and promote insight. Laughter and the confusion that goes with it create an open environment for change to take place (Whitaker & Keith, 1981). If unsuccessful, attempts at humor may alienate the family or some of its members. Therefore, creating humor is an art form that is carefully employed by some experiential family therapists.

Humor is often initiated with families by pointing out the absurdity of their rigid positions or relabeling a situation to make it seem less serious (Carter & McGoldrick-Orfanidis, 1976). In regard to absurdity, a mother might say to a therapist, for example, that she "will die" if her daughter is late for curfew again. A humorous response by the family therapist might be: "Take it easy on your mother. Just paralyze her arm next time."

If the therapist is really into acting out the absurdity, he or she might then ask the daughter to show how she would go about paralyzing her mother's arm. In the interaction following such a strange request, the therapist would probably even engage the mother to help her daughter in such a process. The idea behind this request is to help everyone recognize the distorted power given up by the mother to her daughter. If such insight into this absurdity is developed, a more functional mother/daughter relationship can be formed.

## Touch

Satir, Whitaker, and Kempler are among the most prominent of experiential therapists to use touch to communicate in family therapy sessions. Touch may be putting one's arms around another, patting a person on the shoulder, shaking hands, or even, in an extreme case, wrestling (Napier & Whitaker, 1978). In using touch, experiential family therapists are careful not to violate the personal boundaries of their clients. Physical touch is representative of caring and concern. It loses its potency if it is employed inappropriately or if it is overused.

## Props

Satir used props, such as ropes and blindfolds, in her work with families (Satir & Baldwin, 1983). These props are metaphorical in nature. For instance, a rope may represent how family members are connected to each other. In her work with the family, Satir sometimes literally tied ends of the rope around all members' waists and selectively asked them to move. In this way, the entire family could experience being tied to one other. They also got a feel for how the movement of one family member influenced the rest of the family.

After the props are used, the therapist might ask the family to process the experience and then relate how the experience is similar to and/or different from the dynamics in their present family relationship.

## Family Reconstruction

**Family reconstruction** is a therapeutic innovation developed by Satir in the late 1960s. The purpose of family reconstruction is to help family members discover dysfunctional patterns in their lives stemming from their families of origin. It concentrates on (1) revealing to family members the sources of their old learning, (2) enabling family members to develop a more realistic picture of who their parents are as persons, and (3) setting up ways for family members to discover their own personhood.

Family reconstruction begins with a "**star**" or "**explorer**" (i.e., a central character) who maps his or her family of origin in visually representative ways (Nerin, 1986; Satir, Bitter, & Krestensen, 1988). A **guide** (usually the therapist) can help the star or explorer chart a chronological account of significant family events from paternal, maternal, and family-of-origin histories. The process of family reconstruction attempts to uncover facts about the origin of distorted learning, about parents as people, and about the person as a separate self. "Family maps, the family life fact chronology, and the wheel of influence (Satir & Baldwin, 1983) are the points of entry, the tools, for a family reconstruction" (Satir et al., 1988, p. 202).

1. *Family map.* As shown in Figure 6.1, a **family map** is "a visual representation of the structure of three generations of the star's family" (Satir et al., 1988, p. 202), with adjectives to describe each family member's personality. Circles represent people on the map and lines suggest relationships within the family.

2. *Family life fact chronology.* The **family life fact chronology** is the next tool employed in family reconstruction (see Figure 6.2).

> The star creates the chronology by listing all significant events in his or her life and that of the extended family. Chronologies begin with the births of each set of grandparents. All events having an impact on the people in the family, all significant com-

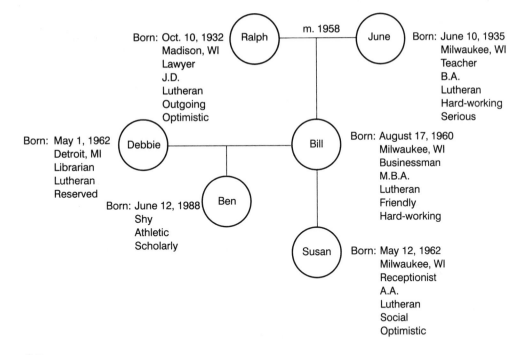

**Figure 6.1**
Basic family map of a star.

From "Family Reconstruction: The Family Within-a-Group Experience" by V. Satir, J. R. Bitter, and K. K. Krestensen, 1988. *Journal for Specialists in Group Work, 13*, p. 202. © ACA. Reprinted with permission. No further reproduction authorized without written permission of the American Counseling Association.

ings and goings, are then listed in order. The family life fact chronology includes the demographic information already on the family map as well as noting illnesses, geographical moves from one place to another, a father going off to war, a sister's teenage pregnancy, or the long-term alcoholism of a family member. When appropriate, historical events associated with given dates are noted to ground the event in time and place. (Satir et al., 1988, p. 203)

3. *Wheel or circle of influence.* A **wheel or circle of influence** representing those who have been important to the star or explorer is the final tool employed in family reconstruction (see Figure 6.3). The star is shown in the middle of those who have had either positive or negative impacts on him or her. A spoke is drawn for every relationship important to the star. The thicker the line, the more important or closer the relationship. "When completed, the wheel of influence displays the star's internalized strengths and weaknesses, the resources on which he or she may rely for new and, it is hoped, more effective ways of coping" (Satir et al., 1988, p. 205).

The final aspect of family reconstruction is to have the star or explorer give life to the events he or she has discovered. This is done by working with a group of at least 10 people, aided by a leader guide (i.e., a therapist), to enact important family scenes. Members

| Date | Event | Relation | Location |
|------|-------|----------|----------|
| **Paternal** | | | |
| 1–1–1918 | John S. born | Star's paternal grandfather | Hastings, MN |
| 2–27–1921 | Martha R. born to rich family | Star's paternal grandmother | Minneapolis, MN |
| 1941 | John S. is 4F | Star's paternal grandfather | Minnesota draft board |
| 1944? | John S. courts & wins rich man's daughter; married Martha R. | Star's paternal grandparents | Minneapolis, MN war in Europe |
| 8–8–1946 | Thomas born | Star's father | Minneapolis, MN |
| 10–1–1946 | John S. goes to work for father-in-law | Star's paternal grandfather | Minneapolis, MN |
| 4–18–1949 | Sam S. born | Star's paternal uncle | Minneapolis, MN |
| **Maternal** | | | |
| 12–4–1918 | Hugh G. born | Star's maternal grandfather | Homer, NY |
| 10–9–1930 | Emma B. born | Star's maternal grandmother | Oshkosh, WI |
| 1943 | Hugh seriously wounded in war & returns home | Star's maternal grandfather | Homer, NY |
| 12–1–1947 | Janice born out of wedlock | Star's mother | Milwaukee, WI |
| 5–1–1948 | Hugh moves to start sales job; meets Emma 1st day | Star's maternal grandfather | Oshkosh, WI |
| 9–9–1948 | Hugh marries Emma | Star's maternal grandparents | Milwaukee, WI |
| 1949? | Hugh, Emma, & Janice move to escape gossip | Star's mother's family | Saint Paul, MN |
| **Family of Origin** | | | |
| 9–22–1961 | Thomas & Jan meet and fall in love | Star's parents | Minneapolis, MN |
| 9–22–1968 | Thomas & Jan marry | Star's parents | Minneapolis, MN |
| 3–9–1970 | Annie is born | Star | Mankato, MN |
| 2–3–1979 | Thomas & Jan divorce | Star's parents | Mankato, MN |
| 1–1–1982 | Thomas dies of sudden heart attack | Star's father | Mankato, MN |
| 9–5–1987 | Annie enters college; lives at home with mom | Star | Mankato, MN |

**Figure 6.2**
Reconstruction of the star's family.

From "Family Reconstruction: The Family Within—A Group Experience" by V. Satir, J. R. Bitter, and K. K. Krestensen, 1988. *Journal for Specialists in Group Work, 13*, p. 204. © ACA. Reprinted with permission. No further reproduction authorized without written permission of the American Counseling Association.

**Figure 6.3**
Wheel of influence.

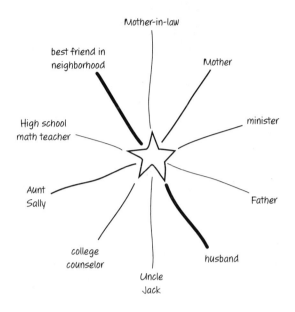

of the group play key figures in the star's life or the life of his or her family. The idea behind this procedure is to help the star or explorer gain a new perspective on family characteristics and patterns. "It is a time when significant questions can receive straight answers, when old, distorted messages can be cleared up, and when understanding can replace judgment and blame" (Satir et al., 1988, p. 207).

## Family Drawings

Experiential family therapists have at their disposal many variations on the technique of family drawings. One is the **joint family scribble** in which each family member makes a brief scribble. After these scribbles have been made, the whole family incorporates their scribbles collectively into a unified picture (Kwiatkowska, 1967). In this procedure, family members get a feel for what it is to work both individually and together. The advantages and disadvantages of each can be talked about, as well as what was produced in each case.

Another drawing approach is known as **conjoint family drawing**. In this procedure, families are given the instruction to "draw a picture as you see yourself as a family" (Bing, 1970). Each member of the family makes such a drawing and then shares through discussion the perceptions that emerge. For example, a younger son might see his older brother as being closer to their parents. His drawing would reflect this spatial difference. On the other hand, a parent in the same family might see all the family members as being equally close to one another and portray that perception in his or her drawing.

Still another type of family drawing is the **symbolic drawing of family life space** (Geddes & Medway, 1977). In this projective technique, the therapist draws a large circle and instructs family members to include within the circle everything that represents the family and to place outside of the circle those people and institutions that are not a part of the family. After this series of drawings, the family is asked to symbolically arrange themselves, through drawing, within a large circle, according to how they relate to one another. An example of symbolic drawing of family life space is shown in Figure 6.4.

Discussion should follow all of these types of drawing techniques. Family members can discuss what was drawn and why, as well as the dynamics of their life as seen from the perspective of the individual members and the family as a whole. In addition, different ways of interacting can be explored with the therapist and illustrated in another drawing.

## Puppet Interviews

In this procedure, the therapist asks one of the family members to make up a story using puppets (Irwin & Malloy, 1975). The idea is that family difficulties can be displayed in the story and the therapist can gain valuable insight in an indirect manner. In the case, for example, of a 4-year-old girl who is having nightmares, the story might be one of a child who is taken by a witch to a land of dragons, where she is constantly threatened and helpless. Actual circumstances could relate, for example, to the child's day-care arrangement in which personnel are scaring children into behaving. Through acting out the scene with puppets, the child can begin to feel safe enough to talk about what is happening in real life.

Family therapists who utilize this process need to be sure they have a variety of puppets for family members to use. In actual practice, this technique is limited. Adults may resist expressing themselves through puppets because they prefer verbal interaction. Children may make up stories that have little or no relationship to what is occurring in their actual

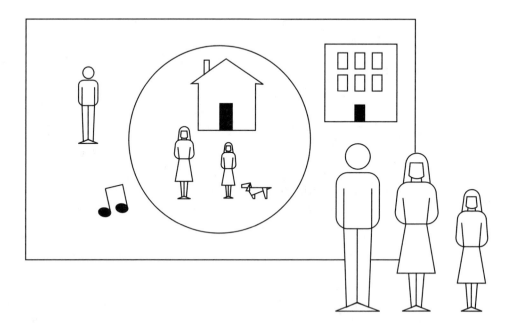

**Figure 6.4**
Symbolic drawing of family life space.

lives. However, a puppet technique may be employed effectively in situations in which young children, shy children, or selectively mute children are being treated who will not or cannot relate much about family dynamics in other ways.

# Role of the Therapist

The role of the experiential family therapist from the more structured tradition is best described as that of being a facilitator and resource person. In these roles, therapists help family members understand themselves and others better. Furthermore, they help families discover their innate abilities and help promote clear communication. The therapist makes use of him- or herself in interacting with the family and, thus, "the therapist enters into relationship with each of the family members, uses his or her feelings as guides toward intervention, and models effective interactional styles" (Kane, 1994, p. 256).

From the less structured tradition, an experiential family therapist assumes the role of active participant, a whole person—not a director or teacher. To be effective in this capacity, the therapist can use a *cotherapist*. According to Whitaker and other symbolic-experiential therapists, the presence of a cotherapist allows greater utilization of intuition (Napier & Whitaker, 1978). Feedback and supervision can also be utilized beneficially in this process.

Generally, experiential therapists try to assist family members in discovering their individuality and in finding fulfilling roles for themselves. They do this by establishing an environment that communicates warmth, acceptance, respect, hope, and an orientation toward improvement and change (Woods & Martin, 1984). A warm environment promotes a willingness to take risks and open up. In such a setting, therapists help families take the first step toward change by **verbalizing presuppositions** of hope that the family has. They also help family members to clarify their goals and to use their natural abilities.

In addition to creating an atmosphere that encourages change, experiential family therapists promote growth through stimulating experiences that provide opportunities for personal existential encounters. Through these encounters, it is hoped that awareness and authenticity will increase and lead "to a reintegration of repressed or disowned parts of the self" (Costa, 1991, p. 122). Experiential family therapists who follow Whitaker's lead at times engage in spontaneous and absurd activities, such as falling asleep in a therapy session or having a dream about a family and reporting back to the family what they dreamed. This use of the absurd can result in raised emotions, anxiety, and, often, insight (Keeney, 1986). It can also break down rational defenses.

More structured experiential family therapists use props or other objects, such as ropes, to metaphorically represent distances and interaction patterns between people in families (Satir & Baldwin, 1983). Experiential therapists who follow the tradition of Satir concentrate on being a model of effective communication (Simon, 1989).

Overall, experiential family therapists are likely to behave as real, authentic people. In contrast to psychoanalytic therapists, they do not encourage projection or act as blank screens for their families. The more involved, energetic, and creative experiential family therapists are, the greater chance they have of making a major impact on the families with whom they work. Experiential family therapy is an approach to working with families that helps both the families and the therapists gain self-awareness and growth. It requires not only commitment but also active risk taking to be an effective experiential family therapist. For instance, experiential family therapists must ask their client families to try new ways of interacting without knowing the ultimate effect of these behaviors.

# Process and Outcome

During experiential family therapy, family members should become more aware of their own needs and feelings. They should share these impressions with each other. This illustrates the inside-out process of change promoted by experiential therapists (Duhl, 1983). Through therapy, family members become more attuned to their emotions and more capable of autonomy and real intimacy. Treatment is generally designed to help individual family members find fulfilling roles for themselves, without an overriding concern for the needs of the family as a whole. However, as in filial therapy, systemic changes occur (Johnson et al., 1999).

Many experiential family therapists concentrate on whoever comes to therapy. However, others insist on having the whole family in treatment. In fact, they request that three generations be present during each session (Whitaker, 1976). Even though the entire family is present, most experiential family therapists usually do not treat the family as a systematic unit. Rather, the emphasis is on the impact of what the therapist and other members of the family do in the sessions. Therapists believe this knowledge is more powerful when shared with everyone present than when it is conveyed to others in the family indirectly.

The process of family therapy differs for each experiential family therapist. Whitaker described family therapy as a process that "begins with a blind date and ends with an empty nest" (Whitaker & Bumberry, 1988, p. 53). For Whitaker, therapy occurred in three phases: (1) engagement, (2) involvement, and (3) disentanglement. During these phases, the therapist increases, in a caring way, the family's anxiety. The idea is to escalate pressure in order to produce a breakdown and breakthrough, both among family members and in the functioning of the family itself. Therapists use themselves, as well as planned and spontaneous actions, to intensify the sane and crazy elements within the family (Whitaker & Keith, 1981). Through these means, they get the family to move toward change.

**Engagement** consists of therapists becoming personally involved with their families through the sharing of feelings, fantasies, and personal stories. During this time, therapists encourage families to become invested in making needed changes within a structured environment. If all goes smoothly, therapists are able to demonstrate their caring attitude to client families. Next, during the **involvement** stage, therapists concentrate on helping families try new ways of relating through the use of playfulness, humor, and confrontation. The emphasis in this stage is on families' broadening their horizons and trying new behaviors. Once constructive action is taken and roles and rules are modified, therapists disengage from families and become their consultants.

Similarly, Satir's approach has three phases of intervention. In Satir's Human Validation Process Model, the three stages are (1) making contact, (2) chaos, and (3) integration. These phases are present in each interview and in the therapy as a whole. In the first stage**, making contact**, Satir would shake each person's hand and focus her attention on that person, in an attempt to raise the level of the person's self-esteem and self-worth.

Satir (1988) compared self-worth with a pot. When "the pot of self-worth is high," people are vitally alive and have faith in themselves. The opposite is true when the "pot of self-worth is low." The establishment of trust and hope takes place during this first 45- to 60-minute nonjudgmental session as well. Family members would be asked what they hoped would come out of the therapy. Then through active techniques, Satir would begin to make interventions.

During the second stage, chaos and disorder among family members is prevalent. Individuals are engaged in tasks, take risks, and share their hurt and pain. This stage is unpredictable, as family members open up and work on issues in a random order.

In the last stage, integration and closure are worked on in regard to issues raised in the second stage. The third stage is often an emotional one. However, Satir would interject cognitive information at this time to help members understand themselves and issues more thoroughly. For example, she might have said to a man grieving the loss of his father with whom he was always distant: "You now understand through your hurt how your father kept all people, including you, from getting close to him."

The family is terminated when transactions can be completed and when family members can see themselves as others do. It is vital that family members be able to share with each other honestly. It is a positive sign when members can argue and disagree and make choices by taking responsibility for outcomes. The sending and receiving of clear communication is a further indicator that the family is ready to end treatment (Satir, 1964). For example, if family members can tell each other that they would rather go somewhere different on vacation than back to the same beach they visited last year, progress has been made.

Regardless of the techniques employed in the experiential approach, the primary goal of therapy is growth, especially in the areas of sensitivity and the sharing of feelings. Therapists and families focus on growing. Growth is usually accomplished through the therapist winning the battle for structure and client families winning the battle for initiative (Napier & Whitaker, 1978). In the battle for structure, the therapist sets up the conditions (e.g., the length of sessions and/or the order of speaking) under which the family will proceed. In the battle for initiative, the family becomes actively involved and responsible for making changes that help them as individuals and as a family (e.g., several family members express a desire to work through a disagreement that has continued to keep them angry and apart). If the battle for structure is won, chances are improved that the battle for initiative will go well. An ideal outcome for experiential family therapists is to help individuals gain congruence between their inner experiences and outward behaviors.

# Unique Aspects of Experiential Family Therapy

## Emphases

The unique qualities of the experiential approach are found on several levels that involve both people and processes. A major uniqueness developed by Virginia Satir and by Bernard and Louise Guerney is the training programs set up to educate others in their approaches to family therapy. The **Avanta Network** (2104 S.W. 152nd Street, #2, Burien, Washington 98166) now carries on the interdisciplinary work of training therapists in Satir's methods.

The Guerneys' training program in filial therapy is known as the **National Institute of Relationship Enhancement** (4400 East-West Highway, Suite 28, Bethesda, Maryland 20814-4501) and carries out regular training sessions in this approach.

A second novel element of the experiential approach relates to research. Although Satir gave consent for only her model and methods to be used in one research project, this study (Winter, 1989), which compared her work with that of Bowen and Haley, produced very favorable results on both a multiple-family group level and with individual family units. Their results, plus her own demonstration of work before large audiences of professionals, have given her approach, and the experiential school of therapy in general, credibility, with the possibility that more will be gained in the future through the generation of data (Satir & Bitter, 2000). Likewise, the filial therapy approach of the Guerneys has distinguished itself in regard to research (Johnson et al., 1999).

Whitaker, on the other hand, has been unique in his stance that empirical research, just like theory, can get in the way of helping a family. Whitaker reported numerous examples of how he conducted family therapy. However, he insisted that because each family is different, each treatment plan should be different and, therefore, cannot really be used for research. In essence, Whitaker is impossible to imitate, as are his therapeutic sessions (Framo, 1996).

The length of treatment and the focus of therapists practicing experiential family therapy represent a third unique aspect of it. Experiential family therapy focuses on immediate experiences and the uniqueness of every family. Treatment tends to be of shorter duration and often more direct than with historical-based approaches.

A fourth quality of experiential family therapy is that it calls attention to emphasizing people as well as structures within the change process. As a theory, experiential family therapy places a great deal of attention on persons within families. It emphasizes that families are composed of individuals. For family systems to change, those who are a part of them must alter their behaviors (Duhl, 1983).

## Comparison with Other Theories

Experiential family therapy is often seen as hard to conceptualize and, therefore, hard to compare with other approaches. However, experiential approaches can be contrasted with other types of family therapy both directly and indirectly.

One comparative aspect of many of the experiential approaches is their dependence on sensitive and charismatic therapists. Virginia Satir and Carl Whitaker, pioneers in the family therapy movement, both fit this profile. Additionally, they were both rather large framed. They encouraged family members to participate physically in activities, for example, by using props, in the case of Satir, and by using their person (e.g., as in arm wrestling contests), in the case of Whitaker. Both had a spontaneous theatrical style that was uniquely their own and made them difficult to emulate. Whitaker especially has been hard to model, partly because of his encouragement of intuitive action by a therapist and partly because of the need for a therapist to do an apprenticeship with him in order to really learn his approach (Sugarman, 1987).

Unlike psychodynamic or Bowenian family treatment, experiential family therapies focus on the present rather than on the past. Such an emphasis can keep therapists and families from dealing with historical patterns or events. By neglecting historical information, therapists could miss data that sheds light on patterns that, if properly understood, could be altered and thereby help alleviate problems. In this last respect, however, experiential and most other family therapies are the same.

Further, experiential family therapies promote individual growth and intrapersonal change as opposed to family growth and interpersonal change. Although personal development is an admirable and noteworthy goal, it may not be sufficient in some cases to help families alter their dysfunctional behaviors. For instance, individual members who have become healthier during treatment may leave the family, or if the family stays together, more dysfunctional family members may work hard to return the family to the way it was before therapy.

Finally, experiential approaches emphasize dealing with feelings in the here and now rather than concentrating on guidance for now and the future. Some theorists criticize making therapeutic interventions without offering family members education about how to help themselves in the future. This critique of the experiential therapies, however, has not altered the overall emphasis of the approach (Duhl & Duhl, 1981).

## CASE ILLUSTRATION

### THE SMITH FAMILY

When Fred first bumped into Heather, it was literally in a car. The accident was minor, but the mutual interest between the divorced man and the widow soon grew. In 6 months, Fred had proposed, and the wedding took place on the anniversary of their collision. Fred's 16-year-old son, Stan, was reluctantly his father's best man; and Heather's 8- and 9-year-old daughters, Ann and Mary, respectively, were her bridesmaids.

Heather's daughters quickly accepted Fred as their new father. (Their biological father had died of cancer when they were 4 and 5.) Stan was not as accepting, and told Heather prior to the wedding ceremony that he already had a mother, Judy. Judy and his father had divorced in a nasty civil suit 2 years previously.

Although Stan has been disrespectful to Heather in subtle ways since, Heather worries more about her daughters' behavior in regard to Fred. They frequently manipulate him into buying them clothes and toys that the family budget cannot afford. Fred reassures Heather that his behavior with respect to the girls is temporary, but she thinks otherwise. Fred is 40, the oldest in his family of origin, which was composed of him, his 8-years-younger sister, Emily, and his parents, both hardworking school teachers. Heather thinks he should be wiser and more appropriate in his interactions with her daughters. Lately, Heather has started scolding Fred and then withdrawing into silence. According to Fred, she is acting more like a 3-year-old than like the 33-year-old woman that she is.

#### Conceptualization of Family: Experiential Perspective

As a remarried family, the Smiths are encountering difficulties in becoming a functioning unit. Some of it is on a conscious, overt level; and some of it appears unconscious and covert. Stan is openly withdrawn from his stepmother and Heather has begun an emotional withdrawal from Fred. At the same time, Fred is being drawn into a relationship with Heather's daughters, who are manipulating him into buying them things they want. Fred is treating them well on the surface, but it is difficult to tell whether he has anything more than a superficial interaction with them. Furthermore, it is interesting to note that Fred has continued his behavior with Heather's daughters despite her disapproval.

There is stress in the marital unit, as well as between the generations. It appears individual members of the family are having problems, too. Clear communication is lacking. In fact, family members seem to hurt themselves and others when they try to make a point (e.g., by giving one another the "cold shoulder").

### Process of Treatment: Experiential Family Therapy

To help the Smiths become a more functional family, an experiential family therapist would go through three phases of treatment, and most likely would use a number of procedures. If the therapist followed Whitaker's symbolic-experiential approach, he or she might initially show care and concern for the family through expressing feelings about individual family members. In this process, the therapist would address remarks to one member of the family at a time. However, it is the manner in which the therapist's remarks are conveyed that establishes trust among all members.

The therapist following Satir's model would likewise focus initially on making contact with family members on a personal level. In such a scenario, the therapist would use "I" statements, for example, "Heather, I really hear that you are feeling hurt and angry about Fred's behavior." The emphasis in such a first session would be on making sure family members felt validated and affirmed as members of the family unit.

After this preliminary engagement/contact, the therapist would move the family into involvement. For a therapist following Whitaker's symbolic-experiential approach, involvement is getting the family to win the battle for initiative by working on problematic areas. In the case of the Smiths, these behaviors range from the proper expression of affection to the expression of anger. To make the family more aware of the importance of the issues involved, a symbolic-experiential therapist might do something absurd, such as sharing a daydream with the family about their situation. Through such a process, some unconscious aspects of the family's life would become more obvious. In most cases, the therapist would also try to get individuals talking to one another about their feelings and how they have handled them previous to this family situation. An opportunity would then be given for family members to try new behaviors.

In the Satir model, the middle part of the therapeutic process might involve chaos, out of which would come clarity. This middle phase would involve such procedures as sculpting, choreography, or art, in which members would get an opportunity to express their feelings in direct and indirect ways. Props might be used in these situations to enhance the quality of the affect that is generated. There would be an emphasis at this stage on exploring, through activities, concerns such as individual self-worth and their family life together (Satir, 1972).

In the final stage of the experiential process, a symbolic-experiential therapist would disengage from the Smith family by encouraging family members to speak more to each other. Likewise, in the Satir model, the therapist would help the Smith family integrate what they learned through their enactments and come to closure.

A more cognitive focus would eventually be emphasized by Satir, after emotions concerning the therapeutic experience were expressed.

# Summary and Conclusion

Experiential family therapy grew out of the humanistic-existential psychology movement of the 1960s. Its original founders were involved with experimental and experiential forms of treatment. They concentrated on immediate personal interactions and sometimes conducted their family sessions like a group by treating all members of the family as equals. Above all, they stressed the importance of taking risks and expressing emotions.

Some of the founders of this approach, such as Virginia Satir and Peggy Papp, developed highly structured treatment methods, such as using "I" messages, sculpting, and family reconstruction. Other practitioners within this theoretical camp, such as Carl Whitaker, relied more on their personality, creativity, and spontaneity to help them make timely and effective interventions. Most clinicians (e.g., Bernard and Louise Guerney) who favor this approach today lean toward the former method of treatment just described rather than the latter.

Some of the major roles of experimental family therapists are to act as facilitators and resource persons. Therapists encourage change and set up a warm and accepting environment in which such a process is possible. Experiential family therapists use a wide variety of techniques that are both concrete and metaphorical. They act as models of clear communication in the hope of promoting intimacy and autonomy. It is assumed that if individuals within families find proper roles for themselves, the family as a whole will function well.

Some of the pioneers of family therapy, such as Virginia Satir and Carl Whitaker, are among the best-known experiential family therapists. Although the therapy they helped develop is valued for its emphasis on stressing the importance of affect in families, it is perceived as weak from a traditional research perspective, except in the area of filial therapy. Furthermore, focusing on persons within the family, instead of the family as a whole, could make systemic change difficult. Complicating the matter still further is the emphasis from the experiential perspective of concentrating on the here and now at the expense of teaching families how to work better in the future. Overall, many forms of experiential family therapy are seen as less viable than previously because of the accountability that is linked with therapeutic treatment. However, this approach continues to be attractive to many practitioners and the institutes set up by Satir and the Guerneys hold promise for its continued development and growth.

# Summary Table
## Experiential Family Therapy

### Major Theorists

| | | |
|---|---|---|
| Virginia Satir | Carl Whitaker | Fred Duhl |
| Bunny Duhl | Bernard Guerney | Louise Guerney |
| Walter Kempler | Augustus Napier | David Keith |
| Leslie Greenberg | Susan Johnson | Peggy Papp |

### Premises of the Theory

Family problems are rooted in suppression of feelings, rigidity, denial of impulses, lack of awareness, emotional deadness, and overuse of defense mechanisms.

### Treatment Techniques

The focus is on individuals and couple dyads, except for Whitaker, who concentrated on three generational families. It is assumed that families will benefit if the individuals within them receive help.

The goals of treatment are

- to promote growth, change, creativity, flexibility, spontaneity, and playfulness
- to make the covert overt
- to increase emotional closeness of spouses and disrupt rigidity
- to unlock defenses, enhance self-esteem, and recover potential for experiencing

Therapeutic techniques of the experiential approach include:

- Sculpting
- Choreography
- Modeling and teaching clear communication skills
- Play therapy
- Filial therapy
- Humor
- Puppet interviews
- Art therapy
- Role playing
- Reconstruction
- Disregarding theory and emphasizing intuitive spontaneity
- Sharing feelings and creating an emotionally intense atmosphere
- Having the therapist win the battle for structure and the family win the battle for initiative
- Making suggestions and giving directives

### Role of the Therapist

Therapists use their own personalities.

Therapists must be open, spontaneous, empathic, sensitive, and demonstrate caring and acceptance.

They must be willing to share and risk, be genuine, and increase stress within the family and its members.

They must deal with regression therapeutically and teach family members new skills in clearly communicating their feelings.

### Process and Outcome

Family members become more aware of their needs and feelings.

Therapy for Satir occurs in three stages: making contact, chaos, and integration.

Therapy for Whitaker occurs in three phases: engagement, involvement, and disentanglement.

Therapists and families focus on growing and winning the battles for structure and initiative respectfully.

## Unique Aspects of Experiential Family Therapy

Experiential family therapy emphasizes:

- creativity and spontaneity in families
- changing roles and increased understanding of self and others
- treating all members of the family as equal in status
- increased awareness of feelings within and among family members
- the breakdown of defenses within the family and among family members through structured exercises
- growth

### Comparison with Other Theories

In experiential family therapy, with the exception of filial therapy, there is little interest in research or data on results of using the theory.

Much of the practice of experiential family therapy is not systems oriented.

The experiential approach can overemphasize emotion.

Experiential family therapy may be too advice oriented and individualistic.

Experiential family therapists use a lot of borrowed techniques that have not been tested empirically.

Much of the effectiveness of experiential family therapy depends on the spontaneity, creativity, and timing of the therapist.

# References

Andolfi, M. (1996). Let it flow: Carl Whitaker's philosophy of becoming. *Journal of Marital and Family Therapy, 22,* 317–319.

Beels, C., & Ferber, A. (1969). Family therapy: A view. *Family Process, 8,* 280–332.

Bing, E. (1970). The conjoint family drawing. *Family Process, 9,* 173–194.

Carter, E. A., & McGoldrick-Orfanidis, M. (1976). Family therapy with one person and the family therapist's own family. In P. J. Guerin, Jr. (Ed.), *Family therapy* (pp. 119–219). New York: Gardner.

Costa, L. (1991). Family sculpting in the training of marriage and family counselors. *Counselor Education and Supervision, 31,* 121–131.

Duhl, B. (1983). *From the inside out and other metaphors.* New York: Brunner/Mazel.

Duhl, B. S., & Duhl, F. J. (1981). Integrative family therapy. In A. S. Gurman & D. P. Kniskern (Eds.), *Handbook of family therapy* (pp. 483–513). New York: Brunner/Mazel.

Duhl, F. J., Kantor, D., & Duhl, B. S. (1973). Learning, space, and action in family therapy: A primer of sculpture. In D. A. Bloch (Ed.), *Techniques of family psychotherapy* (pp. 69–76) New York: Grune & Stratton.

Framo, J. L. (1996). A personal retrospective of the family therapy field: Then and now. *Journal of Marital and Family Therapy, 22,* 289–316.

Geddes, M., & Medway, J. (1977). The symbolic drawing of family life space. *Family Process, 16,* 219–228.

Gladding, S. T. (1992). *A life in a day of aging.* Unpublished manuscript.

Guerney, L. (1991). Parents as partners in treating behavior problems in early childhood settings. *Topics in Early Childhood Special Education, 11,* 74–90.

Irwin, E., & Malloy, E. (1975). Family puppet interview. *Family Process, 14,* 179–191.

Jefferson, C. (1978). Some notes on the use of family sculpture in therapy. *Family Process, 17,* 69–76.

Johnson, L., Bruhn, R., Winek, J., Krepps, J., & Wiley, K. (1999). The use of child-centered play therapy and filial therapy with Head Start families: A brief report. *Journal of Marital and Family Therapy, 25,* 169–176.

Kane, C. M. (1994). Family making: A Satir approach to treating the H. family. *The Family Journal: Counseling and Therapy for Couples and Families, 2,* 256–258.

Kaplan, D. M. (2000). Who are our giants? *The Family Digest, 12*(4), 1, 6.

Keeney, B. P. (1986). Cybernetics of the absurd: A tribute to Carl Whitaker. *Journal of Strategic and Systemic Therapies, 5,* 20–28.

Keith, D. V. (1987). Intuition in family therapy: A short manual on post-modern witchcraft. *Contemporary Family Therapy, 9,* 11–22.

Keith, D. V., & Whitaker, C. A. (1982). Experiential/symbolic family therapy. In A. M. Horne & M. M. Ohlsen (Eds.), *Family counseling and therapy* (pp. 43–74). Itasca, IL: F. E. Peacock.

Kempler, W. (1968). Experiential psychotherapy with families. *Family Process, 7,* 88–89.

Kwiatkowska, H. Y. (1967). Family art therapy. *Family Process, 6,* 37–55.

Moreno, J. L., & Elefthery, D. G. (1975). An introduction to group psychodrama. In G. M. Gazda (Ed.), *Basic approaches to group psychotherapy and group counseling* (pp. 69–100). Springfield, IL: Thomas.

Napier, A. Y., & Whitaker, C. A. (1978). *The family crucible.* New York: Harper & Row.

Nerin, W. F. (1986). *Family reconstruction: Long day's journey into light.* New York: Norton.

Nichols, M. P., & Schwartz, R. C. (1995). *Family therapy: Concepts and methods* (3rd ed.). Boston: Allyn & Bacon.

Papp, P. (1976). Family choreography. In P. J. Guerin, Jr. (Ed.), *Family therapy* (pp. 465–479). New York: Gardner.

Satir, V. M. (1964). *Conjoint family therapy.* Palo Alto, CA: Science and Behavior Books.

Satir, V. M. (1972). *Peoplemaking.* Palo Alto, CA: Science and Behavior Books.

Satir, V. M. (1982). The therapist and family therapy: Process model. In A. M. Horne & M. M. Ohlsen (Eds.), *Family counseling and therapy.* Itasca, IL: F. E. Peacock.

Satir, V. (1986). A partial portrait of a family therapist in process. In H. C. Fishman & B. L. Rosman (Eds.), *Evolving models for family change: A volume in honor of Salvador Minuchin* (pp. 278–293). New York: Guilford Press.

Satir, V. M. (1988). *The new peoplemaking.* Mountain View, CA: Science and Behavior Books.

Satir, V., & Baldwin, M. (1983). *Satir step by step.* Palo Alto, CA: Science and Behavior Books.

Satir, V. M., & Bitter, J. R. (2000). The therapist and family therapy: Satir's human validation process model. In A. M. Horne

(Ed.), *Family counseling and therapy* (3rd ed., pp. 62–101). Itasca, IL: F. E. Peacock.

Satir, V., Bitter, J. R., & Krestensen, K. K. (1988). Family reconstruction: The family within—a group experience. *Journal for Specialists in Group Work, 13,* 200–208.

Satir, V., Stachowiak, J., & Taschman, H. A. (1975). *Helping families to change.* New York: Aronson.

Sauber, S. R., L'Abate, L., & Weeks, G. R. (1985). *Family therapy: Basic concepts and terms.* Rockville, MD: Aspen.

Simon, R. (1984, November/December). Stranger in a strange land: An interview with Salvador Minuchin. *Family Therapy Networker, 8,* 20–31.

Simon, R. (1985, September/October). Take it or leave it: An interview with Carl Whitaker. *Family Therapy Networker, 9,* 27–34.

Simon, R. (1989, January/February). Reaching out to life: An interview with Virginia Satir. *Family Therapy Networker, 13,* 36–43.

Stoltz-Loike, M. (1992). Couple and family counseling. In R. L. Smith & P. Stevens-Smith (Eds.), *Family counseling and therapy* (pp. 80–108). Ann Arbor, MI: ERIC/CAPS.

Sugarman, S. (1987). Teaching symbolic-experiential family therapy: The personhood of the teacher. *Contemporary Family Therapy, 9,* 138–145.

VanFleet, R. (1994). *Filial therapy: Strengthening parent–child relationships through play.* Sarasota, FL: Professional Resource Press.

Whitaker, C. A. (1975). Psychotherapy of the absurd: With a special emphasis on the psychotherapy of aggression. *Family Process, 14,* 1–16.

Whitaker, C. A. (1976). The hindrance of theory in clinical work. In P. J. Guerin, Jr. (Ed.), *Family therapy: Theory and practice.* New York: Gardner.

Whitaker, C. A. (1989). *Midnight musings of a family therapist.* New York: W. W. Norton.

Whitaker, C. A. (1990). 'I had to learn because I wasn't being taught.' *Contemporary Family Therapy, 12,* 181–183.

Whitaker, C. A., & Bumberry, W. M. (1988). *Dancing with the family: A symbolic-experiential approach.* New York: Brunner/Mazel.

Whitaker, C. A., & Keith, D. V. (1981). Symbolic-experiential family therapy. In A. Gurman & D. Kniskern (Eds.), *The handbook of family therapy* (pp. 187–225). New York: Brunner/Mazel.

Winter, J. (1989). *Family research project: Treatment outcomes and results.* Unpublished manuscript, The Family Institute of Virginia, Richmond.

Woods, M. D., & Martin, D. (1984). The work of Virginia Satir: Understanding her theory and technique. *American Journal of Family Therapy, 12,* 3–11.

# Behavioral and Cognitive–Behavioral Family Therapies

They trade insults and accusations like children
afraid to be vulnerable and scared not to be.

Underneath all the words and bravado
is a backlog of bitter emotion
dormant so long that like dry kindling
it burst into flames when sparked.

Through the dark and heated fights
points are made that leave a mark.

In the early morning, she cries silently
into black coffee grown cold with age
while he sits behind a mahogany desk
and experiences the loneliness of depression.

*Gladding, 1991*

**B**ehaviorism is one of the oldest traditions in the helping professions. It developed from the research and writings of Ivan Pavlov, John B. Watson, and B. F. Skinner. Initially, it focused on observable behavior and concentrated on assisting individuals modify dysfunctional behaviors. Since the 1970s, the impact of **cognitions** (i.e., thoughts) have become incorporated into behaviorism, an approach known as *cognitive-behavioral therapy.*

**Behavioral family therapy** is a fairly recent treatment methodology that had its origins in research involving the modification of children's actions by parents (Horne & Sayger, 2000). The initial work in this area was conducted at the Oregon Social Learning Center under the direction of Gerald Patterson and John Reid in the mid-1960s. It involved training parents and significant adults in a child's environment to be agents of change (Patterson, 1975; Patterson & Gullion, 1971). Treatment procedures were based on **social learning theory** (Bandura & Walters, 1963), which stressed the importance of modeling new behaviors. Techniques included "the use of rewards such as candy, but quickly moved toward using basic point systems, modeling, time out, and contingent attention" (Horne & Sayger, 2000, p. 457). The emphasis in this program gradually shifted toward working with families in their natural settings.

From this rather structured beginning in which observers recorded family problems on a checklist that was linear in nature (i.e., "A" caused "B"), behavioral family therapy grew to embrace a more interactional style of explaining family behavior patterns and treating family behavior problems (Falloon, 1988). A type of behavioral family therapy that is basically systemic is **functional family therapy** (Alexander & Parsons, 1982; Barton & Alexander, 1981).

Likewise, **cognitive-behavioral family therapy** is a fairly new treatment, although the importance of thoughts have been stressed throughout history. Cognitive-behavioral theorists postulate that "cognitions such as irrational beliefs, arbitrary inference, dichotomous reasoning, and overgeneralization can be primary factors in causing, or at least maintaining, maladaptive behaviors and psychological disorders in individuals" (Sullivan & Schwebel, 1995, p. 298). Since the 1970s a concerted effort has been made to apply cognitive-behavioral theory and procedures to couples and families (e.g., Baucom & Epstein, 1990; Beck, 1976; Dattilio & Bevilacqua, 2000; Ellis, 2000; Schwebel & Fine, 1994). Unfortunately, cognitive-behavioral approaches to working with families are not as fully developed as behavioral therapies, or even as advanced as cognitive-behavioral couple therapy (Ellis, 1993). Some of the leading proponents of cognitive-behavioral marital and family therapy are Aaron Beck, Frank Dattilio, Albert Ellis, Norman Epstein, and Andrew Schwebel.

This chapter examines the major forms of behavioral and cognitive-behavioral family therapy.

# Major Theorists

There are many well-known behavior and cognitive-behavioral theorists. Early pioneers in this area were John B. Watson, Mary Cover Jones, and Ivan Pavlov. It was not, however, until the emergence of B. F. Skinner that behaviorism gained national prominence. Skinner was the first to use the term *behavior therapy.* He argued convincingly that behavior problems can be dealt with directly, not simply as symptoms of underlying psychic conflict. Skinner was also the originator and a proponent of **operant conditioning.** This viewpoint says that people learn through rewards and punishments to respond behaviorally to their environments in certain ways. For instance, if a man smiles at a woman and she smiles back, he may voluntarily approach and talk with her because his initial action was reinforced. Skinner publicized his ideas on operant conditioning in such scholarly texts as *Science and Human Behavior* (1953) and in popular books such as *Walden Two* (1948).

It is on the work of Skinner, combined with that of Joseph Wolpe and Albert Bandura, that much of behavioral family therapy and cognitive-behavioral family therapy were built. Other significant contributions in this area have come from Gerald Patterson, Richard Stuart, Norman Epstein, Neil Jacobson, John Gottman, Walter Mischel, Robert Weiss, Ed Katkin, Gayola Margolin, Michael Crowe, Albert Ellis, Aaron Beck, Frank Dattilio, David Burns, and Donald Meichenbaum. Gerald Patterson and Neil Jacobson are highlighted here as representatives of this approach.

## Gerald Patterson

Gerald Patterson is often credited as being the primary theorist who began the practice of applying behavioral theory to family problems in the 1960s. His work at the Oregon Social Learning Center, especially in training parents to act as agents of change in their children's environment, led to the identification of a number of behavior problems and corrective interventions. Among the interventions utilized in helping parents and children are **primary rewards,** such as the use of candy, and innovative techniques involving modeling, point systems, time-out, and contingent attention (Patterson & Brodsky, 1966; Patterson, Jones, Whittier, & Wright, 1965; Patterson, McNeal, Hawkins, & Phelps, 1967). Through their observations of parents and children in laboratories and natural environments (such as homes, neighborhoods, and schools), Patterson and his associates have developed a family observational coding system to use in assessing dysfunctional behaviors.

Patterson (1975) has also been instrumental in writing **programmed workbooks for parents** to employ in helping their children, and ultimately their families, modify behaviors. Overall, Patterson is credited as playing a critical role in the extension of learning principles and techniques to family and marital problems. His practical application of social learning theory has had a major impact on family therapy. He has influenced other behaviorists to work from a systemic perspective in dealing with families.

## Neil Jacobson

Neil Jacobson, like a number of prominent theorists in behavioral family therapy, began his work in the 1970s. As a graduate student in psychology at the University of North

Carolina in 1972, he initially intended to be a psychoanalytic and humanistic-oriented clinician. However, after reading Albert Bandura's (1969) *Principles of Behavior Modification*, he "became a born-again behavior therapist" (Hines, 1998, p. 244). The appeal of behaviorism according to Jacobson was not the theory itself but the accountability, empiricism, and methodologies associated with the theory. Jacobson pursued behaviorism with a passion, reading books and articles by Albert Bandura, Walter Mischel, Richard Stuart, Gerald Patterson, and Bob Weiss and arranged to meet some of these individuals at the conferences of the Association for the Advancement of Behavior Therapy (Wood & Jacobson, 1990).

After completing his doctorate, Jacobson settled into an academic career at the University of Washington in 1979. There he developed a clinical practice based on research. His practice helped refine his theoretical contributions to behavioral marital therapy and domestic violence. His graduate students also kept him focused on theory and challenged him to refine it. According to Jacobson, while behaviorism is at the base of his theory, the clinical application of his approach is more eclectic (Hines, 1998). Jacobson crusaded to bridge the gap between "academic statistical research and in-the-trenches, clinical-outcome research" (Wylie, 1999, p. 16).

Jacobson, until his untimely death on June 2, 1999, was on the leading edge of the family therapy field. He was involved in longitudinal research on couples and was constantly making discoveries, some of which were controversial. For example, Jacobson and his colleagues found that 20% of male batterers, whom he designated as Type I or "cobras," have lower (i.e., decelerated) heart rates during times of physical assault, not higher as had previously been assumed (Jacobson, Gottman, & Wu Shortt, 1995). Jacobson, along with his research team, also found that acceptance, that is, loving your partner as a complete person and not focusing on differences, may lead to an ability to overcome fights that continuously focus on the same topic (Christensen & Jacobson, 2000). In addition, such a strategy may promote change.

Jacobson's findings and insights have challenged marital and family therapy practitioners to be more innovative and effective in their work. His nearly 200 research papers and articles as well as nine books are still widely cited and emulated as standards of scholarly and pragmatic writing (Wylie, 1999). Overall, Jacobson's research is a legacy that has contributed greatly to clinicians' understanding of couple interactions and ways of promoting positive family relationships.

# Premises of the Theory

In its simplest forms, behavioral family therapy is based on the theoretical foundations of behavioral therapy in general. An assumption underlying this premise is that all behavior is learned and that people, including families, act according to how they have been previously reinforced. Behavior is maintained by its consequences and will continue unless more rewarding consequences result from new behaviors (Patterson, 1975).

A second major principle of this approach is that maladaptive behaviors, and not underlying causes, should be the targets of change. The primary concern of behaviorists is with changing present behavior, not dealing with historical developments. Ineffective behaviors can be extinguished and replaced with new sequences of behavior patterns. To do this, continuous assessment of treatment is recommended. Tangible behavior changes in the present are the focus of behaviorally based family therapists.

A third premise behind behavioral family therapy is the belief that not everyone in the family has to be treated for change to occur. In fact, many behavioral family therapists work with only one member of a couple or family. In most reported cases involving one individual, the targeted person is the wife. The reason is that women have traditionally been more open to therapy and therapeutic interventions than men. Regardless, in the therapeutic process, behaviorists teach this person new, appropriate, and functional skills, such as **assertiveness** (i.e., asking for what one wants) and **desensitization** (i.e., overcoming unnecessary and debilitating anxiety associated with a particular event) (Goldiamond, 1965; Lazarus, 1968). Behavioral family therapists who are more systemic concentrate on dyadic relationships, such as a parent and child or the couple system (Dattilio, 1998; Gordon & Davidson, 1981; Stuart, 1980, 1998). The idea behind this procedure is that the correction of dysfunctional behaviors in key members of a family results in significant, measurable positive changes in the family as a whole.

Because of its focus on identifiable, overt behavioral changes with individuals sometimes apart from the family as a unit, the behavioral approach is not usually considered a systemic approach to working with families in the fullest sense of the term. However, behaviorism does share with systems theory an emphasis on the importance of "family rules and patterned communication processes, as well as a functional approach to outcome" (Walsh, 1982, p. 17). Furthermore, a number of behaviorally based family therapists, known as functional family therapists, operate from a systemic perspective (e.g., Alexander & Parsons, 1982; Barton & Alexander, 1981).

Regardless of its degree of systems orientation, behavioral family therapy emphasizes the major techniques within a behavioral theory approach, such as stimulus, reinforcement, shaping, and modeling. In addition, some practitioners of this approach incorporate **social exchange theory** (Thibaut & Kelley, 1959), which stresses the rewards and costs of relationships in family life according to a behavioral economy. For example, individuals stay in marital relationships because the rewards they receive are equal to or greater than the cost to them in time, effort, and resources. Otherwise, they leave. A major focus behind the idea of social exchange is mutual reciprocity, for example, pleasantness begets pleasantness.

Many behavioral therapists also emphasize cognitive aspects of treatment (Dattilio & Bevilacqua, 2000; DiGuiseppe, 1988; Epstein, Schlesinger, & Dryden, 1988). In the cognitive-behavioral approach, attention focuses on what family members are thinking, as well as how they are feeling and behaving. The premise behind cognitive-behavioral theory is that "the relationship-related cognitions individuals hold, shape how they think, feel, and behave in couple and family relationships" (Sullivan & Schwebel, 1995, p. 298). Relationship-related cognitions held by individuals concern assumptions about how relationships work and the roles people play in them; expectations and perceptions regarding what particular events occur in relationships; and standards about how individuals in relationships should behave and how relationships ought to work.

In cognitive-behavioral family therapy, there are health promoting relationship-related cognitions that promote growth and negative relationship-related cognitions that lead to distress and conflict. In healthy relationships, partners might believe, for example, that it takes work to build a relationship; that both partners' needs are important; and that relationships are not always going to be free of conflict. Conversely, partners in unhealthy relations might believe that they do not have to work at relationships, that one partner's needs are more important than the other's, and that good relationships are free of conflict.

In addition, therapists must deal with irrational beliefs on the part of resistant family members. Examples of such irrational beliefs (Ellis, 1985, p. 32) include:

- "I must do well at changing myself, and I'm an incompetent, hopeless client if I don't."
- "You [the therapist and others] must help me change, and you're rotten people if you don't."
- "Changing myself must occur quickly and easily, and it's horrible if it doesn't."

# Types of Behavioral and Cognitive-Behavioral Family Therapies

Behaviorism (with or without a cognitive component) has more specific forms of treatment than any other form of family therapy, with the exception of strategic family therapy. The most prevalent forms of behavioral and cognitive-behavioral family therapy are behavioral parent training, behavioral and cognitive-behavioral marriage therapy and education, treatment of sexual dysfunctioning, and functional family therapy.

## Behavioral Parent Training

Behavioral parent training is sometimes referred to as **parent-skills training**. In this model, the therapist serves as a social learning educator whose prime responsibility is to change parents' responses to a child or children, both through thoughts and actions. By effecting such a change in parents, children's behavior is altered. This type of treatment is linear in nature, and therapists who utilize it are precise and direct in following a set procedure.

For example, one of the initial and main tasks of the therapist is to define a specific problem behavior. The behavior is monitored in regard to its antecedents and consequences. The parents are then trained in social learning theory (Bandura, 1969). Parent-training procedures usually include verbal and performance methods. Verbal methods involve didactic instruction as well as written materials. The aim is to influence thoughts and messages. Performance training methods may involve role playing, modeling, behavioral rehearsal, and prompting. Their focus is on improving parent/child interactions. Regardless of the form of the training, parents are asked to chart the problem behavior over the course of treatment. Successful efforts are rewarded through encouragement and compliments by the therapist.

## Marriage/Couples Therapies and Education

The initial efforts in behavioral marital/couple therapy were initiated by Robert Liberman (1970) and Richard Stuart (1969). Liberman expressed his approach to couples in the language of behavioral analysis and worked with families to define specific behavioral goals. His initial efforts to help couples were based on operant conditioning and included such techniques as positive reinforcement, shaping, and modeling. Later, he and his colleagues devised a more sophisticated behavioral approach that included aspects of social learning theory and communications theory (Liberman, Wheeler, deVisser, Kuehnel, & Kuehnel, 1980). This more refined focus helped couples recognize and increase their positive interactions while eliminating negative interactions. The approach also focused on problem solving, building communication skills, and teaching couples how to use contingency contracts in order to negotiate the resolution of persistent problems.

Stuart's early initiatives in marital/couple therapy were described as an operant interpersonal approach. He assumed that, as in exchange theory (Thibaut & Kelley, 1959), the interactions between spouses at any one time were the most rewarding of alternative possibilities. He also believed, like Don Jackson, that successful relationships were based on a quid pro quo formula (i.e., something for something). To take advantage of the positive basis of relationships, Stuart proposed that couples make explicit reinforcement contracts with each other that were of a positive nature. He later refined his theory to include an eight-step model designed to accelerate positive behavioral change (Stuart, 1980, 1998).

Among the most creative of Stuart's techniques to increase consistent pleasure within marriages is one called **caring days.** In this procedure, one or both marital partners act as if they care about their spouse regardless of the other's action(s). This type of technique, which is at the heart of Stuart's approach, embodies the idea of a **positive risk,** which is a unilateral action that is not dependent on another for success. Stuart has been quite detailed in describing his behavioral theory and methods in couple treatment, as indicated by the caring days contract shown in Figure 7.1.

Overall, behavioral marital/couple therapy typically includes four basic components (Hahlweg, Baucom, & Markman, 1988):

1. *A behavioral analysis of the couple's marital distress.* This analysis is based on interviewing, administering self-report questionnaires, and making behavioral observations.
2. *The establishment of positive reciprocity.* This type of behavior is generated through techniques such as "caring days" and contingency contracts.
3. *Communication skills training.* In this type of training, couples learn to use **"I" statements** to express their feelings. They also learn to stick to here-and-now problems, rather than dwell on the past. Furthermore, they begin to describe their spouse's specific behavior rather than apply a label to it, such as "lazy," "aloof," or "frigid." Finally, in this type of training, couples are taught how to provide positive feedback to their significant other in response to similar behavior from that person.
4. *Training in problem solving.* This component of behavioral marital therapy helps equip couples with new problem-solving skills, such as specifying what they want, negotiating for it, and making a contract.

A more recent form of behavioral marital/couple therapy is **integrative behavioral couple therapy (IBCT),** which emphasizes promoting acceptance into the traditional focus of behavioral couple therapy on overt behavioral change (Cordova, Jacobson, & Christensen, 1998). The idea is "that not all aspects of a couple's relationship are amenable to negotiated change. . . . In general, promoting acceptance helps couples identify those aspects of their relationship that are unlikely to change [**unresolvable problems**] and coaches them in ways of coming to terms with those problems" (p. 439).

| Bill | Agreements | Jocelyn |
|---|---|---|
| 9/3  9/4  9/6  9/7  9/8  9/9<br>9/10 9/11 9/12 9/14<br>9/17 9/20 9/21 | Ask how I spent the day. | 9/3  9/4  9/6  9/7  9/8  9/9<br>9/10 9/12 9/14 9/16<br>9/20 9/21 9/23 |
| 9/3  9/4  9/9<br>9/10 9/14 9/16<br>9/20 9/21 9/22 9/23 | Offer to get the cream or sugar for me. | 9/4  9/9<br>9/12 9/15<br>9/23 |
| 9/3  9/7  9/9<br>9/15<br>9/21 9/23 | Listen to "mood music" when we set the clock radio to go to sleep. | 9/3  9/7  9/9<br>9/15<br>9/21 9/23 |
| 9/7  9/8<br>9/11<br>9/19 | Hold my hand when we go for walks. | 9/7  9/8<br>9/11 9/16<br>9/19 9/21 9/23 |
| 9/9<br>9/14 9/16<br>9/23 | Put down the paper or your book and look at me when we converse. | 9/4  9/6  9/7  9/8<br>9/10 9/13 9/14 9/16<br>9/18 9/20 9/21 9/22 9/24 |
| 9/4  9/7<br>9/11 9/12 9/14 9/16<br>9/21 9/23 | Rub my back. | 9/5  9/8<br>9/10 9/14 9/15<br>9/19 |
| 9/3  9/4  9/5  9/7  9/8<br>9/11 9/16<br>9/19 | Tuck in the sheets and blankets before we go to bed. | 9/6  9/9<br><br>9/23 |
| 9/3  9/8<br>9/15<br>9/17 | Call me during the day. | 9/5  9/6  9/7  9/8  9/9<br>9/11 9/13 9/14 9/16<br>9/18 9/20 9/21 9/22 9/23 |
| 9/4  9/6<br>9/13<br> | Offer to play short games with the children when my friends drop in for a few minutes. | 9/8<br>9/12 9/15<br>9/21 |
| 9/7<br>9/11 9/16<br>9/23 | Offer to read the rough drafts of my reports and offer comments. | 9/9<br><br>9/20 |
| 9/5  9/7  9/8  9/9<br>9/11 9/14 9/17<br>9/18 9/21 | Sit down with me when I have coffee even if you don't want any, just for the company. | 9/7<br>9/10 9/13<br>9/23 |
| 9/7<br>9/12<br>9/20 9/23 | Call my folks just to say "hello." | 9/9<br><br>9/23 |
| 9/6  9/7<br>9/15<br>9/18 9/20 9/23 | Fold the laundry. | 9/9<br>9/10 9/14 9/15<br>9/20 |
| 9/4  9/7  9/9<br>9/13<br>9/18 | Buy me a $1 present. | 9/8  9/9<br>9/12 9/14<br>9/21 9/23 |

**Figure 7.1**

Caring days agreement.

From *Helping Couples Change: A Social Learning Approach to Marital Therapy* (p. 200) by R. B. Stuart, 1980, New York: Guilford. Reprinted by permission of the publisher.

Results show more nonblaming descriptions of problems and more **soft emotions** (for example, hurt, loneliness, insecurity, fear) that reveal personal vulnerability and that are more likely to evoke empathy from one's partner as well as emotional closeness.

As mentioned earlier, cognitive-behavioral approaches to working with couples are also strong. For example, Ellis uses rational emotive behavior therapy (REBT) to help couples dispute irrational thoughts they have about themselves, their spouses, or their marriages. In this **ABC procedure**, A stands for the event, B stands for the thought, and C stands for the emotion. The event might be, for example, forgetting a spouse's request to get something from the store. The other spouse might react negatively and think, for example, that "he doesn't love me anymore," which could lead to depression or other unhealthy emotions. Through disputation, the therapist could help the spouse and the couple to learn to think about events either neutrally (e.g., "He did not bring home what I requested.") or positively (e.g., "Because my spouse did not get what I requested, I can now ask for more, and I am sure he/she will be more sensitive this time.").

Other methods cognitive-behavioral family therapists use with couples are teaching them **cognitive distraction** (thinking of other than negative things), **self-control strategies** such as how to employ rational coping statements, and **psychoeducational methods** (i.e., reading books, attending workshops, and listening to audiovisual material) (Ellis, 1993, 2000; Lazarus, 2000). Other than self-control strategies, another type of self-control strategy is known as **relapse prevention** (RP). This cognitive-behavioral approach "enables clients to learn self-control strategies to prevent relapse" and has been applied to the areas of substance abuse, sex offenders, and anger as well as family therapy (Curich & Stone, 1998, p. 328). In the psychoeducational method, individuals are taught to be more aware of their relationship-related cognitions and the benefits and deficits of these thoughts. This strategy shows promise in reducing the divorce rate for participants (Gottman & Silver, 2000; O'Leary & Smith, 1991). It also could have a favorable effect on couple and family units (Schwebel & Fine, 1994).

## Treatment of Sexual Dysfunctioning

The behavioral treatment of sexual dysfunctionality came of age in the United States in the late 1960s and early 1970s with the publication of Masters and Johnson's *Human Sexual Response* (1966) and *Human Sexual Inadequacy* (1970). Prior to these publications, "people with sexual dysfunctions relied primarily on folk cures or saw psychodynamically oriented therapists, who offered long-term insight-oriented treatment with questionable results" (Piercy & Sprenkle, 1986, p. 94).

Masters and Johnson (1970) were not original in all of their contributions, but from their research and clinical observations, they delineated **four phases of sexual responsiveness:** excitement, plateau, orgasm, and resolution. They also discovered the importance of learning in the remediation of sexual dysfunctioning and the importance of behavioral techniques. In their approach to the treatment of sexual dysfunctionality, techniques are tailored to specific problems. In almost all cases, however, couples are taught to relax and enjoy touching and being touched. Then, through *in vivo* desensitization, they learn how to gradually become more intimate with one another and how to feel comfortable either asking for sex or refusing it. For couples who have specific problems, specialized treatments are used. For example, in treating premature ejaculation, the **squeeze technique** (in which the woman learns to stimulate and stop the ejaculation urge in a man through physically stroking and firmly grasping his penis) is used. Other treatments, such as the **teasing technique** (in which a woman starts and stops stimulating a man) are also employed to overcome performance anxiety.

Masters and Johnson stressed the conjoint treatment of couples using a dual-sex therapy team. A basic assumption in the Masters and Johnson approach is that there is no such thing as an uninvolved partner in a relationship in which some form of sexual inadequacy exists. To tailor a treatment plan for a couple, Masters and Johnson (1966, 1970) took an extensive sexual history on each partner, a practice that is still followed. Their work from beginning to end is systemic.

In addition to Masters and Johnson, Helen Singer Kaplan (1974) developed direct behavioral treatment strategies to work with couples and combined this approach with psychoanalytic techniques. Unlike Masters and Johnson, Kaplan's approach employs an outpatient treatment practice. According to Kaplan, couple sexual dysfunctioning can result from one force or a combination of forces, for example, **intrapsychic conflict** (e.g., guilt, trauma, or shame), **interpersonal couple conflict** (e.g., marital discord, distrust), and **anxiety** (e.g., pressure to please, fear of failure).

Joseph LoPiccolo (1978) and associates have also reported success with behavioral sex therapy techniques. In analyzing the success of heterosexual couples in behavioral sex therapy, Heiman, LoPiccolo, and LoPiccolo (1981) reported that behavioral approaches had the following elements in common:

- the reduction of performance anxiety
- sex education including the use of sexual techniques
- skill training in communications
- attitude change methodologies

Overall, the behavioral treatment of sexual dysfunctioning is rich in pragmatic and specific techniques. It includes the modification of thoughts (e.g., attitudes, beliefs), as well as behaviors.

## Functional Family Therapy

For functional family therapists, all behavior is adaptive and serves a function. Behaviors represent an effort by the family to meet needs in personal and interpersonal relationships. Ultimately, behaviors help family members achieve one of three interpersonal states (Alexander & Parsons, 1982):

1. *Contact/closeness (merging).* In the contact/closeness state, family members are drawn together (e.g., in their concern over the delinquent behavior of a juvenile).
2. *Distance/independence (separating).* In this state, family members learn to stay away from each other for fear of fighting.
3. *A combination of 1 and 2 (midpointing).* In this situation, family members fluctuate in their emotional reactions to each other so that individuals are both drawn toward and repelled from each other.

Functional family therapy, which is systemic, is a three-stage process. In the first stage, assessment, the focus is on the function that the behavioral sequences serve. The question is "Do behavioral sequences promote closeness, create distances, or help the family achieve a task?" The therapist determines this through gathering information about the family both by asking questions and by observing.

The second stage of therapy involves change. The purpose is to help the family become more functional. It is carried out by:

- clarifying relationship dynamics
- interrelating thoughts, feelings, and behaviors of family members
- interpreting the functions of current family behavior
- relabeling behavior so as to alleviate blame
- discussing how the removal of a behavior will affect the family
- shifting the treatment from one individual to the entire family

The third and final stage of functional family therapy, maintenance, focuses on educating the family and training them in skills that will be useful in dealing with future difficulties. Specific skills taught during this stage of therapy are those dealing with effective communication, team building, and behavioral management (e.g., contracting).

# Treatment Techniques

As a rule, behavioral and cognitive-behavioral family therapists use a variety of learning theory techniques to bring about change in families. Originally devised for treating individuals, these techniques are modified and applied to problems encountered by couples and families. Among the most well known of these procedures are positive reinforcement, extinction, shaping, desensitization, contingency contracts, and cognitive/behavior modification. These techniques and others are described in the following sections. They are usually applied in combination so that family members learn individually and/or collectively how to give recognition and approval for desired behavior, instead of rewarding maladaptive actions.

> A review of behavioral-family-therapy practice reveals that a relatively small number of interventions tend to form the basis for most therapeutic plans across a broad range of settings. They include education, communication and problem-solving training, operant conditioning approaches, and contingency management. (Falloon, 1991, p. 81)

## Education

Education includes the use of didactic lectures, visual aids, books, handouts, and intimate discussions. These educational methods are intended to help family members learn more about how relationships work as well as see the rationale behind the strategies employed in helping them relate better to one another. For instance, Lazarus (2000) points out that research indicates that the difference between happy and dysfunctional couples is not related to the intensity of their disagreements, but to the frequency and types of negative behaviors during such times, for example, criticism, contempt, defensiveness, and stonewalling (Gottman, Coan, Carrere, & Swanson, 1998). Couples who are informed about this matter can try to alter their behavior accordingly. Similarly, couples and families can read books, such as Fay's (1999) *Making It As a Couple* or Gottman and Silver's (2000) *The Seven Principles for Making Marriage Work* and learn more about relationship traps and tools to repair relationships. Overall, Lazarus (2000) advocates the use of "didactic and pedagogical strategies" (p. 226) in working with couples and families. Such methods help couples and families help themselves.

## Communication and Problem-Solving Strategies

Communication and problem-solving strategies and techniques are intended to help families develop mutually enhancing social exchanges. "Instruction, modeling, and positive reinforcement (e.g., praise) are used to enhance communication skills until a level of competence has been achieved that satisfies the family and therapist" (Falloon, 1991, p. 82). Problem solving is directed at the resolution of conflict within the family.

## Operant Conditioning

Operant conditioning is employed mostly in parent/child relationships. "The most common approach involves teaching parents to use shaping and time out procedures to increase the desirable behavior patterns in children" (Falloon, 1991, p. 83).

## Contracting

**Contracting** is used when family interactions have reached a severe level of hostility. Contracts build in rewards for behaving in a certain manner. A **token economy** is one type of contract; but in many cases, more sophisticated ways of earning points and reinforcing appropriate behavior are used.

The following sections highlight more specific techniques used in the four behavioral and cognitive-behavior family therapy approaches. Almost all of these techniques are used frequently in various forms of behavioral and cognitive-behavioral family therapy. They have the common characteristics of being operationally definable, precise, and measurable. They are applicable to psychological and, in some cases, sexual situations. Furthermore, they foster change through having clients try new forms of acting. Overall, they are able to bring about fairly rapid and significant change in a short period of time. (Meichenbaum's self-instructional training and stress inoculation techniques are particularly suited for children.)

## Classical Conditioning

**Classical conditioning** is the oldest form of behaviorism. In it, a stimulus that is originally neutral is paired up with another event to elicit certain emotions through association. In the case of Pavlov's dogs, the ringing of a bell was paired with the presenting of food so that the sound of the bell elicited a salutary response in the dogs. In families, classical conditioning is used to associate a person with a gratifying behavior, such as a pat on the back or a kind word. For instance, when a preschool child gets dressed, a parent might gently touch and praise him or her immediately after the task is completed. Through such a timely and rewarding interaction, the child may come to view the parent in a different and more positive way, that is, one that represents a pleasant association. Therefore, the relationship becomes more valued.

## Coaching

In **coaching,** a therapist helps individuals, couples, or families make appropriate responses by giving them verbal instructions. For example, the therapist might say: "Sally, when you want John to make eye contact with you and he is looking around, gently touch him on the knee. John, that will be your signal to look directly at Sally." Just as athletes excel through coaching, individuals, couples, and families do best when they are informed about what to do and then have an opportunity to practice their new responses.

## Contingency Contracting

In **contingency contracting** (see Figure 7.2) "a specific, usually written schedule or contract [describes] the terms for the trading or exchange of behaviors and reinforcers between two or more individuals" (Sauber, L'Abate, & Weeks, 1985, p. 34). One action is contingent, or dependent, on another. For example, a child and her parent may write up an agreement whereby the daughter will receive an allowance of 5 dollars a week upon taking the garbage out every day after supper. The way this type of contract is assessed is known as contingency management.

## Extinction

**Extinction** is the process by which previous **reinforcers** of an action are withdrawn so that behavior returns to its original level. For example, a child is ignored by a parent when having a temper tantrum. Similarly, a spouse may not be rewarded by his mate for saying unkind remarks. In almost all cases of extinction, it is important that a replacement behavior be positively reinforced to take the place of the behavior that is being extinguished. For example, in the case of the child or the spouse just mentioned, attention should be given to appropriate or pleasing behaviors.

Contingency Contract
week one
(must earn 5 points for a reward)

| | make bed | clean room | hang up clothes | pick up toys | set table | read a book | Goal |
|---|---|---|---|---|---|---|---|
| George | ✓ | ✓ | | ✓ | ✓ | ✓ | Pizza |
| Will | | ✓ | | ✓ | | | Baseball game |
| Ann | ✓ | ✓ | ✓ | ✓ | ✓ | ✓ | Spend-the-night party |

**Figure 7.2**
Contingency contract.

## Positive Reinforcement

A **positive reinforcer** is usually a material (e.g., food, money, or medals) or a social action (e.g., a smile or praise) that increases desired behaviors. For a reinforcer to be positive, the person involved must be willing to work for it. For example, children are often willing to perform certain actions when the reward is money, candy, or tokens. Adults may be prone to work for verbal or physical recognitions such as praise or smiles.

## Quid pro Quo

Literally translated, the Latin phrase *quid pro quo* means "something for something." Behavioral marital contracts are often based on quid pro quo—that is, a spouse agrees to do something as long as the other spouse does something comparable. For example, in maintaining a house, one spouse may agree to do the dishes if the other does the laundry. In a quid pro quo arrangement, everyone wins. When quid pro quo arrangements are in written form, they often take the form of contingency contracts.

## Reciprocity

The concept of **reciprocity** involves "the likelihood that two people will reinforce each other at approximately equitable rates over time" (Piercy & Sprenkle, 1986, p. 76). Many marital behavior therapists view marriage as based on this principle (Stuart, 1969). When spouses are not reinforced reciprocally, one of them will often leave the relationship either emotionally or physically. For example, if a spouse feels he or she is doing most of the couple's work, such as paying the bills and keeping the house, but is not receiving adequate appreciation, he or she may stop taking care of these duties.

## Shaping

The process of learning in small, gradual steps is called **shaping.** It is often referred to as "successive approximation" (Bandura, 1969). For example, during potty training, children are reinforced in small steps from "running to the potty," to "pulling down their pants," to "sitting on the potty," to "having a bowel movement in the potty." Gradually, children put all of these actions together. In a similar fashion, couples learn to say and act in routine ways that help them bond. For instance, he fixes breakfast in the morning while she takes a shower and gets dressed; then they share a meal and conversation together; then she fixes his lunch and starts the car while he gets dressed; and, finally, they leave for work together.

## Systematic Desensitization

The process of **systematic desensitization** is one in which a person's dysfunctional anxiety is reduced or eliminated through pairing it with incompatible behavior, such as muscular or mental relaxation. This is a gradual procedure in which progressively higher levels of anxiety are treated one step at a time (Wolpe, 1969). This treatment is one of the main approaches to several forms of sexual disorders, such as vaginismus. It may also be used to help individuals feel less anxious about stating what they need from other members of the family. In all such instances, a hierarchy of troublesome behaviors is set up and worked through (see Figure 7.3).

| Targeted Behavior: Speaking to others without being anxious | |
|---|---|
| *Event* | *Anxiety Rating* |
| Speaking in public to a large audience (20 people or more) | 100% |
| Speaking in public to a small audience (e.g., my scout troop) | 90% |
| Speaking with a group of strangers | 80% |
| Speaking casually with someone in a public place | 70% |
| Speaking to someone at a social event | 55% |
| Speaking casually with someone when we are alone | 40% |
| Speaking with my friends when I have an idea | 30% |
| Speaking with my friends in casual conversation | 15% |
| Speaking with my family | 5% |
| Being alone | 0% |

**Figure 7.3**
Hierarchy of a troublesome behavior.

## Time-Out

The process of **time-out** involves the removal of persons (most often children) from an environment in which they have been reinforced for certain actions. Isolation, or time-out, from reinforcement for a limited amount of time (approximately 5 minutes) results in the cessation of the targeted action. For example, a child who is biting his sibling during play has to sit down in a separate room and face a wall for 5 minutes each time it happens.

> Time outs can be used to shape the behaviors of normal children as well as the maladaptive behaviors of problem children. Time outs are best accompanied by a retraining program in which rewards are given when the undesirable behavior is absent for an agreed-upon period of time or if a competing new desirable behavior occurs several times a day. (Thomas, 1992, p. 288)

## Charting

The procedure of **charting** involves asking a client or clients to keep an accurate record of the problematic behavior (Katkin, 1978). The idea is to get the family member to establish a **baseline** (i.e., a recording of the occurrence of targeted behaviors before an intervention is made). From this baseline, modifications can be made to reduce problem behaviors. For instance, a couple might be asked to make a chart of the number of fights they have a day and the type of fights that occur. Similarly, a child may be asked to keep a chart of the number of fights he or she has with parents and when they occur.

## Premack Principle

The **Premack principle** is a behavioral intervention in which family members must first do less pleasant tasks before they are allowed to engage in pleasurable activities (Premack, 1965). For example, a child having problems with schoolwork would be required to do his or her homework before going outside to play. This technique may have as a by-product closer parent/child relationships because parents serve as reinforcers for their children's task accomplishment.

## Disputing Irrational Thoughts

**Disputing irrational thoughts** through the use of an *ABC* format (*A* stands for the event, *B* stands for the thought, and *C* stands for the emotion) was discussed previously. It is crucial to realize that in disputing—for example, with couples—the absurdity of irrational thoughts is often stressed by cognitive-behavioral family therapists with remarks such as "Where is it written that you should have all your needs filled in marriage?" (Ellis et al., 1989). It is hoped that through disputing, couples and families will develop more rational thoughts and behaviors.

## Thought Stopping

The technique of **thought stopping** is used when a family member unproductively obsesses about an event or person. The therapist teaches the individual, or even in unusual cases the whole family, how to stop this repetitive and unhealthy behavior. This is done through inviting the person or persons involved to begin ruminating on a certain thought, for example, "My life is unfair." In the midst of this rumination, the therapist yells, "Stop!" This unexpected response disrupts the person's or family's thought process. Instruction is then given to those involved on how to move from an external disruption like the one they just had to an internal process. As in the case of disputation, neutral or healthy thoughts are substituted for those that have been nonproductive or unhealthy.

## Self-Instructional Training

Self-instructional training is a form of self-management that focuses on people instructing themselves (Meichenbaum, 1977). It is assumed that self-instruction affects behavior and behavioral change. Thus, problems may be based on maladaptive self-statements. In self-instructional training, a self-statement can serve as a practical clue in recalling a desirable behavioral sequence, or it can interrupt automatic behaviors or cognitive thought chains and thereby encourage more adaptive coping strategies. In families, spouses can use this approach in dealing with each other; however, it is more often employed in helping impulsive children "modulate their impulsivity through deliberate and task-oriented 'self-talk'" (Schwebel & Fine, 1994, p. 26).

## Modeling and Role Playing

**Modeling** and **role playing** can take many forms (Bandura, 1977). In certain situations, family members might be asked to "**act as if**" they were the person they wanted to be ideally. In other cases, family members might practice a number of behaviors to see which work best. Feedback and corrective action, which are a part of modeling and role playing, can be given by the therapist or by other family members.

"Shame attack," a process within role playing, occurs when a family member does something he or she has previously dreaded (Ellis, 2000), for example, asking for an allowance.

Individuals who use this technique find that when they do not get what they asked for, they are not worse off for having asked. Similarly, family members may steel themselves for what lies ahead through a **stress inoculation** (Meichenbaum, 1985). In this process, members break down potentially stressful events into manageable units that they can think about and handle through problem-solving techniques. Then the units are linked together so that the entire possible event can be envisioned and handled appropriately.

# Role of the Therapist

In behavioral and cognitive-behavioral family therapies, the therapist is the expert and teacher (Schwebel & Fine, 1992). He or she helps families identify dysfunctional behaviors and then works with these families to set up behavioral and cognitive-behavioral management programs that will assist them in bringing about change. Part of the process of teaching new behaviors to families includes modeling, giving corrective feedback, and learning how to assess behavior modification.

To be effective, the therapist has to learn to play many roles and be flexible. This process has been described as the **Anatomy of Intervention Model (AIM)** (Alexander, 1988). AIM delineates five phases in therapy: (1) introduction, (2) assessment, (3) motivation, (4) behavior change, and (5) termination. "Each phase has different goals, central tasks, needed skills of the therapist, and therapeutic activities or techniques" (Thomas, 1992, p. 289). In addition to utilizing structural skills to achieve the goals of each phase, a therapist must also be able to exhibit relationship skills such as warmth, humor, nonblaming, and self-disclosure. From a behavioral and cognitive-behavioral perspective, the effective treatment of a family is complex.

Cognitive-behavioral family therapists, in particular, concentrate on modifying or changing family members' cognitions as well as their interactions (Dattilio & Bevilacqua, 2000; Schwebel & Fine, 1992). For instance, a negative thought by a son about his father might be "He cares more about his work than he does me." Such a cognition might be modified to "He cares about me, but he has to work long hours and sometimes cannot give me the type of attention I want." To make changes in thoughts and consequently behaviors, cognitive-behavioral family therapists spend more time discussing issues with family members than do strictly behavioral family therapists.

Being a behavioral or cognitive-behavioral family therapist means taking an active part in designing and implementing specific strategies to help families. Such a process can help members eliminate dysfunctional behaviors and replace them with more effective ways of relating. Behavioral and cognitive-behavioral family therapists must have persistence, patience, knowledge of learning theory, and specificity in working with family members. Therapeutic interventions require a great deal of energy and investment.

# Process and Outcome

If behavioral and cognitive-behavioral family therapy is successful, family members will learn how to modify, change, or increase certain behaviors and/or cognitions in order to function more effectively. Simultaneously, they will learn how to eliminate or decrease maladaptive or undesirable behaviors, including negative thoughts. Behavioral and cognitive-behavioral family therapies stress the employment of specific techniques aimed at particularly important actions. For example, a behavioral approach used in marital therapy might concentrate on communication skills in which a couple is taught to listen, to make requests using "I" statements, to give positive feedback, to use immediate reinforcement, and to clarify through questioning the meaning of verbal and nonverbal behaviors (Stuart, 1980).

Behavioral family therapy focuses in particular on increasing parenting skills, facilitating positive couple communication and interaction, and improving sexual behaviors. Cognitive-behavioral family therapy is most powerful in helping families deal with stress (Freeman & Zaken-Greenberg, 1989), addiction (Schlesinger, 1988), and adult sexual dysfunctions (Walen & Perlmutter, 1988). In practice, blending of the behavioral and cognitive-behavioral techniques often occurs.

By the end of treatment, couples and individuals should be able to modify their own maladaptive behaviors and/or cognitions. They should also be able to lower their anxieties about troublesome situations by using relaxation procedures, such as desensitization or thought stopping.

# Unique Aspects of Behavioral and Cognitive-Behavioral Approaches

Behavioral and cognitive-behavioral family therapies, like other therapeutic approaches, have both unique and universal points. Practitioners who are considering using these approaches need to be sure they are aware of the commonalties and differences imbedded in their theory and practice. In this way, they can ensure themselves and others of the best possible outcome.

## Emphases

One unique characteristic of behavioral and cognitive-behavioral family therapies involves the theory behind these approaches. The behavioral and cognitive-behavioral approaches utilize learning theory, which is a well-formulated and highly researched way of working with people. Learning theory focuses on pinpointing problem behaviors and making use of behavioral and cognitive techniques, such as setting up contingency contracts, reinforcement, punishment, and extinction.

Another emphasis of behavioral and cognitive-behavioral family therapy approaches is research. The results of applying learning theory to families indicate that such a process gives parents a management tool that works at home and has a carryover effect at school. Behavioral family therapy aimed at one child's dysfunctional behavior seems to generalize in many cases so as to positively influence interactions with other children, especially siblings. Parental self-esteem and the family's ability to function seems to improve adequately as well (Gurman, Kniskern, & Pinsof, 1985).

A third aspect of these approaches involves continued evolvement. Behavioral family therapy has evolved from a focus on parent management to a focus on the family as a system (i.e., functional family therapy). In addition, behavioral family therapy has incorporated many ideas from cognitive approaches in its handling of families (Falloon, 1988). Because of their considerable flexibility, behavioral and cognitive-behavioral family therapies are able to focus on a variety of problems and concerns, from promoting changes within individuals in families to altering family interaction styles. Likewise, the procedures and processes within behavioral and cognitive-behavioral family therapies have influenced other approaches, such as the structuralists in their treatment of anorexia nervosa (Minuchin, Rosman, & Baker, 1978).

A fourth unique quality of behavioral and cognitive-behavioral family therapies is that treatment is short term. Therapists who work from these perspectives "take presenting problems seriously and examine them in their interpersonal context" (Fish, 1988, p. 15). Thus, on a more microscopic level, the therapist is able to break down the problem into definable parts and then target strategies to either teach skills or extinguish behaviors associated with difficulties.

A fifth emphasis of behavioral and cognitive-behavioral family therapies is that they reject the medical model of abnormal behavior. "Behavior therapists believe many problems result from inadequate personal, social, or work-related skills . . . [and that] inadequately skilled clients need training" (Fish, 1988, p. 15). Time is not spent on looking for biological or chemical causes of behavior or cognition, nor is time spent on examining the history of the client. Because of an immediate focus, problems can be addressed more directly and efficiently without labeling (Atwood, 1992).

Overall, "behavioral family therapy has been demonstrated to have specific benefits in the treatment of conduct disorders of childhood and adolescence" (Falloon, 1991, p. 88). Combined with cognitive processes, it is useful in the management of many adult mental disorders, such as depression. Overall, behavioral and cognitive-behavioral family therapies can be useful on a number of levels as long as they are employed as part of a comprehensive treatment plan that takes into account the uniqueness of families.

## Comparison with Other Theories

Compared with other ways of working with families, behavioral and cognitive-behavioral family therapies are less systemic. The orientation of learning theory, on which these approaches are based, is to bring about linear changes in individuals or subunits of the family. Such a perspective often hinders the introduction of a complete family change process. For example, in behavior parent training, a child may be viewed as "the problem" that the therapist needs "to fix." With such a view, modification of behaviors and/or cognitions that would benefit everyone in the family, such as learning to communicate more clearly, are not addressed.

Another distinction of behavioral family therapy is that some behavioral family therapists do not focus on the affective components of behavior, such as feelings. Instead, they look primarily at behaviors and secondarily at thoughts (i.e., cognitive-behaviors) (Piercy & Sprenkle, 1986). Thus, some family members who have been through this type of treatment may act properly but not feel or think differently. In such cases, the operational procedures are successful, but a price is paid in regard to helping the recipients of the services access their emotions and thoughts.

A third distinct aspect of behavioral and cognitive-behavioral family therapies compared with others is their preciseness. Some therapists who use these approaches think they need to be rigid in their application. Their lack of spontaneity and dependence on techniques may result in their losing rapport with families. In such cases, both the family and therapist end up becoming frustrated, and the therapy is not as effective as it might be otherwise (Wood & Jacobson, 1990).

A fourth aspect of behavioral and cognitive-behavioral family therapies compared with other approaches is the consideration of historical data. Although it is true that as behaviorists Masters and Johnson (1970) emphasize the importance of sexual histories, their approach is more the exception than the rule. By not attending to the past, users of behavioral and cognitive-behavioral family theory may misunderstand family patterns and dynamics. Once a symptomatic behavior is eliminated, another one may appear out of habit or tradition. For example, alcoholism may be brought under control while workaholism emerges.

A final comparable dimension of the behavioral and cognitive-behavioral perspective in family therapy is that these approaches generally stress family action over family insight. As a result, too much emphasis may be given to the employment of methods that facilitate change without ensuring family members' comprehension. For instance, in a situation in which a child has been acting out, parents might learn to use behavioral techniques, such as time-out; but they might not comprehend the dynamics that led to the child's misbehavior in the first place.

## CASE ILLUSTRATION

### THE BROWN FAMILY

Bob Brown, age 50, has reached a stalemate with his wife, Amy, age 47. They are a dual-career couple and have been highly successful financially. Yet Bob is tired of being on the road three nights a week and wants to take an early retirement. Amy, who loves her in-home computer job, cannot imagine such a situation. Bob, a former football athlete, has always had plenty of energy and drive. His early retirement would mean he would be around the house more and probably interfere with her business and routine. As an only child, Amy values her space and privacy. Now that Bob, Jr., age 17, is ready to go to college, she thinks that her husband should "stick it out" for at least 4 or 5 more years for the good of the family.

Bob disagrees. He has a history of heart trouble, and his father died of a heart attack at age 62 during Bob's senior year of college. He wants to quit his job now. He believes that if he stays on much longer, he will become very unhappy and distressed. Open fights that last late into the night began about a month ago. No one in the family is saying anything constructive to anyone else. The tension is as thick as an early morning fog.

### Conceptualization of Family: Behavioral and Cognitive-Behavioral Perspective

The Browns both have strong beliefs about what should occur. Yet, they lack the proper skills to negotiate and settle their dispute. Bob thinks he has worked hard and deserves a rest. He also thinks he will endanger his health by continuing in his present position. Amy thinks if he quits now, he will get in her way and, in addition, not be able to help their son through college. Neither one is reinforcing the other. The result is disruptive behavior and fights that are growing in intensity.

### Process of Treatment: Behavioral and Cognitive-Behavioral Family Therapies

To help the Browns, a behavioral or cognitive-behavioral family therapist would work with the couple to set up a quid pro quo relationship. This would most likely mean drawing up a contingency contract that would describe the terms for exchanging behaviors and reinforcers. For example, if Bob is going to give up his job, he might agree to do it gradually, instead of all at once. Furthermore, regardless of the manner in which he quit his job, he would come to an agreement with Amy as to how much time per day he would spend around the house and with her. On Amy's part, she would be explicit about what time she would like to have Bob at home. Beliefs as well as wishes would be aired.

Once decisions regarding Bob's job and time together were settled, the couple would concentrate with the therapist on the extinction of negative behaviors, such as fights and irrational thoughts. For instance, they might use thought stopping or disputation to deal with the underlying cognitions that lead to their conflict. At the same time, the couple would work on the establishment of reinforcing behaviors, for example, establishing enough time alone for Amy and adequate time together for Bob. Specific rewards could be built into the contingency contract, and the contract itself could be prominently displayed on the refrigerator or some other mutually agreed on setting.

To help the couple and the family as a whole, the therapist might need to help shape their behaviors toward one another and give them a means to disengage from negative interactions, such as the use of time-out. Through all of this action, the couple and therapist would chart the behaviors displayed and refine the process of working with each other on a weekly basis.

# Summary and Conclusion

Behavioral and cognitive-behavioral family therapies are relatively recent phenomena that are based on one of the most thoroughly researched approaches in the helping professions—learning theory. The origin of the theory can be traced back to the beginning of the 20th century. It included such luminaries as Ivan Pavlov, John B. Watson, and B. F. Skinner.

Behavioral family therapy has four basic forms: behavioral parent training, behavioral marital therapy, treatment of sexual dysfunctionality, and functional family therapy. These emphases often utilize cognitive-behavioral methods. All except the last approach are linear and stress individual or dyadic relationships. Many of the interventions used in behavioral and cognitive-behavioral family therapies are the same as those employed in individual treatment. Reinforcement, shaping, modeling, role playing, thought stopping, and extinction are common. However, aspects of behavioral and cognitive-behavioral family therapies also include novel implementations such as contingency contracts, unilateral contracts, and behaviors based on the principle of quid pro quo.

In their therapeutic role, both the behaviorist and cognitive-behaviorist are the experts, teachers, and trainers. The instructions of the therapist are usually carried out by an individual, a couple, or a family, and are carefully monitored. Overall, the therapist is quite powerful and rewards positive behaviors and thoughts as often as possible. In his or her central role, the therapist helps clients learn how to reinforce themselves as well.

If all goes well during the treatment process, the results will be measurable. Traditionally, this has included the emergence of overt behaviors such as parent/child interactions. In more recent times, treatment has focused on the modification of cognitive processes as well, such as the elimination of negative self-statements.

At their best, behavioral and cognitive-behavioral family therapies are concrete and readily applicable to helping parents, couples, and families change. A branch of this approach, functional family therapy, is systemic. The basic concepts on which treatment is based have been well researched. Of all the family therapies, behavioral and cognitive-behavioral family approaches are the most scientific.

On the other hand, behavioral and cognitive-behavioral family therapies, for the most part, still continue to rely too heavily on a linear and limited view of families. These approaches assume that if treatment is applied to one unit in the family and to symptoms, the other aspects of the family will change.

# Summary Table

## Behavioral and Cognitive-Behavioral Family Therapies

### Major Theorists

| | | |
|---|---|---|
| B. F. Skinner | John Watson | Richard Stuart |
| Norman Epstein | Neil Jacobson | Andrew Christensen |
| Gerald Patterson | Robert Weiss | Gayola Margolin |
| Albert Ellis | Albert Bandura | Walter Mischel |
| William Masters | Virginia Johnson | Frank Dattilio |
| John Gottman | Joseph Wolpe | Aaron Beck |
| Donald Meichenbaum | Helen Singer Kaplan | Ed Katkin |

### Premises of the Theory

Behavior is maintained or eliminated by consequences.
Maladaptive behaviors can be unlearned or modified. Adaptive behaviors can be learned.
Likewise, cognitions are either rational or irrational. They can be modified and, as a
    result, bring about a change in couple or family behaviors and interactions.

### Treatment Techniques

In behavioral family therapy, the focus is on parent training, behavioral marriage therapy,
    couple communication, and the treatment of sexual dysfunctions. Cognitive-behav-
    ioral family therapy also emphasizes working with those under stress in the same ways.

Dyads and individuals are seen more than families. The emphasis is on dyadic interactions, except in functional family therapy.

In behavioral family therapy, the emphasis is to bring about behavioral changes by modifying the antecedents or consequences of an action. Special attention is paid to modifying the consequences. Emphasis is on elimination of undesirable behavior and acceleration of positive behavior. Teaching social skills and preventing problems from reoccurring is stressed, too. Promoting competence in individuals and/or couples and fostering an understanding of the dynamics of behavior is highlighted.

In cognitive-behavioral family therapy, the focus is on modifying irrational or unproductive beliefs and the behaviors that go with them.

Behaviorists and cognitive-behaviorists rely primarily on:

- Operant conditioning
- Classical conditioning
- Social learning theory
- Cognitive-behavioral strategies

Techniques include:

- Operant conditioning
- Contracting
- Communication and problem-solving strategies
- Classical conditioning
- Coaching
- Contingency contracting
- Shaping
- Time-out
- Charting
- Premack principle
- Disputing irrational thoughts
- Thought stopping
- Self-instructional training
- Role playing
- Systematic desensitization
- Positive reinforcement
- Intermittent reinforcement
- Generalization
- Fading
- Extinction
- Modeling
- Reciprocity
- Punishment
- Token economies
- Quid pro quo exchanges
- Problem-solving training
- Rational coping statements
- Reframing

- Cognitive distraction
- Psychoeducational methods

### Role of the Therapist

The therapist uses direct and careful assessment and intervention. He or she is a teacher and an expert, as well as a reinforcer. Presenting problems are the focus.

### Process and Outcome

Family members learn to modify, change, or increase/decrease certain behaviors and/or thoughts in order to function more effectively.

Family members eventually are able to modify their own behaviors and cognitions without the aid of a therapist.

### Unique Aspects of Behavioral and Cognitive-Behavioral Approaches

Behavioral and cognitive-behavioral family therapies emphasize:

- straightforwardness with attention paid to observations, measurements, and use of the scientific theory
- the treatment of presenting symptoms and problems
- teaching new social skills and eliminating dysfunctional ones
- positive controls and enlightened education procedures rather than punishment
- with regard to behaviorism: a simple and pragmatic intervention with a variety of workable techniques, such as use of contracts; with regard to cognitive-behaviorism: a straightforward approach that can be pragmatically employed
- research data that accompany these approaches and measure their effectiveness
- short-term treatment

*Comparison with Other Theories*

Many behaviorists operate from a linear perspective and work on individual rather than system concerns. The exception is functional family therapy. Cognitive-behavioral therapy, for example, REBT, is somewhat systemic, but primarily linear.

Behaviorism and cognitive-behaviorism disregard the use of historical data in the treatment of families.

Some behavioral and cognitive-behavioral procedures are mechanical and may become sterile or inefficient when used by certain practitioners.

Some critics of behavioral and cognitive-behavioral family therapies claim there is too much emphasis on action in these approaches and not enough attention to family dynamics.

Behaviorism does not focus attention on affective responses or deal with emotional problems. Cognitive-behaviorism is more attuned to affect and emotion but emphasizes that affect is dependent on thoughts.

# References

Alexander, J. F. (1988). Phases of family therapy process: A framework for clinicians and researchers. In L. C. Wynne (Ed.), *The state of the art in family therapy research: Controversies and recommendations* (pp. 175–188). New York: Family Process Press.

Alexander, J., & Parsons, B. V. (1982). *Functional family therapy.* Pacific Grove, CA: Brooks/Cole.

Atwood, J. D. (1992). The field today. In J. D. Atwood (Ed.), *Family therapy: A systemic behavioral approach* (pp. 29–58). Chicago: Nelson-Hall.

Bandura, A. (1969). *Principles of behavior modification.* New York: Holt, Rinehart, & Winston.

Bandura, A. (1977). *Social learning theory.* Upper Saddle River, NJ: Prentice Hall.

Bandura, A., & Walters, R. H. (1963). *Social learning and personality development.* New York: Rinehart & Winston.

Barton, C., & Alexander, J. F. (1981). Functional family therapy. In A. S. Gurman & D. P. Kniskern (Eds.), *Handbook of family therapy* (pp. 403–443). New York: Brunner/Mazel.

Baucom, D. H., & Epstein, N. (1990). *Cognitive-behavioral marital therapy.* New York: Brunner/Mazel.

Beck, A. T. (1976). *Cognitive therapy and the emotional disorders.* New York: International Universities Press.

Christensen, A., & Jacobson, N. S. (2000). *Reconcilable differences.* New York: Guilford Press.

Cordova, J. V., Jacobson, N. S., & Christensen, A. (1998). Acceptance versus change interventions in behavioral couple therapy: Impact on couples' in-session communication. *Journal of Marital and Family Therapy, 24,* 437–455.

Curich, M. S., & Stone, M. H. (1998). The targeted dysfunctional behavior cycle applied to family therapy. *The Family Journal: Counseling and Therapy for Couples and Families, 6,* 328–333.

Dattilio, F. M. (Ed.). (1998). *Case studies in couples and family therapy: Systemic and cognitive perspectives.* New York: Guilford.

Dattilio, F. M., & Bevilacqua, L. J. (2000). A cognitive-behavioral approach. In F. M. Dattilio & L. J. Bevilacqua (Eds.). *Comparative treatments for relationship dysfunction* (pp. 137–159). New York: Springer.

DiGuiseppe, R. (1988). A cognitive-behavioral approach to the treatment of conduct disorder in children and adolescents. In N. Epstein, S. E. Schlesinger, & W. Dryden (Eds.), *Cognitive-behavioral therapy with families* (pp. 183–214). New York: Brunner/Mazel.

Ellis, A. (1985). *Overcoming resistance: Rational-emotive therapy with difficult clients.* New York: Springer.

Ellis, A. (1993). The rational-emotive therapy (RET) approach to marriage and family therapy. *The Family Journal: Counseling and Therapy for Couples and Families, 1,* 292–307.

Ellis, A. (2000). Rational-emotive behavior marriage and family therapy. In A. M. Horne (Ed.), *Family counseling and therapy* (3rd ed., pp. 489–514). Itasca, IL: F. E. Peacock.

Ellis, A., Sichel, J. L., Yeager, R. J., DiMattia, D. J., & DiGuiseppe, R. (1989). *Rational-emotive couple therapy.* New York: Pergamon.

Epstein, N., Schlesinger, S. E., & Dryden, W. (1988). Cognitive-behavioral family therapy: Summary and future directions. In N. Epstein, S. E. Schlesinger, & W. Dryden (Eds.), *Cognitive-behavioral therapy with families* (pp. 361–366). New York: Brunner/Mazel.

Falloon, I. R. (1988). *Handbook of behavioral family therapy.* New York: Guilford.

Falloon, I. R. H. (1991). Behavioral family therapy. In A. S. Gurman & D. P. Kniskern (Eds.), *Handbook of family therapy* (Vol. II, pp. 65–95). New York: Brunner/Mazel.

Fay, A. (1999). *Making it as a couple.* Essex, CT: FMC Books.

Fish, J. M. (1988, July/August). Reconciling the irreconcilable. *Family Therapy Networker, 12,* 15.

Freeman, A., & Zaken-Greenberg, F. (1989). A cognitive-behavioral approach. In C. R. Figley (Ed.), *Treating stress in families* (pp. 97–121). New York: Brunner/Mazel.

Gladding, S. T. (1991). *The fight.* Unpublished manuscript.

Goldiamond, I. (1965). Self-control procedures in personal behavior problems. *Psychological Reports, 17,* 851–868.

Gordon, S. B., & Davidson, N. (1981). Behavioral parent training. In A. S. Gurman & D. P. Kniskern (Eds.), *Handbook of family therapy.* New York: Brunner/Mazel.

Gottman, J. M., & Silver, N. (2000). *The seven principles of making marriage work.* New York: Three Rivers Press.

Gottman, J. M., Coan, J., Carrere, S., & Swanson, C. (1998). Predicting marital happiness and stability from newlywed interactions. *Journal of Marriage and the Family, 60,* 5–22.

Gurman, A. S., Kniskern, D. P., & Pinsof, W. N. (1985). Research on the process and outcome of family therapy. In S. L. Garfield & A. E. Bergin (Eds.), *Handbook of psychotherapy and behavior change* (3rd ed., pp. 525–623). New York: Wiley.

Hahlweg, K., Baucom, D. H., & Markman, H. (1988). Recent advances in therapy and prevention. In I. R. H. Falloon (Ed.), *Handbook of behavioral family therapy.* New York: Guilford Press.

Heiman, J. R., LoPiccolo, L., & LoPiccolo, J. (1981). The treatment of sexual dysfunction. In A. S. Gurman & D. P. Kniskern (Eds.), *Handbook of family therapy.* New York: Brunner/Mazel.

Hines, M. (1998). Acceptance versus change in behavior therapy: An interview with Neil Jacobson. *The Family Journal: Counseling and Therapy for Couples and Families, 6,* 244–251.

Horne, A., & Sayger, T. V. (2000). Behavioral approaches to couple and family therapy. In A. M. Horne (Ed.), *Family counseling and therapy* (3rd ed., pp. 454–488). Itasca, IL: F. E. Peacock.

Jacobson, N. S., Gottman, J. M., & Wu Shortt, J. (1995). The distinction between Type I and Type II batterers—Further considerations. *Journal of Family Psychology, 9,* 272–279.

Kaplan, H. S. (1974). *The new sex therapy.* New York: Quadrangle Books.

Katkin, E. S. (1978). Charting as a multipurpose treatment intervention in family therapy. *Family Process, 17,* 465–468.

Lazarus, A. A. (1968). Behavior therapy and group marriage counseling. *Journal of the American Society of Medicine and Dentistry, 15*, 49–56.

Lazarus, A. A. (2000). Working effectively and efficiently with couples. *The Family Journal: Counseling and Therapy for Couples and Families, 8*, 222–228.

Liberman, R. P. (1970). Behavioral approaches to family and couple therapy. *American Journal of Orthopsychiatry, 40*, 106–118.

Liberman, R. P., Wheeler, E., deVisser, L. A. J. M., Kuehnel, J., & Kuehnel, T. (1980). *Handbook of marital therapy: A positive approach to helping troubled relationships.* New York: Plenum.

LoPiccolo, J. (1978). Direct treatment of sexual dysfunction. In J. LoPiccolo & L. LoPiccolo (Eds.), *Handbook of sex therapy.* New York: Plenum.

Masters, W. H., & Johnson, V. E. (1966). *Human sexual response.* Boston: Little, Brown.

Masters, W. H., & Johnson, V. E. (1970). *Human sexual inadequacy.* Boston: Little, Brown.

Meichenbaum, D. H. (1977). *Cognitive-behavior modification: An integrative approach.* New York: Plenum.

Meichenbaum, D. H. (1985). *Stress inoculation training.* New York: Pergamon.

Minuchin, S., Rosman, B. L., & Baker, L. (1978). *Psychosomatic families.* Cambridge, MA: Harvard University Press.

O'Leary, K. D., & Smith, D. A. (1991). Marital interactions. *Annual Review of Psychology, 42*, 191–212.

Patterson, G. R. (1975). *Families: Applications of social learning to family life.* Champaign, IL: Research Press.

Patterson, G. R., & Brodsky, A. (1966). A behavior modification programme for a child with multiple behavior problems. *Journal of Child Psychology and Psychiatry, 7*, 277–295.

Patterson, G. R., & Gullion, M. E. (1971). *Living with children: New methods for parents and teachers* (rev. ed.). Champaign, IL: Research Press.

Patterson, G. R., Jones, R., Whittier, J., & Wright, M. (1965). A behavior modification technique for a hyperactive child. *Behavior Research and Therapy, 2*, 217–226.

Patterson, G. R., McNeal, S., Hawkins, N., & Phelps, R. (1967). Reprogramming the social environment. *Journal of Child Psychology and Psychiatry, 8*, 181–195.

Piercy, F. P., & Sprenkle, D. H. (1986). *Family therapy sourcebook.* New York: Guilford Press.

Premack, D. (1965). Reinforcement theory. In D. Levine (Ed.), *Nebraska symposium on motivation.* Lincoln, NB: University of Nebraska Press.

Sauber, R. S., L'Abate, L., & Weeks, G. R. (1985). *Family therapy: Basic concepts and terms.* Rockville, MD: Aspen.

Schlesinger, S. E. (1988). Cognitive-behavioral approaches to family treatment of addiction. In N. Epstein, S. E. Schlesinger, & W. Dryden (Eds.), *Cognitive-behavioral therapy with families* (pp. 254–291). New York: Brunner/Mazel.

Schwebel, A. I., & Fine, M. A. (1992). Cognitive-behavioral family therapy. *Journal of Family Psychotherapy, 3*, 73–92.

Schwebel, A. I., & Fine, M. A. (1994). *Understanding and helping families: A cognitive behavioral approach.* Hillsdale, NJ: LEA Press.

Skinner, B. F. (1948). *Walden two.* New York: Macmillan.

Skinner, B. F. (1953). *Science and human behavior.* New York: Macmillan.

Stuart, R. B. (1969). Operant-interpersonal treatment of marital discord. *Journal of Consulting and Clinical Psychology, 33*, 675–682.

Stuart, R. B. (1980). *Helping couples change: A social learning approach to marital therapy.* New York: Guilford.

Stuart, R. B. (1998). Updating behavior therapy with couples. *The Family Journal: Counseling and Therapy for Couples and Families, 6*, 6–12.

Sullivan, B. F., & Schwebel, A. I. (1995). Relationship beliefs and expectations of satisfaction in marital relationships: Implications for family practitioners. *The Family Journal: Counseling and Therapy for Couples and Families, 3*, 298–305.

Thibaut, J., & Kelley, H. H. (1959). *The social psychology of groups.* New York: Wiley.

Thomas, M. B. (1992). *An introduction to marital and family therapy.* New York: Macmillan.

Walen, S., & Perlmutter, R. (1988). Cognitive-behavioral treatment of adult sexual dysfunctions from a family perspective. In N. Epstein, S. E. Schlesinger, & W. Dryden (Eds.), *Cognitive-behavioral therapy with families* (pp. 325–360). New York: Brunner/Mazel.

Walsh, F. (1982). Conceptualizations of normal family functioning. In F. Walsh (Ed.), *Normal family processes* (pp. 3–44). New York: Guilford.

Wolpe, J. (1969). *The practice of behavior therapy.* New York: Pergamon Press.

Wood, L. F., & Jacobson, N. S. (1990). Behavioral marital therapy: The training experience in retrospect. In F. W. Kaslow (Ed.), *Voices in family psychology* (Vol. 2, pp. 159–174). Newbury Park, CA: Sage.

Wylie, M. S. (1999, September/October). Neil S. Jacobson, 1949–1999. *Family Therapy Networker, 23*(5), 14, 16–18.

# C H A P T E R 8

# Structural Family Therapy

She flips through a magazine on the blue-striped couch
sometimes entertained but often bored,
while he gulps down popcorn and televised football,
feeling occasionally excited yet often empty.

At midnight when the lights go off
and the news of the day and the games are decided,
She lays in anticipation, but without hope, of his touch
while he tackles fullbacks in his sleep
and ignores inner needs.

Alone, they together form a couple,
together, all alone, they long for a relationship.

*Gladding, 1991*

Structural family therapy was initially based on the experiences of Salvador Minuchin and his colleagues at the Wiltwyck School, a residential facility in New York for inner-city delinquents. The treatment was created out of necessity. Long-term, passive, and historically based approaches to working with the families of these children proved unsuccessful (Piercy, Sprenkle, & Wetchler, 1997). The active and often aggressive nature of family members at the Wiltwyck School and their tendencies to blame others and react immediately meant therapists had to be powerful and quick. Minuchin soon discovered that dramatic and active interventions were necessary to be effective.

Since its conception, structural family therapy has grown in popularity and use. It was refined at the Philadelphia Child Guidance Clinic in the 1960s and 1970s. Today, its numerous practitioners are found in many mental health settings, with Philadelphia continuing to be a major center for this approach. **Structural family therapy's major thesis** is that an individual's symptoms are best understood when examined in the context of family interactional patterns. A change in the family's organization or structure must take place before symptoms can be relieved. This idea about the impact of family structure and change on the lives of individuals has continued to be influential in the current practice of many family therapists, even those outside of a structural family therapy orientation.

# Major Theorists

There are several prominent theorists in structural family therapy, including Braulio Montalvo, Bernice Rosman, Harry Aponte, and Charles Fishman. The best known, however, is the founder of the theory, Salvador Minuchin.

## Salvador Minuchin

Salvador Minuchin was born in 1921 to Russian Jewish emigrants in Argentina. He never felt total allegiance to Argentina, but he did learn the rituals of Latin pride and ways of defending his honor against anti-Semitic remarks (Simon, 1984). He completed a medical degree in Argentina, but in 1948, he joined the Israeli army as a doctor and spent the next 18 months in this position. In 1950, Minuchin came to the United States with the intention of studying with Bruno Bettelheim in Chicago. However, he met Nathan Ackerman in New York and chose to stay there. After another 2-year return to Israel, Minuchin returned to the United States for good. In 1954, he began studying psychoanalysis; a few years later, he took the position of medical director of the Wiltwyck School.

Through his experiences at Wiltwyck, Minuchin became a systems therapist and, along with Dick Auerswald and Charles King in 1959, began developing a three-stage approach to working with low-socioeconomic-level black families. As time progressed, the Minuchin team "developed a language for describing family structure and methods for getting families to directly alter their organization" (Simon, 1984, p. 24). It was his innovative work at Wiltwyck that first gained Minuchin widespread recognition. The essence of the method used was published in *Families of the Slums* (Minuchin, Montalvo, Guerney, Rosman, & Schumer, 1967).

In 1965, Minuchin became the director of the Philadelphia Child Guidance Clinic. He transformed the clinic into a family therapy center. In the process, he gained a reputation as a tough and demanding administrator. Minuchin was always creating ideas. One of the most innovative of these was the Institute for Family Counseling, a training program for community paraprofessionals that proved to be highly effective in providing mental health services to the poor.

Minuchin worked closely in Philadelphia with Braulio Montalvo and Jay Haley, who he hired from California. "Probably Minuchin's most lauded achievement at the Clinic was his development of treatment techniques with psychosomatic families, particularly those of anorectics" (Simons, 1984, p. 24). In 1974, Minuchin published *Families and Family Therapy*, one of the most clearly written and popular books in the family therapy field. This work propelled Minuchin into widespread notoriety. In 1975, he stepped down as director of the clinic, but he remained its head of training until 1981.

Since 1981, Minuchin has studied normal families, written several plays and books, and commented on the overall field of family therapy. In addition, he set up the Family Studies Institute in New York City. He still continues to give workshops and to train therapists from all over the world. He remains an expert on working with families from diverse cultures and settings. He is passionately committed to social justice and is involved in the foster care system in New York. Overall, even in retirement, Minuchin remains a force in the field of family therapy.

# Premises of the Theory

The structural approach as a theory is quite pragmatic. Minuchin's theoretical conceptualization was influenced by the philosophy of Ortega y Gasset, who emphasized individuals interacting with their environment.

One of the primary premises underlying structural family therapy is that every family has a **structure**. This structure is revealed only when the family is in action. In other words, structure is an invisible set of functional demands by which family members relate to each other (Minuchin, 1974).

Structure influences families for better or worse. In some families, structure is well organized in a hierarchical pattern and members easily relate to each other. In other families, there is little structure and few arrangements are provided by which family members can easily and meaningfully interact. In both cases, developmental or situational events increase family stress, rigidity, chaos, and dysfunctionality, throwing the family into crisis (Minuchin, 1974). However, families that have an open and appropriate structure recover more quickly and function better in the long term than families without such an arrangement.

The structural approach emphasizes the family as a whole, as well as the interactions between subunits of family members. In some dysfunctional families, coalitions arise (Minuchin, Rosman, & Baker, 1978). A **coalition** is an alliance between specific family members against a third member. A *stable coalition* is a fixed and inflexible union (such as a mother and son) that becomes a dominant part of the family's everyday functioning. A *detouring coalition* is one in which the pair hold a third family member responsible for their difficulties or conflicts with one another, thus decreasing the stress on themselves or their relationship.

Furthermore, a major thesis of structural theory is that a person's symptoms are best understood as rooted in the context of family transaction patterns. The family is seen as the client. The hope is that through structuring or restructuring the system all members of the family and the family itself will become stronger (Minuchin, 1974). Families are conceptualized from this perspective as living systems. They operate in an ever-changing environment in which communication and feedback are important (Friedlander, Wildman, & Heatherington, 1991). Consequently, lasting change is dependent on altering the balance and alliances in the family so that new ways of interacting become realities.

Subsystems are another important aspect of the theory. Subsystems are smaller units of the system as a whole. They exist to carry out various family tasks. Without subsystems the overall family system would not function. They are best defined by the boundaries and rules connected with them. Subsystems are formed when family members join together to perform various functions. Some of these functions are temporary, such as painting a room. Others are more permanent, such as parenting a child. Of particular significance are the spousal, parental, and sibling subsystems (Minuchin & Fishman, 1981).

The spousal subsystem is composed of the marriage partners. In families where there are two such individuals, the way they support and nurture each other has a lot to do with how well structured the family is and how functionally it runs. Spousal subsystems work best when there is "complementarity of functions." In such circumstances, a husband and wife, for example, would operate as a team and accept their interdependency.

The parental subsystem is made up of those responsible for the care, protection, and socialization of children. As with the spousal subsystem, the parental subsystem is considered healthy if it does not function in a cross-generational way. A **cross-generational alliance** in a family contains members of two different generations within it. For example, if a parent and child collude to obtain certain objectives or needs, such as love or power, they have entered into a cross-generational alliance. Parental subsystems must change as children grow. The rules that are applicable, for example, at age 8 do not work at age 18. Therefore, parents are constantly challenged to define appropriate, clear, and permeable boundaries that help family members gain access to each other without becoming fused or distanced.

The sibling subsystem is that unit within the family whose members are of the same generation. For example, brothers and sisters are considered to be a sibling subsystem. In some families, the sibling subsystem is composed of those born of the same parents. In other families, such as in remarried arrangements (i.e., stepfamilies), the sibling subsystem is made up of unrelated children. Age differences may affect how well sibling subsystems function. Subsystems of siblings are often composed of those children who are relatively close to each other in age, for example, 2 or 3 years apart. They are generally closer to one another psychologically because of their opportunities to interact together. The larger the age gap between siblings, the less likely they will become allies (i.e., a subsystem).

A third major aspect of structural family therapy is the issue of boundaries. Basically, boundaries are the physical and psychological factors that separate people from one another and organize them. "For proper family functioning, the boundaries of subsystems must be clear" (Minuchin, 1974, p. 54). The strength of boundaries is represented in structural family mapping systems by broken, solid, and dotted lines. There are three major types of boundaries: clear (represented by a broken horizontal line, i.e., - - - - - ); rigid (represented by a solid line, i.e., _____ ); and diffuse (represented by a separated dotted line, i.e.,. . . . .).

**Clear boundaries** consist of rules and habits that allow family members to enhance their communication and relationships with one another because they encourage dialogue. In families with clear boundaries, members freely exchange information and give and receive corrective feedback. For example, in such a family, only one person at a time talks. With clear boundaries, negotiation and accommodation can successfully occur in families. These processes facilitate change, but still maintain the stability of the family. Parents and children feel a sense of belonging, but nevertheless individuate. For a functional two-parent family with children, clear boundaries might be represented as shown in Figure 8.1(a).

**Rigid boundaries** are inflexible and keep people separated from each other. In families with rigid boundaries, members experience difficulty relating in an intimate way to one another, and therefore, individuals become emotionally detached or cut off from other family members. For example, a family in which a husband and wife are detached from each other is represented in Figure 8.1(b).

In the case of **diffuse boundaries,** there is not enough separation between family members. In this arrangement, some family members are said to be "fused." Instead of creating independence and autonomy within individuals, as with clear boundaries, diffused boundaries encourage dependence. A two-parent family with children in which diffused boundaries exist is represented in Figure 8.1(c).

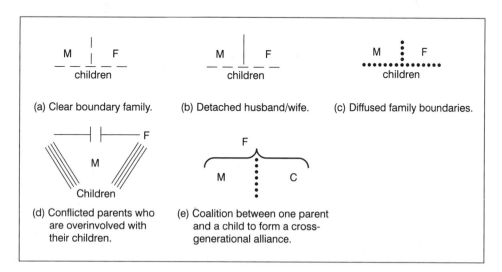

(a) Clear boundary family.

(b) Detached husband/wife.

(c) Diffused family boundaries.

(d) Conflicted parents who are overinvolved with their children.

(e) Coalition between one parent and a child to form a cross-generational alliance.

**Figure 8.1**
Types of family boundaries.

Other symbols are also used to show how families relate. Among the most common are these:[1]

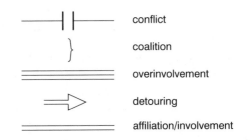

A two-parent family with children in which there is conflict and overinvolvement is represented in Figure 8.1(d). In such families, triangulation exists, and the relationships between the parents and children become closer as the conflict between the parents intensifies. Another family in which a coalition between a parent and children exists is represented in Figure 8.1(e). In this situation, a child becomes parentified as the parents disengage from one another.

In the development of families, boundaries may change regardless of the type of family. It is crucial not to mistake normal family development and growing pains for pathological patterns (Minuchin, 1974). It is also important to realize that during the course of family life over time alignments are formed. **Alignments** are the ways family members join together or oppose one another in carrying out a family activity.

In addition to structure, subsystems, and boundaries, structural family therapy is based also on (1) roles, (2) rules, and (3) power (Figley & Nelson, 1990). In regard to *roles*, therapists need to understand the roles under which families are operating (Kaplan, 2000). Families experiencing difficulties have members who relate to each other according to certain expectations that are either outdated or ineffective. The inefficiency of these families includes "little or no expectations that anyone will hear or be affected by what they say [and] little or no expectation of reward for appropriate behaviors" (McWhirter & McWhirter, 1989, p. 23). For instance, the youngest member of such a family may constantly be placed in the role of "the baby" and never be taken seriously by anyone.

Similarly, *rules* that the family first developed may be adhered to regardless of the changes that have occurred in the family's lifestyle or outside circumstances. For example, a family in which the chief wage earner is laid off may still insist on buying clothes at expensive stores. Such a rule, when adhered to, is to the detriment of the family as a functioning unit. Overall, rules in families "may be explicit or implicit." More functional families generally have more explicit rules. Regardless, rules "provide the family . . . with structure"—an organized pattern that becomes predictable and manifests itself in repeated patterns (Friesen, 1985, p. 7).

*Power* is the ability to get something done. In families, power is related to both authority and responsibility (or the one who makes and the one who carries out the decisions).

[1]Source: Reprinted by permission of the publishers from *Families and Family Therapy* by Salvador Minuchin, Cambridge, MA: Harvard University Press. Copyright © 1974 by the President and Fellows of Harvard College.

Structural family therapists observe that in dysfunctional families, power is vested in only a few members. The ability of family members to provide input in the decision-making process that governs the family is limited. Disenfranchised family members may either cut themselves off from the family, become enmeshed with stronger members, or battle to gain some control in an overt or covert way. The structural family therapist, after noting how power is distributed in the family, will often use his or her skills to unbalance the family and help them learn new ways of dealing with situations that are power based.

# Treatment Techniques

Structural family therapy is sometimes referred to as a way of looking at families. According to Minuchin (1974), dysfunctionality results from the development of *dysfunctional sets*. Dysfunctional sets are the family reactions, developed in response to stress, that are repeated without modification whenever there is family conflict. For example, one spouse might verbally attack the other, bringing charges and countercharges, until the fight escalates into physical violence or the couple withdraws from each other.

A number of procedures are associated with the structural family therapy approach (Friesen, 1985; Minuchin & Fishman, 1981). These techniques are sometimes employed in a sequential manner, or they may be combined. They are basically divided into those "that are primarily used in the formation of a therapeutic system," that is, techniques for joining, and those that are "more directly aimed at provoking disequilibrium and change" (Colapinto, 2000, p. 152). The most frequently used structural treatment methods are highlighted in the following sections.

## Joining

Joining is defined as "the process of 'coupling' that occurs between the therapist and the family, leading to the development of the therapeutic system" (Sauber, L'Abate, & Weeks, 1985, p. 95). It involves the therapist making contact with each family member. In the process, the therapist allies with family members through expressing interest in them as individuals and working with and for them (Minuchin & Fishman, 1981). In this leadership role, the therapist helps initiate the treatment process. Joining is considered one of the most important prerequisites to restructuring. It is a contextual process that is continuous. It's particularly important to join powerful family members, as well as angry ones. Special care and attention must be taken to accept the point of view of the father who thinks therapy is a waste of time and money or of the angry teenager who feels victimized. It is also important to reconnect with such people at frequent intervals during the therapy, particularly during times of overt tension or anger.

The structural family therapy approach joins families in one of four ways. The first is by **tracking.** In tracking, the therapist follows the content of the family (i.e., the facts). For instance, the therapist might say to a woman: "So as I understand this situation, you and your husband were married last May and had your first child this past March. You do not think you had enough time to establish a relationship with your spouse before you were required to start one with your baby."

During tracking, judgments are not made by the therapist (at least not overtly). Rather, information is gathered by means of open-ended questions to inquire about the interests and concerns of family members. Tracking is best exemplified when the therapist gives a family feedback.

The second way of joining is through **mimesis.** In mimesis, the therapist becomes like the family "in the manner or content of their communications, for example, joking with a jovial family, or talking slowly or sparsely with a slow-talking family" (Sauber et al., 1985, p. 107). Or, if a family frequently uses road metaphors to describe what is occurring between its members, a therapist would do likewise by stating: "I want to help you find a highway you can travel that leads somewhere and that everyone enjoys."

A third way of joining is through confirmation. The process of **confirmation of a family member** involves using an affective word to reflect an expressed or unexpressed feeling of that family member. It may also be accomplished through a nonjudgmental description of the behavior of the individual. For example, a therapist might say to a daughter who stares at the floor when addressing her father: "I sense that your looking at the floor when you talk to your father is connected with some depression you feel inside."

The final way to join with a family is by **accommodation.** In accommodation, the therapist makes personal adjustments in order to achieve a therapeutic alliance. For example, the therapist would remove his or her coat if the family came to the session in shirt sleeves (Minuchin, 1974).

## Disequilibrium Techniques

As indicated earlier disequilibrium techniques are interventions that are aimed at changing a system. "Some of them, like enactment and boundary making, are primarily employed in the creation of a different sequence of events, whereas others, like reframing, punctuation, and unbalancing, tend to foster a different perception of reality" (Colapinto, 2000, p. 154).

### Reframing

The technique of **reframing** involves changing a perception by explaining a situation from a different context. In this activity, the facts of an event do not change, but the meaning of the situation is examined from a new perspective (Sherman & Fredman, 1986). Through this process, a negative situation can sometimes be viewed in a more favorable light. This type of change is crucial to the promotion of movement in family therapy. For example, if disruptive behavior is reframed by the therapist as being "naughty" instead of "incorrigible," family members can find ways to modify their attitudes toward the "naughty" person and even help him or her make changes.

### Punctuation

**Punctuation** is a universal phenomenon and is characteristic of all human interaction. It is the way a person describes a situation, that is, begins and ends a sentence, due to a selective perspective or emotional involvement in an event. In structural family therapy, punctuation is "the selective description of a transaction in accordance with a therapist's goals" (Colapinto, 2000, p. 158). For example, if a therapist is trying to show that a mother has competence in controlling the behavior of her children, the therapist may declare her competent when she corrects or disciplines a child. By punctuating a particular situation at a specific moment in time, the perception of everyone involved is changed. Punctuation enhances possibilities for new competencies and behaviors in the future.

### Unbalancing

**Unbalancing** (or allying with a subsystem) is a procedure wherein the therapist supports an individual or subsystem against the rest of the family. For instance, a therapist may sit next to a daughter who is being accused of not living up to the family's tradition. In this position, the therapist can also take up for the daughter against the family and give reasons why it is important for the daughter to create new ways of behaving. Family members, individually and as a group, are then forced to act differently with the person or subsystem. They have to expand their roles and functions. When this technique is used to support an underdog in the family system (as it usually is), a chance for change within the total hierarchical relationship is fostered (Sauber et al., 1985).

## Enactment

The process of **enactment** consists of families bringing problematic behavioral sequences into treatment by showing them to the therapist in a demonstrative transaction. For example, a family that frequently argues about how they are going to spend their Saturdays is asked to have a heated argument in front of the therapist instead of waiting for the fight to occur at another time. The idea is to see how family members interact with one another and to challenge their existing patterns and rules. This method can also be used to help family members gain control over behaviors they insist are beyond their control. It puts an end to members' claims that they are helpless in controlling their actions, thoughts, and feelings. The result is that family members experience their own transactions with heightened awareness (Minuchin, 1974). In examining their roles, members often discover more functional ways of behaving.

## Working with Spontaneous Interaction

Working with spontaneous interaction is similar to being a lighting expert who focuses the spotlight of attention on some particular behavior. It occurs whenever families display actions in sessions that are disruptive or dysfunctional, such as members yelling at one another or parents withdrawing from their children. In these cases, therapists can see firsthand the dynamics within a family's interactions. On such occasions, therapists can point out the dynamics and sequencing of behaviors. The focus is on process not content. It is crucial that therapists use such occasions to help families recognize patterns of interaction and what changes they might make to bring about modification.

## Boundary Making

A boundary is an invisible line that separates people or subsystems from each other psychologically (Minuchin, 1974). To function effectively, families need different types of boundaries at distinct times of stage development. "Each stage brings demands, forcing the family members to accommodate to new needs as family members grow up or age, and circumstances change" (Minuchin, 1993, p. 40). For example, families may need more rigid boundaries during stages when children are young in order to make sure that everyone is taken care of and more flexible boundaries during the time when there are teenagers in the house in order to meet the demands of different schedules. "Part of the therapeutic task is to help the family define, redefine, or change the boundaries within the family. The therapist also helps the family to either strengthen or loosen boundaries, depending upon the family's situation" (Sauber et al., 1985, p. 16).

## Intensity

**Intensity** is the structural method of changing maladaptive transactions by using strong affect, repeated intervention, or prolonged pressure. The tone, volume, pacing, and choice of words used by a therapist can raise the affective intensity of statements. For example, intensity is manifested if a therapist keeps forcefully telling a family to "do something different" (Minuchin & Fishman, 1981). The persistence employed in this technique breaks down family patterns of equilibrium and challenges the family's perception of reality. Intensity works best if therapists know what they want to say and do so in a direct, unapologetic manner that is goal specific.

## Restructuring

The procedure of **restructuring** is at the heart of the structural approach. In fact, the goal of this approach to family therapy is structural change. Restructuring involves changing the structure of the family. The rationale behind restructuring is to make the family more functional by altering the existing hierarchy and interaction patterns so that problems are not maintained. It is accomplished through the use of enactment, unbalancing, and boundary formation.

For instance, if a father dominates to the point where children feel intimidated, the therapist may ask the family to enact a "father-dominated scenario." As it occurs, the therapist may instruct the rest of the family members to behave in a certain way, for example, uniformly refusing to do what the father requests without getting something in return. If these instructions are carried out, the family behaves differently and change becomes possible. If change occurs, members generally feel more enfranchised and invested in the family.

## Shaping Competence

In the process of **shaping competence,** structural family therapists help families and family members become more functional by highlighting positive behaviors. For example, therapists may reinforce parents who make their children behave, even if the parents succeed only momentarily in accomplishing this feat. In effect, shaping competence is a matter of therapists not acting as experts all of the time. Instead, therapists reinforce family members for doing things right or making their own appropriate decisions (Minuchin, Lee, & Simon, 1997). As a result, positive abilities are highlighted and appropriate alternative ways of working with problems are produced.

## Diagnosing

One of the main tasks of structural family therapists is to diagnose the family in such a way as to describe the systematic interrelationships of all family members. This type of mapping, as shown in Figure 8.1, allows therapists to see what needs to be modified or changed if the family is going to improve. For example, therapists may note disruptive coalitions or triangles among family members.

Diagnosing is done early in the therapeutic process before the family can induct the therapist as a part of their system. By diagnosing interactions, therapists become proactive, instead of reactive, in promoting structural interventions.

## Adding Cognitive Constructions

Although structural family therapy is primarily action oriented, it does include verbal components in the form of words to help families help themselves. The multiple aspects of the technique of **adding cognitive constructions** include advice, information, pragmatic fictions, and paradox. *Advice* and *information* are derived from experience and knowledge of families in therapy. They are used to calm anxious family members and to reassure them about certain actions. They may occasionally include explanations about structure within the family. For example, if a family member says, "I'll bet you've never seen a family as messed up as we are," the therapist might reply, "Your family is unique in quite a few ways, but many of your concerns and behaviors are common among families I see."

**Pragmatic fictions** are pronouncements that help families and family members change. For instance, therapists may occasionally tell children that they are acting younger than their years. **Paradox,** on the other hand, is a confusing message meant to frustrate or confuse families and motivate them to search for alternatives. For example, a family that is resistant to instructions and change may be told not to follow the therapist's instructions and not to change. Given this permission to do as they wish, families may defy the therapist and become better, or they may explore reasons why their behaviors are as they are and make changes in the ways they interact.

# Role of the Therapist

The structural family therapist is both an observer and an expert who is active in making interventions to modify and change the underlying structure of the family. Successful structural family therapists require high energy and precise timing (Minuchin et al., 1967).

The therapist's role changes over the course of therapy (Minuchin, 1974). For example, in the first phase of treatment, the therapist joins the family and takes a leadership position. In phase two, the therapist mentally maps out the family's underlying structure. In the final phase, the therapist helps transform family structure. Thus, during treatment the therapist watches "the family 'dance' and then enters ('joins') and leaves the interactional field at will in order to transform it therapeutically" (Friedlander et al., 1991, p. 397).

The therapist uses a number of techniques to accomplish the goal of change, including unbalancing (e.g., siding with one member of the family), praise, challenges, direct orders, and judgments (Fishman, 1988; Minuchin & Fishman, 1981). An implicit, if not explicit, assumption is that the therapist has a "correct" interpretation of what is happening within the family and powerful tools for helping the family construct and maintain a more functional system.

In some cases, the therapist acts dramatically (if this is the only way to get the attention of the family) (Simon, 1984). For instance, the therapist may say to a withdrawn or denying family member: "Admit it, through your actions and passivity you are playing a major role in how this family operates." At other times, the therapist is low key and notices repetitive interactions, such as a young girl clinging to her mother. On such occasions, the therapist may or may not mention the actions. Regardless, the therapist works to change the structure of the family at crucial times so that family members can unite in a healthy and productive way.

# Process and Outcome

The process of change within structural family therapy is probably best described as gradual but steady. It is geared to the cultural context of the family but follows some general patterns. When successful, this approach results in symptom resolution and structural changes. Usually, significant changes occur after a few sessions because the therapist uses specific techniques to help family members interact in new ways. These techniques are often used in an overlapping manner in order to help the family to become less homeostatic. The idea is to emphasize action over insight. Family members are given homework (i.e., activities to do outside of the session) in addition to the work they do within their therapeutic time.

In successful treatment, the overall structure of the family is altered and reorganized. This change in structure enables family members to relate to one another in a more functional and productive manner. As a part of this process, dated and outgrown rules are replaced by those more related to the family's current realities. In addition, parents are in charge of their children, and a differentiation between distinct subsystems emerges (Piercy et al., 1997).

# Unique Aspects of Structural Family Therapy

## Emphases

One strong aspect of structural family therapy is its versatility. The structural approach has proven successful in treating families experiencing difficulties with juvenile delinquents, alcoholics, and anorexics (Fishman, 1988). It is as appropriate for low-socioeconomic-level families (Minuchin, Colapinto, & Minuchin, 1999) as for high-income families. It can be adapted for use with minority and cross-cultural populations as well (Boyd-Franklin, 1987; Jung, 1984). In essence, structural family therapy is suitable for a wide variety of client families. It is sensitive to the effect of culture on families.

A second characteristic of this approach is its emphasis on terminology and ease of application. Basically, structural family therapy has clearly defined terms and procedures. Treatment methods and techniques are described in such a way that novice therapists can easily conceptualize what they are to do and when to do it (Minuchin & Fishman, 1981). The process is clear because of the clarity of the theory.

A third attribute of structural therapy is that it helped make family therapy as a whole acceptable to medicine in general and psychiatry in particular (Simon, 1984). As a psychiatrist, Minuchin was able to make a case with the medical community for his approach and for family therapy treatment. Without this recognition and implicit endorsement, family therapy would be more of an intellectual exercise and a mystery.

A fourth aspect of the structural approach is its emphasis on symptom removal and reorganization of the family. "Changes in family structure contribute to changes in behavior and the inner psychic processes of the members of the system" (Minuchin, 1974, p. 9). Families have a different emphasis as a result of treatment and are able to cope better. Members experience their families in new and positive ways.

A fifth dimension of structural family therapy is its pragmatic, problem-solving emphasis. Therapists are active in bringing about change (Colapinto, 2000). For example, by using reframing, a structural family therapist can help a family conceptualize a situation as being "depressive" rather than "hopeless." By seeing the difficulty in this way, the family can take steps to cope with or address depression and thereby gain greater control over themselves and their environment. In essence, structural family therapy was born out of necessity. It has not deviated from its origins.

## Comparison with Other Theories

Structural family therapy is a well-developed, action-oriented, and pragmatic approach to working with families. It has been as well articulated and illustrated as any other family therapy. However, critics charge that the theory is not complex or profound enough to address the complexity of family life to any great extent.

A second point of comparison is based on the accusation by some clinicians that the focus of the theory lends itself to reinforcing sexism and sexual stereotypes (Simon, 1984). These critics stress that Minuchin encourages husbands to take on executive roles and wives to take on expressive roles in the family so that everyone does not suffer (Luepnitz, 1988). They contend that mothers should be encouraged and supported to become more effective. In fairness, it must be said that Minuchin developed his theory with low-income families in which husbands had hidden or indirect power and would undermine the efforts of their spouses.

A third distinction of the structural approach is that it focuses on the present. Past patterns and history are not emphasized (Minuchin, 1974). Structural family therapy basically ignores historical data. For example, structuralists mentally map the present configuration of the family rather than pay attention to the historic or developmental landmarks of the family over time.

A fourth aspect of structural family therapy is that it is sometimes hard to distinguish from strategic family therapy (Friesen, 1985; Stanton, 1981). In both approaches, there is a pragmatic emphasis on identifying and blocking present behaviors that are destructive and repetitive. There is also a focus on the process, as opposed to the content, of sessions. The therapist takes a great deal of responsibility for initiating change through such techniques as enactments or homework assignments. In both approaches, the time frame for treatment is relatively short term—less than 6 months.

A final distinction of structural family therapy is that families may not become as empowered because the therapist is active and in control of the process (Friesen, 1985).

This aspect of treatment may be helpful to families who would not have taken any initiative by themselves, but for others it may hinder the speed of progress.

---

## CASE ILLUSTRATION

### THE JOHNSON FAMILY

Melinda Johnson, age 28, is the mother of four children: Bill, age 12, Sally, age 8, Holly Jean, age 5, and Michael, age 2. Her common law husband, George, lives with the family on occasions but usually stays away because he fears Melinda's social worker will cut off government support if he is discovered in her apartment. Because of George's frequent absence and his financial inability to contribute to the family, Melinda and her children often go without needed food and medical care. Their apartment in "the projects" is in serious disrepair.

Melinda recently told her social worker that Bill has been sneaking out late at night. She is unable to control him, and the social worker is considering removing him from the family. Melinda fears the effects of such a process and is equally distressed at the thought that Bill may become part of a gang and endanger her and the younger children. Her social worker wants specific detailed information on what Bill is doing. Melinda's mother, age 45, who lives nearby, is urging Melinda to "do something and do it quickly."

### Conceptualization of Family: Structural Perspective

From a structural perspective, the Johnson family is unorganized and problematic. It lacks resources. Melinda does not have a supportive relationship with either George or her mother. The fact that Bill is beginning to act out is indicative of this lack of a hierarchy and the effects of poverty. Power is being usurped by Bill because the boundaries within the family unit are diffused. If the family structure is not strengthened soon, Bill will most likely become triangulated.

### Process of Treatment: Structural Family Therapy

To help the Johnsons, a structural family therapist would first join with all members of the family that come for treatment. The therapist would then urge all members of the family, including George and Melinda's mother, to attend most, if not all, sessions. The therapist would next mentally map the family after they are seated and notice who sits next to whom and the verbal interactions that take place. Then, to help the family begin to help itself, the therapist would move members around until natural subsystems within the family are grouped together, such as parents and children. With the Johnsons, the therapist would concentrate also on mimesis and match the family's feeling mood, most likely hopelessness.

After the therapist "joins" and "accommodates" the family, he or she would begin to take a leadership role in the family. First, he or she would unbalance the family by allying with the parent subsystem. By doing so, the therapist emphasizes the importance of a strong couple subsystem, that is, both Melinda and George. The therapist might then work with spontaneous interactions within the session itself.

For example, if Melinda and George ask Bill to sit down and he does not, the therapist might insist through the use of an intensity method of repetition and would keep trying until successful. Then, even if only momentarily, the therapist would note the success and in so doing shape competence. The therapist might also use reframing, for example, state that Melinda's mother, through her overinvolvement in pressuring her daughter to act, is "quite concerned" about her daughter and the family's well-being.

In this approach, the therapist would always begin an intervention with the parent subsystem in order to clarify and emphasize boundaries. As treatment progresses each session, the therapist would seek to put less attention on Bill and more on family dynamics and processes as influenced by structure. Bill would lose his status as the identified patient and the family would become the treated unit. As boundaries and structure are changed, power would regress to the parent subsystem. At this time, the therapist would share with Melinda and George some pragmatic and cognitive knowledge to help them stay on top of the family situation.

# Summary and Conclusion

Structural family therapy was formed out of necessity in the 1960s by Salvador Minuchin and his colleagues at the Wiltwyck School in New York. It was begun because traditional methods of treatment, especially psychoanalysis, were not effective in serving the needs of inner-city ghetto boys from low-income families, who were the primary residents of this facility. It was refined at the Philadelphia Child Guidance Clinic in the 1970s and 1980s. It continues to be a major theoretical approach to helping families change.

Like most systems theorists, the structural family therapists are interested in how the components of a system interact, how balance or homeostasis is achieved, how family feedback mechanisms operate, and how dysfunctional communication patterns develop. A particular emphasis of the structural approach is that all families have structures that are revealed through member interactions. Some family structures are more functional than others. Families that have a hierarchy that is well organized adjust better to their environment and crises than families that are not set up in this manner. Of special interest to structural family therapists are spouse, parent, and sibling subsystems and the clearness of boundaries between them. In addition, roles, rules, and power within the family are emphasized.

A number of innovative techniques and procedures have come from structural family therapy. Among the best known and most effective are joining, reframing, unbalancing, enacting, working with spontaneous interaction, boundary formation, intensity, restructuring, shaping competence, and adding cognitive constructions. Like an artist, structural family therapists time the intensity and emphasis of their inputs. On some occasions, they "map" family interactions; on others, they intervene in dramatic fashion. This unpredictability can be a powerful feature of the approach.

If all works well, families leave structural family treatment with more functional ways by which members can interact and with clearer boundaries. Families may not have insight into their new behaviors, but they have new ways of relating. Structural family therapy is versatile in the types of families with which it can be used. It is also easily combined with other family therapy approaches, such as strategic family therapy. Critics of the approach claim it concentrates too much on surface issues and that it may be implicitly sexist. Yet, as a treatment methodology, structural family therapy remains popular.

# Summary Table
## Structural Family Therapy

### Major Theorists

| | | |
|---|---|---|
| Salvador Minuchin | Braulio Montalvo | Charles Fishman |
| Bernie Rosman | Harry Aponte | Duncan Stanton |
| Thomas Todd | | |

### Premises of the Theory

Family functioning involves family structure, subsystems, and boundaries.

Overt and covert rules, hierarchies, and interpersonal accommodation must be understood and changed, if necessary, to keep the family flexible and adjusted to new situations.

### Treatment Techniques

The family is treated as a system or a subsystem. However, individual needs are not ignored.

One goal of treatment is to bring problematic behaviors out in the open so therapists can observe and help change them.

Another goal is to bring about structural changes within families, such as organizational patterns, hierarchies, and sequences.

Therapeutic techniques include the following:

- Joining
- Accommodating
- Restructuring
- Working with interaction (enactment, spontaneous behaviors)
- Intensifying messages
- Unbalancing
- Reframing
- Shaping competence
- Making boundaries

### Role of the Therapist

Therapists mentally "map" their families and work actively in counseling sessions. They instruct families to interact through enactments and spontaneous sequences. Therapists are like theater directors.

### Process and Outcome

Action is emphasized over insight with the therapist using specific techniques to help family members interact in new ways.

Family members are given homework to do outside of therapy sessions.
The overall structure of the family is altered and reorganized.

### Unique Aspects of Structural Family Therapy

Structural family therapy emphasizes the following:

- The approach was the first developed for low-socioeconomic-level families and is very pragmatic.
- It was one of the first developed exclusively for families.
- It was influential in getting the profession of psychiatry to respect family therapy as an approach to treatment.
- The tenets and techniques of the therapy are clearly stated by Minuchin, Fishman, Stanton, and others.
- Treatment has proven effective in working with families of addicts, eating disorders, and suicidals.
- The therapy is well researched, systemic, problem focused in the present, and relatively short term (generally less than 6 months).
- Therapists and families are active during the sessions.
- Homework is sometimes assigned in between sessions.

### Comparison with Other Theories

The theory is as well developed and well articulated as any approach in the family therapy field.

Some feminists believe the theory promotes gender stereotypes by emphasizing traditional paternal roles, but that is not Minuchin's focus.

The theory is not as strong in explaining family dynamics and development as the practice of this approach is in fostering change.

The therapist must be active and creative. He or she is highly influential in the change process and may inadvertently prevent maximum family interaction and employment.

Structural family theory and strategic family theory are sometimes conceptualized as one in the same, which makes it hard for some therapists to discern the unique aspects of each. The result is often a failure to appreciate the contributions of structural family therapy or to use it appropriately.

# References

Boyd-Franklin, N. (1987). The contribution of family therapy models to the treatment of black families. *Psychotherapy, 24,* 621–629.

Colapinto, J. (2000). Structural family therapy. In A. M. Horne (Ed.), *Family counseling and therapy* (3rd ed., pp. 140–169). Itasca, IL: F. E. Peacock.

Figley, C. R., & Nelson, T. S. (1990). Basic family therapy skills, II: Structural family therapy. *Journal of Marital and Family Therapy, 16,* 225–239.

Fishman, C. H. (1988). *Treating troubled adolescents: A family therapy approach.* New York: Basic Books.

Friedlander, M. L., Wildman, J., & Heatherington, L. (1991). Interpersonal control in structural and Milan systemic family therapy. *Journal of Marital and Family Therapy, 17,* 395–408.

Friesen, J. D. (1985). *Structural-strategic marriage and family therapy.* New York: Gardner.

Gladding, S. T. (1991). *Monday nights.* Unpublished manuscript.

Jung, M. (1984). Structural family therapy: Its application to Chinese families. *Family Process, 23,* 365–374.

Kaplan, D. M. (2000). Who are our giants? *The Family Digest, 12*(4), 1, 6.

Luepnitz, D. A. (1988). *The family interpreted: Feminist theory in clinical practice.* New York: Basic Books.

McWhirter, J. J., & McWhirter, E. H. (1989). Poor soil yields damaged fruit: Environmental influences. In D. Capuzzi & D. R. Gross (Eds.), *Youth at risk* (pp. 19–40). Alexandria, VA: American Counseling Association.

Minuchin, P., Colapinto, J., & Minuchin, S. (1999). *Working with families of the poor.* New York: Guilford.

Minuchin, S. (1974). *Families and family therapy.* Cambridge, MA: Harvard University Press.

Minuchin, S. (1993). *Family healing: Tales of hope and renewal from family therapy.* New York: Free Press.

Minuchin, S., & Fishman, C. H. (1981). *Family therapy techniques.* Cambridge, MA: Harvard University Press.

Minuchin, S., Lee, W.-Y., & Simon, G. M. (1997). *Mastering family therapy: Journeys of growth and transformation.* New York: Wiley.

Minuchin, S., Montalvo, B., Guerney, B. G., Rosman, B. L., & Schumer, F. (1967). *Families of the slums.* New York: Basic Books.

Minuchin, S., Rosman, B., & Baker, L. (1978). *Psychomatic families: Anorexia nervosa in context.* Cambridge, MA: Harvard University Press.

Piercy, F. P., Sprenkle, D. H., & Wetchler, J. L (1997). *Family therapy sourcebook* (2nd ed.). New York: Guilford.

Sauber, S. R., L'Abate, L., & Weeks, G. R. (1985). *Family therapy: Basic concepts and terms.* Rockville, MD: Aspen.

Sherman, R., & Fredman, N. (1986). *Handbook of structural techniques in marriage and family therapy.* New York: Brunner/Mazel.

Simon, R. (1984, November/December). Stranger in a strange land: An interview with Salvador Minuchin. *Family Therapy Networker, 8,* 21–25.

Stanton, M. D. (1981). An integrated structural/strategic approach to family therapy. *Journal of Marital and Family Therapy, 7,* 427–439.

# C H A P T E R 9

# Strategic and Systemic Family Therapies

After giving birth to Nathaniel
you asked for a Wendy's shake and fries.

I can still remember as if yesterday
the words that broke the silence
surrounding the miracle of new life:
"I'm hungry."

Walking from your room still dazed,
through the Sunday streets of Birmingham,
I brought you back your first request from labor.

That cold November morning is now a treasure in my mind
as are you and the child that you delivered.

*Gladding, 1993*

**S**trategic and systemic family therapies are method oriented and brief in duration. In this chapter, the essence of these theories is examined and compared. Strategic and systemic therapies are indebted to the work of Milton Erickson, whose work influenced their founders. Erickson's goal in treatment was change. He believed in utilizing the resources of his clients and designing a "strategy for each specific problem" (Madanes, 1991, p. 396). Erickson then worked with his clients to help them become active in assisting themselves. He did so through giving them directives and indirect suggestions. He did not care if people gained insight as long as their actions produced beneficial results. "If Freud was a philosopher-priest from Vienna, Erickson was a samurai warrior from Wisconsin" (Wylie, 1990, p. 28).

Despite sharing a common heritage—both obtained ideas from Erickson and used some of the same methods (e.g., seeing families for a limited period of time)—strategic and systemic family therapies are distinct. The differences between these approaches have been articulated by theorists from:

- the Mental Research Institute (MRI), 555 Middlefield Road, Palo Alto, CA 94301 (i.e., strategic family therapists)
- the Washington School of Jay Haley and Cloe Madanes (i.e., strategic family therapists)
- the Milan Systems Group (i.e., systemic family therapists)

The MRI form of strategic family therapy is the oldest of these therapeutic approaches. It is a descendent of the Bateson communications studies group, which was conducted in Palo Alto from 1952 to 1962. Among the most active modern proponents of this approach are Paul Watzlawick and John Weakland. Other figures connected with this branch of strategic family therapy are Lynn Hoffman, Peggy Penn, and Richard Rabkin.

A second type of strategic family therapy is that articulated by the Washington School of thought, most notably Jay Haley and Cloe Madanes. This school of thought was organized in the mid-1970s (Keim, 2000). Haley, Madanes, and their followers have influenced other theories, theorists, and teams of researchers, including those in the MRI Palo Alto group.

The third group of theorists considered here is from Milan, Italy. The genesis of this branch of family therapy, which is usually referred to as *systemic family therapy,* was formulated by a team of practitioners whose members originally included Mara Selvini Palazzoli, Luigi Boscolo, Gianfranco Cecchin, and Guiliana Prata (Campbell, Draper, & Crutchley, 1991, p. 325). The team leader of this effort was Selvini Palazzoli. In 1967, she established the Milan Center for the Study of the Family. Previous to this landmark event, Selvini Palazzoli had devoted her life to the study and treatment of anorexia nervosa, with limited success (Selvini Palazzoli, 1974). Systemic family therapy has been characterized as **long brief therapy** because of the amount of time that lapses between sessions (usually a month) and the duration of treatment (up to a year) (Tomm, 1984a).

The format of this chapter consists of discussions of the underlying principles of strategic and systemic theories as unique but related approaches. Included in this examination is a brief description of major professionals involved in formulating these theories. The primary assumptions and underpinning techniques of these positions are highlighted. The foci of therapists using these orientations are then discussed. Finally, the process and outcome of these theories are described along with their unique contributions to the field of family therapy.

# ◢ Strategic Family Therapy ◣

The strategic family therapy approaches have a history that is both long and distinguished. Jay Haley (1963, 1973) coined the term **strategic therapy** to describe the work of Milton Erickson. Erickson conducted therapy by paying extreme attention to details of the symptoms his clients presented. His focus, like that of most present-day strategic therapists, was to change behavior by manipulating it and not to instill insight into those with whom he worked.

Erickson achieved his objectives in therapy by:

- accepting and emphasizing the positive (i.e., he framed all symptoms and maladaptive behaviors as helpful)
- using indirect and ambiguously worded directives
- encouraging or directing routine behaviors so that resistance is shown through change and not through normal and continuous actions (Haley, 1963)

## Major Theorists

The strategic family therapy approaches have many well-known practitioners, such as Paul Watzlawick, John Weakland, and Cloe Madanes. However, as a representative of these approaches, the background of Jay Haley is highlighted here.

### Jay Haley

Haley influenced the Bateson group and the MRI group as a founding member of each and set up the Family Therapy Institute of Washington, D.C., with Cloe Madanes in 1974. His theoretical writings and techniques have also had a powerful impact on the Milan systems approach originated by Selvini Palazzoli.

As implied previously, Jay Haley is one of the most distinguished and controversial pioneers in the field of family therapy. He has served as an effective communicator between people and groups and has been a strong advocate of family therapy in public and professional settings. Haley's development is unique among family therapists. He learned from and with the three people who had the most influence on the evolution of family therapy: Milton Erickson, Gregory Bateson, and Salvador Minuchin.

Haley began his career with Gregory Bateson in 1952. Because he had a master's degree in communications, his chief responsibility in the research team Bateson assembled was to take a lead in diagnosing communication patterns in schizophrenic families. As a result of his work, Haley became interested in studying the hypnotherapy communication process of Milton Erickson. He learned hypnosis from Erickson in 1953 and later taught and practiced it (Simon, 1982). He incorporated much of Erickson's ideas into his own concepts about how to do therapy. Erickson supervised him as he learned to become a therapist. Basically, he adopted and modified Erickson's individual emphasis so that it would work with families.

In 1962, after the Bateson team dissolved, Haley joined the Mental Research Institute staff, where he worked until 1967. It was at this time that he stopped doing therapy and became primarily involved in "family research and the observation of therapy" (Simon, 1982, p. 20). He also became the first editor of the initial journal in the field of family therapy, *Family Process*, a position he held from 1962 to 1969. Haley became even more involved in supervision when he moved east to join Salvador Minuchin at the Philadelphia Child Guidance Center in 1967. With Minuchin, he organized "the **Institute for Family Counseling** (IFC), a project training people from the Philadelphia ghetto, who had no formal education beyond high school, to be family therapists" (Simon, 1982, p. 20). This process further established his prominence.

In 1976, he moved to the Washington, D.C., area to establish the Family Therapy Institute with Cloe Madanes. After this move, he published two of his most influential books, *Problem Solving Therapy* (1976) and *Leaving Home* (1980). These books spelled out the essence of strategic family therapy as Haley views it, an approach that distinguishes itself by its emphasis on power and hierarchy. He is described as having the skills of a power broker and a military strategist and having made these skills "respectable therapeutic techniques" (Wylie, 1990, p. 28). Haley retired in 1995 and currently lives in La Jolla, California.

# Premises of the Theory

As a group, strategic family therapies follow Ericksonian principles. They emphasize short-term treatment, about 10 sessions. Often strategic therapies are characterized as brief therapy. The term *brief*, used in this way, is misleading. Brief therapy has to do more with the clarity about what needs to be changed rather than with time. "A central principle of brief therapy is that one evaluates which solutions have so far been attempted for the patient's problem" (Priebe & Pommerien, 1992, p. 433). After the evaluation, different solutions in therapy are tried. These solutions are often the opposite of what has already been attempted (Watzlawick, 1978).

For instance, if parents have begged a daughter to make good grades, treatment might focus on having the parents ask the daughter to show them how she manages to do so poorly in school. They may even instruct her to continue what she has been doing. "Brief therapists hold in common the belief that therapy must be specifically goal-directed, problem-focused, well-defined, and, first and foremost, aimed at relieving the client's presenting complaint" (Wylie, 1990, p. 29).

In general strategic family therapists concentrate on the following dimensions of family life:

- **Family rules:** the overt and covert rules families use to govern themselves, such as "you must only speak when spoken to"

- **Family homeostasis:** the tendency of the family to remain in its same pattern of functioning unless challenged to do otherwise, for example, getting up and going to bed at the same time
- **Quid pro quo:** the responsiveness of family members to treating others in the way they are treated, that is, something for something
- **Redundancy principle:** the fact that a family interacts within a limited range of repetitive behavioral sequences
- **Punctuation:** the idea that people in a transaction believe that what they say is caused by what others say
- **Symmetrical relationships** and **complementary relationships:** the fact that relationships within a family are both among equals (symmetrical) and unequals (complementary)
- **Circular causality:** the idea that one event does not "cause" another but that events are interconnected and that the factors behind a behavior, such as a kiss or a slap, are multiple

# Treatment Techniques

As a group, strategic family therapists are very innovative. They believe that telling people what they are doing wrong is not helpful. The same is true concerning the encouragement of catharsis (Haley, 1976). If families are going to change, alterations in the ways their members act must precede new perceptions and feelings. This goal can be accomplished in an almost endless number of ways. For example, some problems can be resolved by not treating them as problems, such as not becoming overly concerned when a 2-year-old throws a temper tantrum because that is typical behavior at that age.

Each intervention in strategic therapy is tailored to the idiosyncrasies of persons and problems. The customization makes strategic therapies some of the most technique driven of all family therapies. Among the various schools of strategic family therapy, different concepts and methods are highlighted here. In general, strategic family therapists emphasize reframing, directive, paradox, ordeals, pretend, and positioning techniques.

## Reframing

Reframing involves the use of language to induce a cognitive shift within family members and alter the perception of a situation. In reframing, a different interpretation is given to a family's situation or behavior. In this process, a circumstance is given new meaning and, as a consequence, other ways of behaving are explored. Reframing does not change a situation, but "the alteration of meaning invites the possibility of change" (Piercy & Sprenkle, 1986, p. 35). For instance, "depression" may be conceptualized as "irresponsibility" or "stubbornness."

Overall, reframing helps establish rapport between the therapist and the family and breaks down resistance. Through the use of reframing, what was once seen as out-of-control behavior may become voluntary and open to change.

## Directive

A **directive** is an instruction from a family therapist for a family to behave differently. "The directive is to strategic therapy what the interpretation is to psychoanalysis. It is the basic tool of the approach" (Madanes, 1991, p. 397). Many types of directives can be given in strategic therapy, including nonverbal messages (e.g., silence, voice tone, and posture), direct and indirect suggestions (e.g., "go fast" or "you may not want to change too quickly"), and assigned behaviors (e.g., when you think you won't sleep, force yourself to stay up all night). The purpose of these "outside of therapy" assignments is to help people to behave differently so that they can have different subjective experiences. Directives also increase the influence of the therapist in the change process and give the therapist information about how family members react to suggested changes.

An example of a directive is to tell a family to "go slow" in working to bring about change. In this situation, their resistance to change may dissolve as they attempt to disobey the directive. On the other hand, if they follow the directive, the therapist can gain more influence in their lives.

## Paradox

One of the most controversial and powerful techniques in strategic family therapy is paradox (Sexton & Montgomery, 1994). Although fine distinctions can be made between them, this process is very similar to **prescribing the symptom**. It gives client families and their members permission to do something they are already doing and is intended to lower or eliminate resistance. Jay Haley (1976) is one of the best-known proponents of this technique. Paradox takes many forms, including the use of restraining, prescribing, and redefining:

1. In **restraining,** the therapist tells the client family that they are incapable of doing anything other than what they are doing. For example, a therapist might say: "In considering change, I am not sure you can do anything other than what you are presently doing."
2. In **prescribing,** family members are instructed to enact a troublesome dysfunctional behavior in front of the therapist. For instance, parents may be asked to show how they argue with their 16-year-old about when he will be allowed to get a driver's license. They are to continue the argument for about the same amount of time the argument usually takes and to come up with the same impasses.
3. **Redefining** is attributing positive connotations to symptomatic or troublesome actions. The idea is that symptoms have meaning for those who display them whether such meaning is logical or not. In the case of a school-phobic child, the therapist might redefine her behavior as an attempt to keep her parents together in the marriage through focusing their attention on her.

## Ordeals

The **ordeals** technique involves helping the client to give up symptoms that are more troublesome to maintain than they are worth (Haley, 1984). In this method, the therapist assigns a family or family member(s) the task of performing an ordeal in order to eliminate a symptom. The ordeal is a constructive or neutral behavior that must be performed before engaging in the undesirable behavior. For example, an ordeal might be to exercise before the onset of depression or to give a present to a despised person or group. In essence, the ordeal is always healthy, but is not an activity that those directed to do it want to engage in. The hope is that those involved will give up the symptom in order to avoid performing the constructive behavior.

## Pretend

The **pretend technique** is a more gentle and less confrontive technique than most of the other procedures used in strategic family therapy. Cloe Madanes (1981, 1984) is identified as the creator of this concept. Basically, the therapist asks family members to pretend to engage in a troublesome behavior, such as having a fight. The act of pretending to fight helps individuals change through experiencing control of a previously involuntary action.

## Positioning

The act of **positioning** by the therapist is one that involves acceptance and exaggeration of what family members are saying (Piercy & Sprenkle, 1986). If conducted properly, it helps the family see the absurdity of what they are doing. They are thereby freed to do something else. For example, if a family member states that her relationship with her father is "difficult," the therapist might respond: "No, it is hopeless" (Watzlawick, 1983).

# Role of the Therapist

The roles of strategic therapists differ among their subschools. However, those who work within this methodology share a belief in being active and flexible with their family clients. It is the therapist's responsibility in these family therapy approaches to plan strategies to resolve family problems. Therapists often proceed quickly and specifically in their focus on resolving presenting problems and virtually ignore family histories and personal diagnoses (Wylie, 1990). "They are symptom focused and behaviorally oriented" (Snider, 1992, p. 20).

"The first task of the therapist is to define a presenting problem in such a way that it can be solved" (Madanes, 1991, p. 396). Although the problem can be conceptualized in a number of ways, the therapist usually tries to define it as one that the family has voluntary control over and that involves a power struggle. In defining the problem in such a manner, the therapist sets out to help family members make changes that alter the family dynamics from a competitive stance (in which there are winners and losers) to a cooperative position (in which everyone wins) (Watzlawick, 1983).

Most strategic therapists are overtly active. For instance, Haley (1990) believes it is essential to make changes in people and families within the first three sessions. Thus, he works hard at reframing client's perceptions and presenting complaints. He also strives to come up with a unique innovative method to use in each case. He tailors his approach for each family in the same way as Milton Erickson, one of his mentors, and in the same way a surgeon would plan an operation.

Overall, strategic family therapists try to use presenting problems as ways to bring about change in families by giving them tasks that are usually carried out between sessions, that is, homework. "Therapists also use structural interventions such as attempting to unbalance family systems by joining with one or more members on a conflictual point, fortifying generational boundaries, and supporting members at particular times to accomplish a specific objective" (Snider, 1992, p. 20).

# Process and Outcome

The goal of strategic family therapy is to resolve, remove, or ameliorate the problem the family agreed to work on (Snider, 1992). In addition, the family must learn, at least indirectly, how to address other problems in a constructive manner. Often, resolving family difficulties involves a multitude of interventions or steps. Four common procedures for ensuring a successful outcome include:

1. defining a problem clearly and concisely
2. investigating all solutions that have previously been tried
3. defining a clear and concrete change to be achieved
4. formulating and implementing a strategy for change (Watzlawick, 1978)

Overall, the emphasis in strategic therapy (as in systemic family therapy) is on process rather than content. The methods used in bringing about change focus on breaking up vicious cycles of interaction and replacing them with virtuous cycles that highlight alternative ways of acting (Friesen, 1985).

# Unique Aspects of Strategic Family Therapy

## Emphases

A major emphasis of strategic family therapy is its flexibility as a viable means of working with a variety of client families. This approach has been successfully used in treating families and their members who display such dysfunctional behaviors as enmeshment, eating disorders, and substance abuse (Haley, 1980; Stanton, Todd, & Associates, 1982).

A second characteristic of this approach is that, with the exception of a few true believers, most therapists who use it "now concede that real change is possible at the individual and dyadic level—that the entire system need not always be involved in lower-order change" (Fish, 1988, p. 15). Because significant change can be brought about without having the entire family involved in treatment sessions, the chances of obtaining a desirable outcome are increased.

A third emphasis of strategic family therapy is its focus on innovation and creativity. As previously mentioned, strategic therapists trace their lineage to Milton Erickson, who was especially potent in devising novel ways to help his clients. Many of today's strategic family therapy practitioners, especially Cloe Madanes (1990), are a part of this tradition. For example, Madanes has devised a 16-step procedure for working with sex offenders and their victims. This approach is notable for its concreteness in obtaining clear facts, its linkage in connecting sexuality with spirituality, and its power in persuading the offender to seek forgiveness from the victim on his knees.

As a group, strategic family clinicians view the major goal of therapy as changing the perception and, hence, the interaction of families. Through their "introduction of the novel or unexpected, a frame of reference is broken and the structure of reality is rearranged" (Papp, 1984, p. 22).

A fourth quality of strategic family therapy is the way it can be employed with a number of other therapies, particularly the behavioral and structural family therapy schools of thought (Alexander & Parsons, 1982; Fish, 1988; Haley, 1976; Steinberg, Sayger, & Szykula, 1997). One reason this quality is so prevalent in strategic therapy is that one of its codevelopers, Jay Haley, worked at the Philadelphia Child Guidance Clinic in a structural setting and incorporated parts of that theory into his version of strategic treatment. Another reason is that behavioral family therapy focuses on defining, clarifying, and changing specific interactional patterns in a parallel manner to the strategic approach (Fish, 1988). A final reason is that many influential therapists have a historical or personal connection with strategic therapy. Consequently, they continue to be influenced in their thoughts and actions by dialogue and debate among and with strategic family therapists.

## Comparison with Other Theories

One aspect of strategic family therapy, especially of the MRI group, that set it apart from other family therapies early in its development is that it concentrates on one problem. Basically, a strategic family therapist focuses on one problem and helps families marshal their resources in dealing with an identified difficulty quickly and efficiently (Snider, 1992).

A second point of comparison is based on the accusation that strategic family therapy is too "cookbookish" and "mechanical" (Simon, 1984). This charge is the result of prescribed methods of treatment by the MRI and Jay Haley. In fairness, however, there is considerable flexibility among therapists who embrace this theory.

A third comparable quality associated with strategic family therapy is the controversial view about schizophrenia proposed by one of its leading proponents, Jay Haley. Haley, in essence, denies the existence of schizophrenia.

A fourth comparative feature of strategic family therapy involves the skill necessary to implement some of its methods. For instance, the use of paradox can be powerful in the hands of a skilled clinician, but its use can be a catastrophe if employed in a naive way (Friesen, 1985). Some strategic family therapy approaches demand considerable training of practitioners before they can be implemented properly.

A fifth comparative factor of strategic family therapy concerns time and emphasis. All subschools within this orientation restrict the number of therapeutic sessions. Although this format motivates families to work, it is limiting. For example, the seriousness or extent of problems may not be dealt with adequately (Wylie, 1992). It is hoped that by resolving one specific situation, families will learn problem-solving skills. Although this is the case for some families, it is not universal.

A final comparable quality of strategic family therapy is its lack of collaborative input from client families. Some strategic family therapy models, such as those devised by Haley, emphasize power techniques and the expertness of the therapist. All stress the creativeness of the therapist to find a solution for the family. Much like a physician, the strategic therapist who does not produce the desired results in clients usually takes the blame. This type of procedure is the antithesis of most other forms of family therapy.

A comparison between strategic and structural family therapies is shown in Figure 9.1. In some instances, the two approaches are so compatible that theorist Duncan Stanton (1981) has suggested they be integrated into a single approach. (Stanton's idea is not universally shared.) Although some professionals experience confusion over the differences between the two therapies, rules and guidelines are available to help either combine the

### Common View of the Family
- People are seen as interacting within a context that they influence and are influenced by.
- The family life cycle and developmental stages are important in the assessment of families and their members.
- Symptoms are system maintained and maintain the system.
- The family can change its behavior if the overall context in which they live is changed.

### Overlap in Therapy Process
- Treatment is viewed from a pragmatic perspective, although structural family therapy follows a more detailed plan of action in providing services than strategic family therapy.
- The emphasis is on the present, not the past.
- Repetitive and destructive patterns of behavior are focused on as targets of change.
- The emphasis of intervention is on family process not content.
- Both structural and strategic families therapies are symptom oriented.
- The family therapist is active in helping families change and often directs the process.
- Contracts for change are negotiated between the family and the therapist and are aimed at presenting problems and goals of treatment.
- Reframing is emphasized, not insight.
- Considerable effort is made by the therapist in "joining" the family and establishing rapport.
- The therapist assigns homework and tasks to be completed outside of the therapy sessions.
- The total time of treatment is relatively short, about 6 months.

### Distinctions Between Strategic and Structural Family Therapies
- "Structuralists emphasize the importance of system role relationships . . . whereas strategists emphasize mainly function or process" (Fraser, 1982, p. 14). In essence, the structuralists strive to help a family member change his or her position; the strategic family therapists concentrate on breaking up or changing dysfunctional repetitive patterns.
- "Structural views are centered around negative feedback cycles and breaking homeostatic bonds, whereas strategic views focus on positive feedback cycles and interrupting vicious cycles to create virtuous ones" (Fraser, 1982, p. 14). A negative feedback loop is one that maintains homeostasis. Structural family therapists try to break the status quo through restructuring, for example, by helping the family create new rules for an adolescent because rules that worked for him or her as a child are no longer appropriate. On the other hand, strategic family therapists seek to help families do less, not more, of a particular activity, for example, arguing. In the beginning of a family's history, arguing may have resolved some issues, so arguing continued (a positive feedback loop) with the expectation that more issues would be resolved. However, the results were negative (a vicious cycle). In strategic family therapy, attention is paid to positive deviations that are adaptable (a virtuous cycle).
- "The unit of intervention in structural therapy is the entire family unit and its subunits as they function now. . . . The Strategic unit of intervention may be with a subsystem of the family system" including an individual (Fraser, 1982, p. 14).

**Figure 9.1**

Distinctions and similarities in strategic and structural family therapy.

Sources: Adapted from "Structural and Strategic Family Therapy: A Basis for Marriage, or Grounds for Divorce?" by J. S. Fraser, 1982, *Journal of Marital and Family Therapy, 8*(2), 13–22. Copyright 1982, American Association for Marriage and Family Therapy. Reprinted by permission; and "An Integrated Structural/Strategic Approach to Family Therapy" by M. D. Stanton, 1981, *Journal of Marital and Family Therapy, 7*(4), 427–439. Copyright 1981, American Association for Marriage and Family Therapy. Reprinted with permission.

two approaches or sequence them in a complementary manner. For example, a general rule is that when structural interventions fail, therapists should try strategic methods because these methods were developed on more highly resistant clients (Friesen, 1985).

# ◾ Systemic (Milan) Family Therapy ◾

Systemic (Milan) family therapy is sometimes confused with the overall concept of "systemic" as an approach to family therapy. *Systemic* as a general term is inclusive and encompassing. It describes a therapeutic approach with interrelated elements. **Systemic family therapy**, also known as the Milan approach, stresses the interconnectedness of family members while also emphasizing the importance of second-order change in families (Tomm, 1984a, 1984b).

# Major Theorists

## Mara Selvini Palazzoli

Like many well-known therapists in the family therapy field, Mara Selvini Palazzoli was initially trained as a psychoanalyst. In her native Italy, she specialized in working with patients who had eating disorders, but she became increasingly frustrated with the results (Selvini Palazzoli, 1974). In 1967, she became the leader of a group of eight psychiatrists who were the forerunners in applying psychoanalytic ideas to working with families. Later they discovered the ideas of Bateson, Haley, Watzlawick, and others and began to modify their approach. By 1971, there was a systemic factioning of the group. Selvini Palazzoli, Boscolo, Cecchin, and Prata formed the Center for the Study of the Family in Milan, where they developed the Milan model (Wylie & Cooper, 2000).

The Milan team split up in 1980. Selvini Palazzoli and Prata continued to do family systems research until 1982. At that time, Selvini Palazzoli formed a new group to work with families of schizophrenics and anorectics (Selvini, 1988). Simultaneously, her conceptual ideas underwent change, and she began to describe her client families as engaged in a series of **games**. When families are engaged in games, the children and parents stabilize around disturbed behaviors in an attempt to benefit from them. To break up these games, family therapists must first meet with families and then with parents separately to give them an invariant or variant prescription (explained later in the techniques section) that is designed to produce a clear and stable boundary between generations.

Palazzoli died June 21, 1999, in Milan, Italy, at the age of 83. She was one of the family therapy field's "most unconventional and charismatic personalities" (Wylie & Cooper, 2000, p. 11).

# Premises of the Theory

Systemic family therapy is premised on the idea that therapists will take a systemic (circular) view of problem maintenance and a strategic (planned) orientation to change. Symptoms serve a purpose. Individual distress, anguish, or acting out is seen as the "thermometer of family functioning" (Snider, 1992, p. 13). Aberrant behaviors by one member of the family suggest a disturbance within the entire family. Therefore, systemic therapies concentrate on the consequences of family communication patterns and conflict between competing hierarchies. They shy away from doing anything more than accepting the symptoms as described by the family or family members.

The concept of neutrality is one of the main pillars underlying the Milan family systems approach (Selvini Palazzoli, Boscolo, Cecchin, & Prata, 1980). It is referred to as **therapeutic neutrality**. It keeps the therapist from being drawn into family coalitions and disputes and gives the therapist time to assess the dynamics within the family. This type of neutrality also encourages family members to generate solutions to their own problems (Boscolo, Cecchin, Hoffman, & Penn, 1987).

# Treatment Techniques

Systemic (Milan) therapists have created and utilized a number of therapeutic treatment techniques. In addition to paradox (described earlier) these five techniques are widely utilized: hypothesizing, positive connotation, circular questioning, invariant/variant prescriptions, and rituals.

## Hypothesizing

**Hypothesizing** is central to the Milan approach. It involves a meeting of treatment team members before the arrival of a family in order to formulate and discuss aspects of the family's situation that could be generating a symptom. During this pre-session, the team members attempt to prepare themselves for treating the family. Their belief is that they must come up with ideas about how a particular family operates, or the family will define the problem and treatment in a faulty way. Hypotheses are modified as treatment continues. Circularity throughout the family system is stressed.

## Positive Connotation

A **positive connotation** is a type of reframing in which each family member's behavior is labeled as benevolent and motivated by good intentions. For example, if a mother is overinvolved with her daughter, the therapist might label her behavior as one of concern. By giving positive connotations to behaviors, therapists simultaneously reduce resistance to treatment by the family and establish rapport.

## Circular Questioning

Circular questioning originated with the Milan team (Selvini Palazzoli et al., 1980). It focuses attention on family connections through framing every question so that it addresses differences in perception by family members about events or relationships. For example, each family member might be asked to state how he or she perceived the family dealing with a crisis situation. The intent is to highlight information, differences, and circular processes within the family system. It gives the family clear information while breaking down the idea of individual causes and helping family members raise questions.

## Invariant/Variant Prescriptions

An **invariant prescription** involves a specific kind of ritual, and it is given to parents with children who are psychotic or anorexic in an attempt to break up the family's dirty game (i.e., power struggle between generations sustained by symptomatic behaviors) (Selvini Palazzoli, 1986; Simon, 1987). The invariant prescription requires parents to unite so that children cannot manipulate them or stereotype them as "winners" or "losers" and thereby side with them.

The essence of this technique is that parents tell their symptomatic children that they have a secret, but they never reveal what the secret is. In addition, they record the reactions of family members to the fact that the parents have a secret. They then go out together for varying periods of time (some of them quite long) without telling their children where they are going or when they will return. This mysterious type of behavior allies parents in a new way and gives them an opportunity to observe and discuss the family's reactions. In the process, changes within the parents themselves and the family as a whole are noted. Constructive changes are preserved.

A **variant prescription** is given for the same purpose as an invariant one. The difference is that a variant prescription is tailored to a particular family and considers unique aspects of that family.

## Rituals

The assignment of **rituals** is an attempt to break up dysfunctional rules in the family (Selvini Palazzoli, Cecchin, Prata, & Boscolo, 1978). In essence, rituals are specialized directives that are meant to dramatize positive aspects of problem situations (Boscolo et al., 1987). Rituals occur daily at mealtime, bedtime, and during chores. They can occur, for example, when sitting down to a meal together or when saying "goodnight" to everyone before bed. They include five components essential to family health: membership, belief expression, identity, healing, and celebration (Imber-Black, 1988, 1989, 1999). In essence, a ritual is a type of prescription that directs the members of the family to change their behavior under certain circumstances. By changing the actions of the family members, the therapist hopes to change the cognitive map or meaning of the behavior. When prescribing a ritual, the therapist should state a specific time when the ritual is to be carried out.

Effective rituals are specific in describing what is to be done, who is to do it, and how it is to be done. For example, an anorexic girl might be given the assignment of saying to her dying grandmother every night: "I love you so much that I did not want my parents to feel much pain about your impending death, so I am starving myself to cause them to worry about me." The grandmother would respond: "Thank you, but your parents are strong enough to handle my situation and still love you."

# Role of the Therapist

In the Milan family systems approach, the therapist is both an expert and "a co-creator of the constantly evolving family system" (Friedlander, Wildman, & Heatherington, 1991, p.

397). The therapist in these roles takes a nonblaming stance, gives directives, and is neutral to the point of even avoiding the use of the verb "to be" (Boscolo et al., 1987). Thus, the Milan family systems therapist does not usually try overtly to challenge or change families. Instead, the therapist takes a paradoxical position of being a change agent who argues against change (Simon, 1987). As such, the therapist uses circular questioning and other indirect forms of intervention to bring about family transformation. The therapist stresses the positive connotations of a behavior and explains to the family how even the most troublesome symptom is "ultimately in the service of family harmony" (Simon, 1987, p. 19).

# Process and Outcome

When successful, systemic family therapy results in symptom resolution in a relatively short period of time (10 or fewer sessions). In addition, family dynamics change. The family experiences how family members are interlinked. The connection between what family members do and how the health of every member influences the others becomes evident. In addition, one member of the family stops being the focus of the family's problems, that is, the scapegoat. Further, nonproductive interactions and "games" change. As the family evolves and discards the **old epistemology,** or dated ideas, that do not fit their current situation, more productive and appropriate behaviors emerge (Tomm, 1984a). Perhaps most importantly, families make changes that are directed to their particular circumstance. For example, a family that was centered around eating problems can now become focused on affirmation of one another and clear communication.

In addition, if the therapy is successful, the process of growth within families continues after they formally terminate therapy. Growth continues because the family has experienced a pattern of change on which they can build; they have moved from a vicious to a virtuous cycle of interaction with renewed energy and focus.

# Unique Aspects of Systemic Therapy

## Emphases

One characteristic of systemic family therapy is its flexibility in being a viable means of working with a variety of client families. This approach has been successfully used in treating families and their members who display such dysfunctional behaviors as enmeshment, eating disorders, and substance abuse (Selvini Palazzoli, 1981).

A second aspect of systemic (Milan) family therapy is that therapists work in teams to help families solve problems. With few exceptions, systemic family therapists work with some team members present with the family and others behind a one-way mirror (Simon, 1986). The team approach is monetarily expensive, but it is effective. The team concept has been borrowed and modified by a number of other schools of family therapy and has proven especially popular as a format to use in educating novice family therapists.

The team approach is especially powerful in the hands of skilled clinicians, such as Peggy Papp (1980), who has devised a form of it known as the **Greek chorus.** In this format observers of a family treatment session (i.e., the team) may do such things as debate the merits of what a therapist is doing to bring about change. Families are helped to acknowledge and feel their ambivalence.

A third aspect of systemic therapy is its concentration on one problem over a short period of time. In so doing, systemic therapy helps families marshal their resources in dealing with an identified difficulty (Snider, 1992). Therapists who follow this approach might help a family find ways to share free time together so that members are not in competition with one another. Once that problem has been resolved, the family and therapist might spend their time and resources in more productive ways.

## Comparison with Other Theories

A major contrast of the Milan school with other theories is its "European bias toward non-intervention" (Simon, 1984, p. 28). The roots of the nonintervention approach, according to Salvador Minuchin, come from the European experience of Hitler and Nazi Germany. "In Europe, there is a great respect for people's individual boundaries" (Simon, 1984, p. 28). This same type of view is not shared worldwide, and the mentality of this approach is not universal.

A second comparable quality associated with systemic family therapy is the controversial view about schizophrenia proposed by one of its leading proponents, Mara Selvini Palazzoli. It is Selvini Palazzoli's contention that "schizophrenia always begins as a child's attempt to take sides in the stalemated relationship between . . . parents" (Simon, 1987, p. 19). Although Selvini Palazzoli's view is not exactly the same as that of Jay Haley in this matter, it is interesting that Selvini Palazzoli, who was influenced by Haley, holds such a view because, as previously discussed, Haley's position on schizophrenia is controversial.

A final comparative feature of the Milan systemic approach is that, similar to strategic family therapy, there is an attempt in this treatment to tailor interventions to the specifics of a family. Therapists working as a team are responsible for creating innovative treatment plans. Like strategic and structural family therapies, systemic family therapy takes on some of the most outwardly difficult families with which to work.

## CASE ILLUSTRATION

### THE WILSON FAMILY

Bo and Harriet Wilson have been married for 15 years and are the parents of Rich, age 12, and Ryan, age 11. Rich has a learning disability and is in a special school. He also has a physical handicap, having been born with dislocated hips. He requires frequent medical attention from physicians and is described as "a source of worry" by his parents. He wears braces. Ryan, on the other hand, is bright, attractive, and full of energy. He loves sports and is a member of a number of youth teams, including soccer, basketball, and baseball. He seems to have little interest in his brother's condition and is quite demanding on his parents, insisting that they "take him" to games and play with him.

Bo is a painter and his work is seasonal. During the winter months, he has more time for his family and himself. He has tended to drink heavily during the winter months, but during the past 3 years, he has begun drinking heavily all year round. As a result, he misses work, gets fired from jobs, and is not paid regularly. He has lost the medical benefits he once had. Harriet is a waitress. She initially worked only during the lunch shift, but during the past year, she has begun working breakfast and dinner shifts as well. She is physically drained at the end of the day but has to do housework when she is home. She is concerned that none of the males in her life are doing well and that the family is "falling apart." She made the call for the therapy appointment.

### Conceptualization of Family: Strategic and Systemic Perspective

The Wilsons are disengaged interpersonally and are under a lot of financial and physical stress. They are displaying a number of repetitive patterns, such as excessive drinking and overwork, that are not benefiting family members individually or the family as a whole. The children are demanding physically and psychologically. Harriet is overfunctioning; Bo is underfunctioning.

### Process of Treatment: Strategic and Systemic Therapies

To treat the Wilsons, strategic and systemic family therapists would convey to them initially that treatment would consist of a limited number of sessions, for example, 10. The family would be asked before treatment began to define their problem/concern in a solvable format, for example, "to decrease the amount of friction, that is, the number of fights/arguments, between family members." Removal of the problem/concern would be seen as an index of change (Bodin, 1981). Regardless of what the problem/concern was, it would be accepted and seen by the therapist as serving some useful function.

In treatment, it would be ideal if the whole family could be seen. The therapist, in any of these approaches, would initiate actions and interventions and would clearly be in charge. The therapist would first gather information through such procedures as circular questioning or direct observations of nonverbal behaviors. During this process, the problem of friction would be reframed as behaviors associated with concern by family members for the well-being of the family as a whole. Attention would be focused on creating a specific approach that would help the Wilson family make needed transitions and second-order change. Some of the initial interventions of strategic and systemic family therapists might go as follows:

1. In the MRI form of strategic therapy, a directive might initially be given to break up the family's homeostasis: "Spend an hour with each other doing a mutually decided activity, such as playing board games like checkers and monopoly." The rules of the game, as well as the rules of the family (e.g., how decisions are made to play games), would be discussed when the family returned for its next appointment.

2. In the Washington School (i.e., Haley/Madanes) form of strategic therapy, the use of pretend might be employed. This would require members of the family to pretend to care for each other in some specific way, such as giving one another imaginary gifts of traits/characteristics (e.g., bravery, assertion) or needed necessities. Thus, activity would take place in the presence of the therapist. If such an approach were not utilized, an ordeal might be

employed. For example, a son might be required to give his mother money before he would be allowed to argue with her.

3. In the Milan format, the therapist along with the observation/treatment team might have the family engage in a ritual, such as eating dinner together in silence, for an extended period of time. At the conclusion of the meal, each member of the family would have to convey to the rest of the family how isolated and lonely he or she felt, and the others would simply acknowledge what they heard.

Regardless of their initial intervention, strategic and systemic family therapists would be active in sessions with this family and look for ways to bring about rapid change. With the Wilsons, a focus might be to get the parents more involved with each other and with their children. This might mean further treatment for the alcoholism and workaholism in Bo and Harriet, respectively. It might also mean finding ways for Rich and Ryan to cooperate with each other and with their parents. Ryan, for instance, might be able to focus some of his attention on tutoring Rich academically and athletically; Rich could concentrate on encouraging and supporting Ryan in his practices and games.

# Summary and Conclusion

Strategic and systemic family therapies are among the most popular approaches to working with families. They are short term, specific, positive, and appealing to families that have difficulty with organization and development. Inherent in their techniques are directives designed to change behaviors and thoughts, which are often overlooked by other therapeutic approaches (Perry, 1992).

The Mental Research Institute, following the creative genius of Milton Erickson, formulated the innovative foundation of the strategic therapy model in the 1960s. Members of this Palo Alto institute limited to ten the number of sessions they would agree to see families. They also consented to accept for treatment the problems families wished to work on, as long as they were clearly definable. Instead of trying to change families as they saw fit, these pioneers in family therapy focused on working with symptomatic behavior(s) and viewed dysfunctional behavior as having an underlying positive and beneficial basis. The MRI version of strategic family therapy has stood the test of time and is still being both refined and utilized.

The MRI therapeutic approach was later modified by Jay Haley, one of its initial participants. Haley's particular contributions include his ways of working with young adults and their families who conspire to keep them from leaving home. His partner at their Washington institute, Cloe Madanes, is among the most creative therapists anywhere. Both versions of strategic family therapy have similarities and differences related to structural family therapy. They have influenced a wide variety of therapeutic approaches.

Strategic family therapy, particularly the MRI approach, was one of the influences in the original Milan, Italy, systemic family therapy treatment team. The Milan group originally concentrated on treating eating disorders, but from its study of strategic family therapy, it broadened its base.

Systemic family therapy has been both praised and criticized for its treatment procedures. Overall, some of the techniques employed in strategic and systemic family therapies—for example, hypothesizing, utilization of teams, invariant prescriptions, circular questioning, and the use of paradox—are among the most creative ever formulated. These therapeutic approaches appear to be strong. They are applauded for making necessary and sufficient changes that help families work better. However, these brief-oriented family therapies are criticized for not dealing extensively enough with family problems. Overall, strategic and systemic family therapies are well-defined, specific, and goal-directed treatments that employ a variety of techniques.

# Summary Table
## Strategic and Systemic Family Therapies

### Major Theorists

*Strategic*

| | | |
|---|---|---|
| Milton Erickson | Mental Research Institute | Paul Watzlawick |
| John Weakland | Richard Fisch | Washington School |
| Jay Haley | Cloe Madanes | James Keim |

*Systemic*

| | | |
|---|---|---|
| Mara Selvini Palazzoli | Luigi Boscolo | Gianfranco Cecchin |
| Guiliana Pata | Karl Tomm | Lynn Hoffman |
| Peggy Papp | Olga Silverstein | Peggy Penn |
| Richard Rabkin | Joel Bergman | Carlos Sluzki |
| James Coyne | | |

### Premises of the Theory

People and families can change quickly.

Treatment should be simple and pragmatic.

The concentration is on changing symptomatic behaviors and rigid rules.

With hard work and the use of techniques such as enactment, ordeals, paradox, pretend, and rituals, families can change their unhealthy behaviors.

### Treatment Techniques

Although these approaches can be selectively used with dyads and individuals, the family is treated as a system.

The focus of treatment is on resolving present problems and bringing about change. Definable behavioral goals are targeted. Insight is minimized.

Therapeutic techniques include the following:

- Reframing (including positive connotation)
- Using directives

- Using compliance-based and defiance-based paradox (including prescribing the symptoms)
- Using invariant and variant prescriptions (to disrupt dirty games)
- Promoting second-order change
- Discouraging interpretation
- Pretending
- Using cooperative hierarchies
- Assigning ordeals
- Assigning rituals
- Utilizing teams
- Using circular questioning

### Role of the Therapist

The therapist is responsible for overcoming resistance in the family and designing strategies for solving problems that are novel. One way to overcome resistance is to positively accept whatever problem the family brings.

The therapist is much like a physician in taking responsibility for the success of treatment.

The therapist must plan ahead and develop strategies for helping families change.

### Process and Outcome

Family therapist uses multiple outcomes.

Four common procedures used are defining a problem clearly, investigating all solutions previously tried, defining concrete change, and implementing a strategy for change.

Change focuses on breaking up vicious cycles of interaction and replacing them with virtuous cycles.

### Unique Aspects of Strategic and Systemic Family Therapies

Strategic and systemic therapies emphasize:

- seeing symptoms in a positive way
- short-term treatment (usually 10 or fewer sessions)
- changing present problematic behavior
- tailor-made techniques for each family
- innovative treatments
- flexible, evolving, and creative approaches (that combine easily with other theories)

### Comparison with Other Theories

Historical patterns of family interaction are ignored.

The medical model, that is, expertise, is emphasized.

The use of teams, such as in the Milan approach, is featured.

The employment of paradox is widely used.

Families can change in treatment but not understand why.

Some confusion exists about the differences between strategic and structural family therapy.

# References

Alexander, J., & Parsons, B. (1982). *Functional family therapy.* Pacific Grove, CA: Brooks/Cole.

Bodin, A. (1981). The interactional view: Family therapy approaches to the Mental Research Institute. In A. S. Gurman & D. P. Kniskern (Eds.), *Handbook of family therapy* (Vol. I, pp. 267–309). New York: Brunner/Mazel.

Boscolo, L., Cecchin, G., Hoffman, L., & Penn, P. (1987). *Milan systemic family therapy.* New York: Basic Books.

Campbell, D., Draper, R., & Crutchley, E. (1991). The Milan systemic approach to family therapy. In A. S. Gurman & D. P. Kniskern (Eds.), *Handbook of family therapy* (Vol. II, pp. 325–362). New York: Brunner/Mazel.

Fish, J. M. (1988, July/August). Reconciling the irreconcilable. *Family Therapy Networker, 12,* 15.

Fraser, J. S. (1982). Structural and strategic family therapy: A basis for marriage or grounds for divorce? *Journal of Marital and Family Therapy, 8,* 13–22.

Friedlander, M. L., Wildman, J., & Heatherington, L. (1991). Interpersonal control in structural and Milan systemic family therapy. *Journal of Marital and Family Therapy, 17,* 395–408.

Friesen, J. D. (1985). *Structural-strategic marriage and family therapy.* New York: Gardner.

Gladding, S. T. (1993). *Milestones.* Unpublished manuscript.

Haley, J. (1963). *Strategies of psychotherapy.* New York: Grune & Stratton.

Haley, J. (1973). *Uncommon therapy.* New York: Norton.

Haley, J. (1976). *Problem-solving therapy.* San Francisco: Jossey-Bass.

Haley, J. (1980). *Leaving home: The therapy of disturbed young people.* New York: McGraw-Hill.

Haley, J. (1984). *Ordeal therapy.* San Francisco: Jossey Bass.

Haley, J. (1990). Interminable therapy. In J. Zeig & S. Gilligan (Eds.), *Brief therapy: Myths, methods, and metaphors.* New York: Brunner/Mazel.

Imber-Black, E. (1988). *Families and larger systems: A family therapist's guide through the labyrinth.* New York: Guilford.

Imber-Black, E. (1989, July/August). Creating rituals in therapy. *Family Therapy Networker, 13,* 39–47.

Imber-Black, E. (1999). Creating meaningful rituals for new life cycle transitions. In B. Carter & M. McGoldrick (Eds.), *The expanded family life cycle* (3rd ed., pp. 202–214). Boston: Allyn & Bacon.

Keim, J. (2000). Strategic family therapy. In A. Horne (Ed.). *Family counseling and therapy* (3rd ed., pp. 170–207). Itasca, IL: F. E. Peacock.

Madanes, C. (1981). *Strategic family therapy.* San Francisco: Jossey-Bass.

Madanes, C. (1984). *Behind the one-way mirror: Advances in the practice of strategic therapy.* San Francisco: Jossey-Bass.

Madanes, C. (1990). *Sex, love, and violence.* New York: Norton.

Madanes, C. (1991). Strategic family therapy. In A. S. Gurman & D. P. Kniskern (Eds.), *Handbook of family therapy* (Vol. II, pp. 396–416). New York: Brunner/Mazel.

Papp, P. (1980). The Greek chorus and other techniques of paradoxical therapy. *Family Process, 19,* 45–57.

Papp, P. (1984, September/October). The creative leap. *Family Therapy Networker, 8,* 20–29.

Perry, V. (1992). *An examination of attention deficit disorders without hyperactivity: A case study from a strategic family systems perspective.* Unpublished master's research report, Wake Forest University, Winston-Salem, North Carolina.

Piercy, F. P., & Sprenkle, D. H. (1986). *Family therapy sourcebook.* New York: Guilford.

Priebe, S., & Pommerien, W. (1992). The therapeutic system as viewed by depressive inpatients and outcome: An expanded study. *Family Process, 31,* 433–439.

Selvini Palazzoli, M. (1988). *The work of Mara Selvini Palazzoli.* Northvale, NJ: Jason Aronson.

Selvini Palazzoli, M. (1974). *Self-starvation.* London: Human Context Books.

Selvini Palazzoli, M. (1981). *Self-starvation: From the intrapsychic to the transpersonal approach to anorexia nervosa.* New York: Aronson.

Selvini Palazzoli, M. (1986). Towards a general model of psychotic family games. *Journal of Marital and Family Therapy, 12,* 339–349.

Selvini Palazzoli, M., Boscolo, L., Cecchin, G., & Prata, G. (1980). Hypothesizing-circularity-neutrality. *Family Process, 19,* 73–85.

Selvini Palazzoli, M., Cecchin, G., Prata, G., & Boscolo, L. (1978). *Paradox and counterparadox.* New York: Jason Aronson.

Sexton, T. L., & Montgomery, D. (1994). Ethical and therapeutic acceptability: A study of paradoxical techniques. *The Family Journal: Counseling and Therapy for Couples and Families, 2,* 215–228.

Simon, R. (1982, September/October). Behind the one-way mirror: An interview with Jay Haley. *Family Therapy Networker, 6,* 18–25, 28–29, 58–59.

Simon, R. (1984, November/December). Stranger in a strange land: An interview with Salvador Minuchin. *Family Therapy Networker, 8,* 20–31.

Simon, R. (1986, September/October). Behind the one-way kaleidoscope: An interview with Cloe Madanes. *Family Therapy Networker, 10,* 19–29, 64–67.

Simon, R. (1987, September/October). Good-bye paradox, hello invariant prescription: An interview with Mara Selvini Palazzoli. *Family Therapy Networker, 11,* 16–33.

Snider, M. (1992). *Process family therapy.* Boston: Allyn & Bacon.

Stanton, D., Todd, T., & Associates. (1982). *The family therapy of drug abuse and addiction.* New York: Guilford.

Stanton, M. R. (1981). An integrated structural/strategic approach to family therapy. *Journal of Marital and Family Therapy, 7,* 427–439.

Steinberg, E. B., Sayger, T. V., & Szykula, S. A. (1997). The effects of strategic and behavioral family therapies on child behavior and depression. *Contemporary Family Therapy, 19,* 537–551.

Tomm, K. M. (1984a). One perspective on the Milan approach: Part I. Overview of development, theory, and practice. *Journal of Marital and Family Therapy, 10,* 113–125.

Tomm, K. M. (1984b). One perspective on the Milan approach: Part II. Description of session format, interviewing style, and interventions. *Journal of Marital and Family Therapy, 10,* 253–271.

Watzlawick, P. (1978). *The language of change.* New York: Basic Books.

Watzlawick, P. (1983). *The situation is hopeless but not serious.* New York: W. W. Norton.

Wylie, M. S. (1990, March/April). Brief therapy on the couch. *Family Therapy Networker, 14,* 26–35, 66.

Wylie, M. S. (1992, January/February). The evolution of a revolution. *Family Therapy Networker, 16,* 17–29, 98–99.

Wylie, M. S., & Cooper, G. (2000, March/April). Remembering Mara Selvini Palazzoli. *Family Therapy Networker, 24,* 11.

# CHAPTER 10

# Solution-Focused and Narrative Family Therapies

He changed
giving her small compliments at breakfast such as:
"I like the way your hair looks" or
"Nice dress."

She wondered:
"What is he doing?"
But she also knew she liked his words.

So as the days continued
she responded
and acts of kindness became more common.

He changed
She changed
They changed
And it was for the better.

*Gladding, 1996*

The most recent theoretical development in the field of family therapy is the creation of solution-focused and narrative family therapies. Solution-focused family therapy grew out of strategic therapy, particularly the MRI model. Yet, it also represents a departure from that tradition by concentrating on finding solutions instead of dealing with problems. Narrative family therapy originated in Australia and New Zealand and focuses on helping families solve difficulties by depersonalizing them and rewriting their own family stories.

The two most experienced and elegant spokespersons for solution-focused family therapy are Steve deShazer and Bill O'Hanlon, both of whom studied with Milton Erickson. The model appeared in its earliest form in the writings of Steve deShazer and his associates at their Brief Family Therapy Center in Milwaukee, Wisconsin (deShazer, 1982, 1985, 1988, 1991). The writings and work of Bill O'Hanlon and his associates also are solution focused (O'Hanlon & Weiner-Davis, 1989; O'Hanlon & Wilk, 1987). Present advocates of the solution-focused theoretical position include Patricia O'Hanlon Hudson (Hudson & O'Hanlon, 1991), Michele Weiner-Davis, Alan Gurman, Eve Lipchik, and Scott Miller.

Michael White and David Epston (1990) formulated narrative therapy. While the focus of this approach is on engaging families in solution-oriented therapeutic processes, it is distinct from the approaches of deShazer and O'Hanlon in its origin, having been derived from the research and writings of Gregory Bateson, Edward Bruner, and Michel Foucault (Monk, 1998). Difficulties are externalized and families are asked to work together as a team to develop strategies for overcoming problems. Yet, just as solution-focused therapy has a Midwest origin with a worldwide application, so narrative family therapy has a Pacific Rim genesis with a global usefulness.

In this chapter, solution-focused family therapy is examined first, followed by an examination of narrative family therapy.

# ◼ Solution-Focused Family Therapy ◼

## Major Theorists

Many of the major figures in solution-focused therapy originally worked with one another at the Brief Family Therapy Center in Milwaukee. Notables attached to the center at one time or another include the husband/wife team of Steve deShazer and Insoo Berg and also Michele Weiner-Davis and Eve Lipchik. Even though Bill O'Hanlon was never a part of this group, he has been influenced by the Brief Family Therapy Center at least indirectly in his collaborative writing with Weiner-Davis. DeShazer and O'Hanlon are highlighted here.

## Steve deShazer

Steve deShazer began his career by working at the Mental Research Institute in the mid-1970s. In the late 1970s, deShazer and a group of individuals in Milwaukee established the Brief Family Therapy Center (Kaplan, 2000). He first gained national attention as director of the center and began to emerge and gain recognition as a major theorist in family therapy in the 1980s. Initially, deShazer was considered to be a strategic family therapist who was influenced by the work of not only Milton Erickson but also Gregory Bateson, and the staff of the MRI. Yet, during the 1980s and into the present, the writings and presentations of deShazer and Berg have become distinct from the mainstream of the strategic family therapy approach.

DeShazer (1982) identifies his theory as *brief family therapy*, sometimes called just *brief therapy*, and describes it as an ecosystemic approach. His approach, like that of the Milan group, employs a team whenever possible. The team, collectively known as consultants, transmits messages to the therapist at a designated break time in the session. They observe from behind a one-way mirror. Thus, the family in treatment is sometimes the beneficiary of multiple inputs. As with any theory, deShazer has devised special terms to describe the techniques that make his approach unique.

## Bill O'Hanlon

Bill O'Hanlon entered family therapy because of his interest in his own life experiences. As an adolescent, he was unhappy and shy. As a college student, he was isolated and uncomfortable in the world. He reports that he felt "like all exposed nerve—no skin—everything hurt" (Krauth, 1995, p. 24). He experimented with drugs and noticed that "the reality we all take for granted could be changed by a couple of micrograms of something introduced into one's body" (Bubenzer & West, 1993, p. 366). He also contemplated suicide, but changed his mind when a friend offered him hope by promising him a lifetime of free rent on a Nebraska farm she would inherit, if he would stay alive. That possibility changed his outlook on life and led to his interest in therapeutic work beyond repairing damage or dealing with pathology.

Later, after earning a tailor-made master's degree from Arizona State University in family therapy, he went on to receive special tutelage under Milton Erickson in exchange for being Erickson's gardener. The influence of Erickson on O'Hanlon was profound and shifted his attention to focusing on solutions. O'Hanlon was also influenced by the work done at the Mental Research Institute.

In 1980, O'Hanlon set out to become a major proponent of solution-focused therapy, which he now prefers to call **possibility therapy** (Bubenzer & West, 1993; Krauth, 1995). His motivation was to shift the focus of family therapy from problems to solutions. He characterizes his approach as one that is pragmatic and full of Midwest values.

# Premises of the Theory

Solution-focused family treatment is built on the philosophy of social constructionism, that is, family therapy includes the social context, or cultural context, of a family. Because culture influences the way families view the world, the philosophy of constructivism also must be considered in working with families. **Constructivism** states that reality is not an objective entity, but a reflection of observation and experience (Maturana & Varela, 1987; Simon, Stierlin, & Wynne, 1985).

In addition, solution-focused therapy shares some of the same premises about families as the MRI strategic and Milan systemic approaches. At the foundation of this approach is the belief that dysfunctional families get "stuck" in dealing with problems (deShazer, 1985). These families basically use an unsatisfactory method to solve their difficulties, that is, they rely on patterns that do not work (Bubenzer & West, 1993). Solution-focused family therapy is aimed toward breaking such repetitive, nonproductive behavioral patterns by deliberately setting up situations in which families take a more positive view of troublesome situations and actively participate in doing something different. "It is not necessary to know the cause of the complaint or even very much about the complaint itself in order to resolve it" (Cleveland & Lindsey, 1995, p. 145). Rather, the presenting problem is seen as the problem for which a solution needs to be worked out (Kaplan, 2000). Therefore, there is no need for extensive analysis.

Identifying what is a problem versus what is not a problem is a key component in the solution-focused perspective (deShazer, 1988). Exceptions to general ways of behaving and viewing situations are emphasized (O'Hanlon & Wilk, 1987). The aim is to help families unlock their set views, to be creative, and to generate novel approaches that may be applicable in a number of circumstances. It is believed that all families have resources and strengths with which to resolve complaints (Cleveland & Lindsey, 1995). The task is simply getting them to use the abilities they already have. Therefore, the focus is on solutions, not problems. To increase motivation and expectation, solution-focused family therapy, like strategic and systemic therapy, emphasizes short-term treatment, between 5 and 10 sessions.

As a theory, solution-focused family therapy does not focus on a detailed family history of problems. Such a process is believed to be unhelpful (deShazer, 1985; O'Hanlon & Weiner-Davis, 1989). A foundational belief of this approach is that causal understanding is unnecessary. To stress this point, O'Hanlon and Wilk (1987) state that every psychotherapy office should have a couch for therapists, instead of clients, because "every now and then, in the course of a session, a hypothesis might accidentally enter the therapist's head, and the best remedy for it is to lie down until it goes away" (p. 98).

Another premise of solution-focused family therapy is that families really want to change. As a way of underscoring this idea, deShazer (1984) has declared the death of resistance as a concept. Thus, when families do not follow therapists' directions, they are "cooperating" by teaching therapists the best way to help them.

A final concept underlying solution-focused family therapy is that only a small amount of change is necessary. An analogy that is used to illustrate this point is that a one-degree error in flying across the United States will result in a plane being considerably off course in the end (deShazer, 1985). Small amounts of change can also be reinforcing to families in helping them realize they can make progress. It boosts confidence and optimism and, in effect, creates a "ripple effect" (Spiegel & Linn, 1969).

# Treatment Techniques

Solution-focused therapy constructs solutions in collaboration with the client (Kiser, Piercy, & Lipchik, 1993). One subtle but primary treatment technique is to co-create a problem with a family. For the therapeutic process to be productive, initially, an agreement must be made as to which problem they want to solve. For example, a therapist and a family must agree that a family's failure to discipline a child properly is the difficulty that needs to be addressed.

A second key component in treatment is to ask a family for a hypothetical solution to their situation. Such a process is often achieved by asking the **miracle question;** for example, "If a miracle happened tonight and you woke up tomorrow and the problem was solved, what would you do differently?" (Walter & Peller, 1993, p. 80). Such a question invites family members to suspend their present frames of reference and enter a reality that they wish to achieve. A miracle question is asked only after the therapist has gained enough background information on a family and the family itself has demonstrated its ability to respond positively to treatment and to notice exceptions to its complaints.

Another novel technique in solution-focused therapy related to the first two emphases is to **focus on exceptions,** that is, to look for "negative" or "positive" space (or time when a family goal may be happening) (Krauth, 1995). "In a practical sense, exceptions do not exist in the real world of clients; they must be cooperatively invented or constructed by both the client and the therapist while exploring what happens when the problem does not occur" (Fleming & Rickord, 1997, p. 289). For example, a family that is quarrelling a lot might find that they are peaceful whenever they sit down to eat. At such times, they may agree to disagree and actually have civil conversations with one another. By examining the dynamics of the family at this time, members may learn something about themselves and the dynamics of their relationship and in the process become different. "Inventing exceptions to problems deconstructs the client's frame: I am this way, or it always happens that way" (Fleming & Rickord, 1997, p. 289).

Solution-focused family therapists following deShazer and Berg's approach use the technique of scaling, too. In **scaling**, questions are asked using a scale of 1 (low) to 10 (high) to help move clients toward their goals. For example, the therapist might say: "On a scale of one to ten, how far do you think you have come in solving your problem?" If the client family replies "six," the therapist would then challenge them to think what it would take to move them to "seven." By answering the question, the client family could reach a new understanding in regard to their goal and what immediate, realistic, and measurable steps they would have to take to get there (Fleming & Rickord, 1997).

Yet a fifth emphasis in this approach involves second-order (qualitative) change, or a qualitatively different way of doing something. The goal is to change the family's organization and structure. This change can be accomplished through planning interventions in accordance with the order of events within a family's life or by altering the frequency and duration of a dysfunction (O'Hanlon, 1987). For example, a family that has been having long fights at dinner might agree to finish their meal before arguing and then limit their disagreement time to 15 minutes. This type of change in the structure and length of events is likely to alter family dynamics.

Another intervention is to give the family a **compliment**. For solution-focused therapists, especially deShazer (1982), a compliment is a written message designed to praise a family for its strengths and build a "yes set" within it. A compliment consists of a positive statement with which all members of a family can agree. For example, the therapist might say: "I am impressed with your hard work to bring about change and the way all of you are discussing what needs to happen next." A compliment is always planned as a lead-in to giving a family a task or assignment.

A seventh major technique is to provide the family with a **clue,** or an intervention that mirrors the usual behavior of a family. It is intended to alert a family to the idea that some behavior is likely to continue (deShazer, 1982). For example, the intervention of the therapist might be: "Don't worry about working too hard in trying to spend time together talking, because conversation is something that regularly occurs in your environment and you can do it naturally." The idea behind clueing is "to build mutual support and momentum for carrying out later interventions" (Sauber, L'Abate, & Weeks, 1985, p. 23).

A final treatment intervention is to use procedures that have worked before and that have a universal application. These **skeleton keys** will help families unlock a variety of problems (deShazer, 1985). For instance, deShazer has refined five interventions that have been useful to him in a number of situations (deShazer, 1985; deShazer & Molnar, 1984):

1. "Between now and next time we meet, we (I) want you to observe, so that you can tell us (me) next time, what happens in your (life, marriage, family, or relationship) that you want to continue to happen" (deShazer, 1985, p. 298). Such a request encourages a client family to look at the stability of the problems on which they wish to work.

2. "Do something different" (p. 300). This type of request encourages individuals and the family to explore the range of possibilities they have, rather than to continue to do what they believe is correct. DeShazer gives an example of a woman who complained that her husband, a police detective, was staying out late every night with his friends. The message she received from the deShazer team was that her husband might want more mysterious behavior from her. Therefore, one night she hired a babysitter, rented a motel room, and stayed out until 5 A.M. Her husband came in at 2 A.M. Nothing was said, but her husband began staying home at night.

3. "Pay attention to what you do when you overcome the temptation or urge to . . . perform the symptom or some behavior associated with the complaint" (p. 302). This instruction helps families to realize that symptoms are under their control.

4. "A lot of people in your situation would have . . . " (p. 302). This type of statement again helps family members realize they may have options other than those they are exercising. Through such awareness, they can begin to make needed changes.

5. "Write, read, and burn your thoughts." This experience consists of writing about past times, such as times spent with an ex-spouse, and then reading and burning the writings the next day.

Overall, solution-focused therapy interventions help the client family to view their situation differently. These interventions can also give them hope, thereby assisting clients in powerful ways (Bubenzer & West, 1993). To use the words of deShazer and Molnar (1984): "It now appears to us that the therapists' ability to see change and to help the clients to do so as well, constitutes a most potent clinical skill" (p. 304). Families become more empowered as a result of participating in solution-focused therapy.

# Role of the Therapist

One of the first roles of a solution-focused therapist is to determine how active a client family will be in the process of change. Clients usually fall into one of three categories: visitors, complainants, or customers. **Visitors** are not involved in the problem and are not part of the solution. **Complainants**, as their name implies, complain about situations but can be observant and describe problems even if they are not invested in solving them. Finally, **customers** are not only able to describe a problem and how they are involved in it, but are willing to work to solve it. If a therapist is working with customers or can help visitors and complainants evolve into customers, intervention strategies can be developed (Fleming & Rickord, 1997).

In the process of helping the client family become involved in therapy, a solution-focused family therapist becomes a "facilitator of change, one who helps clients access the resources and strengths they already have but are not aware of or are not utilizing" (Cleveland & Lindsey, 1995, p. 145). To do so, solution-focused practitioners focus attention on complaints that families want to change and work with families in helping them gain a different perspective on a problem. They accomplish this goal partly through their words. Language becomes important (West, Bubenzer, Smith, & Hamm, 1997). Positive assumptions about change are constantly conveyed by the therapist. For example, the therapist might ask a "presuppositional question" such as "What good thing happened since our last session?" "By selecting a specific verb tense, or implying the occurrence of a particular event, the family is led to believe that a solution will be achieved" (Gale, 1991, p. 43). Likewise, when an improvement occurs, therapists use "positive blame" and recognition of competence through such questions as "How did you make that happen?" (Fleming & Rickord, 1997).

Solution-focused family therapists believe that it is important to "fit" therapeutic interventions into the context of family behavior. The fit of a solution has been particularly articulated by deShazer (1985). He contends that a solution does not have to be as complex as the presenting problem and need not include everyone in the family. He uses the metaphor of locks and keys to illustrate what he means. Locks may be complex, but opening them does not require a similar complexity of keys. In fact, several keys may fit the lock (or problem) well enough *to open the door to change.* Skeleton keys (i.e., standardized therapeutic techniques) can be helpful in dealing with most locks regardless of complexity.

To obtain a proper solution fit for a family, deShazer (1985) uses a team to begin **mapping** or sketching out the course of successful intervention. From the mapping experience, multiple perspectives about the family's problem are given. It is up to the family to define what they wish to achieve; the therapist then helps them define clear, specific goals that can be conceptualized concretely (deShazer, 1985; O'Hanlon & Weiner-Davis, 1989). It is through this process that families and therapists begin to create solutions, that is, desired behaviors. "Therapy is over when the agreed upon outcome has been reached" (O'Hanlon & Wilk, 1987, p. 109).

Solution-focused family therapists encourage families to make small changes and to do so rapidly (deShazer, 1985; O'Hanlon & Weiner-Davis, 1989). The therapist encourages the family to focus on changes in their behaviors, changes in their perceptions, and the recognition and use of family resources/strengths that can be brought to bear on a problematic situation (Cleveland & Lindsey, 1995). One way of making such change is through a "gender solution-focused genogram to help clients identify the beliefs and behaviors related to their presenting problems" especially those involving gender role messages from the past that have negatively influenced their present behaviors (Softas-Nall, Baldo, & Tiedemann, 1999, p. 179). Regardless of the method used, once small change is achieved, the therapist gets out of the way and lets the "beneficial difference amplify itself naturally" (Fleming & Rickord, 1997, p. 289).

In solution-focused family therapy, the therapist does not distinguish between short-term and long-term problems, because such a difference is irrelevant. Some problematic behaviors endure longer than others because often the right solutions have not been tried. Solution-focused therapists are always challenging families to envision a "future that has possibilities of change" (Bubenzer & West, 1993, p. 372). This type of focusing on how things will be different in the future "provides hope and expands the options for solutions" (Erdman, 2000, p. 100).

# Process and Outcome

Solution-focused family therapy concentrates on encouraging client families to seek solutions and tap internal resources. It encourages, challenges, and sets up expectations for change. The concept of pathology does not play a part in the treatment process. Rather, solution-focused therapists see client families as cooperative. They frequently commend the family on an aspect of a member's behavior, even if the behavior seems negative to the family. Solution-focused therapy takes the Ericksonian position that change is inevitable; it is only a matter of when it will happen. This type of therapy is oriented toward the future and helps client families change their focus and reframe their situations positively. By stressing that the family can change, finding incidents where the family acts differently than usual, asking optimistic questions, and reinforcing small but specific movement, solution-focused family therapy helps its families resolve difficulties and make needed changes.

# Unique Aspects of Solution-Focused Family Therapy

## Emphases

As a group, solution-focused family therapies concentrate on and are directed by a family's theory (i.e., their story). Before any attempt is made to help families change, their experiences are accepted. O'Hanlon compares this type of approach with the Rogerian concept of first listening attentively to how people are feeling before trying to implement change (Bubenzer & West, 1993).

A second characteristic of solution-focused therapy is that therapists assist families in defining their situations clearly, precisely, and with possibilities. "The defined problem should be achievable" (Todd, 1992, p. 174). Sometimes success is measured in the elimination of problems. Often, therapy is significant if the family changes its perception of a situation or discovers exceptions to troublesome times. Regardless, whatever the family brings to therapy is examined from a broad context. The past is not emphasized, except when it calls attention to the present.

A third emphasis is that solution-focused therapy does not focus on clinical understanding of the family situation by the family or the therapist. Rather, the focus is on change. The therapist's job is to produce change by helping the family to focus on what they see as solutions to the problems they have reported. For example, families should look at exceptions to behaviors. Therapists also produce changes in families by challenging their world view, by asking them appropriate questions, and by giving them skeleton keys, which are, as discussed earlier, universal tasks that have the power to help families find ways to unlock their potential.

A fourth quality of solution-focused family therapy is that it is empowering and meant to assist families in assessing and utilizing their resources. Formula tasks, such as "Do something different," and awareness exercises, such as "Find times when symptoms do not occur," help families help themselves. Families "are encouraged to imagine a future without the problem(s) so that they can identify what they will be doing (solutions)" (Kok & Leskela, 1996, p. 398).

Finally, achievable goals are emphasized, such as small changes in behavior. These changes are seen as the basis for larger systemic changes. Therapists encourage and reinforce any type of family change. The idea is that once change starts, it will continue. "Solution-focused brief therapy further asserts that change is inevitable and that clients want to change" (Kok & Leskela, 1996, p. 398).

## Comparison with Other Theories

Unlike Bowen or psychoanalytic theory, virtually no attention is paid to history with solution-focused therapy. Rather, perception and minimal change are the focus. If families change their views on situations, they behave differently or more functionally (Bubenzer & West, 1993). Likewise, if a family begins to interact differently, they begin to see their situation from a new perspective.

Like strategic and systemic family therapy, solution-focused family therapy is brief in regard to the situation focused on and the amount of time allotted to it. Structuring the sessions in a way that emphasizes the therapist's expectations regarding doing something differently encourages rapid change. Difficulties lose their potency. Sometimes this results in a one-session treatment. However, deShazer (1989, 1991) has found that most clients (80.37%) meet their goals or make significant progress in an average of 4.5 sessions. Milton Erickson's influence on rapid changes is an obvious factor in all solution-focused approaches.

Therapy ends when an agreed-on behavioral goal is reached, rather than when a hypothetical therapeutic issue is discussed (O'Hanlon & Wilk, 1987). If there is no complaint or objective, there is no need for treatment. In this respect, solution-focused family therapy is similar to many forms of behavioral family therapy, in that it concentrates on resolving a concrete objective.

Like systemic (Milan) family therapy, some proponents of solution-focused therapy, mainly deShazer and Berg, use a team in helping the family help itself. Therefore, the expense of treatment may be high even though there are generally fewer sessions than in some other approaches, such as psychoanalytic therapy.

Like MRI strategic therapy, solution-focused therapy aims to help client families change their thoughts or actions so that they become more satisfied with their lives. However, solution-focused therapists trust and utilize family resources more than MRI strategic therapists.

---

## CASE ILLUSTRATION

### THE ROBERTS FAMILY

After 25 years of marriage and the raising of two children, Don and Kathy Roberts are contemplating a divorce. This crisis has led them to family therapy. Since the children left home 2 years ago, they have been drifting apart. Both Don, a computer analyst, and Kathy, a school superintendent, think they have little in common anymore. Thus, they work long hours, take separate vacations, spend the weekends with friends or by themselves, and basically just share space in their house. The couple is saddened by the fact that their marriage is no longer vibrant, but they are proud of their children and what they accomplished while the children were young.

#### Conceptualization of Family: Solution-Focused Perspective

Don and Kathy are at a critical stage in their personal, professional, and couple life. They have focused on their children and activities outside the marriage to the extent that they have failed to cultivate common interests and activities. Both seem to have taken a fatalistic view that their marriage is over. Yet, by coming to therapy, they have some hope that perhaps their relationship can be saved.

There is a long history on which to build in working with this couple. Finding patterns and exceptions are real possibilities. The couple has some motivation and considerable ability given their jobs and past successes. A drawback to this situation is that the couple may be operating in the cognitive domain. Also, the spouses are presently detached from each other.

#### Process of Treatment: Solution-Focused Therapy

In working with the Roberts, a solution-focused family therapist would first listen to their concerns. In this case, a lack of closeness and common interests would most likely surface. From the first session, the therapist would begin to discuss with the Roberts exceptions to their complaint, that is, times when they were close and shared common interests. For example, they may have both shared a love for knowledge at the beginning of their marriage and throughout the time of raising their children.

In the deShazer model of solution-focused therapy, the therapist might take a break after listening to the complaints and exceptions. At the break, the therapist would either consult with a team of other professionals watching the session or think alone about setting up a homework assignment for the Roberts. When the therapist returned, he or she would lead off with a compliment to build a "yes set" and then give the homework assignment. In the O'Hanlon model, this structure (especially the break and the possible use of a team) would not be implemented. Instead, the therapist would focus on giving the couple a task to either make a small change or increase what they have been doing less of (i.e., make a second-order change).

In either form of solution-oriented therapy, the emphasis would be on working with the couple to do something different. In the deShazer version of this model, the couple would be asked on return appointments to check on clues (i.e., "What is different this week from last week?"). There would also be an emphasis on scaling (i.e., ranking the concern on a scale of 1 [bad] to 10 [good]). The idea behind this method would be to get the Roberts to become increasingly aware of their improvement in therapy and to give them hope that their situation could be better. In both forms of solution-focused therapy, considerable emphasis would be placed on the strengths of the Roberts, for example, their intelligence, hardworking spirit, motivation, and past success. Considerable talk would also revolve around change. In the deShazer model, the therapist might employ the miracle question to encourage more thought about change and elicit solution-focused information, if the therapeutic process did not proceed smoothly or efficiently.

The total number of sessions needed to work with the Roberts or a typical client family would be between five and six. By the end of therapy, the Roberts should have made changes in their lifestyle and have skills to take with them should they drift apart again.

# ▪ Narrative Family Therapy ▪

## Major Theorists

The most prominent professionals associated with narrative family therapy are Michael White (who is highlighted here), the codirector of the Dulwich Centre in Adelaide, South Australia, and David Epston, the codirector of the Family Therapy Centre in Auckland, New Zealand. Other professionals include associates of White and Epston, such as Michael Durrant and Gerald Monk.

### Michael White

Michael White began his work as a family therapist in the 1970s in Australia. He was initially attracted to the work of Gregory Bateson and Bateson's explanatory model of systems analysis, but later, almost by accident, he discovered Edward Bruner's ethnographic work in library research (Monk, 1998). From Bruner, White took the idea that stories are not just descriptive but are constitutive as well. Furthermore, lived experiences, that is, narratives, may be overshadowed by dominant problem-saturated stories. Thus, a task of therapists is to co-construct with a client an alternative, more favored story line.

White then discovered the writings of Michel Foucault (1980, 1982, 1984), a French intellectual who formulated theories of knowledge and power. "Foucault described how people are constantly evaluating their worth in relation to widely accepted societal norms" (Monk, 1998, p. 3). This act of subjecting oneself or others to comparison and evaluation becomes the source of many problems in life. Problems can thus be addressed when a culture's values and ideas are questioned or challenged. Overall, White has read extensively outside the field of family therapy and has drawn heavily from literary theory, anthropology, and critical theory. He has also been influenced by feminist theory (Bubenzer, West, & Boughner, 1994).

In recent years, White has increasingly turned toward the narrative metaphor and away from systems thinking. He sees people's problems as related to the stories they have about themselves, which in turn often reflect oppressive cultural practices. One uniqueness about White's narrative approach, compared with others based on constructivism, is that White does not see one description of reality as better than any other. Instead, values play a role in actions, such as action against abuses of power, against neglect, against cruelty, and against injustice (White, 1993).

# Premises of the Theory

Narrative family therapy is based on a liberation philosophy consistent with postmodernism and social constructionism. It eschews attempts to formulate universal, generic principles. Indeed, the creators of this theory base much of their approach on the writings of Michel Foucault (1965, 1980), who asserts that human sciences (including social sciences like family therapy) generally characterize, classify, and specialize along a scale that objectifies people. As such, human sciences repress personal experiences and stories. The result is that people internalize and judge themselves in a logical and normative way that limits their options.

Thus, the narrative therapy approach distinguishes between **logico-scientific reasoning,** which is characterized by empiricism and logic, and **narrative reasoning,** which is characterized by stories, substories, meaningfulness, and liveliness. According to the narrative family viewpoint, "people live their lives by stories" (Kurtz & Tandy, 1995, p. 177). Therefore, the emphasis in this approach is shifted to a narrative way of conceptualizing and interpreting the world. Narrative therapy emphasizes empowering client families to develop their own unique and alternative stories about themselves in the hope that they will come up with novel options and strategies for living. By reauthoring their lives, families are enabled to change in ways not possible before (Bubenzer et al., 1994; Hodas, 1994; White, 1995).

In the process of changing their lives by changing their stories, client families are urged to **externalize problems** in order to solve them. Externalization breaks the habitual reading and retelling of the complaint-saturated story as residing in the person. In externalization "the problem becomes a separate entity" (White & Epston, 1990, p. 38). Family members reduce their arguments about who owns a problem and ideally form a team and enter into dialogue about problem solving.

# Treatment Techniques

Many narrative family treatment techniques are quite innovative. The most prevalent are highlighted here.

## Externalization of the Problem

As previously implied, through externalization, therapists seek to separate problems from people. The result is usually (1) a decrease in unproductive conflict between persons, (2) a lessening of the sense of failure an unresolved problem has on persons, (3) an increase of cooperation among family members to problem solve and dialogue with each other, (4) an opening up of new possibilities for action, and (5) a freeing of persons to be more effective and less stressed in approaching problems (White & Epston, 1990).

In externalization, the problem is the problem. As such, it becomes objective and can be addressed in unique ways (White, 1991). In some cases, the problem can be described in such a way that it takes on a personality of its own, such as encopresis being given the name "Sneaky Poo" (White, 1989). In situations like this, all family members can relate to what is facing them. They may then become consultants to the therapist helping to solve the problem and not themselves defined by the problem itself (Bitter, 2000).

## Influence (Effect) of the Problem on the Person

The goal of asking how a problem has influenced a person is to increase the person's awareness and objectivity. This type of awareness can best be generated by the therapist asking each family member to give a detailed, no-holds-barred account of how the problem has affected him or her (e.g., dominated his or her life). A typical question in this process might be: "How has the problem influenced you and your life and your relationships?"

## Influence (Effect) of the Person on the Problem

The purpose of asking family members how they have influenced a problem is twofold. First, it makes them increasingly aware of their response to a problem. Second, it helps them realize their strengths or potential in facing such a situation. In essence, this technique is the opposite of the influence of the problem on the person (see preceding section). Again, this type of treatment breaks a fixed perception or behavior pattern and creates a new possible way to combat or stand up against a problem.

## Raising Dilemmas

The effect of raising dilemmas is to get client families to examine possible aspects of a problem before the need arises. For instance, parents might be asked in relation to their misbehaving son how they would cope with "Worry" if the son's behavior became better, worsened, or remained the same. They might also be asked to consider how they would handle "Worry" if their youngest sibling began misbehaving as well.

## Predicting Setbacks

Setbacks in family therapy are almost inevitable. Narrative family therapy takes the approach that setbacks are best dealt with when they are planned for or anticipated (White, 1986). By doing so, families can decide ahead of time how they will act in the face of adversity. For instance, in regard to "Worry," narrative therapists might ask a family what they would do if, once they appear to have resolved their problem, "Worry" reappeared. In other words, would they give up and let "Worry" reenter their lives or would they fight back and drive "Worry" away?

## Using Questions

Through the use of questions, therapists can challenge families to examine the nature of the difficulties they bring to therapy and what resources they have and can use to handle their problems. Questions can take a variety of forms but two of the most prevalent types are those that explore exceptions and those that deal with significance.

*Exceptions questions* are directed toward finding instances when a situation reported to be a problem was not true. For instance, if a family reports they are in chaos, an exceptions question would be aimed at finding examples of times when the family was not chaotic. The idea behind such questions is to challenge the family's view of the world and to offer them hope that their lives can be different because some change has already taken place. Most exceptions questions begin with *when* or *what*. Research on exceptions questions reveals that blaming statements decrease and positive statements increase during exceptions questions conditions (Meidonis & Bry, 1995).

*Significance questions* are "unique redescription questions, they search for and reveal the meanings, significance, and importance of the exceptions" (Kurtz & Tandy, 1995, p. 189). For example, a family might be asked: "Now that you are more aware of how you acted in this situation, to what do you attribute that behavior?"

## Letters

Writing letters to families after therapy sessions is an important part of narrative therapy. According to Epston (1994), "words in a letter don't fade or disappear the way a conversation does. . . . A client can hold a letter in hand, reading and rereading it days, months, and years after the session" (p. 31). Thus, letters can serve as a medium for continuation of the dialogue between the therapist and family members and as a reminder of what has occurred in therapy session. For Epston, letters are case notes. Through them, he attempts to be transparent and congruent in his statements to families while they are in therapy.

## Celebrations and Certificates

Celebrations and certificates are a unique and important part of narrative therapy and are used to bring closure to therapy. They serve as tangible affirmations of the defeat of a problem. They also mark the beginning of a new description of a family (White & Epston, 1990). Celebrations can and should take on a festive air and include cakes, cookies, punch, and other goodies that signify a victory or an achievement.

Certificates can and should be tailored for the family and the situation they have faced. Certificates are best when printed and affixed with a logo. For instance, in regard to a family that has defeated "Apathy," a certificate might read:

> This certificate is awarded to the Fong Family in recognition of their conquest of Apathy and its insidious effect upon their lives. Family members are commended for their persistence in the face of inertia and their ability to mobilize their energy to do something about troublesome situations rather than wait for them to go away.

# Role of the Therapist

The narrative family therapist works in a number of ways. Like therapists in other traditions, narrative family therapists engage their clients and use the basic relationship skills of attending, paraphrasing, clarifying, summarizing, and checking to make sure they hear the client's story or problem correctly (Monk, 1998). The therapist does not assume that symptoms serve a function for families. In fact, just the opposite is true. Problems are seen as oppressive for families. They need to be addressed and eliminated as rapidly as possible. Therefore, the narrative therapist is a questioner who works to find unique outcomes or exceptions when families experience problems. The therapist is also notable for examining the meaning of situations for families.

To help families, the therapist assists them in separating themselves from old, problem-saturated stories by constructing new stories in which they, instead of their problems, are in control. This procedure is called *reauthoring* (White, 1992, 1995). It involves the redefining of lives and relationships in a new narrative. Sometimes this process can be accomplished creatively such as through the use of music and verse (Hodas, 1994). At other times, it is accomplished through a series of questions and the careful use of language. Regardless, family members and families as a whole are successful when they organize to help themselves and escape the power of oppressive influences.

# Process and Outcome

The process of narrative family therapy is one in which individuals and families are aided in learning to value their own life experiences and stories. In therapy, individuals and families are challenged to examine exceptions to problems they bring in and to change their behaviors so that they collectively address difficulties by externalizing them. The history of a problem is not as important as making the effort to reconstruct or reauthor a story so that problems are less dominant and significant in a family's life. Questions are raised that are aimed at finding exceptions to the dominant influence of problems. The externalization of the problem unites the family in attacking it and, thus, helps the family to avoid scapegoating. By marshaling family resources, expecting setbacks, and raising dilemmas, narrative family therapists help families construct new stories and meaning in their lives without falling into old and unproductive patterns of perception and behavior.

Narrative family therapy has been applied to the following problems: couple relationships, substance abuse, adolescent sexual offenders, schizophrenia, post-traumatic stress disorder (PTSD), AIDS, learning disabilities, temper problems within a family, anorexia/bulimia, and grief. Most of the outcome studies on its effectiveness have been in the form of case reports. For an example, see Merscham (2000).

Overall, narrative therapy is a social constructionism approach that is eclectic and uses the literary metaphors of storytelling and writing. Therapeutic relationships are collaborative. It emphasizes co-creating differences, new stories, and new realities. Problems are investigated in terms of exceptions and meaning rather than causes. There is a focus on societal influences on people.

# Unique Aspects of Narrative Family Therapy

## Emphases

Narrative family therapy emphasizes the reauthoring by families of their life stories. According to White (1992), a key component of family therapy is a **deconstruction**, which involves "procedures that subvert taken-for-granted realities and practices" (p. 121). Using questions is one way of employing deconstruction as a therapeutic tool. For instance, the therapist might ask: "Does this problem or situation invite you to react in certain ways?" or "What ideas do you have about _____ that explain why you acted that way?" (Monk, 1998, p. 5). Through deconstruction, the client is helped to move beyond symptom-maintaining myths to create a more vital story. Family problems are externalized to increase cooperation among family members to problem solve and create new possibilities for action.

In narrative family therapy, the individuals and families are asked to look for exceptions to the difficult situations they are experiencing. The idea is to focus on solutions, which are the exceptions, rather than problems, which are the rule. Questions are used extensively.

The expectation of setbacks and the raising of dilemmas are built into narrative family therapy so that the people involved can realize ahead of time some of the problems they might have in creating new lifestyles. Expecting setbacks may be especially helpful in lowering resistance to making changes.

Letters are sent to families about their progress. Celebrations are held and personalized certificates are issued when goals are achieved.

## Comparison with Other Theories

Both solution-focused and narrative family therapy are based on postmodern, social constructionist points of view (Freedman & Combs, 1996). As such they are among the most cerebral and intellectual of any of the family therapy approaches. Furthermore from a narrative family therapy perspective, there is no normative family pattern that should be achieved. Rather, meaning, purposefulness, and health are determined by each family based on their own life history and culture.

Narrative family therapy pays particular attention to the use of language. This emphasis on the importance of verbal behavior is similar to most other forms of family therapy.

Little attention is paid in narrative family therapy to the history of the concern (or complaint) brought by the family. In this regard, narrative family therapy is similar to solution-focused, strategic, systemic, and behavioral therapies in its focus on the present rather than the past. Like systemic family therapy, the origins of narrative family therapy began outside the United States. Narrative family therapy focuses on collaborative therapeutic relationships, which is similar to solution-focused and systemic family approaches. However, narrative family therapy is not a systems-oriented approach to working with families.

Overall, narrative therapy takes

> a strong stand against the functionalist elements of both family systems and psychoanalytic models that led therapists to believe that problems are inherent in individuals (as psychoanalysis would have it) or in families (as family systems would have it). Instead, they believe that problems arise because people are induced by our culture into subscribing to narrow and self-defeating views of themselves and the world. (Schwartz, 1999, p. 264)

### CASE ILLUSTRATION

### THE BEARCLAW FAMILY

David Bearclaw married Claire Standback in a civil ceremony after a whirlwind courtship lasting 3 months. David, age 23, was new to city life and missed the comfort of friends and family on the reservation where he grew up. Claire, age 22, was away from her family for the first time. The couple shared a high hope for their marriage and a physical attraction for one another, but their cultural backgrounds were different as were their expectations for the relationship. David expected to be a good provider and to head the household. Claire, although not opposed to these roles, expected to have a say in the way the family functioned, especially after the birth of their daughter, Rose, now age 5, and their son, Hunter, now age 3. The trouble was that David worked construction and was often between jobs. During these times, he would insist that Claire not work and that she use the money they had saved to pay the bills and keep creditors from bothering them. David also would isolate himself from Claire during these times of unemployment and would leave home to meditate. Claire became depressed but continued going to church and nurturing her children.

### Conceptualization of Family: Narrative Perspective

The 6-year-old marriage of David and Claire is stressed due to economic concerns, a lack of common strategies for problem solving, the stress of preschool children, and other external and internal pressures. The couple has had time to get to know one another, but it appears they do not. They live according to rigid and passive gender roles that do not serve them or their family well. Their lack of outside social support and their tendency to retreat from talking with each other during times of heightened stress contribute to their difficulties.

### Process of Treatment: Narrative Therapy

To help the Bearclaws, narrative family therapists would first listen to their story and help them rank order the difficulties they face. In this case, financial stress would be rated number one and the therapist would then work with the Bearclaws to externalize the problem and give it a name, such as "Money." After externalizing the problem, the Bearclaws would be asked by the therapist to state how the problem has affected them and how they have influenced the problem as well.

The therapist would then use questions to help the Bearclaws find times when there were exceptions to their present way of acting and how that behavior impacted on them. For instance, the therapist would compliment the Bearclaws on their ability to buy necessary items on sale and on their agreement to make and keep a budget that allowed for some savings during times of employment. The therapist would make case notes in a letter to the Bearclaws on these exceptions and their work on the troublesome problem of "Money." The therapist would raise dilemmas during treatment on aspects of "Money" the Bearclaws may not have considered and would predict setbacks in the Bearclaws solving their "Money" trouble, too.

Through all of the sessions, the narrative therapist would encourage the Bearclaws to create a new story of their lives, such as switching roles when David is out of work and letting Claire bring home "Money" by working for a temporary employment agency while David takes care of the children. In such a story, the Bearclaws could be more united and less concerned about "Money." The result should lead to a celebration and new strategies for living as a family.

# Summary and Conclusion

In the 1980s, but especially in the 1990s, the work of deShazer and O'Hanlon brought national attention to solution-focused therapy. This approach concentrates on bringing change to a wider range of client family problems. It is short term, specific, positive, and concentrates on bringing about small changes in the process of facilitating larger ones. Both deShazer and O'Hanlon have been greatly influenced by Milton Erickson.

In the 1990s, narrative family therapy emerged as another strong approach that continues today. Like solution-focused therapy, it is based on a postmodern, social constructionist view of the world that emphasizes the subjective nature of reality and the importance of families making their own meaning in the world by creating stories that are not problem centered. In this approach, difficulties are externalized and, like solution-focused therapies, exceptions to problems are noted and utilized to help families change their behaviors for the better.

Both solution-focused and narrative family therapies are concerned with changing present behaviors, not examining past histories. They both stress that families have untapped resources that can and should be marshaled in helping them help themselves. Likewise, these therapies are creative in innovative ways that go beyond traditional forms of family therapy, such as emphasizing that change is inevitable. Together, solution-focused and narrative family therapies represent the best of the developing, dynamic family therapy approaches that continue to develop.

# Summary Table

## Solution-Focused and Narrative Family Therapies

### Solution-Focused Therapy

*Major Theorists*

| | | |
|---|---|---|
| Steve deShazer | Insoo Berg | Bill O'Hanlon |
| Michele Weiner-Davis | Eve Lipchik | Alan Gurman |
| Scott Miller | Patricia O'Hanlon Hudson | |

*Premises of the Theory*

Reality is seen as a reflection of observation and experience not as objective reality.
Focus is on exceptions to dysfunctionality, hypothetical solutions, and small changes.
Exceptions to patterns are highlighted.
The present is emphasized.
The family is viewed as an ally that wants to change.

*Treatment Techniques*

The unit of treatment is the family as a system, although solution-focused approaches can be selectively used to help dyads and individuals make changes.
The goals of treatment are

- to help the family to seek solutions and tap internal resources

- to help the family perceive the world differently, especially in regard to the inevitability of change and the importance of making small changes

The therapeutic techniques include:

- Joining
- Listening and accepting
- Noting of patterns and exceptions
- Awareness exercises
- Hypothetical solutions, particularly the "miracle question"
- Making small changes
- Skeleton keys
- Task assignments
- Compliments
- Scaling
- Clues
- Mapping

### Role of the Therapist

The solution-oriented family therapist initially determines the motivation of families and their members, that is, are they visitors, complainants, or customers? Then the therapist works as a facilitator with families, asking them questions and talking to them about expectations of change. Simple and universal solutions are emphasized by the therapist whenever possible.

### Process and Outcome

Families are presented with the Ericksonian position that change is inevitable. Families are asked optimistic questions and reinforced for small but specific movement. Families are encouraged to seek solutions and tap internal resources.

### Unique Aspects of Solution-Focused Therapy

Unique aspects of solution-focused therapy include:

- the acceptance of a family's situation through listening
- an emphasis on the present and clear definition of a family's situation
- the noting of exceptions to family patterns and raising of awareness (including family resources)
- a focus on small changes through completion of an assigned task or through observation within the family

### Comparison with Other Theories

Unlike Bowen or psychoanalytic approaches, no attention is paid to history.

Like strategic and systemic family therapies, solution-focused therapy is brief (usually five to six sessions).

Like behavioral therapy, treatment ends when goals are achieved. However, universal solutions may be utilized in the process of fostering change.

Like systemic family therapy, a team is sometimes used in treatment (deShazer).

Like MRI strategic therapy, solution-focused therapy is aimed at helping families think and act differently.

### Narrative Family Therapy

*Major Theorists*

| | | |
|---|---|---|
| Michael White | David Epston | Michael Durrant |
| Gerald Monk | Associates of White and Epston | |

*Premises of the Theory*

Narrative therapy is based on a postmodern and social constructionist perspective that rejects classification systems based on empiricism and promotes empowering persons and families through emphasizing their stories.

Problems are seen as external to persons and families.

Problems should be attacked in a cooperative manner by families who work as teams and utilize their resources.

*Treatment Techniques*

Narrative therapy treats family units, subunits, and individuals.

The goal of treatment is on helping families reauthor their lives and bring about change so that they and not their problems dominate.

Narrative therapy treatment techniques include:

- Externalization of the problem
- Influence (effect) of the problem on the person
- Influence (effect) of the person on the problem
- Raising dilemmas
- Predicting setbacks
- Use of questions (exceptions and significance questions)
- Letters
- Celebrations and certificates

*Role of the Therapist*

The therapist views problems as oppressive to families and in need of elimination.

The therapist works to find unique outcomes, that is, exceptions, to families' problems.

The therapist uses questions and helps families create new stories where they, and not their problems, are in control.

*Process and Outcome*

Individuals and families are challenged to reconstruct and reauthor their lives.

Problems are externalized and attacked by the whole family.

Problems are investigated in terms of meaning and exceptions rather than causes.

*Unique Aspects of Narrative Family Therapy*

Unique aspects of narrative family therapy include:

- families learn to value their own life experience and stories and to reauthor their lives
- families learn to find exceptions to their regular patterns of living

- problems are externalized and worked on cooperatively
- expectations of setbacks and the raising of dilemmas help lower resistance
- letters to families by their therapists are sent regarding their progress
- celebrations by families and therapists are held when goals are reached

### Comparison with Other Theories

Narrative therapy is postmodern and based on social constructionist viewpoint like solution-focused therapy.

The theory originally developed outside of the United States, like that of systemic therapy.

The emphasis of therapy is on the present as compared with the historical emphasis of Bowen and psychoanalytic approaches.

The focus of the approach is on collaborative effort of families and therapists, like strategic and solution-focused family therapies.

# References

Bitter, J. R. (2000). Dissolving a problem: Structuring externalization interviews with couples. In R. E. Watts (Ed.), *Techniques in marriage and family counseling* (pp. 91–94). Alexandria, VA: American Counseling Association.

Bubenzer, D. L., & West, J. D. (1993). William Hudson O'Hanlon: On seeking possibilities and solutions in therapy. *The Family Journal, 1*, 365–379.

Bubenzer, D. L., West, J. D., & Boughner, S. R. (1994). Michael White and the narrative perspective in therapy. *The Family Journal, 2*, 71–83.

Cleveland, P. H., & Lindsey, E. W. (1995). Solution-focused family interventions. In A. C. Kilpatrick & T. P. Holland (Eds.), *Working with families* (pp. 145–160). Boston: Allyn & Bacon.

deShazer, S. (1982). *Patterns of brief family therapy*. New York: Guilford.

deShazer, S. (1984). The death of resistance. *Family Process, 23*, 11–21.

deShazer, S. (1985). *Keys to solution in brief therapy*. New York: W. W. Norton.

deShazer, S. (1988). *Clues: Investigating solutions in brief therapy*. New York: W. W. Norton.

deShazer, S. (1989). Resistance revisited. *Contemporary Family Therapy, 11*, 227–233.

deShazer, S. (1991). *Putting differences to work*. New York: W. W. Norton.

deShazer, S., & Molnar, A. (1984). Four useful interventions in brief family therapy. *Journal of Marital and Family Therapy, 10*, 297–304.

Epston, D. (1994). Extending the conversation. *Family Therapy Networker, 18*, 30–37, 62–63.

Erdman, P. (2000). Bringing a symbol: An experiential exercise for systematic change. In R. E. Watts (Ed.), *Techniques in marriage and family counseling* (pp. 99–102). Alexandria, VA: American Counseling Association.

Fleming, J. S., & Rickord, B. (1997). Solution-focused brief therapy: One answer to managed mental health care. *The Family Journal, 5*, 286–294.

Foucault, M. (1965). *Madness and civilization: A history of insanity in the use of reason*. New York: Random House.

Foucault, M. (1980). *Power/knowledge: Selected interviews and other writings*. New York: Pantheon Books.

Foucault, M. (1982). The subject and power. In H. Dreyfus & P. Rabinow (Eds.), *Michel Foucault: Beyond structuralism and hermeneutics*. Chicago: University of Chicago Press.

Foucault, M. (1984). Space, knowledge and power. In P. Rabinow (Ed.), *The Foucault reader*. New York: Pantheon.

Freedman, J., & Combs, G. (1996). *Narrative therapy: The social construction of preferred reality*. New York: Norton.

Gale, J. E. (1991). *Conversion analysis of therapeutic discourse: The pursuit of a therapeutic agenda*. Norwood, NJ: Ablex.

Gladding, S. T. (1996). *Small change*. Unpublished manuscript.

Hodas, G. R. (1994). Reversing narratives of failure through music and verse in therapy. *The Family Journal, 2*, 199–207.

Hudson, P. O., & O'Hanlon, W. H. (1991). *Rewriting love stories: Brief marital therapy*. New York: Norton.

Kaplan, D. M. (2000). Who are our giants? *The Family Digest, 12*(4), 1,6.

Kilpatrick, A. C., & Holland, T. P. (1995). *Working with families* (pp. 175–197). Boston: Allyn & Bacon.

Kiser, D. J., Piercy, F. P., & Lipchik, E. (1993). The integration of emotion in solution-focused therapy. *Journal of Marital and Family Therapy, 19,* 233–242.

Kok, C. J., & Leskela, J. (1996). Solution-focused therapy in a psychiatric hospital. *Journal of Marital and Family Therapy, 22,* 397–406.

Krauth, L. D. (1995, December). Strength-based therapies. *Family Therapy News, 26,* 24.

Kurtz, P. D., & Tandy, C. C. (1995). Narrative family interventions. In A. C. Kilpatrick & T. P. Holland (Eds.), *Working with families* (pp. 177–197). Boston: Allyn & Bacon.

Maturana, H., & Varela, F. (1987). *The tree of knowledge.* Boston: New Science Library.

Meidonis, G. G., & Bry, B. H. (1995). Effects of therapist exceptions questions on blaming and positive statements in families with adolescent behavior problems. *Journal of Family Psychology, 9,* 451–457.

Merscham, C. (2000). Restorying trauma with narrative therapy: Using the phantom family. *The Family Journal, 8,* 282–286.

Monk, G. (1998). Narrative therapy: An exemplar of the postmodern breed of therapies. *Counseling and Human Development, 30*(5), 1–14.

O'Hanlon, W. H. (1987). *Taproots: Underlying principles of Milton Erickson's therapy and hypnosis.* New York: W. W. Norton.

O'Hanlon, W. H., & Weiner-Davis, M. (1989). *In search of solutions: A new direction in psychotherapy.* New York: W. W. Norton.

O'Hanlon, W. H., & Wilk, J. (1987). *Shifting contexts: The generation of effective psychotherapy.* New York: Guilford Press.

Sauber, S. R., L'Abate, L., & Weeks, G. R. (1985). *Family therapy: Basic concepts and terms.* Rockville, MD: Aspen.

Schwartz, R. C. (1999). Narrative therapy expands and contracts family therapy's horizons. *Journal of Marital and Family Therapy, 25,* 263–267.

Simon, F., Stierlin, H., & Wynne, L. (1985). *The language of family therapy.* New York: Family Process Press.

Softas-Nall, B. C., Baldo, T. D., & Tiedemann, T. R. (1999). A gender-based, solution-focused genogram case: He and she across the generations. *The Family Journal, 7,* 177–180.

Spiegel, H., & Linn, L. (1969). The "ripple effect" following adjunct hypnosis in analytic psychotherapy. *American Journal of Psychiatry, 126,* 53–58.

Todd, T. (1992). Brief family therapy. In R. L. Smith & P. Stevens-Smith (Eds.), *Family counseling and therapy* (pp. 162–175). Ann Arbor, MI: ERIC/CAPS.

Walter, J., & Peller, J. (1993). Solution-focused brief therapy. *The Family Journal, 1,* 80–81.

West, J. D., Bubenzer, D. L., Smith, J. M., & Hamm, T. L. (1997). Insoo Kim Berg and solution-focused therapy. *The Family Journal, 5,* 346–354.

White, M. (1986). Negative explanation, restraint, and double description: A template for family therapy. *Family Process, 25,* 169–184.

White, M. (1989). *Selected papers.* Adelaide, South Australia: Dulwich Centre Publications.

White, M. (1991). Deconstruction and therapy. *Dulwich Center Newsletter, 3,* 21–40.

White, M. (1992). Deconstruction and therapy. In M. White & D. Epston (Eds.), *Experience, contradiction, narrative, and imagination* (pp. 109–151). Adelaide, South Australia: Dulwich Centre Publications.

White, M. (1993). The histories of the present. In S. Gilligan (Ed.), *Therapeutic conversations.* New York: W. W. Norton.

White, M. (1995). *Re-authoring lives.* Adelaide, South Australia: Dulwich Centre Publications.

White, M., & Epston, D. (1990). *Narrative means to therapeutic ends.* New York: Norton.

# PART THREE

# Special Populations in Family Therapy

# CHAPTER 11

# Working with Single-Parent Families

She talks about her unborn
as three small children noisily play
in the dusty red dirt around her cluttered yard
with hand-me-down toys
from their richer peers in Buena Vista.

Amid the chaos and bleakness,
I wonder how she survives summer's heat
or manages a smile in the face of stress
as her bills pile up like unwashed clothes
in a house without running water.

But in the silence,
as the noise of that scene fades in my mind,
at the end of a day filled with mental struggles
I hear the strength of resolve in her voice,
remember her caring eyes and toughness,
and in it all I know, though pained, she will prevail.

*Gladding, 1993*

**S**ingle-parent families are those either headed by a mother or a father, a sole parent, responsible for taking care of herself or himself and a child or children (Walsh, 1991). The term has been applied to a number of different family forms. The families covered under this designation include those created as a result of divorce, death, abandonment, unwed pregnancy, and adoption. As a type of American family, single-parent families make up ever-growing proportions of families in the United States (Kleist, 1999). They differ in regard to dynamics and vary in their interactions depending on the number of people within the unit, the background and resources of the members, and the stage of the individual and family life cycle at the time the unit was formed. Thus, there is no prototype of a single-parent family.

The number of single-parent families in the United States has increased sharply in recent years. They are increasingly common across all socioeconomic groups (Coates, 1996). Prior to 1970, about one family in ten (10%) was headed by a single parent, usually the mother (Seward, 1978). By the turn of the twenty-first century, however, "almost one third of the 35 million households with children in the United States" were headed by a single parent (Krauth, 1995, p. 14). This increase has affected some groups more than others but all cultural groups in the United States have changed in regard to the number of two-parent and single-parent households within their population.

Historically, most single-parent families had been created by the death or desertion of a spouse. In the 1950s, a new trend began: The percentage of single-parent families created by divorce started to exceed those created by death (Levitan & Conway, 1990). Further, the decision of many unmarried women to bear and raise children by themselves, which began in the 1970s, also increased the number of single-parent families. The number of births "to unmarried mothers hit a record high in 1990 of 1,165,384." Approximately "20 percent of white births, 37 percent of Hispanic births, and 67 percent of black births" were to unmarried women (Associated Press, 1993a, p. 2). While this trend has subsided in recent years, more than half a million children are still born out of wedlock each year, the majority to teenage girls.

This chapter examines three distinct single-parent family lifestyles: those created by divorce, death, and election to bear children alone. It also examines the dynamics underlying and affecting these types of single-parent families, as well as single-parent families in general. The common strengths and challenges associated with the single-parent family life styles are highlighted. Finally, therapeutic approaches for working with single-parent families that experience difficulties are discussed from selected theoretical and self-help perspectives. The role of the family therapist and expected outcomes are highlighted.

# Types of Single-Parent Families

Single-parent families vary greatly. Their development occurs over time, whether they are planned or unplanned. Three major types of single-parent families are those that develop as a result of divorce, death, or intentionality. A common dimension of all single-parent families is that the process in their development is one that has definable stages.

## Single Parenthood as a Result of Divorce

The underlying factors contributing to divorce are complex. They range from infidelity to incompatibility. Regardless of the reasons, however, "divorce does not end family life, although it changes its shape" (Barnes, 1999, p. 436). In the United States "two of every three divorces are now initiated by women" (Silverstein & Levant, 1996, p. 18). Despite who initiates the action, when single-parent families begin as a result of divorce, two subunits are formed (except in some cases of joint custody arrangements). One subunit involves the custodial single parent and his or her interactions with the ex-spouse and children. The other subunit includes the noncustodial single parent and his or her relationships with the ex-spouse and children (Carter & McGoldrick, 1988).

Both parental/child arrangements for single-parent families of divorce experience stresses and rewards (Blaisure & Geasler, 2000). For custodial parents in such situations, stressors include rebuilding financial resources and social networks, with the most stressful time for these families being during their first 3 years (Morrison, 1995). A major benefit for successful custodial parents is a renewed sense of confidence in oneself. For the noncustodial parent in such a family, stressors include finding ways to continue to be involved with one's children as a parent and the rebuilding of social networks. When successful, noncustodial parents experience rewards. The rewards include devising creative problem-solving methods and gaining renewed self-confidence. Carter and McGoldrick (1988, p. 22) conceptualize the stages of single-parent families formed through divorce as shown in Table 11.1.

## Single Parenthood as a Result of Death

In single-parent families that begin as a result of death, the stages of development have not been as specifically delineated as in those single-parent families resulting from divorce. However, it is clear that death has an overall impact on family life and that reestablishment of one's life and the family are major tasks (Brown, 1988; Moody & Moody, 1991; Pulleyblank, 1996).

The family's development may involve three stages, as shown in Table 11.2. The first stage is mourning, which takes time and cannot be forced (Rotter, 2000). It is vital in the mourning stage for surviving family members to release both positive and negative feelings about the deceased because "death ends a life, not a relationship" (Albom, 1997, p. 174). This type of catharsis makes it possible to move to the second stage—readjustment. The readjustment stage involves learning to do new tasks, dropping old tasks, and/or reassigning duties previously done by the ex-spouse to other members of the family (Murdock, 1980). When this stage is completed, the family can move into a final stage—renewal and accomplishment—in which family members, and the family as a whole, can concentrate on finding and engaging in new growth opportunities. This last stage, which may or may not be achieved, results in new collective and individual identities and relationships.

## Single Parenthood by Intent

The final way in which single-parent families begin involves intentionality. The actions associated with intent are (1) purposefulness in conceiving a child out of wedlock, (2)

**Table 11.1**

Dislocations of the Family Life Cycle Requiring Additional Steps to Restabilize and Proceed Developmentally

| Phase | Emotional Process of Transition Prerequisite Attitude | Developmental Issues |
|---|---|---|
| *Divorce* | | |
| 1. The decision to divorce | Acceptance of inability to resolve marital tensions sufficiently to continue relationship | Acceptance of one's own part in the failure of the marriage |
| 2. Planning the breakup of the system | Supporting viable arrangements for all parts of the system | a. Working cooperatively on problems of custody, visitation, and finances<br>b. Dealing with extended family about the divorce |
| 3. Separation | a. Willingness to continue cooperative coparental relationship and joint financial support of children<br>b. Work on resolution of attachment to spouse | a. Mourning loss of intact family<br>b. Restructuring marital and parent–child relationships and finances; adaptation to living apart<br>c. Realignment of relationships with extended family; staying connected with spouse's extended family |
| 4. The divorce | More work on emotional divorce: Overcoming hurt, anger, guilt, etc. | a. Mourning loss of intact family: giving up fantasies of reunion<br>b. Retrieval of hopes, dreams, expectations from the marriage<br>c. Staying connected with extended families |
| *Post-divorce family* | | |
| 1. Single-parent (custodial household or primary residence) | Willingness to maintain financial responsibilities, continue parental contact with ex-spouse, and support contact of children with ex-spouse and his or her family | a. Making flexible visitation arrangements with ex-spouse and spouse's family<br>b. Rebuilding own financial resources<br>c. Rebuilding own social network |
| 2. Single-parent (noncustodial) | Willingness to maintain parental contact with ex-spouse and support custodial parent's relationship with children | a. Finding ways to continue effective parenting relationship with children<br>b. Maintaining financial responsibilities to ex-spouse and children<br>c. Rebuilding own social network |

From "Overview: The Changing Family Life Cycle: A Framework for Family Therapy," by B. Carter and M. McGoldrick, in *The Changing Family Life Cycle* (2nd ed., p. 22) by B. Carter and M. McGoldrick, 1988, New York: Gardner. Reprinted by permission of Allyn & Bacon, Boston.

**Table 11.2**
Single-Parent Families Created by Death

| Stage | Task | Result |
|---|---|---|
| Mourning | Emotional catharsis | Resolution of past relationship |
| Readjustment | Learning/dropping of duties | Performance of essential duties |
| Renewal and accomplishment | Personal and family development | Acquiring of new skills and interests |

deciding to carry a child to term after accidentally becoming pregnant out of wedlock, or (3) adopting a child as a single adult. The unique aspect of this type of single-parent family is that the parent has time to prepare before the child arrives. Furthermore, it is clear to the parent in these situations that there will usually be no other support outside of the parent's resources. In these cases, single-parent families go through the stages, processes, and outcomes listed in Table 11.3.

In general, the formation of these types of single-parent families occurs over time. No one type of single-parent family works best in all situations. Also, time lines must be kept flexible when considering single-parent family development. Different circumstances within each type of family require adjustment considerations that are unique. Two years after the family first develops, however, reality (as opposed to idealization) should be present in all of these types of families (Freeman, 1985).

# Dynamics Associated with the Formation of Single-Parent Families

In defining how single-parent families are formed, we need to examine the roots from which they spring: divorce, death, and intentionality. By understanding the dynamics

**Table 11.3**
Single-Parent Families Created by Intention

| Stage | Task | Result |
|---|---|---|
| Planning | Preparing for the arrival of the child | Marshaling of resources Mental expectation of change |
| Arrival | Creating a parent and child relationship | Physical and emotional bonding |
| Adjustment and achievement | Resolving situational and development needs | Growth of family and individual |

underlying these diverse ways of establishing single-parent families, therapists can make better decisions in formulating treatment strategies.

## Dynamics of Single-Parent Families Formed Through Divorce

Numerous factors influence the decision for couples to divorce. Among the top three considerations affecting the dissolution of marriages are social, personal, and relationship issues (Bornstein & Bornstein, 1986).

On a social level, the pace of American life has changed rapidly, especially since World War II (Levitan & Conway, 1990). Major changes include new technology, more alternatives, less stability, and the opportunity for greater frustration, fulfillment, and alienation. Women's roles have changed; and the alliance between men and their work has weakened. In addition, the mobility of society has contributed to an acceptance of options, transitions, and a new openness to mores and laws. Divorce is more acceptable today (Bumpass, 1990).

A second reason for not staying married involves personal issues. People marry at different levels of psychological maturity and with varied expectations. If they are immature, their decisions and actions will most likely reflect it (Bowen, 1978). Some relationships are doomed to failure before they even begin because of the personalities of those involved. In these marriages, the individuals involved are probably best served when the relationship dissolves, especially if they seek help in becoming more autonomous and mature.

Interpersonal issues are a third variable related to divorce. Marriage and family life involve give-and-take interactions (i.e., a quid pro quo, or something for something). People often do not stay married when they perceive that they are giving more than they are receiving (Klagsbrun, 1985). There are ways to rectify such situations, but frequently couples do not seek help or seek it too late. The result is the splitting of a relationship.

In all of these situations, men or women who become single parents following divorce and separation deal with the following issues (Garfield, 1982):

- resolution of the loss of the marriage
- acceptance of new roles and responsibilities
- renegotiation and redefinement of relationships with family and friends
- establishment of a satisfactory arrangement with one's ex-spouse

The transition is not easy. In fact, "divorce is much more devastating than people who go into the process anticipate" (Moody, 1992, p. 171). Individuals who have ample resources in the form of psychological or financial aid/support find the difficulties less intense but still formidable. "Loss is an issue of great significance with regard to how adults and children experience divorce" regardless of financial or psychological support (Arditti & Prouty, 1999, p. 63). Added to these difficulties is the fact that society still disapproves of and stigmatizes those who divorce. Little wonder then that at least 10% of individuals who experience marital separation or divorce see a therapist or counselor (Sweet, Bumpass, & Call, 1988).

## Dynamics of Single-Parent Families Formed Through Death

Even when death is expected, it is still a shock. This reaction is especially prevalent if a person is survived by a spouse and child(ren). "About 800,000 spouses . . . die every year"

(McGoldrick, 1986, p. 30), leaving behind millions of immediate family members to mourn the loss. It is important that survivors of these deaths properly grieve. Such a process may be difficult because of the lack of mourning rituals in modern society. Yet if family members, especially widows and widowers, do not appropriately grieve for their former spouses, their chances of reestablishing themselves or establishing a healthy single-parent family are greatly lessened.

Therefore, it is crucial that family members talk to one another and others, such as neighbors, extended kin, or counselors, after the death of a spouse/parent. By doing so, they release their feelings and are able to see the dead person as mortal instead of superhuman. Such a perspective helps family members deal with their feelings and external demands productively and realistically.

## Dynamics of Single-Parent Families Formed Through Choice

The number of people, especially women, who raise a family by themselves is large and growing. It cuts across racial, social, and economic divisions in American society (Associated Press, 1993b). Some of the reasons for this pattern are due to tradition, some to change and acceptance by society, and some to choice. Each reason is examined here briefly.

Historical tradition is one factor that helps explain why certain groups of women have children out of wedlock. In some subcultures, a maternally oriented society has evolved in which children have been raised by single-parent mothers. In these subcultures, many young women and men are inclined to avoid marriage and to follow the pattern they grew up in, especially if they are not exposed to other role models. The socioeconomic milieu in such cases has a strong influence that can prove detrimental to the subculture and simultaneously give it a distinction and even, ironically, pride. Racism, ignorance, and socioeconomic crises also contribute to such a pattern of maternal single parenting and make it hard to break the cycle (Strong, DeVault, & Sayad, 2001).

Acceptance is a second reason women elect to have children out of wedlock. The upheavals in American society following World War II helped break down stigmas and taboos. The turbulence of the 1960s further eroded some traditional norms and patterns, such as ostracizing women who bore children out of wedlock. Since the 1970s there has been an increase in the number of women who have elected to have children out of wedlock (National Center for Health Statistics, 1991). In 1992, the percentage of women ages 18 to 44 giving birth outside of marriage was 24%. Most were between ages 25 and 39 and most were nonwhite: 56% for African-American women, 33% for Hispanic women, 15% for white women, and 7% for Asian women (Erbe, 1993). "Society is not frowning on them any more" (Associated Press, 1993b, p. 2).

A final factor that has influenced the increased number of women bearing children out of wedlock is a choice. A small percentage of women who thoughtfully decide to bear and raise children by themselves are well educated; about 33% are high school graduates; and over 8% hold a managerial or professional position (Associated Press, 1993b). In addition, the number of prominent older women who thoughtfully decided to raise a baby by themselves increased beginning in the 1980s. Two well-publicized examples are Mia Farrow and Goldie Hawn (Erbe, 1993).

Furthermore, the dramatization of the lives of fictitious women who choose parenthood outside of marriage as seen in movies, such as *The Big Chill,* or television programs, such as *Murphy Brown,* has been extensive. Whether one agrees or disagrees with their decisions, the fact is that more mothers over age 25 are deciding to have babies outside of marriage; "about one quarter in 1980 compared with about one third in 1988," with no slow down in the trend expected (Bray, 1993, p. 95).

Although not a complete parallel, the reasons for unmarried women choosing to adopt babies have some similarity to those who become pregnant (Pavao, 1998). For instance, it is more socially acceptable for unwed women to adopt babies than it was in the past. Furthermore, because of resources and desire, many professional women are electing to adopt and raise children by themselves. Two major differences between single women who adopt and those who elect to biologically have a baby are timing and resources. Women who adopt can more precisely pick the time when they wish to become a parent. Many of the women are affluent. Like other single women, they are not encumbered by the demands of a marital relationship and can therefore give more time and nurturance to their child(ren) (Groze, 1991).

# Single-Parent Mothers and Fathers

Gender issues can have an impact on how single-parent families function. To understand the life and needs of these families, it is necessary to be aware of how they differ according to who is parentally in charge. Although single-parent families are formed in a number of different temporary and permanent ways, they are ultimately headed by either a mother or father (Hill, 1986).

## Families of Single-Parent Mothers

Historically, between 85% and 90% of children in single-parent households live with their mothers (Glick, 1988; Krauth, 1995). This figure varies from year to year and in some subgroups it is higher than others. For instance, about 45% of African-American families (or 3.8 million households) were led by women without partners present in 1999, while approximately 13% of European American families in the same year were headed by women alone (Associated Press, 2000).

In regard to single-parent mothers and finances, research shows contrasts. Children whose single-parent mothers engage in full-time, paid work report "more positive self-esteem and daily affect and arousal" than those whose mothers do not engage in paid work (Duckett & Richards, 1995, p. 427). In addition, employment has been found to contribute to single mothers' health. However, because women are paid, on average, lower wages than men, these single-parent mothers and their children generally have fewer resources than most families in the United States. For instance, the median income of a married couple with children in 1990 was $41,260, as compared with a single-parent father's income of $25,211 and a single-parent mother's income of $13,092 (Ward, 1993). Although the figures have changed in the twenty-first century, the pattern has not: single-parent mothers as a group are still poorer than their counterparts.

Single-parent mothers who have been married may potentially collect either insurance or child support. However, "nearly 70 percent of noncustodial fathers become delinquent within a few years of child support" (Levitan & Conway, 1990, p. 18). When there is regular child support, it does not usually come without some restrictions. Noncustodial fathers who pay support often wish and have the right to be involved in decisions made regarding the welfare of their children (Melli, 1986). Unwed mothers, particularly if they are adolescents themselves, find it difficult to obtain enough financial support to make ends meet. Violence and abuse are unfortunately associated with mother-only homes at the poverty level (Gelles, 1989, 1997).

In addition to limited financial assets and the drawbacks that come with them, single-parent mothers may also be pressed for time (Murdock, 1980). Often they sacrifice time in personal care activities, including sleep and rest, in order to take care of their families (Sanik & Mauldin, 1986). They also have new time demands to take care of, such as work duties or school obligations. For some there is the difficulty of dealing with a former spouse's family. These families may want to visit with the child(ren) on occasions, regardless of whether it is convenient for the custodial parent. This type of time demand may interfere with the welfare of the single-parent family as a whole, but it may especially affect the mother.

Furthermore, there is the problem of identity or establishing a different identity. Young single-parent mothers are frequently in need of care, support, and guidance. As a group, they usually have low in self-esteem and little work experience and education (Levitan & Conway, 1990). In addition to difficulties involving identity and functioning, the parent within these households frequently lacks knowledge about how to obtain medical and psychological services. Women over 40, especially if they have mainly worked inside the home, have an extremely hard time rebuilding their lives socially, psychologically, and economically (Wallerstein, 1986).

Overall, the health and well-being of households headed by single-parent mothers depends on the age and stage of the parent and her children, as well as her level of education, income, and social support. Conditions are often perilous. For example, "children raised by single-parent mothers drop out of high school twice as often as children from two-parent households, and their daughters are twice as likely to become teen mothers" (Krauth, 1995, p. 14). Yet, despite numerous difficulties, there are many mother-headed single-parent families that function quite well.

## Families of Single-Parent Fathers

An increasing number of men are seeking and gaining custody of their children (Bumpass & Sweet, 1989; Davis & Borns, 1999). Therefore, single-parent families headed by fathers are growing fast numerically and as a percentage of families headed by single parents. "Between 1985 and 1989 alone, the number . . . soared from 1.3 million to 1.8 million, three times the rate of female-headed families" (Elias, 1992, p. 1A). If this rate continues, single-parent families headed by men may well exceed the historical rate of 10% to 15%.

One advantage fathers have as single parents is that they usually have access to more than twice the financial resources of women (Elias, 1992). This monetary strength allows them flexibility in what they do with their children. It also enables them to hire more caretakers as a group than single-parent women and take much needed breaks from the duties of raising children. Thus, these parents can afford to choose when to be close to their children and be good role models for them. What they give up, however, is time with their offspring. Quality time alone seldom brings closeness to a relationship the way that a combination of qualitative and quantitative time does. In addition, children of single-parent fathers who hire domestic help to take care of them may find that their children have incorporated the help's value system into their lives.

An advantage of single-parent fathers in general is that most feel comfortable and competent as single parents (Riseman, 1986). This characteristic seems to hold true regardless of the reason for custody or the father's financial status. However, societal norms and personal traditions dictate that men should generally place work responsibilities above parenting duties. This means single-parent fathers may be absent from their children more than single-parent mothers. Otherwise, they have to take less desirable and demanding jobs, which reduces their financial resources and stops or regresses their career advancement.

A final factor associated with single-parent families headed by fathers involves time and social life. Like single-parent mothers, single-parent fathers are frequently pressed for time and may experience exhaustion at the end of the day, with no relief from others. Socially and parentally, single-parent fathers are sometimes hindered by fatigue (Davis & Borns, 1999). The plight of Dustin Hoffman as a single-parent father in the movie *Kramer vs. Kramer* is a good example of all the factors and dilemmas facing men who opt for such a lifestyle.

# Effects of Divorce and Death on Children

Estimates have been made that approximately 50% of all children under age 18 will spend some time growing up in a single-parent household (Casto & Bumpass, 1989). Most of the children will live in single-parent households created by divorce and death. Their adjustment will vary but is strongly influenced by the functioning of the family and the children before the divorce or death, experiences surrounding the creation of the single-parent household, and the resources available to children afterward.

## Children of Divorce

Children whose parents divorce tend to do best if their mothers and fathers continue or resume their parenting roles, manage to put differences aside, and allow children to have a continuing relationship with both of them (Barnes, 1999; Wallerstein, 1992). "Children who experience a positive relationship with their parents show fewer behavioral problems regardless of family structure" (Duckett & Richards, 1995, p. 419). Good sibling relationships, social support from adults outside the immediate family, such as teachers, positive friendships, and someone to openly talk to and confide in are most helpful also (Barnes, 1999). Unfortunately, many children do not experience such an atmosphere. As a result, these children suffer mental and emotional anguish long after their parents divorce and may act out behaviorally.

In a 15-year follow-up of children whose parents divorced, Wallerstein (1990) found that children had vivid memories of their parents' separation. Ironically, those who were most distressed during the time of the breakup, preschoolers, were best adjusted as a group at the time of follow-up. Those who were adolescents during the time of divorce were the most pained as a group at the time of follow-up, when they were young adults. They felt physically and emotionally abandoned. Overall, Wallerstein concluded that "divorce is not an event that stands alone in children's or adults' experience. It is a continuum" (1992, p. 167). For instance, children from families disrupted by divorce are less likely to do well educationally including applying to, being admitted to, and enrolling at more select colleges (Gose, 1996). They are also less prone to form strong adult attachment bonds in later life, a finding that cuts across racial/ethnic groups (Lopez, Melendez, & Rice, 2000).

One of the primary tasks for society in the years ahead is to strengthen families, not by turning back the clock, but by helping children feel as socially, economically, and emotionally secure as possible. Otherwise, children who emerge from particularly conflictual divorces may become what Nurse (1996, p. 22) calls "cardboard kids . . . good surface, but nobody knows the depth, or if in fact there is any depth, or authentic self." Suggestions from Glang and Betis (1993) for helping children through the divorce process include:

- having both parents tell the children about the divorce with care and concern
- giving children advanced warning before a parent moves out
- ensuring that children do not feel they are being divorced from either parent
- explaining divorce to children in words they understand
- giving children space of their own both physically and psychologically
- helping children look forward to the visit of a noncustodial parent (which includes realizing and accepting the fact that children often wish their parents to reconcile)

In addition, it is important for children in the long term to have continued contact with noncustodial parents, usually fathers. Children who do best after the actual event of a divorce perceive their fathers as accepting, supportive, and trustworthy regardless of marital status (Arditti & Prouty, 1999). They sense that their fathers will be there for them as well as financially provide for them.

## Children Who Lose a Parent by Death

Children who experience death within the family, especially of a parent, express a number of emotions and behaviors depending on their age and attachment to the deceased. They may become anxious, hope for a reunion, blame themselves or others, and become overly active (Olowu, 1990). To cope, they need to be given accurate information on what happened and the support of the surviving parent. These children also need to go through three distinct stages of bereavement: protest, despair, and detachment.

Adolescents have some of the same reactions to the death of a parent as younger children. Support from the surviving parent and peers is generally helpful to them (Gray, 1988, 1989). In addition, their grief and response is influenced by their adjustment prior to the parent's death and their religious beliefs (Gray, 1987).

# Strengths and Challenges Connected with Single-Parent Families

Embedded within the structure of single-parent families are inherent strengths and challenges. Sometimes these two aspects of family life are ironically the same. For example, the freedom that single-parent families have to interact with a wide variety of people can also be a detriment to them because of the resources such types of relationships demand. Despite this irony, some unique aspects of single-parent families are mainly positive or negative.

## Strengths of Single-Parent Families

A strength of single-parent families as a whole is that they tend to be more democratic than most family types (Wallerstein & Kelly, 1980; Weiss, 1979). An informal way of relating to each other is developed out of necessity. This aspect of family life often helps children and their parents interact in unique ways. When decisions have to be made, the needs of all parties, parent and child(ren), are usually taken into consideration.

Another strength of single-parent families relates to roles and rules. Because of limited resources, many single-parent families are flexible in regard to which members will perform what tasks. For example, in single-parent families, any member can wash dishes, sweep the floor, or work in the garden. Adjustability in regard to members' responsibilities is essential and usually occurs.

A third unique quality of single-parent families is the pace at which members go through developmental stages. In single-parent families, children often learn how to take responsibility for their actions at an early age (Wallerstein & Kelly, 1980). They also learn essential skills, such as finding a bargain or saving money, faster than most children. This behavior often endears these individuals to the parent with whom they live and gives them a certain maturity beyond their years in relating to adults.

The final area in regard to assets of single-parent families is the matter of resources. On the positive side, the children of single parents, and the adults themselves, often are creative in locating and utilizing needed materials for their overall well-being. They learn to survive through being frugal as well as innovative. Single-parent family members realize quite realistically the value of commodities, such as money and time, that other families take for granted (Ahrons & Rodgers, 1987).

## Challenges of Single-Parent Families

A challenge of single-parent families involves the defining or refining of boundaries and roles (Glenwick & Mowrey, 1986). Troublesome areas include boundary disputes between former spouses and between children and their custodial parent or joint custody parents. Boundary issues with former spouses involve everything from visitation situations to sexuality (Goldsmith, 1982). Within single-parent families, the democratic nature of these families may blur needed boundary distinctions between a parent and child. In either of these cases, if boundaries are not clear and enforced, chaotic and confusing interactions may result and children may get out of control (Glenwick & Mowrey, 1986). Unfortunately, children who grow up in single-parent households often exhibit behavior problems as a result of boundary issues. They are more than twice as likely to have emotional and behavioral problems as those who grow up in intact families (Blaisure & Geasler, 2000).

Role delineation is likewise a hurdle that must be overcome. Although role flexibility may prove useful and valuable in helping single-parent families accomplish tasks, it may add stress and work onto select members of these families. They in turn may experience role reversal or role overload (Weiss, 1979). In fact, fatigue and burnout on the part of one or more members of the family unit is often the outcome of this type of open operating procedure.

Another challenge for single-parent families, especially when they result from divorce, is educational achievement. Children have noticeable academic difficulties during the first 18 months of their parent's divorce (Benedek & Benedek, 1979). These effects may be long lasting. For instance, children reared in single-parent families, especially boys, are likely to receive reduced schooling (Krein, 1986). "On the average, children of divorced parents are less educated than others their age and are less likely to graduate from high school than are children of similar backgrounds who grow up in intact families" (Carlson & Sperry, 1993, p. 6).

A third challenge for single-parent families is connected with identity. Many children, especially those who have been raised in a single-parent family as a result of divorce, have difficulty establishing a clear and strong identity and relating to others of the opposite gender. "Children of divorce leave home earlier than others, but not to form families of their own. They are far more likely than their peers to cohabit before they marry, and when they do marry, they also are more likely to divorce" (Carlson & Sperry, 1993, p. 6). They may not experience childhood to the fullest. In adulthood they may come to resent growing up so fast and may consciously or unconsciously display less personal maturity.

A fourth potential problem for single-parent families is poverty. As a group, single-parent families are financially less well off than other family forms. For instance, they are six times as likely to be poor when compared with nuclear families (Urschel, 1993). Part of the disparity in income is due to the disproportionate number of female-headed single-parent families. Approximately 90% of these families are led by women who in general earn less than men. In addition to generally lower wages earned by women, the lack of child support has further strained the financial resources of these families. Data by the Center for the Study of Social Policy shows that of the single-parent families headed by a female that receive child support or alimony, 43% are white, 18% are Hispanic, and 17% are African American (McLean, 1993). Overall, 50% of children living in single-parent households live below the poverty line (Walsh, 1991).

A final challenge that a single-parent family usually faces relates to emotions. The psychological feelings expressed by parents and children in these families include helplessness, hopelessness, frustration, despair, guilt, depression, and ambivalence (Baruth & Burgraff, 1991; Goldsmith, 1982; Murdock, 1980). These feelings come with the awareness that one has not resolved matters with a significant other, such as a former spouse or parent. These feelings are complicated when one does not have ready access to the needed person. With time, these feelings increase and stress intensifies. They keep the person within the single-parent family "hooked" emotionally to historical times and situations. It usually takes 2 or more years for single-parent family members to resolve their plethora of emotions and to form into a functional unit (Goldenberg & Goldenberg, 1998).

# Approaches for Treating Single-Parent Families

Several family therapy approaches work well with single-parent families (Westcot & Dries, 1990). All are dependent on therapists taking the time and effort to get to know the unique aspects of each family. Assessment of the unique as well as universal aspects of a single-parent family always precedes therapeutic interventions. To treat single-parent families effectively, therapists must help them work together as a team systematically.

## Family Theory Approaches

Six family theories most often employed with single-parent families are (1) structural, (2) strategic, (3) solution-focused, (4) Bowenian, (5) experiential, and (6) narrative.

Structural family therapy appears to be popular because it deals with common concerns of single-parent families such as structure, boundaries, and power (Minuchin & Fishman, 1981). The interventions of structural family therapists seek to restructure or redefine family systems (Minuchin, 1974). For example, this approach is designed to put the parent in charge of the way the family functions. As such, the family moves from being a system in which there is a **parentified child** or an equalized relationship among parents and children to one in which power is vested in a custodial parent.

Strategic family therapies are utilized frequently with single-parent families because they focus on immediate problem solving in connection with a particular problem, such as acting out behavior (Westcot & Dries, 1990). The interventions of these approaches may be direct, but often they are more subtle, for example, as in reframing, the use of paradox, and prescribing symptoms. One strategic method that may be particularly effective is reframing. For instance, a reframe may be used to describe a child's behavior as "depressed" instead of "hostile." In such a case, single-parent family members can rally around the child rather than make accusations and continually argue about the child's behavior.

Solution-focused therapy may be particularly helpful to single-parent families because it helps them focus on new aspects of their lives by finding exceptions to difficult situations and doing something different (deShazer, 1991; O'Hanlon & Weiner-Davis, 1989). The emphasis on making small changes is ideally suited to the beginning developmental phase of single-parent family life in which there is much unrest, and the ability to participate in therapeutic work is limited because of demands and fatigue. When family members perceive they are in harmony with each other, even for a short period, they can then focus their energy and efforts on cultivating these exceptional times and in the process make significant and healthy changes.

Bowenian family therapy is employed because of its emphasis on resolving the past and examining historical family patterns (Bowen, 1978). Through the construction of a genogram, single-parent families may come to notice and deal with the absent person or persons that have influenced them positively or negatively previously. For example, a solo parent may realize he is still trying to live up to the words of his mother who admonished him to "stay married at all costs" and "always put your children's needs before your own." In the process of constructing a genogram, such "ghosts" from the past lose their power to interfere with the family's present interactions because they are recognized as historical figures over which one has control.

Experiential family therapy, especially as advocated by Virginia Satir (1967), is useful for single-parent families in helping their members enact metaphorically—through sculpting and choreography—troublesome and unresolved situations. The feelings that arise in connection with these symbolic experiences often help family members work through emotions and experience affective relief from circumstances they can no longer influence or control.

Finally, narrative family therapy can be helpful to single-parent families both at the initial time of forming the family, especially if through divorce, and in resolving other routine and special difficulties associated with being a single-parent family. If the family is formed due to a divorce, the narrative technique of externalizing the problem may be useful (White & Epston, 1990). Such a process helps family members pull together and combat emotions such as fear, anger, and anxiety that might otherwise take a toll on them individually. Future stories created by children or the parent(s) involved in a single-parent household can also be therapeutic and provide hope and direction for the family in regard to relationships, meaning, and development (Arditti & Prouty, 1999).

Regardless of what theoretical approach is employed with single-parent families, therapists should keep in mind that a number of children and parents in these units have already formed opinions about treatment. The reason is that "children in single-parent families are twice as likely to have behavior problems and undergo professional help for these problems than are children in nuclear families" (Bray, 1993, p. 95). Therefore, although these families are in need, they may have mixed feelings—ranging from prejudice to negative expectations—about entering treatment. If complicating and detrimental factors are not addressed, families may not be helped.

## Other Approaches for Treating Single-Parent Families

Several other strategies work well in helping single-parent families. These nontheory strategies are especially useful if they are employed simultaneously.

One approach is to help family members communicate clearly and frequently with each other. Clear family communication patterns are associated with the well-being of single-parent families (Hanson, 1986). A forum family therapists can use in this way is the Adlerian concept of a weekly family conference (Baruth & Burgraff, 1991). This type of meeting in which all members are present and talk about their concerns encourages families to resolve problems and plan for the future.

A second way of working with single-parent families involves linking family members and the family as a whole to needed sources of social support. The work of Nagy, which emphasized community connectedness, is the underpinning for this functional approach (Boszormenyi-Nagy, 1987). For example, **Parents Without Partners** is a national organization that helps single parents and their children deal with the realities of single-parent family life in educational and experiential ways (Murdock, 1980). Single parents also need the positive involvement and care of extended family and friends whenever possible (Gladow & Ray, 1986).

A third nontheory way of working with single-parent families involves assisting them in getting their financial matters resolved. As a general rule, most single-parent families have economic problems (Norton & Glick, 1986). Financial counseling through, for example, United Way agencies or volunteers can be quite beneficial for these families. Job training and educational opportunities connected with advancement also can help. Through these types of assistance, family members can best utilize their resources.

A final approach to working with single-parent families is through educational methods, such as providing them with reading resources (Blaisure & Geasler, 2000). One particular helpful means of working with these families is through bibliotherapy (Gladding,

1998; Pardeck & Pardeck, 1997). Bibliotherapy involves the reading by a family or members of a family of literature and the processing of the reading experience with the therapist. A number of appropriate books written for all members of single-parent families and for the families themselves can help individuals involved realize they are not alone in what they are experiencing. For example, *This Is Me and My Single Parent* (Evans, 1989) is a discovery type of workbook that children (ages 4 to 12) and single parents can work on together. In addition, even a simple newsletter that provides educational information and emotional support can make a difference in the adjustment and well-being of single-parent families (Nelson, 1986).

# Role of the Therapist

The role of family therapists in working with single-parent families parallels in some ways their role in helping other types of families. For instance, therapists must deal with issues related to boundaries, hierarchies, and engagement/detachment. However, both subtle and obvious differences exist that must be taken into consideration when treating single-parent families. These distinctions are related to the uniqueness of these families as well as their commonness with other families. As a general rule, family therapists "should not be guided by the intact family model and attempt to replicate a two-parent household" (Walsh, 1991, p. 533). Single-parent families are socially, psychologically, and economically unique.

In working with single-parent families, therapists must lay aside personal prejudices and biases. The ability to avoid making judgments and criticisms is especially difficult if therapists have not resolved their own personal problems (e.g., a divorce) that might involve the issue of a single-parent family. To be effective, family therapists must deal directly with people, hierarchies, and circumstances of these families, not myths (Bray, 1993). Likewise, therapists must assist single-parent families in giving up any negative stereotypes of themselves.

A second area family therapists must address, especially with those who have become single parents due to divorce, involves emotional volatility. "Interactional conflict between former spouses is the norm" (Walsh, 1991, p. 532). Therapists must help their clients "distinguish between emotional divorce issues and legal divorce issues and to understand that the emotional issues must be set aside at times in order to make mature and reasonable legal decisions" (Oliver, 1992, p. 41). Getting single parents to separate their feelings from their functions is at best difficult. It requires that therapists stay focused and balanced in their interactions with family members.

A third role of family therapists in working with single-parent families is to help members and the family as a whole tap their own inner resources as well as utilize support groups (Juhnke, 1993). Many single-parent families are caught up in their problems and biased against themselves. In these situations, members become discouraged and unable to perceive successful problem-solving methods. For instance, a single-parent mother may find through treatment that she is better at achieving results with her children when she listens to them instead of yelling at them. The talent to tap this resource may go unused if the family therapist does not help the parent discover and utilize it. Similarly, in assisting the family, the therapist needs to be aware of both formal and informal support groups, such as friends in the neighborhood. Through such groups, parents and children may find encouragement, relief from each other, and renewal through interacting with different people and ideas.

# Process and Outcome

Single-parent families that are successful in family therapy show a variety of improvements. Four of the most important are highlighted here, with the realization that other changes may be unique to particular families.

First, as a result of therapeutic interventions, single-parent families manifest more confidence and competence in themselves (Baruth & Burgraff, 1991). Often single-parent families and their members lose self-esteem and exhibit dependence, helplessness, and hopelessness. Single-parent mothers may feel especially overloaded in performing their executive tasks as head of these families (Weltner, 1982). If treatment has been beneficial, family members rely more on themselves and extended networks of family and friends. They function with greater efficiency. They also have a better knowledge of a number of agencies or networks from which they can get the help they need. Furthermore, these families as units experience fewer behavior problems and less stress, and they see an increase in relationship skills, especially between parent and child(ren) (Soehner, Zastowny, Hammond, & Taylor, 1988).

A second expected outcome of family treatment with single-parent families is that members within these units are helped to have clear and functional boundaries (Westcot & Dries, 1990). Single-parent families are frequently enmeshed with cross-generational alliances and nonproductive structures (Glenwick & Mowrey, 1986). When a family breaks up, the custodial parent must help himself or herself, as well as any children involved, adjust to a new hierarchy. Ideally, this type of structure allows for the interaction between the new single-parent family and others (Minuchin & Fishman, 1981). In the case of divorce, an amiable relationship between children and both former marriage partners is needed whether or not there is joint custody.

When these outcomes do not occur, children and adults are forced to operate in inappropriate ways (Juhnke, 1993). For example, when single-parent families are enmeshed, a child, usually the oldest, is often "parentified" (Minuchin, Montalvo, Guerney, Rosman, & Schumer, 1967). Parentified children are forced to give up their childhoods and act like adult parents even though they lack the necessary knowledge and skills. When freed from intergenerational enmeshment, the parentified child's role is no longer necessary and can be given up. If all goes well in family therapy, members of single-parent families gain a clearer perspective on their lives, the dynamics of their families, and appropriate behaviors.

A third area of improvement involves the ability to make informed decisions regarding remarriage. Research shows there is a strong tendency for single parents to move into new marital relationships too quickly. The majority of single parents are single for less than 5 years. Yet, remarriage is a move that "often compounds problems rather than leading to resolution" (Carlson & Sperry, 1993, p. 6). Remarriages have a higher probability of dissolving than first marriages (Levine, 1990). Counseling can help single parents and their children examine more thoroughly the pros and cons of remarriage options. Through such a process, single parents can make better decisions, and children can work through their feelings before instead of after the marriage.

Finally, families are able to utilize resources in the community better and make use of their own resources to the fullest. Improvements are seen in financial and personal management areas. Negative feelings accumulated through past experiences begin to dissipate. And, the development of friends, the tapping of family, and the pulling together of family members within the single-parent family unit should occur.

# Summary and Conclusion

Single-parent families have a lifestyle that is both temporary and permanent. Although there have always been single-parent families, the growth in their number within the United States has increased drastically since World War II. The reasons for the quantitative rise are varied and complex but include such factors as history, choice, and detrimental circumstances, such as death or divorce. In the 1950s, divorce became the leading cause of the formation of single-parent families. It continues to be a driving force, along with death of a spouse and choice.

Single-parent families come in many forms. They include at least one parent who is biologically related to the child (or the children) or who has assumed such a role through adoption. Because of the structure of single-parent households, a less structured and more democratic setup is created. This type of atmosphere may promote psychological bonding but may also blur needed boundary lines and lead to some confusion and frustration. As a group, single-parent families are less affluent than other family forms, and the majority of them are headed by women.

The possibilities and problems of single-parent families are numerous. As a group, single-parent families may find it easier to relate to a variety of family types and individuals. Most of these families are flexible in their form and functionality. On the other hand, finding resources to support themselves and finding time together (or alone) to enjoy each other (or themselves) is difficult. Many single-parent families live in or close to poverty. They are often adversely affected by such environments.

Through therapeutic interventions, family therapists can help these families maximize their potential and minimize their problems. In working with single-parent families, therapists utilize mainstream theories, such as structural, strategic, solution-focused, Bowen, experiential, and narrative family therapies. They also employ communication procedures, bibliotherapy, and linkage with relevant outside groups, such as Parents Without Partners and financial counselors. The role of the family therapist is to be an advocate for these families in finding resources within themselves and others. To do so, therapists must lay aside prejudices and deal with volatile emotions.

If therapy is successful, single-parent families should show a number of improvements. These improvements include more confidence and competence, better efficiency, clear and functional boundaries and structures, and better decision-making ability in regard to considerations such as remarriage and finances.

# Summary Table

## Working with Single-Parent Families

The term *single-parent families* is applied to a number of different family forms such as those created by divorce, death, abandonment, unwed pregnancy, and adoption.

A common thread of single parenthood is that one parent is primarily responsible for himself/herself and a child or children.

Single-parent families compose over 30% of today's families with children.

Historically most single-parent families were created by death or divorce.

One reason single-parent families are increasing, however, is that many single women are choosing to bear and raise children themselves.

### Types of Single-Parent Families

Single-parent families that form as a result of divorce contain both custodial and noncustodial parents. Each parent faces challenges individually and in connection with her or his child(ren).

Single-parent families that form as a result of death face the task of having all members go through the stages of mourning, readjustment, and achievement.

Single-parent families formed as a result of intentionality must deal with planning, arrival, and adjustment stages of development.

Generally, all types of single-parent families require time (about 2 years) to form into functional units.

### Dynamics Associated with Single-Parent Families

By understanding the dynamics underlying the formation of single-parent families, therapists can best help them.

Single-parent families that form as a result of divorce have spouses who have generally been influenced by rapid change, personality compatibility factors, and unequal distribution of power.

Members must deal with the loss of the marriage, new roles, redefinement of relationships, and establishment of a satisfactory arrangement with the ex-spouse or noncustodial parent.

Single-parent families formed as a result of the death of a spouse must deal with shock, grief, a new family reality, and internal/external demands.

Single-parent families that form as a result of intentionality must successfully combat societal pressures. Furthermore, they must justify their decision, and marshal their resources.

### Single-Parent Mothers and Fathers

Families headed by single-parent mothers make up between 85% and 90% of all single-parent households. They face problems associated with finances, role overload, extended family or ex-spouse interference, and parental identity. Conditions are often perilous.

Families headed by single-parent fathers make up between 10% and 15% of all single-parent households. They are usually more affluent than those of single-parent mothers. In addition, confidence and competence in single-parent fathers is high. Negatives of these families are job/career limitations, social restrictions, and physical fatigue.

### Effects of Divorce and Death on Children

Children's reactions to divorce or death in a family setting are sometimes delayed or inhibited.

Children of divorce do best if their custodial parents allow relationships with both parents to continue and put aside differences.

Regardless of adjustment, children whose parents divorce have memories of it. Their later reactions depend on their ages at the time of separation and the support they receive in working through their feelings about the divorce.

Children who face the death of a parent must deal with their grief through proper mourning and not become overanxious, blameful, or overactive. Detachment is the final stage of the grief process after bereavement and despair. Surviving parents and peer support groups are most helpful.

### Strengths and Challenges Connected with Single-Parent Families

Single-parent families often have the following strengths:

- They are more democratic.
- They have flexible roles and rules.
- The children mature and take responsibility earlier.
- They are creative in locating needed resources.

Single-parent families often face the following challenges:

- They have unclear or undefined boundaries and roles.
- They have overall limited academic achievement by children.
- The children contend with identity confusion.
- The children may have difficulty relating to the opposite gender.
- They live with poverty.
- They cope with depression and other negative emotional residue.

### Approaches for Treating Single-Parent Families

Theories that work with single-parent families are:

| | | |
|---|---|---|
| structural | strategic | solution-focused |
| Bowenian | experiential (Satir) | narrative |

In addition to theories, family therapists can utilize:

- communication methods (e.g., Adlerian family council)
- social support groups (e.g., Parents Without Partners)
- financial counseling services
- bibliotherapy

### Role of the Therapist

The role of the family therapist includes dealing with boundaries, hierarchies, and engagement/detachment.

Family therapists must lay aside personal biases/prejudices.
Family therapists must deal with emotional volatility of the family.
Family therapists must help foster inner resources and support groups for family members.

### Process and Outcome

If single-parent family therapy is successful, families should:

- manifest more competence and confidence in themselves
- have clear and functional boundaries
- make better financial and remarriage decisions
- utilize their own and community resources more fully

# References

Ahrons, C. R., & Rodgers, R. H. (1987). *Divorced families: A multi-disciplinary developmental view.* New York: Norton.

Albom, M. (1997). *Tuesdays with Morrie.* New York: Doubleday.

Arditti, J. A., & Prouty, A. M. (1999). Change, disengagement, and renewal: Relationship dynamics between young adults and their fathers after divorce. *Journal of Marital and Family Therapy, 25,* 61–81.

Associated Press. (1993a, February 26). Single mothers growing in number. *Winston-Salem (NC) Journal,* p. 2.

Associated Press. (1993b, July 14). Study: More unwed women having babies. *Winston-Salem (NC) Journal,* p. 2.

Associated Press (2000, February 14). Half of black homes headed by single women. *Winston-Salem (NC) Journal,* p. A8.

Barnes, G. G. (1999). Divorce transitions: Identifying risk and promoting resilience for children and their parental relationships. *Journal of Marital and Family Therapy, 25,* 425–441.

Baruth, L. G., & Burgraff, M. Z. (1991). Counseling single-parent families. In J. Carlson & J. Lewis (Eds.), *Family counseling: Strategies and issues* (pp. 157–173). Denver, CO: Love Publishing.

Benedek, R., & Benedek, E. (1979). Children of divorce. Can we meet their needs? *Journal of Social Issues, 35,* 155.

Blaisure, K. R., & Geasler, M. J. (2000, March). Divorce interventions. *AAMFT Clinical Update, 2*(2), 1–8.

Bornstein, P. H., & Bornstein, M. T. (1986). *Marital therapy: A behavioral-communications approach.* New York: Pergamon.

Boszormenyi-Nagy, I. (1987). *Foundations of contextual therapy.* New York: Brunner/Mazel.

Bowen, M. (1978). *Family therapy in clinical practice.* New York: Jason Aronson.

Bray, J. H. (1993). Families in demographic perspective: Implications for family counseling. *The Family Journal: Counseling and Therapy for Couples and Families, 1,* 94–96.

Brown, F. H. (1988). The impact of death and serious illness on the family life cycle. In B. Carter & M. McGoldrick (Eds.),

*The changing family life cycle* (2nd ed., pp. 457–482). New York: Brunner/Mazel.

Bumpass, L. L. (1990). What's happening to the family? Interactions between demographic and institutional change. *Demography, 27,* 483–498.

Bumpass, L., & Sweet, J. A. (1989). Children's experience in single-parent families: Implications of cohabitation and marital transitions. *Family Planning Perspectives, 6,* 256–260.

Carlson, J., & Sperry, L. (1993, January/February). The future of families: New challenges for couple and family therapy. *Family Counseling and Therapy, 1,* 1–14.

Carter, B., & McGoldrick, M. (1988). Overview: The changing family life cycle: A framework for family therapy. In *The Changing Family Life Cycle* (2nd ed., p. 22). New York: Gardner.

Casto, M. T., & Bumpass, L. L. (1989). Recent trends in marital disruption. *Demography, 26,* 37–51.

Coates, J. F. (1996, September/October). What's ahead for families: Five major forces of change. *The Futurist,* pp. 27–35.

Davis, R. F., & Borns, N. F. (1999). *Solo dad survival guide: Raising your kids on your own.* New York: NTC/Contemporary Publishing.

deShazer, S. (1991). *Putting differences to work.* New York: W. W. Norton.

Duckett, E., & Richards, M. H. (1995). Maternal employment and the quality of daily experience for young adolescents of single mothers. *Journal of Family Psychology, 9,* 418–432.

Elias, M. (1992, June 19–21). Parenting turns men's lives on end. *USA Today,* pp. 1A, 2A.

Erbe, B. (1993, July 19). Stop surge of unwed mothers. *USA Today,* p. 11A.

Evans, M. (1989). *This is me and my single parent.* New York: Brunner/Mazel.

Freeman, M. G. (1985). *The concepts of love and marriage* (film). Atlanta, GA: Emory University.

Garfield, R. (1982). Mourning and its resolution for spouses in marital separation. In J. C. Hansen & L. Messinger (Eds.), *Therapy with remarriage families* (pp. 1–16). Rockville, MD: Aspen.

Gelles, R. J. (1989). Child abuse and violence in single-parent families: Parent absence and economic deprivation. *American Journal of Orthopsychiatry, 59*, 492–501.

Gelles, R. J. (1997). *Intimate violence in the family* (3rd ed.). Thousand Oaks, CA: Sage Publications.

Gladding, S. T. (1993). *Birth and Resolve*. Unpublished manuscript.

Gladding, S. T. (1998). *Counseling as an art: The creative arts in counseling* (2nd ed.). Alexandria, VA: American Counseling Association.

Gladow, N. W., & Ray, M. P. (1986). The impact of informal support systems on the well-being of low income single-parents. *Family Relations, 35*, 113–123.

Glang, C., & Betis, A. (1993). Helping children through the divorce process. *PsychSpeak, 13*, 1–2.

Glenwick, D. S., & Mowrey, J. D. (1986). When parent becomes peer: Loss of intergenerational boundaries in single-parent families. *Family Relations, 35*, 57–62.

Glick, P. C. (1988). The role of divorce in the changing family structure: Trends and variations. In S. A. Wolchik & P. Karoly (Eds.), *Children of divorce: Empirical perspectives on adjustment* (pp. 3–34). New York: Gardner.

Goldenberg, H., & Goldenberg, I. (1998). *Counseling today's families* (3rd ed.). Pacific Grove, CA: Brooks/Cole.

Goldsmith, J. (1982). The postdivorce family system. In F. Walsh (Ed.), *Normal family processes* (pp. 297–330). New York: Guilford.

Gose, B. (1996, July 12). Study finds children of divorced parents less likely to enroll at selective colleges. *Chronicle of Higher Education, XLII*, A35–A36.

Gray, R. E. (1987). Adolescent response to the death of a parent. *Journal of Youth and Adolescence, 16*, 511–525.

Gray, R. E. (1988). The role of school counselors with bereaved teenagers: With and without peer support. *The School Counselor, 35*, 185–193.

Gray, R. E. (1989). Adolescent's perceptions of social support after the death of a parent. *Journal of Psychosocial Oncology, 7*, 127–144.

Groze, V. (1991). Adoption and single-parents: A review. *Child Welfare, 70*, 321–332.

Hanson, S. M. (1986). Healthy single-parent families. *Family Relations, 35*, 125–132.

Hill, R. (1986). Life cycle stages for types of single-parent families: Of family developmental theory. *Family Relations, 35*, 19–29.

Juhnke, G. A. (1993). *Effective family counseling: Applications for school counselors*. Paper presented at the 66th annual convention of the North Carolina Counseling Association, Raleigh, NC.

Klagsbrun, F. (1985). *Married people*. New York: Bantam.

Kleist, D. M. (1999). Single-parent families: A difference that makes a difference? *The Family Journal, 7*, 373–378.

Krauth, L. D. (1995, December). Single-parent families: The risk to children. *Family Therapy News, 26*(6), 14.

Krein, S. F. (1986). Growing up in a single-parent family: The effects on education and earnings of young men. *Family Relations, 35*, 161–168.

Levine, A. (1990, January 29). The second time around: Realities of remarriage. *U.S. News and World Report*, pp. 50–51.

Levitan, S. A., & Conway, E. A. (1990). *Families in flux*. Washington, DC: Bureau of National Affairs.

Lopez, F. G., Melendez, M. C., & Rice, K. G. (2000). Parental divorce, parent–child bonds, and adult attachment orientation among college students: A comparison of three racial/ethnic groups. *Journal of Counseling Psychology, 47*, 177–186.

McGoldrick, M. (1986, November/December). Mourning rituals. *Family Therapy Networker, 10*, 29–30.

McLean, E. A. (1993, April 8). Who gets child support. *USA Today*, p. 1A.

Melli, M. S. (1986). The changing legal status of the single-parent. *Family Relations, 35*, 31–35.

Minuchin, S. (1974). *Families and family therapy*. Cambridge, MA: Harvard University Press.

Minuchin, S. , & Fishman, H. C. (1981). *Family therapy techniques*. Cambridge, MA: Harvard University Press.

Minuchin, S., Montalvo, B., Guerney, B., Rosman, B., & Schumer, F. (1967). *Families of the slums*. New York: Basic Books.

Moody, F. (1992). Divorce: Sometimes a bad notion. In O. Pocs (Ed.), *Marriage and family 92–93* (pp. 171–176). Guilford, CT: Dushkin.

Moody, R. A., & Moody, C. P. (1991). A family perspective: Helping children acknowledge and express grief following the death of a parent. *Death Studies, 15*, 587–602.

Morrison, N. C. (1995). Successful single-parent families. *Journal of Divorce and Remarriage, 22*, 205–219.

Murdock, C. V. (1980). *Single parents are people too*. New York: Butterick.

National Center for Health Statistics. (1991). *Advanced report of final natality statistics, 1989* (Monthly vital statistics report). Hyattsville, MD: Public Health Service.

Nelson, P. T. (1986). Newsletters: An effective delivery mode for providing educational information and emotional support to single-parent families? *Family Relations, 35*, 183–188.

Norton, A. J., & Glick, P. C. (1986). One parent families: A social and economic profile. *Family Relations, 35*, 9–17.

Nurse, A. R. (1996, Spring). The cardboard kids. *The Family Psychologist, 13*, 22–23.

O'Hanlon, W. H., & Weiner-Davis, M. (1989). *In search of solutions: A new direction in psychotherapy.* New York: W. W. Norton.

Oliver, C. J. (1992). Legal issues facing families in transition: An overview for counselors. *New York State Journal for Counseling and Development, 7,* 41–52.

Olowu, A. A. (1990). Helping children cope with death. *Early Child Development and Care, 61,* 119–123.

Pardeck, J. T., & Pardeck, J. A. (1997). Recommended books for helping young children deal with social and developmental problems. *Early Child Development and Care, 136,* 57–63.

Pavao, J. M. (1998). *The family of adoption.* Boston: Beacon Press.

Pulleyblank, E. (1996, January/February). Hard lessons. *Family Therapy Networker,* 42–44, 46, 49.

Riseman, B. J. (1986). Can men "mother"? Life as a single father. *Family Relations, 35,* 95–102.

Rotter, J. C. (2000). Family grief and mourning. *The Family Journal, 8,* 275–277.

Sanik, M. M., & Mauldin, T. (1986). Single versus two parent families: A comparison of mothers' time. *Family Relations, 35,* 53–56.

Satir, V. (1967). *Conjoint family therapy.* Palo Alto, CA: Science and Behavior Books.

Seward, R. (1978). *The American family: A demographic history.* Newbury Park, CA: Sage Publications.

Silverstein, L. B., & Levant, R. F. (1996, Spring). Children need fathers not patriarchs. *The Family Psychologist, 13,* 18–19

Soehner, G., Zastowny, T., Hammond, A., & Taylor, L. (1988). The single-parent family project: A community-based, preventive program for single-parent families. *Journal of Child and Adolescent Psychiatry, 5,* 35–43.

Strong, B., DeVault, C., & Sayad, B. W. (2001). *The marriage and family experience* (8th ed.). Belmont, CA: Wadsworth.

Sweet, J. A., Bumpass, L. L., & Call, V. (1988). *The design and content of the National Survey of Families and Households* (Working paper NSFH-1). Madison, WI: University of Wisconsin, Center for Demography and Ecology.

Urschel, J. (1993, April 8). Stopping high-risk marriages. *USA Today,* p. 12A.

Wallerstein, J. S. (1986). Women after divorce: Preliminary report from a 10-year follow up. *American Journal of Orthopsychiatry, 56,* 65–77.

Wallerstein, J. S. (1990). *Second chances.* New York: Ticknor & Fields.

Wallerstein, J. S. (1992). Children after divorce. In O. Pocs (Ed.), *Marriage and family 92–93* (pp. 163–168). Guilford, CT: Dushkin.

Wallerstein, J. S., & Kelly, J. (1980). *Surviving the breakup: How children actually cope with divorce.* New York: Basic Books.

Walsh, F. (1991). Promoting healthy functioning in divorced and remarried families. In A. S. Gurman & D. P. Kniskern (Eds.), *Handbook of family therapy* (Vol. II, pp. 525–545). New York: Brunner/Mazel.

Ward, S. (1993, May 6). Median income of families with children. *USA Today,* p. D1.

Weiss, R. (1979). *Going it alone: The family life and social situation of the single parent.* New York: Basic Books.

Weltner, J. S. (1982). A structural approach to the single-parent family. *Family Process, 21,* 203–210.

Westcot, M. E., & Dries, R. (1990). Has family therapy adapted to the single-parent family? *American Journal of Family Therapy, 18,* 363–372.

White, M., & Epston, D. (1990). *Narrative means to therapeutic ends.* New York: Norton.

# CHAPTER 12

# Working with Remarried Families

They were a trio,
a mother and young adolescents
scared and scarred.

Learning to sing songs without a bass
while opening jars and opportunities
through the strength of sheer persistence.

He became a part of them,
breaking through boundaries with clumsy actions
while exposing his feelings with caring words.

Slowly, through chaos, a family emerged
as a group, like a jazz quartet.

Through improvisation
they developed a syncopated rhythm.

In an atmosphere of hope,
came the sounds of harmony.

*Gladding, 1992*

**M**any terms are used to describe **remarried families** including *stepfamilies, reconstituted families, recoupled families, merged families, patched families,* and *blended families.* Regardless of the terminology used, these families "consist of two adults and step-, adoptive, or foster children" (Pearson, 1993, p. 51). Although most prevalent among European Americans because of their high divorce and remarriage rate, remarried families are found among all cultural groups within the United States. They have become the norm in American society (Howell, Weers, & Kleist, 1998).

Remarried families have always been a part of American family life. However, the way they are formed has changed, and their numbers have increased dramatically in recent years. For example, in the 1880s, the divorce rate for first marriages was only 7%, and the most prevalent reason for forming remarried families was due to the death or desertion of a spouse (Martin & Bumpass, 1989). These figures shifted in the decades that followed. After World War II, the divorce rate in the United States began to rise rapidly. The 1960s and the 1970s saw divorce reach an unprecedented height quantitatively, with approximately 50% of all marriages ending in divorce (Levitan & Conway, 1990). These decades also marked the beginning of a large remarriage movement (Braver et al., 1993).

By the beginning of the twenty-first century, 1 million of the 2 million marriages in the United States each year involved at least one formerly married person. Reasons for the growth of this type of family are associated with the fact that approximately three out of every four people who divorce eventually remarry (Carter & McGoldrick, 1999). In addition, more than 40 million adults had been or were stepparents by this time. Furthermore, it was estimated that "about a third of all Americans" would "remarry at least once in their lives" (Levine, 1990, p. 50).

As a result of the remarried family trend, approximately 40% of all children born in the 1980s and 1990s have lived in such an arrangement before reaching the age of 18 (Glick, 1989). Indeed, the growth of remarried families is one of the major reason that during the last half of the twentieth century the perception of what was "normal" or "common" in family life changed.

This chapter examines the dynamics and life cycle of remarried families. These families share unique and universal qualities with other types of families. It is important to delineate and address the issues faced by these families if therapists are going to work with them effectively. By understanding the nature of remarried families, family therapists can assess areas of distinction and commonness (Hayes & Hayes, 1991). "One of the difficulties" of remarried families is that they are fairly new as a common entity and "we have neither terminology to discuss" them "nor do we have research that explains the complex nature" of them (Pearson, 1993, p. 51). In addition, there is still too little information in the professional literature about clinically working with remarried families (Darden & Zimmerman, 1992). Thus, remarried families are a professional challenge. The issues surrounding them, however, are understandable.

# Forming Remarried Families

Many possible configurations of remarried families exist. Compared with "first-marriage families, the structures are more complex" (Bray, 1994, p. 67). Remarried families are most commonly formed when a person whose previous marriage ended in death, divorce, or abandonment marries either another previously married person or someone who has never been married. The result is a new combination of people, histories, issues, and interactions that are unique to that particular relationship. Unique opportunities arise from this complex joining of personalities and families. However, in this section an emphasis is placed on the most common concerns of remarried families, because they are the issues therapists deal with frequently.

## Common Concerns of Remarried Families

Establishing a remarried family is a more complicated process than creating a nuclear family (Visher & Visher, 1993). Remarried families face many situational and developmental tasks that are quite different from those found in other family lifestyles. They must systemically deal with complex kinship networks, define ill-defined goals, develop patterns of interaction that assist them in being cohesive, and reach consensual goals (Bernstein & Collins, 1985; Roberts & Price, 1986). As a way of understanding remarried families and the issues they encounter, Carter and McGoldrick (1988) have formulated a table (see Table 12.1) that outlines the stages, prerequisite attitude, and developmental issues of these family forms.

## Dealing with the Death of a Parent

Before the twentieth century, one out of every two adults died before age 50. "Families had to face the possibility that neither parent would survive to raise children to maturity. Not more than a third of the population had a single marriage last more than 10 years. Fifty percent of the time, children lost a parent before reaching maturity" (McGoldrick, 1986, p. 30). "The fundamental uncertainty of life was much harder for families to avoid" (McGoldrick, 1986, p. 29). Life-shortening events included women dying in childbirth and men dying in accidents. The result was a blending of families and kinship networks. Another consequence of such times was that families developed rituals, such as wearing black for a year and visiting a grave on anniversaries, to deal with death and move on with life.

Today, a death is denied or covered up in many families. Death often occurs in hospitals away from all family members. Funeral services usually include a closed coffin, and those who have died are often described in vague expressions (e.g., "departed" or "passed on") that fail to adequately describe the realities of death. This type of experience with death is particularly true of American families of European descent but much less true for other groups such as African-American families. Therefore, forming a remarried family after the death of a spouse is more difficult for some cultural groups than others because grief may not have been adequately expressed or processed. In these cases, "family members may refuse to accept a new member who is seen as replacing the deceased" (McGoldrick & Walsh, 1999, p. 187). The situation is further complicated by the fact that there are no established guidelines for couples and their offspring to follow in coming together. Indeed, "new roles and

**Table 12.1**
Remarried Family Formation: A Developmental Outline

| Steps | Prerequisite Attitude | Developmental Issues |
|---|---|---|
| 1. Entering the new relationship | Recovery from loss of first marriage (adequate "emotional divorce") | Recommitment to marriage and to forming a family with readiness to deal with the complexity and ambiguity |
| 2. Conceptualizing and planning new marriage and family | Accepting one's own fears and those of new spouse and children about remarriage and forming a stepfamily<br><br>Accepting need for time and patience for adjustment to complexity and ambiguity of:<br>1. Multiple new roles<br>2. Boundaries: space, time, membership, and authority<br>3. Affective issues: guilt, loyalty conflicts, desire for mutuality, unresolvable past hurts | a. Work on openness in the new relationships to avoid pseudo-mutuality<br>b. Plan for maintenance of cooperative coparental relationships with ex-spouses<br>c. Plan to help children deal with fears, loyalty conflicts, and membership in two systems<br>d. Realignment of relationships with extended family to include new spouse and children<br>e. Plan maintenance of connections for children with extended family of ex-spouse(s) |
| 3. Remarriage and reconstitution of family | Final resolution of attachment to previous spouse and ideal of "intact" family; acceptance of a different model of family with permeable boundaries | a. Restructuring family boundaries to allow for inclusion of new spouse—stepparent<br>b. Realignment of relationships throughout subsystems to permit interweaving of several systems<br>c. Making room for relationships of all children with biological (non-custodial) parents, grandparents, and other extended family<br>d. Sharing memories and histories to enhance stepfamily integration |

From *The Changing Family Life Cycle* (2nd ed., p. 24), edited by B. Carter and M. McGoldrick, 1988, New York: Gardner. Reprinted with permission from Allyn & Bacon, Boston.

rules need to be worked out, relationships developed and maintained, and a working relationship created between households" (Visher & Visher, 1994, p. 208). The process differs in kind and degree from establishing such a family after a divorce (Visher & Visher, 1988).

## Dealing with the Divorce of a Couple

Divorce has become a common experience in American culture. As mentioned previously, more than 50% of first marriages end in divorce and some demographers argue that the actual divorce rate is greater than 50% (McGoldrick & Carter, 1999; Castro-Martin & Bumpass, 1989). This rate has held steady since the late 1980s. Thus, it is estimated that if you include couples who separate but never file for divorce, the number of first marriages that end in divorce or separation may be as high as 66% (Walker, 1990).

Divorces occur for numerous reasons, including affairs and conflicting role expectations. Gottman and Carrere (Peterson, 2000) have found through longitudinal research of couples that there are several key predictors of couples most likely to divorce. These predictors include "a husband's unwillingness to be influenced by his wife, who is often the one trying to solve marital problems; and the wife starting quarrels 'harshly' and with hostility" (p. A1). A dynamic of this type tends to escalate into bigger conflicts and ultimately the dissolution of the marriage.

Interestingly, two thirds of divorces occur in the first 10 years of marriage. Thus, the median duration of marriage in the United States is 7 years (National Center for Health Statistics, 1988). Two prevalent times of breakup occur during the first few years of a couples' marital relationship. The first is when newlyweds are adjusting to each other and decide that the relationship they have entered is not working. The second is after the birth of a child, when the family becomes unsettled and stressful as new routines are established and disrupted because of infant needs. The National Center for Health Statistics reports that the ages of men and women who divorce has risen slightly since the 1970s and is today approximately 37.3 years for men and 34.8 years for women. However, these figures are more a reflection of later first marriages than increased marriage/family stability (Mullins, 1993).

Another factor associated with the dissolution of a marriage is that most people who go through this experience eventually remarry. In fact, approximately "two thirds of divorced women and three fourths of divorced men" marry again (Bray & Hetherington, 1993, p. 3). The divorce rate among divorcees is slightly higher than for couples that have never been married. Remarried couples that do best have extended family that approve or accept the new union, with those who do second best having extended family that disapprove of the remarriage (McGoldrick & Carter, 1999). Indifference or being cut off from one's extended family is the worst thing that can happen.

A final phenomenon associated with marriage breakup is that ethnic groups experience the consequences of this activity differently. For instance, when compared with European Americans, African-American couples are more likely to separate and stay separated longer before obtaining a divorce. They are also less likely to remarry once separated (Cherlin, 1992). A greater percentage of African-American children (75%), as opposed to European American children (40%), will experience their parents divorce or separation by age 16 (Bumpass & Sweet, 1989).

An outcome of marital dissolvement is that contact between nonresidential parents and their children declines over the years (Bray, 1994; Seltzer, 1991). Noncustodial mothers (about 10% to 15% of nonresidential parents) maintain better contact with their children than do nonresidential fathers (Furstenberg, 1990). Boys are particularly impacted in a negative way when their nonresidential fathers fail to maintain contact with them (Depner & Bray, 1993; Hetherington, 1990; Weiss, 1979). As a group, they become less competent and exhibit more behavioral problems than do children in other types of family arrangements.

# Making Healthy Adjustments in Remarried Families

Making healthy adjustments in remarried families is easier to conceptualize than to achieve. It takes dedication and work. If remarried families are to achieve a sense of harmony and stability, family members must concentrate on taking care of their own individual issues, as well as family issues (Roberts & Price, 1986). They must learn to relate productively to others with whom they now interact in a manner that connects them as a system. The two subunits that must make this systemic change are children and parents (Bray, 1993).

## Transitions for Children in Remarried Families

Issues for children who are making the adjustment to remarried families revolve around liabilities and benefits that result from such arrangements. Resolving issues surrounding the death of a parent takes time. It is a loss in which the normal grief period is from 6 to 36 months. Divorce for children also takes time. Divorce is a psychological death, as opposed to a physical death, of an intimate relationship. "The ways in which children perceive and respond to their parents' divorce vary by age, gender, parental conflict, pre- and postseparation, caretaking arrangements, individual resiliency characteristics, and the availability of emotional support" (Schwartz, 1992, p. 324). Liabilities for children may include losing the closeness of a previous parent relationship, losing one's ordinal position from a previous family experience (especially seniority), moving into a new house and/or neighborhood, and having to relate to stepsiblings and a stepparent (Wald, 1981; Wallerstein & Kelly, 1980).

Despite the loss of a family member, benefits for children in remarried families may be significant. For instance, children may gain a closeness with their biological parents as well as their stepparent. They may also be the recipients of increased positive attention from known and new relatives and relations. A third advantage for children in remarried families is they may find areas of common interest among their new stepsiblings and develop lasting friendships. Finally, moving (if it occurs) may provide children in remarried families with the opportunity to establish a different identity that is more congruent with who they wish to become (Kitson & Holmes, 1992; Visher & Visher, 1988).

## Transitions for Parents and Stepparents in Remarried Families

Parenting and stepparenting have drawbacks and attractions associated with them. One unattractive aspect of stepparenting is uncertainty. "There are no accepted social roles for stepparents" (Bray, 1994). In the case of a new stepparent, he or she may find that his or her new spouse and stepchildren have established routines that are difficult to modify or break. Therefore, a previously unmarried parent may have to work especially hard to make a place for himself or herself within the family system. In the process, these individuals may alienate or create friction among the ones with whom they are trying to relate (Bray, 1993).

For previously married spouses, the difficulties of forming a remarried family involve expectations and realities. These individuals may expect their reformed family to act similarly to their previous one. The reality may be quite different and a source of consternation. In addition, previously married spouses may have unpleasant memories, or unpleasant present encounters, involving an ex-spouse. These types of situations may magnify the stress under which formerly married spouses operate in reestablishing themselves in a new family (Visher & Visher, 1985). The nature of the relationship between ex-spouses is a significant predictor of intimacy in the remarried spouses (Gold, Bubenzer, & West, 1993). It has an impact on their children too with those children who do best having parents who form an ongoing parental alliance (Whiteside, 1998).

# Dynamics Associated with Remarried Families

It is sometimes said that remarried families are born out of loss and hope. As previously indicated, most adults and children who form this type of union have experienced a divorce, an abandonment, or a death. They wish, as well as expect, the remarried family to be a different and better experience. A characteristic of remarried family members is that they often carry a positive fantasy with them about what family life can be like (Schulman, 1972). For the most part, adults who form a remarried family believe marriage and family life can be good. Most children who come into these relationships share a similar belief (Visher & Visher, 1993).

Before a remarriage can develop, however, previous experiences in life, especially those associated with a former family, must be resolved. Adults and children of these former unions are often in mourning and must work through their feelings before they can emotionally join a new family. The extent to which loss is resolved or hope fulfilled makes a major difference in how the people in such arrangements adjust (Pill, 1990).

Another factor that influences the dynamics of remarried families is structure. Remarried families have structural characteristics that make them unique (Galvin & Brommel, 1986; Visher & Visher, 1979). Structural distinctions of remarried families include:

- a biological parent elsewhere
- a relationship in the family between an adult (parent) and at least one child that predates the present family structure
- at least one child who is a member of more than one household
- a parent who is not legally related to at least one child
- a couple that begins other than simply as a dyad
- a complex extended family network

The structure of most remarried families initially is "a weak couple subsystem, a tightly bonded parent–child alliance, and potential 'interference'" (Martin & Martin, 1992, p. 23).

A third dynamic characterizing remarried families is that they are **binuclear,** that is, two interrelated family households that comprise one family system (Ahrons, 1979; Piercy & Sprenkle, 1986). As a remarried (REM) family form, these families have multiple subsystems that include an entourage of adults, children, and legally related persons such as cousins and stepgrandparents (Sager et al., 1983). They have **quasi kin** who are a "formerly married person's ex-spouse, the ex-spouse's new husband or wife, and his or her blood kin" (Ihinger-Tallman & Pasley, 1987, p. 43). These people are a part of the extended kin network of remarried spouses' families. They make communications and relations among family members difficult.

# Issues Within Remarried Families

Many issues arise in remarried families. Because each family is unique, the importance of these concerns varies. Among the most prominent that surface, according to Carter and McGoldrick (1988), are those that center around:

- resolving the past
- alleviating fears and concerns about stepfamily life
- establishing or reestablishing trust
- fostering a realistic attitude
- becoming emotionally/psychologically attached to others

In addition, a major issue in remarried families is finding time to consolidate the couple relationship (Pill, 1990). Research shows that children below the age of 9 accept a step-parent more readily than those above this age (Hetherington, Cox, & Cox, 1981). At the same time, young children are more physically demanding on parents than older children. They may keep the new couple from adequately bonding. Likewise the presence of older children may complicate the bonding process, because of the needs of adolescents to establish identities through interactions that can often take the form of rebellion or disruption (Schwartzberg, 1987). Less cohesion in remarried families is more common during the early years of a family's formation (Bray, 1994).

A second factor that becomes an issue in reconstituting a remarried family is that of feelings. The life circumstances surrounding the dissolution of the previous marriage and the adjustment and life experiences of present family members since that time must be worked through. Romantic and negative feelings must be sorted out in a timely and appropriate way. Sometimes partners in a remarried family do not think through the feelings they bring into the relationship until after it is formed (Pill, 1990). What they expect in regard to closeness may therefore be shattered. Likewise, when members of a newly formed family are still mourning the loss of a previous relationship, they may not be adaptable or open to changes. In either of these cases, the past relationships and present realities are issues that inhibit or facilitate the adjustment and satisfaction of these families as units (Pill, 1990).

A third issue that occurs in remarried families is the integration of members into a cohesive family unit. "Cohesion and adaptability represent two pivotal dimensions of family behavior related to family function" (Pill, 1990, p. 186). In the professional literature, "stepfamilies are described as less cohesive, more problematic, and more stressful than first-marriage families" (Bray & Hetherington, 1993, p. 5). Both stepparent/child and sibling relationships are characterized as less warm and intimate than those in first-marriage families. Most members of remarried families have to work harder than those in nuclear or extended families to create interpersonal connectedness and rapport with other family members. The process of relating in remarried families is often troubled in stepfather/daughter interactions, especially when the arrangement involves preadolescent children (Hetherington, 1991). Many other arrangements of children and stepfathers are also bothersome (Ahrons, 1996; Grove & Haley, 1993; Stern, 1978; Visher & Visher, 1978). A relatively high percentage of stepchildren have behavioral problems in remarried families during the first 6 months of the new union (Bray, 1988).

On average it takes approximately 2 to 5 years for stepparents to form an in-depth relationship with stepchildren and to achieve the role of being a primary parent (Dahl, Cowgill, & Asmundsson, 1987). This 2- to 5-year forming period parallels that of the first stage of the newly married couple (DuVall, 1977). According to Visher and Visher (1986), the eight tasks listed in Figure 12.1 must be completed in order to develop a stepfamily identity.

# Strengths and Challenges of Remarried Families

Remarried families come in many forms. They share some universal qualities, but they also have unique situational and developmental factors that either help or hinder them in their total functioning and interpersonal relationships.

## Strengths of Remarried Families

The strengths of blended families are important to the stability and survival of these units. Sometimes they are overlooked. However, if utilized, remarried families grow stronger in both their relationships and their overall functioning.

### Life Experience

One of the strongest assets of remarried family members is their life experience. For instance, sometimes a stepparent can offer a new spouse or stepchildren something that was not there before, such as a common interest or opportunity unavailable in the original family of origin (Marino, 1996). In addition, both adults and children who form blended families have survived a number of critical incidents that have usually taught them something about themselves and others (Hetherington, 1991). This life knowledge can help them understand their environments in different and potentially healthy ways. It can assist members in being empathic toward new family members, and it can influence individual and family resilience in adverse situations.

### Kin and Quasi-Kin Networks

A second strength of remarried families is the kin and quasi-kin networks that they establish. Remarried couples and families are sometimes isolated and frustrated when dealing with societal events, such as father/son or mother/daughter events in community clubs, associations, or educational institutions (Martin & Martin, 1992). Through kin and quasi-kin networks, remarried family members can help one another in a variety of ways, such as offering moral support, guidance, or physical comfort.

### Creativity and Innovativeness

A third positive facet of remarried families is their creativity and innovation. Sometimes remarried family members are able to generate new ideas, perceptions, and possibilities because they realize that what they have tried before has not worked. As in gestalt therapy, remarried families who develop these abilities are able to see and act on their perceptions of relationships involving present situations (i.e., figure) and less important present situations or those in the future (i.e., ground) (Papernow, 1993). For example, a step-

1. Dealing with losses and changes
2. Negotiating different developmental needs
3. Establishing new traditions
4. Developing a solid couple bond
5. Forming new relationships
6. Creating a "parenting coalition"
7. Accepting continual shifts in household composition
8. Risking involvement despite little societal support

1. Dealing with losses and changes
   - Identifying/recognize losses for all individuals
   - Support expressions of sadness
   - Help children talk and not act out feelings
   - Read stepfamily books
   - Make changes gradually
   - See that everyone gets a turn
   - Inform children of plans involving them
   - Accept the insecurity of change
2. Negotiating different developmental needs
   - Take a child development and/or parenting class
   - Accept validity of the different life-cycle phases
   - Communicate individual needs clearly
   - Negotiate incompatible needs
   - Develop tolerance and flexibility
3. Establishing new traditions
   - Recognize ways are *different*, not right or wrong
   - Concentrate on important situations only
   - Stepparents take on discipline enforcement slowly
   - Use family meetings for problem solving and giving appreciation
   - Shift "givens" slowly whenever possible
   - Retain/combine appropriate rituals
   - Enrich with new creative traditions
4. Developing a solid couple bond
   - Accept couple as primary long-term relationship
   - Nourish couple relationship
   - Plan for couple "alone time"
   - Decide general household rules as a couple
   - Support one another with the children
   - Expect and accept different parent–child and stepparent–stepchild feelings
   - Work out money matters together

**Figure 12.1**
Tasks that must be completed to develop a stepfamily identity.

5. Forming new relationships
   - Fill in past histories
   - Make stepparent–stepchild one-to-one time
   - Make parent–child one-to-one time
   - Parent make space for stepparent–stepchild relationship
   - Do not expect instant love and adjustment
   - Be fair to stepchildren even when caring not developed
   - Follow children's lead in what to call stepparent
   - Do fun things together

6. Creating a "parenting coalition"
   - Deal directly with parenting adults in other household
   - Keep children out of the middle of parental disagreements
   - Do not talk negatively about adults in other household
   - Control what you can and accept limitations
   - Avoid power struggles between households
   - Respect parenting skills of former spouse
   - Contribute own "specialness" to children
   - Communicate between households in most effective manner

7. Accepting continual shifts in household composition
   - Allow children to enjoy their households
   - Give children time to adjust to household transitions
   - Avoid asking children to be messengers or spies
   - Consider teenager's serious desire to change residence
   - Respect privacy (boundaries) of all households
   - Set consequences that affect own household only
   - Provide personal place for nonresident children
   - Plan special times for various household constellations

8. Risking involvement despite little societal support
   - Include stepparents in school, religious, sports activities
   - Give legal permission for stepparent to act when necessary
   - Continue stepparent–stepchild relationships after death or divorce of parent when caring has developed
   - Stepparent includes self in stepchild's activities
   - Find groups supportive of stepfamilies
   - Remember that all relationships involve risk

From *Stepfamily Workshop Manual* (pp. 235–236) by E. B. Visher and J. S. Visher, 1986, Baltimore, MD: Stepfamily Association of America. Reprinted by permission of the publisher.

mother and daughter in a remarried family might decide to throw a surprise birthday party for their husband/father, rather than doing routine shopping. By doing so, they create a memory of a shared experience that strengthens the relationship bonds between them. The result may be a synergistic flow of energy and enthusiasm that lasts a lifetime.

### Appreciation and Respect for Differences

Another strength of remarried families is their ability to appreciate and respect differences in people and ways of living (Crohn, Sager, Brown, Rodstein, & Walker, 1982). Through experiencing stepparents and new siblings, children especially can benefit. For instance, they learn that mothering or fathering can take on several forms. In the process of obtaining this insight, they pick up new habits from their stepsiblings that may benefit them. Remarriage makes it possible for individuals to observe a richer variety of models for emulating than they may have typically experienced.

### Making the Most of Situations

Still another strength of remarried families is their ability to make the most of situations and in the process teach other families how to have fulfilling relationships (Martin & Martin, 1992). Not all remarried families and their members learn how to cope with difficulties, such as loss, or how to promote care and open communication within a new context. However, in remarried families that develop these abilities, the insight they bring to other families in distress can be rewarding and enabling. It is a dynamic that therapists and educators must utilize whenever possible.

## Challenges of Remarried Families

Challenges and potential problems exist in remarried families that need to be resolved. Some of these difficulties revolve around psychological phenomena, such as competing for attention; others center on physical realities, such as the fact that remarried families move three times as often as dual-parent households (Krauth, 1995).

### Loss of an Important Member

One challenge almost all remarried families face is the loss of an important member(s) of the former family. For example, even though a noncustodial parent may be physically absent from a household, such a person may retain a "tremendous impact," both directly and indirectly, on the remaining family members (Braver et al., 1993, p. 9). The loss of significant others is complicated when difficulties arise concerning feelings about these individuals who are unavailable. The result is a ripple effect throughout the family. All members of the family can be affected by one individual's unresolved personal issues related to loss.

### Establishment of a Hierarchy

Another significant challenge for remarried families is the establishment of a hierarchy. Children may have difficulty in this area because they can lose status in regard to their ordinal position in the family. For example, a sibling can become the middle child instead of the oldest, and in the process lose his or her leadership role and privileges. This loss of place and power may be complicated even further if the children involved do not particularly like their new stepsiblings or stepparent. Because working out relationships among children takes time and is not always amiable, newly formed remarried families with children are vulnerable to disruption and volatile outbreaks of emotional, if not physical, struggle (White & Booth, 1985). Adults must give up myths and unrealistic expectations in order to rectify this potential problem area (Bray, 1994).

### Boundary Difficulties

A third challenge sometimes endemic to remarried families concerns boundaries. "Unlike biological families in which family membership is defined sanguinely, legally, and spatially and is characterized by explicit boundaries, the structure of a stepfamily is less clear" (Pasley, Rhoden, Visher, & Visher, 1996, p. 344). The result is that children who are a part of two families may experience boundary ambiguity, which results in loyalty conflicts and feelings of guilt about belonging simultaneously to two households. Overall,

> boundary difficulties include issues of:
> 1. Membership (Who are the "real" members of the family?)
> 2. Space (What space is mine? Where do I really belong?)
> 3. Authority (Who is really in charge? Of discipline? Of money? Of decisions? etc.)
> 4. Time (Who gets how much of my time and how much do I get of theirs?)
>    (McGoldrick & Carter, 1988, pp. 406–407)

Often, stepfamily members who have boundary problems characterize their relationships as chaotic (Pill, 1990). They are unsure of who and what is involved in making their lives adaptable. To resolve issues around the confusion in boundaries, most remarried families need time, flexibility, and commitment (Ihinger-Tallman & Pasley, 1987). They must deal with issues in a straightforward manner, including those involving sexuality between unrelated siblings or parents and siblings. Members can and should discuss and negotiate how they would like their blended family to function.

### Resolving Feelings

The fourth challenging area remarried families must address is related to feelings. In some remarried families, especially those in which members have been in denial, emotions remain unresolved. These emotions include guilt, loyalty, and anger. A typical response for some remarried family members is to suppress their emotions when they begin to recognize that such affect is related to unresolved feelings. For example, a teenage boy might deny his anger toward his stepmother especially if he still has unresolved anger toward his mother. An equally destructive way of handling these emotions is to project them onto others. For instance, some remarried family members may act in such a manner that stepsiblings or stepparents become negatively characterized or stereotyped (Marino, 1996). In such a situation, a stepmother might be seen as a "witch."

### Economic Problems

Another potential challenge remarried families encounter is economic. As a group, blended families are less affluent than other family types except single-parent families. The lack of money adds additional stress to family members and the family as a whole

(Coleman & Ganong, 1989). In addition, many remarried families have expenses, such as child support or the cost of maintaining two residences, that other families do not have. Such families may have a difficult time making ends meet.

# Approaches for Treating Remarried Families

"Many stepfamilies seek therapy when emotional tensions are high, integration seems impossible, and the family is functioning in ways that increase rather than reduce stress" (Pasley et al., 1996, p. 344). Fortunately, a number of approaches work when helping remarried families. These approaches range from educational to theoretical interventions (Visher & Visher, 1994; Woestendiek, 1992).

## Guidance in Retaining Old Loyalties

First of all, remarried family members must be helped to recognize that they do not have to give up old loyalties in order to form new ties (Visher & Visher, 1988). Too often individuals, especially children, believe that they must not think or talk about their past lives. This type of repression is likely to lead to resentment, exclusion, isolation, and depression rather than adjustment and growth. In addition, often the new stepparent is treated like an "outsider." This situation can cause the stepparent to feel angry and frustrated, which in turn can lead to complete withdrawal or violence. The important thing is that family members learn through interaction with the therapist to be inclusive rather than exclusive. This may mean that the therapist draws instructional diagrams for the family of how they are operating and also challenges them to participate in cooperative interactive events, such as picnics or board games.

## Focus on Parental Involvement

Another way of helping remarried families is to focus on parental involvement. Stepparents need to maintain a balance in their involvement with their natural children (if any), new children (if any), former spouse (where applicable), and present spouse. The more children and spouses in one's past, the harder this task is to accomplish. Therefore, before and after their wedding, stepparents should spend time discussing the impact of past relationships on new relationships (Martin & Martin, 1992). They can then work with a family therapist to overcome unresolved issues and, thus, learn to contribute to the well-being of all family members.

## Provide Education

Education is one of the best ways to help remarried families to adapt, adjust, and grow. For example, remarried family members need to understand the differences between a stepfamily and a non-stepfamily system (Pasley et al., 1996). Learning what to expect and having guidelines for handling typical situations is rated high by remarried families (Visher & Visher, 1994). Stepparents are often unsure, for example, of how to discipline the other spouse's children (Woestendiek, 1992). Likewise, children brought into remarried families are frequently confused about how to relate to their new parent and stepsiblings.

A number of popular books and pamphlets are available for individuals in newly created blended families to read and discuss with members of their new family. For instance, the Family Service Association of America publishes materials that are helpful in developing effective stepparenting skills (Larson, Anderson, & Morgan, 1984). Likewise, a program has been devised for building remarried family strengths (Duncan & Brown, 1992). Numerous books that can be utilized in a bibliotherapeutic way are available for children (Pardeck & Pardeck, 1987). An example is a book authored by Richard Gardner (1971) entitled *The Boys and Girls Book About Stepfamilies*. It is a work meant to be read and responded to verbally by stepparents and children (Gardner, 1984). *This Is Me and My Two Families* (Evans, 1988) is an engaging and therapeutically oriented scrapbook/journal for children ages 4 to 12 living in remarried families.

## Assist in the Creation of Family Traditions and Rituals

A fourth therapeutic way of working with remarried families is through assisting them in devising their own traditions and rituals (Coale, 1994). Rituals facilitate "developmental transitions, maintenance of stability and continuity; healing processes; and connectedness. . . . Healthy ritual life can also serve to buffer families from toxic effects of stress and pathology" (Giblin, 1995, p. 37). The use of rituals has also been found to be powerful in assisting remarried families in thinking through their definition of what makes a family (Peterson, 1992; Whiteside, 1989). Traditions and rituals include ways of celebrating nodal events, such as birthdays and anniversaries. They also include mundane daily transactions, such as when to go to bed, when to get up, and who will do what chores. When these situations are worked out, new and predictable ways of interacting are established that give family members predictability and stability. Such a process provides time for fun while allowing family members to experience security.

In addition to their celebration and enjoyment functions, rituals may facilitate:

- the forming of relationships
- the resolution of ambiguous boundaries
- the healing of loss
- the settling of hierarchy and power struggles
- the creating of beliefs
- the beginnings of changes (Coale, 1994; Roberts & Imber-Black, 1992)

For instance, by gathering all members of a new family together once a week for "game night," a stepmother may help family members learn more about each other and develop friendships. The overall impact is one that is likely to result in the building of trust and care.

## Apply Structural Family Therapy

A particularly effective theoretical approach for working with remarried families is structural family therapy. The reason is that structural family therapy concentrates on setting up a clear hierarchy within the family and on establishing boundaries (Minuchin, 1974). If remarried families do not structurally readjust boundaries after the new family unit is formed, the family may experience conflict that is prone to escalation in negative outcomes such as anger or abuse (Friesen, 1985).

In working from a structural perspective, it is crucial that the family be encouraged to set up an open system "with permeable boundaries between current and former spouses and their families" (Goldenberg & Goldenberg, 1990, p. 141). The reason for such an arrangement is that it facilitates coparenting relationships and prevents children from exerting a type of inappropriate power to decide important parental prerogatives such as remarriage, custody, or visitation.

### Apply Experiential Family Therapy

Another approach for helping remarried families is experiential family therapy. Some of the methods associated with the work of Virginia Satir may be especially useful (Satir, Banmen, Gerber, & Gomori, 1991). For example, sculpting and choreography may help family members see the closeness or distance of relationships and the interrelatedness of certain actions. Role playing also may assist family members to become sensitized to the real and imagined restraints that keep them in dysfunctional patterns. Such information helps them become aware of how they can break out of vicious cycles and make progress in their personal and interpersonal lives.

### Do Transgenerational Work

A final theoretical perspective that is pertinent for remarried families is transgenerational work, especially Bowenian family therapy (Bowen, 1981; Visher & Visher, 1996). In this approach, the use of a three-generational genogram helps families detect patterns that can both inform and assist them in forming a new family unit. By examining the past through a genogram, remarried families can plan for a productive future and avoid previous mistakes. This process is the same as that for other family types.

# Role of the Therapist

Therapists who work with remarried families wear many hats. They must deal with a variety of dynamics and complexities that are more complicated than those found in nuclear families (Visher & Visher, 1996). For example, they must deal with issues involving separation and custody; they must be concerned with the developmental dilemmas that can arise within newly formed families (Bray & Berger, 1992); and they must concentrate on fostering a strong and healthy parental coalition (Visher & Visher, 1994):

> Because stepfamily issues and needs are diverse and often emotionally charged, the ability to be active, to take charge of intensely emotional sessions, and to be flexible and resourceful in the use of different therapeutic modalities contributes to therapists' effectiveness in working with families. (Pasley et al., 1996, p. 347)

In working with remarried families in regard to separation and custody issues, children within the family system must be given special consideration. "Child clients may experience confusion, fear, and depression as they become aware that they are the focal point in a custody, visitation, or child support dispute" (Oliver, 1992, p. 41). To alleviate undue anxiety and distress, family therapists need to be well informed about legal processes as well as psychological ones. For example, they should be aware of legal precedence concerning custody decisions. Family therapists who are knowledgeable about such aspects of family jurisprudence can help all members of families make better decisions. They are enabled and empowered by such legal insight to work in helping the family process information on an emotional and intellectual level so that everyone in the family, including small children, understands what is happening or can happen (Oliver, 1992).

Family therapists must also work with the family in arranging predictable and mutually satisfactory arrangements between former parents and their child or children (if the family was formed as a result of divorce). The continuity and quality of children's relationships with their parents following a divorce is a major factor in determining the children's healthy development (Wallerstein, 1990). Therefore, in some cases, counseling sessions may include the noncustodial parent, as well as the reconstituted family. In these situations, family therapists must focus their attention on helping families negotiate arrangements that will benefit everyone involved.

Fostering strong and healthy parental coalitions means helping stepparents work together to nurture one another and find ways for them to work together to be effective parents. Such a task may involve the couple spending select time together, working with former spouses (if present) to be supportive of them, and finding ways for children in the new family to care for one another physically and psychologically (Visher & Visher, 1994).

Hayes and Hayes (1986) mention four more issues that must be dealt with:

1. *Family members must be encouraged to relinquish personal myths they have carried into the new family relationship.* These myths may take many forms, but often they involve seeing former relationships as idyllic and viewing other people as either saints or devils.
2. *Family members must learn effective ways of communicating with each other.* Effective communication skills used in remarried families are the same as those used in facilitating other counseling relationships. They include paying attention to verbal and nonverbal messages, the use of "I" messages, and concreteness.
3. *Family members need structured programs of parent training and reading lists of materials that are germane to their situation in the new family structure.* Material provided in this bibliotherapeutic process should include research, especially for the adults in the relationship, as well as other books or pamphlets that are more simply formatted.
4. *Family members, especially children, need a forum within the therapeutic setting in which they can mourn the loss of previous relationships and develop relationships in the reconstituted family.*

Overall, the family therapist working with remarried families must focus on external and internal factors that tend to unbalance the family system. Although family therapists dealing with traditional two-parent families concentrate on some of these same factors, the degree and complexity of the dynamics are not the same. Remarried families have more emotional, historical, and internal issues that must be settled.

To be effective, family therapists who work with remarried families must devote large amounts of energy and effort to bringing about multiple-person resolutions. They must join with members of the family in order to understand the frustrations inherent in each person's role while seeking to bring about resolutions to real and potential problems within the family system as a whole. It is not an easy or simple task.

# Process and Outcome

If therapy is successful with remarried families, these families come to understand themselves better as systems. This goal is often disruptive and stressful because remarried families are "an evolving family system in which each member reciprocally influences and is influenced by other family members" (Bray, 1993, p. 272). Yet, the process of better understanding the unity of the family can be achieved in several ways.

One systemic based way of helping remarried families come to terms with themselves is by supporting the new parent and sibling subunits. This type of support stresses the importance of the couple and children learning to work, play, and make mistakes together. If successful, remarried families become aware of themselves as family units composed of subsystems. They begin to gel in age- and stage-appropriate ways. For instance, children within remarried families may unite to ask for special privileges or a raise in their allowance. Similarly, parents may present a unified front as to behaviors that are and are not acceptable.

Effective therapy also helps family members become tolerant of and deal realistically with one another and family life events. This means that persons within reconstituted families must avoid projection and distortions. For instance, "the entrance of a new parent figure is a . . . unique experience" for children who may "displace their anger" onto this person (Walsh, 1991, p. 521). Likewise, all involved in a remarried family must give up romanticizing or idealizing those who are now outside the formal structure of the family, such as a parent who no longer lives with his or her children (Everett & Volgy, 1991).

On a developmental level, effective therapy helps family members find their place in the new family as it is now. In some remarried families, congruence between individual and family developmental issues exists, such as in remarried families with young children. In this case, both parents and children seek cohesion. On the other hand, in other remarried families, divergence between the goals of individuals and families exists, such as in a remarried family with adolescents. In this case, the new couple might be developmentally prone to closeness while the teenagers are ready to separate (Bray, 1993). When family therapy is successful, members become aware that they are in an environment in which novel roles can be explored (Martin & Martin, 1992). Such an environment is one in which family members are safe, and the overall atmosphere is one in which members can deal with their losses, gains, aspirations, and/or regrets.

A fourth dimension of process and outcome involves fostering new traditions, including those dealing with both responsibility and celebrations (Imber-Black, 1988). Many rituals in American society are inadequate as ways of terminating relationships (Everett & Volgy, 1991). Likewise, few models are available for joining family members from different backgrounds (Imber-Black, 1988). Family therapy helps remarried families create new and lasting ways of humanizing relationships. For example, new traditions can be built around a commonly shared meal, such as dinner, in which everyone is given space and time to relate. Similarly, holiday periods can become opportunities for family members to celebrate old and new traditions.

Finally, in working with remarried families, therapists must help them develop a healthy self-concept of themselves as a family. The mass media and even some scholarly journals generally portray remarried families in a negative way. For example, Whitehead (1993) states that research has found "stepfamilies disrupt established loyalties, create new uncertainties, provoke deep anxieties, and sometimes threaten a child's physical safety as well as emotional security" (p. 71). Therefore, to do well, remarried families must first find internal strength, in order to deal with the external pressures and stereotypes that are less than healthy (or accurate).

# Summary and Conclusion

Working with remarried families is a challenging process because of the multitude of variables and personalities involved. Family therapists who work with such families need to realize that remarried families have unique as well as universal characteristics. For example, remarried families have a particular life cycle of their own. They are binuclear in their structure. Many members of remarried families are dealing with loss and grief because their previous relationships ended in death, abandonment, or divorce. The expression of feelings is probably higher than in traditional nuclear families.

On the other hand, like other family forms, members of remarried families must deal with the universal aspects of parent/children and sibling relationships. Members must balance concerns so that neither the individual nor the family suffers or is ignored.

Helping remarried families means that therapists must be sensitive to their own biases and perceptions and flexible in their theoretical approaches. Structural, experiential, and transgenerational (i.e., Bowenian) family therapies are three ways to assist these families in resolving the issues and tasks before them. The use of rituals from a strategic family therapy point of view is also an important therapeutic tool that can be employed. Remarried families need to formulate and practice new traditions in a ritualistic manner. Such behavior helps them bond and overcome physical and psychological barriers that would otherwise hinder them. Bibliotherapy and psychoeducational processes are yet other possible ways to help.

Family therapists who work with remarried families need energy and imagination. They are called on to engage family members in ways that are complex and taxing. At times therapists may need to see significant others in the family outside of those living under one roof. Just as being a successful remarried family requires negotiation skills from members, the same is demanded of family therapists. With the number of remarried families growing, it is doubtful one can be a family therapist without acquiring skills in regard to this population. Therefore, the challenge is to continuously learn about common elements special to remarried families while treating each new remarried family as a one-of-a-kind phenomenon.

# Summary Table
## Working with Remarried Families

A remarried family consists of two adults and step-, adoptive, or foster children. They are most prevalent among European Americans, although they are found among all cultural groups.

Historically, remarried families have always been part of American family life, although their numbers have increased dramatically in recent years.

It is predicted that up to 40% of children born in the 1980s will spend part of their life in a remarried family.

The growth of remarried families is a major reason the perception of what is "normal" in family life has changed.

One of the problems of treating remarried families is that there is no terminology to discuss the complex dynamics within them.

### Forming Remarried Families

A remarried family is most commonly formed when a person from a previous marriage remarries someone who is single or previously married. One or both of the marriage partners comes into this arrangement with children.

Prior to the 1950s, death was the most frequent reason for the ending of a marriage. Rituals helped survivors deal with death. About 800,000 spouses die each year. Many do not mourn their loss appropriately.

More than 1 million divorces occur each year. The actual divorce rate is between 50% and 66%. About two thirds of divorces occur in the first 10 years of marriage. Most who divorce eventually remarry. Ethnic groups experience divorce differently. After divorce, contact between a child and a noncustodial parent usually declines.

### Making Healthy Adjustments in Remarried Families

Healthy adjustment in remarried families depends on members working on both individual and family issues.

Children must deal with real and perceived losses such as parental closeness, seniority privileges, moving, and adjustment to new stepsiblings and a stepparent.

Benefits for children in remarried families include closeness to a new adult parent figure, increased attention, new friendships, and the opportunity to establish a different identity.

Drawbacks for new stepparents include breaking into or modifying established routines, adjusting to expectations and realities, and managing the stress of different relationships.

### Dynamics Associated with Remarried Families

Remarried families are born out of loss and hope.

Most children and adults who become part of a remarried family can have a good experience, but first they must resolve past experiences and modify unrealistic fantasies.

Remarried families have structures that both help and inhibit bonding and alliances. These structures are different from those of nuclear families.

Many remarried families are binuclear and involve the interrelating of two or more households.

### Issues Within Remarried Families

Remarried families face situational and developmental tasks that are different from those of other families. They must resolve the past, alleviate fears, deal with trust, be realistic, and become psychologically/physically attached.

The ages and stages of children and parents influence how many issues remarried families face and how they are resolved.

Integrating members into remarried families is difficult and takes at least 2 years. Some relationships, such as that between children and stepfathers, are bothersome.

### Strengths and Challenges Connected with Remarried Families

Assets remarried family members bring to each other include:

- different life experiences
- kin and quasi-kin networks
- creativity and innovation
- appreciation and respect for differences in living styles
- the ability to make the most of situations and model appropriate coping strategies for other families

Challenges that remarried families must deal with include:

- the loss of an important member (or members) of the former family
- the establishment of a workable family hierarchy
- boundary difficulties
- unresolved emotions
- economic concerns and financial difficulties

### Approaches for Treating Remarried Families

To deal effectively with remarried families, therapists should:

- help families to recognize and deal appropriately with old loyalties and new ties
- help families become involved constructively with significant others, such as a former spouse or new children
- provide families with educational materials
- help families to develop their own rituals and traditions
- apply structural, strategic, Bowenian, and experiential family therapy to deal with issues such as history, boundaries, structure, and feelings

### Role of the Therapist

Therapists who work with remarried families wear many hats. They must help remarrieds deal with separation/custody issues rationally and psychologically.

Therapists must help remarried families to arrange predictable and mutually satisfactory interactional patterns, including relinquishing personal myths, teaching communication skills, offering parent training, and providing a forum for the airing of common and unique concerns.

Overall, family therapists must work with a variety of internal and external issues that tend to unbalance remarried families.

### Process and Outcome

As a result of effective family therapy interventions, remarried families are

- able to understand personal and systemic issues related to this arrangement
- aware of subunits within their families and more tolerant and realistic with each other

- able to find their place within these families and deal effectively with individual and family developmental issues
- able to understand the importance of integrating family members into a working system through creating unique family ways of operating and traditions
- stronger internally and able to withstand negative portrayals of remarried families in the popular press

# References

Ahrons, C. R. (1979). The binuclear family: Two households, one family. *Alternative Lifestyles, 2,* 499–515.

Ahrons, C. R. (1996). *The good divorce: Keeping your family together when your marriage comes apart.* New York: HarperCollins.

Bernstein, B. E., & Collins, S. K. (1985). Remarriage counseling: Lawyers and therapist's help with the second time around. *Family Relations, 34,* 387–391.

Bowen, M. (1981). The use of family theory in clinical practice. In J. Haley (Ed.), *Changing families.* Philadelphia: Grune & Stratton.

Braver, S. L., Wolchik, S. A., Sandler, I. N., Sheets, V. L., Fogas, B., & Bay, R. C. (1993). A longitudinal study of noncustodial parents: Parents without children. *Journal of Family Psychology, 7,* 9–23.

Bray, J. (1988). Children's development during early remarriage. In E. M. Hetherington & J. Arastek (Eds.), *The impact of divorce, single-parenting, & stepparenting on children* (pp. 279–298). Hillsdale, NJ: Lawrence Erlbaum.

Bray, J. H. (1993). Becoming a stepfamily: Developmental issues for new stepfamilies. *The Family Journal, 1,* 272–275.

Bray, J. H. (1994). What does a typical stepfamily look like? *The Family Journal, 2,* 66–69.

Bray, J. H., & Berger, S. H. (1992). Stepfamilies. In M. E. Procidano & C. B. Fisher (Eds.), *Contemporary families: A handbook for school professionals* (pp. 57–79). New York: Teachers College Press.

Bray, J. H., & Hetherington, E. M. (1993). Families in transition: Introduction and overview. *Journal of Family Psychology, 7,* 3–8.

Bumpass, L., & Sweet, J. A. (1989). Children's experience in single-parent families: Implications of cohabitation and marital transitions. *Family Planning Perspectives, 6,* 256–260.

Carter, B., & McGoldrick, M. (1988). Overview: The changing family life cycle—A framework for family therapy. In B. Carter & M. McGoldrick (Eds.), *The changing family life cycle* (2nd ed., pp. 3–28). New York: Gardner.

Carter, B., & McGoldrick, M. (1999). *The expanded family life cycle* (3rd ed.). Boston: Allyn & Bacon.

Castro-Martin, T., & Bumpass, L. (1989). Recent trends and differentials in marital disruption. *Demography, 26,* 37–51.

Cherlin, A. J. (1992). *Marriage, divorce, remarriage* (rev. ed.). Cambridge, MA: Harvard University Press.

Coale, H. W. (1994). Therapeutic use of rituals with stepfamilies. *The Family Journal, 2,* 2–10.

Coleman, M., & Ganong, L. H. (1989). Financial management in stepfamilies. *Lifestyles, 10,* 217–232.

Crohn, H., Sager, C. J., Brown, H., Rodstein, E., & Walker, L. (1982). A basis for understanding and treating the remarried family. In J. C. Hansen & L. Messinger (Eds.), *Therapy with remarriage families.* Rockville, MD: Aspen.

Dahl, A. S., Cowgill, K. M., & Asmundsson, R. (1987). Life in remarriage families. *Social Work, 32,* 40–44.

Darden, E. C., & Zimmerman, T. S. (1992). Blended families: A decade review, 1979–1990. *Family Therapy, 19,* 25–31.

Depner, C. E., & Bray, J. H. (Eds.). (1993). *Nonresidential parents. New vistas in family living.* Newbury Park, CA: Sage Publications.

Duncan, S. F., & Brown, G. (1992). RENEW: A program for building remarried family strengths. *Families-in-Society, 73,* 149–158.

Duvall, E. M. (1977). *Marriage and family development* (5th ed.). Philadelphia: Lippincott.

Evans, M. (1988). *This is me and my two families.* New York: Brunner/Mazel.

Everett, C. A., & Volgy, S. S. (1991). Treating divorce in family-therapy practice. In A. S. Gurman & D. P. Kniskern (Eds.), *Handbook of family therapy* (Vol. II, pp. 508–524). New York: Brunner/Mazel.

Friesen, J. D. (1985). *Structural-strategic marriage and family therapy.* New York: Gardner.

Furstenberg, F. F. (1990). Divorce and the American family. *Annual Review of Sociology, 16,* 379–403.

Galvin, K. M., & Brommel, B. J. (1986). *Family communication: Cohesion and change* (2nd ed.). Glenview, IL: Scott, Foresman.

Gardner, R. A. (1971). *The boys and girls book about stepfamilies.* New York: Bantam.

Gardner, R. (1984). Counseling children in stepfamilies. *Elementary School Guidance and Counseling, 19,* 40–49.

Giblin, P. (1995). Identity, change, and family rituals. *The Family Journal, 3,* 37–41.

Gladding, S. T. (1992). *Blendings.* Unpublished manuscript.

Glick, P. C. (1989). Remarried families, stepfamilies, and stepchildren: A brief demographic profile. *Family Relations, 38,* 24–27.

Gold, J. M., Bubenzer, D. L., & West, J. D. (1993). Differentiation from ex-spouses and stepfamily marital intimacy. *Journal of Divorce and Remarriage, 19,* 83–95.

Goldenberg, H., & Goldenberg, I. (1990). *Counseling today's families.* Pacific Grove, CA: Brooks/Cole.

Grove, D. R., & Haley, J. (1993). *Conversations on therapy: Popular problems and uncommon solutions.* New York: W. W. Norton.

Hayes, R. L., & Hayes, B. A. (1986). Remarriage families: Counseling parents, stepparents, and their children. *Counseling and Human Development, 18*(7), 1–8.

Hayes, R. L., & Hayes, B. A. (1991). Counseling remarried families. In G. Carlson & J. Lewis (Eds.), *Family counseling: Strategies and issues* (pp. 175–188). Denver, CO: Love Publishing.

Hetherington, E. M. (1990). Coping with family transitions: Winners, losers, and survivors. *Child Development, 60,* 1–14.

Hetherington, E. M. (1991). Families, lies and videotapes. *Journal of Research on Adolescence, 1,* 323–348.

Hetherington, E. M., Cox, M., & Cox, R. (1981). The aftermath of divorce. In E. M. Hetherington & R. D. Parke (Eds.), *Contemporary readings in child psychology* (2nd ed., pp. 99–109). New York: McGraw-Hill.

Howell, L. C., Weers, R., & Kleist, D. M. (1998). Counseling blended families. *The Family Journal, 6,* 42–45.

Ihinger-Tallman, M., & Pasley, K. (1987). *Remarriage.* Newbury Park, CA: Sage Publications.

Imber-Black, E. (1988). Normative and therapeutic rituals in couple therapy. In E. Imber-Black, J. Roberts, & R. Whiting (Eds.), *Rituals in families and family therapy.* New York: W. W. Norton.

Kitson, G. C., & Holmes, W. M. (1992). *Portrait of divorce: Adjustment to marital breakdown.* New York: Guilford Press.

Krauth, L. D. (1995, December). Single parent families: The risk to children. *Family Therapy News, 26*(6), 14.

Larson, J. H., Anderson, J. O., & Morgan, A. (1984). *Effective stepparenting.* New York: Family Service Association of America.

Levine, A. (1990, January 29). The second time around: Realities of remarriage. *U.S. News & World Report,* pp. 50–51.

Levitan, S. A., & Conway, E. A. (1990). *Families in flux.* Washington, DC: Bureau of National Affairs.

Marino, T. W. (1996, August). Families often merge onto a highway of frustration. *Counseling Today,* p. 8.

Martin, D., & Martin, M. (1992). *Stepfamilies in therapy.* San Francisco: Jossey-Bass.

Martin, T. C., & Bumpass, L. (1989). Recent trends and differentials in marital disruption. *Demography, 26,* 37–51.

McGoldrick, M. (1986, November/December). Mourning rituals. *Family Therapy Networker, 10,* 29–30.

McGoldrick, M., & Carter, B. (1988). Forming a remarried family. In B. Carter & M. McGoldrick (Eds.), *The changing family life cycle* (2nd ed., pp. 399–429). New York: Gardner.

McGoldrick, M., & Carter, B. (1999). Remarried families. In B. Carter & M. McGoldrick (Eds.), *The expanded family life cycle* (3rd ed., pp. 417–435). Boston: Allyn & Bacon.

McGoldrick, M., & Walsh, F. (1999). Death and the family life cycle. In B. Carter & M. McGoldrick (Eds.), *The expanded family life cycle* (3rd ed., pp. 185–201). Boston: Allyn & Bacon.

Minuchin, S. (1974). *Families and family therapy.* Cambridge, MA: Harvard University Press.

Mullins, M. E. (1993, July 14). Divorcing couples growing older. *USA Today,* p. D1.

National Center for Health Statistics. (1988). Births, marriages, divorces, and deaths for November 1987. *Monthly vital statistics report, 36,* 13.

Oliver, C. J. (1992). Legal issues facing families in transition: An overview for counselors. *New York State Journal for Counseling and Development, 7,* 41–52.

Papernow, P. L. (1993). *Becoming a stepfamily.* San Francisco: Jossey-Bass.

Pardeck, J. T., & Pardeck, J. A. (1987). Using bibliotherapy to help children cope with the changing family. *Social Work in Education, 9,* 107–116.

Pasley, K., Rhoden, L., Visher, E. B., & Visher, J. S. (1996). Successful stepfamily therapy: Clients' perspectives. *Journal of Marital and Family Therapy, 22,* 343–357.

Pearson, J. C. (1993). *Communication in the family* (2nd ed.). New York: HarperCollins.

Peterson, K. S. (1992, November 25). Traditions that put life in context. *USA Today,* pp. D1–2.

Peterson, K. S. (2000, March 30). Sweet nothings help marriages stick. *USA Today,* p. A1.

Piercy, F. P., & Sprenkle, D. H. (1986). *Family therapy sourcebook.* New York: Guilford Press.

Pill, C. J. (1990). Stepfamilies: Redefining the family. *Family Relations, 39,* 186–193.

Roberts, J., & Imber-Black, E. (1992). *Rituals for our times: Celebrating, healing, and changing our lives and our relationships.* New York: HarperCollins.

Roberts, T. W., & Price, S. J. (1986). A systems analysis of the remarriage process: Implications for the clinician. *Journal of Divorce, 9,* 1–25.

Sager, C. J., Brown, H. S., Crohn, H., Engel, T. Rodstein, E., & Walker, L. (1983). *Treating the remarried family.* New York: Brunner/Mazel.

Satir, V., Banmen, J., Gerber, J., & Gomori, M. (1991). *The Satir model: Family therapy and beyond*. New York: Science and Behavior Books.

Schulman, G. L. (1972). Myths that intrude on the adaptation of the stepfamily. *Social Casework, 53*, 131–139.

Schwartz, L. L. (1992). Children's perceptions of divorce. *American Journal of Family Therapy, 20*, 324–332.

Schwartzberg, A. Z. (1987). The adolescent in the remarriage family. *Adolescent Psychiatry, 14*, 259–270.

Seltzer, J. A. (1991). Relationships between fathers and children who live apart: The father's role after separation. *Journal of Marriage and the Family, 53*, 79–101.

Stern, P. N. (1978). Stepfather families: Integration around child discipline. *Issues in Mental Health Nursing, 1*, 50–56.

Visher, E. B., & Visher, J. S. (1978). Common problems with stepparents and their spouses. *American Journal of Orthopsychiatry, 48*, 252–262.

Visher, E. B., & Visher, J. S. (1979). *Stepfamilies: A guide to working with stepfamilies and stepchildren*. New York: Brunner/Mazel.

Visher, E. B., & Visher, J. S. (1985). Stepfamilies are different. *Journal of Family Therapy, 7*, 9–18.

Visher, E. B., & Visher, J. S. (1986). *Stepfamily workbook manual*. Baltimore, MD: Stepfamily Association of America.

Visher, E. B., & Visher, J.S. (1988). *Old loyalties; new ties: Therapeutic strategies with stepfamilies*. New York: Brunner/Mazel.

Visher, E. B., & Visher, J. S. (1993). Remarriage families and stepparenting. In F. Walsh (Ed.), *Normal family processes* (2nd ed., pp. 235–253). New York: Guilford Press.

Visher, E. B., & Visher, J. S. (1994). The core ingredients in the treatment of stepfamilies. *The Family Journal, 2*, 208–214.

Visher, E. B., & Visher, J. S. (1996). *Therapy with stepfamilies*. New York: Brunner/Mazel.

Wald, E. (1981). *The remarried family: Challenges and promise*. New York: Family Service Association of America.

Walker, L. D. (1990). Problem parents and child custody. *American Journal of Family Law, 4*, 155–168.

Wallerstein, J. S. (1990). *Second chances*. New York: Ticknor & Fields.

Wallerstein, J. S., & Kelly, J. B. (1980). *Surviving the break up: How children and parents cope with divorce*. New York: Basic Books.

Walsh, F. (1991). Promoting healthy functioning in divorced and remarried families. In A. S. Gurman & D. P. Kniskern (Eds.), *Handbook of family therapy* (Vol. II, pp. 525–545). New York: Brunner/Mazel.

Weiss, R. S. (1979). *Going it alone*. New York: Basic Books.

White, L. K., & Booth, A. (1985). The quality and stability of remarriages: The role of children. *American Sociological Review, 50*, 689–698.

Whitehead, B. D. (1993). Dan Quayle was right. *The Atlantic Monthly, 271*, 47–84.

Whiteside, M. F. (1989). Family rituals as a key to kinship connections in remarried families. *Family Relations, 38*, 34–39.

Whiteside, M. F. (1998). The parental alliance following divorce: An overview. *Journal of Marital and Family Therapy, 24*, 3–24.

Woestendiek, J. (1992, August 15). You are not my mother. *Winston-Salem (NC) Journal*, pp. 22–23.

# CHAPTER 13

# Working with Culturally Diverse Families

She works cleaning clothes and ironing sheets,
a person of color in a bland and bleached world
where there is little emotion amid the routine
as the days fade like memories into each other.

He struggles trimming hedges and mowing grass,
a solitary white man surrounded by people
whose skin is darker than his.

Sometime when discouraged she struggles
to stop her dreams from slipping away,
like the fresh steam from her always hot iron,
by giving them vividness in her mind
and calling her hopes by name.

He too concentrates on the future
amid the tedium of routine and long hours
as he imagines scenes of those who love him
and conjures up pictures of home.

*Gladding, 1992*

**D**istinct cultures and culturally diverse families have been a part of American society since its inception. In fact, "every family's background is multicultural. All marriages are to a degree cultural intermarriages. No two families share exactly the same cultural roots" (McGoldrick & Giordano, 1996, p. 6).

It was not until the civil rights struggles of the 1960s, however, that the majority of people in the United States began to recognize and accept cultural pluralism (Lee & Richardson, 1991). Before this time, many Americans were cut off from the mainstream of society because of racial, language, or custom differences. These barriers to accessibility resulted in many new immigrants and cultural minorities isolating themselves in order to establish a sense of community, preserve traditional values, and be protected. In most major cities, enclaves still exist of Italians, Haitians, Poles, Ukrainians, Irish, Koreans, Nigerians, Cubans, Vietnamese, Mexicans, and others distinct family groups who live physically and psychologically apart from other cultures. This type of separation, along with the societal tradition of often ignoring or exaggerating differences, has made it hard for family therapists to understand culturally distinct families and their issues. Thus, compassionate and effective treatment has been, until recently, almost nonexistent for these families.

As the population of the United States becomes more diverse, family therapists must gain knowledge about different family types and skills in treating them. Increasingly, family therapists are "finding themselves working with families in multicultural context" (Goldberg, 1993, p. 1). Indeed, "the families of today—postmodern families—are characterized by diversity, not only diversity of structure but also diversity along class, ethnic, culture, and gender lines" (Ahrons, 1992, p. 3). Thus, now instead of looking at actions in the context of isolated individuals, therapists view persons as a part of families and their behaviors as a part of a sociocultural context (Falicov, 1983). Put another way, therapists strive to understand individuals and families "in the context of the family's culture" and the culture at large (Gushue, 1993, p. 489).

Different culturally diverse families have much to teach each other, and therapists. For instance, situations that encompass the life span, from dealing with health to reacting to death, are treated differently by distinct cultural groups (Brown, 1988; Hines, Preto, McGoldrick, Almeida, & Weltman, 1999). Thus, in working with families, therapists must take into account how different cultures instill in family members attitudes and actions, such as social and communication patterns (Goldenberg & Goldenberg, 1993; Thomas, 1998).

When family therapists do not comprehend the values and characteristics of specific cultures and their families, the behaviors associated with these beliefs and traditions are likely to be undervalued, misunderstood, and/or pathologized (Billingsley, 1968; McGoldrick & Giordano, 1996). This misunderstanding is associated with cultural prejudices, flaws in collecting data about minorities, stereotyping, and unrecognized economic differences (Hampson, Beavers, & Hulgus, 1990).

Therefore, culturally diverse families need to be seen in regard to their strengths and liabilities both collectively and individually. One way to do this is to study culturally diverse families from the perspective of their competencies, social class, and observed family styles (Billingsley, 1992; Hampson et al., 1990). This type of approach makes it more likely that significant differences and similarities of families from various backgrounds will be reported accurately and fairly.

This chapter discusses numerous aspects of culturally diverse families. The emphasis is on the dynamics that are common to a broad range of families. Issues involved in working from a multicultural point of view are stressed. In addition, some special aspects of conducting family therapy with culturally diverse families are highlighted. Matters pertaining to working with gay and lesbian families are addressed first since this family form is found to some extent within all cultures and until recently has been "invisible." Then, issues in working with more identifiable cultural groups, that is, African-American, Asian-American, Hispanic/Latino-American, and Native American families are dealt with. In discussing cultural groups, we must stress that it is easy to stereotype groups according to cultures and that therapists must take extreme care not to get caught in this trap. Instead, they must realize that within-group differences are greater than outside differences in cultures and be open to working with the uniqueness that is every family.

# What Is a Culture?

To tackle the issues involved in multicultural family therapy, we must first define *culture* and distinguish it from race and ethnicity. Such a procedure helps clarify concepts and the interrelatedness of terms. It is a difficult process and one for which there is no universal agreement.

**Culture** can be defined in numerous ways, but it is generally considered to be "the customary beliefs, social forms, and material traits of a racial, religious, or social group" (*Webster's*, 1989, p. 314). "This broad definition implies that culture is a multidimensional concept that encompasses the collective realities of a group of people" (Lee, 1991, p. 11). As such, culture is made up of behaviors and traditions that have been cultivated over a long period of time. It may be a conscious aspect of a family's identity, such as taking pride in ancestry, or it may consist of unconscious practices that family members perform and never question. Both conscious and unconscious practices of culture involve seeing and being in the world through a persistence to continue to live a certain way despite information to the contrary (Watzlawick, 1976).

A culture includes diverse groups of people who may differ in regard to race, religion, or social status but who identify themselves collectively in a particular way. For instance, it is possible to speak about Jewish, Christian, Buddhist, Hindu, or Muslim cultures that encompass people from a wide range of social classes. It is also appropriate to talk about specific countries and their cultures, such as Japanese, Egyptian, Kenyan, or Indian. Culture may be spoken of in regard to those who are racially in either the majority or the minority. The point is that cultures operate on many levels, that is, inclusive and exclusive, specific and general. Many cultures are open to people of various backgrounds who identify with them and act in accordance with their traditions and values. Some are closed. In a pluralistic society such as the United States, "a complex melange of cultural influences" exists that impacts families and their members (Szapocznik & Kurtines, 1993). "Cultural values define behaviors and therefore establish norms for attitudes and behaviors within families" (Thomas, 1998, p. 24).

*Racial groups* and *ethnicity* are not so broadly defined. A racial group is "a family, tribe, people, or nation belonging to the same stock" (*Webster's*, 1989, p. 969). It may include an ethnic group, but "*race* is primarily a biological term" (Lee, 1991, p. 12). Ethnic groups are "large groups of people classed according to common racial, national, tribal, linguistic, or cultural origin or background" (*Webster's*, 1989, p. 427). Ethnic identity "is anything but homogenous" (Giordano & Carini-Giordano, 1995, p. 352). In describing ethnic groups, the term *ethnicity* is used to reflect a sociological concept (Lee, 1991). "Ethnicity . . . influences the kinds of messages that people learn . . . for example, Scandinavian patterns for expressions of intimacy may differ greatly from Italian and Greek messages" (Mason, 1991, p. 481). Therefore, ethnic family customs influence a group's "fit" within an overall culture, just as race does.

Although race and ethnicity may be used synonymously at times to refer to people who share similar traits or characteristics, they differ when employed in their most precise form. Therefore, the term *culture* is more widely utilized when discussing a group of people with similar backgrounds, beliefs, and behaviors. The broadness of *culture* is the primary reason it is employed in this chapter as a modifier of family diversity.

# Dynamics Associated with Culturally Diverse Families

Culturally diverse families are affected by the same social pressures that impact other families. These families must learn to cope with the stressors associated with money, work, children, aging, death, success, and leisure (Turner, 1993). However, the ways in which families from different cultural backgrounds view and respond to life events differ. For instance, some general and striking characteristics of Jewish families are to marry within the group, to encourage children, to value education, and to use guilt as a way of shaping behavior. On the other hand, some general characteristics of Italian families are to place importance on expressiveness, personal connectedness, enjoyment of food and good times, and traditional sex roles (McGoldrick & Rohrbaugh, 1987). Regardless, minority culture families are affected both quantitatively and qualitatively in regard to life experiences in ways that members of majority families are not (Sue & Sue, 1999). "Certain moments in the family life cycle will represent greater crisis for one culture than for another" (Gushue, 1993, p. 489). For instance, in Irish families, "death is generally considered the most significant life cycle transition and members will go to great lengths not to miss a wake or a funeral" (McGoldrick, 1986, p. 31). On the other hand, "because of the stress on interdependence in Puerto Rican culture, the loss of a family member is experienced as an especially profound threat to the family's future and often touches off reactions of extreme anxiety" (Garcia-Preto, 1986, p. 33).

In addition, culturally diverse families who are in the minority must also contend with overt as well as covert criticism of their patterns of family interaction that may not be universally accepted (Tseng & Hsu, 1991). For example, if women are treated by certain families as inferior or subservient, these families and their culture may be taken to task by others. Likewise, a majority culture may ignore important civic or religious holidays in particular culture groups and both directly and indirectly convey to members of these groups their disinterest or disdain in them as people.

Another difficulty for culturally diverse families is appearance. Members of some families may be recognized by their distinct skin color, physical features, or dress. Therefore, they must deal with subtle and blatant prejudice and discrimination on an almost continuous basis (Ho, 1987). As a result of discrimination or hatred based on outward appearance, some families are faced with the task of nurturing and protecting each other in ways unknown to majority culture families.

A fourth dynamic that affects culturally diverse families involves their access to mental health services (Sue & Sue, 1999). The location of mental health services, their formality, and the way they advertise their services is often a turnoff for culturally diverse families. For example, Native American Indians may have to drive miles for treatment and then find that the clinic operation hours are not convenient to their lifestyle. This kind of situation is known as an **institutional barrier**. Other institutional barriers include the use of a language not understood by minority families and the lack of culturally diverse practitioners.

A final factor influencing culturally diverse families involves economics (Arnold & Allen, 1995). To function well in society, families must have one or more persons earning wages that make it possible to live beyond a survival level. Minority cultures are often excluded from certain jobs and their employment opportunities can be limited by events in society such as the rise of technology and service industries and the shrinkage of the working class in the United States. These events have resulted in many heads of minority households being cut out of employment opportunities that paid good wages and falling into the ranks of the working poor and underclass.

# Issues Within Culturally Diverse Families

A number of critical issues are involved in working with culturally diverse families. These issues center around attitudes, skill, and knowledge. No family therapist can be an expert on all cultures (Hines et al., 1999). However, most family therapists can acquire general abilities that enable them to be effective in helping a wide variety of families. Such factors as sensitivity, experience, acceptance, ingenuity, specificity, and intervention often determine whether family therapists are successful or not.

## Sensitivity

The issue of sensitivity is one with which all helping professionals must deal. "Sensitivity and respect for the beliefs and world view of the client/family is crucial" (Santisteban & Szapocznik, 1994, p. 22). If family therapists are not sensitive to the similarities and differences between themselves and the families they work with, they may make assumptions that are incorrect and unhelpful (Boynton, 1987). Professionals who are insensitive have been described as **culturally encapsulated counselors** (Wrenn, 1962, 1985). They tend to treat everyone the same, and in so doing, make mistakes. For instance, every Hispanic/Latino family differs in regard to its makeup and the strategies members use to resolve problems. If therapists are not sensitive to this fact, they may try the same methods with all Hispanic/Latino families and get mixed results.

## Experience

The issue of experience refers to that of the family therapists as well as that of the families they treat. Professionally, a family therapist may find it hard to work with a family of a diverse background if the therapist has not had some life experiences with members of that culture. For instance, a family therapist who has been socially isolated in a white, middle-class culture may become lost when trying to help a newly immigrated Vietnamese family resolve family conflict.

Also important is the experience of specific culturally diverse families. If a family of Hispanic/Latino descent has a history of affluence and acceptance within mainstream society, a family therapist needs to recognize and respect the socioeconomic factors that influence that family. Specific cultural backgrounds are often influenced by a family's experiences in the larger society. Such families and their members often find themselves in conflict because of their inheritance of two different cultural traditions (Ho, 1987; Sue & Sue, 1999).

## Acceptance

The issue of acceptance encompasses therapists' personal and professional comfortableness with a family. If therapists cannot openly accept culturally diverse families, they are likely to display overt or covert prejudice that negatively impacts the therapeutic process. Therefore, it is of utmost importance that therapists assess their thoughts and feelings about the families that are before them. The question of racism must be raised early if the family and therapist are of different racial backgrounds (Franklin, 1993). Social, behavioral, and economic differences need to be examined also to assess whether the family and therapist are a good match. Models for examining therapists' values in regard to families and self have been developed by Ho (1987) (see Table 13.1).

## Ingenuity

To be effective in treating culturally diverse families, therapists must use their ingenuity. Most cultural settings provide natural help-giving networks (Sue & Sue, 1999). Effective family therapists utilize these networks and are innovative as well. Instead of trying to treat some families within the confines of an office, therapists act as consultants to agencies and persons who can best work with certain families. For example, in the African-American community, churches and ministers have traditionally been a source of strength and help. Thus, therapists may act in conjunction with and in direct and open collaboration with these sources in treating a family in context (Boszormenyi-Nagy, 1987). On the other hand, with traditional Asian Americans, subtlety and indirectness may be called for rather than direct confrontation and interpretation (Sue & Sue, 1999).

## Specificity

Specificity is necessary because each family is unique and must be treated differently. Family therapists must assess the strengths and weaknesses of individual families and design

**Table 13.1**
Cultural Value Preferences of Middle-Class White Americans and Ethnic Minorities: A Comparative Summary

| Area of Relationships | Middle-Class White Americans | Asian/Pacific Americans | American Indian, Alaskan Native | African Americans | Hispanic Americans |
|---|---|---|---|---|---|
| Man to nature/environment | Mastery over | Harmony with | Harmony with | Harmony with | Harmony with |
| Time orientation | Future | Past-present | Present | Present | Past-present |
| Relations with people | Individual | Collateral | Collateral | Collateral | Collateral |
| Preferred mode of activity | Doing | Doing | Being-in-becoming | Doing | Being-in-becoming |
| Nature of man | Good and bad | Good | Good | Good and bad | Good |

From *Family Therapy with Ethnic Minorities* (p. 232) by M. K. Ho, 1987, Newbury Park, CA: Sage. Copyright © 1987 by Sage Publications, Inc. Reprinted by permission of Sage Publications, Inc.

and implement specific procedures for each. For instance, "in families that expect therapy to be a growth experience . . . the therapy must be presented in this light. Conversely, in families that expect a no-nonsense, problem-solving approach, therapy should be presented as having concrete, attainable, short-term goals . . . " (Santisteban & Szapocznik, 1994, p. 22). Although strategic family therapy (Haley, 1973, 1976) and solution-focused therapy (deShazer, 1988) pride themselves on devising approaches that address the needs of specific families, other family therapy models also modify their goals, guidelines, and interventions, depending on the particular families they are treating.

In practical terms, family therapists must realize, for example, that the needs and issues of first-generation families differ from those of more acculturated families. Contrary to popular belief, as families become acculturated, they do not drop former cultural ways but instead add new ones and synthesize "both the new and the old in a creative manner" (Newlon & Arciniega, 1991, p. 202). The issue of specificity is a reminder that the application of treatment needs to be congruent with and tailored to families' experiences.

## Intervention

A final aspect of being an effective counselor with culturally diverse families involves the challenge of intolerance within systems. Such a goal is accomplished when a counselor assumes the role of a systematic change agent (Lee, Armstrong, & Brydges, 1996). In this type of role, a counselor tries to intervene on behalf of families in unhealthy and intolerant systems. There are two types of unhealthy systems. One involves a "passive insensitivity to diversity" (Lee et al., 1996, p. 5), that is, the plight of people outside one's culture is simply ignored. The other intolerant system is "one characterized by an active and intentional insensitivity to diversity" (Lee et al., 1996, p. 5). This latter type of system fosters active discrimination that is easier to identify. Bringing about change in either type of system takes courage, persistence, and time.

# Approaches for Treating Culturally Diverse Families

Culturally diverse families share some characteristics in common. For example, the importance and influence of the extended family and kinship ties are almost universal in families from all cultural backgrounds (Johnson, 1995). However, all families have unique characteristics that must be considered when working with them. Therapists will find it important, for example, to consider that "the definition of *family*, as well as the timing of life cycle phases and the importance of different transitions, varies depending on a family's cultural background" (Carter & McGoldrick, 1988, p. 25). With that in mind, the following sections highlight some common aspects of and therapeutic issues surrounding the "invisible family" form composed of gays and lesbians and four distinct culturally diverse minority family groups in the United States: African Americans, Asian Americans, Hispanic/Latino Americans, and Native Americans.

## Gay and Lesbian Families

Family therapists are seeing increasing numbers of gay and lesbian couples and families (Chen-Hayes, 1997; Laird, 1993). By understanding the dynamics surrounding these relationships, family therapists can overcome negative and detrimental stereotypes associated with this population and at the same time be able to provide proper and needed services.

Until recently there has not been much research on gay and lesbian families. In fact, the gay and lesbian family form has been all but "invisible" in family therapy research and this population has been mainly studied in regard to individuals (Laird, 1993). However, a number of facts are known about gay and lesbian families.

First, as a group, gay and lesbian families are intergenerational. "Each partner, child, and other family member is influenced by and must come to terms with the specific history and culture of his or her own family of origin in its sociocultural context" (Laird, 1993, p. 285).

Second, there is a cycle to gay and lesbian family life and issues at each stage are crucial to understand if these families are to be understood. Like other families, gay and lesbian families "must decide who will do what, when, where, and how in order to meet the particular needs of the family as a whole and of individual family members, whose interests at times may conflict or compete" (Laird, 1993, p. 308).

Third, gay and lesbian families are varied within as a group. Thus there is no "typical" gay or lesbian family form any more than there is a typical family form for any other cultural group.

Finally, as much as any minority group, gay and lesbian families have suffered from a lack of affirming role models and social support. They still face discrimination on all levels and are stigmatized within society in general (Sayger, Homrich, & Horne, 2000).

### Therapeutic Treatment of Gay and Lesbian Families

The place most family therapists need to start when working therapeutically with gay and lesbian families is with themselves, especially in sorting out their feelings in regard to this population (May, 1994). Most family therapists are heterosexuals and carry conscious and unconscious negative thoughts and feelings about those who are not. Thus to be effective with gay and lesbian families, family therapists need to stay open, aware, and acknowledging of their beliefs and biases as well as studious regarding current scientific knowledge and clinical issues regarding gay and lesbian lifestyles (Sayger et al., 2000).

After working on themselves and sharpening their clinical abilities to be therapeutic with members of this population, family therapists must address both external and internal issues associated with being a gay or lesbian couple or family. Externally, gay and lesbian families face a world of obstacles including cultural and societal homophobia. Therefore, family therapists need to be familiar with "local, state, and national laws" affecting gays and lesbians, "as well as community and psychoeducative resources" available to them and their families-of-origin (Sayger et al., 2000, p. 34). Another external issue is that some parents and relatives of gays and lesbians have difficulty accepting the sexual orientation and lifestyle of their kin. Therefore, therapeutic treatment may involve working with the extended family members of this population so that at least an understanding, if not an acceptance, of the gay and lesbian family can be gained.

A challenge that is continuous for family therapists is dealing with the diversity of gay and lesbian family lifestyles and subcultures (Snead, 1993). Treatment for gay and lesbian families that may be appropriate in one case may not be appropriate in another. For example, some forms of these families have "fluid boundaries and flexible composition" (Patten, 1992, p. 34) while others do not.

Finally, family therapists face the challenge of helping these families relate positively to the heterosexual families from which most came, to the communities in which they live, and to themselves and their partners. The process is a two-way street; and in working with gay and lesbian families, therapists often have to work with society at large and its institutions (May, 1994). All of these processes take time, support, and creativity.

## African-American Families

Until displaced by Hispanic Americans (Grieco & Cassidy, 2001), African Americans were the largest minority group in the United States (Sue & Sue, 1999). There were approximately 34.4 million African Americans in 1998, according to the Census Bureau (Associated Press, 1999). Their families are diverse in regard to background and traditions. However, they share a commonness in that many of their ancestors were brought to America as slaves and their black skin color differentiates them from the majority of people in the United States. These two characteristics have kept them at an extreme disadvantage in acculturating and being accepted in society (Walsh, 1982). In addition, African-American families have had to face continuous racism, poverty, and discrimination. As a group, they have faced many socioeconomic disadvantages and a great deal of stress (Kazdin, Stolar, & Marciano, 1995). On popular television shows and in films, African Americans have been depicted as being wise and witty (e.g., *The Cosby Show*), middle-class (e.g., *Laural Avenue*), violent and unruly (e.g., *Boyz N the Hood*), and heroic (e.g., *Passenger 57*). In truth, African-American families vary, just like other types of families.

In regard to strengths, African-American families are known for being "strong" in the areas of kinship bonds. Most African-American families "are embedded in a complex kinship and social network" that includes both blood relatives and close friends (Lambie & Daniels-Mohring, 1993, p. 74). Another strength is their religious orientation and spirituality; they often utilize the resources of their clergy and churches (Richardson, 1991). Cooperation, strong motivation to achieve, caring parenting, and work orientation are other positive characteristics that describe African Americans (Hill, 1972; Olson, 2000). Finally, African Americans are "adaptable" in their family roles. Members of such families are less likely to stereotype each other into roles based on gender (Ericksen, Yancey, & Ericksen, 1979).

Despite their strengths, African-American families face a number of negatives. Internally, African-American male–female relationships have "become more problematic, conflictual, and destructive" (Willis, 1990, p. 139). "Census figures show that 35% of Americans between 24 and 34 have never married. For African-Americans that figure is 54%" (Peterson, 2000, p. 8D). The reasons for this phenomenon are complex and relate to factors—such as mistrust, insecurity, unemployment, socialization, and rage—that are the conscious and unconscious legacies of slavery and a changing society. Regardless of the underlying dynamics, the result is that despite their belief in the institution of marriage and an increase in affluence, fewer African Americans marry today than at any time in history (Cherlin, 1992). Out of wedlock births account for two out of three first births to African-American women under age 35 (Ingrassia, 1993).

In addition, African-American families must deal with outside pressures, such as racism, prejudice, poverty, and discrimination (Lee, 1995). The social and economic turmoil surrounding the civil rights movement, the women's movement, and the Vietnam

War changed the overall makeup of African-American families. Two of the best aspects of change that occurred in African-American families in the 1970s were financial and social upward mobility. Employment and educational opportunities, previously closed because of racial barriers, opened. Housing and social options became more available. The opposite side of the upward mobility movement was the poverty and hopelessness of the African Americans left behind, especially in inner-city ghettos. These African Americans tended to be poorer and less educated, and to have less opportunity to advance. Unemployment rose in general among African-American men from the late 1950s on because of the elimination of many working-class jobs (Gaston, 1996). The consequence was that a large economic underclass of African Americans developed. Within this class was a loosening of family ties because of the stress and strain associated with single parenting, high unemployment, and living in or near the poverty level. With this phenomenon came social frustration and anger that led to an increase in violence and the incarceration of a large percentage of young black men who dropped out as potentially available marriage partners and constructive citizens (Jones, 1993; Olson, 2000).

These external factors influence the inner realities affecting family dynamics today (Franklin, 1993). Such stress within any group takes its toll on family life and individuals within these families. Boys and young men in African-American communities seem to have been especially negatively impacted.

### Therapeutic Treatment of African-American Families

The concept of family therapy is new to most African-American families (Willis, 1988; Wilson & Stith, 1991). Traditionally, African Americans have relied on extended family networks to take care of their needs. African-American men have, as a group, been particularly reluctant to share their most intimate thoughts and feelings because of socialization patterns that have taught them not to share pain and frustration (Peterson, 2000). Yet, many African-American families may benefit from time-specific therapy approaches that are problem focused or multigenerational in nature (Boyd-Franklin, 1993). For example, structural, Bowenian, and strategic family therapy theories have been found appropriate in working with African-American families (Boyd-Franklin, 1987). In addition, psychoeducation, especially with single-parent African-American women, can be effective (Lee, 1995). However, in treating African-American families, there is "no prescriptive approach" that can be applied universally in the helping process (Newlon & Arciniega, 1991, p. 192).

To be successful, family therapists need to understand the historical and social background of African-American families in the United States. They must also appreciate the issue of trust that arises between African-American families and non-African-American family therapists (Willis, 1988). An important point for family therapists to comprehend is that many African-American families first need to perceive treatment as a form of social support that can benefit them. Then, they can more readily accept it.

Therefore, working with African-American families requires that therapists have an understanding of **multigenerational family** systems (Hines, Garcia-Preto, McGoldrick, Almeida, & Weltman, 1992). In addition, they must be sensitive to the importance of respect for elderly family members. Often family therapy is begun by African-American families because therapists have emphasized to older family members that therapy can be of value.

Therapists must assure African-American families that through the therapeutic process they can learn how to handle many of their own problems. Through "education about various issues (e.g., parental rights in educational systems) and concrete skills training," confidence and competence may be enhanced in African-American families so they can advocate on their own behalf (McGoldrick, Preto, Hines, & Lee, 1991, p. 561). For instance, Lee (1995) describes how single African-American mothers may be empowered to effectively deal with their children and extreme environmental hardships through helping these women foster a positive culture identity in their children. In addition, these women can be assisted by helping them appreciate parenthood from an Afrocentric perspective.

Finally, in working with African-American families, therapists need to address social and institutional issues that have adversely affected African Americans. This includes working in an outreach fashion to marshal support of institutions, such as governments and churches, that can lend support to African-American families and help change policies that may have a detrimental effect on these families. The presentation of positive role models of African-American families can also make a difference (Stovall, 2000).

## Asian-American Families

In 1998, Asian Americans constituted about 4% of the population of the United States or 10.5 million people (Associated Press, 1999). However, by 2010, they are expected to make up about 10% of the nation's population. Asian Americans trace their cultural heritages to countries such as China, Japan, Vietnam, Cambodia, India, Korea, the Philippines, and the Pacific islands. The backgrounds of Asian Americans are diverse, "with as many as 32 different Asian ethnic groups now identified in the U.S." (Cheng, 1996, p. 8). They differ in regard to language, history, and socioeconomic factors. Yet, Asian Americans share many cultural values, such as a respect and reverence for the elderly, extended family support, family loyalty, and a high value on education (Olson, 2000). They also place a strong emphasis on self-discipline, order, social etiquette, and hierarchy (Hong, 1989; London & Devore, 1992).

"Traditional Asian/Pacific values governing family life have been heavily influenced by Confucian philosophy and ethics, which strongly emphasizes specific roles and proper relationships among people in those roles" (Ho, 1987, p. 25). Three main relationship roles that are stressed within the family are father/son, husband/wife, and elder/younger siblings (Keyes, 1977). In these relationships, there are feelings of obligation and shame. If a member of a family behaves improperly, the whole family loses face. Buddhist values also are prevalent in many Asian-American families. These values stress harmonious living and involve "compassion, a respect for life, and moderation of behavior; self-discipline, patience, modesty, and friendliness" (Ho, 1987, p. 25).

As Asian-American families have moved into mainstream American society, they have had to contend with a number of problems that are both unique and universal to other families. For instance, like other families, Asian-American families have had to face the fact that geographically and emotionally, families are moving further apart. This is a trend in American society that places more emphasis on the individual than the family (Sue & Morishima, 1982). In addition, substance abuse is on the rise in some Asian-American populations (Mercado, 2000). Unique to Asian-American family culture is the reality that "parents can no longer expect complete obedience, as families become more democratic and move away from the patriarchal system of the past" (London & Devore, 1992, p. 368). In many ways, Asian-American families and other U.S. families appear to be similar, but the dynamics underlying them differ substantially.

## Therapeutic Treatment of Asian-American Families

In working with Asian-American families, therapists must take acculturation into account. First-generation Asian-American families, for instance, may need assistance from family therapists in learning how to interrelate properly to other families and societal institutions. They may likewise face problems involving social isolation, adjustment difficulties to a particular location, and language barriers (Hong, 1989). The role of the therapist in such cases is primarily educational and avocational rather than remedial. It is directed toward outreach efforts (Cheng, 1996).

On the other hand, many established Asian-American families need help in resolving intrafamily difficulties, such as intergenerational conflicts, role confusion, and couple relationships (McGoldrick et al., 1991). For instance, there may be an acculturation gap (i.e., different rates of acculturation) between immigrant parents and U.S.-raised children that "complicates the normal generation gap, resulting in greater misunderstandings, miscommunications, and eventual conflicts among family members" (Lee, Choe, Kim, & Ngo, 2000, p. 211). In these cases, therapists work according to both specific cultural norms as well as universal treatment model procedures.

Like African-American families, Asian-American families seem to do best in family therapy when the focus of sessions is problem or solution oriented and when the family is empowered to help itself through its own and community resources. Most Asian-American families are reluctant to initiate family therapy; and if therapists are to be of assistance to these families, they must do the following:

- Orient them and educate them to the value of therapy.
- Establish rapport quickly through the use of compassion and self-disclosure.
- Emphasize specific techniques families can use in improving their relationships and resolving their problems.

Problematic to Asian-American families, and all recognizable ethnic minority families, is racism, which may disrupt their internal family dynamics as well as outside relationships (Sue & Morishima, 1982). In such situations, family therapists not only work to address societal changes but also focus with family members on assessing the values and skills within the family for dealing with prejudice and discrimination. This type of work utilizes family cultural strengths and family therapy strengths.

Overall, in working with families of Asian origin, therapists need to recognize that they may be most effective if they are knowledgeable about Asian philosophers, such as Lao Tzu and Confucius. They are also usually at their best when they seek "to create a safe and nurturing environment that mirrors a supportive and caring family and where each participant is respected, and without fear, can explore relevant problems and concerns" (Cheng, 1996, p. 8).

## Hispanic/Latino-American Families

"The term *Hispanic,* or *Latino,* refers to people who were born in any of the Spanish-speaking countries of the Americas (Latin America), from Puerto Rico, or from the U.S. who trace their ancestry to either Latin America or to Hispanic people from U.S. territories that were once Spanish or Mexican" (Cohen, 1993, p. 13). Over one in ten residents (11%) of the United States is of Hispanic/Latino origin, with a combined population of 30.3 million. Preliminary data from the 2000 Census (Grieco & Cassidy, 2001) indicate that Hispanics have become the nation's largest minority, surpassing African Americans. Original projections were that this change would take place by 2010 (Benedetto, 1992), when the Hispanic/Latino-American population was estimated to be about 40 million people (Puente, 1993). The majority (76%) of Hispanic/Latino-American families are those whose ancestry is Mexican, Cuban, or Puerto Rican.

Considerable diversity exists among Hispanics/Latinos and the families they create. Most wish to be in the mainstream of society in the United States, and a majority do not support "traditional" roles for women (Benedetto, 1992). As a group, Hispanics/Latinos also tend to be family oriented. However, differences in distinct groups of Hispanics/Latinos means that each family is unique, sharing both common and special qualities when compared with others.

As a group, Hispanic/Latino families have the following difficulties (Puente, 1993; Usdansky, 1993):

- They have a higher unemployment rate than non-Hispanic/Latinos.
- They live below the poverty line at over twice the rate of non-Hispanic/Latinos.
- They lag behind non-Hispanic/Latinos in earning high school diplomas and college degrees.

However, Hispanic/Latino families have a number of assets and strengths. For instance, as a group, they are very family oriented, with unwavering love and loyalty to their families (Ponce, 1995; Ruiz, 1981). "Family members are viewed as interdependent, and no sacrifice is seen as too great for the family" (Lambie & Daniels-Mohring, 1993, p. 73). Parents appear to be especially dedicated in Hispanic/Latino families. Children, in turn, show gratitude through submitting to family rules. In addition, the extended family plays a positive part in Hispanic/Latino families in the teaching "of such traditional values as *dignidad* (dignity), *orgullo* (pride and self-reliance), *confianza* (trust and intimacy), and *respecto* (respect)" (Johnson, 1995, p. 319).

### Therapeutic Treatment of Hispanic/Latino Families

In working with Hispanic/Latino families, it is helpful for family therapists to develop a basic knowledge about cultural traditions before attempting to employ treatment modalities. For example, traditional rituals, such as religious festivities, *Quinceanos* (when a daughter is presented to society as a woman), engagements, weddings, and funerals, are highly valued in Hispanic/Latino culture and bring families together (Ponce, 1995, p. 7). In addition, "Hispanic/Latino individuals are interested in getting to know someone as a person rather than assessing a person based on external factors such as occupational or socioeconomic status" (Cooper & Costas, 1994, p. 32). Furthermore, as a group, Hispanic/Latinos tend to be "physically expressive, such as gesturing with their hands and face (e.g., eyes/eyebrows and mouth) while they talk" (Ponce, 1995, p. 7).

This type of cultural information can be obtained through specific academic courses as well as through direct observation, interactions with Hispanics/Latinos, and continuing education opportunities. Educational information helps therapists learn as well as, if not better than, case-by-case supervision (Inclan, 1990). Regardless of the approach family therapists employ, several unique factors must be taken into consideration when helping Hispanic/Latino families.

The first factor is external. A disproportionate number of Hispanic/Latino families live at or below the poverty level (Facundo, 1990). More than 40% of Hispanic/Latino children live in poverty, with the proportion of Puerto Rican children especially high (57%) (Usdansky, 1993). Stress related to economic factors and working conditions often contributes to intrafamily difficulties. Serving as an advocate and a resource is a crucial role family therapists sometimes need to play in helping poor Hispanic/Latino families help themselves.

Another area that family therapists need to address with Hispanic/Latino families relates to acculturation (LeVine & Padilla, 1980; Olson, 2000). As a group, Hispanics/Latinos seek to fit into the larger U.S. culture as rapidly as possible. However, family members may do so at different rates. For instance, school-age children may become "Americanized" at a faster and easier rate than grandparents. The older Hispanic/Latino family members may fear the loss of their children and traditions to a new culture and, hence, may become isolated and depressed because of rapid changes and loss (Baptiste, 1987). Therefore, in working with Hispanic/Latino families, therapists should consider how the pressure for acculturation may contribute to family turmoil, especially as it relates to family loyalty (Hines et al., 1992). Language factors, especially bilingualism, must also be explored (Sciarra & Ponterotto, 1991).

Another consideration in treating Hispanic/Latino families involves outside sources and internal beliefs. An institution that encompasses both of these helpful dimensions is the Catholic Church, especially for Mexican Americans and Puerto Ricans (Johnson, 1995). Historically, the Catholic Church has provided social, economic, and emotional support to Hispanic/Latino families when few other community services were available.

A fourth area that needs to be addressed in Hispanic/Latino families is the family hierarchy and roles. "By accepting therapy, the Hispanic father may feel . . . humiliated and shown to be ineffective" (Santisteban & Szapocznik, 1994, p. 21). Therefore, from the point of first contact, the therapist "must send the message that the father is a central figure in the family" (p. 21). Similarly, Hispanic/Latino women may present themselves as self-sacrificing and victims of other family members. The therapist will do best not to immediately challenge this assumption but rather to redirect this behavior "to fit the needs . . . of getting other family members into therapy" (p. 22).

Finally, the length of therapy and its focus must be considered when working with Hispanics/Latinos. Because Hispanic/Latino families are accustomed to being treated by physicians, they generally expect mental health services to be similar. Therefore, family therapists need to be active and employ direct and short-term theories. Two family therapy approaches that appear to be best suited for use with this population are behavioral family therapy and structural family therapy (Canino & Canino, 1982; Juarez, 1985; Ponterotto, 1987). Structural family therapy can be especially useful in addressing problems of extreme enmeshment—that is, "when several generations live in the same household, causing problems like lack of privacy, undefined boundaries in the family structures, and confusion as to who gives the discipline at home" (Ponce, 1995, p. 11).

## Native-American Families

Approximately 2.4 million Native Americans Indians, Eskimos, and Aleuts live in the United States (Associated Press, 1999). They are an extremely diverse group belonging to 517 state-recognized tribes (321 in the lower 48 states and 196 in Alaska) (Herring, 1991). Collectively, Native American life has been built around cultures that emphasize harmony, acceptance, cooperation, sharing, and a respect for nature and family. "Family, including extended family, is of major importance, and the tribe and family to which one belongs provide significant meaning" (Newlon & Arciniega, 1991, p. 196).

Difficulties within this population vary. Because the extended family is important in most Native-American cultures, one prevalent problem is the breakup or dysfunctionality of these families (Herring, 1989). Some historical practices of the U.S. government have resulted in "between 25% and 55% of all Native-American children" being separated from their family of origin "and placed in non-Native-American foster homes, adoption homes, boarding homes, or other institutions" (Herring, 1991, pp. 39–40). Many Native Americans who have had such experiences have suffered both a confusion about their identity and a trauma about their relationships to others. Families have likewise been negatively affected.

Another problematic family concern centers on geography and culture. Many Native Americans are torn between living with their families on a reservation or trying to adjust to life in the dominant culture of the United States. Cultural connectedness with other like-minded individuals is important to Native Americans, as is a relationship with the land. Yet, there are more Native Americans living in urban areas than on reservations. Urban life is stressful and is often not conducive to maintaining good mental health. For Native-American families as a group, isolation from their roots presents multiple difficulties in terms of functionality.

A final problem of Native-American families involves substance abuse, particularly alcoholism (Hill, 1989). In some family groups, drinking is encouraged as a form of socialization (Manson, Tatum, & Dinges, 1982). The results are manifest in higher death and disorder rates. Suicide, cirrhosis of the liver, and fetal alcohol syndrome are three examples of alcohol-related problems within Native-American families.

### Therapeutic Treatment of Native-American Families

Treating Native-American families requires sensitivity, cultural knowledge, and innovation. Outsiders, including family therapists, do not gain entrance into the family easily (Ho, 1987). To be accepted and be effective with Native Americans, therapists who treat these families should recognize that some techniques work better than others. For example, indirect forms of questioning and open-ended questions lead to responses. Direct forms of questioning and closed-ended questions do not (Tafoya, 1994).

Therapists should also know and utilize certain symbols. For example, the circle is considered sacred and represents unity and reciprocal relationships (Tafoya, 1994). This symbol, and others like it, can be used metaphorically as models for relationships (Tafoya, 1989). Finally, the admission by therapists that they may make mistakes in treatment because of cultural ignorance can go a long way toward establishing rapport and trust (Tafoya, 1989).

One approach for working with Native-American families is to use **home-based therapy** (Schacht, Tafoya, & Mirabla, 1989). This method requires that family therapists be with a family before attempting to help them. Thus, therapists spend more time than usual with families and may actually do chores with them before discussing troublesome areas of family life. From a pragmatic point of view, this approach does not appear to be the most efficient use of time. However, by devoting one's self to home-based therapy, essential services can be offered to families who would not otherwise receive them.

Another approach to working with Native-American families is to combine structural family therapy with traditional healing modalities. In both structuralism and traditional healing, the concepts of spontaneity, joining, and complementarity are utilized (Napoliello & Sweet, 1992). Family therapists can therefore employ concepts that transcend two cultures in order to promote change and resolution. This type of family therapy recognizes the importance of the fit between a therapeutic ideology and a family/cultural tradition (Hodges, 1989).

Finally, the "importance of visual mode should be noted—for a number of Native-American languages, the verb 'to learn' is a combination of the verbs 'to see' and 'to remember'" (Tafoya, 1994, p. 28). Therefore, concrete and active behavior, rather than insight, is stressed in traditional Native-American healing. In working with Native-American families, therapists would be wise to use therapeutic approaches that are directive but open ended, such as those that are strategically oriented.

# Guidelines for Selecting Treatment Approaches in Working with Culturally Diverse Families

Two main approaches are used in working with culturally diverse families. The first is the culture-specific model; the second is the universal perspective model. The culture-specific model emphasizes the values, beliefs, and orientation of different ethnic cultural groups (Sue, 1994). Most courses offered in higher education reflect this model. In such an approach, students memorize cultural variations among groups. Although this knowledge may be extremely valuable for therapists working with some families, it has its drawbacks. Basically, the culture-specific model may become unwieldy and may lead to stereotyping in which group characteristics, instead of unique characteristics, are singled out.

The universal perspective model is more general. It assumes that counseling approaches already developed can be applied with minor changes to different cultural groups. Thus, cultural differences are recognized from a family systems perspective. This approach also attempts to "identify human processes that are similar, regardless of ethnicity or cultural backgrounds" (Sue, 1994, p. 19). The only problem is that this way of working with culturally diverse families may be too general to be of any real use to a therapist.

In essence, the task of finding one approach that is always useful in working with culturally diverse families is impossible. However, a number of general guidelines can help family therapists choose an appropriate approach for working with specific families.

A broad guideline for therapists to use in selecting an intervention strategy is to assess whether the family's difficulties are mainly internal or external. If the problems are primarily internal, such as a failure to communicate effectively, well-established theoretical approaches may be employed. On the other hand, if the concerns are external, such as racism, the therapist may need to shift to a culture-specific way of helping.

Another guideline is to determine the family's degree of acculturation. Families that are more "Americanized" are generally open to a wider range of theoretical approaches than are the families of those who are new immigrants or only second generation.

A third guideline to use in working with culturally diverse families is to explore their knowledge of family therapy and their commitment to resolving their problems or finding solutions. If the family is unsophisticated about mental health services and pressed for time, the therapist is wise to use both educational and/or direct, brief theory-driven treatments, such as behavioral family therapy, solution-focused therapy, or structural family therapy. Otherwise, a culture-specific approach may be employed.

A fourth guideline for choosing an approach for culturally diverse families is to find out what has been tried and what is preferred. By determining what has been tried, therapists can devise methods that are appropriate and that overcome resistance. Preference is important to the establishment of rapport and effectiveness of treatment. "There are certain culture-preferred patterns for families to cope with problems" (Tseng & Hsu, 1991, p. 107). For instance, upwardly mobile African-American families gravitate toward dependence on extended family members during times of high stress (McAdoo, 1982). Therefore, in working with these families, therapists should include extended family members.

# Role of the Therapist

For family therapists to be competent in working with culturally diverse families, they must examine their own biases and values. This examination must be conducted on both an intellectual and an emotional level (Sue & Sue, 1999). For instance, research indicates that some white therapists may minimize or avoid the impact of societal expectations on cultural minority families (Rowe, Bennett, & Atkinson, 1994). Therefore, it is crucial for these family therapists to examine their thinking and feelings in regard to families whose cultural heritage differs from theirs. In general, culturally skilled family therapists are

- aware and sensitive to their own cultural heritage and to valuing and respecting differences
- comfortable with differences that exist between themselves and their clients in terms of race and beliefs
- sensitive to circumstances (personal biases, stage of ethnic identity, sociopolitical influences, etc.) that may dictate referral of a family
- knowledgeable of their own racist attitudes, beliefs, and feelings (Sue & Sue, 1999)

After family therapists have dealt constructively with themselves, they are then able to fulfill vital roles in working with culturally diverse families.

> One obvious question is how different styles of family therapy (e.g., more or less active, directive, collaborative, strategic, interpretive, etc.) intersect with the cultural or ethnic values that families bring to the therapy room. It is reasonable to expect that cultural values differentially affect family members' expectations for the therapist's behavior, their communication patterns in the session, and their perceptions of the therapeutic alliance. (Friedlander, Wildman, Heatherington, & Skowron, 1994, p. 411)

An initially important role of family therapists is to be concurrently culturally sensitive and open to themselves and to the families with whom they work (Franklin, 1993). If family therapists are not attuned and responsive to specific aspects of families, stereotyping may occur to the detriment of everyone involved (Tseng & Hsu, 1991). A lack of openness restricts the topics that can be discussed and the good that can be achieved through family therapy.

A second role of family therapists is to help culturally diverse families acknowledge and deal with their thoughts and emotions. For example, many of these families suppress anger and manifest depression. Although white, Anglo-Saxon, Protestant (WASP) families are most known for the suppression of thoughts and feelings, other cultural groups, such as Asian Americans, also utilize this approach (Tseng & Hsu, 1991). It is important that where and when appropriate, cognitions and emotions are expressed and therapeutically dealt with.

A third role of family therapists is to help culturally diverse families acknowledge and celebrate their heritages. "It is essential for clinicians to consider how ethnicity intersects with the life cycle and to encourage families to take active responsibility for carrying out the rituals in their ethnic or religious group(s) to mark each phase" (Carter & McGoldrick, 1988, p. 25). By being true and loyal to their pasts, culturally diverse families can deal better with the present.

A fourth role of family therapists is to help culturally diverse families move through and adjust to family life stages in the healthiest way possible. This means helping them become aware of, accept, and function in new family life cycle roles, whether in a nuclear or extended family.

Overall, to be effective with culturally diverse families, family therapists would do well to remember the acronym **ESCAPE** (Boynton, 1987). This symbolic word stands for four major investments therapists must make: (1) **e**ngagement with families and process, (2) **s**ensitivity to **c**ulture, (3) **a**wareness of family **p**otential, and (4) knowledge of the **e**nvironment.

# Process and Outcome

The process of family therapy with culturally diverse families is one that takes into consideration the uniqueness and common components of each family and culture. Process has an impact on outcome. Similarly, cultural patterns and traditions have an impact on families, and families have an influence on cultures (Tseng & Hsu, 1991).

## Initial Phase of Working with Culturally Diverse Families

Working with culturally diverse families requires that the family therapist first establish rapport. This may be done in a number of ways, but it could be problematic because many "ethnic minority Americans find it difficult to trust a family therapist who represents the majority system" (Ho, 1987, p. 255). One way to broach this barrier is for family therapists to define their roles clearly and early in the initial session. By so doing, they set the stage for future relationships.

A second way to establish rapport is through office furnishings and decorations. If family therapists show they have a broad knowledge and appreciation for cultural differences, families who exemplify these characteristics will feel much more comfortable. They are also likely to be more trusting.

A third way of helping culturally diverse families is for family therapists to respect the family hierarchy (Minuchin, 1974). This means talking to the person of highest status first, usually the husband/father, and then to others in the family. Such a procedure demonstrates an appropriate personal/family interest.

A final way to help culturally diverse families become a part of the therapeutic process is for therapists to set the rules of operation (Napier & Whitaker, 1978). This type of action alleviates anxiety and gives families an indication of where therapy will lead.

## Middle Phase of Working with Culturally Diverse Families

After family therapists have earned the respect, trust, and faith of culturally diverse families, they can begin to help these families deal with their problems. This middle phase of the process involves setting a mutually agreed on focus and goal for families. This process usually involves families and therapists working together in a consensual manner. In this phase, therapists must be patient and help family members be as specific as possible.

A number of techniques can be employed at this time to help families reach a productive outcome, for example, stressing family values, using reframing, or even employing a therapist-helper, such as a grandparent or family friend (Ho, 1987). All of these techniques are meant to utilize resources within families for promoting change without violating their cultural heritage.

## Final Phase of Working with Culturally Diverse Families

In the last phase of process and outcome, family therapists evaluate with culturally diverse families what has been achieved and what still needs to be accomplished. This phase focuses on the abilities that family members have to work in harmony with each other to accomplish a task. It draws families closer together through formal or informal celebrations. The ways in which families made their changes is highlighted so that the model of interacting can be utilized again.

# Summary and Conclusion

The multidimensional aspects of working with culturally diverse families were covered in this chapter. As the United States becomes a country of increased diversity, family therapists will find it critical to become competent in helping families from many backgrounds. This does not mean that family therapists must learn specific information about all cultures, for cultures are broad-based entities. However, it does mean that therapists must be aware of where to find appropriate information and guidelines to follow in being of assistance to families that clearly differ from them.

Culturally diverse families face most of the same life situations other families encounter. The difference is that in addition to expected stress, these families often encounter barriers, such as prejudice or access to services, in resolving these dilemmas. Thus, the dynamics affecting culturally diverse families differ from those that other families face.

In working with culturally diverse families, therapists must be sensitive to their own backgrounds and those of their client families. Furthermore, they must become innovative and experienced in applying theories to specific situations. They should obtain supervision and specialized educational training when needed. Family therapists must also be accepting of themselves and others. Otherwise, culturally diverse families are labeled pathological and are not helped. Successful treatment of most culturally diverse families depends on their ability to tap nontraditional centers of help. Using extended family members or institutions, such as the church or a club, may provide families with a sense of empowerment and connectedness as well as assistance. Finally, therapists need to be guided by specificity so that they make appropriate cultural interventions.

Gay and lesbian families are emerging from being invisible to being families therapists will work with and help. The gay and lesbian culture is imbedded in most other family cultures. African-American, Asian-American, Hispanic/Latino-American, and Native-American families are visible minority culture families that all share common and unique concerns. In selecting approaches to employ with these families, therapists need to consider the degree of acculturation, the individual/family life stages, and the level of understanding and commitment to family therapy.

The role of the therapist is to be sensitive and sensible when working with culturally diverse families. Also, family therapists need to realize that the process of assisting these types of families is a process that has a beginning, middle, and final phase in which some interventions are more appropriate than others in achieving a positive outcome. Overall, "family therapy has a great deal of promise in working with ethnic minority families, but it needs to be modified to include a comprehensive understanding of the diverse entities we call families" (Sue, 1994, p. 21).

# Summary Table

## Working with Culturally Diverse Families

Culturally diverse families have always been a part of American society, but often they have been cut off physically and psychologically from mainstream society.

As American culture becomes more diverse, family therapists must learn to work with families within their cultural context.

When culture is ignored families are misunderstood or pathologized.

### What Is a Culture?

*Culture* is a broadly defined term referring to the customary beliefs, social forms, and traits of a group.

*Race* is more narrowly defined as primarily a biological term.

*Ethnicity* is a sociological concept that is used to classify people according to a common origin or background.

### Dynamics Associated with Culturally Diverse Families

Culturally diverse families face the same pressures as other families, but they are affected in qualitatively and quantitatively different ways.

Certain family life cycle events have more impact on some families than others.

Unique traditions, distinctions in appearance, and access to mental health services can adversely affect culturally diverse families.

## Issues Within Culturally Diverse Families

Family therapists cannot become experts in all cultures. Instead they must acquire more general abilities to work with culturally diverse families. The following factors determine the effectiveness of family therapists:

- sensitivity (i.e., the ability to be open, rather than "culturally encapsulated")
- experience (i.e., social life experience with and knowledge of specific cultural backgrounds)
- acceptance (i.e., personal/professional comfortableness)
- ingenuity (i.e., the willingness to try innovative methods)
- specificity (i.e., the ability to access the strengths/weaknesses of a particular family)
- intervention (i.e., the active involvement of challenging intolerance with systems)

## Approaches for Treating Culturally Diverse Families

### Gay and Lesbian Families

Gay and Lesbian families are becoming increasing visible in American society.

These families must overcome negative and detrimental stereotypes.

Until recently not much research had been conducted on these families.

As a group, gay and lesbian families are intergenerational. There is also a cycle to gay and lesbian family life.

Gay and lesbian families vary greatly and, as with other minority culture groups, these families suffer from a lack of affirmative role models and social support.

Therapy with gay and lesbian families must start with therapists examining themselves in regard to conscious and unconscious thoughts and feelings about these families since most therapists are heterosexual.

Externally, family therapists should help gay and lesbian families deal with homophobia and restrictive laws as well as their family networks.

Internally, family therapists should help family members explore their relationships and community resources.

Overall, family therapists must be flexible and work on multiple levels, including societal, in treating gay and lesbian families.

### African-American Families

Commonalities among African-American families include slave history, skin color, and past discrimination treatment (i.e., racism).

Strengths associated with African-American families include kinship bonds, social networks, religion, cooperation, work orientation, and adaptability.

Weaknesses associated with African-American families include internal stresses (e.g., male–female relationships) and external pressures (e.g., discrimination, poverty, single parenting, less education, high unemployment).

The weaknesses associated with African-American families have a negative systemic impact on these families as a whole and increase prejudice.

African-American families generally benefit when treatment is time specific, problem focused, and multigenerational.

Structural, Bowenian, and strategic family therapies are often used with African-American families, but there is no prescriptive approach.

Developing trust, understanding African-American culture (including the importance of extended families), and assuring families that therapy is useful in self-help are keys to successful treatment.

*Asian-American Families*

Asian-American families come from diverse cultural heritages with different languages, histories, and values.

Most of these families have reverence for the family and the elderly.

Confucian and Buddhist philosophies influence roles and relationships.

Family strengths include an emphasis on self-discipline, patience, modesty, and friendliness.

Acculturation into mainstream society is associated with problems in Asian-American families, including issues of loyalty.

Therapy with Asian-American families must take into consideration problems associated with acculturation, such an intergenerational conflict and role confusion. Racism must also be addressed.

Asian-American families usually respond best to treatment when it is problem focused and empowering.

Family therapists do best when they orient themselves to Asian-American values, establish rapport quickly, and emphasize relationship enhancement and problem-solving therapies.

*Hispanic/Latino-American Families*

Hispanic/Latino families, the largest minority, trace their roots to Spanish-speaking countries.

Hispanic/Latino families wish to acculturate, do not support traditional roles for women, and are family oriented.

Weaknesses associated with Hispanic/Latino families include high unemployment, poverty, and low educational attainment.

Strengths associated with Hispanic/Latino families include family loyalty and parent/child dedication.

The treatment of Hispanic/Latino families includes developing a knowledge about their culture, assessing the relationship between financial factors and intrafamily difficulties, and addressing acculturation.

Family therapists work best with Hispanic/Latino families when they are active and direct, and therapy is short term. Structural and behavioral family therapies are usually appropriately employed.

*Native-American Families*

Native-American families are diverse, belonging to 517 recognized tribes.

Strengths of these families include an emphasis on harmony, acceptance, cooperation, sharing, and respect for nature/family.

Weaknesses include alcoholism and dysfunctional families as a result of government policies regarding the removal of children.

Successful treatment of Native-American families requires sensitivity, cultural knowledge, innovation, and use of certain symbols, for example, the circle.

Indirect questions work best with Native-American families. Home-based approaches and a variation of structural family therapy and native healing modalities have also been utilized.

### Guidelines for Selecting Treatment Approaches in Working with Culturally Diverse Families

Specific approaches for working with culturally diverse families include those that are culture specific and those that are based on a universal perspective. Other general guidelines family therapists need to master include:

- determining if difficulties are primarily internal or external
- determining the degree of a family's acculturation
- exploring a family's knowledge of family therapy and commitment to problem
- finding out what has been tried

### Role of the Therapist

Family therapists must examine their own biases and values before beginning to work with culturally diverse families.

Effective family therapists are aware of their own heritage, comfortable with differences, sensitive to circumstances, and knowledgeable of feelings/attitudes.

Family therapists must be open to themselves and to families to avoid stereotyping.

Family therapists must help families acknowledge their emotions when appropriate.

Family therapists must help families celebrate their cultural heritage.

Family therapists must assist families in dealing successfully with events in the family life cycle.

### Process and Outcome

Process has an impact on outcome, just as culture has an influence on families.

In the initial phase of the therapy process, the therapist establishes rapport, builds trust, defines his role clearly, makes the family comfortable, shows respect for the family hierarchy, and sets the rules for operation.

In the middle phase of the therapy process, the therapist helps the family focus on goals and achievement of a productive outcome through the use of specific family therapy techniques that are mainstream and innovative.

In the final phase of the therapy process, the therapist helps the family evaluate achievements and celebrate changes.

# References

Ahrons, C. R. (1992, October). 21st-Century families: Meeting the challenges of change. *Family Therapy News, 23,* 3, 16.

Arnold, M. S., & Allen, N. P. (1995). Andrew Billingsley: The legacy of African American families. *The Family Journal, 3,* 77–85.

Associated Press. (1999, September 15). Hispanic population in U.S. grew quickly in 1990s, report says. *Winston-Salem Journal*, pp. A1, A5.

Baptiste, D. A. (1987). Family therapy with Spanish-heritage immigrant families in cultural transition. *Contemporary Family Therapy, 9*, 229–251.

Benedetto, R. (1992, December 16). Hispanics feeling at home. *USA Today*, p. 5A.

Billingsley, A. (1968). *Black families in White America*. Upper Saddle River, NJ: Prentice Hall.

Billingsley, A. (1992). *Climbing Jacob's ladder: The enduring legacy of African American families*. New York: Simon & Schuster.

Boszormenyi-Nagy, I. (1987). *Foundations of contextual therapy*. New York: Brunner/Mazel.

Boyd-Franklin, N. (1987). The contribution of family therapy models to the treatment of black families. *Psychotherapy, 24*, 621–629.

Boyd-Franklin, N. (1993, July/August). Pulling out the arrows. *Family Therapy Networker, 17*, 54–56.

Boynton, G. (1987). Cross-cultural family therapy: The ESCAPE model. *American Journal of Family Therapy, 15*, 123–130.

Brown, F. H. (1988). The impact of death and serious illness on the family life cycle. In B. Carter & M. McGoldrick (Eds.), *The changing family life cycle* (2nd ed., pp. 457–482). New York: Gardner.

Canino, I., & Canino, G. (1982). Cultural syntonic family for migrant Puerto Ricans. *Hospital and Community Psychiatry, 33*, 299–303.

Carter, B., & McGoldrick, M. (1988). Overview: The changing family life cycle—A framework for family therapy. In B. Carter & M. McGoldrick (Eds.), *The changing family life cycle* (2nd ed., pp. 3–28). New York: Gardner.

Chen-Hayes, S. F. (1997). Counseling lesbian, bisexual, and gay persons in couple and family relationships: Overcoming the stereotypes. *The Family Journal, 5*, 236–240.

Cheng, W. D. (1996, Spring). Pacific perspective. *Together, 24*, 8.

Cherlin, A. (1992). *Marriage, divorce, remarriage*. Cambridge, MA: Harvard University Press.

Cohen, E. (1993, August). Who are Latinos? *Family Therapy News, 24*, 13.

Cooper, C., & Costas, L. (1994, Spring). Ethical challenges when working with Hispanic/Latino families: Personalismo. *The Family Psychologist, 10*, 32–34.

deShazer, S. (1988). *Clues: Investigating solutions in brief therapy*. New York: W. W. Norton.

Ericksen, J. A., Yancey, W. L., & Ericksen, E. P. (1979). The division of family roles. *Journal of Marriage and the Family, 41*, 301–313.

Facundo, A. (1990). Social class issues in family therapy: A case study of a Puerto Rican migrant family. *Journal of Strategic and Systemic Therapies, 9*, 14–34.

Falicov, C. J. (Ed.). (1983). *Cultural perspectives in family therapy*. Rockville, MD: Aspen.

Franklin, A. J. (1993, July/August). The invisibility syndrome. *Family Therapy Networker, 17*, 32–39.

Friedlander, M. L., Wildman, J., Heatherington, L., & Skowron, E. A. (1994). What we do and don't know about the process of family therapy. *Journal of Family Psychology, 8*, 390–416.

Garcia-Preto, N. (1986, November/December). Puerto Rican families. *Family Therapy Networker, 10*, 33–34.

Gaston, J. (1996, July 8). Roots of disunion. *Winston-Salem Journal*, pp. D1–D2.

Giordano, J., & Carini-Giordano, M. A. (1995), Ethnic dimensions in family treatment. In R. H. Mikesell, S. H. McDaniel, & D-D. Lusterman (Eds.), *Integrating family therapy* (pp. 347–356). Washington, DC: American Psychological Association.

Gladding, S. T. (1992). *Differences in awareness*. Unpublished manuscript.

Goldberg, J. R. (1993, August). Is multicultural family therapy in sight? *Family Therapy News, 24*, 1, 7, 8, 16, 21.

Goldenberg, H., & Goldenberg, I. (1993). Multiculturalism and family systems. *Progress: Family Systems Research and Therapy, 2*, 7–12.

Grieco, E. M., & Cassidy, R. C. Overview of race and Hispanic origin, Census 2000. brief. http://www.census.gov/prod/2001pubs/cenbr01-1.pdf

Gushue, G. V. (1993). Cultural-identity development and family assessment: An interactive model. *The Counseling Psychologist, 21*, 487–513.

Haley, J. (1973). *Uncommon therapy*. New York: Norton.

Haley, J. (1976). *Problem-solving therapy*. San Francisco: Jossey-Bass.

Hampson, R. B., Beavers, W. R., & Hulgus, Y. (1990). Cross-ethnic family differences: Interactional assessment of white, black, and Mexican-American families. *Journal of Marital and Family Therapy, 16*, 307–319.

Herring, R. D. (1989). The Native American family: Dissolution by coercion. *Journal of Multicultural Counseling and Development, 17*, 4–13.

Herring, R. D. (1991). Counseling Native American youth. In C. C. Lee & B. L. Richardson (Eds.), *Multicultural issues in counseling: New approaches to diversity* (pp. 37–47). Alexandria, VA: American Counseling Association.

Hill, A. (1989). Treatment and prevention of alcoholism in the Native American family. In G. W. Lawson & A. W. Lawson (Eds.), *Alcoholism and substance abuse in special populations* (pp. 247–272). Rockville, MD: Aspen.

Hill, R. (1972). *The strengths of black families*. New York: Emerson-Hall.

Hines, P. M., Garcia-Preto, N., McGoldrick, M., Almeida, R., & Weltman, S. (1992). Intergenerational relationships across cultures. *Families in Society: The Journal of Contemporary Human Services, 73,* 323–338.

Hines, P. M., Preto, N. G., McGoldrick, M., Almeida, R., & Weltman, S. (1999). Culture and the family life cycle. In B. Carter & M. McGoldrick (Eds.), *The expanded family life cycle* (3rd ed., pp. 69–87). Boston: Allyn & Bacon.

Ho, M. K. (1987). *Family therapy with ethnic minorities.* Newbury Park, CA: Sage.

Hodges, M. (1989). Culture and family therapy. *Journal of Family Therapy, 11,* 117–128.

Hong, G. K. (1989). Application of cultural and environmental issues in family therapy with immigrant Chinese Americans. *Journal of Strategic and Systemic Therapies, 8,* 14–21.

Inclan, J. (1990). Understanding Hispanic families: A curriculum outline. *Journal of Strategic and Systemic Therapies, 9,* 64–82.

Ingrassia, M. (1993, August 30). Endangered family. *Newsweek,* pp. 17–27.

Juarez, R. (1985). Core issues in psychotherapy with Hispanic children. *Psychotherapy, 22,* 441–448.

Johnson, A. C. (1995). Resiliency mechanisms in culturally diverse families. *The Family Journal, 3,* 316–324.

Jones, C. (1993, April 12). Alone: Marriage rate for blacks is declining. *Winston-Salem Journal,* pp. 43–44.

Kazdin, A. E., Stolar, M. J., & Marciano, P. L. (1995). Risk factors for dropping out of treatment among white and black families. *Journal of Family Psychology, 9,* 402–417.

Keyes, C. (1977). *The golden peninsula.* New York: Macmillan.

Laird, J. (1993). Lesbian and gay families. In F. Walsh (Ed.), *Normal family processes* (2nd ed., pp. 282–328). New York: Guilford.

Lambie, R., & Daniels-Mohring, D. (1993). *Family systems within educational contexts.* Denver: Love Publishing.

Lee, C. C. (1991). Cultural dynamics: Their importance in multicultural counseling. In C. C. Lee & B. L. Richardson (Eds.), *Multicultural issues in counseling: New approaches to diversity* (pp. 11–17). Alexandria, VA: American Counseling Association.

Lee, C. C. (1995). Empowering the African American family: New perspectives on single parenthood. *The Family Digest, 8,* 1, 3, 11.

Lee, C. C., Armstrong, K. L., & Brydges, J. L. (1996). The challenges of a diverse society: Counseling for mutual respect and understanding. *Counseling and Human Development, 28*(5), 1–8.

Lee, C. C., & Richardson, B. L. (1991). Promise and pitfalls of multicultural counseling. In C. C. Lee & B. L. Richardson (Eds.), *Multicultural issues in counseling: New approaches to diversity* (pp. 3–9). Alexandria, VA: American Counseling Association.

Lee, R. M, Choe, J., Kim, G., & Ngo, V. (2000). Construction of the Asian American family conflicts scale. *Journal of Counseling Psychology, 47,* 211–222.

LeVine, E., & Padilla, A. (1980). *Cross cultures in therapy: Pluralistic counseling for the Hispanic.* Pacific Grove, CA: Brooks/Cole.

London, H., & Devore, W. (1992). Layers of understanding: Counseling ethnic minority families. In R. L. Smith & P. Stevens-Smith (Eds.), *Family counseling and therapy* (pp. 358–371). Ann Arbor, MI: ERIC/CAPS.

Manson, S. M., Tatum, E., & Dinges, N. G. (1982). Prevention research among American Indian and Alaska Native communities: Charting further courses for theory and practice in mental health. In S. M. Manson (Ed.), *New directions in prevention among American Indian and Alaska Native Communities* (pp. 1–61). Portland, OR: Oregon Health Sciences University.

Mason, M. J. (1991). Family therapy as the emerging context for sex therapy. In A. S. Gurman & D. P. Kniskern (Eds.), *Handbook of family therapy* (Vol. II, pp. 479–507). New York: Brunner/Mazel.

May, K. M. (1994, Winter). Gay and lesbian families. *The Family Digest, 7,* 1, 3.

McAdoo, H. P. (1982). Stress absorbing systems in black families. *Family Relations, 31,* 479–488.

McGoldrick, M. (1986, November/December). Irish families. *Family Therapy Networker, 10,* 31.

McGoldrick, M., & Giordano, J. (1996). Overview: Empathy and family therapy. In M. McGoldrick, J. Giordano, & J. K. Pearce (Eds.), *Ethnicity and family therapy* (2nd ed., pp. 1–27). New York: Guilford.

McGoldrick, M., Preto, N. G., Hines, P. M., & Lee, E. (1991). Ethnicity and family therapy. In A. S. Gurman & D. P. Kniskern (Eds.), *Handbook of family therapy* (Vol. II, pp. 546–582). New York: Brunner/Mazel.

McGoldrick, M., & Rohrbaugh, M. (1987). Researching ethnic family stereotypes. *Family Process, 1,* 89–100.

Mercado, M. M. (2000). The invisible family: Counseling Asian American substance abusers and their families. *The Family Journal, 8,* 267–272.

Minuchin, S. (1974). *Families and family therapy.* Cambridge, MA: Harvard University Press.

Napier, A. Y., & Whitaker, C. (1978). *The family crucible.* New York: Bantam Books.

Napoliello, A. L., & Sweet, E. S. (1992). Salvador Minuchin's structural family therapy and its application to Native Americans. *Family Therapy, 19,* 155–165.

Newlon, B. J., & Arciniega, M. (1991). Counseling minority families: An Adlerian perspective. In J. Carlson & J. Lewis (Eds.), *Family counseling: Strategies and issues* (pp. 189–223). Denver, CO: Love.

Olson, D. H. (2000). *Marriage and the family: Diversity and strengths* (3rd ed.). Mountain View, CA: Mayfield Publishing.

Patten, J. (1992, October). Gay and lesbian families. *Family Therapy News, 23,* 10, 34.

Peterson, K. S. (2000, March 8). Black couples stay the course. *USA Today,* p. 8D.

Ponce, A. (1995, Winter). The Hispanic family. *The Family Digest, 7,* 7, 11.

Ponterotto, J. G. (1987). Counseling Mexican-Americans: A multimodal approach. *Journal of Counseling and Development, 65,* 308–312.

Puente, M. (1993, July 16). Hispanics debating their "destiny" in USA. *USA Today,* p. 10A.

Richardson, B. L. (1991). Utilizing the resources of the African American church: Strategies for counseling professionals. In C. C. Lee & B. L. Richardson (Eds.), *Multicultural issues in counseling: New approaches to diversity* (pp. 65–75). Alexandria, VA: American Counseling Association.

Rowe, W., Bennett, S. K., & Atkinson, D. R. (1994). White racial identity models: A critique and alternative proposal. *The Counseling Psychologist, 22,* 129–146.

Ruiz, A. (1981). Cultural and historical perspectives in counseling Hispanics. In D. W. Sue (Ed.), *Counseling the culturally different: Theory & practice* (pp. 186–215). New York: Wiley.

Santisteban, D. A., & Szapocznik, J. (1994). Bridging theory, research and practice to more successfully engage substance abusing youth and their families into therapy. *Journal of Child & Adolescent Substance Abuse, 3,* 9–24.

Sayger, T. V., Homrich, A. M., & Horne, A. M. (2000). Working with a family focus. In A. M. Horne (Ed.), *Family Counseling and Therapy* (3rd ed., pp. 12–40). Itasca, IL: F. E. Peacock.

Schacht, A. J., Tafoya, N., & Mirabla, K. (1989). Home-based therapy with American Indian families. *American Indian and Alaska Native Mental Health Research, 3,* 27–42.

Sciarra, D. T., & Ponterotto, J. G. (1991). Counseling the Hispanic bilingual family: Challenges to the therapeutic process. *Psychotherapy, 28,* 473–479.

Snead, E. (1993, July 13). Lesbians in the limelight. *USA Today,* pp. D1, D2.

Stovall, T. (2000). *A love supreme: Real-life stories of black love.* New York: Warner.

Sue, D. (1994, Spring). Incorporating cultural diversity in family therapy. *The Family Psychologist, 10,* 19–21.

Sue, D. W., & Sue, D. (1999). *Counseling the culturally different* (3rd ed.). New York: Wiley.

Sue, S., & Morishima, J. K. (1982). *The mental health of Asian Americans.* San Francisco: Jossey-Bass.

Szapocznik, J., & Kurtines, W. M. (1993). Family psychology and cultural diversity: Opportunities for theory, research, and application. *American Psychologist, 48,* 400–407.

Tafoya, T. (1989). Circles and cedar: Native Americans and family therapy. *Journal of Psychotherapy and the Family, 6,* 71–98.

Tafoya, T. (1994, Spring). Epistemology of native healing and family psychology. *The Family Psychologist, 10,* 28–31.

Thomas, A. J. (1998). Understanding culture and worldview in family systems: Use of the multicultural genogram. *The Family Journal, 6,* 24–32.

Tseng, W.-S., & Hsu, J. (1991). *Culture and family.* Binghamton, NY: Haworth.

Turner, W. L. (1993, April). Identifying African-American family strengths. *Family Therapy News, 24,* 9, 14.

Usdansky, M. L. (1993, August 23). Census shows diversity of Hispanics in USA. *USA Today,* p. A1.

Walsh, F. (1982). Conceptualization of normal family functioning. In F. Walsh (Ed.), *Normal family processes* (pp. 3–44). New York: Guilford.

Watzlawick, P. (1976). *How real is real?* New York: Random House.

*Webster's ninth new collegiate dictionary.* (1989). Springfield, MA: Merriam-Webster.

Willis, J. T. (1988). An effective counseling model for treating the Black family. *Family Therapy, 15,* 185–194.

Willis, J. T. (1990). Some destructive elements in African-American male–female relationships. *Family Therapy, 17,* 139–147.

Wilson, L. L., & Stith, S. M. (1991). Cultural sensitive therapy with black clients. *Journal of Multicultural Counseling and Development, 19,* 32–43.

Wrenn, C. G. (1962). The culturally-encapsulated counselor. *Harvard Educational Review, 32,* 444–449.

Wrenn, C. G. (1985). Afterward: The culturally-encapsulated counselor revisited. In P. B. Pedersen (Ed.), *Handbook of cross-cultural counseling and therapy.* Westport, CT: Greenwood Press.

# CHAPTER 14

# Working with Substance-Related Disorders, Domestic Violence, and Child Abuse in Families

As an old dog, he has survived
the marriage of his master to a Nutmeg woman,
the first clumsy steps of sandy-haired toddlers,
and the crises of moves around eastern states.

So in the gentle first light of morning
he rolls leisurely in piles of yesterday's clothes
left over from last night's baths by little boys,
an act of independence.

Then slowly, with a slight limp,
he enters his daily routine,
approaching the kitchen at the breakfast rush hour
to quietly consume spilled cereal
and dodge the congested foot traffic.

Sure of his place in a system of change
he lays down to sleep by an air vent.

A family grows around him.

*Gladding, 1991*

**A**buse of any kind within a family is tragic. Yet, like a plague that cripples and kills, abuse has been pervasive through time and cultures. It has affected families in different life cycles and in distinct ways. It has taken a number of forms, for example, substance-related, spouse, and child abuse, and its impact on lives has been physical, mental, sexual, and economical.

Abuse is an entity from which families may recover, but its presence is a factor that continues to haunt families and their members long after the actions associated with it have ended. In short, abuse is a blight that stains and puts a strain on a family even after it has outwardly disappeared. In this chapter three forms of abuse—substance-related, domestic violence, and child abuse—will be examined in regard to the nature and appropriate treatment of each. Substance-related disorders will be used as an overall model of how to engage families into therapy. However, in treating abuse in families, it must be remembered that each case, like each family, is unique.

# Substance-Related ■ Disorders and Families ■

Substance-related disorders are "disorders related to the taking of a drug of abuse (including alcohol), to the side effects of medication, and to toxin exposure" (American Psychiatric Association [APA], 1994, p. 175). For diagnostic purposes, substances are grouped into 11 classes: "alcohol; amphetamines or similar acting sympathomimetics; caffeine; cannabis; cocaine; hallucinogens; inhalants; nicotine; opioids; phencyclidine (PCP) . . . and sedatives, hypnotics, or anxiolytics" (p. 175).

Substance-related disorders due to the side effects of medication and to toxin exposure will not be covered here because problems regarding substances for most families tend to be associated with the taking of a drug of abuse. Indeed, nearly 60% of the world's production of illegal drugs and a substantial percentage of legal alcohol products are consumed in the United States. Overall, approximately 1 in 11 Americans suffers from severe addictive problems, and "one third of all American families are affected by alcohol problems" (Daw, 1995, p. 19).

In the particular area of alcohol problems there are two general levels or forms of **alcohol use disorders.** The first is **alcohol abuse,** "a problem pattern where the drinking interferes with work, school, or home life" in addition to other difficulties with the law and society (Stanton, 1999, p. 1). The second is **alcohol dependency** where the person is unable to control the drinking even after trying.

Regardless of the level or form, as a group substance-related disorders are considered to be family based and supported with individuals in families abusing various substances for a variety of reasons, for example, as a way of coping with crisis or connecting with one another (Schroeder, 1989). Yet instead of helping family members relate, the substance-related disorders have a profound negative effect on individual and family life cycles. Developmental stages are altered significantly, for example, young adults going off to college may find they are unable to assimilate into the academic and social environment and make necessary adjustments (Cutler & Radford, 1999).

Similarly, families of addicts are often stuck in a lifestyle that promotes dependency of the young and a false sense of identity known as **pseudo-individuation**. Young people in such circumstances lack basic coping skills and fail to achieve real identity. As a result, they become "competent within a framework of incompetence" (Stanton et al., 1982, p. 19). Therefore, they become marginalized in society and noncontributors to it.

# Manifestation of Substance-Related Disorders

Substance-related disorders impact both families and the individuals within them. Thus, while a person with a substance-related disorder may think that taking a substance is only an intrapersonal problem, he or she is wrong. The behaviors that go with substance abuse or dependence permeate and penetrate into other relationships and impact the actions of everyone who comes in contact with the person who has the disorder.

## Family Manifestations

Families deal with substance-related disorders in a number of ways. Unhealthy or dysfunctional methods of working with the situation and person(s) involved are usually tried initially and are displayed through various strategies, including the following.

One way for the family to deal with the seriousness of a substance-related disorder problem is through denial. In such a scenario, the family pretends that the existence of the disorder is not present in their household. For example, a spouse may make excuses for his or her mate by saying that the substance abuser's actions were due to other circumstances, such as fatigue or frivolity. This strategy is somewhat akin to not acknowledging an elephant in one's living room.

Another way a family may deal with the existence of a substance-related disorder is through the expression of negative feelings. In such a scenario members of the family, except for the abuser(s), experience a plethora of unpleasant emotions such as fear, anger, shame, guilt, resentment, insecurity, confusion, and rejection. When a family is caught up in such a whirlwind of affect, they relate to each other and to the outside world in a despondent and anxious manner.

Still a third way for a family to manifest a substance-related disorder is for family members to assume roles that allow them and others to survive. Among these roles, according to Murphy (1984) are the **enabler**, a spouse or other family member on whom the substance abuser is most dependent and who allows a substance abuser to continue and become worse; the **family hero**, an adult or oldest child who functions to provide self-worth for the family; the **scapegoat**, often a child who attempts to distract the family focus away from the substance abuser by acting out in a disruptive manner and being blamed for the family's problems; the **lost child**, usually a child in the family who suffers from rejection and loneliness and who offers a substance abuser family relief; and the **family clown**, who is often the youngest member of the family and whose function is to provide the family with humor and thus reduce tension.

A fourth way for a family to display a substance-related disorder is for it to deteriorate. In these cases members of an entire family may do such things as drink or take drugs together. This type of behavior is not common but it does occur especially as children in families grow into adolescents. Usually, within a family the consumption of a harmful substance is centered around an adult or adults as in the play *Who's Afraid of Virginia Woolf*.

Another pattern that highlights a substance-related disorder is for the family to focus all of their energy on the substance abuser. In this type of reaction, the family as a whole may spend the majority of their time begging, pleading, blaming, or shaming a substance abusing or dependent family member for all of the family's problems. For instance, a son might spend countless hours trying to help his father stay sober in the belief that the family would become a warm and loving entity if that happened.

A final way a substance-related disorder is shown in a family is for parents to misuse or abuse not only the substance in question but also the family resources. As a result the entire family suffers physically because of a lack of money and effort to purchase essential necessities. A popular book of the late 1990s, *Angela's Ashes* (McCourt, 1996) describes the impact of such parental substance abuse, in this case alcohol. *Angela's Ashes* and other literature point out that family members, especially children, may be severely affected in multiple ways because of substance-related disorders.

## Individual Manifestations

In addition to families showing the affects of substance-related disorders, individuals within families also display manifestations. For example, children may behave confused about their self-identity and self-worth. As a result, they may become controlling in their interpersonal relationships as a way of gaining security (Schroeder, 1989). Children who live in an environment where at least one parent is an abuser of alcohol are twice as likely as their counterparts to develop "social and emotional problems," such as low school achievement and trouble with the law (Lawson, 1994, p. 213).

Also, adults who have grown up in families where there was a substance-related disorder may spend considerable time and energy attempting to resolve issues related to the dysfunctional nature of their families of origin. For example, many adults coming from an alcohol abuse family environment struggle in dealing with feelings of numbness, a sense of guilt, confusion, denial, and compulsive behavior (Black, 1990). Their intrapersonal relations with themselves and interpersonal dynamics with others are affected and they may be unable to form long-lasting and intimate relationships.

# Engaging Substance-Related Disorder Families in Treatment

Families with substance-related problems, especially where alcohol is the primary drug, are frequently treated with family therapy (Edwards & Steinglass, 1995). In fact, family therapy is one of the preferred means of working with families who are faced with substance-related disorders. "The consequences of not treating a family that has become dysfunctional by the substance abuse of a family member can be disastrous for the family, the chemically dependent individual, or both" (Murphy, 1984, p. 106). However, getting the family to agree to therapy is often a challenge:

> The task of engaging an entire family unit from the onset is a very difficult, yet critical component of the family therapy process. This may be particularly true when working with minority families because cultural factors can create unique family dynamics that become intertwined with the complex issue of engagement. (Santisteban & Szapocznik, 1994, pp. 9–10)

One way to get the family engaged is to involve **concerned significant others** (CSOs) in the process of treatment. CSOs can be spouses, relatives, or children of the substance abuser or dependent person. The success of such a strategy has proven to be effective in engaging initially unmotivated problem drinkers in treatment (Miller, Meyers, & Tonigan, 1999). Rates of success for such an approach are high (64%) and have proved to be better than interventions from other professional groups. Overall, treatment engagement rates are highest for CSOs who are parents than for spouses.

Another way to engage families in the process of treatment is to widen "the focus of attention from providing therapy once a family brings itself to the clinic to considering that the treatment begins prior to the first clinic visit" (Santisteban & Szapocznik, 1994, pp. 11–12). In this emphasis, the interaction between the therapist and the family is included in the formation of a therapeutic system. A de-emphasis is placed on the therapist as the ally of the family member who made the initial call. Instead, issues in diagnosing potential obstacles to engaging the family include those involving the family system (e.g., characteristics and/or interactional patterns of the family) and issues involving the therapeutic system (e.g., the interface/interaction between the family system and the therapist).

The developmental issue that may present itself most blatantly in this early stage of treatment is the status of the identified patient in the family system. The **identified patient (IP)** is usually an extremely powerful member of the family whose development has been arrested and who is generally resistant to therapy because to engage in the process is to agree to someone else's agenda and weaken one's own position of power. Therefore, if such families are going to be brought successfully into family therapy, especially if the IP is an adolescent, the therapist must contact the identified patient directly and immediately. In this contact, the therapist makes it clear that he or she "would like to explore the IP's goals" (Santisteban & Szapoczik, 1994, p. 16).

To engage a substance-related disorder family to the fullest, the family therapist may also call the person in the family who is most disengaged, often a father, or another family member who is "allegedly unwilling" to enter family therapy. In these cases, a direct conversation may be persuasive in helping such a family member realize that he or she has much to contribute to the therapeutic process. Likewise, if a family is fearful or suspicious of where therapy will lead, the therapist must reframe the process so that the family is in agreement as to the specific nature of what will be worked on so they will feel more in control.

# Approaches for Treating Substance-Related Disorder Families After Engagement

Individuals and families who are engaged in substance-related activities are often difficult to treat. Many have a high degree of resistance to therapy, and relapse may be frequent with up to 90% having one relapse during the first 4 years following treatment (Diamond, 2000). Therefore, to help rehabilitate these individuals and their families once they have been engaged, therapists are wise to realize that recovery is a matter of "phasing" in treatment to fit the developmental readiness of the family (Berenson, 1992). Thus, recovery is a process that occurs in stages.

Areas that must be addressed within families are issues dealing with physical, emotional, social, and vocational impairments. All of these areas influence each other systematically. For example, physical factors, such as excessive drinking and the behaviors that accompany it, such as undue disorderliness, spill over and impact emotional, social, and vocational arenas of the family. The reverse occurs too. Fortunately, there are a number of ways to address these family dynamics (Lewis, 1994).

Probably the most important dimension to initially address in families who are in treatment for substance-related problems is "environmental influences" (Lawson, 1994, p. 213). Environmental influences include the physical aspects of a family's life, such as getting the substance abuse behavior stopped, for example, getting the abuser "dry." This process may involve a detoxification center where the abuser is helped physically and psychologically to give up the substance he or she has been abusing.

Once substance-related behavior, such as abuse, stops, then the family can enter a new phase of treatment such as determining when and where they interact as well as how they engage in activities both within and outside the environment in which they live. These physical influences can be manipulated more easily early on in the therapeutic process and can help the family realize the power of simple change, for example, rearranging times when tasks are done or assigning different individuals to complete essential jobs needed to keep the family functioning.

In addition to making environmental changes, clinicians must help individual family members, as well as the family, with emotional, social, and vocational issues. In situations where an adolescent is the identified patient, a primary role of the family therapist is to make an assessment and decision about the use of the substance an adolescent may be abusing. That task is required for members of this population because drug consumption can take three forms with adolescents: experimenting, dependence, or addiction (Schroeder, 1989). If the adolescent is merely experimenting, issues surrounding consumption can be addressed in an easier and more straightforward manner than if the adolescent has become dependent on or addicted to a substance. In the case of dependence and addiction, dysfunctional behaviors in families arise and professional intervention is both warranted and needed.

Among other issues that must be addressed in families where there are substance-related problems are feelings (e.g., anger, intimacy), defense mechanisms (e.g., denial, projection), and work by individuals in these families. In the process, therapists help the family and its members take responsibility for behaviors that before have been minimized, excused, or enabled (Krestan & Bepko, 1988). In essence, they help the family get back on track as a functional system by getting "involved in the treatment process" and "helping the abusing member overcome . . . addiction, rather than serving as a force that maintains it" (Van Deusen, Stanton, Scott, Todd, & Mowatt, 1982, p. 39).

Ways in which therapists assist families are often tied to specific family theories (Todd & Selekman, 1991). Among the most prominent approaches that have been used with substance-related disorder families are structural-strategic, Bowenian, behavioral, Adlerian, and multifamily therapies. In addition, increased emphasis has been placed on preventive efforts that involve marshaling community resources as well (Bry, 1994).

## Structural-Strategic Family Therapy

Early in its history, family therapy addressed the problem of substance abuse as a family systems problem. The documentation of the effectiveness of family therapy forms of treatment for drug abuse and addiction was particularly well demonstrated in the structural/strategic emphasis of Stanton et al. (1982) and Todd and Selekman (1991). The meticulous work of these researchers underscores the importance of family dynamics in such situations, and the crucial nature of involving the entire family in treatment.

Among the recommended models for treatment and prevention of substance-related family disorders from a structural-strategic approach are the following. Treatment should initially address excessive drinking or other forms of substance abuse in order to get it stopped. Such a process might mean getting inpatient detoxification, enrolling appropriate family members in Alcoholics Anonymous (AA) or Al-Anon, and mobilizing support networks. After the abuse of substances has come to an end, then treatment based on clear thinking and a drug-free mind can begin, using a combination of structural/strategic family therapy methods.

Structural family therapy may be used just by itself as well. For instance, in working with a multigenerational Hispanic stepfamily experiencing alcohol dependence, Wycoff and Cameron (2000) found that "because structural family therapy is action oriented . . . and encourages active participation by the counselor, it lends itself nicely to the educative and supportive facilitation process needed during the early recovery period for the alcohol dependent family" (p. 52). Family mapping, searching for family strengths, the use of praise, and respecting as well as working within cultural traditions produced needed results in the modification of the family structure.

## Bowenian Family Therapy

Effective therapy for alcohol abuse families may also take a Bowenian family therapy approach (Bowen, 1974). Bowenian theory is especially helpful as a component in implementing a program that deals with codependency treatment (Gibson & Donigian, 1993). In **codependency** there is a dynamic in a family of overresponsibility (the codependent family member, usually a spouse) and underresponsibility (the substance abuser) (Morgan, 1998). However, in the Bowenian model of family therapy, emphasis is placed on the differentiation of oneself and achieving an interplay between two counterbalancing life forces–individuality and togetherness. Thus, the family therapist works with both the substance-related abuser and codependent in the family to help them and the family become balanced. This process is often worked out by toning down the functioning of the overre-sponsible member (i.e., the codependent), since it is easier to do so than to boost up the behavior of the underresponsible member of the family.

In reaching a balanced state of being, individuals, especially those with low self-esteem such as codependents, learn to distinguish between subjective feelings and objective thoughts. Thus, they become more flexible, adaptable, and independent. Through the use of genograms, "I" position statements, and reconnections of emotional cutoffs, codependents gain a greater awareness and understanding of how family patterns developed and have been maintained (Gibson & Donigian, 1993). Thereby, they gain a greater freedom to change how they relate to all family members and to stop behaving in ways that either make them dependent or that enable someone in the family to be a substance-related abuser.

## Behavioral Family Therapy

Behavioral therapies have produced good results in treating families with a substance-related problem, particularly alcohol abuse. A number of behaviors can be specified and modified in behaviorally oriented approaches to treatment by incorporating basic behavioral methods such as reinforcement, modeling, rehearsal, and extinction.

Written behavioral contracts may be particularly effective. These contracts have a number of common elements that make them useful. In these documents the drinking behavior goal is made explicit. Furthermore, specific behaviors that each spouse can incorporate to help achieve this goal are detailed. The contract provides alternative behaviors to negative interactions about drinking, too. "Finally, the agreement decreases the nonalcoholic spouse's anxiety and need to control the alcoholic and his or her drinking" (O'Farrell, 1996, p. 106).

## Adlerian Therapy

The Adlerian approach to working with substance-related abusers in families is premised on the idea that members of such families are discouraged. Treatment then is designed to increase the social interest of family members, particularly those who may be most affected by the abuse (Odom, Snow, & Kern, 1999). The problem of substance-related abuse is reframed also from one that is disease focused to one that is socially focused.

One way to increase social interest and consequently the health and functioning of the family is to work with the parents and children in multiple ways. A major avenue of intervention from this perspective is to get parents involved in a group that helps increase their self-esteem as well as their skills. Systematic Training for Effective Parenting (STEP) is such a group that can help parents increase their understanding of family relations as well as improve their communications with their children (Dinkmeyer & McKay, 1989). A child who may have been parentified because of the dysfunctioning of the family system may also be used and can serve as a cofacilitator in family therapy. As such, the child can both role play situations in the STEP program and otherwise educate or reeducate parents about what works in family relations (Odom et al., 1999).

## Multifamily Therapy

Another way of working with families who have individuals who are substance-related abusers is through multifamily therapy. The idea behind multifamily therapy is to treat several families at the same time (Laqueur, 1976). Such treatment is not only cost effective but is also reported to have a high success rate. In these settings, according to Carl Whitaker, a person may experience his or her dynamics in other families, "whereas the same dynamics could be overwhelming to address in the context of one's own family" (Boylin, Doucette, & Jean, 1997, p. 400).

One of the prime beneficiaries of multifamily therapy are women who often feel more pressure to leave treatment before they are ready because of family obligations. "By attending multifamily therapy, the family gives the client permission to stay in treatment and demonstrates that its members are managing at home without the client" (Boylin et al., 1997, p. 45).

## Use of Community Resources and Prevention

Outside community resources are often essential in helping a substance-related abuse family help itself. These resources can be informative as well as supportive of the family as it wrestles with overcoming substance-related abuse. For example, family members may participate in Alcoholics Anonymous (AA), Narcotics Anonymous (NA), and Al-Anon as complements to almost any therapeutic approach (Berenson, 1992; Morgan, 1998). By participating in such groups, family members gain insight into themselves and how their behaviors affect family functioning. Furthermore, they learn from others who have similar experiences and backgrounds how they are coping with substance-related abuse and what works for them.

Prevention from substance-related abuse is a critical element in treatment as well. Prevention is dependent on both keeping a person or family from engaging in the habitual activity of taking substances and on making other activities with reliable positive outcomes (e.g., art, athletic, hobbies, meaningful work) available and central to their lives (Bry, 1994). At its best, prevention involves the substance-related abuse family in community activities. In such an environment, the family becomes more consistent in its effort and sustains it better. At present, policies in the United States do not encourage prevention on such a level. Thus, more individualized and piecemeal programs prevail. For example, in regard to teen alcohol abuse, forms of prevention that are recommended include:

- giving kids accurate information about alcohol use in an objective way;
- presenting information through a 'teen-respected' source;
- helping kids say yes to life, not just no to drugs;
- parent networking;
- setting strict rules about drinking with kids and
- continued pressure to "take back the communities" (Daw, 1995, p. 19)

While some of these preventive efforts involve networking and the setting up of structure, such as making rules, they are not usually tied to specific organizations. Until or unless more community resources are made available to help "people from outside the family to support parents' efforts to reduce their adolescents' substance abuse," it is doubtful that the preventive efforts under way for primary prevention in this arena will have more than scattered success (Bry, 1994, p. 21).

On the other hand, secondary and tertiary prevention for family members of substance-related abusers and substance-related abusers themselves may be more successful. Recovery and prevention programs such as 12-step programs are aimed at keeping substance-related abusers free from the resumption of the habits that harmed their family

lives. In addition, family programs, such as Al-Anon, assist family members in both understanding the dynamics involved in substance-related abuse and ways of not enabling the
abuser to resume his or her past destructive behavior. Other self-help groups, such as
Rational Recovery or Women for Sobriety, can also provide assistance in offering support
for substance-related abusers and their families (Lawson, 1994).

# ■ Domestic Violence and Families ■

**Domestic violence** refers to "aggression that takes place in intimate relationships, usually
between adults" (Kemp, 1998, p. 225). The topic is referred to in a number of ways,
including "spousal abuse," "partner abuse," and "marital violence." Domestic violence can
take many forms, including physical, sexual, psychological, and economic (see Figure
14.1) (Schecter & Ganley, 1995). The worst form of domestic violence is referred to as
**battering**—"violence which includes severe physical assault or risk of serious injury"
(Kemp, 1998, p. 225).

Increasing attention is being given to domestic violence in the United States. The reason is that "approximately one-third of all married couples experience physical aggression"
(Crespi & Howe, 2000, p. 6). Although some men are the victims of abuse and violence by
their mates, the large majority of those assaulted each year are women. Those who batter
come in "all shapes, sizes, classes, races, and sexual orientation" (Almeida, 2000, p. 23).

About 13% of all murders involve husbands killing their wives, and at least 1.6 million
wives are severely beaten by their husbands each year (Gottman et al., 1995). Even premarital rates of physical violence are high—about 36% (McLaughlin, Leonard, & Senchak, 1992). "Not surprisingly, there is a well-documented association between alcohol
intoxication and battering, with most research indicating a 60% to 70% rate of alcohol
abuse among men who batter" (Wycoff & Cameron, 2000, p. 53).

## Assessment of Domestic Violence

Several barriers impede the assessment of the degree of domestic violence that couples
and families experience. These barriers include those that are legal, such as court orders
that mandate separation of family members from one another, and those that are psychological, such as the stigma that surrounds abuse of this nature.

In assessing domestic violence, one of the first things to realize is that "determining the
level and prevalence of violence within the family is extremely difficult," yet important
and essential (Rotter & Houston, 1999, p. 59). The reason is that without this knowledge, the therapist will not know how best to work with the family. Yet, violent families
will go to almost any lengths to keep this family secret hidden. Furthermore, there is a
tendency is these families to minimize the amount of violence and its impact on the family
and relationships.

However, assessing the level of violence may be done in a number of ways. For example, determining the power imbalance within the family is one place to start. This assessment helps individuals make the transition from violent to nonviolent behavior and

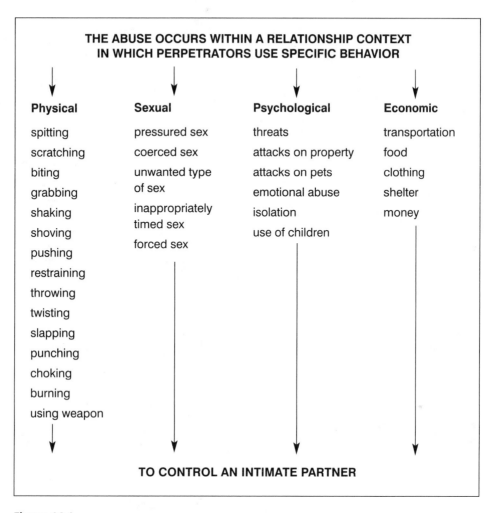

THE ABUSE OCCURS WITHIN A RELATIONSHIP CONTEXT
IN WHICH PERPETRATORS USE SPECIFIC BEHAVIOR

**Physical**

spitting

scratching

biting

grabbing

shaking

shoving

pushing

restraining

throwing

twisting

slapping

punching

choking

burning

using weapon

**Sexual**

pressured sex

coerced sex

unwanted type
of sex

inappropriately
timed sex

forced sex

**Psychological**

threats

attacks on property

attacks on pets

emotional abuse

isolation

use of children

**Economic**

transportation

food

clothing

shelter

money

TO CONTROL AN INTIMATE PARTNER

**Figure 14.1**

Graphic representation of Schecter and Ganley's definition model.

This material was adapted from "Understanding Domestic Violence," by S. Schecter and A. Ganley, in *Domestic Violence: A National Curriculum for Family Preservation Practitioners*, written by Susan Schechter, M.S.W., and Anne L. Ganley, PhD. Copyright © 1995 Family Violence Prevention Fund.

assists them in learning what each is. Pence and Paymar (1993) have created two wheels to illustrate the difference: a "power and control wheel" (Figure 14.2), aimed particularly at men, and an "equality wheel" (Figure 14.3), aimed at promoting positive behaviors such as mutuality, respect, and egalitarianism.

Assessment when conducted in an open manner usually results in obtaining the most information. An open assessment is one where blame is not a primary emphasis and also one where the therapist emphasizes that the expression of violence in the family hurts the

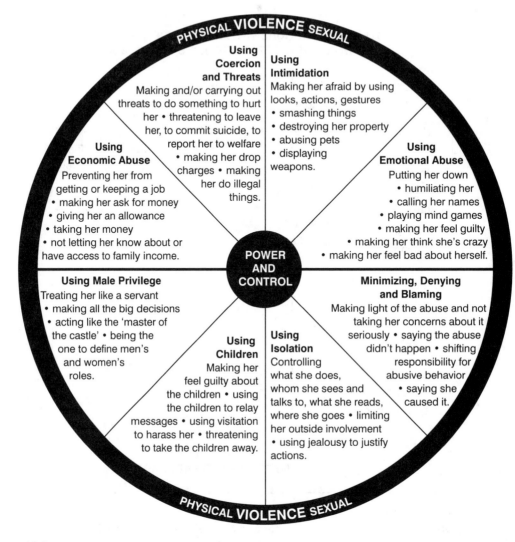

**Figure 14.2**
Power and control wheel.

From *Education Groups for Men Who Batter,* by E. Pence and M. Paymar. Copyright © 1993 Springer Publishing Company, Inc. New York, 10012. Used by permission.

entire family rather than just one person (Almeida, 2000). Therefore, the focus of the assessment centers around dynamics within the family associated with family relationships, such as emotional expression, handling of money, sexuality, and social connections. It is the interconnection of these aspects of interpersonal life that signals whether there is a harmful power imbalance in the family and therefore gives clues as to what can or should be changed and to what degree.

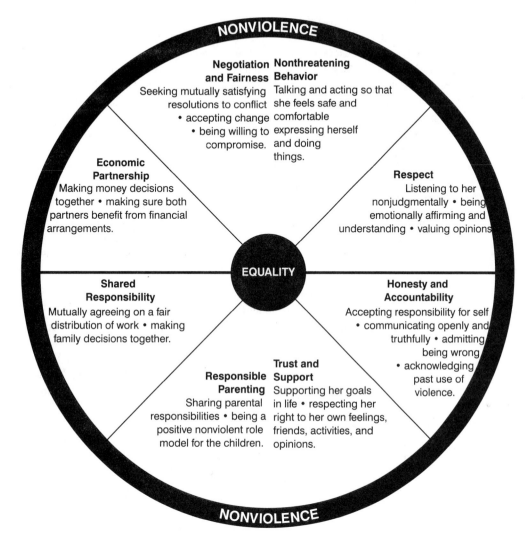

**Figure 14.3**
Equality wheel.

From *Education Groups for Men Who Batter,* by E. Pence and M. Paymar. Copyright © 1993 Springer Publishing Company, Inc. New York, 10012. Used by permission.

# Approaches for Treating Domestic Violence

Once an assessment of domestic violence is made, various treatment options are available, including those that are individually, group, educationally, and family systems focused. In family therapy "two positions have typified popular ideas about responsibility and domestic violence: (1) both parties are equally responsible for the violence; and (2) the perpetuator is unilaterally responsible" (Bograd, 1999, p. 284). The position that a family therapist takes in regard to responsibility influences the type of treatment option chosen.

If the therapist assumes both parties have equal responsibility in spousal abuse and domestic violence cases, then traditional conjoint or couples therapy may be used in some cases. On the other hand, if the perpetuator is seen as having unilateral responsibility, then an intimate justice theory may be employed that is based on an ethics of accountability from the abuser and is employed on an individual and couple level (Jory & Anderson, 2000; Rotter & Houston, 1999). In the intimate justice approach, it is up to the abuser to recognize that abuse and accountability are related and to thereby make needed changes. The benefits and limitations of both approaches are discussed here.

## Conjoint or Couples Therapy

**Conjoint therapy** involves seeing the couple together. "A primary concern about the wisdom of couples therapy is the woman's safety" (Bograd & Mederos, 1999, p. 293). This concern requires an assessment of safety issues. According to Bograd and Mederos (1999) three conditions must be satisfied to ensure safety:

- the man's participation must be voluntary;
- "special agreements about confidentiality must be established," that is, material on domestic violence will not be disclosed by the woman or the therapist until the woman is ready; and
- "an optimal therapeutic stance must be achieved" (p. 294), that is, the therapist must be able to "create a context of self-protection" (p. 296) since working with domestic violence is often emotionally disturbing, dehumanizing, and intimidating.

In such circumstances couple therapy may work if the following criteria are met:

- There has been only a history of minor and infrequent psychological violence or abuse.
- There are no risk factors for lethality, such as prior use or threat of weapons.
- The man admits and takes responsibility for abusive behavior and also demonstrates an ongoing commitment to contain his explosive feelings without blaming others or acting them out (Bograd & Mederos, 1999).

In this approach, the couple talks about their wishes as well as the dynamics currently present in their relationships. Through such communication, agreement can be reached as to new or altered ways of behaving and relating.

## Intimate Justice

**Intimate justice theory** "includes the ethical context of abuse and violence in intimate relationships" (Rotter & Houston, 1999, p. 60). "Intimate justice theory encompasses three ethical dimensions and nine ethical concepts" (Jory & Anderson, 1999, p. 350). See Figures 14.4 and 14.5. Furthermore, the theory "encourages therapists to confront, challenge, explore, and educate clients about abuse of power in emotional systems" (Jory & Anderson, 1999, p. 350).

Overall, intimate justice theory is akin to solution-based approaches and confronts disempowerment and abuses of power in a partnership while challenging internalized beliefs about how one should treat one's partner (Jory, Anderson, & Greer, 1997). The approach

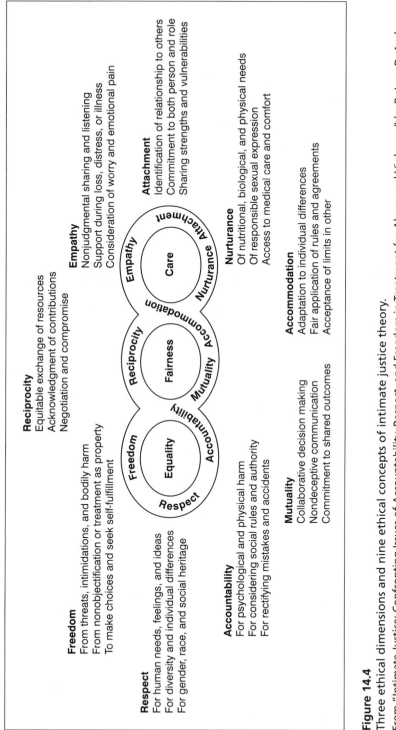

**Freedom**
From threats, intimidations, and bodily harm
From nonobjectification or treatment as property
To make choices and seek self-fulfillment

**Respect**
For human needs, feelings, and ideas
For diversity and individual differences
For gender, race, and social heritage

**Accountability**
For psychological and physical harm
For considering social rules and authority
For rectifying mistakes and accidents

**Mutuality**
Collaborative decision making
Nondeceptive communication
Commitment to shared outcomes

**Reciprocity**
Equitable exchange of resources
Acknowledgment of contributions
Negotiation and compromise

**Empathy**
Nonjudgmental sharing and listening
Support during loss, distress, or illness
Consideration of worry and emotional pain

**Attachment**
Identification of relationship to others
Commitment to both person and role
Sharing strengths and vulnerabilities

**Nurturance**
Of nutritional, biological, and physical needs
Of responsible sexual expression
Access to medical care and comfort

**Accommodation**
Adaptation to individual differences
Fair application of rules and agreements
Acceptance of limits in other

**Figure 14.4**
Three ethical dimensions and nine ethical concepts of intimate justice theory.

From "Intimate Justice: Confronting Issues of Accountability, Respect, and Freedom in Treatment for Abuse and Violence," by B. Jory, D. Anderson, and C. Greer, 1997, *Journal of Marital and Family Therapy, 23,* 350. Copyright 1997, American Association for Marriage and Family Therapy. Reprinted with permission.

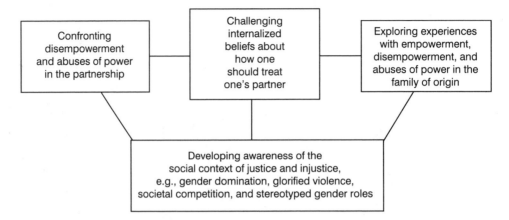

**Figure 14.5**
Confronting, challenging, and educating clients about abuses of power in emotional systems.
From "Intimate Justice: Confronting Issues of Accountability, Respect, and Freedom in Treatment for Abuse and Violence," by B. Jory, D. Anderson, and C. Greer, 1997, *Journal of Marital and Family Therapy, 23*, 350. Copyright 1997, American Association for Marriage and Family Therapy. Reprinted with permission.

also explores experiences with empowerment, disempowerment, and abuses of power in one's family of origin. It has been found to be effective as a treatment for abuse in couples who voluntarily enter therapy (Jory & Anderson, 2000). Through knowledge and insight, both behavioral attitudes and behaviors in couples may be modified.

### Educational Treatment

Educationally, programs based on intimate justice theory and cognitive behavior theory have also been employed with domestic violence families. One such is the Duluth model, which is a cognitive-behavioral model of treatment (Pence & Paymar, 1993). The premise of this model is that people learn violent behaviors because of being reinforced for them in cultural and social circles. They can therefore unlearn these behaviors and learn new ones through cognitive-behavioral means, such as education.

Almeida (2000) argues that social and educational programs that are based on cognitive-behavioral principles are effective in producing rehabilitation in perpetrators if they are long lasting. The term *long lasting,* according to Almeida, means a time span of at least a year. Participants must be held accountable for their actions, too.

# Child Abuse and ◾ Neglect in Families ◾

With the lifestyle changes that have occurred in the forms and behaviors of American families in recent years, concern has increased over the welfare and well-being of children

(Popenoe, 1993). Children face a number of problems in families. Among them are "delinquency and crime (including an alarming juvenile homicide rate), drug and alcohol abuse, suicide, depression, eating disorders, and the growing number of children in poverty" (Popenoe, 1993, p. A48).

Child abuse and neglect are major concerns in American family life that first began to be recognized in the early 1960s (Oates & Bross, 1995). Included in this category of abuse are physical, sexual, and psychological abuse, as well as neglect and abandonment. It should be stressed that abuse is seldom of one type and that families who engage in abuse are usually chaotic in nature and have relationship deficits (Mullen, Martin, Anderson, Romans, & Herbison, 1995).

The effects of child abuse, especially emotional and psychological abuse, may have a powerful influence on adult behavior that is lifelong (Elam & Kleist, 1999). Adults who were abused as children appear to be as a group less satisfied with their lives and prone to suffer from a number of disorders including depression and low self-esteem. However, there is not a causal relationship between abuse and adult symptomatology (Mullen et al., 1995).

**Child physical abuse** resides on a continuum from physical contact that is mild to that which is severe (Kemp, 1998). Severe physical child abuse is manifested in everything from skin injuries to death. In between are physical traumas such as broken bones, soft-tissue swelling, and bleeding. In addition to physical marks, psychological consequences result from physical abuse that range from fearfulness of others to posttraumatic stress responses. Many children who are physically abused become distrustful of others and even depressed. In addition, a number of these children have difficulty forming close, lasting relationships with peers, let alone adults.

Besides physical abuse, one of the most insidious forms of child abuse is **childhood sexual abuse** (CSA). This type of abuse includes unwanted touching, intercourse, oral sex, and photographs taken while nude (Elam & Kleist, 1999). "It is generally believed that sexual abuse of all children is significantly underreported, with sexual abuse of boys being reported least" (Tomes, 1996, p. 55). In sexual abuse situations, "most abuse of boys is done by perpetrators outside the family; girls' abuse is predominantly intrafamilial" (Hutchins, 1995, p. 21). Almost one in three girls is sexually abused by age 18 (Crespi & Howe, 2000). About one in six boys is sexually abused by age 16 (Tomes, 1996).

Child abuse of either a physical or sexual nature has become prominent news, from notorious cases to lesser known court trials (Shapiro, 1993). Yet, the most long-range type of abuse is psychological abuse or emotional neglect. It is both more constant in nature and more damaging throughout life (Elam & Kleist, 1999).

The National Clearinghouse on Child Abuse and Neglect Information (http://www.calib.com/nccanch/index.htm) provides current updates and background on abuse and neglect problems. Still, child abuse and neglect are pervasive problems and ones most family therapists must obtain clinical skills in if they are to confront them effectively.

# Approaches for Treating Child Abuse and Neglect

Treatment of child abuse and neglect is complicated because it involves legal, developmental, and psychological issues (Gladding, Remley, & Huber, 2001; Pistorello & Follette, 1998). All states require mental health workers and other professional helpers to report child abuse and neglect. Thus, before treatment can begin in some cases, legal issues must be resolved. In addition, developmental and psychological matters must be dealt with as well. For instance, when child sexual abuse occurs early in a person's life, the child may blame herself or himself for the abuse just as children of divorce often first find themselves at fault before they come to realize they have been victimized. In addition, child sexual abuse is often not treated until adulthood when other complications, such as couple intimacy, overlay the original problems.

Therefore, family therapists must deal with a plethora of current and historical issues in working with child abuse. Anger and feelings of betrayal on the part of the abuser must often be dealt with before working with the family as a whole in correcting the problem and preventing it from happening again. Furthermore, because of legal issues involved, the abuser in the family may be separated from the family, which makes the job of working with the family even more difficult and challenging.

Nevertheless, when family therapists encounter child abuse cases of any type, they "should not attempt to take the focus off the abuser, as this approach serves only to lead family members and community service agencies to believe that the therapist is excusing the violent acts" (Fenell & Weinhold, 1996, p. 5). Rather, they should concentrate on (1) assisting the abuser in learning how to delay acting impulsively and (2) helping the abuser and the abused family members to recognize and select alternatives other than violence. Motivation for achieving these goals is greatest immediately following abusive behavior, when the family is in crisis and the abuser is usually feeling badly about what has happened.

In working with adult survivors of abuse, clinicians must be able to treat not only issues these individuals have from childhood but also "the specific adult behaviors that may be associated with the history" (Elam & Kleist, 1999, p. 159). In this double emphasis, the clinician needs to understand the context in which the abuse occurred, for instance, in a family that had other relationship deficits, and also needs to realize that children are rarely abused in only one way. The process of treatment in these cases can vary from Bowenian-based family-of-origin work, which explores the dynamics associated with the abuse, to behavioral interventions, which help the client and his or her family modify or change behaviors triggered by memories of the abuse.

Children who have been abused physically or sexually likewise do not have one treatment modality that works best in helping them resolve the traumas of their experiences and make adequate and necessary adjustments (Hyde, Bentovim, & Monck, 1995; Oates & Bross, 1995). Rather, a variety of treatments have been used with members of this population and follow-up studies have, for the most part, not taken place or been inconclusive (Greenwalt, Sklare, & Portes, 1998).

Overall, knowledge is scarce on what treatment works best with survivors of child abuse. It does appear that children and their mothers who attend groups with peers in addition to family/network meetings alone benefit in regard to increased self-esteem and outcome (Hyde et al., 1995). Thus, group work may be an added component that helps children and parents face and talk through problems and possibilities they do not do when in a family context.

# Summary and Conclusion

This chapter has dealt with three types of abuse: substance-related, domestic violence, and child abuse. Unfortunately, all three are found in a number of American families.

These dysfunctional behaviors manifest themselves in many ways, for instance, abuse of alcohol, narcotics, battering, inappropriate usurping of power, neglect, and betrayal of trust and responsibility. They are all "tragic and inexcusable and every effort must be made by couples and family therapists to intervene with the family to stop the abuse and help the family become more supportive" (Elam & Kleist, 1999, p. 159).

To treat any of these maladies, family therapists must first assess what is occurring and then find treatment strategies that have proven effective. Working with just the abuser is usually futile because abuse is a systemic problem that has both its origins and solution within a family and societal context.

In the treatment of substance-related disorders, family therapists have two choices. First, they can work with the family in order to confront the problem that the family is experiencing with substance-related abuse or dependence or second they can work with the family once the abuser is "dry" and more motivated. In some cases, the therapist will work with the family in both ways. Regardless, therapists must realize that those with substance-related disorders have power within a family. Therefore, if they as clinicians are to help the family, they will have to engage the person with the substance-related disorder as well as the family in treatment.

Once the substance-related problem family enters therapy, a number of approaches can be used to help them. Theoretical methods of helping include structural-strategic, Bowenian, behavioral, Adlerian, and multifamily. An emphasis on the use of community resources for both the prevention and treatment of substance-related disordered families is also necessary.

Families that are engaged in domestic violence and child abuse/neglect provide equally difficult challenges for family therapists to handle. In both cases, these families, in order to minimize or excuse their behaviors, may use a number of defense mechanisms, for instance, denial. Complicating both situations from the standpoint of treatment is the fact that legal and psychological barriers must be addressed and worked through often before any therapeutic action can be taken.

In domestic violence, power issues must be confronted and modified. In child abuse and neglect, power issues also prevail as well as those connected with trust. Family therapists can help families in these circumstances by assisting them in learning alternatives to the actions they are currently taking. Changing the dynamics that underlie such behaviors may involve a gamut of treatment strategies from those that explore the family-of-origin to those that are behaviorally based.

# Summary Table
## Working with Substance-Related Disorders, Domestic Violence, and Child Abuse in Families

### Substance-Related Disorders and Families

Substance-related disorders are "related to the taking of a drug of abuse (including alcohol), to the side effects of medication, and to toxin exposure" (APA, 1994, p. 175).

Substance-related disorders that involve taking a drug of abuse were dealt with in this chapter since many families are affected by them and they are a family systems problem.

*Manifestation of Substance-Related Disorders*

Families and individuals manifest substance-related disorders in a number of ways, for example, denial, expression of negative feelings, assumption of roles, deterioration, scapegoating, misuse of resources, confusion about self-worth, and expenditure of time/energy resolving past issues.

*Engaging Substance-Related Disorder Families in Treatment*

Engaging the family in the therapeutic process involves having the therapist contact the least engaged as well as the most engaged member(s) of the family.
Use of significant others, such as parents and siblings, and widening the focus of therapy are helpful.

*Approaches for Treating Substance-Related Disorder Families After Engagement*

Treatment for substance-related disorder families must address issues such as relapse, the environment, and intrapersonal (i.e., emotions) and interpersonal (i.e., social) relations.
Prominent approaches to working with substance-related families consist of a number of proven approaches. Among these are structural-strategic family therapy, Bowenian family therapy, behavioral family therapy, Adlerian family therapy, and multifamily therapy.
Community resources, such as AA and Al-Anon, and prevention activities are a part of treatment too.

## Domestic Violence and Families

Violence against spouses, primarily women, takes many forms: physical, sexual, psychological, and economic.
Violence in families stems from a power imbalance.

*Assessment of Domestic Violence*

Assessment of domestic violence is complicated by legal and psychological barriers.
Assessment of domestic violence is best done in an open manner where emphasis is on how the family is hurt rather than who is to blame.

*Approaches for Treating Domestic Violence*

Family therapists primarily use conjoint family therapy, intimate justice theory, and educational methods, for example, cognitive-behavioral theory, in working with families involved in domestic violence.

## Child Abuse and Neglect in Families

Child abuse and neglect first became a major concern in American society in the 1960s.
Included in child abuse are physical, sexual, and psychological abuse as well as neglect and abandonment.
Emotional/psychological abuse is the most long lasting and damaging.

*Approaches for Treating Child Abuse and Neglect*

Treatment of child abuse is complicated because it involves legal, developmental, and psychological issues.

All states require reporting of child abuse and neglect cases.

Treatment of child abuse and neglect may focus on historical as well as current issues. Bowenian and behavioral family treatments are used as well as peer groups of children and parents.

# References

Almeida, R. (2000, March/April). Probing beyond the bruises. *Family Therapy Networker, 24,* 23–24.

American Psychiatric Association. (1994). *Diagnostic and Statistical Manual of Mental Disorders* (4th ed.). Washington, DC: Author.

Berenson, D. (1992). The therapist's relationship with couples with an alcoholic member. In E. Kaufman & P. Kaufman (Eds.), *Family therapy of drug and alcohol abuse* (pp. 224–235). Boston: Allyn & Bacon.

Black, C. (1990). *Double duty.* New York: Ballantine.

Bograd, M. (1999). Strengthening domestic violence theories: Intersections of race, class, sexual orientation, and gender. *Journal of Marital and Family Therapy, 25,* 275–289.

Bograd, M., & Mederos, F. (1999). Battering and couples therapy: Universal screening and selection of treatment modality. *Journal of Marital and Family Therapy, 25,* 291–312.

Bowen, M. (1974). Alcoholism as viewed through family systems theory and family psychotherapy. *Annals of the New York Academy of Sciences, 233,* 125–132.

Boylin, W. M., Doucette, J., & Jean, M. F. (1997). Multifamily therapy in substance abuse treatment with women. *American Journal of Family Therapy, 25,* 39–47.

Bry, B. H. (1994). Preventing substance abuse by supporting families' efforts with community resources. *Child and Family Behavior Therapy, 16,* 21–26.

Crespi, T. D., & Howe, E. A. (2000, March). Families in crisis: Considerations and implications for school counselors. *Counseling Today, 42*(9), 6.

Cutler, H. A., & Radford, A. (1999). Adult children of alcoholics: Adjustment to a college environment. *The Family Journal: Counseling and Therapy for Couples and Families, 7,* 148–153.

Daw, J. L. (1995, December). Alcohol problems across the generations. *Family Therapy News, 26,* 19.

Diamond, J. (2000, July/August). Making friends with your addiction. *Family Therapy Networker,* pp. 40–47.

Dinkmeyer, D. C., & McKay, G. D. (1989). *STEP: The parents handbook.* Circle Pines, MN: American Guidance Service.

Edwards, M. E., & Steinglass, P. (1995). Family therapy treatment outcomes for alcoholism. *Journal of Marital and Family Therapy, 4,* 475–509.

Elam, G. A., & Kleist, D. M. (1999). Research on the long-term effects of child abuse. *The Family Journal: Counseling and Therapy for Couples and Families, 7,* 154–160.

Fenell, D. L., & Weinhold, B. K. (1996, March). Treating families with special needs. *Counseling and Human Development, 28,* 1–12.

Gibson, J. M., & Donigian, J. (1993). Use of Bowen theory. *Journal of Addiction & Offender, 14,* 25–35.

Gladding, S. T. (1991). *Eli.* Unpublished manuscript.

Gladding, S. T., Remley, T. P., Jr., Huber, C. H. (2001). *Ethical, legal, and professional issues in the practice of marriage and family therapy* (3rd ed.). Upper Saddle River, NJ: Merrill/Prentice Hall.

Gottman, J. M., Jacobson, N. S., Rushe, R. H., Wu Shortt, J., Babcock, J., La Tallade, J. J., & Waltz, J. (1995). The relationship between heart rate reactivity, emotionally aggressive behavior, and general violence in batterers. *Journal of Family Psychology, 9,* 227–248.

Greenwalt, B. C., Sklare, G., & Portes, P. (1998). The therapeutic treatment provided in cases involving physical child abuse: A description of current practices. *Child Abuse and Neglect, 22,* 71–78.

Hutchins, J. (1995, December). Barrett calls for MFT mediation for false memory families. *Family Therapy News, 26,* 21.

Hyde, C., Bentovim, A., & Monck, E. (1995). Some clinical and methodological implications of a treatment outcome study of sexually abused children. *Child Abuse and Neglect, 19,* 1387–1399.

Jory, B., & Anderson, D. (2000). Intimate justice III: Healing the anguish of abuse and embracing the anguish of accountability. *Journal of Marital and Family Therapy, 26,* 329–340.

Jory, B., & Anderson, D. (1999). Intimate justice II: Mutuality, reciprocity, and accommodation in therapy for psychological abuse. *Journal of Marital and Family Therapy, 25,* 349–364.

Jory, B., Anderson, D., & Greer, C. (1997). Intimate justice: Confronting issues of accountability, respect, and freedom in treatment for abuse and violence. *Journal of Marital and Family Therapy, 23,* 399–419.

Kemp, A. (1998). *Abuse in the family: An introduction.* Pacific Grove, CA: Brooks/Cole.

Krestan, J., & Bepko, C. (1988). Alcohol problems and the family life cycle. In B. Carter & M. McGoldrick (Eds.), *The changing family life cycle* (2nd ed., pp. 483–511). New York: Gardner.

Laqueur, H. P. (1976). Multiple family therapy. In P. Guerin (Ed.), *Family therapy*. New York: Gardner.

Lawson, A. W. (1994). Family therapy and addictions. In J. A. Lewis (Ed.), *Addiction: Concepts and strategies for treatment* (pp. 211–232). Gaithersburg, MD: Aspen.

Lewis, J. A. (Ed.), *Addictions: Concepts and strategies for treatment*. Gaithersburg, MD: Aspen.

McCourt, F. (1996). *Angela's Ashes*. New York: Simon & Schuster.

McLaughlin, I. G., Leonard, K. E., & Senchak, M. (1992). Prevalence and distribution of premarital aggression among couples applying for a marriage license. *Journal of Family Violence, 7,* 309–319.

Miller, W. R., Meyers, R. J., & Tonigan, J. S. (1999). Engaging the unmotivated in treatment for alcohol problems: A comparison of three strategies for intervention through family members. *Journal of Consulting & Clinical Psychology, 67,* 688–697.

Morgan, O. J. (1998). Addiction, family treatment, and healing resources: An interview with David Berenson. *Journal of Addiction and Offender Counseling, 18,* 54–61.

Mullen, P. E., Martin, J. L., Anderson, J. C., Romans, S. E., & Herbison, G. P. (1995). The long-term impact of physical, emotional, and sexual abuse of children: A community study. *Child Abuse and Neglect, 20,* 7–21.

Murphy, J. P. (1984). Substance abuse and the family. *Journal for Specialists in Group Work, 9,* 106–112.

Oates, R. K., & Bross, D. C. (1995). What have we learned about treating child physical abuse? A literature review of the last decade. *Child Abuse and Neglect, 19,* 463–473.

Odom, M., Snow, J. N., & Kern, R. M. (1999). Use of the identified patient as the helper in family therapy. *The Family Journal: Counseling and Therapy for Couples and Families, 7,* 181–184.

O'Farrell, T. J. (1996). Marital and family therapy in the treatment of alcoholism. In *Hatherleigh Guide to Treating Substance Abuse,* Part I (pp. 101–127). New York: Hatherleigh Press.

Pence, E., & Paymar, M. (1993). *Education groups for men who batter: The Duluth Model.* New York: Springer Publishing.

Pistorello, J., & Follette, V. M. (1998). Childhood sexual abuse and couples' relationships: Female survivors' reports in therapy group. *Journal of Marital and Family Therapy, 24,* 473–485.

Popenoe, D. (1993, April 14). Scholars should worry about the disintegration of the American family. *Chronicle of Higher Education, XXXIX,* A48.

Rotter, J. C., & Houston, I. S. (1999). Treating family violence: Risks and limitations. *The Family Journal: Counseling and Therapy for Couples and Families, 7,* 58–63.

Santisteban, D. A., & Szapocznik, J. (1994). Bridging theory, research and practice to more successfully engage substance abusing youth and their families into therapy. *Journal of Child & Adolescent Substance Abuse, 3,* 9–24.

Schecter, S., & Ganley, A. (1995). *Domestic violence: A national curriculum for family preservation practitioners.* San Francisco: Family Violence Prevention Fund.

Schroeder, E. (1989). Therapy for the chemically dependent family. *Journal of Chemical Dependency Treatment, 2,* 95–129.

Shapiro, L. (1993, April 19). Rush to judgment. *Newsweek,* pp. 54–60.

Stanton, M. D. (1999, May). Alcohol use disorders. *AAMFT Clinical Update, 1*(3), 1–8.

Stanton, M. D., Todd, T. C., Heard, D. B., Kirschner, S., Kleiman, J. I., Mowatt, D. T., Riley, P., Scott, S. M., & Van Deusen, J. M. (1982). A conceptual model. In M. D. Stanton, T. C. Todd, & Associates (Eds.), *The family therapy of drug abuse and addiction* (pp. 7–30). New York: Guilford.

Todd, T. C., & Selekman, M. D. (1991). *Family therapy approaches with adolescent substance abusers.* Boston: Allyn & Bacon.

Tomes, H. (1996, August). Are we in denial about child abuse? *APA Monitor, 27,* 55.

Van Deusen, J. M., Stanton, M. D., Scott, S. M., Todd, T. C., & Mowatt, D. T. (1982). Getting the addict to agree to involve his family or origin: The initial contact. In M. D. Stanton, T. C. Todd, & Associates (Eds.), *The family therapy of drug abuse and addiction* (pp. 39–59). New York: Guilford.

Wycoff, S., & Cameron, S. C. (2000). The Garcia family: Using a structural systems approach with an alcohol-dependent family. *The Family Journal: Counseling and Therapy for Couples and Families, 8,* 47–57.

# PART FOUR

# Professional Issues and Research in Family Therapy

# Ethical, Legal, and Professional Issues in Family Therapy

He counts the coat hooks up to 39
that line the wall from the door to his classroom.

An unrefined scientist, at the age of four,
he delights in adding up objects
that fill his world with fascination.

*Gladding, 1993*

**P**rofessional issues in family therapy focus on matters pertaining to ethics, law, and identity. In the process of helping families, there is a link between the selection of treatment procedures and the consideration of professional issues (Gladding, Remley, & Huber, 2001). For instance, therapeutic interventions must be based on ethical and legal factors. However, professional issues generally receive less attention than therapeutic ones. Perhaps it is because these former matters are so basic. Regardless, professional matters are usually written about in more mechanical and less appealing ways than those related to treatment. Ethical guidelines, legal standards, and association bylaws are worded in a matter-of-fact, prosaic manner. They are not inviting to read and are not always clear. Yet, the codes, guidelines, and associations that make up family therapy are at the heart of the profession. It is crucial that the issues surrounding the work of family therapy be well understood by clinicians and the public.

Moreover, it is essential that family therapists be vigilant in their pursuit and knowledge regarding ethical, legal, and professional identity issues. If they are not, the result may be clinical or personal actions that are harmful though well intended. Just as the family is a system, so the field of family therapy is systemic. For family clinicians to stay healthy, they and their colleagues must abide in harmony with ethical codes and legal statutes and practice according to the highest standards possible. In addition, they must form a strong identity as family therapists. Membership in an association that nourishes and enriches them professionally is necessary. For the sake of colleagues, and themselves, family therapists must deal with professional issues (Wendorf & Wendorf, 1992).

This chapter examines issues connected with ethics, the law, and family therapists' identities. Ignorance of these aspects of therapy can get practitioners into serious trouble and cost them time and money or possibly their careers.

# Overview of Ethics in Families and Family Therapy

Human experience is a moral enterprise (Doherty, 1995). **Ethics** are moral principles from which individuals and social groups, such as families, determine rules for right conduct. Families and society are governed by "relationship ethics." These ethics are based on two main principles:

1. **equitability** or the proposition "that everyone is entitled to have his or her welfare interests considered in a way that is fair from a multilateral perspective" (Boszormenyi-Nagy & Ulrich, 1981, p. 160), and
2. **caring** or the idea that moral development and principles are centered in the social context of relationships and interdependency (McGoldrick & Carter, 1999).

Ironically, family therapy initially grew up in an atmosphere in which its practitioners believed that the theories and practices involved in working with families were "value free" (Krasner & Houts, 1984). The result was that ethical principles for working with families were rarely discussed by family therapists on a formal or informal basis until the mid-1960s (Grosser & Paul, 1964; Hurvitz, 1967). Even now, ethics in family therapy is sometimes treated lightly and in a nonsystemic manner.

Thus, it is understandable that there is a great deal of uncertainty about ethical decision making in family therapy. When faced with an ethical dilemma, especially if it is complex, many clinicians are quite sure they will be making a big mistake regardless of what path they choose (Hundert, 1987). Yet, despite this historical conflict and present reality, the domain of ethics is part and parcel of the total fabric of family treatment. It needs to be considered in a thoughtful and systemic way. Family therapists probably face more ethical conflicts than any other type of therapist (Morrison, Layton, & Newman, 1982). They must be aware and knowledgeable of current codes of ethics for the profession as well as actively engaged in making suggestions for revisions of these codes (Jordan & Stevens, 1999).

# Ethics and Values

Ethical decision making is based on an awareness and understanding of values. A **value** is "the ranking of an ordered set of choices from the most to the least preferable" (Spiegel, 1971, p. 53). Basically, there are four domains of values: personal, family, political/social, and ultimate. Each has an impact on the other (Thomas K. Hearn, March 23, 1993, personal communication). Family therapy, theoretically and clinically, is a profession that now acknowledges it is based on multiple sets of values (Gladding et al., 2001).

Effective therapists realize the therapeutic process is influenced by the complexity of personal values, client family values, and theoretical values. They examine their own values first. These "are influenced by a therapist's age; marital status; gender; . . . and ethnic, religious, and socio-cultural background" (Aponte, 1992, p. 273). For example, a young, single, Catholic Hispanic/Latino male family therapist from an affluent background may have values different from an older, divorced, Native American who is the parent of two adolescents and has lived in poverty most of her life. Once aware of their values and how they are different and similar to others, family therapists can then begin work with families.

Next, therapists look at the values of their client families. In families, it is clear to see how personal values of members or political/social values make an impact. Inherited values within the family also have an influence (McGoldrick, Gerson, & Shellenberger, 1998). In working with families, their values must be examined from a systemic point of view—that is, how family members' values affect the family as a whole. Such a perspective complicates the matter of dealing with values; but simultaneously, it puts values into a realistic framework and makes the study of them a dynamic enterprise. If therapists and their client families are far apart in regard to espoused core values, negotiations between them or a referral may be needed.

Finally, therapists explore values connected to the theories, processes, and outcomes they embrace (Giblin, 1993). In this last arena, ethical issues in family therapy are seen in relationship to which values in families need to be kept, emphasized, and reinforced and which ones should be changed (Carter, 1986). Some family therapies center their treatment on helping families remove symptoms. Others focus on establishing a new structure or boundaries. Still others concentrate on helping individuals differentiate from their families of origin or find new solutions.

Uninformed practitioners may try to deny the nature or even importance of values. Others may attempt to "use therapy as a means to campaign for the revisions [of values] they favor" (Wendorf & Wendorf, 1992, p. 316). Both approaches are filled with flaws and possible danger. In the long run, values are the driving force behind ethical behavior and the conduct of family therapy.

# How Do Values Influence Ethical Practice?

Values influence ethics in the sense that as "beliefs and preferences," they "undergird the ethical decisions made by individuals and groups. In other words, all ethical issues involve values as grounds for decision making, and all values that deal with social rights and obligations inevitably surface in ethical decisions" (Doherty & Boss, 1991, p. 610). For instance, Jacobson (1994) admonished those studying family violence to focus on action-oriented research, that is, finding solutions to this problem, because he believed that such a focus was the only ethical way to investigate a phenomenon where people were being abused.

In family therapy, some therapists work from an individual therapeutic approach in the presence of the family as a group. This type of treatment raises a value and an ethical question because problems of the family in such an arrangement are not being viewed from their "context as a whole" (Fishman, 1988, p. 5). The result is that recommendations for modifications in the family's way of interacting do not consider the overall complexity of the situation. Because such an approach is limited, it is not clear whether it is of value or ethical when a more effective treatment would work better.

In practice, family therapists are "ethically bound to be honest and forthright with . . . clients, clearly informing them of their choices, [the therapist's] biases, and . . . professional judgments" (Wendorf & Wendorf, 1992, p. 317). The values that family therapists embrace directly affect their clinical practices.

# Guidelines for Making Ethical Decisions

To guard against making unethical decisions, family therapists can use a number of models and resources, once they are aware of what values are involved (Cottone & Claus, 2000). Four of the most prevalent and useful means of making ethical decisions are association codes of ethics, educational resources, professional consultation, and interactions with colleagues and supervisors.

## Codes of Ethics

Primary resources for family therapists to use in ethical decision making are association codes of ethics. "Ethical codes are set up not to prevent what *will* happen, but to prevent what *might* happen" (Kaplan & Culkin, 1995, p. 337). Both the American Association for Marriage and Family Therapy (AAMFT, 2001) (see Appendix A) and the International Association of Marriage and Family Counselors (IAMFC, 1993) (see Appendix B) have codes of ethics, each containing eight sections, that address issues confronting family therapists.

The AAMFT ethics code contains sections on the following topics:

1. responsibility to clients
2. confidentiality
3. professional competence and integrity
4. responsibility to students, employees, and supervisees
5. responsibility to research participants
6. responsibility to the profession
7. financial arrangements
8. advertising

In comparison, the IAMFC ethics code covers the following topics:

1. client well-being
2. confidentiality
3. competence
4. assessment
5. private practice
6. research and publications
7. supervision
8. media and public statements

Family therapists face a number of ethical dilemmas that are discussed in these codes of ethics, as well as some that are not (Green & Hansen, 1989). Many of the most common ethical concerns are those that involve treating the entire family, being current on new family therapy developments, seeing one family member without the others present, and sharing values with clients (Green & Hansen, 1986).

Unfortunately, there are few specific behavioral guidelines in codes of ethics that direct family therapists on what to do and how. As a result, family therapists will sometimes make unethical decisions because they use rationalization or hearsay, such as "other practitioners do this or that" (Pope & Vasquez, 1998). The limitations of ethical codes may become especially pronounced when attempts are made to deal with complicated issues, such as **dual relationships**, that is, relationships that are not built on mutuality and where a therapist assumes a second role, for example, a friend, business associate, and so on (Ryder & Hepworth, 1990). Thus, determining the best course of action from reading an ethical code may be difficult for experienced, as well as beginning, therapists.

## Educational Resources

A second source family therapists can utilize in making informed ethical decisions is educational material. One of the best educational resources is found in the form of case histories related specifically to dilemmas in family therapy. For instance, Peggy Papp (1977) has compiled a book of full-length case studies to which family therapists can refer. In addition, and briefer in format, is the regular column in *The Family Journal: Counseling and*

*Therapy for Couples and Families,* which features case consultations from a particular theoretical view. In each issue, this material highlights a different case and theory. Such educational cases need to be studied on a systematic basis. Knowledge of how family therapists made decisions in the past can be useful to current practitioners, too.

Case studies can also help family therapists reason through the steps needed in making ethically appropriate choices. In ethical decision making, step-by-step processes have been established (Corey, Corey, & Callanan, 1998). These processes emphasize generating a continuum of alternative actions that therapists can take for the good of the family's welfare and to meet their own professional responsibilities. Therapists then evaluate and weigh the consequences of these alternatives. From this process, they make a tentative decision, and implement that decision, after they have double-checked it with supervisors, consultants, or colleagues if they are in doubt. The final step involves documenting what has been done (Mitchell, 1991). Documenting should be based on customary practices or reputable suggested practices that are defensible ethically and legally (Wilcoxon, 1993).

## Professional Consultation

A third resource for making ethical decisions is professional consultation. Professional consultation is the use of experts in an area, such as family therapy ethics, to enhance one's own knowledge and abilities (Kurpius & Fuqua, 1993). Consultation can take many forms. For instance, consultation can be internally or externally oriented, process or outcome focused, and formal or informal.

Internal consultation can take the form of talking with an expert where one works about an ethical matter concerning a family. Outside consultation would involve conversation with a professional outside one's agency or setting. Process consultation refers to conferring with an expert about the ethics of methods one is using with a family, whereas outcome-focused consultation would be centered on the ethics of what the therapist and/or family hopes to accomplish. Finally, formal consultation is input gained from an expert through an appointment or structured meeting, whereas informal consultation may well take the form of talking with an expert in the hallways at a professional therapy conference or some less structured way of interacting.

Whatever the form, the idea is that through consultation services, family therapists can gain a broader view of the principles and case histories associated with specific aspects of ethical codes. In consultation encounters, therapists become consumers of services that are aimed toward prevention, enlightenment, and change.

## Interaction with Colleagues and Supervisors

A final source of support in making ethical decisions is one's colleagues and supervisors. Family therapists need to interact with their peers for many reasons, but mainly to share in the collected wisdom and opinions of these individuals when it comes to matters of ethical conduct. Peers are usually more accessible than consultants and educational materials. Furthermore, the cost of using peers, such as in peer supervision, is inexpensive or free and may actually pay psychological dividends both in knowledge and support. In addition, colleagues can often inform professionals of new trends.

Direct supervision of one's work by noncolleagues is also effective and recommended especially as professionals begin their careers (Cobia & Boes, 2000). Unlike individual supervision, family therapy supervision is systemic and includes a focus on interpersonal as well as intrapersonal issues (Gladding, Wilcoxon, Semon, & Myers, 1992). Furthermore, family therapy supervision places an emphasis on the critiquing of videotapes as well as the use of one-way mirrors for live observation and intervention (Schwartz, Liddle, & Breunlin, 1988). By using various forms of supervisory interaction—such as a supervision team behind a one-way mirror or a **bug-in-the-ear supervision method** (in which the therapist receives messages from a supervisor through a telephone hookup device)—family therapists are less likely to make ethical mistakes through omitting data or avoiding personal/professional issues.

# Common Ethical Concerns

Some conduct in family therapy is considered unethical regardless of the experience of the professional involved. However, some practices are not as clearly defined. Common ethical concerns are examined here.

## Confidentiality

**Confidentiality** is "the ethical duty to fulfill a contract or promise to clients that the information revealed during therapy will be protected from unauthorized disclosure" (Arthur & Swanson, 1993, p. 7). In addition to its ethical focus, confidentiality is a legal matter as well. In a 1996 U.S. Supreme Court decision (*Jaffe v. Redmond*), the high court upheld that a therapist could not be forced to testify about confidential communications in treatment settings (Seppa, 1996). However, if confidentiality is broken during treatment, it may become an ethical and/or legal nightmare. Therefore, family therapists need to take precautions ahead of time.

One of the best strategies for family therapists to initiate is to inform all family members in the initial session that the family is the client and will be treated as such in regard to information conveyed in treatment. This process can be done verbally, but it should also be conveyed in writing through the use of a professional self-disclosure statement. This statement, which contains essential information about therapy and the mutual rights and responsibilities of all involved, is signed by the family and returned to the therapist. A copy is then given to all members of the family and retained by the therapist (see Chapter 4 for an example of a professional self-disclosure statement).

By informing the family that they are the client and using a professional disclosure statement to do this and more, family members are concretely informed about the parameters of therapy including confidentiality. In the process, they are discouraged from seeking individual sessions with therapists unless appropriate. They are also informed that they should not try to persuade therapists to keep their secrets from other family members. This approach basically reinforces a systems perspective, that is, the family is an interrelated unit and what affects one member has an impact on the entire family.

At times, family therapists may have to break confidentiality. These times are dictated by ethical and legal considerations regarding the well-being of the family (Kaplan & Allison, 1993b). In these situations, the question of **privileged communication** comes to the forefront. Privileged communication is "a client's legal right, guaranteed by statute, that confidences originating in a therapeutic relationship will be safeguarded" (Arthur & Swanson, 1993, p. 7). However, if it becomes clear during a session that, for example, a child or older adult in the family is being abused, the therapist has a legal and ethical obligation to report the abuse to an agency responsible for dealing with it, usually a department of social services (Welfel, Danzinger, & Santoro, 2000). All states grant immunity from criminal or civic liability to professionals who report child abuse (Gladding et al., 2001). Family therapists need to check their state regulations and seek advice from colleagues, professional association and ethical guidelines, supervisors, and attorneys if there is ever a question of what they should reveal professionally or legally.

Confidentiality broken through carelessness is another matter. Carelessness can involve an impropriety such as talking about a case in public. However, it can also be more innocent such as using a cellular phone to call a client or an insurance agency. Electronic communication tools (including e-mail and fax) provide no guarantee that information will be received by the person for whom it is intended without being intercepted or read by someone else (O'Malley, 1995). Such situations constitute an ethical violation, and it is possible that a civil suit will follow (Woody, 1988). "Office personnel may need to be trained to think preventively about possible violations of confidentiality that may occur with a computer system" (O'Malley, 1995, p. 9). This type of protection would include placing the computer in a discrete position so that only office staff can view it. Family therapists who use computers to type progress notes must also take care with computer access and display. Client notes and records that are typed on computer disks must be protected in the same way as hardcopy notes. Therefore, proper precautions must be used when employing electronic devices.

## Gender Issues

Gender can be an important ethical issue in conducting family therapy. "Gender is not just a set of behaviors and expectations but rather a principal of social organization that structures relations, especially the power relations, between men and women" (Smith & Stevens-Smith, 1992, p. 436). The genders of the therapist and of those in the family play a part in what issues are addressed during treatment and how they are addressed (Walsh, 1993). In its initial years, family therapy was male focused (Weiner & Boss, 1985). The result was that sometimes social and system issues involving women were ignored or glossed over (Costa & Sorenson, 1993).

Since the 1980s, gender issues have been dealt with extensively in family therapy (Hare-Mustin, 1987). The status of core inequality among individual members within the family, especially women, has been focused on (Carter, 1992; Walters, Carter, Papp, & Silverstein, 1992). Nevertheless, the conduct of many families and that of family therapy have changed only slightly. Males and females who did not grow up in a nonstereotyped environment tend to act and react in the same manner as their caretakers. This behavior has ethical implications because traditional roles have sometimes inhibited the growth, change, and healthy functioning of both genders. For example, women may be shortchanged in therapy if they assume that because of their gender they must be cooperative and make concessions regardless of cost (Nixon, 1993). Likewise, men raised in stereotyped ways may think they cannot make concessions within the family without losing face or power.

Therefore, in working with whole families, therapists must be attuned to such ethical and practical issues as:

- the balance of power between a husband and wife both financially and physically
- the rules and roles played by members of different genders and how these are rewarded
- what a shift in a family's way of operating will mean to the functionality of the family as a whole (McGoldrick, 1999)

A balanced perspective needs to be maintained in regard to gender and change. Urging or implementing change in gender-prescribed behaviors within a family solely because a therapist believes it is right may be quite costly to all involved (Wendorf & Wendorf, 1992). On the other hand, condoning through silence emotional abuse or intimidation that is lethal to the life and functioning of the family is irresponsible, too. Ethical and systemic considerations need to be addressed when discussing gender issues in family therapy (Bograd, 1992). This is especially true when changes in relationship patterns are being contemplated or implemented.

## Sex Between a Therapist and a Family Member

One of the most important ethical taboos in professional family therapy is for a therapist to become sexually involved with a client. Unfortunately, in the history of mental health treatment, blatant cases are seen of sexual affairs between therapists and those they have treated. Movies from *Spellbound* to *The Prince of Tides* have portrayed forbidden intimacy within the confines of analysis (Ansen & Springen, 1992). In the annals of therapeutic history, two publicized cases of sexual involvement with clients are those documented between Carl Jung and a couple of the women he treated who became his mistresses, and Otto Rank who had a long love affair with one of his patients (Beck, Springen, & Foote, 1992).

Noted practitioners in the mental health field have warned against such liaisons. Furthermore, sexual relations between a therapist and client are forbidden in the code of ethics of all family therapy professional associations. Unfortunately, the practice clearly goes on even though "fewer therapists admit to indiscretions these days even in anonymous surveys" (Beck et al., 1992, p. 54).

When it is discovered that this type of conduct is probably occurring, the person receiving the news should confront the accused professional with the evidence in order to verify its truthfulness. If there is a conflict of information between the therapist and client, a written report of the incident by the client should be made. After the complaint is made, the national ethics board that governs the mental health discipline under which the person in question is a member (e.g., AAMFT, American Counseling Association, or American Psychological Association) has the authority to gather evidence, to hear testimony if necessary, and, then, to make a decision.

## Theoretical Techniques

Some theoretical techniques are controversial and should only be used as a last resort and with discretion. For instance, the use of conscious deceit or paradox as applied in strategic family therapy is not recommended when a straightforward approach would work just as well (Henderson, 1987; Solovey & Duncan, 1992). Similarly, the strategic stance of neutrality is of questionable ethical use when violence between family members is occurring. In such cases, family therapists who practice from the strategic point of view should concentrate on actively bringing the violence within the family to cessation and initiate a contract between members for nonviolence (Willbach, 1989). Only by working with the family in such a way can therapists hope to bring about stability and change. Again, legal as well as ethical factors may need to be considered in deciding on a course of action.

## Multicultural Therapy Issues

Another area in which ethical issues commonly arise is in the multicultural domain (Saba, Karrer, & Hardy, 1996). In working with minority culture families, Pedersen (1996) proposes that there are three serious errors, all of which have ethical implications that should be avoided. These errors are a tendency to:

1. overemphasize similarities
2. overemphasize differences
3. make assumptions that either similarities or differences must be emphasized

Instead, family therapists need to take a "culturally relevant perspective that attempts to identify cultural significance from the family's own perspective rather than a prescribed set of cultural characteristics that may or may not be relevant to a family" (Kurilla, 1998, p. 210). Such situations may be difficult to handle, and supervision and/or consultation are recommended as ways to keep perspective and act ethically. For example, family therapists generally avoid touching clients. Yet, Hispanic/Latino family members may openly touch or hug therapists, especially in greeting them (Cooper & Costas, 1994). In a situation where the therapist was with a Hispanic/Latino family where touch was frequent, he or she would face the ethical dilemma of respecting cultural tradition, while at the same time making sure that ethical codes regarding intimacy between the therapist and the family were not violated.

## Use of the Internet for On-Line Therapy

The World Wide Web has opened up possibilities and problems regarding its ethical and legal use as a tool in therapy (Caudill, 2000; Hohenshil, 2000). The Internet is already used by some practitioners to communicate with clients both around their community and around the world (Frame, 1998; Hannon, 1996). In some setups, clients, regardless of where they live, "e-mail a question of no more than 200 words to a counselor who then e-mails a response within 24 to 72 hours" (Frame, 1998, p. 328). A prepayment is required usually by credit card.

A related use of the Internet is in working with families who are hearing impaired or in remote areas where the physical presence of a therapist is not possible. Clinicians working with special populations or in rural and isolated regions may use this means to help families for whom services would not otherwise be available. The length of questions and payment will vary.

In yet a third kind of setup, family therapists simply communicate with families or members of families between regular therapy sessions. Such a practice may provide guidance, clarity issues, or lower anxiety.

The ethical dilemmas associated with the use of the Internet are numerous. They include a lack of security, possible breaches of confidentiality, an inability on the therapist's part to fulfill the duty to either protect the client or warn others of potential danger, and the inability of the therapist to read nonverbal responses and clues. Clients may also misunderstand written communications and, in the first case cited, clients are vulnerable to incompetent practice.

To complicate matters even further, there are few ethical guidelines and virtually no existing laws about the use of technology, specifically the Internet, in conducting marriage and family therapy. One factor does seem clear. The use of Internet and long-distance therapy will increase and there are risks of malpractice associated with it (Caudill, 2000).

# Addressing Unethical Behavior

By reading codes of ethics, consulting with colleagues, studying cases, operating from a theoretical position, developing policies and strategies beforehand, and receiving supervision or peer consultation, family therapists can usually avoid making unethical decisions (Brendel & Nelson, 1999; Gladding et al., 2001). However, at times therapists may notice unethical actions in fellow professionals. When such behavior comes to the attention of a therapist, he or she should address it. The first step in such a process is to discuss the violation directly with the professional in whom it was observed or who allegedly acted in an unethical way.

If the situation is not resolved on this level, the family therapist should report it to an appropriate professional association, such as the AAMFT or IAMFC, as well as inform licensure or certification boards regulating the practice of family counseling. When reported to such agencies, a formal investigation will almost always take place. If found guilty, professionals under the jurisdiction of these agencies are usually admonished and expelled (Kaplan & Culkin, 1995, p. 337).

Addressing unethical behavior in fellow professionals becomes more difficult, however, if the information is conveyed through a client the therapist is seeing. In such cases, the question of confidentiality arises. It then becomes the responsibility of the therapist to check with an attorney or ethics case manager in the profession in which he or she is in to determine whether his or her duty to report overrides the duty to maintain confidentiality. If there is a clear violation, then there are at least three options: "encourage your client to file an ethics complaint with her [or his] professional association or licensure board; file a complaint yourself; or do nothing, if your professional code doesn't require you to report" (Piercy, 2000, p. 21). Each option involves risks and for a client to come forward against a therapist can be a traumatic experience.

# Legal Issues in Family Therapy

"Ethics and law frequently overlap" (Wilcoxon, 1993, p. 3). For instance, if a family requests that they be billed for individual counseling, rather than for the couple therapy that they are receiving, and a family therapist complies, the parties involved are not only violating sections of the AAMFT and IAMFC codes of ethics but also committing insurance fraud (Kaplan & Allison, 1993a; Stevens-Smith & Hughes, 1993). If such a complaint is raised against a therapist, it may be handled by an ethics committee, a state regulatory commission, or a court of law (Woody, 1988).

Because of the interrelatedness of family ethics and law and the prevalence of law in governing interpersonal relationships, family therapists need to be aware of legal issues affecting therapy. Family therapists are not exempt from dealing with the legal system anymore than they are exempt from being involved in ethical decision making. It is important that family therapists "be aware of legislative decisions, legal precedents, and professional practices" connected with the law (Wilcoxon, 1993, p. 3) in case they are called on to participate in the legal system.

# The Legal System

The term **legal** refers to "law or the state of being lawful"; the term **law** refers to "a body of rules recognized by a state or community as binding on its members" (Shertzer & Stone, 1980, p. 386). In contrast to popular belief, "law is not cut and dried, definite and certain, or clear and precise" (Van Hoose & Kottler, 1985, p. 44). Yet, most family therapists are not familiar with American jurisprudence in more than a superficial way. They do not realize the fluidity within the legal system. The reason is largely because the law is a specialty that requires years of study and practice for one to become proficient. However, without becoming an expert in law, family therapists must master certain aspects of the legal system is order to be effective within this domain.

Interestingly, similarities exist between the legal and therapy communities. For example, both are concerned with setting up healthy relationships between people. In addition, both handle cases that involve drama and resolution. Also, ironically, professionals in both fields are sometimes referred to as "counselors."

Yet, the differences between the legal and the therapeutic systems are greater than their areas of overlap. A few of these differences are quite noticeable. For instance, the legal system is concerned with gathering evidence based on facts; and therapy is more interested in processes and making changes. Therefore, attorneys spend more time gathering information and concentrating on content than therapists do. Another distinction is that the legal system relies on adversity (Gladding et al., 2001); and the therapeutic system relies on cooperation. Although some legal decisions may involve compromises, attorneys focus on "winning" cases for their clients. Therefore, lawyers engage in discrediting or disproving other evidence that contradicts their cases. For attorneys, their clients' well-being and rights are based on representation that is singularly focused. Finally, although attorneys represent families as a whole in some legal cases, they do not deal with whole families when there are internal disputes. Rather, in the legal system each family member involved in a dispute is represented by a different legal counselor. In such situations, the focused outcome is on a just settlement rather than family change and resolution.

In recognition of the growing need for marriage and family therapists to have affordable, regular, and up-to-date information about managing legal risks in their practices, the

American Association for Marriage and Family Therapy established a legal and risk management plan in 1995 for its members. Under the plan, clinical members can receive "one free legal consultation per quarter with the AAMFT in-house attorney" (Jester, 1995, p. 6).

# Types of Law

Family therapists should be familiar with several types of law. Some of the most important of these types of law have been defined by Gladding et al. (2001). They are common law, statutory law, administrative (regulatory) law, case law (court decisions), and civil and criminal law.

## Common Law

**Common law** is law derived from tradition and usage. The common law of the United States has its roots in England and the tradition of accepting customs passed down from antiquity. The idea behind common law is that all law does not need to be derived from written sources. For instance, there are common law family matters, such as common law marriages.

## Statutory Law

In contrast to common law, **statutory law** consists of those laws passed by legislative bodies, such as state and national legislatures, and signed by an authorized source, such as a governor or the president. Statutory laws are only valid in the jurisdiction in which they are passed. Some states have laws, for instance, addressing marital rape, and other states do not. In 2000, most states regulated the practice of marriage and family therapy through statutory laws regarding licensure. Unfortunately, becoming licensed or certified as a family therapist in one state does not guarantee recognition of that license or certification by another state.

## Administrative (Regulatory) Law

**Administrative (regulatory) law** consists of specialized regulations passed by authorized government agencies that pertain to certain specialty areas. For example, laws governing the use of federal land are often made under this arrangement. Some regulations in regard to families, such as those dealing with abuse cases, may also fall in this category.

## Case Law (Court Decisions)

As the name implies, **case law** is the type of law decided by decisions of courts at all levels from state to federal. Cases are decided in regard to legal statutes, but many nuances enter the process. Even a minor change in the facts can change the decision of the court. Matters pertaining to child support, for example, may be decided by case law.

## Civil Law Versus Criminal Law

**Civil law** pertains to acts offensive to individuals, **criminal law** to acts offensive to society in general. Most of the law involving family therapists falls into the civil law classification (Hopkins & Anderson, 1990). One of the primary civil legal issues confronting some family therapists is divorce. Therapists who are familiar "with the legal issues facing families in transition can be effective in helping those clients make informed, rational, and realistic decisions" (Oliver, 1992, p. 41). The essential element at such times is being knowledgeable about therapeutic and legal issues.

Some incidents in family therapy involve issues that are legally criminal in scope. In such cases, therapists must be aware of what their duties and responsibilities are and what roles they need to play professionally. Two examples of criminal actions within families are spousal abuse and child abuse. In both cases, family therapists have a duty to take actions that are not usually within their domains, such as reporting their knowledge to a legally responsible agency.

# Legal Situations That Involve Family Therapists

Family therapists can be faced with any number of legal situations. Most of these occur on the state or local level. Some of the most common legal issues that come up in family counseling "revolve around state laws focusing on the reporting of child abuse, maltreatment, and neglect of minors" (Kaplan & Culkin, 1995, p. 337). Therefore, it behooves family therapists to become familiar with their state's legal system and even the courts and judges in their area (Stevens-Smith & Hughes, 1993). "It is difficult to uphold state laws if you don't know what they are" (Kaplan & Culkin, 1995, p. 337).

Therapists may be called on to participate in some legal and legally related situations in the following capacities: expert witness, child custody evaluator, reporter of abuse, and court-ordered witness.

## Expert Witness

As an **expert witness,** family therapists are asked to give testimony about probable causes and recommendations in regard to family members, such as juveniles who are acting out behaviorally. Because courts are adversarial, therapists must prepare themselves before their appearance. They must stay objective and establish their credibility by presenting their credentials and qualifications. They must speak from authoritative sources and be specific. This type of preparation can help them increase their confidence and competence.

## Child Custody Evaluator

As a **child custody evaluator,** family therapists are asked to determine what is in the best interest of a child in custody arrangements. In these cases, "the child custody evaluator represents the children and the courts, not the parents" (Stevens-Smith & Hughes, 1993, p. 27). The evaluation of a child includes home visits, testing, and conversations with the child involved. It requires that family therapists involved have a background and experience in child development, family systems, parenting skills, psychometry, counseling, and witness testimony (Remley & Miranti, 1992).

## Reporter of Abuse

As a reporter of **abuse,** family therapists must break confidentiality. In doing so, therapists are following the Child Abuse Prevention and Treatment Act of 1974, which mandates the reporting of such situations for the greater good of society. Abuse includes all forms of maltreatment whether physical, sexual, or emotional. It is recommended that family therapists advise families when they are obligated to report abuse and explain to these families how the reporting process works (Stevens-Smith & Hughes, 1993).

## Court-Ordered Witness

As a **court-ordered witness,** family therapists must appear before a court to testify on behalf of or against a family or family member. If given a choice, most family therapists "would prefer to refuse to testify because they see problems as being systemic and no one is to blame" (Green & Hansen, 1989, p. 156). However, in cases in which they are subpoenaed, family therapists can help themselves and the persons involved by preparing ahead of time. One way they may do this is to seek the advice of attorneys (Remley, 1991). By learning about trial procedures and role playing possible situations, family therapists come to understand courts of law as they do other systems. Thus, they are able to function more effectively.

# Issues of Law in Family Therapy

Legal issues in family therapy are usually in the background, as opposed to the foreground, of a clinician's practice. Most involve matters germane to the question of **malpractice,** which is "the failure to fulfill the requisite standard of care" (Woody, 1988, p. 2). Malpractice can occur because of "omission (what should have been done, but was not done) or commission (doing something that should not have been done)" (Woody, 1988, p. 2). In both cases, negligence must be proved for a malpractice suit to be brought forward. Such an incidence may happen if the family therapist either fails to report criminal activities [*Missouri v. Beatty,* 770 S.W.2d 387 (Mo. Ct. App. 1989)] or does not inform a family or some of its members that they are in grave danger [*Tarasoff v. Regents of the University of California,* 551 P.2d 334 (Cal. 1976)].

Two other frequent situations that relate to malpractice involve advertising and record keeping. In regard to advertising, most states "place legal limits" on what family practitioners can do to advertise their skills and services (Bullis, 1993, p. 15). These limits take the form of protecting a title. Thus, only professionals who have met the necessary criteria can call themselves "licensed marriage and family therapists." Because state laws vary, family therapists need to become informed of their state's general statutes before they advertise. They must also check professional ethics codes. For instance, the AAMFT has an extensive section in their code on advertising.

In the matter of record keeping, clinical notes should be kept "accurately and professionally" and "separately" from any required business transactions (Hopkins & Anderson, 1990, p. 18). Accuracy encompasses the sequential and cogent nature of what was written. In maintaining accuracy, therapists should "indicate any addendum to records and sign and date such additions. All changes to diagnoses or treatment plans must be made as separate entries" (Marine, 1995, p. 11). Professionalism deals with the legibility and protection of records. "Therapists must always know where their records are and who is responsible for them. Failure to produce records reflects poorly on malpractice litigation"

(Marine, 1995, p. 11). Therefore, family therapists are advised to keep their records locked in filed cabinets that are then secured in locked storage areas. In general, most states require all therapists to keep client records and have stipulations as to the length of time records must be kept. "Because family therapy has a long maturation process for claims (sometimes 10, 15, or 20 years after treatment is terminated), maintaining records is a primary risk management technique" (Marine, 1995, p. 11).

Overall, family therapists can help themselves and their client families by being current on acceptable practices and codes within the family therapy field and by making referrals to other more skilled clinicians when they are beyond their level of competence (Hopkins & Anderson, 1990). Carrying professional liability insurance is a must (Bullis, 1993). Such insurance protects therapists financially from legal claims that they have mishandled family needs or members. The responsibility for legally and ethically protecting client families lies squarely on the shoulders of family therapy professionals.

# Family/Divorce Mediation

**Family/divorce mediation** is related to legal issues in family therapy but differs in its scope and emphasis. It is the process of helping couples and families settle disputes or dissolve their marriages in a nonadversarial way. Mediation is an increasingly utilized alternative to court action (Gladding et al., 2001). As a family/divorce mediator, family therapists are specially trained to function in a legally related role as an impartial, cognitive, neutral, third party to facilitate negotiation between disputing parties, often a husband and wife. The objective is to help those involved make an informed and mutually agreed on decision that resolves differences between themselves in a practical and fair manner (Ferstenberg, 1992; Waxman & Press, 1991). "Mediation involves the resolution of conflict, not merely the cessation of it" (Huber, Mascari, & Sanders-Mascari, 1991, p. 117).

Steps involved in the mediation procedure include the mediator obtaining a brief history of the couple/family including information about children. The family members also disclose to the mediator their assets, incomes, liabilities, and goals, whenever appropriate. Furthermore, they prioritize their most important issues. Where necessary, the mediator may involve or consult with other professionals, such as accountants. However, information, ideas, and decisions are generally limited to the parties involved and the mediator.

In contrast to divorce proceedings, mediation is less time consuming, less costly, less hostile and stressful, and more productive (Ferstenberg, 1992). It protects clients and their records from public scrutiny and helps them problem solve and reconstruct their lives in a reasonable and settled manner. There is an external deadline, and mediation concludes with a negotiated written agreement. The important point that family therapists who function as mediators must remember is that they have to help the parties involved learn how to bargain and come to a fair agreement. In doing so, they function in a role quite apart from that of a family therapist, let alone an attorney.

Organizations family therapists can consult in finding out more about mediation include the Academy of Family Mediators in Lexington, Massachusetts, phone: (617)674-2663; the Association of Family and Conciliation Courts in Madison, Wisconsin, phone: (608)251-4001; the National Institute for Dispute Resolution in Washington, DC, phone:

(202)466-4764; and the Society for Professionals in Dispute Resolution in Washington, DC, phone: (202)783-7277.

# Professional Identification as a Family Therapist

In addition to ethical and legal questions in the practice of family therapy, there is at least one other professional issue: professional identification. A professional's educational background is usually related to his or her identification. This background also influences future professional opportunities, self-esteem, colleagues, and clinical practices. To be a member of an association and/or licensed or certified by a respectable professional group or state is important. Associations and licensure groups establish standards for their members to follow. They also offer a means for those within the public domain to address grievances or concerns related to a practitioner or the profession in general. Belonging to a professional association or being licensed helps clinicians and the public relate to one another on a higher plane and in a better way than would otherwise be possible.

## Organizations Associated with Family Therapy

Before the 1980s, the four major associations dealing with issues connected with family therapy were the American Association for Marriage and Family Therapy (AAMFT), the American Family Therapy Association (AFTA), the Affiliated Council for Marriage Enrichment (ACME), and the National Council on Family Relations (NCFR). Of the four, the AAMFT was dominant in regard to membership and influence.

However, in the 1980s, two new family therapy associations were established. The first was Division 43 (Family Psychology), which was formed within the American Psychological Association in 1984. The second fledgling group established in 1986 was the International Association of Marriage and Family Counselors (IAMFC). The IAMFC has been connected with the American Counseling Association from its beginning.

### American Association for Marriage and Family Therapy

The American Association for Marriage and Family Therapy is the oldest and largest (22,000 members) professional family therapy organization (Nichols, 1992). It was initially established in 1942 as the American Association of Marriage Counselors (AAMC). The driving force behind the forming of this group was Lester Dearborn of Boston, who organized the AAMC like a private club. Some of the most prominent names in the field of marriage counseling were charter members of the AAMC including Emily Mudd, Ernest Groves, and Abraham Stone. (See Chapter 3 on the history of family therapy for more details on the establishment of AAMFT.) From 1942 to 1967 the AAMC was "an elite interest group" that struggled in regard to both its identity and its financial stability (Nichols, 1992, p. 5).

In 1970, the AAMC became the American Association of Marriage and Family Counselors (AAMFC). At the same time, membership standards were lowered and membership (and revenue) increased. It changed its name to the American Association for Marriage and Family Therapy in 1979 and moved its headquarters to Washington, DC, in 1982.

The AAMFT and its affiliate organizations concentrate on accrediting educational programs that meet prescribed standards and advocating for licensure for family therapists on the state level. The AAMFT also produces videos on family therapy and publishes professional literature, including the *Journal of Marital and Family Therapy* and the *Family Therapy News*. It also holds an annual convention. In addition, the AAMFT lobbies for passage of select federal legislation that is in the interest of family therapy, including the recognition of family therapists as "core" mental health providers.

Overall, the AAMFT is a multifaceted, multidisciplinary professional association that is active in positively impacting the health care delivery system in the United States as it affects families.

### American Family Therapy Association

The American Family Therapy Association (AFTA) was founded by Murray Bowen in 1977. Its stated objectives include:

- advancing theories and therapies that regard the entire family as a unit
- promoting research and professional education in family therapy and allied fields
- making information about family therapy available to practitioners in other fields of knowledge and to the public
- fostering the cooperation of all who are concerned with the medical, psychological, social, legal, and other needs of the family
- promoting the science and practice of family therapy

The five categories of AFTA membership are charter, clinical-teacher, research, distinguished, and foreign. Association members represent a wide variety of disciplines. Membership requirements are essentially a terminal professional degree, 5 years of post-degree clinical experience with families, and 5 years of teaching family therapy or performing significant research in the family field. The membership numbers approximately 1,000 family therapy teachers and researchers who meet once a year to share ideas and develop common interests (Kaslow, 1990).

### Division 43 of the American Psychological Association: Family Psychology

Division 43 (Family Psychology) of the American Psychological Association (APA) was established to enable psychologists who worked with families to keep their identity as psychologists (Kaslow, 1990). As a division, Family Psychology includes more than 3,000 practitioners and academicians who are concerned with the science, practice, public interest, and education of psychologists who work with families. Family psychologists are involved in premarital, marital, divorce, and remarriage counseling. They focus on family abuse and violence, pediatrics, geriatrics, and governmental policies connected with family issues.

To become a division member, a professional must hold membership in the APA. Like the AAMFT and AFTA, the Division of Family Psychology sponsors a number of programs in which members may participate, including the annual APA convention. It has established task forces and committees that members may join. A bulletin, *The Family Psychologist,* is published regularly by the division, and many Division 43 members contribute to the APA periodical *Journal of Family Psychology.*

According to L'Abate (1992), family psychology differs from family therapy in three areas. First, "family psychology is interested in the whole functionality-dysfunctionality continuum, while family therapy is mainly concerned with dysfunctionality" (p. 3). Second, "while family psychology focuses reductionistically on the relationship of the individual within the family, family therapy focuses holistically on the family as a whole unit or system" (p. 3). Third, "family psychology stresses objective evaluation and primary and secondary prevention approaches" (p. 3). Family therapy, on the other hand, "stresses the subjective understanding of the family and sees therapy as one type of tertiary prevention" (p. 3). Not all family therapists agree with L'Abate, and the debate about the identity of family psychology continues.

### International Association of Marriage and Family Counselors

The International Association of Marriage and Family Counselors (IAMFC) is a division of the American Counseling Association (ACA). IAMFC membership is interdisciplinary. The major elements common to the approximately 4,000 members include professional training in marriage and family counseling/therapy and an interest/involvement in working with couples and families directly or tangentially. Members participate in regional and national conferences sponsored by the IAMFC and the ACA. In addition, the IAMFC has developed national training standards accepted by its membership and the Council for Accreditation of Counseling and Related Educational Programs.

The IAMFC publishes the *IAMFC Newsletter,* which is devoted to examining current issues related to marriage and family counseling, and *The Family Journal: Counseling and Therapy for Couples and Families,* a quarterly periodical. It also produces videos and publishes books related to family therapy. In addition, the association is involved in credentialing marriage and family counselors/therapists. It is helping to upgrade ethical standards within the ACA on marriage and family counseling/therapy, but maintains its own standards as well.

### National Council on Family Relations

The National Council on Family Relations (NCFR) is the oldest professional association dedicated to working with families. It was established in 1939, and many of its members helped to create and support the AAMFT (Nichols, 1992). Throughout its history, the NCFR has concentrated on education. Its membership is interdisciplinary and includes family life educators, sociologists, family researchers, and family therapists.

A specialty of the NCFR is delineating information about family history, family forms and functions, and family life in a variety of settings. It publishes a variety of publications including the *Journal of Marriage and the Family* and *Family Relations.* It also sponsors annual conventions in which professionals from a wide variety of settings can exchange ideas. One of its major subspecialty groups is devoted to family therapy.

### Affiliated Council for Marriage Enrichment

One of the oldest interdisciplinary associations for marriage enrichment is the Affiliated Council for Marriage Enrichment (ACME), established in 1975. This association, like others, has gone through a number of transitions. Its constituent members are comprised of various enrichment group leaders from across the United States. It is preventive in nature and is sometimes overlooked as a resource for family therapists.

## Education of Family Therapists

Part of professional identity is one's education. The educational programs of family therapists are conducted in collaboration with learned societies and associations. The formal process of education is overseen by representatives from a number of associations, such as the Commission on Accreditation for Marriage and Family Therapy Education (COAMFTE) or the Council on Accreditation of Counseling and Related Educational Programs (CACREP).

In recent years the curriculums for graduating master's degree family therapists have been similar in accredited AAMFT and CACREP programs. Table 15.1 shows the required course work areas for these two programs.

Numerous problems are associated with current educational programs in family therapy. For example, among professional association groups, there is considerable in-fighting for recognition that one method of educating family therapists is superior to others. This type of "turfism" is sometimes conducted in a blind fashion, with some professional groups refusing to recognize other similar groups (Baltimore, 1993).

A second weakness in family therapy education programs as they are presently structured is that "they tend to ignore issues that are controversial and difficult to teach" (Smith & Stevens-Smith, 1992, p. 438). Areas that arouse emotion in regard to therapeu-

**Table 15.1**
Example of Course Work Areas Required for a Master's Degree in AAMFT-Accredited and CACREP-Accredited Programs

| CACREP Curriculum | AAMFT Curriculum |
| --- | --- |
| Human Growth & Development | Introduction Family/Child Dev. |
| Social and Cultural Foundations | Marital & Family Systems |
| Helping Relationships | Intro. Family/Child Development |
| Groups | Dysfunctions in Marriage/Family |
| Lifestyle & Career Development | Advanced Child Development |
| Appraisal/Assessment | Assessment in Marital/Family |
| Research and Evaluation | Research Methods Child/Family |
| Professional Orientation | Professional Issues Family |
| Theoretical Foundation MFT | Theories of MFT |
| Techniques/Treatment MFT | Marriage/Family Pre-Practicum |
| Clinical Practicum/Internship | Clinical Practicum |
| Substance Abuse Treatment | Human Sexual Behavior |
| Human Sexuality | Thesis |
| Electives | Electives |

From "The Training of Marriage and Family Counselors/Therapists: A 'Systemic' Controversy among Disciplines" by Michael Baltimore, 1993, *Alabama Counseling Association Journal, 19,* 40. Copyright 1993, Alabama Counseling Association. Reprinted with permission.

tic content and process need to be examined. For example, divorce, substance abuse, homelessness, teen pregnancies, extramarital affairs, and the impact of AIDS on family life are but a handful of these subjects. They may require specialized courses or they may be explored in different regular course offerings.

## Issues in Professional Identification

As is evident from this overview of professional family therapy associations, practitioners have a wide choice regarding which group or groups they align with. Each association has unique aspects or foci. For instance, the Affiliated Council for Marriage Enrichment concentrates on preventive services (i.e., primary intervention). On the other hand, the National Council on Family Relations is most concerned with education and training (i.e., secondary intervention). The other associations all concentrate to some extent on the promotion of health and on the therapeutic treatment of dysfunctionality (i.e., tertiary intervention). Each of these associations sponsors programs and speakers that address the issues involved in prevention and education, too. They all like to think of themselves as holistic in their approaches, and indeed the case can be strongly made that the AAMFT, IAMFC, AFTA, and Division 43 of APA do follow such a comprehensive model.

Emphasis aside, friction exists among associations that are dedicated to family therapy. In all likelihood, turf issues surrounding this uneasiness will continue in the foreseeable future.

# Summary and Conclusion

Ethical, legal, and professional identity issues are of major importance to family therapists. Ignorance of codes, standards, and associations are no excuse for acting unethically, illegally, and/or unprofessionally.

Family and societal conduct is based on relationship ethics. Family therapy is not value free, either. When faced with a dilemma, family therapists must know their own values, the values ethical codes are based on, and the values of the families with whom they work. They can then make informed ethical decisions. Four of the most useful tools they can use in this process are codes of ethics, educational resources, professional consultation, and interaction with colleagues, including supervisors. Common ethical concerns are related to confidentiality, gender inequality, sexual relationships, therapeutic techniques, multicultural therapy issues, and use of the Internet to provide therapy.

Legal issues often overlap with ethical matters. The law and therapy share some common concerns regarding setting up relationships between people. They differ in their emphases on facts/process and adversarial/cooperative approaches. The most common type of law most family therapists are concerned with is civil law (acts offensive to individuals). However, it is important that therapists know other types of law and local/state statutes related to families. Family therapists are most likely to participate in legal situations as expert witnesses, child custody evaluators, reporters of abuse, and court-ordered witnesses. They must actively protect themselves against malpractice by adhering to commonly accepted and legal ways of handling family therapy cases. Furthermore, they must carry malpractice insurance. Family therapists may act as family mediators if they receive advanced training. Such positions involve the resolution of conflict in a nonadversarial and rational way.

In regard to identity, family therapists generally belong to one or more professional associations including AAMFT, AFTA, Family Psychology (APA), IAMFC, NCFR, and ACME. All of these groups have much to offer that can positively influence the careers of family therapists; however, they sometimes quarrel.

# Summary Table

## Ethical, Legal, and Professional Issues in Family Therapy

Ethics, law, and identity are of major concern to family therapists.

It is crucial for family therapists to be knowledgeable about issues in ethics, law, and identity if they are to practice according to high standards and avoid serious trouble.

### Overview of Ethics in Families and Family Therapy

Families and societies are governed by relationship ethics based on the principle of equitability.

Family therapy is also governed by principles of ethics that have been codified.

Ethics are a part of the total system of family therapy.

Family therapists face more ethical conflicts than other therapists.

### Ethics and Values

Ethical decision making is based on an awareness and understanding of values. A value is a choice that is more or less preferable.

Effective therapists are aware of their own values and those of the families with whom they work. Values have an impact on families and undergird ethical decisions.

Ethical dilemmas in family therapy are related to deciding which values to keep and which to discard. Emphasis of values is of concern.

### How Do Values Influence Ethical Practice?

All ethical issues involve values as grounds for decision making.

The values family therapists embrace directly affect their clinical practice.

### Guidelines for Making Ethical Decisions

Four prevalent resources family therapists use in ethical decision making are

- codes of ethics
- educational resources
- professional consultation
- interactions with colleagues including supervision

Both the AAMFT and the IAMFC have developed codes of ethics.

Ethical codes are sometimes limited by the complexity of issues.

Educational resources include case studies and columns on family therapy ethics. Ethical decision making is a step-by-step process.

Professional consultation involves the use of experts to enhance one's knowledge and abilities.

Interactions with peers, including supervision, help family therapists draw on the wisdom and opinions of others in a systemic manner.

## Common Ethical Concerns

Among the most common ethical concerns are those involving:

- confidentiality (i.e., the revealing to others of information revealed in a therapy session)
- gender issues (e.g., inequality of men and women)
- sex between a therapist and a client
- use of some theoretical techniques (e.g., conscious deceit or neutrality)
- multicultural therapy issues
- use of the Internet for therapy

## Addressing Unethical Behavior

Addressing unethical behavior with fellow professionals accused of violations is the first step in resolving it.

Reporting to professional associations/organizations is a second step.

Complaints by clients to a licensure board is a third step.

## Legal Issues in Family Therapy

Ethics and law frequently overlap, such as with cases involving intentional misdiagnosis.

Family therapists are not immune to dealing with the legal system and must be aware of legal decisions, precedents, and practices.

## The Legal System

*Legal* refers to "law or being lawful." *Law* refers to a body of rules, made on a variety of levels such as state or federal, that are binding in certain locales and under specific situations.

The legal and therapeutic systems are similar in that they both are concerned with setting up healthy relationships and both handle cases that involve drama and resolution.

Differences between legal and therapeutic systems also exist. The legal system is concerned with gathering evidence based on facts, and the therapeutic system is more interested in process and change. In addition, the legal system relies on adversity, and the therapeutic system relies on cooperation.

## Types of Law

The most common types of law are

- common law (law derived from tradition)
- statutory law (rules passed by legislative bodies)
- administrative law (rules made by government agencies)
- case law (court decisions)
- civil versus criminal law (offenses against individuals versus those against society in general)

Therapists who are knowledgeable about the law can help themselves and their client families.

## Legal Situations That Involve Family Therapists

Family therapists may be called on to participate in some legal and legally related situations in the following capacities:

- expert witness (one who gives testimony in the form of recommendations about a family or family member)
- child custody evaluator (one who determines the best interest of a child in a custody hearing)
- reporter of abuse (one who informs members of the legal system about the maltreatment of a family member)
- court-ordered witness (one who is subpoenaed to testify in court about a family seen in treatment)

## Issues of Law in Family Therapy

Malpractice is a major legal issue and can occur through omission as well as commission. In either case, negligence must be proved.

Advertising and record keeping are two other legal issues. The first involves protecting a title and representing one's skills adequately. The second focuses on keeping accurate and professional notes.

Liability insurance is a must if one is going to be legally protected as a family therapist.

## Family/Divorce Mediation

Mediation is the process of helping couples/families settle disputes or dissolve relationships in a nonadversarial way.

Skills associated with mediation include abilities to be cognitive, neutral, impartial, practical, and fair minded.

Steps in the mediation process include taking a brief history of the couple/family and obtaining disclosure of assets, incomes, liabilities, and goals. Prioritizing choices is essential.

Overall, mediation is less time consuming, costly, hostile, and stressful than legal divorce proceedings. It is also more productive.

## Professional Identification as a Family Therapist

A family therapist's education, background, self-perception, and opportunities are associated with professional identity.

The six national professional associations related to family therapy are as follows:

- AAMFT was established in 1942. It is the oldest and largest association devoted to family therapy. Its membership is interdisciplinary.
- AFTA was established in 1977 by Murray Bowen. It is the most focused on teaching and research.
- Family Psychology (APA) was established in 1984 to allow psychology practitioners who work with families to keep their identity as psychologists.
- IAMFC was established in 1986. It is the second largest family therapy association. It parallels many aspects of AAMFT but is more affiliated with counseling as a profession.

- NCFR was established in 1939, but only one group within the association is dedicated to working therapeutically with families.
- ACME is an interdisciplinary association for marriage enrichment groups, like a confederation. It was established in 1975.

Despite areas of overlap, there is still competition and some disagreement among these groups.

# References

American Association for Marriage and Family Therapy. (2001). *AAMFT Code of Ethics*. Washington, DC: Author.

Ansen, D., & Springen, K. (1992, April 13). A lot of not so happy endings. *Newsweek*, p. 58.

Aponte, H. J. (1992). Training the person of the therapist in structural family therapy. *Journal of Marital and Family Therapy, 18*, 269–281.

Arthur, G. L., & Swanson, C. D. (1993). *Confidentiality and privileged communication*. Alexandria, VA: American Counseling Association.

Baltimore, M. (1993). The training of marriage and family counselors/therapists: A "systemic" controversy among disciplines. *Alabama Counseling Association Journal, 19*, 34–44.

Beck, M., Springen, K., & Foote, D. (1992, April 13). Sex and psychotherapy. *Newsweek*, pp. 52–57.

Bograd, M. (1992). Values in conflict: Challenges to family therapists' thinking. *Journal of Marital and Family Therapy, 18*, 245–256.

Boszormenyi-Nagy, I., & Ulrich, D. N. (1981). Contextual family therapy. In A. S. Gurman & D. P. Kniskern (Eds.), *Handbook of family therapy*. New York: Brunner/Mazel.

Brendel, J. M., & Nelson, K. W. (1999). The stream of family secrets: Navigating the islands of confidentiality and triangulation involving family therapists. *The Family Journal: Counseling and Therapy for Couples and Families, 7*, 112–117.

Bullis, R. K. (1993). *Law and the management of a counseling agency or private practice*. Alexandria, VA: American Counseling Association.

Carter, B. (1986). Success in family therapy. *Family Therapy Networker, 10*, 16–22.

Carter, B. (1992). Stonewalling feminism. *Family Therapy Networker, 16*, 64–69.

Caudill, O. B., Jr. (2000, February/March). Long distance liability. *Family Therapy News, 31*(1), 10–12.

Cobia, D. C., & Boes, S. R. (2000). Professional disclosure statements and formal plans for supervision: Two strategies for minimizing the risk of ethical conflicts in post-master's supervision. *Journal of Counseling and Development, 78*, 293–296.

Cooper, C., & Costas, L. (1994, Spring). Ethical challenges when working with Hispanic/Latino families: Personalismo. *The Family Psychologist, 10*, 32–34.

Corey, G., Corey, M. S., & Callanan, P. (1998). *Issues and ethics in the helping professions* (5th ed.). Pacific Grove, CA: Brooks/Cole.

Costa, L., & Sorenson, J. (1993). Feminist family therapy: Ethical considerations for the clinician. *The Family Journal: Counseling and Therapy for Couples and Families, 1*, 17–24.

Cottone, R. R., & Claus, R. E. (2000). Ethical decision-making models: A review of the literature. *Journal of Counseling and Development, 78*, 275–283.

Doherty, W. J. (1995). *Soul searching: Why psychotherapy must promote moral responsibility*. New York: Basic Books.

Doherty, W. J., & Boss, P. G. (1991). Values and ethics in family therapy. In A. S. Gurman & D. P. Kniskern (Eds.), *Handbook of family therapy* (Vol. II, pp. 606–637). New York: Brunner/Mazel.

Ferstenberg, R. L. (1992). Mediation versus litigation in divorce and why a litigator becomes a mediator. *American Journal of Family Therapy, 20*, 266–273.

Fishman, C. H. (1988). *Treating troubled adolescents*. New York: Basic Books.

Frame, M. W. (1998). The ethics of counseling via the Internet. *The Family Journal: Counseling and Therapy for Couples and Families, 5*, 328–330.

Giblin, P. (1993). Values: Family and other. *The Family Journal: Counseling and Therapy for Couples and Families, 1*, 240–242.

Gladding, S. T. (1993). *Nathaniel's entrance*. Unpublished poem.

Gladding, S. T., Remley, T. P., Jr., & Huber, C. H. (2001). *Ethical, legal and professional issues in the practice of marriage and family therapy* (3rd ed.). Upper Saddle River, NJ: Merrill/Prentice Hall.

Gladding, S. T., Wilcoxon, S. A., Semon, M. G., & Myers, P. (1992). Individual and marriage/family counseling supervision: Similarities, differences, and implications for training. *Journal of the Florida Association for Counseling and Development, 1*, 58–71.

Green, S. L., & Hansen, J. C. (1986). Ethical dilemmas in family therapy. *Journal of Marital and Family Therapy, 12*, 225–230.

Green, S. L., & Hansen, J. C. (1989). Ethical dilemmas faced by family therapists. *Journal of Marital and Family Therapy, 15,* 149–158.

Grosser, G. H., & Paul, N. L. (1964). Ethical issues in family group therapy. *American Journal of Orthopsychiatry, 34,* 875–884.

Hannon, K. (1996, May 13). Upset? Try cybertherapy. *U.S. News and World Report,* pp. 81–83.

Hare-Mustin, R. T. (1987). The problem of gender in family therapy theory. *Family Process, 26,* 15–27.

Henderson, M. C. (1987). Paradoxical process and ethical consciousness. *Family Therapy, 14,* 187–193.

Hohenshil, T. H. (2000). High tech counseling. *Journal of Counseling and Development, 78,* 365–368.

Hopkins, B. R., & Anderson, B. S. (1990). *The counselor and the law* (3rd ed.). Alexandria, VA: American Counseling Association.

Huber, C. H., Mascari, J. B., & Sanders-Mascari, A. (1991). Family mediation. In J. Carlson & J. Lewis (Eds.), *Family counseling: Strategies and issues.* Denver, CO: Love.

Hundert, E. M. (1987). A model for ethical problem solving in medicine, with practical applications. *American Journal of Psychiatry, 144,* 839–846.

Hurvitz, N. (1967). Marital problems following psychotherapy with one spouse. *Journal of Consulting and Clinical Psychology, 31,* 38–47.

International Association of Marriage and Family Counselors. (1993). Ethical code for the International Association of Marriage and Family Counselors. *The Family Journal: Counseling and Therapy for Couples and Families, 1,* 73–77.

Jacobson, N. (1994). Rewards and dangers in researching domestic violence. *Family Process, 33,* 81–85.

Jester, S. (1995, December). Legal and risk management plan and *Practice Strategies* newsletter join growing list of AAMFT member benefits. *Family Therapy News, 26,* 7.

Jordan, K., & Stevens, P. (1999). Revising the ethical code of the IAMFC–A training exercise for counseling psychology and counselor education students. *The Family Journal: Counseling and Therapy for Couples and Families, 7,* 170–175.

Kaplan, D., & Allison, M. (1993a). Family ethics. *The Family Journal: Counseling and Therapy for Couples and Families, 1,* 72–77.

Kaplan, D., & Allison, M. (1993b). Family ethics. *The Family Journal: Counseling and Therapy for Couples and Families, 1,* 246–248.

Kaplan, D., & Culkin, M. (1995). Family ethics: Lessons learned. *The Family Journal: Counseling and Therapy for Couples and Families, 3,* 335–338.

Kaslow, F. (1990). *Voices in family psychology.* Newbury Park, CA: Sage.

Krasner, L., & Houts, A. C. (1984). A study of the "value" systems of behavioral scientists. *American Psychologist, 39,* 840–850.

Kurilla, V. (1998). Multicultural counseling perspectives: Culture specificity and implications in family therapy. *The Family Journal: Counseling and Therapy for Couples and Families, 6,* 207–211.

Kurpius, D. J., & Fuqua, D. R. (1993). Fundamental issues in defining consultation. *Journal of Counseling & Development, 71,* 598–600.

L'Abate, L. (1992). Family psychology and family therapy: Comparisons and contrasts. *American Journal of Family Therapy, 20,* 3–12.

Marine, E. (1995, December). Preserving your records. *Family Therapy News, 26*(6), 11.

McGoldrick, M. (1999). Women and the family life cycle. In B. Carter & M. McGoldrick (Eds.), *The expanded family life cycle* (3rd ed., pp. 106–123). Boston: Allyn & Bacon.

McGoldrick, M., & Carter, B. (1999). Self in context: The individual life cycle in systemic perspective. In B. Carter & M. McGoldrick (Eds.), *The expanded family life cycle* (3rd ed., pp. 27–46). Boston: Allyn & Bacon.

McGoldrick, M., Gerson, R., & Shellenberger, S. (1998). *Genograms in family assessment* (2nd ed.). New York: Norton.

Mitchell, R. W. (1991). *Documentation in counseling records.* Alexandria, VA: American Counseling Association.

Morrison, J., Layton, B., & Newman, J. (1982). Ethical conflict in clinical decision making: A challenge for family therapists. In J. Hansen (Ed.), *Values, ethics, legalities and the family therapists.* Rockville, MD: Aspen.

Nichols, W. C. (1992). *Fifty years of marital and family therapy.* Washington, DC: American Association for Marriage and Family Therapy.

Nixon, J. A. (1993). Gender considerations in the case of "The Jealous Husband": Strategic therapy in review. *The Family Journal: Counseling and Therapy for Couples and Families, 1,* 161–163.

Oliver, C. J. (1992). Legal issues facing families in transition: An overview for counselors. *New York State Journal for Counseling and Development, 7,* 41–52.

O'Malley, P. (1995, December). Confidentiality in the electronic age. *Family Therapy News, 26,* 9.

Papp, P. (1977). *Family therapy: Full-length case studies.* New York: Gardner.

Pedersen, P. (1996). The importance of similarities and differences in multicultural counseling: Reaction to C. H. Patterson. *Journal of Counseling and Development, 74,* 236–237.

Piercy, F. P. (2000, March/April). To tell or not to tell? *Family Therapy Networker, 24,* 21.

Pope, K. S., & Vasquez, M. J. T. (1998). *Ethics in psychotherapy and counseling: A practical guide.* San Francisco: Jossey-Bass.

Remley, T. P. (1991). *Preparing for court appearances.* Alexandria, VA: American Counseling Association.

Remley, T. P., Jr., & Miranti, J. (1992). Child custody evaluator: A new role for mental health counselors. *Journal of Mental Health Counseling, 13,* 334–342.

Ryder, R., & Hepworth, J. (1990). AAMFT ethical code: "Dual relationships." *Journal of Marital and Family Therapy, 16,* 127–132.

Saba, G. W., Karrer, B. M., & Hardy, K. V. (Eds.). (1996). *Minorities and family therapy.* New York: Haworth.

Schwartz, R. C., Liddle, H. A., & Breunlin, D. C. (1988). Muddles in live supervision. In H. A. Liddle, D. C. Breunlin, & R. C. Schwartz (Eds.), *Handbook of family therapy training* (pp. 172–182). New York: Guilford.

Seppa, N. (1996, August). Supreme Court protects patient-therapist privilege. *APA Monitor, 27,* 39.

Shertzer, B., & Stone, S. (1980). *Fundamentals of counseling* (3rd ed.). Boston: Houghton Mifflin.

Smith, R. L., & Stevens-Smith, P. (1992). Future projections for marriage and family counseling and therapy. In R. L. Smith & P. Stevens-Smith (Eds.), *Family counseling and therapy* (pp. 433–440). Ann Arbor, MI: ERIC/CAPS.

Solovey, A. D., & Duncan, B. L. (1992). Ethics and strategic therapy: A proposed ethical direction. *Journal of Marital and Family Therapy, 18,* 53–61.

Spiegel, J. (1971). *Transactions: The interplay between individual, family, and society.* New York: Science House.

Stevens-Smith, P., & Hughes, M. M. (1993). *Legal issues in marriage and family counseling.* Alexandria, VA: American Counseling Association.

Van Hoose, W. H., & Kottler, J. (1985). *Ethical and legal issues in counseling and psychotherapy* (2nd ed.). San Francisco: Jossey-Bass.

Walsh, W. M. (1993). Gender and strategic marital therapy. *The Family Journal: Counseling and Therapy for Couples and Families, 1,* 160–161.

Walters, M., Carter, B., Papp, P., & Silverstein, O. (1992). *The invisible web: Gender patterns in family relationships.* New York: Guilford.

Waxman, G. L., & Press, S. (1991). Mediation: Part II. Mediation in Florida. *Nova Law Review, 15,* 1212–1225.

Weiner, J. P., & Boss, P. (1985). Exploring gender bias against women: Ethics for marriage and family therapy. *Counseling and Values, 30,* 9–21.

Welfel, E. R., Danzinger, P. R., & Santoro, S. (2000). Mandated reporting of abuse/maltreatment of older adults: A primer for counselors. *Journal of Counseling and Development, 78,* 284–292.

Wendorf, D. J., & Wendorf, R. J. (1992). A systemic view of family therapy ethics. In R. L. Smith & P. Stevens-Smith (Eds.), *Family counseling and therapy* (pp. 304–320). Ann Arbor, MI: ERIC/CAPS.

Wilcoxon, S. A. (1993, March/April). Ethical issues in marital and family counseling: A framework for examining unique ethical concerns. *Family Counseling and Therapy, 1,* 1–15.

Willbach, D. (1989). Ethics and family therapy: The case management of family violence. *Journal of Marital and Family Therapy, 15,* 43–52.

Woody, R. H. (1988). *Fifty ways to avoid malpractice.* Sarasota, FL: Professional Resource Exchange.

# CHAPTER 16

# Research and Assessment in Family Therapy

As a child of five he played in leaves
his father raked on autumn days,
safe in the knowledge that the yard was home
and that dinner would be served at sunset.

Now middle-aged he examines fences,
where from within his own children frolic
in the deep shadowed light of dusk,
Aware that strong boundaries help create bonds
that extend time and memory beyond the present.

*Gladding, 1992*

Research and assessment are vitally interlinked with family therapy and have a long association with it. From the time the term *family therapy* was first used in the 1950s until now, there has been a focus on assessment and healing among mental health professionals working with families (Baldwin & Huggins, 1998; Shields, Wynne, McDaniel, & Gawinski, 1994). Indeed, "the assessment of individuals and their family relationships has been and is an evolving part of the marriage and family counseling literature" (Sporakowski, 1995, p. 60).

Most of the pioneers in family therapy employed research-based procedures to evaluate and work with families. They were in effect "researcher-clinicians" (Sprenkle & Moon, 1996, p. 3). Although some of their research was "soft" by today's standards, initially, research came first and therapy was a secondary activity. Many early studies of therapeutic changes in families conducted by groups, such as those led by Bateson, Wynne, and Minuchin, excelled in family therapy research and assessment (Wynne, 1983). Historically, in the world of family therapy, there has been "a synergistic interplay among research, theory, and practice" (Sprenkle & Piercy, 1984, p. 226).

It is unfortunate but, after the genesis of family therapy, many practitioners drifted away from research and assessment. This split is most dramatically seen in some influential schools of family therapy whose advocates have gained considerable prominence but whose methods provide little empirical evidence to support their effectiveness (Gurman, Kniskern, & Pinsof, 1986). During the 1960s, therapists and researchers became two distinct groups, a fact lamented by Jay Haley (1978), among others.

In the 1990s, however, interest in both the practice of family therapy and the conducting of research was renewed. Research became so prevalent, in fact, that it was hard to keep up with it (Liddle, 1992). In addition, research by family therapists began to include a multitude of methods such as "surveys, personal interviews, observational studies, and content analysis of historical documents" (Bird & Sporakowski, 1992, p. x). The increase in the volume of family therapy research, and its more sophisticated procedures, added to the power and credibility of family therapy.

In the twenty-first century, family therapy is becoming even more sophisticated in its research and focus on real-life context. For example, Carrere, Buchlman, Gottman, Coan, & Ruckstruhl (2000) have found in studying the longitudinal course of marriages through social psychophysiological observations of marital interactions that they can predict with 81% accuracy what marriages will last at least 5 years. More emphasis is now placed on connecting process and outcome in family therapy research, too (Baldwin & Huggins, 1998), and making the translation of research findings into practical ways of working with dysfunctional families (Liddle, 1992).

Likewise, the assessment of families is becoming stronger. **Assessment** focuses on dimensions of particular families and usually includes the administration of formal or informal tests or evaluation instrument(s) along with behavioral observations. Assessment is dependent on having a theoretical model of how families function and of the ways in which their functioning may go awry. Sometimes this type of information is easily obtained, but often it is not. The field of family assessment is less developed and more complex than that of individual evaluation (Drummond, 2000; Snyder, Cavell, Heffer, & Mangrum, 1995).

Ways of conducting assessment are covered in this chapter, and some of the most common assessment instruments are described. First, however, the most prominent features of family research are considered.

# Importance of Research in Family Therapy

Research is important in family therapy for many reasons, but three of the most important involve accountability, practicality, and uniqueness.

In regard to accountability, research studies provide family therapists with the means to prove they are not "witch doctors, snake oil peddlers, or overachieving do-gooders" (Hubble, 1993, p. 14). Research results are a necessary element in the increasing respectability of family therapy.

On the level of practicality, research also has a payoff. Although research studies sometimes do not yield immediate applicability, they do have "an influence on clinical practice" in the long run (Hubble, 1993, p. 15). Therefore, it is critical that practitioners as well as statisticians become familiar with family therapy research methods and outcomes.

Finally, in regard to uniqueness, it is through research that the field of family therapy establishes its common bond and point of departure with other mental health counseling approaches. In the process of gaining knowledge about treatment methods and approaches, the profession of family therapy establishes itself as a type of entity that can make claims for its theories, practices, and clinicians (Schwartz & Breunlin, 1983). Thus, research is a vital link in the claim that family therapy should and does stand on its own as a type of specialized treatment (Piercy & Sprenkle, 1986).

# Research Findings in Family Therapy

Research on the effectiveness of family therapy is connected to research on the overall effectiveness of all types of psychotherapies. In general, most individuals improve when they receive therapy of any kind, especially when compared with a control group left on its own to resolve problems (Hubble, 1993). Comprehensive reviews of family therapy research indicates specifically that:

1. The improvement rate in family therapy is similar to the improvement rate in individual therapy.
2. The deterioration rate in family therapy is likewise similar to the deterioration rate in individual therapy.
3. "Deterioration may occur because:
   a. The therapist has poor interpersonal skills.

    b. The therapist moves too quickly into sensitive topic areas and does not handle the situation well.

    c. The therapist allows family conflict to become exacerbated without moderating therapeutic intervention.

    d. The therapist does not provide adequate structure in the early stages of therapy.

    e. The therapist does not support family members" (Fenell & Weinhold, 1992, p. 333).

4. Family therapy is as effective as individual counseling for personal problems or family conflict.

5. Brief therapy of 20 sessions or less is as effective as long-term therapy.

6. Participation of fathers in family therapy is much more likely to bring about positive results than family therapy without them.

7. Relationship skills of family therapists are crucial in producing positive outcomes.

8. Less severe forms of mental/psychological distress are more likely to be successfully treated than those that are severe.

9. Psychosomatic problems can be treated successfully with a modified version of structural family therapy.

10. The type of family, its background, and present interactional style relate to the success or failure of family therapy.

Some of the most promising research in the area of family therapy has been conducted by Jose Szapocznik and his associates at the Spanish Family Guidance Center in Miami (Letich, 1993). This clinically based research has concentrated on Hispanic/Latino-American families but has general implications. Among the contributions made by Szapocznik are

- the development of the Strategic Family Systems Rating (SFSR), a research tool that objectively measures and evaluates family functioning on six dimensions: structure, resonance, developmental stage, identified patienthood, flexibility, and conflict resolution (Szapocznik et al., 1991)
- the creation of one-person family therapy (OPFT), in which strategic family therapy is offered to any person who comes to therapy in order to help that person make changes in the family system (Szapocznik, Kurtines, Perez-Vidal, Hervis, & Foote, 1990)
- a comparison of outcome in boys and their families of the efficacy of individual, psychodynamic, child therapy versus family therapy (a landmark study in supporting the family therapy concept of complementarity, that is, if one person gets better without changing the family structure, the rest of the family gets worse (Szapocznik et al., 1989)

Szapocznik's research demonstrates a commitment to rigor and control with an orientation toward practical use. His work represents the best of clinical research. It is often idealized but seldom emulated by those within the field of family therapy.

# Two Types of Family Therapy Research

The two types of family therapy research are qualitative and quantitative. **Qualitative research** is still in its infancy. It is rooted in the traditions of anthropology and sociology (Moon, Dillon, & Sprenkle, 1990). Present interest in qualitative methodology "appears to be part of a larger postmodern turn in the human sciences. Postmodernism represents a general loss of faith in ultimate truth, a 'knowable' reality, certainty, and determinancy" (Kleist & Gompertz, 1997, p. 137).

According to Moon et al. (1990) most qualitative research is characterized by:

- open-ended, discovery-oriented questions that are holistic
- small samples carefully chosen to "fit research goals (criterion-based selection)" or to "help elaborate developing theory (theoretical selection)" (p. 369)
- participant-observer researchers who are subjectively explicit
- visual or verbal data reporting rather than numerical data reporting
- data analysis occurring simultaneously with data collection
- "analytic induction and constant comparison" (p. 369) by researchers who try to discern patterns in analyzing results of time- and labor-intensive investigations
- results that "take the form of theoretical assertions, discovered theory, or categorical systems (taxonomies)" (p. 369)
- reports that are well written, often as books, but with no standardized form
- reliability and validity based on journalistic reflections, thick descriptions of data, audits, comparison analysis, and "participant critiques of research reports" (p. 369)

Qualitative research, at its best, is found in extended interviews and autobiographies. A good example of a qualitative research study is the interview study of 10 couples with children in which both partners worked outside the home (Hochschild, 1989). In this research, written as a book, couples were asked who did what work around the house as well as information about their backgrounds. The researchers detected patterns and then made comments about them. The advantages of qualitative research over quantitative research include a more integrated and holistic view of client families and greater interaction between researcher/clinicians and client families (Sussman & Gilgun, 1997). Qualitative research also increases the flexibility of therapists to meet the needs of families (Hood & Johnson, 1998).

A particular type of qualitative research that is beginning to impact family therapy is participatory evaluation research (Piercy & Thomas, 1998). **Participatory evaluation research** has various forms but it differs from "other qualitative methods in the degree of participants' involvement" (p. 166). Instead of asking clients for information, a participatory researcher "might actually train clients as individual or focus group interviewers and involve them as co-researchers in data analysis interpretation and write-up" (p. 167). Overall, participatory research engages and empowers participants much more in the research process and is more democratic than other types of research.

**Quantitative research** grew out of the scientific traditions of physics, chemistry, and biology, and is the way most research is reported. Quantitative research is characterized by an emphasis on closed-ended questions, such as "Does a certain variable, such as working outside the home, have an impact on a family's happiness?" To answer this type of question, quantitative research utilizes large sample sizes to gather information. Objective researchers then focus on gathering data in a precise form, frequently using standardized instruments. Usually, the data from such studies is reported in a statistical format, such as averages of specific test scores. After the data are collected, they are analyzed and deductive conclusions are made based on the data analysis. The results tend to "prove" or "disprove" theories and assertions that formed the basis for the research in the first place.

A final report is then written in a standard and prosaic form. In it a description of what was done and how it was done is included. The report highlights characteristics of the population used; the reliability and validity of the instruments employed; and the process, conclusions, and recommendations for further research (Gay & Airasian, 2000; Goldman, 1990).

Quantitative research is one reason why family therapy is seen as a science as well as an art. By using quantitative methods, researchers are careful to define what they are doing and to record their results in a precise and scholarly manner. When they present their findings, quantitative researchers are likely to be able to focus on interventions that made a difference overall in their treatment. One example of an empirical study is the investigation of systemic and nonsystemic diagnostic processes by McGuirk, Friedlander, and Blocher (1987) in which they found that "systemic clinicians, in contrast with . . . nonsystemic ones, identified as relevant a greater number of different subsystems, more triads, and fewer monads" (p. 69).

Whether family therapy researchers choose qualitative or quantitative research methods, they must deal with complexities that are usually quite complicated. Family therapy is premised on a systemic perspective that emphasizes circular causality (i.e., A and B affect each other) rather than linear thinking that stresses cause and effect (e.g., A caused B). Thus, the emphasis in treatment and research is on the interaction of family members with each other (West, 1988). Difficulties stemming from this model present themselves in many forms. Questions related to one's choice of **research design,** sampling, instrumentation, and procedure are critical. Theoretical and statistical choices are also important in regard to researching the process and outcome of family therapy.

# Difficulties in Family Therapy Research

Many difficulties are associated with rigorously researching the effectiveness of family therapy. These include, but are not limited to, the complexity of relationships within families. In the study of family relationships, one question is "What within the family is the focus of attention?" For example, family therapy research can concentrate on the identified patient (IP), the marriage, the total family system, cross-generational relationships, and so forth (Gurman & Kniskern, 1981). The problems connected with studying families are further complicated by environmental factors. Are families studied within their environments or in a laboratory setting? Furthermore, the time commitment needed to study the effects of family therapy is great, and the number of personnel who must be devoted to gathering and analyzing data is difficult as well as expensive to sustain over time.

Assuming that the questions of focus and environment can be controlled, it then becomes important to focus attention on another pertinent aspect of research—its design.

## Design

The way in which research is designed ultimately affects the results (Gay & Airasian, 2000). Poorly designed studies yield worthless results; well-designed studies produce reports worth reading. In considering the design of a research study, investigators must make sure the design fits the families to be studied and that it is efficient (Miller, 1986).

Overall, the five categories of research design are exploratory, descriptive, developmental, experimental, and correlational. In exploratory research a qualitative approach is often taken because issues are still being defined. Therefore, many exploratory research designs consist of interviews between researchers and families. In descriptive research, the design is set up to describe specific variables, for example, subpopulations within the United States.

Developmental research designs focus on studying changes over time. The most characteristic of this type of design is a longitudinal study, although some cross-sectional studies are developmental in nature, too. A study focusing on the effects within families in which a member had AIDS is an example of a longitudinal study. Experimental research designs are those that adhere to classic "hard science" methodologies, such as an hypothesis and dependent/independent variables. In an experimental research design, at least one variable is manipulated.

Finally, in correlational research designs, the degree of association or relatedness between two variables is calculated. This type of research is usually *ex post facto* (after the fact) rather than *a priori* (before the fact). With correlational research, unlike experimental research, it is difficult to state in any precise way what factors were most influential and with whom. A correlational study might be one that examined the number of divorces in marriages of children of divorce.

## Sampling

Because it is virtually impossible to study all families within a community, the **sample** that one chooses becomes extremely important. When conducted properly, a randomly chosen sample of families is representative of an entire group of families. "There is no substitute for randomly assigning families to treatment conditions. Without random assignment, group differences are uninterpretable; the study is not worth conducting" (Jacobson, 1985, p. 154).

In a random assignment sampling procedure, every family has an equal chance of being selected. Families are chosen by the luck of the draw. For instance, each family is assigned a number and then those numbers are blindly pulled out of a hat to set up a control and experimental group. The results of such studies are generalizable to the selected population of families as a whole.

When a sample is not chosen wisely, bias and/or misinformation results. Such has been the case with a large number of family studies (Gurman et al., 1986). Several creative ways have been devised to collect samples of families. Two of the most frequently used are those based on probability and those based on nonprobability. "Probability samples are drawn from a known population in such a way that it is possible to calculate the likelihood . . . of each case being included in the sample" (Miller, 1986, p. 70). In this method, it is also possible to estimate the margin of error between the sample data and the entire population. Ways of conducting probability sampling include conducting:

- a simple random sample, in which each family within a population has an equal chance of being selected
- a systematic random sample, in which the first family to be studied is selected at random, and then every *n*th family is automatically included
- a stratified sampling, in which random samples are drawn from different strata or groups of a population, such as families headed by women and families headed by men

Nonprobability samples are the opposite of probability samples. They may be used "when representativeness of a whole population is not as important as the information itself or when probability sampling is not feasible" (Nelson, 1996, p. 454). Despite a reluctance to use nonprobability samples, they "have an important place in marriage and family research" (Miller, 1986, p. 70). This is especially true in studies that "are more exploratory and qualitative, hypothesis generating rather than hypothesis testing" (Miller, 1986, p. 71). Ways of collecting nonprobability samples are through:

- convenience (using local families or those known by the researcher)
- snowballing (asking participating families to refer other families)
- purposiveness (choosing families because they are thought by the researcher to be representative of the study population)

## Instrumentation

The type of instrument used in a study has an influence on what is reported as outcome. For instance, a self-report instrument yields a different result than a behaviorally based observation report. Self-reports have an advantage in family therapy research in that they can be distributed to a large number of families at a relatively low cost. Their scoring is also objective, and this makes it relatively easy to establish external validity (i.e., generalization) (Copeland & White, 1991). In addition, self-report instruments can "provide family members an opportunity to systemically understand what the other members' concerns are" and "to self-disclose through paper and pencil rather than their usual method, which has failed" (Brock & Barnard, 1988, p. 41). On the other hand, self-reports are questionable in regard to construct validity (i.e., measuring what they report to measure).

More open-ended or behaviorally based instruments have an advantage in that they focus on specific actions that can be observed in the present. They also allow researchers an opportunity to establish a baseline by which future interactions can be measured. This type of data is more complete than self-reports. However, it is more complicated to obtain:

> Direct observational assessment is characterized by the use of coders, raters, or judges, who usually are not participants in the interpersonal system being studied and whose task is to unitize and assign meaning to some aspects of the family therapy process. (Alexander, Newell, Robbins, & Turner, 1995, p. 355)

The weaknesses of open-ended and behaviorally based instruments include interrater reliability (i.e., raters may not always agree on what they saw) and other types of bias that may slip into the reports that are made (Copeland & White, 1991). Direct observation of families can also be very expensive and time consuming (L'Abate & Bagarozzi, 1993). One attempt to resolve this problem has been to videotape families and have more than one observer evaluate their actions (Lewis, Beavers, Gossett, & Phillips, 1976).

## Procedure

Procedure involves how families are studied. It can take numerous forms. Keep in mind, however, that research procedures and paradigms are not neutral but instead reflect the **epistemology** (i.e., the world view) of the investigator (Colapinto, 1979). For instance, researchers who are interested in proving the effectiveness of a theory or method generally concentrate on outcome research, that is, what is achieved as a result of a therapeutic intervention. In this type of research, families are exposed to a task or condition, and a measure is made of the impact (i.e., the reaction) (Beavers, 1985). On the other hand, researchers who wish to examine "the 'how' and the 'why' of effective or noneffective therapy" concentrate on doing process research (Diamond & Dickey, 1993, p. 23). Process research is time consuming and labor intensive (Liddle, 1992). However, the results are often enlightening and clinically meaningful. They can inform practitioners of what treatments under what conditions and with what types of clients are most effective. Furthermore, process research "can assess the systemic and contextual processes that characterize family therapy" (Diamond & Dickey, 1993, p. 24).

## Theory

Theory is an important element in research, and the interrelationship between theory, research, and practice is a crucial component in family therapy (Hawley & Geske, 2000). Well-designed research is based on questions that have usually arisen from a theory. Investigators conduct their inquiries to prove or disprove specific theoretical hypotheses, such as the importance of establishing permeable boundaries in family functioning. In using theory as a basis for conducting studies, researchers should pick a strong and relatively simple, clear theory that is logically connected (Shields, 1986). Most family therapy is based on general systems theory. This theory has made specific inquiry into how families change (Reiss, 1988). Some theoretical research, such as that on addicts and their families by Stanton et al. (1982), has been successful because of the careful way it was set up. However, in numerous cases, the questions that have been asked and the answers that have been derived have been insignificant or even harmful.

An example of a group of detrimental inquiries not carefully based on general systems theory is found in some research studies on African-American families that employ "a deficit theoretical underpinning" (Turner, 1993, p. 9). In these studies, the focus is on African-American childhood aggression, within-race violence, household father absence, family disruption, and social/health problems. This type of approach assumes that African-American families can and should be compared with "ideal families" or families from other cultural groups. It "overlooks the political realities that individuals and families are affected by race, economic status, and cultural values" (Turner, 1993, p. 9). Research of this nature fails to view whatever family form or family group is being studied as embedded in larger social systems.

## Statistics

Researchers can be excellent methodologists but weak statisticians. Likewise, statisticians may not be able to design research studies in a scientific manner. Regardless, when research results are reported in a statistical manner, they need to be clinically relevant and readable to practitioners as well as scientists (Gay & Airasian, 2000). One way to do this is to use descriptive statistics as a supplement to other statistical procedures. "By reporting the proportion of clients who improve to a clinically significant degree, the data from family therapy outcome research will be much more useful to family therapists than it will if researchers limit their reports to group means and statistical significance tests" (Jacobson, 1985, p. 151).

In general, statistics can show that a family is improved under the following circumstances:

- "if the posttherapy status places" the family "outside the distribution of dysfunctional clients (or families) and/or within the limits of a functional distribution of clients and
- if the amount of change during the course of therapy exceeds expectations" (Jacobson, 1988, p. 141)

Problems in reporting statistics are related to whether the sample they were based on was skewed or normally distributed.

## Validity/Reliability

The term **validity** "is the extent to which a measuring instrument measures what it was intended to measure" (Miller, 1986, p. 58). There are three main measures of validity:

1. content, which is aimed at actually tapping into representative beliefs or behaviors
2. criterion, which is the degree to which what is measured actually relates to life experience
3. construct, which is the degree to which a measured performance matches a theoretical expectation

**Reliability** refers to the consistency or dependency of a measure. Another way to conceptualize reliability is that it truly measures the differences between families. Perfect reliability is expressed as a correlational coefficient of 1.00, which is seldom achieved. "Measures can be reliable but not valid, but they cannot be valid unless they are reliable" (Miller, 1986, p. 59).

Family therapy research must have strong degrees of validity and reliability in order to be considered substantial. Consumers of research need to focus on the validity and reliability of outcomes in studies as they evaluate results.

# The Importance of Assessing Families

An assessment procedure is any method "used to measure characteristics of people, programs, or objects" (American Educational Research Association, American Psychological Association, & National Council on Measurement in Education, 1985, p. 89). As opposed to testing, which is usually a task in which people are asked to do their maximum best, assessment evaluates typical performances, behaviors, or qualities. It is broader than any test measure. As such, assessment is a vital part of family therapy. Through assessment, therapists gain information that helps them understand (i.e., diagnose) and respond systemically and appropriately to the families with whom they are working (Gold, 1997). For example, in assessment, therapists gain insight into a family's structure (i.e., roles, boundaries); control (i.e., power, flexibility); emotions/needs (i.e., affective expression, affective themes); culture (i.e., social position, cultural heritage); and development (stage of life) (Fisher, 1976).

In the past, the **Diagnostic and Statistical Manual (DSM)**, which is published by the American Psychiatric Association and is the basis on which mental health disorders are assessed, has given little attention to marital and family diagnostic categories. The reason is that most of the key concerns of family therapists have been relationship oriented

(Simola, Parker, & Froese, 1999). Rather than attach a disorder label to a relationship, the DSM's approach has been to use V codes to describe these difficulties. The V code designation means that the condition described is "not attributable to a mental disorder" (American Psychiatric Association [APA], 1994, p. 9).

The fourth edition of the DSM (DSM-IV; APA, 1994) "brings slightly more focus on relational problems, such as parent–child, sibling, and partner relationships and physical and sexual abuse" (Sporakowski, 1995, p. 61). However, a V code diagnosis is not reimbursed by a third-party payer, such as an insurance company, regardless of its seriousness. Nevertheless, despite this obvious drawback, family therapists need to assess and diagnose when possible so that an appropriate treatment plan can be developed and followed (Gold, 1997).

Another advantage of assessment is that families and their members can be helped to understand the dynamics within their relationship better, enabling them to clarify goals, and to gain a sense of perspective (Hood & Johnson, 1998). A final reason for the importance of assessment relates to accountability and professionalism. Therapy requires documentation of services and the reasons behind the services being offered. Family therapy is moving to become more scientific and precise. Family clinicians who wish to improve their skills and serve the public are increasingly likely to rely on assessment. Such reliance is a matter of being responsible.

# Dimensions of Assessing Families

Most assessment with families is based on a systemic approach. This approach

> . . . requires that one utilize the transactions between individuals, rather than the characteristics of each given individual, as primary data. Even when, for one reason or another, attention is focused on one person, his/her behavior is analyzed in terms of its power to affect and shape the behavior of other members of the system and in terms of the variables of the ecosystem that may have affected it. (Sluzko, 1978, p. 366)

Therefore, when questions are asked in therapy sessions, they focus on transactions and relationships more than demographic data. For instance, they might include inquiries such as "When John gets angry, Mary, what do you do?" or "Carole, how do you react when the other children leave you out of their activities?"

Fishman (1988) states that therapists should consider four aspects of assessment: "contemporary developmental pressures on the family, history, structure, and process" (p. 14). He continues:

> The four-dimensional model should give therapists, like cubist painters, a kaleidoscopic view of their subject. It allows therapists to look at a moving system from different perspectives. It also takes into consideration therapists' positions in the process as they move in and out of the system, sometimes as neutral observers, other times as involved protagonists who support a particular family member or suddenly realize the family's control. (p. 14)

This emphasis on processes and therapists' active place in them is what helps define family therapy as a therapy of experience.

# Methods Used in Assessing Families

Assessment techniques available to family therapists "are many and varied" (Sporakowski, 1995, p. 61). Both informal and formal methods are used in the assessment of families. Informal methods include observational data related to either natural or game-playing situations that may or may not be quantified. Formal methods are usually field-tested instruments, some of which are based on a theoretical foundation and some of which are not. (L'Abate & Bagarozzi, 1993).

## Informal Methods of Assessing Families

One of the best informal methods of assessing a family is through using the Family Assessment Form (Piercy, McKeon, & Laird, 1983). This form is succinct. Yet, it provides family therapists of all theoretical orientations with a means for fine-tuning their approach with a particular family. As can be seen from examining the family assessment form shown in Figure 16.1, therapists can gain a lot of knowledge in a relatively short amount of time. They can then tailor clarification questions and possible interventions accordingly.

Another way to informally assess families is through direct observation. In contrast to individual counseling, family therapy "offers the unique opportunity to observe directly the problematic interpersonal exchanges of clients and to contrast these with subjective appraisals of these events" (Snyder et al., 1995, pp. 163–164). Even though this process is complex because of the number of individuals in some sessions and possible expressions of hostility, it is an invaluable tool for picking up information that other instruments cannot provide.

## Formal Methods of Assessing Families

More than 1,000 assessment instruments are available to family therapists (Touliatos, Perlmutter, & Straus, 1990). They cover areas as diverse as intimacy, power, parenthood, and adjustment. "Instruments can enrich the practitioner's and the clients' assessment and treatment process when used in combination" (Thomas, 1995, p. 285). Figure 16.2 lists some of the most widely used assessment measures in marital and family therapy training programs, as reported by Gold (1997).

This text examines some of the best known and refined family and marital tests many of which are on Gold's list. Yet, clinicians need to consult reference works and abstracts for specific measures pertinent to their situations. Likewise, it is important to note that with all assessment instruments, scales used in family therapy must be employed judiciously. Furthermore, these instruments should be scrutinized in regard to the variables being measured, the scales and subscales being reported, the ease or difficulty of scoring directions and interpretation of test results, and the evidence available about validity and reliability (Sprenkle & Piercy, 1984).

Despite availability of an increasing number of family therapy measurement devices, clinicians are reticent to use them. The reasons for this reticence include the fact that using assessment instruments removes family therapists from the cutting edge of innova-

Family Name _____ (Age)_____

Father _____(__) Mother _____(__)

Occupation _____ Occupation _____

Years Married _____

Children: _____(__) _____(__) _____(__)

_____(__) _____(__) _____(__)

Blended Family Relationships (Number of marriages, children by other marriages, etc.)

_____

_____

Referral Source _____

1. Presenting Problem/Change Desired (from each person's perspective)

2. Repetitive Nonproductive Behavioral Sequences (attempted solutions, attempts to maintain homeostatic balance)

3. Family Structure (family map; enmeshment, isolation or individuation, chaos, rigidity or flexibility; power structure; generational boundaries; spousal relationships, alliances, roles played, intrusions, etc.)

4. Communication and Interaction Styles (direct, clear, indirect, confused, vague, double binding, affective, cognitive, positive, supported, negative, aggressive, etc.)

5. Hypotheses Regarding Symptom Maintenance (how might the symptom serve a function)

6. Family Life Stages (courtship, early marriage, child bearing, child rearing, parents of teenagers, launching, middle years, retirement, etc.)

7. Pertinent Family-of-Origin Information (positive or negative influence from past generations)

8. External Sources of Stress and Support (relationships outside immediate family: community, work, friends, relatives)

9. Family Strengths

10. Significant Physical Conditions/Medication

11. Other Information (previous treatment, test results, etc.)

12. Therapeutic Goals:

13. Proposed Therapeutic Interventions (means for reaching goals)

_____    _____

Counselor's Signature           Date

**Figure 16.1**
Family assessment form.

From "A Family Assessment Process for Community Mental Health Clinics" by F. P. Piercy, D. McKeon, and R. A. Laird, 1983, *AMHCA Journal, 5*(3), pp. 94–104. Reprinted by permission of the publisher.

Marital assessment measures ($n = 19$)
  Attitudes Toward Working Women Scale
  Caring Days Inventory
  Couples' Pre-Counseling Inventory
  Dual-Career Family Scale
  Dyadic Adjustment Scale
  Evaluating and Nurturing Relationship Issues, Communication, and Happiness
  Exchange-Orientation Instrument
  Family of Origin Scale
  Locke-Wallace Marital Adjustment Test
  Marital Adjustment Balance Scale
  Marital Communication Inventory
  Marital Evaluation Checklist
  Marital Satisfaction Inventory
  Myers-Briggs Typology Inventory
  Personal Assessment of Intimacy in Relationship
  Sexual Attitudes and Beliefs Inventory
  Sexual Interaction Inventory
  Spouse Observation Checklist
  Waring Intimacy Questionnaire
Parenting assessment measures ($n = 2$)
  Parent-Adolescent Communication Inventory
  Parenting Skills Inventory
Family assessment measures ($n = 8$)
  Beavers-Timberlawn Family Evaluation Scales
  Conflict Tactics Scale
  Family Adaptability and Cohesion Scale
  Family Inventory of Life Events and Change
  Kveback Family Sculpture Test
  McMaster Family Assessment Device
  Quality of Life Scale
  Taylor-Johnson Temperament Analysis

**Figure 16.2**

Widely used assessment measures in marital and family therapy training programs.

From "Assessing Education in Marriage and Family Counseling" by J. M. Gold, 1997, *The Family Journal: Counseling and Therapy for Couples and Families, 5*, 159-163. Copyright © 1997 by Sage Publications, Inc. Reprinted by permission of Sage Publications, Inc.

tive practice (Shields et al., 1994). In addition, many practitioners lack adequate training in family assessment instruments (Thomas & Olson, 1993). Therefore, family therapists who tend to employ measuring devices in their practices most often use individually focused assessment instruments, such as the MMPI-2 and the Myers-Briggs Type Indicator (Boughner, Bubenzer, Hayes, & West, 1993). Table 16.1 examines some conceptual issues and formal assessment techniques across family system levels.

# Family Therapy Scales

To make an informed decision on what assessment instrument(s) would serve their clients best, therapists must conceptually clarify the areas in which they need to obtain information. A brief description of some specific assessment devices in family therapy follows.

### Family-of-Origin Scale

The family-of-origin scale (FOS) was developed to measure self-perceived healthiness in one's family of origin (Hovestadt, Anderson, Piercy, Cochran, & Fine, 1985). The scale is based on a five-point Likert format and contains 40 questions. Outcome scores can range from 40 to 200, with higher scores indicative of better overall family health. The test–retest reliability coefficient has been reported to be 0.97 for undergraduates on whom the scale was normed.

Two subscales of the FOS reflect 10 core constructs of family healthiness, principally derived from Lewis et al. (1976). The Autonomy subscale emphasizes characteristics of healthiness such as clarity of expression, personal responsibility, respect for other family members, and openness to others within and outside the family system. The Intimacy subscale emphasizes characteristics such as expression of feelings, emotional warmth, conflict resolution without undue stress, sensitivity to other family members, and trust (Wilcoxon, Walker, & Hovestadt, 1989, p. 226–227).

The FOS can be used in the context of both family and couple therapy (Hovestadt, 2000). It has been found to distinguish between different cultural groups' (i.e., African Americans, European Americans, and Hispanic Americans) perceptions of their families of origin (Kane & Erdman, 1998). In this study African Americans rated their families of origin significantly higher than European Americans and Hispanic Americans on the major scales of Autonomy and Intimacy and on the Intimacy subscales Range of Feelings, Conflict Resolution, and Empathy. The researchers also found that there were no significant differences between males and females or between European Americans and Hispanic Americans.

### The Personal Authority in the Family System Questionnaire

The Personal Authority in the Family System (PAFS) questionnaire is a self-report questionnaire based on the theoretical work of family systems theorists, such as Bowen, Boszormenyi-Nagy, and Williamson. It assesses relationships in three generational families. It contains 132 items, all of which are scored on a five-point Likert scale. Five subscales measure intergenerational themes such as dependence/independence, intergenerational triangles, intergenerational intimidation, personal authority, and intergenerational fusion/individuation (Bray, Williamson, & Malone, 1984).

Reliability measures range from a test–retest low of 0.55 to an internal consistency of 0.95. Construct and concurrent validity are both solid. Overall, "the PAFS describes an individual's current interaction with his or her family of origin" (West, 1988, p. 176).

### PREPARE/ENRICH

The PREPARE/ENRICH inventories are part of a package of material developed for couples striving to become more aware of or to nourish their relationships (Fredman & Sherman,

**Table 16.1**
Model Conceptual Issues and Formal Assessment Techniques Across Family System Levels

| Modal Conceptual Issues | Formal Assessment Techniques |
|---|---|
| **Individual** | |
| How may cognitive style or abilities influence family members' response to therapy or each other? | Short-form Wechsler administrations (Silverstein, 1990) |
| | Peabody Picture Vocabulary Test–Revised (Dunn & Dunn, 1981) |
| | Attributional Style Questionnaire (Peterson & Villanova, 1988) |
| | Children's Attributional Style Questionnaire (Fielstein et al., 1985) |
| What dimensions of individual emotional or behavioral functioning influence family interaction? Which of these, if any, warrant separate treatment? Which reflect strengths? | Minnesota Multiphasic Personality Inventory–2 (Butcher, Dahlstrom, Graham, Tellegen, & Kaemmer, 1989) |
| | Millon Clinical Multiaxial Inventory–II (Millon, 1987) |
| | NEO Personality Inventory–Revised (Costa & McCrae, 1992) |
| | Schedule for Affective Disorders and Schizophrenia (Endicott & Spitzer, 1978) |
| How should current issues be viewed from a developmental perspective? | Child Behavior Checklist (Achenbach & Edelbrock, 1983) |
| | Personality Inventory for Children (Wirt, Lachar, Klinedinst, & Seat, 1984) |
| | Kiddie-Schedule for Affective Disorders and Schizophrenia (Puig-Antich & Chambers, 1978) |
| **Dyad** | |
| What are the sources and levels of distress or satisfaction in the marriage? In the parent–child relationships? | Marital Satisfaction Inventory (Snyder, 1981) |
| | Sexual Functioning Inventory (Derogatis, 1975) |
| | Parenting Stress Index (Abidin, 1986) |
| What patterns of communication typify these relationships? | Marital Interaction Coding System–Global (Weiss & Toiman, 1990) |
| | Rapid Couples Interaction Scoring System (Krokoff, Gottman, & Hass, 1989) |
| | Parent–Adolescent Interaction Coding System (Robin & Weiss, 1980) |
| How consistent and functional are relationship expectations? How do members view each other's behavior or motives? | Relationship Brief Inventory (Edelson & Epstein, 1982) |
| | Relationship Attribution Measure (Fincham & Bradbury, 1992) |
| | Child's Report of Parental Behavior Inventory (Burger & Armentrout, 1971) |

1987). PREPARE is designated for engaged couples; ENRICH is for already married couples. Both scales are composed of a 125-item inventory that is designed to identify relationship strengths and weaknesses in 10 specific areas of couple/family life. These areas are (1) personality issues, (2) communication, (3) conflict resolution, (4) financial management, (5) leisure activities, (6) sexual relationship, (7) children and marriage, (8) family and friends, (9) egalitarian roles, and (10) religious orientation (Olson, Fournier, & Druckman,

| Modal Conceptual Issues | Formal Assessment Techniques |
|---|---|
| **Nuclear family** | |
| How close do family members feel to each other? How effective is the family in responding to daily challenges and crises? | Family Environment Scale (Moos & Moos, 1986) |
| | Children's Version–Family Environment Scale (Pino, Simons, & Slawinowski, 1984) |
| | Family Assessment Measure–III (Skinner, Steinhauer, & Santa-Barbera, 1984) |
| | Family Adaptability and Cohesion Evaluation Scales III (Olson, Portner, & Lavee, 1985) |
| How is the family organized along dimensions of affect, authority, and control? What strategies do family members use to influence each other? | Child-Rearing Practices Report (Block, Block, & Morrison, 1981) |
| | Family Behavior Interview (Robin & Foster, 1989) |
| | Family Interaction Coding System (Reid, 1978) |
| **Extended system** | |
| To what extent do relationships with extended family, friends, or coworkers serve as sources of support or stress? | Genogram (McGoldrick & Gerson, 1985) |
| | Interpersonal Support Evaluation List (Cohen, Mermelstein, Kamarck, & Hoberman, 1985) |
| | Survey of Children's Social Support (Dubow & Ullman, 1989) |
| | My Family and Friends (Reid, Landesman, Treder, & Jaccard, 1989) |
| How do family members vary in their sources of external stress or support? How are these shared in the marriage or nuclear family? | |
| **Community and culture** | |
| What community resources are available to this family? Are these resources used? How does the community contribute to this family's distress or survival? | Mothers' Activities Checklist (Kelley & Carper, 1988) |
| | Community Interaction Checklist (Wahler, 1980) |
| | Eco-Map (Hartman, 1979) |
| To what extent do family members identify with a particular ethnic heritage? | Behavioral Acculturation Scale (Szapocznik, Kurtines, & Fernandez, 1980) |

From "Marital and Family Assessment: A Multifaceted, Multilevel Approach" by D. K. Snyder, T. A. Cavell, R. W. Heffer, and L. F. Mangrum in *Integrating Family Therapy* (pp. 163–182), edited by R. H. Mikesell, D.-D. Lusterman, and S. H. McDaniel. Copyright © 1995 American Psychological Association. Reprinted with permission.

1987). Each scale also measures idealistic distortion, although PREPARE alone gets a reading on realistic expectations, and ENRICH alone obtains a score on marital satisfaction.

An individual score for each person on every scale is generated, and areas of agreement and disagreement are duly noted. Comparisons are coded as "relationship strength," "possible strength," "possible growth area," or "growth area." PREPARE and ENRICH both have strong reliability and validity scores in most areas. Both also have been found to have some predictive uses. For example, in a 3-year follow-up of couples who took the PREPARE scale, scores were better than 80% accurate in predicting marital happiness versus separation/divorce (Flowers & Olson, 1986).

### Family Adaptability and Cohesion Evaluation Scale III

The Family Adaptability and Cohesion Evaluation Scale III (FACES III) is similar to PREPARE/ENRICH in that it is based on the circumplex model of family functioning (i.e., adaptability and cohesion) (Olson et al., 1985). It is a self-report inventory "designed to measure an insider's perspective on family functioning" (Griffin & D'Andrea, 1998, p. 305). This instrument has undergone considerable refinement since it was introduced in 1978. Basically, it can be taken twice in order to derive ideal and perceived descriptions of a family. The discrepancy between these two outcome scores "provides a measure of family satisfaction with current levels of adaptability and cohesion" (West, 1988, p. 173). Reliability and validity are within acceptable limits.

FACES III has been used in a variety of ways including to investigate perceived family cohesion and adaptability in current relationships and family of origin, to assess cohesion and adaptability in violent couples, to predict future behavior, and to classify the relationship status of battered women (Griffin & D'Andrea, 1998).

### Family Inventory of Life Events and Changes

The purpose of the Family Inventory of Life Events and Changes (FILE) instrument is to "investigate the impact of life stresses on family well-being" (L'Abate & Bagarozzi, 1993, p. 176). As emphasized in this text, families undergo many transitions that affect them for better or worse. Sometimes stress events "pile up" on families and have negative consequences. FILE, as a 71-item self-report instrument, examines the normative and non-normative events that have been experienced by families during a year, including financial, intrafamily, work, legal, loss, illness, marital, moving, and pregnancy/childbearing (Bretherson, Walsh, & Lependorf, 1996; McCubbin, Thompson, Pirner, & McCubbin, 1988). FILE scores can be summed according to family life event score, family-couple life events score, family-couple discrepancy score, family adjustment score, and family-couple readjustment score (Touliatos et al., 1990).

By gathering and scoring information on the family, therapists are more aware of where to address their interventions. The reliability and validity of FILE are high.

### Family Environment Scale

The Family Environment Scale (FES) is "a 90-item, true-false, self-report questionnaire with 10 subscales designed to measure the social and environmental characteristics of a family" (Fredman & Sherman, 1987, p. 82). It is divided into 10 subscales that come under three major categories: (1) relationship (i.e., cohesion, expressiveness, and conflict subscales); (2) personal growth (i.e., independence, achievement orientation, intellectual-cultural orientation, active-recreational orientation, and moral-religious emphasis subscales); and (3) system maintenance (i.e., organization and control subscales).

"The FES can be used to describe and compare family social environments, contrast parent and child perceptions, and examine actual and preferred family milieus" (Moos &

Moos, 1986, p. 11). It is "probably the most widely accepted measure of the family climate" and "among the first" objectively scored methods of family assessment to be developed (Oliver, Handal, Enos, & May, 1988, p. 470). One of the reasons for the popularity of the FES is that it comprehensively addresses all aspects of family environment. It has a Real Form (which measures families' actual perceptions), an Ideal Form (which measures families' perceptions of how they would like their family to be), and an Expectations Form (which measures what people expect their families to be like).

In general, the FES has been shown to have sufficient measures of validity and reliability (Moos, 1990). It has been used in studies examining a wide variety of topics from academic performance to eating disorders.

### Family Assessment Device

The Family Assessment Device (FAD) is a 60-item questionnaire geared toward assessing family functioning. It is based on the McMaster Model of Family Functioning (Epstein, Baldwin, & Bishop, 1983) and takes about 20 minutes to complete. The FAD has been translated into seven different languages and is one of the most researched family assessment tools available. This instrument examines seven dimensions of family functioning: (1) problem solving, (2) communication, (3) roles, (4) affective responsiveness (sharing of affection), (5) affective involvement (emotional sensitivity), (6) behavior control, and (7) general functioning (boundaries). The best use of the FAD is the use of the general functioning subscale as a summary score since FAD subscales overlap substantially and do not assess unique dimensions of family functioning.

### Family Strengths Scale

The Family Strengths Scale is a brief, 12-item inventory developed in 1983. It is appropriate for adults and adolescents (Olson, Larson, & McCubbin, 1985). It measures two areas of family functioning, family pride (e.g., loyalty, optimism, and trust) and family accord (e.g., ability to accomplish certain task, to deal with problems, to get along with one another).

The scale is scored on a five-point Likert index (Giblin, 1996). It is aimed at identifying how happy families resemble one another. Higher scores correlate with a higher level of family functioning. The inventory was initially based on the family strength work of Stinnet (1981), but the final version of the test is less comprehensive. Reliability for the total scale is reported at 0.83.

### Family Coping Strategies Scale

The Family Coping Strategies Scale (F-COPES) is a measure of internal and external family coping strategies (McCubbin, Larsen, & Olsen, 1982). Internal strategies include reframing and passive appraisal; external strategies are those connected with acquiring social support, seeking spiritual support, and mobilizing the family to seek and accept help.

The scale assumes that family coping can potentially achieve the following:

- Decrease the family's vulnerability to stress.
- Strengthen or maintain those family resources that serve to protect the family from the full impact of problems.
- Reduce or eliminate the impact of stressor events.

- Actively influence the environment by changing the social circumstances to make it easier for the family to adjust to the situation.

The reliability of the instrument is in the 0.60 range.

### Self-Report Family Inventory

The Self-Report Family Inventory (SFI) is a 36-item self-report family instrument that measures five family domains: health/competence, conflict resolution, cohesion, leadership, and emotional expressiveness (Beavers & Hampson, 1990). The inventory is based on a five-point Likert scale, except for the final two questions. The SFI has high reliability (between 0.84 and 0.93) and validity (0.62 and better). This instrument also "corresponds well with other self-report family scales measuring conceptually similar domains" (Hampson, Prince, & Beavers, 1999, p. 414). Included in the inventory is a husbands and wives demographic information form and an open-ended questionnaire on the family's evaluation of treatment.

## Marital Therapy Scales

Marital and couple assessment is aimed at obtaining information in a fast and efficient manner so therapists can concentrate on particularly difficult relationship areas. Some of the earliest assessment instruments in the marital and family therapy areas were initially developed for this purpose. Those instruments described here are specifically geared for marital and couple use.

### Locke-Wallace Marital Adjustment Test (MAT)

The Locke-Wallace Marital Adjustment Test (MAT) is one of the oldest and most widely used tests of marital satisfaction. It consists of 15 items that are of a self-report nature. It can be completed in about 10 minutes and is scored by the therapist. Higher scores (above 100 points) differentiate nondistressed from distressed couples (Sullivan, Parch, Eldridge, & Bradbury, 1998). This inventory has been successfully modified for use with premarital couples. It has been reported to have a split-half reliability of 0.90 (Locke & Wallace, 1959). Furthermore, the MAT is the standard by which other marriage adjustment inventories correlate their results (Fredman & Sherman, 1987). The main drawback to the MAT is that a few of its items are now considered out of date.

### Bienvenu Marital Communication Inventory (MCI)

The Bienvenu Marital Communication Inventory (MCI) is a 46-item, self-administered questionnaire that focuses on the perceived quality of marital communication. Each question is graded on a zero- to four-point scale, with a range of scores from 0 to 138. Higher scores are indicative of better perceived couple communication patterns. The split-half reliability is 0.93 (Bienvenu, 1970).

This instrument is used in both marital and premarital counseling and can be interpreted as a measure of perceptions concerning the quality of communication (Schumm, 1983). Only a seventh-grade reading ability is required.

### Dyadic Adjustment Scale

The Dyadic Adjustment Scale (DAS) is a 32-item self-report, pencil-and-paper questionnaire of marital satisfaction (Spanier, 1976). Thirteen consensus items in areas such as household tasks, finances, recreation, friends, religion, and decision making are measured. The DAS possesses good reliability and discriminant validity. It yields an overall score as well as scores for four subscales: dyadic consensus, satisfaction, cohesion, and affectional expression (Kramer & Conoley, 1992).

The usual cutoff point between distressed and nondistressed couples is 100, with higher scores indicating a better relationship (Floyd & Markman, 1983). The range of scores for the DAS is from 0 to 150. The reliability of this instrument is high (0.96). Validity is also quite good (Fredman & Sherman, 1987). The DAS is reportedly the most commonly used self-report measure of marital adjustment (Glenn, 1990). It has been used in more than 1,000 studies, translated into two languages (French and Chinese) and has been revised from a 32- to a 14-item instrument (Prouty, Markowski, & Barnes, 2000).

### Marital Coping Questionnaire

The Marital Coping Questionnaire (MCQ) is an 18-item, self-report questionnaire in which respondents indicate how frequently they engage in each of a set of coping efforts (Fleishman, 1984; Menaghan, 1982; Pearlin & Schooler, 1978). The MCQ is situation specific rather than global in its assessment.

The six most reliable coping factors are as follows:

> (1) seeking advice (e.g., ask the advice of relatives about getting along in marriage); (2) emotional discharge (e.g., yell or shout to let off steam); (3) positive comparison (e.g., how would you compare your marriage to that of most other people like yourself—better, the same, less good); (4) negotiation (e.g., try to find a fair compromise in marital problems); (5) resignation (e.g., just keep hurt feelings to yourself); (6) selective ignoring (e.g., try to ignore difficulties by looking only at good things). (Sabourin, Laporte, & Wright, 1990, pp. 91–92)

### Primary Communication Inventory

The Primary Communication Inventory (PCI) is a 25-item, self-report questionnaire, with a five-point scale designed to measure a couple's verbal and nonverbal communication (Locke, Sabagh, & Thomas, 1956). It is one of the oldest and most frequently used marriage therapy indexes and has been the subject of several significant research studies (L'Abate & Bagarozzi, 1993). It distinguishes satisfied and dissatisfied couples from each other, but has some problems in regard to validity.

### Marital Satisfaction Inventory

The Marital Satisfaction Inventory (MSI) is a 280-item, true–false questionnaire that has been compared with the MMPI because of both its length and number of scales (i.e., 11 scales). It measures couple satisfaction in areas such as childrearing, finances, sexual problems, communication, and family history. It also provides a global distress scale so clinicians can rate the overall level of distress within a marriage relationship (Snyder, 1981; Snyder & Regts, 1982).

The MSI has a test–retest reliability on average of 0.89 for each subscale. It is one of the strongest marital satisfaction measures available in psychometric terms (Fowers, 1990). Overall, the MSI is a well-constructed inventory that is strong in regard to its research and clinical application.

### Marital Instability Inventory

The Marital Instability Inventory (MII) is a paper-and-pencil instrument designed to assess marital instability among intact couples (Booth & Edwards, 1983). It has a 20- and a 5-question form, both of which are scored from 0 (never) to 3 (now). Higher scores are more indicative of marital instability.

The MII is composed of two parts: cognitive (thoughts about the marriage) and behavior (actions based on thoughts about the marital relationship). Both reliability and validity factors are high, with the shorter form of the scale being less reliable.

### Dyadic Trust Scale

The Dyadic Trust Scale (DTS) is an eight-item, pencil-and-paper questionnaire that takes less than 3 minutes to take. Its focus is on trust between marriage partners rather than trust in general (Larzelere & Huston, 1980). It has high internal consistency reliability (0.93), good face validity, and correlates well with scales of love and self-disclosure. The main drawback to this instrument is that its initial sample size was limited and, in norming the test, all participants were volunteers (Fredman & Sherman, 1987).

### Marital Problem-Solving Scale

The Marital Problem-Solving Scale (MPSS) is a nine-item, seven-point Likert scale that measures problem-solving ability (Baugh, Avery, & Sheets-Haworth, 1982). It has strong internal consistency (0.95) and test–retest reliability (0.86). Validity is also good. An interesting aspect about the MPSS is that it "has demonstrated concurrent validity with behavioral coding assessments, enabling one to say that it is just as good as the time-consuming and expensive methods of behavior coding" (L'Abate & Bagarozzi, 1993, p. 145).

### Couple Rating Scale

The Couple Rating Scale (CRS) is "a self-report assessment that encourages relationship insight for couples. Eight common areas of problems, consisting of 31 specific issues, are rated by each partner to assess both current level and desired level of functioning for the self and other" (Cron, 2000, p. 302). The eight areas addressed in the CRS are communication life, home life, work life, love life, sexual life, spiritual life, problem-solving life, and dream for the future life. Each area is rated from 1 to 10.

The CRS (Figure 16.3) is intended to operate on two levels—present reality and desired level of functioning for self and other. It is meant to be a measure that closes the gap in assessment on two specific couple misconceptions: external locus of control (e.g., "if my partner changed everything would be fine") and single-issue focus (e.g., money, sex).

## Couple Rating Scale

Instructions: Rating scale is from 1 to 10, with 1 being the lowest and 10 being the highest. You will rate yourself in the first two columns. In Column 1, rate your current level of each trait. Column 2 is for the level you desire to reach. Columns 3 and 4 are for rating your partner. In Column 3, using your personal perception, rate his or her current level of each trait. In Column 4, rate the level desired by you for him or her to attempt.

| Life Area | Self Current/ Desired | Other Current/ Desired | Life Area | Self Current/ Desired | Other Current/ Desired |
|---|---|---|---|---|---|
| | (1) (2) | (3) (4) | | (1) (2) | (3) (4) |
| **Communication life** | | | **Love life** | | |
| Degree of listening skill | __/__ | __/__ | Degree of acceptance of other | __/__ | __/__ |
| Degree of sensitivity and respect | __/__ | __/__ | Degree of mutual understanding | __/__ | __/__ |
| Degree of honesty | __/__ | __/__ | Degree of trust in other | __/__ | __/__ |
| Degree of openness | __/__ | __/__ | Degree of expressed (spoken) love | __/__ | __/__ |
| Degree of flexibility/ compromise | __/__ | __/__ | Degree of implied (unspoken) love | __/__ | __/__ |
| **Home life** | | | Degree of forgiveness in relationship | __/__ | __/__ |
| Degree of satisfaction with household responsibilities | __/__ | __/__ | **Spiritual life** | | |
| Degree of completing household responsibilities | __/__ | __/__ | Degree of spiritual belief | __/__ | __/__ |
| Degree of role flexibility | __/__ | __/__ | Degree of religious practice | __/__ | __/__ |
| Degree of good parenting skills | __/__ | __/__ | Degree of comfort with spiritual expression | __/__ | __/__ |
| **Work life** | | | **Problem-solving life** | | |
| Degree of fulfillment in own career | __/__ | __/__ | Ability to talk about problems (get them in the open) | __/__ | __/__ |
| Degree of comfort with partner's career | __/__ | __/__ | Ability to work through problems | __/__ | __/__ |
| Degree of balance between work and home life | __/__ | __/__ | Ability to fight fair | __/__ | __/__ |
| **Sexual life** | | | Ability to resolve family-of-origin problems | __/__ | __/__ |
| Degree of frequency | __/__ | __/__ | **Dream for the future life** | | |
| Degree of satisfaction in lovemaking | __/__ | __/__ | Degree that your dream is also his or hers | __/__ | __/__ |
| Degree of excitement in lovemaking | __/__ | __/__ | Degree that your dream is mutually decided | __/__ | __/__ |
| Degree of variety in lovemaking | __/__ | __/__ | | | |

**Figure 16.3**

Couple rating scale.

From "Couple Rating Scale: Clarifying Problem Areas" by E. A. Cron, 2000, *The Family Journal: Counseling and Therapy for Couples and Families, 8*(3), p. 303. Copyright © 2000 by Sage Publications, Inc. Reprinted by permission of Sage Publications, Inc.

# Summary and Conclusion

Family research and assessment efforts have a long history. They began with the genesis of the field and have continued to the present. Research is the backbone of family therapy, because through it family therapists can prove that what they do is beneficial, unique, and practical. Fortunately, family therapy research indicates that treating families is at least equal to that of working with individuals. Particularly encouraging are findings that show the importance of therapists' relationship skills and the critical nature of having certain members of families, such as fathers, participate in treatment. From these data, clinician/researchers, such as Jose Szapocznik, have advanced the field of family therapy even further through innovative research projects.

In examining family therapy research, keep in mind that many difficulties are associated with it because of the systemic nature of family therapy. Among problematic areas are those that involve whether to conduct qualitative or quantitative research. The design of the research, along with sampling procedures and choosing instruments, are also important. Equally crucial are considerations involving whether procedures should focus on process or outcome results, the statistical methods, if any, to employ, and the theoretical base on which to center the study. As the field of family therapy grows, efforts to incorporate research methods and findings into training/educational programs will increase, accompanied by renewed attention on the importance of research to practice (Liddle, 1992).

Like research, assessment is based on systemic theory and has been highlighted more in recent years. Assessment may take "many forms depending on the theory, practice, clients, and personal, professional development of the counselor" (Sporakowski, 1995, p. 63). There are a number of family assessment approaches, from those that consider limited data to those that encompass a broad perspective. Informal as well as formal methods of assessment are available. Formal methods, although well researched, have still not been as utilized by family therapists as some popular, more individualized assessment tools, such as the Myers-Briggs Type Indicator and the MMPI-2. Nevertheless, there is an abundance of assessment instruments that will most likely grow in use and usefulness in the future.

Overall, research and assessment are a vital part of the practice of family therapy. It is essential that clinicians keep current with advancements and related research. Otherwise, they will be handicapped in the treatment of their client families, and all will suffer as a result.

# Summary Table
## Research and Assessment in Family Therapy

Research and assessment has a long association with family therapy that dates back to the 1950s and pioneers in the field such as Bateson, Wynne, and Minuchin.

During the 1960s, therapists and researchers became two distinct groups.

In the 2000s, research in family therapy is growing again and is becoming increasingly sophisticated.

Assessment, which focuses on a family unit rather than a group of families, is also growing.

Good assessment instruments are based on theoretical models.

## Importance of Research in Family Therapy

Empirical data are crucial to the future of treating families. The practitioner/research model needs to be highlighted.

Research is important in family therapy as a result of accountability, practicality, and uniqueness. Research results help family therapy gain respect.

Clinicians gain from research studies in the long run. Research also helps family therapists claim their area as a specialization.

## Research Findings in Family Therapy

Family therapy is as effective as other psychotherapies, according to research.

Deterioration in family therapy is related to poor skills and timing on the therapist's part.

Brief family therapy (20 sessions or less) is as effective as long-term family therapy.

Participation by the father in family therapy makes it more likely to have a positive outcome.

Less severe family problems are most successfully treated.

Some family therapies are more suited to certain types of problems than others.

The research of Jose Szapocznik is a good example of how research results can have practical application.

## Two Types of Family Therapy Research

Qualitative and quantitative research methods are often used in measuring the impact of family therapy.

Qualitative research is characterized by its open-ended approach. It uses small samples, with the participant/observer/researcher gathering and analyzing data simultaneously in a narrative manner. A form of qualitative research, participatory evaluation research, involves participants even more in the research process and empowers them as well.

Quantitative research is characterized by its closed-ended questions, large sample sizes, objective data reporting, and numerical data analysis after the data are collected. Its conclusions are deductive, written in a prosaic form, with reference to standard measures of validity and reliability. It seeks to prove or disprove a theory or hypothesis.

Whether one chooses qualitative or quantitative research methods, studying families is complicated, especially if a systems model is followed.

## Difficulties in Family Therapy Research

Difficulties in family therapy research are associated with:

- where to focus (e.g., on the marriage, the identified patient, etc.)
- what environment to use (natural or laboratory)
- what research design to use (exploratory, descriptive, developmental, experimental, or correlational)
- sampling (random or nonprobable)
- instrumentation (self-report or behavioral open-ended)
- procedure (outcome or process based)
- theory (simple, clear, and systemic or not)
- statistics (descriptive and clinically relevant or not)

- validity (content, criterion, and construct)
- reliability (i.e., the consistency/dependability of a measure)

### The Importance of Assessing Families

Assessment is the evaluation of families in particular cases with specific instruments. It is usually clinically relevant in regard to a family in treatment.

Assessment is related to diagnosis and, consequently, to treatment plans and outcomes.

Assessment is the basis for accountability with third-party providers.

For therapists, assessing families is necessary for survival as well as a matter of being responsible.

### Dimensions of Assessing Families

Most assessment is conducted on a systematic level.

Dimensions of assessment are those related to:

- pressures on the family
- family history
- family structure
- family process

Assessment is a continuous process.

### Methods Used in Assessing Families

Both informal and formal methods are used in assessment.

Informal methods include family assessment forms.

Formal methods include the more than 1,000 assessment instruments available to family therapists.

Family therapy scales used by clinicians include:

- Family-of-Origin Scale (FOS)
- Personal Authority in the Family System Questionnaire (PAFS)
- PREPARE/ENRICH
- Family Adaptability and Cohesion Evaluation Scale III (FACES III)
- Family Inventory of Life Events and Changes (FILE)
- Family Environment Scale (FES)
- Family Assessment Device (FAD)
- Family Strengths Scale
- Family Coping Strategies Scale (F-COPES)
- Self-Report Family Inventory (SFI)

Marital therapy scales used by clinicians include:

- Locke-Wallace Marital Adjustment Test (MAT)
- Bienvenu Marital Communication Inventory (MCI)
- Dyadic Adjustment Scale (DAS)
- Marital Coping Questionnaire (MCQ)
- Primary Communication Inventory (PCI)
- Marital Satisfaction Inventory (MSI)

- Marital Instability Inventory (MII)
- Dyadic Trust Scale (DTS)
- Marital Problem-Solving Scale (MPSS)
- Couple Rating Scale (CRS)

# References

Alexander, J. F., Newell, R. M., Robbins, M. S., & Turner, C. W. (1995). Observational coding in family therapy process research. *Journal of Family Psychology, 9,* 355–365.

American Educational Research Association, American Psychological Association, & National Council on Measurement in Education (1985). *Standards for educational and psychological testing.* Washington, DC: American Psychological Association.

American Psychiatric Association. (1994). *Diagnostic and statistical manual of mental disorders* (4th ed.). Washington, DC: Author.

Baldwin, C., & Huggins, D. (1998). Marital and family therapy research: Outcomes and implications for practice. *The Family Journal: Counseling and Therapy for Couples and Families, 6,* 212–218.

Baugh, C. W., Avery, A. W., & Sheets-Haworth, K. L. (1982). Marital Problem Solving Scale: A measure to assess relationship conflict negotiation ability. *Family Therapy, 9,* 43–51.

Beavers, W. R. (1985). *Successful marriage.* New York: Norton.

Beavers, W. R., & Hampson, R. B. (1990). *Successful families: Assessment and intervention.* New York: Norton.

Bienvenu, M. J. (1970). Measurement of marital communication. *The Family Coordinator, 19,* 26–31.

Bird, G. W., & Sporakowski, M. J. (1992). The study of marriage and the family. In G. Bird & M. J. Sporakowski (Eds.), *Taking sides* (pp. x–xv). Guilford, CT: Dushkin.

Booth, A., & Edwards, J. (1983). Measuring marital instability. *Journal of Marriage and the Family, 45,* 387–393.

Boughner, S., Bubenzer, D. L., Hayes, S., & West, J. (1993). *Use of standardized assessment instruments by marital and family practitioners.* Atlanta, GA: American Counseling Association annual convention.

Bray, J. H., Williamson, D. S., & Malone, P. E. (1984). Personal Authority in the Family System: Development of a questionnaire to measure personal authority in intergenerational family processes. *Journal of Marital and Family Therapy, 10,* 167–178.

Bretherson, I., Walsh, R., & Lependorf, M. (1996). Social support in postdivorce families. In G. R. Pierce, B. R. Sarason, & I. G. Sarason (Eds.), *Handbook of social support and the family* (pp. 345–373). New York: Plenum Press.

Brock, G. W., & Barnard, C. P. (1988). *Procedures in family therapy.* Boston: Allyn & Bacon.

Carrere, S., Buchlman, K. T., Gottman, J. M., Coan, J. A., & Ruckstruhl, L. (2000). Predicting marital stability and divorce in newlywed couples. *Journal of Family Psychology, 14,* 42–58.

Colapinto, J. (1979). The relative value of empirical evidence. *Family Process, 18,* 427–441.

Copeland, A. P., & White, K. M. (1991). *Studying families.* Newbury Park, CA: Sage.

Cron, E. A. (2000). Couple Rating Scale: Clarifying problem areas. *The Family Journal: Counseling and Therapy for Couples and Families, 8,* 302–304.

Diamond, G., & Dickey, M. (1993, Spring). Process research: Its history, intent and findings. *The Family Psychologist, 9,* 23–25.

Drummond, R. J. (2000). *Appraisal procedures for counselors and helping professionals* (4th ed.). Upper Saddle River, NJ: Merrill/Prentice Hall.

Epstein, N. B., Baldwin, L. M., & Bishop, D. S. (1983). The McMaster Family Assessment Device. *Journal of Marital and Family Therapy, 9,* 171–180.

Fenell, D. L., & Weinhold, B. K. (1992). Research in marriage and family therapy. In R. L. Smith & P. Stevens-Smith (Eds.), *Family counseling and therapy* (pp. 331–337). Ann Arbor, MI: ERIC/CAPS.

Fisher, L. (1976). Dimensions of family assessment: A critical review. *Journal of Marriage and Family Counseling, 2,* 367–382.

Fishman, C. H. (1988). *Treating troubled adolescents.* New York: Basic Books.

Fleishman, J. A. (1984). Personality characteristics and coping patterns. *Journal of Health and Social Behavior, 25,* 229–244.

Flowers, B., & Olson, D. (1986). Predicting marital success with PREPARE: A predictive validity study. *Journal of Marital and Family Therapy, 12,* 403–413.

Floyd, F. J., & Markman, H. J. (1983). Observational biases in spouse interaction: Toward a cognitive/behavioral model of marriage. *Journal of Consulting and Clinical Psychology, 51,* 450–457.

Fowers, B. J. (1990). An interactional approach to standardized martial assessment: A literature review. *Family Relations, 39,* 368–385.

Fredman, N., & Sherman, R. (1987). *Handbook of measurements for marriage and family therapy.* New York: Brunner/Mazel.

Gay, L. R., & Airasian, P. (2000). *Educational research: Competencies for analysis and applications* (6th ed.). Upper Saddle River, NJ: Merrill/Prentice Hall.

Giblin, P. (1996). Family strengths. *The Family Journal: Counseling and Therapy for Couples and Families, 4,* 339–348.

Gladding, S. T. (1992). *Past presence.* Unpublished manuscript.

Glenn, N. D. (1990). Quantitative research on marital quality in the 1980s: A critical review. *Journal of Marriage and the Family, 52,* 818–831.

Gold, J. M. (1997). Assessing education in marriage and family counseling. *The Family Journal: Counseling and Therapy for Couples and Families, 5,* 159–163.

Goldman, L. (1990). Qualitative assessment. *The Counseling Psychologist, 18,* 205–213.

Griffin, J. E., & D'Andrea, L. M. (1998). Using FACES II to classify the relationship status of battered women. *The Family Journal: Counseling and Therapy for Couples and Families, 5,* 303–308.

Gurman, A. S., & Kniskern, D. P. (1981). Family therapy outcome research: Knowns and unknowns. In A. S. Gurman & D. P. Kniskern (Eds.), *Handbook of family therapy.* New York: Brunner/Mazel.

Gurman, A. S., Kniskern, D. P., & Pinsof, W. M. (1986). Research on the process and outcome of marital and family therapy. In S. L. Garfield & A. E. Bergin (Eds.), *Handbook of psychotherapy and behavioral change* (3rd ed., pp. 565–624). New York: Wiley.

Haley, J. (1978). Ideas which handicap therapists. In M. M. Berger (Ed.), *Beyond the double bind.* New York: Brunner/Mazel.

Hampson, R. B., Prince, C. C., & Beavers, W. R. (1999). Marital therapy: Qualities of couples who fare better or worse in treatment. *Journal of Marital and Family Therapy, 25,* 411–424.

Hawley, D. R., & Geske, S. (2000). The use of theory in family therapy research: A content analysis of family therapy journals. *Journal of Marital and Family Therapy, 26,* 17–22.

Hochschild, A. (1989). *The second shift: Working parents and the revolution at home.* New York: Viking.

Hood, A. B., & Johnson, R. W. (1998). *Assessment in counseling* (2nd ed.). Alexandria, VA: American Counseling Association.

Hovestadt, A. J. (2000). Unresolved couple conflict: Clinical use of the family of origin scale. In R. E. Watts (Ed.), *Techniques in marriage and family counseling* (pp. 75–80). Alexandria, VA: American Counseling Association.

Hovestadt, A. J., Anderson, W. T., Piercy, F. P., Cochran, S. W., & Fine, M. (1985). A family of origin scale. *Journal of Marital and Family Therapy, 11,* 287–297.

Hubble, M. A. (1993, Spring). Therapy research: The bonfire of the uncertainties. *The Family Psychologist, 9,* 14–16.

Jacobson, N. S. (1985). Family therapy outcome research: Potential pitfalls and prospects. *Journal of Marital and Family Therapy, 11,* 149–158.

Jacobson, N. S. (1988). Guidelines for the design of family therapy outcome research. In L. C. Wynne (Ed.), *The state of the art in family therapy research* (pp. 139–155). New York: Family Process Press.

Kane, C. M., & Erdman, P. (1998). Differences in family-of-origin perceptions among African American, Anglo-American, and Hispanic college students. *The Family Journal: Counseling and Therapy for Couples and Families, 6,* 13–18.

Kleist, D. M., & Gompertz, K. (1997). Current use of qualitative research methodology in couples and family counseling. *The Family Journal: Counseling and Therapy for Couples and Families, 5,* 137–143.

Kramer, J. J., & Conoley, J. C. (Eds.). (1992). *The eleventh mental measurements yearbook.* Lincoln, NE: Buros Institute of Mental Measurement.

L'Abate, L., & Bagarozzi, D. A. (1993). *Sourcebook of marriage and family evaluation.* New York: Brunner/Mazel.

Larzelere, R., & Huston, T. (1980). The Dyadic Trust Scale: Toward understanding interpersonal trust in close relationships. *Journal of Marriage and the Family, 43,* 595–604.

Letich, L. (1993, September/October). A clinician's researcher. *Family Therapy Networker, 17,* 77–82.

Lewis, J. M., Beavers, W. R., Gossett, J. T., & Phillips, V. A. (1976). *No single thread.* New York: Brunner/Mazel.

Liddle, H. A. (1992, October). Assessing research productivity and impact. *Family Therapy News, 23,* 17, 29.

Locke, H. J., Sabagh, G., & Thomas, M. (1956). Correlates of primary communication and empathy. *Research Studies of the State College of Washington, 24,* 116–124.

Locke, H., & Wallace, K. (1959). Short marital adjustment and prediction tests: The reliability and validity. *Marriage and Family Living, 21,* 251–255.

McCubbin, H. I., Larsen, A., & Olson, D. H. (1982). F-COPES: Family coping strategies. In D. H. Olson, H. I. McCubbin, H. I., Barnes, A. Larsen, M. Maxen, & M. Wilson (Eds.), *Family inventories: Inventories used in a national survey of families across the family life cycle* (pp. 101–120). St. Paul, MN: University of Minnesota.

McCubbin, H. I., Thompson, A. I., Pirner, P. A., & McCubbin, M. A. (1988). *Family types and strengths: A life cycle and ecological perspective.* Edina, MN: Burgess.

McGuirk, J. G., Friedlander, M. L., & Blocher, D. H. (1987). Systemic and nonsystemic diagnostic processes: An empirical comparison. *Journal of Marital and Family Therapy, 13,* 69–76.

Menaghan, E. (1982). Measuring coping effectiveness: A panel analysis of marital problems and coping efforts. *Journal of Health and Social Behavior, 23,* 220–234.

Miller, B. C. (1986). *Family research methods*. Beverly Hills, CA: Sage.

Moon, S. M., Dillon, D. R., & Sprenkle, D. H. (1990). Family therapy and qualitative research. *Journal of Marital and Family Therapy, 16*, 357–374.

Moos, R. H. (1990). Conceptual and empirical approaches to developing family-based assessment procedures: Resolving the case of the family environment. *Family Process, 29*, 199–208.

Moos, R. H., & Moos, B. S. (1986). *The family environment scale manual* (rev. ed.). Palo Alto, CA: Consulting Psychologists Press.

Nelson, T. S. (1996). Survey research in marriage and family therapy. In D. H. Sprenkle & S. M. Moon (Eds.), *Research methods in family therapy* (pp. 447–468). New York: Guilford.

Oliver, J. M., Handal, P. J., Enos, D. M., & May, M. J. (1988). Factor structure of the family environment scale: Factors based on items and subscales. *Educational and Psychological Measurement, 48*, 469–477.

Olson, D. H., Fournier, D. G., & Druckman, J. M. (1987). *Counselor's manual for PREPARE/ENRICH* (rev. ed.). Minneapolis, MN: PREPARE/ENRICH Inc.

Olson, D. H., Larsen, A. S., & McCubbin, H. I. (1985). Family strengths. In D. Olson, H. McCubbin, H. Barnes, A. Larsen, M. Muxen, & M. Wilson (Eds.), *Family inventories* (rev. ed.). St Paul, MN: Family Social Science, University of Minnesota.

Olson, D. H., McCubbin, H. I., Barnes, H., Larsen, A., Muxen, M., & Wilson, M. (1985). *Family inventories: Inventories used in a national survey of families across the family life cycle*. St Paul, MN: Family Social Science, University of Minnesota.

Pearlin, L. T., & Schooler, C. (1978). The structure of coping. *Journal of Health and Social Behavior, 19*, 2–21.

Piercy, F. P., McKeon, D., & Laird, R. A. (1983). A family assessment process for community mental health clinics. *AMHCA Journal, 5*, 94–104.

Piercy, F. P., & Sprenkle, D. H. (1986). *Family therapy handbook*. New York: Guilford.

Piercy, F. P., & Thomas, V. (1998). Participatory evaluation research: An introduction for family therapists. *Journal of Marital and Family Therapy, 24*, 165–176.

Pinsof, W. M., & Wynne, L. C. (2000). Toward progress research: Closing the gap between family therapy practice and research. *Journal of Marital and Family Therapy, 26*, 1–8.

Prouty, A. M., Markowksi, E. M., & Barnes, H. L. (2000). Using the Dyadic Adjustment Scale in marital therapy: An exploratory study. *The Family Journal: Counseling and Therapy for Couples and Families, 8*, 250–257.

Reiss, D. (1988). Theoretical versus tactical inferences. In L. C. Wynne (Ed.), *The state of the art in family therapy research* (pp. 33–46). New York: Family Process Press.

Sabourin, S., Laporte, L., & Wright, J. (1990). Problem solving self-appraisal and coping efforts in distressed and nondistressed couples. *Journal of Marital and Family Therapy, 16*, 89–97.

Schumm, W. R. (1983). Theory and measurement in marital communication training programs. *Family Relations, 32*, 3–11.

Schwartz, R. C., & Breunlin, D. (1983). Research: Why clinicians should bother with it. *Family Therapy Networker, 7*, 22–27, 57–59.

Shields, C. G. (1986). Critiquing the new epistemologies: Toward minimum requirements for a scientific theory of family therapy. *Journal of Marital and Family Therapy, 12*, 359–372.

Shields, G., Wynne, L. C., McDaniel, S. H., & Gawinski, B. A. (1994). The marginalization of family therapy: An historical and continuing problem. *Journal of Marital and Family Therapy, 20*, 117–138.

Simola, S. K., Parker, K. C. H., & Froese, A. P. (1999). Relational V-code conditions in a child or adolescent population do warrant treatment. *Journal of Marital and Family Therapy, 25*, 225–236.

Sluzko, C. E. (1978). Marital therapy from a systems theory perspective. In T. J. Paolino & B. C. McCrady (Eds.), *Marriage and marital therapy*. New York: Brunner/Mazel.

Snyder, D. K. (1981). *Marital Satisfaction Inventory manual*. Los Angeles: Western Psychological Services.

Snyder, D. K., & Regts, J. M. (1982). Factor scales for assessing marital disharmony and disaffection. *Journal of Consulting and Clinical Psychology, 50*, 736–743.

Snyder, D. K., Cavell, T. A., Heffer, R. W., & Mangrum, L. F. (1995). Marital and family assessment: A multifaceted, multilevel approach. In R. H. Mikesell, D.-D. Lusterman, & S. H. McDaniel (Eds.), *Integrating family therapy* (pp. 163–182). Washington, DC: American Psychological Association.

Spanier, G. B. (1976). Measuring dyadic adjustment: New scales for assessing the quality of marriage and similar dyads. *Journal of Marriage and the Family, 38*, 15–28.

Sporakowski, M. J. (1995). Assessment and diagnosis in marriage and family counseling. *Journal of Counseling & Development, 74*, 60–64.

Sprenkle, D. H., & Moon, S. M. (1996). Toward pluralism in family therapy research. In D. H. Sprenkle & S. M. Moon (Eds.), *Research methods in family therapy* (pp. 3–19). New York: Guilford.

Sprenkle, D. H., & Piercy, F. P. (1984). Research in family therapy: A graduate level course. *Journal of Marital and Family Therapy, 10*, 225–240.

Stanton, M. D., Todd, T. C., & Associates (1982). *The family therapy of drug abuse and addiction*. New York: Gardner Press.

Stinnet, N. (1981). In search of strong families. In N. Stinnet, B. Chesser, & J. DeFrain (Eds.), *Building family strengths: Blueprints for action*. Lincoln, NE: University of Nebraska Press.

Sullivan, K. T., Parch, L. A., Eldridge, K. A., & Bradbury, T. N. (1998). Social support in marriage: Translating research into practical applications for clinicians. *The Family Journal: Counseling and Therapy for Couples and Families, 6*, 263–271.

Sussman, M., & Gilgun, J. F. (Eds.).(1997). *The methods and methodologies of qualitative family research*. New York: Haworth.

Szapocznik, J., Kurtines, W., Perez-Vidal, A., Hervis, O., & Foote, F. (1990). One person family therapy. In R. A. Wells & V. A. Gianetti (Eds.), *Handbook of brief psychotherapies* (pp. 493–510). New York: Plenum.

Szapocznik, J., Rio, A., Hervis, O., Kurtines, W., Faraci, A. M., & Mitrani, V. (1991). Assessing change in family functioning as a result of treatment: The structural family systems rating scale (SFSR). *Journal of Marital and Family Therapy, 17*, 295–310.

Szapocznik, J., Rio, A., Murray, E., Cohen, R., Scopetta, M., Rivas-Vasquez, A., Hervis, O., Posada, V., & Kurtines, W. (1989). Structural family therapy versus psychodynamic child therapy for problematic Hispanic boys. *Journal of Consulting and Clinical Psychology, 57*, 571–578.

Thomas, V. (1995). The clinical report: Integrating family assessment instruments into family counseling practice. *The Family Journal: Counseling and Therapy for Couples and Families, 3*, 284–297.

Thomas, V., & Olson, D. H. (1993). Problem families and the circumplex model: Observational assessment using the Clinical Rating Scale (CRS). *Journal of Marital and Family Therapy, 19*, 159–175.

Touliatos, J., Perlmutter, B. F., & Straus, M. A. (Eds.) (1990). *Handbook of family measurement techniques*. Newbury Park, CA: Sage.

Turner, W. L. (1993, April). Identifying African-American family strengths. *Family Therapy News, 24*, 9, 14.

West, J. D. (1988). Marriage and family therapy assessment. *Counselor Education and Supervision, 28*, 169–180.

Wilcoxon, S. A., Walker, M. R., & Hovestadt, A. J. (1989). Counselor effectiveness and family-of-origin experiences: A significant relationship? *Counseling and Values, 33*, 225–229.

Wynne, L. C. (1983). Family research and family therapy: A reunion? *Journal of Marital and Family Therapy, 9*, 113–117.

# Appendix A

## AAMFT Code of Ethics

### Preamble

The Board of Directors of the American Association for Marriage and Family Therapy (AAMFT) hereby promulgates, pursuant to Article 2, Section 2.013 of the Association's Bylaws, the Revised AAMFT Code of Ethics, effective July 1, 2001.

The AAMFT strives to honor the public trust in marriage and family therapists by setting standards for ethical practice as described in this Code. The ethical standards define professional expectations and are enforced by the AAMFT Ethics Committee. The absence of an explicit reference to a specific behavior or situation in the Code does not mean that the behavior is ethical or unethical. The standards are not exhaustive. Marriage and family therapists who are uncertain about the ethics of a particular course of action are encouraged to seek counsel from consultants, attorneys, supervisors, colleagues, or other appropriate authorities.

Both law and ethics govern the practice of marriage and family therapy. When making decisions regarding professional behavior, marriage and family therapists must consider the AAMFT Code of Ethics and applicable laws and regulations. If the AAMFT Code of Ethics prescribes a standard higher than that required by law, marriage and family therapists must meet the higher standard of the AAMFT Code of Ethics. Marriage and family therapists comply with the mandates of law, but make

known their commitment to the AAMFT Code of Ethics and take steps to resolve the conflict in a responsible manner. The AAMFT supports legal mandates for reporting of alleged unethical conduct.

The AAMFT Code of Ethics is binding on Members of AAMFT in all membership categories, AAMFT-Approved Supervisors, and applicants for membership and the Approved Supervisor designation (hereafter, AAMFT Member). AAMFT members have an obligation to be familiar with the AAMFT Code of Ethics and its application to their professional services. Lack of awareness or misunderstanding of an ethical standard is not a defense to a charge of unethical conduct.

The process for filing, investigating, and resolving complaints of unethical conduct is described in the current Procedures for Handling Ethical Matters of the AAMFT Ethics Committee. Persons accused are considered innocent by the Ethics Committee until proven guilty, except as otherwise provided, and are entitled to due process. If an AAMFT Member resigns in anticipation of, or during the course of, an ethics investigation, the Ethics Committee will complete its investigation. Any publication of action taken by the Association will include the fact that the Member attempted to resign during the investigation.

### Principle I: Responsibility to Clients

#### 1. Responsibility to Clients

*Marriage and family therapists advance the welfare of families and individuals. They respect the rights of those persons seeking their assistance, and make reasonable efforts to ensure that their services are used appropriately.*

**425**

1.1 Marriage and family therapists provide professional assistance to persons without discrimination on the basis of race, age, ethnicity, socioeconomic status, disability, gender, health status, religion, national origin, or sexual orientation.

1.2 Marriage and family therapists obtain appropriate informed consent to therapy or related procedures and use language that is reasonably understandable to clients. The content of informed consent may vary depending upon the client and treatment plan; however, informed consent generally necessitates that the client: (a) has the capacity to consent; (b) has been adequately informed of significant information concerning treatment processes, procedures, risks and benefits; (c) has freely and without undue influence expressed consent; and (d) has provided consent that is appropriately documented. When persons, due to age or mental status, are legally incapable of giving informed consent, marriage and family therapists obtain informed permission from a legally authorized person, if such substitute consent is legally permissible.

1.3 Marriage and family therapists are aware of their influential positions with respect to clients, and they avoid exploiting the trust and dependency of such persons. Therapists, therefore, make every effort to avoid conditions and multiple relationships with clients that could impair professional judgment or increase the risk of exploitation. Such relationships include, but are not limited to, business or close personal relationships with a client or the client's immediate family. When the risk of impairment or exploitation exists due to conditions or multiple roles, therapists take appropriate precautions.

1.4 Sexual intimacy with clients is prohibited.

1.5 Sexual intimacy with former clients is likely to be harmful and is therefore prohibited for two years following the termination of therapy or last professional contact. In an effort to avoid exploiting the trust and dependency of clients, marriage and family therapists should not engage in sexual intimacy with former clients after the two years following termination or last professional contact. Should therapists engage in sexual intimacy with former clients following two years after termination or last professional contact, the burden shifts to the therapist to demonstrate that there has been no exploitation or injury to the former client or to the client's immediate family.

1.6 Marriage and family therapists comply with applicable laws regarding the reporting of alleged unethical conduct.

1.7 Marriage and family therapists do not use their professional relationships with clients to further their own interests.

1.8 Marriage and family therapists respect the rights of clients to make decisions and help them to understand the consequences of these decisions. Therapists clearly advise the clients that they have the responsibility to make decisions regarding relationships such as cohabitation, marriage, divorce, separation, reconciliation, custody, and visitation.

1.9 Marriage and family therapists continue therapeutic relationships only so long as it is reasonably clear that clients are benefiting from the relationship.

1.10 Marriage and family therapists assist persons in obtaining other therapeutic services if the therapist is unable or unwilling, for appropriate reasons, to provide professional help.

1.11 Marriage and family therapists do not abandon or neglect clients in treatment without making reasonable arrangements for the continuation of such treatment.

1.12 Marriage and family therapists obtain written informed consent from clients before videotaping, audio recording, or permitting third-party observation.

1.13 Marriage and family therapists, upon agreeing to provide services to a person or entity at the request of a third party, clarify, to the extent feasible and at the outset of the service, the nature of the relationship with each party and the limits of confidentiality.

## Principle II: Confidentiality

### 2. Confidentiality

*Marriage and family therapists have unique confidentiality concerns because the client in a therapeutic relationship may be more than one person. Therapists respect and guard the confidences of each individual client.*

2.1 Marriage and family therapists disclose to clients and other interested parties, as early as feasible in their professional contacts, the nature of confidentiality and possible limitations of the clients' right to confidentiality. Therapists review with clients the circumstances where confidential information may be requested and where disclosure of confidential information may be legally required. Circumstances may necessitate repeated disclosures.

2.2 Marriage and family therapists do not disclose client confidences except by written authorization or waiver, or where mandated or permitted by law. Verbal authorization will not be sufficient except in emergency situations, unless prohibited by law. When providing couple, family or group treatment, the therapist does not disclose information outside the treatment context without a written authorization from each individual competent to execute a waiver. In the context of couple, family or group treatment, the therapist may not reveal any individual's confidences to others in the client unit without the prior written permission of that individual.

2.3 Marriage and family therapists use client and/or clinical materials in teaching, writing, consulting, research, and public presentations only if a written waiver has been obtained in accordance with Subprinciple 2.2, or when appropriate steps have been taken to protect client identity and confidentiality.

2.4 Marriage and family therapists store, safeguard, and dispose of client records in ways that maintain confidentiality and in accord with applicable laws and professional standards.

2.5 Subsequent to the therapist moving from the area, closing the practice, or upon the death of the therapist, a marriage and family therapist arranges for the storage, transfer, or disposal of client records in ways that maintain confidentiality and safeguard the welfare of clients.

2.6 Marriage and family therapists, when consulting with colleagues or referral sources, do not share confidential information that could reasonably lead to the identification of a client, research participant, supervisee, or other person with whom they have a confidential relationship unless they have obtained the prior written consent of the client, research participant, supervisee, or other person with whom they have a confidential relationship. Information may be shared only to the extent necessary to achieve the purposes of the consultation.

## Principle III: Professional Competence and Integrity

### 3. Professional Competence and Integrity

*Marriage and family therapists maintain high standards of professional competence and integrity.*

3.1 Marriage and family therapists pursue knowledge of new developments and maintain competence in marriage and family therapy through education, training, or supervised experience.

3.2 Marriage and family therapists maintain adequate knowledge of and adhere to applicable laws, ethics, and professional standards.

3.3 Marriage and family therapists seek appropriate professional assistance for their personal problems or conflicts that may impair work performance or clinical judgment.

3.4 Marriage and family therapists do not provide services that create a conflict of interest that may impair work performance or clinical judgment.

3.5 Marriage and family therapists, as presenters, teachers, supervisors, consultants and researchers, are dedicated to high standards of scholarship, present accurate information, and disclose potential conflicts of interest.

3.6 Marriage and family therapists maintain accurate and adequate clinical and financial records.

3.7 While developing new skills in specialty areas, marriage and family therapists take steps to ensure the competence of their work and to protect clients from possible harm. Marriage and family therapists practice in specialty areas new to them only after appropriate education, training, or supervised experience.

3.8 Marriage and family therapists do not engage in sexual or other forms of harassment of clients, students, trainees, supervisees, employees, colleagues, or research subjects.

3.9 Marriage and family therapists do not engage in the exploitation of clients, students, trainees, supervisees, employees, colleagues, or research subjects.

3.10 Marriage and family therapists do not give to or receive from clients (a) gifts of substantial value or (b) gifts that impair the integrity or efficacy of the therapeutic relationship.

3.11 Marriage and family therapists do not diagnose, treat, or advise on problems outside the recognized boundaries of their competencies.

3.12 Marriage and family therapists make efforts to prevent the distortion or misuse of their clinical and research findings.

3.13 Marriage and family therapists, because of their ability to influence and alter the lives of others, exercise special care when making public their professional recommendations and opinions through testimony or other public statements.

3.14 To avoid a conflict of interests, marriage and family therapists who treat minors or adults involved in custody or visitation actions may not also perform forensic evaluations for custody, residence, or visitation of the minor. The marriage and family therapist who treats the minor may provide the court or mental health professional performing the evaluation with information about the minor from the marriage and family therapist's perspective as a treating marriage and family therapist, so long as the marriage and family therapist does not violate confidentiality.

3.15 Marriage and family therapists are in violation of this Code and subject to termination of membership or other appropriate action if they: (a) are convicted of any felony; (b) are convicted of a misdemeanor related to their qualifications or functions; (c) engage in conduct which could lead to conviction of a felony, or a misdemeanor related to their qualifications or functions; (d) are expelled from or disciplined by other professional organizations; (e) have their licenses or certificates suspended or revoked or are otherwise disciplined by regulatory bodies; (f) continue to practice marriage and family therapy while no longer competent to do so because they are impaired by physical or mental causes or the abuse of alcohol or other substances; or (g) fail to cooperate with the Associa-

tion at any point from the inception of an ethical complaint through the completion of all proceedings regarding that complaint.

## Principle IV: Responsibility to Students and Supervisees

### 4. Responsibility to Students and Supervisees

*Marriage and family therapists do not exploit the trust and dependency of students and supervisees.*

4.1 Marriage and family therapists are aware of their influential positions with respect to students and supervisees, and they avoid exploiting the trust and dependency of such persons. Therapists, therefore, make every effort to avoid conditions and multiple relationships that could impair professional objectivity or increase the risk of exploitation. When the risk of impairment or exploitation exists due to conditions or multiple roles, therapists take appropriate precautions.

4.2 Marriage and family therapists do not provide therapy to current students or supervisees.

4.3 Marriage and family therapists do not engage in sexual intimacy with students or supervisees during the evaluative or training relationship between the therapist and student or supervisee. Should a supervisor engage in sexual activity with a former supervisee, the burden of proof shifts to the supervisor to demonstrate that there has been no exploitation or injury to the supervisee.

4.4 Marriage and family therapists do not permit students or supervisees to perform or to hold themselves out as competent to perform professional services beyond their training, level of experience, and competence.

4.5 Marriage and family therapists take reasonable measures to ensure that services provided by supervisees are professional.

4.6 Marriage and family therapists avoid accepting as supervisees or students those individuals with whom a prior or existing relationship could compromise the therapist's objectivity. When such situations cannot be avoided, therapists take appropriate precautions to maintain objectivity. Examples of such relationships include, but are not limited to, those individuals with whom the therapist has a current or prior sexual, close personal, immediate familial, or therapeutic relationship.

4.7 Marriage and family therapists do not disclose supervisee confidences except by written authorization or waiver, or when mandated or permitted by law. In educational or training settings where there are multiple supervisors, disclosures are permitted only to other professional colleagues, administrators, or employers who share responsibility for training of the supervisee. Verbal authorization will not be sufficient except in emergency situations, unless prohibited by law.

## Principle V: Responsibility to Research Participants

### 5. Responsibility to Research Participants

*Investigators respect the dignity and protect the welfare of research participants in research and are aware of applicable laws and regulations and professional standards governing the conduct of research.*

5.1 Investigators are responsible for making careful examination of ethical acceptability in planning studies. To the extent that services to research participants may be compromised by participation in research, investigators seek the ethical advice of qualified professionals not directly involved in the investigation and observe safeguards to protect the rights of research participants.

5.2 Investigators requesting participants' involvement in research inform them of all aspects of the research that might reasonably be expected to influence willingness to participate. Investigators are especially sensitive to the possibility of diminished consent when participants are also receiving clinical services, have impairments which limit understanding and/or communication, or when participants are children.

5.3 Investigators respect each participant's freedom to decline participation in or to withdraw from a research study at any time. This obligation requires special thought and consideration when investigators or other members of the research team are in positions of authority or influence over partic-

ipants. Marriage and family therapists, therefore, make every effort to avoid multiple relationships with research participants that could impair professional judgment or increase the risk of exploitation.

5.4 Information obtained about a research participant during the course of an investigation is confidential unless there is a waiver previously obtained in writing. When the possibility exists that others, including family members, may obtain access to such information, this possibility, together with the plan for protecting confidentiality, is explained as part of the procedure for obtaining informed consent.

## Principle VI: Responsibility to the Profession

### 6. Responsibility to the Profession

*Marriage and family therapists respect the rights and responsibilities of professional colleagues and participate in activities that advance the goals of the profession.*

6.1 Marriage and family therapists remain accountable to the standards of the profession when acting as members or employees of organizations. If the mandates of an organization with which a marriage and family therapist is affiliated, through employment, contract or otherwise, conflict with the AAMFT Code of Ethics, marriage and family therapists make known to the organization their commitment to the AAMFT Code of Ethics and attempt to resolve the conflict in a way that allows the fullest adherence to the Code of Ethics.

6.2 Marriage and family therapists assign publication credit to those who have contributed to a publication in proportion to their contributions and in accordance with customary professional publication practices.

6.3 Marriage and family therapists do not accept or require authorship credit for a publication based on research from a student's program, unless the therapist made a substantial contribution beyond being a faculty advisor or research committee member. Coauthorship on a student thesis, dissertation, or project should be determined in accordance with principles of fairness and justice.

6.4 Marriage and family therapists who are the authors of books or other materials that are published or distributed do not plagiarize or fail to cite persons to whom credit for original ideas or work is due.

6.5 Marriage and family therapists who are the authors of books or other materials published or distributed by an organization take reasonable precautions to ensure that the organization promotes and advertises the materials accurately and factually.

6.6 Marriage and family therapists participate in activities that contribute to a better community and society, including devoting a portion of their professional activity to services for which there is little or no financial return.

6.7 Marriage and family therapists are concerned with developing laws and regulations pertaining to marriage and family therapy that serve the public interest, and with altering such laws and regulations that are not in the public interest.

6.8 Marriage and family therapists encourage public participation in the design and delivery of professional services and in the regulation of practitioners.

## Principle VII: Financial Arrangements

### 7. Financial Arrangements

*Marriage and family therapists make financial arrangements with clients, third-party payors, and supervisees that are reasonably understandable and conform to accepted professional practices.*

7.1 Marriage and family therapists do not offer or accept kickbacks, rebates, bonuses, or other remuneration for referrals; fee-for-service arrangements are not prohibited.

7.2 Prior to entering into the therapeutic or supervisory relationship, marriage and family therapists clearly disclose and explain to clients and supervisees: (a) all financial arrangements and fees related to professional services, including charges for canceled or missed appointments; (b) the use of collection agencies or legal measures for nonpayment; and (c) the procedure for obtaining payment from the client, to the extent allowed by law, if payment is denied by the third-party payor. Once ser-

vices have begun, therapists provide reasonable notice of any changes in fees or other charges.

7.3 Marriage and family therapists give reasonable notice to clients with unpaid balances of their intent to seek collection by agency or legal recourse. When such action is taken, therapists will not disclose clinical information.

7.4 Marriage and family therapists represent facts truthfully to clients, third-party payors, and supervisees regarding services rendered.

7.5 Marriage and family therapists ordinarily refrain from accepting goods and services from clients in return for services rendered. Bartering for professional services may be conducted only if: (a) the supervisee or client requests it, (b) the relationship is not exploitative, (c) the professional relationship is not distorted, and (d) a clear written contract is established.

7.6 Marriage and family therapists may not withhold records under their immediate control that are requested and needed for a client's treatment solely because payment has not been received for past services, except as otherwise provided by law.

## Principle VIII: Advertising

### 8. Advertising

*Marriage and family therapists engage in appropriate informational activities, including those that enable the public, referral sources, or others to choose professional services on an informed basis.*

8.1 Marriage and family therapists accurately represent their competencies, education, training, and experience relevant to their practice of marriage and family therapy.

8.2 Marriage and family therapists ensure that advertisements and publications in any media (such as directories, announcements, business cards, newspapers, radio, television, Internet, and facsimiles) convey information that is necessary for the public to make an appropriate selection of professional services. Information could include: (a) office information, such as name, address, telephone number, credit card acceptability, fees, languages spoken, and office hours; (b) qualifying clinical degree (see subprinciple 8.5); (c) other earned degrees (see subprinciple 8.5) and state or provincial licensures and/or certifications; (d) AAMFT clinical member status; and (e) description of practice.

8.3 Marriage and family therapists do not use names that could mislead the public concerning the identity, responsibility, source, and status of those practicing under that name, and do not hold themselves out as being partners or associates of a firm if they are not.

8.4 Marriage and family therapists do not use any professional identification (such as a business card, office sign, letterhead, Internet, or telephone or association directory listing) if it includes a statement or claim that is false, fraudulent, misleading, or deceptive.

8.5 In representing their educational qualifications, marriage and family therapists list and claim as evidence only those earned degrees: (a) from institutions accredited by regional accreditation sources recognized by the United States Department of Education, (b) from institutions recognized by states or provinces that license or certify marriage and family therapists, or (c) from equivalent foreign institutions.

8.6 Marriage and family therapists correct, wherever possible, false, misleading, or inaccurate information and representations made by others concerning the therapist's qualifications, services, or products.

8.7 Marriage and family therapists make certain that the qualifications of their employees or supervisees are represented in a manner that is not false, misleading, or deceptive.

8.8 Marriage and family therapists do not represent themselves as providing specialized service unless they have the appropriate education, training, or supervised experience.

# Appendix B

# Ethical Code for the International Association of Marriage and Family Counselors

## Preamble

The IAMFC (The International Association of Marriage and Family Counselors) is an organization dedicated to advancing the practice, training, and research of marriage and family counselors. Members may specialize in areas such as: premarital counseling, intergenerational counseling, separation and divorce counseling, relocation counseling, custody assessment and implementation, single parenting, stepfamilies, nontraditional family and marriage life-styles, healthy and dysfunctional family systems, multicultural marriage and family concerns, displaced and homeless families, interfaith and interracial families, and dual career couples. In conducting their professional activities, members commit themselves to protect and advocate for the healthy growth and development of the family as a whole, even as they conscientiously recognize the integrity and diversity of each family and family member's unique needs, situations, status, and member's unique needs, situations, status, and condition. The IAMFC member recognizes that the relationship between provider and consumer services is characterized as an egalitarian process emphasizing co-participation, co-equality, co-authority, co-responsibility, and client empowerment.

This code of ethics promulgates a framework for ethical practice by IAMFC members and is divided into eight sections: client well-being, confidentiality, competence, assessment, private practice, research and publications, supervision, and media

Reprinted from *The Family Journal*, Vol. 1, January 1993, pp. 73–77. © ACA. Reprinted with permission.

and public statements. The ideas presented within these eight areas are meant to supplement the ethical standards of the American Counseling Association (ACA), formerly the American Association for Counseling and Development (AACD), and all members should know and keep to the standards of our parent organization. Although an ethical code cannot anticipate every possible situation or dilemma, the IAMFC ethical guidelines can aid members in ensuring the welfare and dignity of the couples and families they have contact with, as well as assisting in the implementation of the Hippocratic mandate for healers: Do no harm.

## Section I: Client Well-Being

A. Members demonstrate a caring, empathic, respectful, fair, and active concern for family well-being. They promote client safety, security, and place-of-belonging in family, community, and society. Due to the risk involved, members should not use intrusive interventions without a sound theoretical rationale and having thoroughly thought through the potential ramifications to the family and its members.

B. Members recognize that each family is unique. They respect the diversity of personal attributes and do not stereotype or force families into prescribed attitudes, roles, or behaviors.

C. Members respect the autonomy of the families that they work with. They do not make decisions that rightfully belong to family members.

D. Members respect cultural diversity. They do not discriminate on the bases of race, sex, disability, religion, age, sexual orientation, cultural background, national origin, marital status, or political affiliation.

E. Members strive for an egalitarian relationship with clients by openly and conscientiously sharing information, opinions, perceptions, processes of decision making, strategies of problem solving, and understanding of human behavior.

F. Members pursue a just relationship that acknowledges, respects, and informs clients of their rights, obligations, and expectations as a consumer of services, as well as the rights, obligations, and expectations of the provider(s) of services. Members inform clients (in writing if feasible) about the goals and purpose of the counseling, the qualifications of the counselor(s), the scope and limits of confidentiality, potential risks and benefits associated with the counseling process and with specific counseling techniques, reasonable expectations for the outcomes and duration of counseling, costs of services, and appropriate alternatives to counseling.

G. Members strive for a humanistic relationship that assists clients to develop a philosophy of meaning, purpose, and direction of life and living that promotes a positive regard of self, of family, of different and diverse others, and of the importance of humane concern for the community, nation, and the world at large.

H. Members promote primary prevention. They pursue the development of clients' cognitive, moral, social, emotional, spiritual, physical, educational, and career needs, as well as parenting, marriage, and family living skills, in order to prevent future problems.

I. Members have an obligation to determine and inform all persons involved who their primary client is—i.e., is the counselor's primary obligation to the individual, the family, a third party, or an institution? When there is a conflict of interest between the needs of the client and counselor's employing institution, the member works to clarify his or her commitment to all parties. Members recognize that the acceptance of employment implies that they are in agreement with the agency's policies and practices, and so monitor their place of employment to make sure that the environment is conducive to the positive growth and development of clients. If, after utilizing appropriate institutional channels for change, the member finds that the agency is not working toward the well-being of clients, the member has an obligation to terminate his or her institutional affiliation.

J. Members do not harass, exploit, coerce, engage in dual relationships, or have sexual contact with any current or former client or family member to whom they have provided professional services.

K. Members have an obligation to withdraw from a counseling relationship if the continuation of services is not in the best interest of the client or would result in a violation of ethical standards. If a client feels that the counseling relationship is no longer productive, the member has an obligation to assist in finding alternative services.

L. Members maintain accurate and up-to-date records. They make all file information available to clients unless the sharing of such information would be damaging to the status, goals, growth, or development of the client.

M. Members have the responsibility to confront unethical behavior conducted by other counselors. The first step should be to discuss the violation directly with the counselor. If the problem continues, the member should first use procedures established by the employing institution and then those of the IAMFC. Members may wish to also contact any appropriate licensure or certification board. Members may contact the IAMFC executive director, president, executive board members, or chair of the ethics committee at any time for consultation on remedying ethical violations.

## Section II: Confidentiality

A. Clients have the right to expect that information shared with the counselor will not be disclosed to others and, in the absence of any law to the contrary, the communications between clients and marriage and family counselors should be viewed as privileged. The fact that a contact was made with a counselor is to be considered just as confidential as the information shared during that contact. Information obtained from a client can only be disclosed to a third party under the following conditions.

1. The client consents to disclosure by a signed waiver. The client must fully understand the nature of the disclosure (i.e., give informed consent), and only information described in the waiver may be disclosed. If more than one person is receiving counseling, each individual who is legally competent to execute a waiver must sign.
2. The client has placed him- or herself or someone else in clear imminent danger.
3. The law mandates disclosure.
4. The counselor is a defendant in a civil, criminal, or disciplinary action arising from professional activity.
5. The counselor needs to discuss a case for consultation or education purposes. These discussions should not reveal the identity of the client or any other unnecessary aspects of the case and should only be done with fellow counseling professionals who subscribe to the IAMFC ethical code. The consulting professional counselor has an obligation to keep all shared information confidential.

B. All clients must be informed of the nature and limitations of confidentiality. They must also be informed of who may have access to their counseling records, as well as any information that may be released to other agencies or professionals for insurance reimbursement. These disclosures should be made both orally and in writing, whenever feasible.

C. All client records should be stored in a way that ensures confidentiality. Written records should be kept in a locked drawer or cabinet and computerized record systems should sue appropriate passwords and safeguards to prevent unauthorized entry.

D. Clients must be informed if sessions are to be recorded on audio- or videotape and signed a consent form for doing so. When more than one person is receiving counseling, all persons who are legally competent must give informed consent in writing for the recording.

E. Unless alternate arrangements have been agreed upon by all participants, statements made by a family member to the counselor during an individual counseling or consultation contact are to be treated as confidential and are not disclosed to other family members without the individual's permission. If a client's refusal to share information from individual contacts interferes with the agreed upon goals of counseling, the counselor may have to terminate treatment and refer the clients to another counselor.

## Section III: Competence

A. Members have the responsibility to develop and maintain basic skills in marriage and family counseling through graduate work, supervision, and peer review. An outline of these skills is provided by the Council for Accreditation of Counseling and Related Educational Programs (CACREP) *Environmental and Specialty Standards for marriage and Family Counseling/Therapy*. The minimal level of training shall be considered a master's degree in a helping profession.

B. Members recognize the need for keeping current with new developments in the field of marriage and family counseling. They pursue continuing education in forms such as books, journals, classes, workshops, conferences, and conventions.

C. Members accurately represent their education, areas of expertise, training, and experience.

D. Members do not attempt to diagnose or treat problems beyond the scope of their abilities and training.

E. Members do not undertake any professional activity in which their personal problems might adversely affect their performance. Instead, they focus their energies on obtaining appropriate professional assistance to help them resolve the problem.

F. Members do not engage in actions that violate the moral or legal standards of their community.

## Section IV: Assessment

A. Members utilize assessment procedures to promote the best interests and well-being of the client in clarifying concerns, establishing treatment goals, evaluating therapeutic progress, and promoting objective decision making.

B. Clients have the right to know the results, interpretation, and conclusions drawn from assessment interviews and instruments, as well as how this information will be used.

C. Members utilize assessment methods that are reliable, valid, and germane to the goals of the client. When using computer-assisted scoring, members obtain empirical evidence for the reliability of the methods and procedures used.

D. Members do not use inventories and tests that have outdated test items or normative data.

E. Members do not use assessment methods that are outside the scope of their qualifications, training, or statutory limitations. Members using tests or inventories have a thorough understanding of measurement concepts.

F. Members read the manual before using a published instrument. They become knowledgeable about the purpose of the instrument and relevant psychometric and normative data.

G. Members conducting custody evaluations recognize the potential impact that their reports can have on family members. As such, they are committed to a thorough assessment of both parents. Therefore, custody recommendations should not be made on the basis of information from only one parent. Members only use instruments that have demonstrated validity in custody evaluations and do not make recommendations based solely on test and inventory scores.

H. Members strive to maintain the guidelines in the *Standards for Educational and Psychological Testing,* written in collaboration by the American Educational Research Association, American Psychological Association, and National Council on Measurement in Evaluation, as well as the *Code of Fair Testing Practices,* published by the Joint Committee on Testing Practices.

## Section V: Private Practice

A. Members assist the profession and community by facilitating, whenever feasible, the availability of counseling services in private settings.

B. Due to the independent nature of their work, members in private practice recognize that they have a special obligation to act ethically and responsibly, keep up to date through continuing education, arrange consultation and supervision, and practice within the scope of their training and applicable laws.

C. Members in private practice provide a portion of their services at little or no cost as a service to the community. They also provide referral services for clients who will not be seen pro bono and who are unable to afford private services.

D. Members only enter into partnerships in which each member adheres to the ethical standards of their profession.

E. Members should not charge a fee for offering or accepting referrals.

## Section VI: Research and Publications

A. Members shall be fully responsible for their choice of research topics and the methods used for investigation, analysis, and reporting. They must be particularly careful that findings do not appear misleading, that the research is planned to allow for the inclusion of alternative hypotheses, and that provision is made for discussion of the limitations of the study.

B. Members safeguard the privacy of their research participants. Data about an individual participant are not released unless the individual is informed about the exact nature of the information to be released and gives written permission for doing so.

C. Members safeguard the safety of their research participants. Members receive approval from, and follow guidelines of, any institutional research committee. Prospective participants are informed, in writing, about any potential risk associated with a study and are notified that they can withdraw at any time.

D. Members make their original data available to other researchers.

E. Members only take credit for research in which they make a substantial contribution, and give credit to all such contributors. Authors are listed from greatest to least amount of contribution.

F. Members do not plagiarize. Ideas or data that did not originate with the author(s) and are not common knowledge are clearly credited to the original source.

G. Members are aware of their obligation to be a role model for graduate students and other future researchers and so act in accordance with the highest standards possible while engaged in research.

## Section VII: Supervision

A. Members who provide supervision acquire and maintain skills pertaining to the supervision process. They are able to demonstrate for supervisees the application of counseling theory and process to client issues. Supervisors are knowledgeable about different methods and conceptual approaches to supervision.

B. Members who provide supervision respect the inherent imbalance of power in the supervisory relationship. They do not use their potentially influential positions to exploit students, supervisees, or employees. Supervisors do not ask supervisees to engage in behaviors not directly related to the supervision process, and they clearly separate supervision and evaluation. Supervisors also avoid dual relationships that might impair their professional judgement or increase the possibility of exploitation. Sexual intimacy with students or supervisees is prohibited.

C. Members who provide supervision are responsible for both the promotion of supervisee learning and development and the advancement of marriage and family counseling. Supervisors recruit students into professional organizations, educate students about professional ethics and standards, provide service to professional organizations, strive to educate new professionals, and work to improve professional practices.

D. Members who provide supervision have the responsibility to inform students of the specific expectations surrounding skill building, knowledge acquisition, and the development of competencies. Members also provide ongoing and timely feedback to their supervisees.

E. Members who provide supervision are responsible for protecting the rights and well-being of their supervisees' clients. They monitor their supervisees' counseling on an ongoing basis, and create procedures to protect the confidentiality of clients whose sessions have been electronically recorded.

F. Members who provide supervision strive to reach and maintain the guidelines provided in the *Standards for Counseling Supervisors* published by the ACA Governing Council (cf. *Journal of Counseling & Development*, 1990, Vol. 69, pp. 30–32).

G. Members who are counselor educators encourage their programs to reach and maintain the guidelines provided in the CACREP *Environmental and Specialty Standards for Marriage and Family Counseling/Therapy.*

## Section VIII: Media and Public Statements

A. Members accurately and objectively represent their professional qualifications, skills, and functions to the public. Membership in a professional organization is not to be used to suggest competency.

B. Members have the responsibility to provide information to the public that enhances marriage and family life. Such statements should be based on sound, scientifically acceptable theories, techniques, and approaches. Due to the inability to complete a comprehensive assessment, and provide follow-up, members should not give specific advice to an individual through the media.

C. The announcement or advertisement of professional services should focus on objective information that allows the client to make an informed decision. Providing information such as highest relevant academic degree earned, licenses or certifications, office hours, types of services offered, fee structure, and languages spoken can help clients decide whether the advertised services are appropriate for their needs. Members advertising a specialty within marriage and family counseling should provide evidence of training, education, and/or supervision in the area of specialization. Advertisements about workshops or seminars should contain a description of the audience for which the program is intended. Due to their subjective nature, statements either from clients or from the counselor about the uniqueness, effectiveness, or efficiency or services should be avoided. Announcements and advertisements should never contain false, misleading, or fraudulent statements.

D. Members promoting psychology tapes, books, or other products for commercial sale make every effort to ensure that announcements and advertisements are presented in a professional and factual manner.

Reader's Note: Mary Allison, R. P. Ascano, Edward Beck, Stuart Bonnington, Joseph Hannon, David Kaplan (chair), Patrick McGrath, Judith Palais, Martin Ritchie, and Judy Ritterman are members of the IAMFC ethics committee who formulated the IAMFC code of ethics.

# Glossary

**ABC procedure** a procedure in Ellis's theory for disputing emotions where A stand for an event, B stands for the thought, and C stands for the emotion.

**absurdity** statements that are half-truths and even silly if followed to a conclusion. Whitaker and symbolic-experiential family therapists often work with families by using absurdities.

**abuse** all forms of maltreatment within a family, such as physical, sexual, or emotional.

**accommodation** a process of joining in which the therapist makes personal adjustments in order to achieve a therapeutic alliance with a family.

**act as if** a role-playing strategy where persons act as if they are the persons they want to be ideally.

**adding cognitive constructions** the verbal component of structural family therapy, which consists of advice, information, pragmatic fictions, and paradox.

**administrative (regulatory) law** specialized regulations that pertain to certain specialty areas that are passed by authorized government agencies, for example, laws governing the use of federal land.

**affect** feelings or emotions.

**aging family** a family headed by those 65 years old and above.

**alcohol use disorder** a term for alcohol problems that include two levels: **alcohol abuse**, a problem with drinking that interferes with work, school, and home life, and **alcohol dependency**, a disorder in which persons are unable to control their drinking of alcohol.

**alignments** the ways family members join together or oppose one another in carrying out a family activity.

**Anatomy of Intervention Model (AIM)** a cognitive-behavioral strategy where the therapist learns to play many roles and be flexible.

**anxiety** mental and physical nervousness associated with pressure to please and fear of failure.

**assertiveness** asking for what one wants in a timely and appropriate manner.

**assessment** the administration of formal or informal tests or evaluation instrument(s) along with behavioral observations.

**autonomy** a designation for the level of differentiation in a person according to Bowen which signals the ability to think through a situation clearly.

**Avanta Network** an association that carries on the interdisciplinary work of training therapists in Satir's methods.

**baseline** a recording of the occurrence of targeted behaviors before an intervention is made.

**battering** violence that includes severe physical assault or risk of serious injury.

**battle for initiative** the struggle to get a family to become motivated to make needed changes.

**battle for structure** the struggle to establish the parameters under which family therapy is conducted.

**behavioral family therapy** an approach to treating families that focuses on dealing with behaviors directly in order to produce change. *See also* **cognitive-behavioral family therapy.**

**binuclear family** a term that describes two interrelated family households that comprise one family system, such as a remarried family.

**blamer** according to Satir, a person who attempts to place blame on others and not take responsibility for what is happening.

**boundaries** the physical and psychological factors that separate people from one another and organize them.

**brief therapy** an approach to working with families that has to do more with the clarity about what needs to be changed rather than time. A central principle of brief therapy is that one evaluates which solutions have so far been attempted and then tries new and different solutions to the family's problem, often the opposite of what has already been attempted.

**bug-in-the-ear supervision method**   a supervision model where the therapist working with a family receives messages from a supervisor through a telephone hookup device.

**captitated contract**   a managed care method of cutting costs in which providers agree to provide treatment for a per-person, per-year fee.

**caring**   the idea that moral development and principles are centered in the social context of relationships and interdependency.

**caring days**   part of a behavioral marital procedure in which one or both marital partners act as if they care about their spouse regardless of the other's action(s). This technique embodies the idea of a "positive risk"—a unilateral action not dependent on another for success.

**case law (court decisions)**   the type of law decided by decisions of courts at all levels from state to federal.

**centrifugal**   literally, directed away from a center. It describes how people move away from their family (i.e., family disengagement).

**centripetal**   literally, directed toward a center. It describes a tendency to move toward family closeness.

**charting**   a procedure that involves asking clients to keep an accurate record of problematic behaviors. The idea is to get family members to establish a baseline from which interventions can be made and to show clients how the changes they are making work.

**child custody evaluator**   a family therapist who acts on behalf of a court to determine what is in the best interest of a child in a custody arrangement.

**child physical abuse**   the physical abuse of a child that ranges from mild to severe.

**childhood sexual abuse**   unwanted touching, intercourse, oral sex, and photographs taken while nude of children by adults.

**childless family**   a couple who consciously decides not to have a child or who remains childless as a result of chance, such as infertility.

**choreography**   a process in which family members are asked to symbolically enact a pattern or a sequence in their relationship to one another. Choreography is similar to mime or a silent movie.

**circular causality**   the idea that actions are part of a causal chain, each influencing and being influenced by the other.

**circular questioning**   a Milan technique of asking questions that focus attention on family connections and highlight differences among family members. Every question is framed so that it addresses differences in perception about events or relationships by various family members.

**civil law**   that part of the law that pertains to acts offensive to individuals. Law involving family therapists pertains primarily to civil law—for example, divorce.

**classical conditioning**   the oldest form of behaviorism, in which a stimulus that is originally neutral is paired up with another event to elicit certain emotions through association.

**clear boundaries**   rules and habits that allow and encourage dialogue and thus help family members to enhance their communication and relationships with one another.

**clue**   an intervention in deShazer's brief therapy approach that mirrors the usual behavior of a family. It is intended to alert a family to the idea that some of their present behavior will continue.

**coaching**   a technique by which a therapist helps individuals, couples, or families make appropriate responses by giving them verbal instructions.

**coalition**   an alliance between specific family members against a third member. *See also* **detouring coalition; stable coalition.**

**codependency**   a dynamic within a family where one member of the family underfunctions (such as a substance abuser) while another member of the family overfunctions (such as the codependent family member).

**cognitions**   thoughts.

**cognitive-behavioral family therapy** an approach to working with families that takes into account the impact of cognitions (i.e., thoughts) and behaviors families have incorporated into their lives.

**cognitive distraction** thinking of other than what one normally thinks of.

**cohabitation** the living together of a couple without being married.

**common law** law derived from tradition and usage.

**communication stance** an experiential family therapy procedure of Satir's in which family members are asked to exaggerate the physical positions of their perspective roles in order to help them "level." *See also* **leveling.**

**communications theory** an approach to working with families that focuses on clarifying verbal and nonverbal transactions among family members. Much communication theory work is incorporated in experiential and strategic family therapy.

**complainant** a solution-focused term to describe a client who complains about and describes a situation or problem.

**complementarity** the degree of harmony in the meshing of family roles.

**complementary relationship** relationships based on family member roles or characteristics that are specifically different from each other (e.g., dominant versus submissive, logical versus emotional). If a member fails to fulfill his or her role, such as be a decision maker or a nurturer, other members of the family are adversely affected.

**compliment** a written message used in brief family therapy designed to praise a family for its strengths and build a "yes set" within it. A compliment consists of a positive statement with which all members of a family can agree.

**computer** or **rational analyzer** according to Satir, a person who interacts only on a cognitive or intellectual level.

**concerned significant others (CSOs)** spouses, relatives, or children of a substance abuser who work to engage initially unmotivated problem abusers into treatment.

**confidentiality** the ethical duty to fulfill a contract or promise to clients that the information revealed during therapy will be protected from unauthorized disclosure.

**confirmation of a family member** a process that involves using a feeling word to reflect an expressed or unexpressed feeling of that family member or using a nonjudgmental description of the behavior of the individual.

**confrontation** a procedure through which the therapist points out to families how their behaviors contradict or conflict with their expressed wishes.

**conjoint couple therapy (dual therapy)** a form of therapy devised by Whitaker.

**conjoint family drawing** a procedure in which families are initially given the instruction "Draw a picture as you see yourself as a family." Each member of the family makes such a drawing and then shares through discussion the perceptions that emerge.

**conjoint therapy** the involvement of two or more members of a family in therapy together at the same time.

**constructivism** a philosophy that states reality is a reflection of observation and experience, not an objective entity.

**content** the details and facts.

**contingency contracting** a procedure in which a specific, usually written, schedule or contract describes the terms for the trading or exchange of behaviors and reinforcers between two or more individuals. One action is contingent, or dependent, on another.

**contracting** creating a formal agreement, often in writing, that describes what and when behavioral changes will be made. It is used when family interactions have reached a level of severe hostility. The contract contains built-in rewards for behaving in a certain manner.

**courage** the ability to take calculated risks without knowing the exact consequences.

**court-ordered witness** the role a family therapist assumes when he or she must appear before a court to testify on behalf of or against a family or family member.

**criminal law** that part of the law that deals with acts offensive to society in general.

**crisis resolution** a treatment modality used in crisis situations where the therapist focuses most on supporting defenses and clarifying communication in order to help a family.

**cross-generational alliance (coalition)** an inappropriate family alliance that contains members of two different generations within it, for example, a parent and child collusion.

**culturally encapsulated counselors** professional therapists who treat everyone the same and, in so doing, ignore important differences.

**culture** the customary beliefs, social forms, and material traits of a racial, religious, or social group.

**customers** a solution-focused term for clients who are not only able to describe a problem and how they are involved in it but who are willing to work to solve it.

**cybernetics** a type of systemic interrelatedness governed by rules, sequences, and feedback. The term was introduced as a concept to family therapy by Gregory Bateson. *See also* **new epistemology.**

**deconstruction** a narrative family therapy procedure that uses questions as a therapeutic tool to help clients more closely examine taken-for-granted realities and practices.

**desensitization** a behavioral approach to overcoming unnecessary and debilitating anxiety associated with a particular event.

**detouring coalition** a coalition in which a pair holds a third family member responsible for their difficulties or conflicts with one another.

**detriangulation** the process of being in contact with others and, yet, emotionally separate.

**development** predictable physical, mental, and social changes over life that occur in relationship to the environment.

**developmental crises** times of change in the life span, often accompanied by turmoil and new opportunity.

**developmental stressors** stressful events that are predictable and sequential, such as aging.

**Diagnostic and Statistical Manual (DSM)** a manual, now in its fourth edition, published by the American Psychiatric Association, that codifies psychiatric disorders.

**differentiation (of self)** a level of maturity reached by an individual who can separate his or her rational and emotional selves. Differentiation is the opposite of **fusion.**

**diffuse boundaries** arrangements that do not allow enough separation between family members, resulting in some members becoming fused and dependent on other members.

**DINK** an acronym meaning *dual income, no kids.*

**directive** an instruction from a family therapist for a family to behave differently. A directive is to strategic therapy what the interpretation is to psychoanalysis—that is, the basic tool of the approach.

**disengaged** the state of being psychologically isolated from other family members.

**disputing irrational thoughts** a cognitive-behavioral strategy in which irrational beliefs about an event are challenged.

**distancing** the isolated separateness of family members from each other, either physically or psychologically.

**distractor** according to Satir, a person who relates by saying and doing irrelevant things.

**domestic violence** aggression that takes place in intimate relationships usually between adults.

**double-bind** the theory that states that two seemingly contradictory messages may exist at the same time on different levels and lead to confusion, if not schizophrenic behavior, on the part of an individual who cannot comment on or escape from the relationship in which this is occurring.

**dual-career families** those in which both marital partners are engaged in work that is developmental in sequence and to which they have a high commitment.

**dual relationship** a relationship that is not built on mutuality and where a therapist assumes a second role, for example, being a friend, business associate, lover, and so on.

**dual therapy (conjoint couple therapy)** a form of therapy devised by Whitaker.

**emotional deadness**   a condition that exists when individuals in families either are not aware of or suppress their emotions.

**emotionally cut off**   a Bowenian concept used to describe a family in which the members avoid each other, either physically or psychologically, because of an unresolved emotional attachment.

**emotionally overinvolved**   *See* **fusion.**

**empty nest**   a term that describes couples who have launched their children and are without childrearing responsibilities.

**enabler**   a spouse or other family member on whom a substance abuser is most dependent and who allows the abuser to continue and become worse.

**enactments**   the actions of families that show problematic behavioral sequences to therapists, for example, having an argument instead of talking about one.

**engagement**   where experiential therapists become personally involved with their families through the sharing of feelings, fantasies, and personal stories.

**enmeshment**   loss of autonomy due to overinvolvement of family members with each other, either physically or psychologically.

**epistemology**   the study of knowledge.

**equitability**   the proposition that everyone is entitled to have his or her welfare interests considered in a way that is fair from a multilateral perspective. Equitability is the basis for relationship ethics.

**ESCAPE**   an acronym that stands for four major investments therapists must make: (1) engagement with families and process, (2) sensitivity to culture, (3) awareness of families' potentials, and (4) knowledge of the environment.

**ethics**   the moral principles from which individuals and social groups, such as families, determine rules for right conduct. Families and society are governed by relationship ethics.

**expected event**   a predictable event that occurs such as getting married.

**experiential symbolic family therapy**   the approach to working with families created by Carl Whitaker.

**expert witness**   the role assumed by a family therapist who is asked to give testimony in regard to the probable causes of certain negative behaviors and to make recommendations in regard to a family member (e.g., an uncontrollable juvenile) displaying these behaviors.

**externalize problems**   a method of treatment in narrative therapy devised by White and Epston in which the problem becomes a separate entity outside of the family. Such a process helps families reduce their arguments about who owns the problem, form teams, and enter into dialogue about solving the problem.

**extinction**   the process by which previous reinforcers of an action are withdrawn so that behavior returns to its original level. It involves the elimination of behavior.

**family**   those persons who are biologically and/or psychologically related, who are connected by historical, emotional, or economic bonds, and who perceive themselves as a part of a household.

**family adaptability**   the ability of a family to be flexible and change.

**family clown**   a member of a substance abuse family whose function is to provide the family with humor and thus reduce tension.

**family cohesion**   emotional bonding within a family.

**family dance**   the verbal and nonverbal way a family displays its personality.

**family development and environmental fit**   a concept that states that some environments are conducive to helping families develop and resolve crises, and others are not.

**family/divorce mediation**   the process of helping couples and families settle disputes or dissolve their marriages in a nonadversarial way.

**family group therapy**   a treatment approach that conceptualizes family members as strangers in a group. Members become known to each other in stages similar to those found in groups.

**family hero**   an adult or child who functions to provide self-worth for the family of a substance abuser.

**family homeostasis**   the tendency of the family to remain in its same pattern of functioning and resist change unless challenged or forced to do otherwise.

**family life cycle**   developmental trends within the family over time.

**family life fact chronology**   a tool employed in family reconstruction in which the "star" creates a listing of all significant events in his or her life and that of the extended family having an impact on the people in the family.

**family map**   a visual representation of the structure of three generations of the "star's" family, with adjectives to describe each family member's personality.

**family of origin**   the family a person was born or adopted into.

**family projection**   the tendency of couples according to Bowen to produce offspring at the same level of differentiation as themselves.

**family reconstruction**   a therapeutic innovation developed by Satir to help family members discover dysfunctional patterns in their lives stemming from their families of origin.

**family rules**   the overt and covert rules families use to govern themselves, such as "you must only speak when spoken to."

**feedback**   the reinsertion of results of past performances back into a system. Negative feedback maintains the system within limits; positive feedback signals a need to modify the system.

**feminist family therapy**   an attitude and body of ideas, but not clinical techniques, concerning gender hierarchy and its impact on conducting family therapy. Feminists recognize the overriding importance of the power structure in any human system.

**filial therapy**   a hybrid form of child-centered play therapy in which parents (or other primary caregivers) engage in play therapy with their own child in order to address the child's problem in the context of the parent/child relationship.

**first-order change**   the process whereby a family that is unable to adjust to new circumstances often repetitiously tries the same solutions or intensifies nonproductive behaviors, thus assuring that the basic organization of the family does not change.

**focus on exceptions**   a technique utilized by brief family therapists to help families realize that their symptoms are not always present and that they have some power in what they are presently doing to make changes.

**four phases of sexual responsiveness**   excitement, plateau, orgasm, and resolution.

**frame**   a perception or opinion that organizes one's interactions.

**functional family therapy**   a type of behavioral family therapy that is basically systemic.

**fusion**   the merging of intellectual and emotional functions so that an individual does not have a clear sense of self and others. Fusion is the opposite of **differentiation.**

**games**   a Milan concept that stresses how children and parents stabilize around disturbed behaviors in an attempt to benefit from them.

**gay/lesbian family**   a same-sex couple with or without children from a previous marriage or artificial insemination.

**general systems theory**   *See* **systems theory.**

**genogram**   a visual representation of a person's family tree depicted in geometric figures, lines, and words; originated by Bowen.

**going home again**   a Bowenian technique in which the family therapist instructs the individual or family members with whom he or she is working to return home in order to better get to know the family in which they grew up. By using this type of information, individuals can differentiate themselves more clearly.

**good enough mother**   a mother who lets an infant feel loved and cared for and thereby helps the infant develop trust and a true sense of self.

**Greek chorus**   the observers/consultants of a family treatment session (i.e., the team) as they debate the merits of what a therapist is doing to bring about change. They send messages about the process to the therapist and family. Through this process, the family is helped to acknowledge and feel their ambivalence.

**guide**   a family therapist who helps the star or explorer, during family reconstruction, chart a chronological account of family events that include significant events in the paternal and maternal families, and the family of origin.

**health** an interactive process associated with positive relationships and outcomes.

**Hispanic or Latino** a person born in any of the Spanish-speaking countries of the Americas (Latin America), Puerto Rico, or the United States who traces his or her ancestry to either Latin America or to Hispanic people from U.S. territories that were once Spanish or Mexican.

**historical time** the era in which people live. Historical times consist of forces that affect and shape humanity at a particular point in time, such as during an economic depression or a war.

**home-based therapy** a method of treatment that requires family therapists to spend time with families before attempting to help them.

**homeostasis** the tendency to resist change and keep things as they are, in a state of equilibrium.

**homework** tasks clients are given to do outside of therapy session.

**horizontal stressors** stressful events related to the present, some of which are developmental, such as life cycle transitions, and others of which are unpredictable, such as accidents.

**hypothesizing** a technique central to the Milan approach that involves a meeting of the treatment team before the arrival of a family in order to formulate and discuss aspects of the family's situation that may be generating a symptom. Through hypothesizing, team members prepare themselves for treating the family.

**"I" statements** statements that express feelings in a personal and responsible way that encourages others to express their opinions.

**identified patient (IP)** a family member who carries the family's symptoms.

**individual time** the span of life between one's birth and death. Notable individual achievements are often highlighted in this perspective, for example, when recognized as "teacher of the year."

**informed consent brochure** a brochure that includes all the information in a self-disclosure statement about therapy as well as a place for clients to sign off that they understand the policies and procedures involved.

**Institute for Family Counseling** an early intervention program at the Philadelphia Child Guidance Center for community paraprofessionals that proved to be highly effective in providing mental health services to the poor.

**institutional barrier** any hardship that minority populations must endure to receive mental health services, such as the inconvenient location of a clinic, the use of a language not spoken by one's family, and the lack of diversified practitioners.

**integrative behavioral couple therapy (IBCT)** an approach that emphasizes the promotion of acceptance into the traditional focus of behavioral couple therapy.

**intensity** the structural method of changing maladaptive transactions by having the therapist use strong affect, repeated intervention, or prolonged pressure with a family.

**interlocking pathology** a term created by Ackerman to explain how families and certain of their members stay dysfunctional. In an interlocking pathology, an unconscious process takes place between family members that keeps them together.

**interpersonal couple conflict** aspects within a marriage such as distrust or discord that get in the way of couple functioning.

**intimate justice theory** a theory of ethics that is used in the treatment of abuse and violence in intimate relationships. The theory confronts disempowerment abuses of power in a partnership while challenging internalized beliefs on how one should treat one's partner.

**intrapsychic conflict** emotions such as guilt, trauma, or shame that keep a person from functioning well.

**invariant/variant prescription** a specific kind of ritual given to parents with children who are psychotic or anorexic in an attempt to break up the family's **dirty game** (i.e., power struggle between generations sustained by symptomatic behaviors). An *invariant prescription* requires parents to unite so that children cannot manipulate them as "winners" or "losers" and thereby side with them. A *variant prescription* is given for the same purpose as an invariant one. The difference is that a variant prescription is tailored to a particular family and considers unique aspects of that family.

**invisible loyalties**  unconscious commitments that grown children make to help their families of origin, especially their parents.

**involvement**  a stage in experiential family therapy where therapists concentrate on helping families try new ways of relating through the use of playfulness, humor, and confrontation.

**joining**  the process of "coupling" that occurs between the therapist and the family, leading to the development of the therapeutic system. A therapist meets, greets, and forms a bond with family members during the first session in a rapid but relaxed and authentic way and makes the family comfortable through social exchange with each member.

**joint family scribble**  an experiential family therapy technique in which family members individually make a brief scribble. Then, the whole family incorporates their scribbles collectively into a unified picture.

**law**  a body of rules recognized by a state or community as binding on its members.

**legal**  the law or the state of being lawful.

**leveling**  "congruent communication" in which straight, genuine, and real expressions of one's feelings and wishes are made in an appropriate context.

**life cycle**  the events in life (individual or family) from birth to death.

**linear causality**  the concept of cause and effect—that is, forces being seen as moving in one direction, with each action causing another. Linear causality can be seen in, for example, the firing of a gun.

**logico-scientific reasoning**  a way of thinking characterized by empiricism and logic.

**long brief therapy**  another name for systemic family therapy. *Long brief therapy* refers to the length of time between sessions (usually a month) and the duration of treatment (up to a year).

**lost child**  a child in a substance abuse family who suffers from rejection and loneliness.

**making contact**  the first stage in Virginia Satir's human validation process model where attention is focused on each member of the family in an attempt to raise the level of the person's self-esteem and self-worth.

**malpractice**  the failure to fulfill the requisite standard of care either because of omission (what should have been done, but was not done) or commission (doing something that should not have been done). In either case, negligence must be proved.

**managed health care**  a wide range of techniques and structures that are connected with obtaining and paying for medical care, including therapy. The most common are preferred provider organizations (PPOs) and health maintenance organizations (HMOs).

**mapping**  in brief therapy, the sketching out of a course of successful intervention; in structural family therapy, a mental process of envisioning how the family is organized.

**marital schism**  overt marital conflict that is pathological.

**marital skew**  a dysfunctional marriage in which one partner dominates the other.

**marriage and family enrichment**  the concept that couples and families stay healthy or get healthier by actively participating in certain activities, usually in connection with other couples.

**metachange**  a changing of rules sometimes referred to as a change of change.

**metacommunication**  the implied message within a message, typically conveyed nonverbally.

**mimesis**  a way of joining in which the therapist becomes like the family in the manner or content of their communications—for example, when a therapist jokes with a jovial family.

**miracle question**  a brief therapy technique in which a therapist poses a question such as "If a miracle happened tonight and you woke up tomorrow and the problem was solved, how would you know?"

**modeling**  observational learning.

**multigenerational families** households that include a child, a parent, and a grandparent.

**multigenerational transmission process** the passing on from generation to generation in families of coping strategies and patterns of coping with stress. In poorly differentiated persons, problems may result, including schizophrenia.

**mystification** the actions taken by some families to mask what is going on between family members, usually in the form of giving conflicting and contradictory explanations of events.

**narrative reasoning** a form of reasoning which is characterized by stories, substories, meaningfulness, and liveliness. Narrative reasoning is the basis on which narrative family therapy is built and is the opposite of empirical and logico-scientific reasoning.

**National Institute of Relationship Enhancement** the Guerneys' training program in filial therapy.

**new epistemology** the idea that the general systems approach of Bateson, sometimes referred to as **cybernetics,** must be incorporated in its truest sense into family therapy with an emphasis on "second-order cybernetics" (i.e., the cybernetics of cybernetics). Basically, such a view stresses the impact of the family therapist's inclusion and participation in family systems.

**nonevent** the nonmaterialization of an expected occurrence (e.g., the failure of a couple to have children).

**nuclear family** a core unit of husband, wife, and their children.

**object** a significant other (e.g., a mother) with whom children form an interactional, emotional bond.

**object relations theory** a psychoanalytic way of explaining relationships across generations. According to this theory, human beings have a fundamental motivation to seek objects (i.e., people) in relationships, starting at birth.

**old epistemology** dated ideas that no longer fit a current situation.

**old old** that group of individuals aged 75 to 84.

**oldest old** that group of individuals aged 85 and over.

**ontology** a view or perception of the world.

**operant conditioning** a tenet of Skinner's behavioral theory that people learn, through rewards and punishments, how to respond to their environments.

**ordeal** a technique in which a therapist assigns a family or family member(s) the task of performing a specific activity (i.e., an ordeal) any time the family or individuals involved display a symptom they are trying to eliminate. The ordeal is a constructive or neutral behavior (e.g., doing exercise), but disagreeable to the person directed to engage in it.

**organism** a form of life composed of mutually dependent parts and processes standing in mutual interaction.

**paradox** a form of treatment in which therapists give families permission to do what they were going to do anyway, thereby lowering family resistance to therapy and increasing the likelihood of change.

**parallel relationships** relationships in which both complementary and symmetrical exchanges occur as appropriate.

**parentified child** a child who is forced to give up childhood and act like a parent, even though lacking the knowledge and skills to do so.

**parent-skills training** a behavioral model in which the therapist serves as a social learning educator whose prime responsibility is to change parents' responses to a child or children.

**Parents Without Partners** a national organization that helps single parents and their children deal with the realities of single-parent family life in educational and experiential ways.

**participatory evaluation research** a type of research in which clients are trained as individuals or focus groups to be involved as coresearchers in data analysis interpretation and write-up.

**patterns of communication** the ways in which family members relate to one another, for example, double messages, withholding information, overgeneralization.

**placater** according to Satir, a person who avoids conflict at the cost of his or her integrity.

**planful competence** when adolescents have a reasonably realistic understanding of their intellectual abilities, social skills, and personal emotional responses in interrelationship with others.

**play therapy** a general term for a variety of therapeutic interventions that use play media such as toys as the basis for communicating and working with children.

**positioning** acceptance and exaggeration by the therapist of what family members are saying. If conducted properly, it helps the family see the absurdity in what they are doing.

**positive connotation** a type of reframing in which each family member's behavior is labeled as benevolent and motivated by good intentions.

**positive reinforcer** a material (e.g., food, money, or medals) or a social action (e.g., a smile or praise) that individuals are willing to work for.

**positive risk** a unilateral action that is not dependent on another for success.

**possibility therapy** another name for Bill O'Hanlon's solution-focused family therapy.

**power** the ability to get something done. In families, power is related to both *authority* (the decision maker) and *responsibility* (the one who carries out the decision).

**pragmatic fictions** pronouncements that help families and family members change, such as when a therapist tells children that they are acting younger than their years.

**Premack principle** a behavioral intervention in which family members must first do less pleasant tasks before they are allowed to engage in pleasurable activities.

**prescribing** a technique in which family members are instructed to enact a troublesome dysfunctional behavior in front of the therapist and to work it out past the point where they usually get stuck.

**prescribing the symptom** a type of paradox in which family members are asked to continue doing as they have done. This technique makes families either admit they have control over a symptom or give it up.

**pretend technique** a technique originated by Cloe Madanes in which the therapist asks family members to pretend to enact a troublesome behavior, such as having a fight. Through this procedure, individuals transform an involuntary action into one that is under their control.

**primary rewards** reinforcers that people will naturally work for, such as food.

**privileged communication** a client's legal right, guaranteed by statute, that confidences originating in a therapeutic relationship will be safeguarded.

**process** how information is handled in a family or in therapy.

**professional self-disclosure statement** a statement given to the family by the therapist that outlines treatment conditions related to who will be involved, what will be discussed, the length and frequency of sessions, and fees.

**programmed workbooks for parents** instrumental behavioral books parents may employ to help their children, and ultimately their families, modify behaviors.

**pseudo-individuation/pseudo-self** a pretend self. This concept involves an attempt by young people who lack an identity and basic coping skills to act as if they had both.

**pseudomutuality** the facade of family harmony that many dysfunctional families display.

**psychoeducational methods** a cognitive-behavioral strategy that involves educational methods such as reading books, attending workshops, and listening to audiovisual material.

**punctuation** the way a person describes a situation, that is, beginning and ending a sentence, due to a selective perception or emotional involvement in an event.

**qualitative research** research that is characterized by an emphasis on open-ended questions and the use of extended interviews with small numbers of individuals/families. Results are written up in an autobiographical form. This research is often used in theory building.

**quantitative research** research that is characterized by an emphasis on closed-ended questions and the use of large sample sizes to gather information. Data are gathered in a precise form, frequently using standardized instruments, and reported in a statistical format. Analyzed and deductive conclusions are made that tend to "prove" or "disprove" theories and assertions.

**quasi kin** a formerly married person's ex-spouse, the ex-spouse's new husband or wife, and his or her blood kin.

**quid pro quo** literally, something for something.

**reciprocity** the likelihood that two people will reinforce each other at approximately equitable rates over time. Many marital behavior therapists view marriage as based on this principle.

**redefining** attributing positive connotations to symptomatic or troublesome actions. The idea is that symptoms have meaning for those who display them, whether such meaning is logical or not. Redefining is one way of lowering resistance.

**redundancy principle** the fact that a family interacts within a limited range of repetitive behavioral sequences.

**reframing** a process in which a perception is changed by explaining a situation from a different context. Reframing is the art of attributing different meaning to behavior.

**reinforcer** a consequence of an action that increases its likelihood of occurring again.

**relapse prevention** cognitive-behavioral strategies clients learn to gain self-control and prevent relapse.

**reliability** the consistency or dependency of a measure.

**remarried families** families that consist of two adults and step-, adoptive, or foster children. Sometimes, they are referred to as *stepfamilies, reconstituted families, recoupled families, merged families,* and *blended families.*

**research design** the way a research study is set up. Five commonly used categories are (1) exploratory, (2) descriptive, (3) developmental, (4) experimental, and (5) correlational.

**resistance** anything a family does to oppose or impair progress in family therapy.

**restraining** telling the client family that they are incapable of doing anything other than what they are doing. The intent is to get them to show they can behave differently.

**restructuring** changing the structure of the family. The rationale behind restructuring is to make the family more functional by altering the existing hierarchy and interaction patterns.

**rigid boundaries** inflexible rules and habits that keep family members separated from each other.

**rituals** specialized types of directives that are meant to dramatize significant and positive family relationships or aspects of problem situations.

**role playing** procedures in which family members are asked to "act as if" they were the persons they ideally wanted to be. Members practice a number of behaviors to see which work best. Feedback is given and corrective actions are taken.

**roles** prescribed and repetitive behaviors involving a set of reciprocal activities with other family members or significant others; behaviors family members expect from each other and themselves.

**rules** implicit or explicit guidelines that determine behaviors of family members.

**sample** a limited number of families representative of an entire group of families.

**sandwich generation** couples who have adolescents and their aging parents to take care of and are squeezed psychologically and physically.

**scaling** a solution-focused technique of asking questions using a scale of 1 (low) to 10 (high) to help clients assess situations.

**scapegoat** a family member the family designates as the cause of its difficulties (i.e., the identified patient).

**schism** the division of the family into two antagonistic and competing groups.

**sculpting** an experiential family therapy technique in which family members are molded during the session into positions symbolizing their actual relationships to each other as seen by one or more members of the family.

**second-order change** a qualitatively different way of doing something; a basic change in function and/or structure.

**second-order cybernetics** the cybernetics of cybernetics, which stresses the impact of the family therapist's inclusion and participation in family systems.

**self-control strategies** various ways individuals can help themselves cope, such as employing rational coping statements.

**shaping** the process of learning in small gradual steps; often referred to as successive approximation.

**shaping competence** the procedure in which structural family therapists help families and family members become more functional by highlighting positive behaviors.

**single-parent family** families that include at least one parent who is biologically related to a child (or children) or who has assumed such a role through adoption. This parent is primarily alone in being responsible for taking care of self and a child (or children). Such families are created as a result of divorce, death, abandonment, unwed pregnancy, and adoption.

**situational stressors** stressful events that are unpredictable, such as interpersonal relationships that are emotional.

**skeleton keys** in deShazer's brief therapy approach, those interventions that have worked before and that have a universal application.

**skew** *See* **marital skew.**

**social constructionism** a philosophy that states experiences are a function of how one thinks about them instead of objective entities.

**social exchange theory** an approach that stresses the rewards and costs of relationships in family life according to a behavioral economy.

**social learning theory** a theory that stresses the importance of modeling and learning through observation as a primary way of acquiring new behaviors.

**social time** time characterized by landmark social events such as marriage, parenthood, and retirement. Family milestones are a central focus in social time.

**societal regression** the deterioration or decline of a society struggling against too many toxic forces (e.g., overpopulation and economic decline) countering the tendency to achieve differentiation.

**soft emotions** those emotions like hurt, insecurity, loneliness, and fear that reveal personal vulnerability.

**splitting** viewing object representations as either all good or all bad. The result is a projection of good and bad qualities onto persons within one's environment. Through splitting, people are able to control their anxiety and even the objects (i.e., persons) within their environment by making them predictable.

**squeeze technique** an approach used in sexual therapy in which a woman learns to stimulate and stop the ejaculation urge in a man through physically stroking and firmly grasping his penis.

**stable coalition** a fixed and inflexible union (such as that of a mother and son) that becomes a dominant part of a family's everyday functioning.

**stages** an identifiable period in an individual's or family's life.

**star** or **explorer** a central character in family reconstruction who maps his or her family of origin in visually representative ways.

**statutory law** that group of laws passed by legislative bodies, such as state and national legislatures, and signed by an authorized source, such as a governor or the president.

**stepfamily** a family created when two people marry and at least one of them has been married previously and had a child.

**strategic therapy** a term coined by Jay Haley to describe the therapeutic work of Milton Erickson in which extreme attention was paid to details of client symptoms and the focus was to change behavior by manipulating it and not instilling insight.

**stress inoculation** a process in which family members break down potentially stressful events into manageable units that they can think about and handle through problem-solving techniques. Units are then linked so that possible events can be envisioned and handled appropriately.

**structural family therapy's major thesis** a thesis stating that an individual's symptoms are best understood when examined in the context of family interactional patterns. A change in the family's organization or structure must take place before symptoms can be relieved.

**structure** an invisible set of functional demands by which family members relate to each other.

**subsystems**   smaller units of the system as a whole, usually composed of members in a family who because of age or function are logically grouped together, such as parents. They exist to carry out various family tasks.

**symbolic drawing of family life space**   a projective technique in which the therapist draws a large circle and instructs family members to include within the circle everything that represents the family and to place outside of the circle those people and institutions not a part of the family. After this series of drawings, the family is asked to symbolically arrange themselves, through drawing, within a large circle, according to how they relate to one another.

**symmetrical relationship**   a relationship in which each partner tries to gain competence in doing necessary or needed tasks. Members within these units are versatile. For example, either a man or a woman can work outside the home or care for children.

**system**   a set of elements standing in interaction. Each element in the system is affected by whatever happens to any other element. Thus, the system is only as strong as its weakest part. Likewise, the system is greater than the sum of its parts.

**systematic desensitization**   a process in which a person's dysfunctional anxiety is reduced or eliminated through pairing it with incompatible behavior, such as muscular or mental relaxation. This procedure is gradual, with anxiety treated one step at a time.

**systemic family therapy**   an approach, sometimes known as the Milan approach, that stresses the interconnectedness of family members as well as the importance of second-order change in families.

**systems theory**   a theory, sometimes known as *general systems theory*, that focuses on the interconnectedness of elements within all living organisms, including the family. It is based on the work of Ludwig von Bertalanffy.

**teasing technique**   a sexual therapy approach in which a woman learns how to start and stop sexually stimulating a man.

**therapeutic neutrality**   accepting and nonjudgmental behavior by family therapists that keeps them from being drawn into family coalitions and disputes and gives them time to assess the dynamics within the family. Neutrality also encourages family members to generate solutions to their own concerns.

**thought stopping**   a cognitive-behavioral technique in which family members are taught how to stop unproductive obsession about an event or person through overt mental procedures.

**time-out**   a process that involves the removal of persons (most often children) from an environment in which they have been reinforced for certain actions. Isolation, or time out, from reinforcement for a limited amount of time (approximately 5 minutes) results in the cessation of the targeted behavior.

**token economy**   a type of contract for earning points and reinforcing appropriate behavior, most often employed with children.

**tracking**   a way of joining in which the therapist follows the content of the family (i.e., the facts).

**transference**   the projection onto a therapist of feelings, attitudes, or desires.

**triadic questioning**   asking a third family member how two other members of the family relate.

**triangle**   the basic building block of any emotional system and the smallest stable relationship system in a family.

**triangulating**   projecting interpersonal dyadic difficulties onto a third person or object (i.e., a scapegoat).

**unbalancing**   therapeutically allying with a subsystem. In this procedure, the therapist supports an individual or subsystem against the rest of the family.

**undifferentiated family ego mass**   according to Bowen, an emotional "stuck togetherness," or fusion, within a family.

**unresolvable problems**   aspects of a couple's relationship that are unlikely to change.

**utilization review**   the process in managed health care by which a therapist submits a written justification for treatment along with a comprehensive treatment plan to a utilization reviewer for approval.

**validity** the extent to which an instrument measures what it was intended to.

**values** the ranking of an ordered set of choices from the most to the least preferable. Basically, there are four domains of values: personal, family, political/social, and ultimate. Each has an impact on the other. Ethics is based on values.

**variant prescription** *See* **invariant/variant prescription.**

**verbalizing presuppositions** an experiential technique in which a therapist helps a family take the first step toward change by talking of the hope that the family has.

**vertical stressors** events dealing with family patterns, myths, secrets, and legacies. These are stressors that are historical and that families inherit from previous generations.

**visitors** a solution-focused term to describe clients who are not involved in a problem and are not part of a solution.

**wheel or circle of influence** that circle of individuals who have been important to the star or explorer through family reconstruction.

**worked through** when insights are translated into new and more productive ways of behaving and interacting.

**young old** that group of individuals aged 65 to 74.

# Author Index

# Subject Index